# THE CHRISTENSEN BROTHERS

## Choreography and Dance Studies

A series of books edited by Muriel Topaz and Robert P. Cohan, C.B.E.

**Please see the back of this book for other titles in the Choreography and Dance Studies series**

# THE CHRISTENSEN BROTHERS

## AN AMERICAN DANCE EPIC

Debra Hickenlooper Sowell
*Brigham Young University, Utah, USA*

**harwood academic publishers**
Australia • Canada • China • France • Germany • India
Japan • Luxembourg • Malaysia • The Netherlands
Russia • Singapore • Switzerland • Thailand
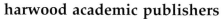

Copyright © 1998 OPA (Overseas Publishers Association) Amsterdam B.V.
Published under license under the Harwood Academic Publishers imprint,
part of The Gordon and Breach Publishing Group.

Amsteldijk 166
1st Floor
1079 LH Amsterdam
The Netherlands

**British Library Cataloguing in Publication Data**
Sowell, Debra Hickenlooper
   The Christensen brothers: an American dance epic. –
   (Choreography and dance studies; v. 16)
   1. Christensen, Harold – Career in ballet  2. Christensen,
   Willam – Career in ballet  3. Christensen, Lew – Career in
   ballet  4. Ballet dancers – United States – Biography
   5. Choreographers – United States – Biography
   I. Title
   792.8'0922

3 8471 00168 2326

ISBN 90-5755-029-6

Cover illustration: Willam, Lew, and Harold Christensen. Courtesy of
Special Collections, University of Utah Marriott Library.

# CONTENTS

# INTRODUCTION TO THE SERIES

*Choreography and Dance Studies* is a book series of special interest to dancers, dance teachers and choreographers. Focusing on dance composition, its techniques and training, the series will also cover the relationship of choreography to other components of dance performance such as music, lighting and the training of dancers.

In addition, *Choreography and Dance Studies* will seek to publish new works and provide translations of works not previously published in English, as well as to publish reprints of currently unavailable books of outstanding value to the dance community.

Muriel Topaz
Robert P. Cohan

# LIST OF PLATES

# PREFACE

Sometime in the late 1970s George Dorris, coeditor of *Dance Chronicle*, suggested that since I was moving to Utah I should write the story of the state's native sons – Willam, Harold, and Lew Christensen. His chance remark took root years later when, as a New York University graduate student, I faced the prospect of a dissertation. I was drawn to the Christensens for several reasons, not the least of which was the family angle. With members of four generations deeply involved in music and dancing, the Christensens are indisputably America's closest equivalent to the European tradition of dance dynasties, such as the Vestris and Taglioni clans. I wondered how family ties affected their careers, how the brothers interacted in the professional arena, and how they coexisted in a world as competitive as that of ballet.

Another reason for pursuing this topic was that time and time again I found confusion, even among dance historians, over the individual contributions of each brother. The accomplishments of one were often credited to another, or all three brothers were lumped together with little understanding of their personal differences. Clearly, the record needed to be set straight.

I also found that some of the Christensens' associates believed Willam to be the truly "great" brother, while others championed Lew just as strongly. I have largely avoided the temptation to make pronouncements of comparative greatness, preferring instead to show the individual attributes and accomplishments of each. The purpose of this career biography is to reveal the tradition from which the brothers came, establish the broad outlines of their lives in dance, and preserve the differences in their personalities, abilities, and outlooks.

Perhaps because the Christensens worked primarily in the West, far from the power center of New York City, their contribution to American ballet has received little scholarly attention. The published information on their careers is limited to occasional articles in dance magazines, a few interviews, essays in Cobbett Steinberg's *San Francisco Ballet: The First Fifty Years*, and occasional critical analyses of their works – the most notable being Marcia Siegel's treatment of Lew's *Filling Station* in her volume *Shapes of Change*. This paucity of published materials undermines our understanding of the history of ballet in America, not only because it leaves us largely ignorant of what the brothers accomplished in the West but also because the Christensens' careers intersected with the plans and ambitions of movers and shakers of the larger dance world, including Lincoln Kirstein, George Balanchine, Sol Hurok, and the Ford Foundation's W. McNeil Lowry. A thorough accounting of the Christensen tradition significantly enlarges our understanding of dance in America since the 1930s.

Writing a triple biography presented the inevitable problem of handling simultaneous events in the brothers' sometimes divergent lives. Because Willam was the oldest and because he so often struck out first in some new direction that would later become the context of his brothers' efforts, the structure of the book usually follows him to a new setting and then brings Harold and Lew up to date. The women in the brothers' lives, and important supporting characters in their careers, admittedly receive short shrift in this recounting, primarily due to limits on the length of the manuscript. Another conscious choice was to skew the text toward the brothers' early history, for this is the information at greatest risk of being lost to future dancers. It was a time of limited opportunities and few conveniences for ballet dancers – the period before nylon tights, when, as Gisella Caccialanza Christensen recalls, dancers warming up in silk stockings before the curtain rose dared not sink into a deep *plié* because "it was permitted to have baggy knees at the end of a performance but not at the beginning."

In the interest of preserving the narrative flow, I have not mentioned in the body of the text each work choreographed by Willam and Lew; instead, all works are listed chronologically in the appendices. In-depth choreographic analysis and extended study of the Christensens' ballets does not fall within the purview of this biography. Rather, this book is intended to establish a foundation for the analysis of the brothers' *oeuvre*, which I see as the next logical step in Christensen studies.

This project could not have been completed without the assistance of many individuals who shared memories and materials that allowed me to reconstruct the Christensens' lives and the context in which their careers unfolded. My first acknowledgment must be to the San Francisco Performing Arts Library and Museum, which, in cooperation with the San Francisco Ballet Association and the William F. Christensen Foundation, gave me a generous grant to write the story of the Christensens' careers. Project coordinator Stephen Cobbett Steinberg encouraged my efforts with unfailing interest in the topic and belief in its importance. I appreciate the support of SF PALM Director Margaret Norton, head librarians Barbara Geisler and Kirsten Tanaka, and the staff, who made the collection's holdings available to me. Recognition of the importance of that collection would not be complete without saluting the years of effort contributed by its founder, Russell Hartley, whose scrapbook history of the San Francisco Ballet was the starting point of much of my historical research.

Other archival repositories that furnished significant amounts of information include the Dance Research Collection of The New York Public Library; the Ballet Society; the Municipal Theatre Association of St. Louis; the Manuscripts Division of the Special Collections Department of the University of Utah Marriott Library, where Nancy Young and her staff gave me full access to the Utah Ballet Archives collection indexed so competently by Susan White; and the Ford Foundation Archives, where archivist Sharon Laist graciously allowed me to consult grant application files and assistant archivist Faith Coleman guided me capably through the maze of forms. W. McNeil Lowry also opened his personal files to me and and shared memories and insights during several interviews.

The terms of my agreement with the San Francisco Performing Arts Library and Museum included a massive oral history effort in which I taped interviews with surviving members of the Christensen family and their professional associates. These narratives contributed largely to the shape of the resulting volume and to my decision to style the work as a family saga. As I studied the oral histories and analyzed their distinctive contributions, I was grateful for the insights contained in Deborah Tannen's *You Just Don't Understand* (New York: Ballantine Books, 1990), which helped me recognize patterns in recounted experiences.

I owe an enormous debt of gratitude to the Christensens themselves: to Willam, who submitted to months of interviews and scoured his closets and chests for photographs and souvenirs; to his wife Florence, who shared her perspective and welcomed my visits; and to his daughter Roxanne, who helped me understand the family context of Willam's career; to Harold, who seemed to enjoy reminiscing and never complained of the pain he was enduring in his battle against cancer; to Ruby Asquith Christensen, who made time in her busy schedule to explain her memories with penetrating insight; and to Gisella Caccialanza Christensen and her son Chris, for helping me to understand Lew, the brother I never had the fortune to meet. All welcomed me into their homes and shared many details of their personal lives with the hope that I would do justice to the brothers' careers. And last but far from least was the contribution of unofficial Christensen family historian Delome S. Billings, who generously shared with me scrapbooks and family records documenting the first two generations of Christensens in Utah. Without her invaluable assistance, I never could have written the first chapter in the form it assumes today.

I am also extremely grateful to the many colleagues, students, and professional associates of the Christensen brothers who shared memories and insights, anecdotes, and understanding. Their names are listed at the beginning of the Bibliography under the category "Interviews and Letters." After completing the oral history portion of my research, which resulted in over 120 hours of taped interviews, I found that only a fraction of the stories they shared could be included in the final manuscript. Tapes and transcripts of a majority of those interviews are now on deposit at the San Francisco Performing Arts Library and Museum for the benefit of future researchers.

In Salt Lake City, Sterling McMurrin and Boyer Jarvis took time to explain the intricacies surrounding Willam's tenure at the University of Utah, and Kirk Baddley steered me to informative records in the University's archives. In New York, Francis Mason made available unpublished interviews with the Christensen brothers, and Barbara Cohen-Stratyner shared her expertise on the Ballet Caravan period and read drafts of two chapters. Janet R. Davis aided my search for Lew's lost work for the BBC. Many others, including William Huck, Lynn Garafola, and Trudy McMurrin, gave encouragement and shared valuable insights. A generous grant from the William F. Christensen Foundation made the desired illustrations possible, and Genevieve Oliver helped in the massive effort of collecting photograph copyright permissions.

I extend heartfelt gratitude to my primary dissertation advisor, Marcia B. Siegel, for years of patient encouragement and guidance as I worked through the issues and information contained herein. I appreciate the insights expressed by Brooks McNamara and Martha Davis, who also graciously made time to be on my committee. My sincere thanks also go to outside readers George Dorris and Selma Jeanne Cohen for perceptive responses to the manuscript as well as encouragement and inspiration over many years. I benefited from the wisdom of the late Martin B. Hickman, who shared insights on the art of biography. My sincerest appreciation also extends to those who read drafts and made helpful comments, including Madison U. Sowell, Lynn Garafola, Linda Hunter Adams, Elizabeth Finch Hedengren, Janice Ross, and anonymous reviewers.

Finally, I express my gratitude for the love and unflagging support of my husband and family, which made the completion of this manuscript possible.

*They could call us fools or pioneers, but we did things with a dream, not knowing the result of the dream.*

*Willam Christensen*

**1** Studio portrait of Lew, Willam, and Harold Christensen, ca. 1950. Photograph by Cristof, courtesy of San Francisco Performing Arts Library and Museum

# PROLOGUE

*A tall, blond Adonis steps out on the stage to go into his amazing
leaps and turns with all the vitality of an American athlete and
the grace of a Nijinsky. This is Lew Christensen of the American
Ballet Caravan, leading dancer and ballet master.*[1]

So the youngest of the three dancing Christensen brothers was
perceived by audiences in the late 1930s: handsome, technically skilled, and radiating strength and grace of motion. Still
today, many balletomanes and historians link the Christensen
reputation, as preserved in the writings of Lincoln Kirstein, to
Lew's star quality and his prominence in George Balanchine's
early New York City companies. But there is much more to the
Christensen story than Lew's tenure as a star in Balanchine's
firmament. The larger view of these extraordinary brothers
encompasses their Mormon pioneer heritage, the circumstances that led them to enter show business with a balletic
vaudeville act, and the rise and fall of companies with which
they were associated during six decades of lives dedicated to
ballet.

Recognition of the brothers' contributions to dance in
America peaked between 1973, when they shared the coveted
*Dance Magazine* Award with Rudolph Nureyev, and 1984,
when the Christensens jointly received the equally distin-
guished Capezio Award. In view of the companies the broth-
ers built and the dozens of dancers they trained over the years
(including Janet Reed, Jocelyn Vollmar, Suki Schorer, Cynthia
Gregory, Conrad Ludlow, Michael Smuin, Finis Jhung, Kent
Stowell, Bart Cook, and Jay Jolley), the distinguished critic of
*The New Yorker* Arlene Croce asserted that "Ballet west of the

---

[1] "Christensen, Balletmaster," no paper credited, clipping hand-dated November
1939, probably in Calgary, Alberta, from the collection of reviews in the American
Ballet Caravan Scrapbooks, Clippings-Announcement, 1933–1941, microfilm, Box 1,
Dance Research Collection of the New York Public Library.

Mississippi is pretty much the creation of the Christensen brothers – Willam, Harold, and Lew – of Utah."[2]

Croce's hyperbole catches the spirit if not the letter of the Christensens' contribution. Certainly, in terms of geography, the Christensens' story provides an alternative view to New York-oriented histories of American dance. It shows the fortunes of a family from the West and how their interconnected efforts cut through the hard economic times of the Great Depression, the tumult of world war, the confident expansion of the postwar era, and the growing number and professionalism of dance companies during the "Dance Boom" of the 1960s and 1970s. The Christensen saga is also the tale of a family ballet business and how it changed over the course of several decades, resulting eventually in artistic corporations beyond familial control.

In the context of American dance history, the story of the Christensen brothers is doubly fascinating because members of the same family exemplify diverse models of how Americans pursued careers in ballet before the United States was dotted by companies. Willam represents one approach: trained in the technique of ballet by an Italian master but not nurtured on the classical repertory, he functioned largely as an independent agent. Unlike many Americans of his generation, he did not go to Europe to study and his career did not spring from beginnings in an established company. With little more than his passion for dance and a strong determination to succeed, Willam developed companies and repertory by the sheer force of his personality, absorbing a pragmatic understanding of ballet's literature as his career progressed. Lew began in this tradition, under family tutelage, but while still young he aligned himself with Balanchine and Kirstein, and that made all the difference. By absorbing Balanchine's attitudes and methods, and performing in the Russian's early New York companies, Lew left his brother's independent world and entered the mainstream of America's understood,

[2] Arlene Croce, *Going to the Dance* (New York: Alfred A. Knopf, 1982), 311.

New York-oriented ballet history. When Willam's and Lew's professional careers intersected in San Francisco at the beginning of the 1950s, the esthetic assumptions underlying those models clashed. The outcome of that conflict assured that Balanchine's influence would prevail in the city by the bay.

On the personal level, the Christensen story is one of unlikely beginnings, naiveté erased by experience, opportunities won and lost, and often unappreciated effort. While the three brothers shared many of their lives' circumstances, their gifts, interests, and personalities diverged wildly. It was Willam's inner drive for glory that first spurred the brothers on to performing careers and his entrepreneurial gift that fueled the family business. Harold, the "middle child" of the three, had the most formal education and enjoyed the least limelight. Lew, introspective and known for the ironic twist of his wit, was the favored "kid brother" whose talents elicited his brothers' nurturing instincts as well as occasional fraternal competition. In his later years he would be credited by Balanchine with training "the best male aspirants on the continent."[3]

Harold and Lew are now dead. Willam, age ninety-four, continues to teach in Salt Lake City. To understand how three brothers from a small Utah community could alter the landscape of American dance, one must turn first to their pioneer heritage, where the Christensen story rightly begins.

December 1996

---

[3] Lincoln Kirstein, *Thirty Years: The New York City Ballet* (New York: Alfred A. Knopf, 1978), 301.

# 1

## FAMILY BEGINNINGS

"Behold this day what dancing can be," exhorted a 1939 advertisement for Lars Peter Christensen's "Le Christ School of Dancing" in Salt Lake City, Utah. The youngest surviving son of the family patriarch who established the Danish American family in Utah, Lars Peter (or L.P., as he was known) was the figure in the family chain who induced members of the third generation, Willam, Harold, and Lew, to pursue careers in ballet. The first two generations of the Christensen clan have received scant recognition, but their varying visions of "what dancing could be" established the context in which the talents of the third generation would be nurtured.

### The First Generation

Like many Utah families, the Christensens of ballet fame descended from Scandinavian immigrants who sought religious freedom and a new life along the western ranges of the Rocky Mountains. Lars Christian Christensen (1825–1908) left Denmark for America in the early 1850s. As converts to The Church of Jesus Christ of Latter-day Saints, commonly referred to as the "Mormon" faith because members accept the Book of Mormon as companion scripture to the Bible, Lars and his wife Jensina endured a lengthy journey fraught with the type of misfortunes of which family legends are made. They buried a son at sea, were quarantined during a cholera epidemic while traveling up the Mississippi River, and laid an infant daughter to rest in Lars's violin case along the trail west.[1]

---

[1] Details of the journey are based on Harold's knowledge of family history (see Interview with Harold F. Christensen, San Anselmo, California, September 22, 1987) and on an account of Lars's life written by his granddaughter Iris Carver, in the possession of Delome Sorenson Billings, Bountiful, Utah. Olga Maynard's article

Six feet tall, broad-shouldered, and of robust build, Lars had blue eyes, a ruddy complexion, and long fingers suited to jobs requiring precision. His instinctive mechanical aptitude was wedded to an unassuming manner and a personality characterized by patience and devotion to his newfound religion. The skills the thirty-year-old brought with him to the New World included approximately one year of formal education, training as a stonemason, and a working knowledge of the violin he had received as a child.

Not long after arriving in the western territory, Lars and Jensina were sent sixty miles north of Salt Lake to Brigham City, a nascent community named after Brigham Young, the church's president, who sent immigrants to colonize the intermountain region. The Christensens were probably part of the group of fifty carefully chosen families who accompanied the Mormon apostle Lorenzo Snow to establish a self-sufficient community on the banks of Box Elder Creek. Lars applied his training as a mason to the production of adobe bricks from local soil. Eventually he was able to build a home, with a parlor large enough to host parties and dances which he accompanied on his violin. He also played the horn in Brigham City's first brass band and figured in the fourteen piece orchestra that accompanied the settlement's amateur theatrical company.

In marked contrast to many other religious groups, the Mormons considered music and dancing beneficial forms of recreation, as long as the dancing parties did not involve drinking or fraternizing with undesirable elements in a way that would lead to moral transgression.[2] Brigham Young rejected the traditional Protestant fire-and-brimstone view of dancing and stated explicitly:

> *I had not the chance to dance, when I was young, and never heard the enchanting tones of the violin, until I was eleven years of age, and then I thought I was on the highway to Hell, if I suffered*

---

"The Christensens: An American Dance Dynasty" (*Dance Magazine*, June 1973: 44–56) includes many of the same details.

[2] For a balanced discussion of the church's stand on dancing, see Michael Hicks, *Mormonism and Music* (Urbana: University of Chicago Press, 1989), 74–90.

*myself to linger and listen to it. I shall not subject my little children to such a course of unnatural training, but they shall go to the dance, study music, read novels, and do anything else that will tend to expand their frames, add fire to their spirits, improve their minds, and make them feel free in body and mind.*[3]

Thus Mormon pioneers danced in the evenings around campfires as they crossed the great plains. At the temporary settlement of Winter Quarters, Nebraska, where planting crops for future wagon companies was the top priority, a dancing school enrolled over 400 participants.[4]

Dancing was a source of relaxed diversion in the cooperative community of Brigham City, but the primary focus of these pioneering years was the forging of a self-sufficient society that could provide for the needs of its citizens and at the same time welcome and help newcomers. In 1864, Brigham City became an economic cooperative, with a general store in which virtually all the inhabitants ultimately held stock. Operating on the assumption that the community could progress more rapidly by coordinating the efforts of its citizens than it could if each family's enterprise struggled under a free-market economy, the Brigham City Cooperative Association organized and oversaw the development of dozens of enterprises to make the farming community less dependent on outside suppliers. At its height, the Brigham City Mercantile and Manufacturing Company, incorporated in 1870, produced its own form of currency as a means of bartering goods and services and oversaw over thirty "departments": a tannery, along with boot- and shoe-making shops; a woolen mill with a large sheep herd for a dependable supply of wool; a dairy that exported butter and cheese; various farms, mills, and machine shops; several textile enterprises, including a millinery shop and a silk factory; furniture and blacksmith shops; even a "tramp department," which made sure that transients coming through had an opportunity

---

[3] M. R. Werner, *Brigham Young* (New York: Harcourt, Brace & Company, 1925), 225.

[4] Debra Hickenlooper Sowell, "Theatrical Dancing in the Territory of Utah, 1848–1868," *Dance Chronicle* 1.2 (1977–1978): 97.

to work and receive sustenance.[5] Lars's talents thrived in this context. He built and supervised a mill that processed sugar cane into molasses, and his mechanical abilities were utilized in building equipment and fixing looms for the cooperative's woolen mills. Lars also taught himself to repair watches and clocks. When he was not actively overseeing work at the mill, he ran a watch and jewelry repair business out of one room in his home. When a several ton clock arrived for the tower of the county courthouse, Lars was entrusted with the task of installing it and keeping it in working order.

Like many other Mormon men of that era, Lars participated in the then-sanctioned practice of plural marriage, a controversial institution that at least provided homes for the influx of female immigrants who arrived in the frontier settlements with no means of support. While Jensina was still living, Lars took a second wife, a Danish immigrant many years his junior named Elsa Kjerstine (or "Christina") Bjerregaard (1839–1911).[6] She bore him ten children, of whom four died before reaching maturity. Of the remaining six, five would figure prominently in the territory's intersecting circles of music and dance.

Lars saw to the musical education of his children, probably with support from Elsa, the wife from whom the musical branch of the family descends. Their children received training on the piano and often accompanied their father when he played the violin for dances in neighboring settlements. When the town cooperative failed in the 1880s (its bankruptcy spurred by drought and a legal challenge to the home scrip), Lars expanded his watch and jewelry repair business to include the sale and repair of musical instruments.

---

[5] Leonard J. Arrington, "Cooperative Community in the North: Brigham City, Utah," *Utah Historical Quarterly* 33.3 (Summer 1965): 198–217. Arrington points out that the success of the Brigham City Cooperative brought it to the attention of English socialists, and Edward Bellamy studied it in person while writing *Looking Backward*.

[6] Family records indicate that Lars had seven children by a third wife, Melvina, and that he also married Ingeborg Lee. Like many other Mormon men of this era, he was imprisoned for a brief season for polygamy.

Although his musical training was limited (he played chiefly by ear), Lars was responsible for the first instrument sales in Brigham City and, according to one local historian, "did much to encourage high class music" in the small community.[7]

Lars was part of a group that was conscious of creating a new society on the frontier. The Mormon pioneers who settled the arid Great Basin region were aware of the biblical prophecy that in the last days a desert would "blossom as the rose" (Isaiah 35:1). They strove to fulfill that vision not only by fostering agriculture and industry but also by devoting individual talents to improving their community's quality of life. In this spirit of consecrating one's efforts to the betterment of society, Lars played his violin at parties and dances without remuneration. And by teaching the younger generation traditional Danish dances, he enriched the community while perpetuating an aspect of his cultural heritage in his new homeland. Lars's satisfactions late in life included playing for the children's Christmas party each year and watching his sons' orchestra accompany local dances. The chief memories his grandsons Willam and Harold had of Lars were of a bearded octagenarian who proudly maintained the courthouse clock.[8]

## The Second Generation

The first son of Lars and Elsa to live to maturity, Christian B. Christensen (1865–1940), known as Chris, was trained on the violin by his father. He sold guitars while working as a railroad laborer one summer and used that income to pay for further musical studies with Willard Weihe, the concertmaster of Salt Lake City's first symphony orchestra.[9] Succeeding

---

[7] Lydia Walker Forsgren, ed., *History of Box Elder County* (Utah: Ca. 1937), 181.

[8] Interview with Harold Christensen, San Anselmo, California, September 22, 1987, and interview with Willam Christensen, Salt Lake City, Utah, March 9, 1987.

[9] Interview with Harold Christensen, San Anselmo, California, September 22, 1987. Weihe is mentioned in Conrad B. Harrison, *Five Thousand Concerts* (Salt Lake City: Utah Symphony Society, 1986), 25.

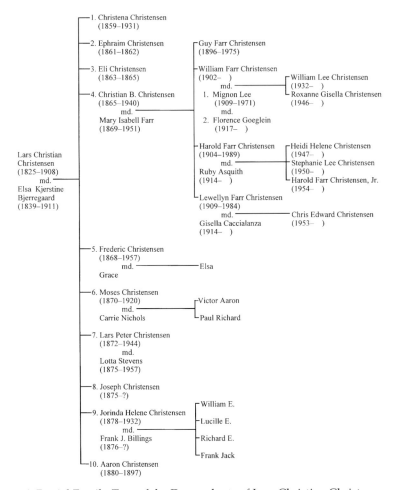

**2**   A Partial Family Tree of the Descendants of Lars Christian Christensen.

children followed Chris's example. Frederic (1868–1957) learned to play the 'cello; Moses (1870–1920) mastered the viola; and L.P. (1872–1944) joined Chris on the violin, completing a fraternal string quartet.[10] The boys and their sister

---

[10] Frederic[k]'s name appears alternately spelled, sometimes with the "k" and sometimes without it, in family records and newspaper clippings. I have chosen the shorter form, which he appeared to use professionally.

Jorinda (1878–1932) were also trained on the piano and the school organ. A fifth brother, Aaron (1880–1897), studied the flute before dying of appendicitis in his teens.

With the children's training in music came instruction in the social dances of their father's youth. Lars taught them minuets and quadrilles, the polka and the schottische. They learned proper steps and positions, correct deportment, and the polite way to ask a young lady to dance. Etiquette had an accepted place in Mormon pioneer society, which, although located on the western frontier, preserved a more formal tone than that of California's rowdy mining towns. Lars's sons also learned how to "call" a dance, to direct others through traditional figures such as "Right and left to places," "Eight hands over," and "Promenade all."[11]

L.P.'s career on the violin was cut short by sudden tragedy. One day while he was feeding sugar cane into his father's mill his left hand got caught between the heavy rollers, and his fingers were irrevocably crushed. This searing experience triggered a period of bitterness and frustration in which he gave up all thoughts of a career in music. But the pull of family tradition was strong, and L.P. eventually found his way back into the circle of sibling musicians by taking up the cornet, which he could hold and play with his right hand. For the rest of his life, he wore a kid leather covering to protect the stump of his left hand.

In 1885 the four older brothers, Chris, Frederic, Moses, and L.P., and a clarinetist, Ernest W. Nichols, formed the Christensen Orchestra. They traveled throughout northern Utah, playing at the social gatherings and dances that were such an integral part of pioneer life. In 1890, ambitious for more professional opportunities, the brothers moved twenty miles south to the larger community of Ogden. An important railroad terminus located near the junction of the Union and Central Pacific lines, Ogden had a population of nearly fifteen thousand (compared to the two thousand inhabitants of

---

[11] Forsgren, 172–73.

**3**   The Christensen Orchestra. Left to right: Lars Peter, Chris, Frederic, and Moses Christensen, and Ernest W. Nichols.
Photograph by Amundsen, courtesy of Willam F. Christensen

Brigham City) and was second only to Salt Lake in size and commercial importance within the territory. There the brothers secured engagements in the opera house and became partners with the owners of a dance hall.[12] Local reports insist that "they created a furore by their splendid playing and gentlemanly conduct."[13]

---

[12] Delome S. Billings, compiler, "History of Lars Peter Christensen," submitted to the Daughters of the Utah Pioneers, February 16, 1983, in Christensen Family Papers and Scrapbooks, in the possession of Delome Sorenson Billings, Bountiful, Utah.

[13] "Christensen's Orchestra – Success! Success! Success!" Unattributed newspaper clipping on the history of the Christensen Orchestra, probably published in Salt Lake City between 1900 and 1905, in the collection of Christensen Family Papers and Scrapbooks, in the possession of Delome Sorenson Billings, Bountiful, Utah.

Encouraged by this success, the brothers moved once again in 1893, settling permanently in Salt Lake City, the region's religious and cultural center. There they enlarged their orchestra to ten players and swiftly worked their way into the social fabric of the city. That summer the Christensens joined a select group of musicians chosen to accompany the 250 voice Mormon Tabernacle Choir during its engagement at the Chicago World's Fair. Beginning the following year, the Christensen Orchestra was hired annually to furnish the music at the Saltair pavilion, a pleasure resort on the shores of the Great Salt Lake (the territory's answer to Coney Island). In 1896, when the territory celebrated its newly acquired statehood, the Christensen Orchestra joined with a local band to provide the music for the new governor's Inaugural Ball. Sister Jorinda, who was well schooled in the social dances of the day, was chosen to be the dancing partner of Colonel Tatlock, Governor Heber M. Wells' personal representative at the ball.[14]

The Christensens further solidified their presence in the community by opening a Christensen Dancing Academy. The academy included a spacious and elegantly appointed ballroom large enough to accommodate two hundred couples at a time, as well as a large reception room, cloakrooms, and dressing rooms for each sex. Here the brothers followed the tradition of nineteenth-century American dancing masters, teaching deportment and social dances according to correct formula. Christensen family papers include pamphlets from the M. B. Gilbert School in Boston for the years 1901 and 1903, and fragmentary correspondence suggests that at least Moses, and perhaps Frederic or L.P., took summer courses there. This exposure to Gilbert, who edited the 1897–98 dance journal *The Director* and was a strong advocate of training for social dance teachers, suggests that the second generation of Christensens took dance technique seriously in a way their

---

[14] Frank Jack Billings, "Utah's First Inaugural," *Salt Lake Tribune*, January 23, 1977, in Christensen Family Papers and Scrapbooks, in the possession of Delome Sorenson Billings, Bountiful, Utah.

father probably never considered. Lars's sons turned their father's pastime into a profession; they benefited from his example but went far beyond the borders of Brigham City to develop their talents and further their careers in music and dancing.

Around the turn of the century, Chris and his brothers began to go their separate ways, with the understanding that they would reassemble in Salt Lake for major events. This branching out coincided with the second generation's desire to marry and establish their own families. Chris married Mary Isabell Farr (1869–1951), daughter of the founder of Ogden, and their first child, Guy, was born in 1896.[15] A dutiful eldest son, Chris returned to Brigham City in deference to his father's wish that one of the boys return "home." There Chris took over his father's music and jewelry business, established a local dance orchestra, and eventually directed Brigham City's Military Brass Band.

Frederic went as far northwest as Seattle, where his wife Grace assisted him in running a Christensen School of Dancing in that city.[16] By 1904 he was one of two cellists in the Seattle Symphony Orchestra.[17]

Mose (who disliked his biblical name and consistently dropped the second "s") settled first in Boise, Idaho, where he and a partner built a large pleasure hall known as the Riverside Pavilion. Events at Mose's ballroom were described in detail in local society columns, with lists of those in

---

[15] Isabell did not use her first name, Mary, and often went by a shortened form of her second, "Belle." Family records alternately spell her name "Isabelle" and "Isabell," but the latter spelling appears on her tombstone.

[16] One of the pieces of lore sometimes attached to Fredric's history is that Merce Cunningham once studied in the former's Seattle school. According to Cunningham Foundation Archivist David Vaughan, Merce remembers watching Fredric's classes but insists he "didn't actually study there." Telephone conversation with David Vaughan, May 26, 1988.

[17] A photograph with the caption "Seattle Symphony Orchestra" lists Erwin Gastel and Frederic Christensen as the symphony's two cellists, *Seattle Sunday Times*, January 24, 1904. Clipping included in Scrapbook of Moses and Carrie Christensen, in the possession of Delome Sorenson Billings, Bountiful, Utah.

attendance and notices of alterations or flourishes in the ballroom's decor. Eventually, Mose and his wife, Carrie Nichols, left Boise for Portland, Oregon, where they opened yet another ballroom. Mose continued to play the viola seriously. Family tradition holds that during visits to New York he played in string quartets with the famous cellist, conductor, and operetta composer Victor Herbert.[18] In Oregon, Mose was the driving force behind the founding of the Portland Symphony Orchestra, an ensemble that premiered in 1911 with fifty-six unpaid musicians. Mose was the symphony's first president and conductor. Demonstrating promotional skills that would surface again in the family's third generation, Mose won the support of local business leaders and curried the favor of the state legislature by giving complimentary concerts at state institutions.[19] As a conductor, Mose was largely self-taught, studying scores for months at a time in preparation for the group's early, infrequent concerts. In Mose's career, music and dance went hand-in-hand; programs for the symphony he conducted also carried advertisements for the Christensen Ballroom in Portland.

L.P. remained in Salt Lake City, where his sister Jorinda served as his accompanist and housekeeper until he married Lotta Stevens. L.P. became an arbiter of taste in the Mormon capital and an outspoken opponent of "degraded" dances such as the Bunny Hug and the Bowery Rassle. Demonstrating an inflexible attitude toward innovation in social dance forms, he admonished his readers that no matter what fads might reign at Coney Island, "the laws of gracefulness

---

[18] When in New York, Mose also played with the Euterpe Symphony Society, a group of seven musicians conducted by Henry Schradieck. A card for the "Euterpe Symphony Society of New York City, Henry Schradieck, Conductor," with Mose's name among the players, is found in the Scrapbook of Mose and Carrie Christensen in the possession of Delome Sorenson Billings, Bountiful, Utah. The other players listed on the card are George McNeice, President; Chas. Seger, Sam'l Lehman, Valentine Drescher, Fred. Blodgett, and Adolph Bernstein, Jr.

[19] "Portland, Ore., Succeeding with Symphony Orchestra," *Christian Science Monitor*, May 20, 1914, in Christensen Family Papers and Scrapbooks, in the possession of Delome Sorenson Billings, Bountiful, Utah.

and propriety are fixed and unalterable."[20] His ballroom
remained a center of circumspect social activity and often
hosted events sponsored by fraternal organizations in the
community. L.P. was also involved in the musical life of the
city. When the Utah-born soprano Emma Lucy Gates left her
New York career to return home and to stage operas in Salt
Lake City, L.P. choreographed her productions of *Faust* and
*Carmen*.[21] On occasion he sold instruments to the Salt Lake
Philharmonic, an early forerunner of the Utah Symphony.[22]
L.P. also instituted an instrumental music program in the
public schools and formed the Puck's Boys Band, composed
of the city's less privileged boys. The group performed in the
Mormon Tabernacle and as far afield as Denver.[23]

In the summer of 1910, Frederic and Mose took a step
that was to have a profound impact upon the family's next
generation. The two brothers traveled to New York City and
joined the American National Association, Masters of Dancing (ANAMD), which was meeting at the Duryea Dancing
School on West 72nd Street. In this organization they found
an outlet for their theories about proper dancing and a
network of professional associates with similar interests.
Showing no hesitation, Frederic and Mose seized the opportunity to lobby the nearly seventy members present on the
subject of waltz tempi, arguing that the slow tempi allowed

---

[20] Prof. L. P. Christensen, "'Hoodlumism' among Salt Lake Dancers," *Deseret Evening News*, January 16, 1904, in Scrapbook of Mose and Carrie Christensen, in the possession of Delome Sorenson Billings, Bountiful, Utah.

[21] Interview with Willam F. Christensen, Salt Lake City, Utah, February 20, 1987. The operatic career of Emma Lucy Gates, including her Utah productions, is chronicled in John Louis Coray, "Emma Lucy Gates (Bowen), Soprano," M.A. thesis, Brigham Young University, 1956.

[22] By the early 1920s, the ensemble was paying Mose $20 a month to rehearse in his ballroom. Conrad B. Harrison, *Five Thousand Concerts: A Commemorative History of the Utah Symphony* (Salt Lake City: Utah Symphony Society, 1986), 20, 25, 49.

[23] "Juvenile Band Will Give Concert at Tabernacle This Evening," *Salt Lake Herald*, no date, copy attached to Delome Sorenson Billings's "History of Lars Peter Christensen," submitted to the Daughters of the Utah Pioneers, February 16, 1983. Christensen Family Papers and Scrapbooks, in the possession of Delome Sorenson Billings, Bountiful, Utah.

by some masters "obliterated the poetry of motion" of that dance.[24] To Mose and his brothers, dancing was a form of social entertainment that could be morally uplifting when practiced correctly but that nonetheless required careful regulation. In establishing "correct" tempi, abolishing dances considered lewd or immoral, and preventing dancers from doing the steps of one dance to the music of another, dancing masters such as the Christensens attempted to exercise firm control over social custom. They attended conventions each year to take home the latest dances to teach in their ballrooms, but they took home only the approved versions.

In the mid-1940s, the dance writer Ann Barzel observed that ninety per cent of American dance schools taught ballroom dancing in addition to theatrical dance:

> *The tie-up between these two entirely different forms of dance remains a fixed idea in the mind of the public. It is not merely because the same word covers both fields. Their histories really overlap at most points in the United States.*[25]

---

[24] This incident is preserved in a tongue-in-cheek account entitled "Dancing Masters Fix Waltz Time," *New York Times*, June 14, 1910. According to the *Times*, Mose jumped to his feet and declared that "too great laxity" had been allowed in the waltz; its tempo needed to be "governed by an iron rule." Arguing that waltzing as slowly as forty measures to the minute "obliterated the poetry of motion" of that dance, he urged the dancing masters to enforce faster speeds. A woman in the back of the room rose to suggest what today would be taken for granted, "that it might be just as well to have a waltz played to the different tempos." Frederic, prepared for such a challenge, took his watch to the piano, and a young woman played a waltz from *The Dollar Princess* at the various speeds under discussion. Finally convinced, a dance teacher heretofore silent on the matter moved that the medium fifty-five measures be adopted, and the motion carried. Another teacher took courage from the Christensens' example and stood to discuss abuses of the two-step, but "the discussion on the waltz seemed to have exhausted the dancing masters, many of whom were removing their coats and collars," and the two-step was abandoned in favor of a "lesson on aesthetics" by the organization's host, Oscar Duryea. Clipping found in the Scrapbook of Mose and Carrie Christensen, in the possession of Delome Sorenson Billings, Bountiful, Utah. At the same convention, Mose also introduced a new dance, "The Hobble," inspired by the sight of women in tight skirts as they climbed into their automobiles at the carriage entrance of the Plaza Hotel.

[25] Ann Barzel, "European Dance Teachers in the United States," *Dance Index* 3 (April–June 1944): 59.

This was certainly true in the case of the Christensens, for whom the activities of the ANAMD provided a bridge from social to theatrical dance. Mose and L.P. probably arrived in New York for the 1910 ANAMD convention too late to witness Anna Pavlova's debut at the Metropolitan Opera that March, but through the association they were doubtless exposed to the teachings of Louis Chalif. Chalif's background included training in the ballet in Odessa, Russia, and a brief career at the Metropolitan Opera. Beginning in 1906 he specialized in teaching dance instructors a watered down form of ballet that he spread through a series of textbooks on simplified dance technique.

As a result of this exposure, Mose became possessed with a desire to find a "scientific" approach to dance training, a system with an established "nomenclature" and discipline as exacting of the body as musical training was on an instrument.[26] The Christensens apparently had no interest in the "poses plastique" taught by Maud May Babcock, a Delsarte-trained elocution teacher, at the University of Utah in the 1890s and early 1900s; when barefoot "esthetic dancing" was added to the curriculum in the 1910s, L.P. made fun of the Duncanesque pageantry in front of his impressionable nephews.[27] Instead, as Mose learned about ballet, he decided that here was a kind of dance based on a formalized technique, a technique even stricter and more comprehensive than that taught by the most skilled social dance teacher. His initial ignorance of what that technique was, or how to acquire it, was not unusual in America at that time, for the United States did not enjoy an established tradition of classical dance parallel to the ballet schools attached to opera houses throughout

---

[26] In telling Mose's story, Willam stresses the notion of "scientific" training; when Harold explains it, he stresses that Mose wanted a system of movement with "nomenclature." See interview with Willam Christensen, Salt Lake City, Utah, March 9, 1987, and interview with Harold Christensen, San Anselmo, California, September 22, 1987.

[27] For more information on forms of dancing taught at the University of Utah in the early decades of this century, see Erna Persch Olsen, "An Historical Study of Physical Education for Women at the University of Utah," M.A. thesis, University of Utah, 1949.

Europe. According to Barzel, two Italian ballet teachers were instrumental in introducing Americans to undiluted classical technique: "Luigi Albertieri and Stefano Mascagno were the first popular teachers to teach correct technique and make many teachers aware of the synthetic quality of their previous training."[28] Once again the Christensens provide Barzel a case in point. Intent on finding a rigorous teacher while in the East, Mose combed the dance studios of Manhattan until he discovered Mascagno, whose father had been a soloist at La Scala. Mascagno himself had been a student of Giovanni Lepri (who was in turn a student of the great nineteenth-century Italian ballet theorist and pedagogue Carlo Blasis) and had trained in the San Carlo Opera Ballet in Naples.[29] When Mose expressed the desire to study ballet, the Italian was doubtful; why would a grown man, especially one who was already a teacher, want to take his ballet classes? But Mose insisted, and Mascagno became his mentor in ballet. And so it happened that despite their heritage, the Christensens' first ballet training was in the Italian, not the Danish, tradition.

Fueled by commitment to ANAMD's *raison d'etre* and a natural leader among the brothers, Mose was elected president of the organization in 1916. His most significant contribution as president was the decision to sponsor, for the first time, a month-long Normal School (or teacher-training course) to precede the following summer's convention.[30] Mose guaranteed the association against financial liability: if they lost money on the project, he would make it up, and if

---

[28] Barzel, 81.

[29] References to Ernesto Mascagno's appearances at La Scala may be found in Giampiero Tintori, *Cronologia: Opere-balletti-concerti 1778–1977* (Gorle [Bergamo] Italy: Grafica Gutenberg Editrice, 1979), 191–92. More information about Stefano Mascagno may be found in Barzel, 82.

[30] This was a significant step in the organization's history. Leona Lucille Mellen's history of the Dancing Masters of America mentions the inauguration of the Normal School in 1917 but does not include any names of those responsible or involved; see Mellen, "History of the Dancing Masters of America, Inc.," *Foreword* 18 (November 1930): 5.

they made money, the association would keep it.[31] The plan was announced as the "founding [of] a ballet school for standard technique, to be known as the American National Ballet School."[32] This ambitious project was to include instruction in the "best points in all the ballet schools of the old world."[33] Dissatisfied with Chalif's methods, Mose chose Mascagno to be principal of the school and to teach classes in ballet technique. Thus it was through Mose that Mascagno acquired the position that would earn his place in history; Barzel writes that "Stefano Mascagno's great influence was due to his long connection with the dancing masters of America."[34]

While the Normal School fell short of creating a national school of ballet in the United States, it did become a traditional part of the dancing masters' annual conventions. Mascagno taught the ballet classes for nine years, after which that position was filled by the former Bolshoi dancer Ivan Tarasoff. As the youngest Christensen of his generation, L.P. gained the most from Mascagno's teaching. But even L.P. started ballet too late in life to perform; he studied it so that he could pass the technique on to his pupils in Salt Lake City.[35]

---

[31] Interview with Harold Christensen, San Anselmo, California, September 22, 1987.

[32] "Convention Decides to Reform Dancing," *Salt Lake Tribune*, September 5, 1917, among the family papers in the possession of Delome Sorenson Billings, Bountiful, Utah.

[33] *Ibid.*

[34] Barzel, 82.

[35] Mose's leadership in the American National Association, Masters of Dancing, which later joined with the International Association of Masters of Dancing to become Dance Masters of America, set a family precedent. L.P. affiliated with the Utah Association Teachers of Dancing, which met in his studio in the late '20s. And in 1927 Frederic wrote an open letter published in *American Dancer* (the forerunner to *Dance Magazine*) advocating a western association of dancing masters. It was costly and time-consuming, reasoned Frederic, for dance teachers in the West to travel to New York and Europe regularly for new material. Why not unite to facilitate the exchange of ideas, break down "selfish competition," and protect their shared interests? (August 1927 issue, 26). The magazine's editor Ruth Eleanor Howard picked up on Frederic's idea and invited other teachers to send in their views on the subject, and L.P. was among those whose supporting comments made it into print. L.P. was for a strict, not a "sentimental" organization, and he advocated bringing the "incomparable Mascagno" out to instruct the western teachers, who should "be careful and not grow too self important" (January 1928, 16, 27).

Of the four brothers, Chris was least involved in the dancing masters' association. In Brigham City he was caught between two worldviews: his father's, in which music and dancing were adornments to a rugged life and talents were gifts from God to be shared freely with one's fellow pioneers in accordance with church policies, and his brothers' more professional outlook, in which skills in music and dance were tools with which to earn one's livelihood. These two views collided in 1903, when Chris's dance orchestra was dismissed from Brigham City's church-run opera house and a smaller, less expensive group was brought in to play for the Saturday night youth dances. Isabell was furious; she insisted hotly that her husband had built up a good business and that he had the right to use his musical skills to provide for his family. So Chris and an associate, C. O. Anderson, decided to open their own dancing establishment, and that summer they erected a large open-air pavilion that sponsored weekly dances in competition with those at the opera house.

As church members of good standing, Chris and his partner informed local ecclesiatical authorities of their professional plans. Despite this polite gesture, those authorities took a dim view of the new commercial enterprise. Although Brigham City had converted to a market economy and individuals were free to earn their living as they pleased, loyalty to church programs and activities was still expected in the predominantly Mormon community. Placing oneself or one's business in direct competition with church activities was frowned upon despite statements from the highest leaders that the Church did not interfere with the private business of its members.[36]

---

[36] For documentation of the controversy over the Brigham City pavilion, see clippings entitled "War at Brigham City" and "The Pavilion Matter to Date" in a file containing background information on the Christensens in the Christensen-Caccialanza Collection, San Francisco Performing Arts Library and Museum. See also "The Pavilion Question," *Box Elder News*, June 25, 1903; "Stake Presidency Explains," *Box Elder News*, July 2, 1903; and "Harmony Is Restored," *Box Elder News*, August 6, 1903.

Dances at the pavilion may have drawn fire from ecclesiastical leaders by allowing an increased number of round dances as part of each evening's activities. The dance tradition among the Mormon pioneers had consisted chiefly of square and line dances, quadrilles and cotillions, in which partners executed figures and formations with limited body contact. In round dances such as the waltz, partners embraced each other (rather than just holding hands) and then upset the decorum of the ballroom by whirling dizzily around the floor. Considered morally suspect, waltzes were usually limited to two or three per evening at church dances, a point of contention in Mormon society because the younger generation wanted only to waltz and had little interest in the dances of the previous generation. Chris and his partner could easily have attracted the youth of Brigham City by offering more waltzes than the church-sponsored dances did. Newspaper reports indicate that nearly three hundred young people frequented the pavilion one Saturday night, shortly after which the opera house changed its dances from Saturday night to Friday to avoid waging a losing battle.

The round dance issue resolved itself with the passage of time; the waltz and the two-step were granted official approval for church dances by 1910, the polka shortly thereafter.[37] But during this transition period, in which Brigham City's civic leaders also tended to be men who held prominent church positions, Chris found himself out of favor in the insular community. In a gesture of defiance, he further distanced himself and his family from the Mormon church by obtaining financial backing and opening a permanent school, the Box Elder Academy of Music and Dancing.

Naturally, the Christensen Orchestra accompanied all classes and dances at the new school, where the "Polite Art of Dancing" was taught as a branch of learning whose objects included "strength, agility, gracefulness of motion,

---

[37] Davis Bitton, "'These Licentious Days': Dancing among the Mormons." *Sunstone* 2.1 (Spring 1977): 25.

ease of manners and politeness."[38] To reassure the parents of prospective students, the Academy's brochure insisted, "Our school is strictly one for dancing, where nothing of promiscuous or public character is allowed."[39] The rules of decorum forbade "loud conversation, profanity, stamping of the feet, whistling, writing on the wall, smoking, spitting, or throwing anything on the floor."[40] With the independent Academy in place, Chris continued to make a living as a musician and music dealer, running his business during weekday hours, teaching ballroom dance classes for adults and children on weekends, and sponsoring dances on Saturday nights, regardless of conflicts with church activities. He maintained high standards of conduct at his ballroom and even bowed to local custom by allowing participants to open activities with prayer, but his activities and policies led to a personal rift with the church that was never reversed.

## The Third Generation

As Lars Christian Christensen's sons married and established separate careers, they carried on the tradition of music and dancing within their own families in different ways. Frederic and Grace had one child, a daughter named Elsa who grew up in the family tradition to the extent that she studied ballet and helped her father by demonstrating social dances at his Seattle school. Because L.P. and his wife Lotta, who assisted him in demonstrating dances and ran the business affairs of the school, had no children, they shared their talents liberally with the young people of Salt Lake City and were especially attentive to their nieces and nephews. L.P. and Lotta were particularly helpful to Jorinda, who married a railroad man, Frank Billings, and was abandoned by him after bearing four

[38] Souvenir Program of the Opening of the Box Elder Academy of Music and Dancing, Season of 1903–1904, 2. Christensen-Caccialanza Collection, San Francisco Performing Arts Library and Museum.

[39] *Ibid.*, 14.

[40] *Ibid.*, 18.

children. Jorinda's son Richard Billings studied with L.P. and specialized in ballroom and tap dancing. Dick Billings, as he was known, would later play a significant role in the life of his cousin Willam.

Mose and Carrie had two sons: Aaron Victor and Paul Richard. The latter died as a child, drowning in an irrigation ditch near the Boise pavilion one summer while Mose was in the East. Carrie reacted to this tragedy by channeling her remaining energies into Victor's training on the violin. She spent a year with him in Brussels, where he studied with Oscar Back and was singled out by the Brussels correspondent of the *Musical Courier* for his rendition of the Paganini Concerto in D Major.[41] The fourteen-year-old was hailed as a child prodigy when he returned to Salt Lake City the summer of 1913; after a triumphant recital, Willard Weihe (who had trained Chris) presented the young teen with a gold medal.[42] Prevented by the outbreak of World War I from returning to Europe, Victor next studied in Manhattan with Leopold Lichtenberg, a former student of the legendary violinist Henri Wieniawsky. Temporarily in Portland with his parents in 1919, Victor played first violin in a string quartet formed by his father Mose (who was violist). Shortly afterwards Victor went to Seattle with a contract to play in that city's symphony orchestra. Ultimately, however, Victor returned to Portland to help run the family ballroom. He followed his father's example and was active in the ANAMD, in which he was elected to national office in 1931.[43]

Chris and Isabell insisted on piano and 'cello lessons for their son Guy and were disappointed when he did not take music seriously and excel as did Mose's son Victor.

---

[41] Two clippings from unspecified Salt Lake papers quote an excerpt from the *Musical Courier*: "Boy Violinist Will Give Concert Tonight" and "Concert by Boy Violinist," probably dated mid-July, 1913; collected in a scrapbook devoted to the career of Victor Christensen in the possession of Delome Sorenson Billings, Bountiful, Utah.

[42] "Youthful Violinist Gives Fine Recital," no paper, no date, probably July 16, 1913, in scrapbook on Victor Christensen, in the possession of Delome Sorenson Billings, Bountiful, Utah.

[43] Mellen, 7.

Instead, Guy married in his late teens and started a family, making the serious development of his musical gifts impractical.

Three more sons were born to Chris and Isabell after they settled in Brigham City. The first was named Christian William Christensen at his birth, August 27, 1902, but the strong-willed Isabell changed his name to William Farr Christensen to include her maiden name.[44] (Later, as a professional dancer and ballet master in San Francisco, William would drop the second "i" from his name and go by "Willam," which he thought sounded more suitable for a dancer in an art form still considered an import from Europe or Russia.) Harold Farr Christensen was born December 25, 1904. So naturally limber that he could stand in a perfect fifth position without strain, he would later joke that he got his perfect turnout for Christmas. The last child, Lewellyn Farr Christensen, was born May 6, 1909, and was named after the doctor who delivered him. The boy rebelled against his first name and went by a shortened version, "Lew," throughout his life.

[44] Conversation with Willam F. Christensen, Salt Lake City, Utah, March 25, 1988.

# 2

## EARLY TRAINING

Willam, Harold, and Lew grew up on Brigham City's Main Street, where the family resided in living quarters behind and above Chris's music store. The family owned a fruit orchard a few blocks away, property inherited from Chris's father Lars. The boys took turns at chores, such as weeding the vegetable garden, picking fruit, and rising at 3:00 a.m. for middle-of-the-night irrigation shifts. In addition to love of God and one's neighbor, Mormon culture espoused industry, thrift, and self-reliance; hard work was a fact of life.

Other values acquired by the brothers at an early age included integrity, sacrifice, and loyalty to family. Heterosexuality and marital fidelity were assumed to be the only acceptable structuring principles for human life and family relations. Although divorced from the immediate influence of the LDS church as a result of her husband's disagreement with local authorities, Isabell reared her sons with strictness according to these ingrained standards. Not given to displays of emotion, Isabell covered sensitive feelings with a brittle outer crust, scoffing at "soft" behavior such as open demonstrations of affection. Harold would inherit her formality, and Lew, her undemonstrative emotional manner.

Musical training fell under the category of developing one's God-given talents. Thus, Chris and Isabell reared their three younger boys in an artistic environment but not a permissive one. Willam spent long hours at the piano when he would rather have been outside playing softball with the neighborhood boys. He also studied the alto horn, on which he performed in the Brigham City Band, and played the drum in his father's orchestra at dances.[1] Harold was instructed on

---

[1] Don McDonagh interview with Willam Christensen, Salt Lake City, Utah, February 26, 1986.

4 Family Portrait. Top: Guy, Chris, and Isabell Christensen. Bottom: Willam, Harold, and Lew Christensen.
Photograph by Amundsen, courtesy of Willam F. Christensen

a child-sized violin by his father, who patiently wrote out notes and demonstrated correct bowing technique. Chris was encouraged by his son's correct form and position in holding the instrument, but Harold ducked out of practicing as often as possible, prepared to endure his mother's scolding and a spanking. Like Chris and Isabell's oldest son Guy, Lew studied the 'cello.

On Saturday afternoons the boys were rounded up, cajoled into serge knickers, white shirts, and gloves, and taken to Chris's children's class at the Academy of Music. Here they learned old-fashioned dances Chris had learned from his father – minuets, quadrilles, and a Danish "Finger Polka" – as well as the two-step and the latest in approved social dances. They mastered the Castle Walk with the knowledge that their uncles knew the famed exhibition ballroom dancers Vernon and Irene Castle. Erect posture and ballroom etiquette were drummed into the boys as part of this training. The Academy's published Rules of Etiquette directed:

> *When a gentleman is about to dance with a lady, he should first execute the proper bow, and if the dance be a quadrille extend the right arm and conduct the lady to the position he has provided for her; when the dance is finished he should lead the lady to her seat, and unless he chooses to sit beside her, bow and withdraw.*[2]

Such courtesies, learned at an early age, formed the basis of chivalrous treatment of women during the brothers' dating years. (Over seventy years later, Jacques d'Amboise, waxing enthusiastic over the Christensens' accomplishments, observed that Balanchine had always liked Willam because he had such perfect manners.[3]) Willam went along with the dancing lessons more graciously than Harold, who hated the "sissy" activity.[4]

In high school Willam developed a taste for jazz music, and towards the end of World War I he formed a Dixieland band with some returning GIs. Willam's enthusiasm for jazz was a thorn in his father's side; Chris could not understand how his son could abandon the musical standards with which the children had been raised. The popularity of the new music also presented a very real threat to business at the Box Elder Academy of Music and Dancing, where social dancing was done to Strauss and Lehar, not jazz.

At the end of World War I the old schism between Chris and local church authorities broke out anew, creating a tension in the small community to which Chris's family became increasingly sensitive. This was particularly upsetting to Isabell, who was a cousin of one of the Mormon apostles, George Albert Smith. The Academy's business declined, and Chris's financial backers decided to replace his orchestra with a band that would play more popular tunes. Ultimately Chris

---

[2] Souvenir of the Opening of the Box Elder Academy of Music and Dancing, Season of 1903–1904, 17.

[3] Interview with Jacques D'Amboise, New York, New York, January 12, 1989.

[4] Interview with Harold F. Christensen, San Anselmo, California, September 22, 1987.

lost his share of the business and had to sell his property to pay taxes. He escaped emotionally from the awful reality of his financial situation by withdrawing to a back room in the family home and playing the violin for hours at a time. Isabell, who had never liked provincial Brigham City, dealt with the situation more decisively. Concluding that the family should move south to Ogden, where her people had figured prominently in the community since its founding, she took the boys and moved, leaving Chris to follow when he could. By 1920 or 1921 the family had completed the transition.[5]

Willam's strong entrepreneurial streak manifested itself early in his teens, when he persuaded Harold to raise pigs with him one summer for spending money. Now graduated from high school, he worked in a dry goods store and got another Dixieland band going to help make ends meet. He also corralled Harold into another moneymaking scheme; this time they sold sheet music outside of theaters, where they caught audiences on their way out and enticed them with songs related to the movie they had just seen.[6] In the wake of Chris's financial problems in Brigham City, Willam gradually assumed the role of *paterfamilias*, bearing much of the responsibility of providing for the family and looking out for his younger brothers.

In Brigham City, Chris's sons had been introduced to ballet technique when L.P.'s students came from Salt Lake to give demonstrations. After Chris and Isabell moved to Ogden, ballet training became part of their sons' lives because L.P., "Uncle Pete" to the boys, maintained a branch of his Salt Lake dancing school in Ogden. Lew recalled later in life that his career in ballet sprang not from any personal desire but because his father took him to L.P.'s studio and admonished,

---

[5] Harold claims the family moved to Ogden in 1918. Willam states that they moved there after World War I, perhaps 1919, but he also clarifies that Isabell took the boys to Ogden before Chris came and made the move permanent. The first printed document that gives evidence of the family's presence in Ogden is the *Utah State Gazetteer and Business Directory* published in 1921.

[6] Interview with Harold Christensen, San Anselmo, California, September 22, 1987.

"Do what your uncle tells you to do."[7] Lew, the baby of the family (seven years younger than Willam, and five younger than Harold), was ten or eleven at the beginning of his formal ballet training. Because he started dancing seriously at a younger age than either of his brothers, Lew profited most from L.P.'s instruction.

Under L.P.'s influence in Ogden, Willam's thinking underwent a gradual evolution. Through dancing he reimmersed himself in classical music and began to feel a bit embarrassed about his Dixieland band. In 1921 he (and probably Lew) saw Anna Pavlova and Alexandre Volinine perform at the Salt Lake Theater. Later that year Mascagno came to Salt Lake City in conjunction with the meetings of the western division of the ANAMD.[8] Members of the Christensen clan came from Seattle and Portland for the occasion.[9]

In anticipation of Mascagno's visit that summer, Chris and L.P. decided that Harold should study with the master as he was the most likely of the boys to succeed in ballet. Lew was still young and inexperienced, and Willam was wrapped up in his music, but Harold had good posture and was blessed with perfect turn-out. Unfortunately, Harold had no intention of studying ballet and flatly refused. Instead, Willam agreed to represent the family.

During that summer workshop, Mascagno taught the best students of the local teachers, while the teachers watched from the sidelines. The master would set up a line of chairs

---

[7] Craig Palmer interview with Lew Christensen for KQED documentary.

[8] There is little evidence concerning exactly which years Mascagno taught in Utah, although it is clear that he came several times. Newspaper clippings document one visit in 1921 and another in 1925. Josephine McKendrick, who was born in 1917, insists that Mascagno came when she was twelve, in 1929, and various interviews suggest that Mascagno returned to teach for Lars Peter and actually lured away some of his students in 1929–1930, during the early part of the Depression.

[9] Mose's son Victor and Fred's daughter Elsa had their pictures in the newspaper with Mascagno, demonstrating the latest popular dance steps. "Here is Official Guide to Newest Dances," *Deseret News*, September 10, 1921, Christensen Family Papers and Scrapbooks, in the possession of Delome Sorenson Billings, Bountiful, Utah.

**5**   Stefano Mascagno with the students of Lars Peter Christensen, Salt Lake City, early 1920s.
Courtesy of San Francisco Performing Arts Library and Museum

behind which those not good enough to do the exercises could work on their own. One day when Willam was unable to perform a combination Mascagno gave, the master banished him to the area behind the chairs. Frederic counseled his nephew, "You'd better practice your *assemblés*."[10] The seriousness with which Uncle Fred offered this advice struck Willam forcefully. To this point he had enjoyed the challenge of ballet, but in a casual sort of way. He had never pursued the mastery of ballet steps with discipline and persistence. That night he did indeed work on his *assemblés*, and the next day Mascagno allowed him back in front of the chairs.

After this experience Willam pursued ballet technique with new commitment. L.P.'s classes, based on his work with

---

[10] Interview with Willam Christensen, Salt Lake City, March 9, 1987. This anecdote is also found in Don McDonagh's interview with Willam Christensen, Salt Lake City, Utah, February 26, 1986.

Mascagno, followed a format recognizable to ballet students today. Exercises recorded by one of his students show that after "bends and stretches," assorted *battements, ronds de jambes,* and *développés* at the barre and in center, Christensen students were taught a respectable variety of allegro combinations demanding strength in the legs. These combinations, done "slow and big" as well as "fast and small," included such standard elements as *échappés, sautés, pas de bourrée, assemblés, jetés* and *jetés brisés, glissades, pas de chat, gorgolades, pas de Basque, cabrioles, sissonnes, royales, entre-chat quatres* and *cinqs, tours jetés, temps de cuisses,* and "petite cabriole front and back continuously with sauté," eight times to each side. *Port de bras* exercises, a variety of turns ("ankle spins," "toe assemblé spins," "arabesque spins," and so on), and "toe work" also had their place. Although most of the recorded exercises are comparable to ballet training today, a few contain instructions that puzzle the contemporary reader; one *développé* combination concludes, "End Grecian runner – floor incovation to front and recover with arm undulations."[11] The directions also indicate a period practice in which girls held the hems of their skirts in their fingers; the preparation for one *port de bras* exercise reads, "Attention take skirts and pose." Records of L.P.'s musical accompaniments indicate a surprisingly heavy reliance on melodies by John Philip Sousa, reflecting perhaps L.P.'s background as a cornet player and his emphasis on allegro combinations.[12] Although some of the embellishments are foreign, these teaching records attest that L.P.'s nephews received a thorough grounding in the balletic vocabulary, a fact that some colleagues questioned later upon

---

[11] All references to L.P.'s exercises are taken from a typescript record in the possession of Delome Sorenson Billings of Bountiful, Utah. Delome Billings studied with L.P., married one of his nephews, and made this record in anticipation of moving away from Utah and setting up her own studio.

[12] Of the forty-three exercises for which the accompaniment is indicated, John Philip Sousa leads the composers with fifteen instances. Strauss places a respectable second with ten, Waldteufel and Lehar have a few each, and a scattering of other composers (of which Tchaikovsky, Grieg, Chopin, and Dvorak are the best known) have one mention each.

learning that the Christensens came from a small town in Utah.

As Willam improved, L.P. insisted that his nephew take over the Ogden branch of his school, which seemed an overwhelming responsibility given that some of the other students were nearly as proficient as Willam himself. He relied heavily on his uncle, using many of the same exercises that L.P. used. When Willam needed music for his accompanist, he would borrow pen and paper and copy his L.P.'s class music onto staff paper note by note. Another resource at Willam's disposal was his uncle's copy of Friedrich Zorn's *Grammar of the Art of Dancing*, a late nineteenth-century treatise that had been reissued in 1905 for the members of the ANAMD.

At age twenty, Willam went to New York by himself to study with Mascagno.[13] Lessons with the "Maestro," as Mascagno's students addressed their teacher, followed strict rules of protocol. Mascagno's Manhattan studio had a dressing room for the girls only, so the boys would change into their practice clothes – full shirts open at the neck, satin knickers and sashes, stockings, and ballet slippers – in the studio itself and then fold their street clothes neatly and hide them under the pillows of the window seat. The students then waited outside in the hall until music within the studio provided their cue to enter. The girls entered and curtsied, the boys entered and bowed, all took their places at the barre, and no one moved until Mascagno tapped his cane.

Following this introductory ritual, Mascagno gave a set barre approximately twenty minutes long, followed by port de bras exercises and the repetition of the entire barre sequence in center to improve the students' balance. Then came adagio combinations (slow sustained movement),

---

[13] Nigel S. Hey reports that Willam went to New York to study at age twenty in "Professor in Ballet Slippers," *Dance Magazine*, May 1963, 48. The exact dates and number of times Willam accompanied Lars Peter to summer Normal Schools is uncertain, although Willam recalls going several times and Harold asserts that Willam and Lew went annually; see interview with Harold Christensen, San Anselmo, California, September 22, 1987.

mezzo-allegro and allegro work, pointe work for the girls, and turns. The latter included circles of *chaîné* turns and multiple circles of *coupés jetés*. One of Mascagno's specialties was a *grand renversé* in which the dancer's working leg whipped around in a high arc from the front to the back of body, causing the dancer to spin on the supporting leg while his arms opened overhead. The Italian was also known for his skill in teaching pirouettes.[14] At the conclusion of the ninety-minute class, the students bowed formally before leaving the studio – the traditional ballet *révérence*. Mascagno's teaching may have reflected the Italian style that Barzel describes as "much foot work, stiff backs, and no extension work."[15] Certainly, he was more concerned with developing strength in the legs than with flexibility or high extensions. In this era the Christensens were satisfied that in Mascagno's teaching they had an authentic tie to the European balletic tradition.

During the years that Willam was seriously pursuing a career in ballet, Harold took a separate path. In the fall of 1922 he went to Seattle, where he lived with the recently divorced Uncle Fred. There Harold completed his junior year in high school and assisted in Frederic's ballroom dance classes. At the end of that year, Harold returned to Ogden. He joined the R.O.T.C., in which he achieved the rank of a major, and graduated from Ogden High School in 1924. In the inscription under his yearbook picture, he predicted, "I will be the leader of an army or a band, or sit at a desk." The army was apparently his first choice, and he was thrilled when he won an appointment to West Point.

Harold was the most academically inclined of the three brothers, and he disapproved of the way Willam pushed Lew's ballet studies. Willam, driven by his own enthusiasm for ballet and realizing Lew's potential, would get his youngest brother out of school early and put the two of them

---

[14] Ann Barzel, "European Dance Teachers in the United States," *Dance Index* 3 (April–June 1944): 82.

[15] Barzel, 78.

through demanding workouts before the other students arrived at the studio for afternoon classes. This angered Lew's teachers and the high school principal, who did not understand why the boy should not finish high school properly and then dance if he wished.[16] But Willam, who had started ballet training late, understood the necessity of molding a body while it was still young and flexible, and he oversaw Lew's training with a sense of urgency. When Lew was deemed old enough, Willam took him along to the ANAMD's summer Normal School sessions to train with Mascagno.

Harold went off to West Point in the fall of 1924. His strict personal discipline and the erect bearing that accentuated his six foot two inch height gave him a distinguished air and augured well for a career in the military. He endured the customary hazing without difficulty but suffered emotionally over the death of his high school sweetheart. Unfortunately, his secondary education had not prepared him adequately for the rigors of the military academy. At the end of his first year, Harold failed an English class and was dismissed. According to West Point policy, he could have made up the course and reapplied for admission, but he was too discouraged to do so.[17] Certainly, he received little encouragement in this direction from his parents. Chris and Isabell were not oriented to higher education, and Chris considered college a waste of time for performers, who (he reasoned) were better off polishing their talents than filling their heads with book learning. Rather than earning readmittance to West Point, Harold quietly acquiesced to his father's original desires and entered the family business. He taught

---

[16] Although a photograph shows Lew in a high school R.O.T.C. group, existing Ogden High School records and yearbooks give no evidence that Lew either attended or graduated from high school.

[17] Conversation with Diane McGhee, Registrar's Office, West Point Military Academy, November 14, 1989. There is some confusion over when Harold's girlfriend died, whether it was before or after he left for West Point, but the loss affected him greatly. He mentioned it as one of the reasons he did not do well academically. Another reason might be that the Brigham City schools had not prepared him adequately in the area of writing and grammar.

ballroom dancing in the Ogden school and continued his education as he could by enrolling in business courses at the local college.[18] He also began taking ballet classes, not from Uncle Pete but from his brother Willam.[19]

In Ogden, the Christensens were exposed to a variety of dance acts that came through on the vaudeville circuit. The most common form of dance in vaudeville was the so-called "adagio act," in which a strong man would lift and throw his female partner around the stage in striking positions. Such acts were more acrobatic than balletic but often incorporated classical poses or lifts. Another hybrid dance act to come through Ogden was that of Lola Menzeli, a protégé of Elizabetta Menzeli, who combined classical technique with Spanish dancing.[20] After seeing a Russian act that included continuous *tours en l'air*, jumping straight up and turning around before landing, several times in rapid succession, Willam and Lew experimented in the studio until they mastered the feat.[21] The enterprising Willam was always on the lookout for performers whom he could invite to give master classes in the family's school. When the Russian song and dance act of Louis Berkoff came through Ogden, Willam paid Berkoff to come to the school and give classes in Russian character dancing.

As Willam's technique and confidence increased, he expanded the activities and ambitions of the Christensen School of Dancing in Ogden, of which he was the acknowledged "Principal" by age twenty-three. By the time Harold

---

[18] Harold enrolled at Weber Academy during the 1925–1926 academic year.

[19] Interview with Harold Christensen, San Anselmo, California, September 22, 1987.

[20] Willam claims she wore pointe shoes augmented by red-and-black heels so that she could run across the stage on the tips of her toes and then break out into Flamenco-style stamping! He describes this act variously in his interview with the author, Salt Lake City, March 9, 1987, and in the Don McDonagh interview with Willam Christensen, Salt Lake City, February 26, 1986. Joe Laurie, Jr., reports that Menzeli, known as "Girlie" in the act "Bankoff & Girlie," was "once picked by Adele Genee as one of the best dancers in the world." Joe Laurie, Jr., *Vaudeville: From the Honky-Tonks to the Palace* (New York: Henry Holt and Company, 1953), 46.

[21] Interview with Willam Christensen, Salt Lake City, Utah, February 20, 1987.

**6** Lew Christensen and Frances Peddlar with students of the Ogden school. Diagonal left to right: Jeanette Reeder, Millicent Neil, Dorothy Young, Martha Boyer, Ruth Paine, Oretel Aadneson, Mignon Lee, Josephine Watson.
Photograph by Ford Studio, courtesy of San Francisco Performing Arts Library and Museum

committed himself to the family school in Ogden (1925), Willam had built up a thriving business and had instituted annual "Dance Revues" to showcase the students' talents. The school recitals, which usually took place in a local vaudeville house, were family productions in every respect. Chris, the school's music director, conducted an orchestra composed of local musicians. Isabell, who regularly tended to matters of student fees and enrollments as the school's secretary, designed the costumes. L.P. contributed choreography, while Willam danced and rehearsed the students with assistance from Harold and a tap dance teacher, Gene Robinson. Lew was a featured performer; one year Uncle Pete even set a version of Fokine's *Spectre de la Rose* as a vehicle for Lew's growing abilities.[22] (Family tradition maintains that Mose and L. P. saw Nijinsky perform with Diaghilev's Ballets Russes; family papers include a souvenir program from the company's 1916–1917 American tour.)

Willam's chief competition in Ogden was an established teacher named Sophia Reed, who had studied with Chalif and was in charge of physical education in the public schools. Reed considered Willam an undesirable upstart and berated him for running a school when he himself had no college education. Willam was not overly concerned about such criticism because his goal was not to teach but to perform. He saw teaching as a necessary but temporary solution to the family's financial situation. In retrospect, the family school under Willam's direction might be considered just another one of his moneymaking schemes, but this time all the pieces fit together; each family member contributed to the successful functioning of the whole according to his or her individual talents. The family dance business under Willam provided dependable income at a time when Chris and Isabell had no practical alternative.

During the summer of 1925, Mascagno came to Salt Lake again to give master classes for two weeks following the annual meeting of the ANAMD in Los Angeles. In Utah he informed the press of his extreme dissatisfaction with the dancing masters' organization, from which he had just resigned (after teaching its Normal School nine summers running). Asserting that ballet was "the foundation of all legitimate dancing," he proclaimed that it was "folly to think that a teacher can give instruction in any form of social dancing without some understanding of ballet."[23] Mascagno

---

[22] Interview with Willam Christensen, Salt Lake City, Utah, March 9, 1987. According to Willam, Lew fell from a tree the day of the performance, and Willam had to step in at the last minute. Unused to the part, Willam got tangled in his cape during the performance.

[23] "Dance Masters to Organize: Three Utahns Will Take Active Part in New Ballet Organization," unattributed clipping in a family scrapbook in the possession of Willam Christensen.

was clearly exasperated with the social dance teachers, who evinced little serious interest in mastering classical technique. The idealistic goals expressed at the founding of the summer Normal School in 1917, including the hope that it would further a National School of Ballet, remained unmet. So Mascagno resigned from the dancing masters' association in protest and founded a new organization: The Ballet Teachers Association of America.[24] Frederic, L.P., and Willam withdrew from ANAMD along with Mascagno to join the new association. In view of the Christensens' involvement, Mascagno decided the organization should be headquartered in Salt Lake City. L.P. composed an impassioned plea for a National Ballet school on the grounds that America was the only nation rich enough to nurture this "art of arts."[25]

In retrospect, it is easy to sympathize with Mascagno's impatience with social dance teachers he considered dilettantes. From today's vantage point, the hopes he and the Christensens expressed for nurturing the growth of ballet in America sound logical enough. Balletic activity had increased significantly during the fifteen years since Pavlova's 1910 debut at the Metropolitan Opera. Gertrude Hoffman had presented a "Saison Russe" in New York (1911); Mikhail Mordkin had toured with a group called the Russian Imperial All-Star Ballet (1911–1912); Diaghilev's Ballets Russes had toured major cities (1916–17); Adolph Bolm had organized his Ballet Intime (1917); Michel Fokine had opened a school in New York (1919) and had staged various productions; and John Alden Carpenter's *Krazy Kat*, with choreography by

---

[24] In addition to the sketchy information on this attempt available from newspaper clippings in Utah, confirmation comes from Ann Barzel's 1944 *Dance Index* article on European Dancing Masters in the United States. On p. 82, Barzel states, "At one time Mascagno and his friends the Christensens . . . considered forming a ballet teachers' association that would eliminate the difficulties experienced in trying to teach artistic ballet work in a mixed organization. Another project in which Maestro was active was the attempt, together with Veronine Vestoff and Desiree Lubovska, to start a National American Ballet."

[25] "Makes Plea for Ballet: Dancing Master Says America Should Develop This Art," unattributed clipping in a family scrapbook in the possession of Willam Christensen.

Bolm, had premiered in 1922.[26] Chicago had witnessed the debut of Carpenter's *Skyscrapers*, "a ballet of modern American life in six scenes" (1920), while the company of Andreas Pavley and Serge Oukrainsky touted itself the "first American ballet and official ballet of Chicago Civic Opera."[27] "American ballet" was a tag readily appropriated by interested parties. When Fokine and his wife, Vera, organized a student company, they termed it "American Ballet" (1924). And the Hungarian born, Viennese-trained ballerina Albertina Rasch, who had made her American debut at the New York Hippodrome in 1910 and who directed groups of highly trained girls in vaudeville and Broadway revues, would publish her theories on American ballet just two years later (1927), when she and her troupe toured under the banner "Albertina Rasch and her American Ballet."[28] Clearly, Mascagno and the Christensens were not the only ones interested in furthering the art of ballet in America. Conditioned by the tradition of teacher associations, they assumed that an organization of American ballet teachers was the most direct path to this goal. But the hoped-for Ballet Teachers Association of America, which one might interpret as the product of Mascagno's purist ideals, seconded by L.P., and Willam's ambition, never got off the ground. Whether or not Mascagno made a real effort to contact ballet teachers in other cities, the decision to make Salt Lake City the headquarters was hardly a politic move given the limited communications systems of that era. A different set of circumstances would produce an organization named the School of American Ballet and would work to further ballet as an American art form, and a Christensen would be involved, but not in this way, not at this time.

---

[26] For more on balletic activity in the United States during this period, see George Amberg, *Ballet* (New York: New American Library, 1949), 191–92, and Suzanne Carboneau Levy, "The Russians Are Coming: Russian Dancers in the United States, 1910–1933" (Ph.D. diss, New York University, Graduate School of Arts and Science, 1990).

[27] Amberg, op.cit.

[28] For more on Rasch's theories of American ballet, see Frank W. D. Ries, "Albertina Rasch: The Concert Career and the Concept of the American Ballet," *Dance Chronicle* 7.2 (1984): 159–97.

Willam's commitment to ballet did not preclude an active participation in popular culture. The same year he resigned from ANAMD, his Ogden school sponsored a city-wide Charleston contest boasting four evenings of eliminations and a grand sweepstakes, complete with cash prizes and trophies. During the 1925–1926 season he and his brothers, supported by advanced students from the school, began appearing in movie "prologues," staged presentations shown in conjunction with films and usually on a related topic. A group from the Christensen school performed a "barefoot ballet" before showings of *The Loves of Pharaoh*. In "Indian Courtship," the prologue to Zane Grey's *The Vanishing American*, Willam, costumed as a Native American, fell to the stage and died with his feet in first position, much to the amusement of kids in the balcony.[29] The brothers also performed in Salt Lake in revues of L.P.'s school, where Willam and Lew were members of the "professional class." For a prologue to be shown with *The Ten Commandments*, Uncle Pete set a bacchanale in which Harold in the role of Moses stood and recited the ten commandments while the other dancers rushed about the stage in idolatrous worship of the golden calf.[30]

Such performing opportunities whetted Willam's desire for a career in show business. He had not grown up with preconceived ideas about ballet being an aristocratic art form suited only to opera house settings; instead, he had faith in ballet's ability to appeal to mass audiences, assuming it were presented correctly. On the other hand, he was well aware of the prevailing sentiment in America that ballet was a foreign art form. When the family's Ogden school moved to new premises in 1926, he changed its name to the Le Crist School of Dancing, citing "professional reasons," and the feelings of school graduates going on to performing careers.[31]

---

[29] Conversation with Willam F. Christensen, Salt Lake City, Utah, April 27, 1987.

[30] Unfortunately, Harold got flustered during the performances and was never able to get past the eighth commandment. Interview with Harold Christensen, San Anselmo, California, September 22, 1987.

[31] "Dance School Forging Ahead," unattributed clipping, probably from the *Ogden Standard Examiner*, in a family scrapbook in the possession of Willam Christensen.

While Willam had a passion for the physical challenge of ballet, Lew was fascinated with the world of the theater in general. As a child he built model stages and experimented with how to light them. He studied the local vaudeville house, saw how it was rigged, and learned how the wings related to the stage area.[32] At age seventeen he acted in a production of *Everybody's Husband*, a fantasy by Gilbert Cannon that the Drama Club Players of Ogden performed in Salt Lake. Willam was away studying with Mascagno at the time, and Lew wrote his older brother earnestly that although he was not being paid, it was good experience.[33] The Le Crist School's recitals also gave Lew a chance to consolidate his knowledge of practical stagecraft, as he helped set up lights and give cues. When the time came to leave Ogden for a performing career, Lew was well versed in how to run a show.

By 1927, Willam was anxious to quit teaching and to dance professionally. Nearly twenty-five years old, he had not given up his social life, endured countless train rides to Salt Lake, crossed the country repeatedly to study with Mascagno, and submitted to several years of physically grueling training only to spend what he felt were his best years teaching beginners in the family school. Lew, now eighteen, had no interest in higher education and saw vaudeville as a ticket out of Utah. By that summer, circumstances were beginning to look favorable: Harold now had enough experience with the family school that he could be prevailed upon to take it over, thus freeing Willam to leave.[34]

Of the three brothers, Harold was the most like his mother; his personality could be stern on the surface, but underneath the bluster he was generous and even self-sacrificing. When Willam asked Harold to give up the college

[32] "Lew Christensen," in Barbara Newman, *Striking a Balance: Dancers Talk About Dancing* (London: Elm Tree Books, 1982), 41.

[33] Don McDonagh interview with Willam Christensen, Salt Lake City, Utah, February 26, 1986.

[34] Harold had by this time acquired enough ballet technique to take over the school. He recalls having studied with a former Bolshoi ballerina, Julietta Mendez, sometime during this era, perhaps the summer of 1926. Interview with Harold Christensen, San Anselmo, California, September 22, 1987.

**7** Harold Christensen, late 1920s.
Photograph by Hanshaw, courtesy of Special Collections, University of
Utah Marriott Library

classes he had enrolled in and to assume responsibility for the Ogden school (arguing that he could always go back to school later), Harold protested but stepped in to fill the need.

Willam made inquiries about breaking into vaudeville and began putting together an act comprised of himself, Lew, and three of the school's most advanced female students – Catherine O'Donnell, Yvonne Mack, and Frances Peddlar. Adopting the name of the school, they called themselves the "Le Crist Revue." It was agreed that Chris would travel with them and conduct their music, while Isabell would remain in Ogden with Harold and the school. Thus the family organization, spurred on by Willam, divided and reformed itself to pursue new opportunities.

Chris and Isabell's oldest son, Guy, and his wife had moved to Ogden when the rest of the family relocated there. Guy's daughter Carol took dancing lessons at the Christensen school, but he continued to pursue a separate existence. Guy worked for the utility company and later went back to school, studied accounting, and got a job as a bookkeeper working for the state. Because Guy was several years older than the rest of the sons, because he married young and eventually moved away, and especially because he was the only one not to pursue a career in dance, the three younger brothers did not feel as close to Guy as they did to each other. Guy did not figure in the course of their careers, and few of their professional associates were even aware that there was a fourth brother. Visits with Guy were infrequent, and for the most part the three younger brothers' lives played out as if Guy had never existed.[35]

---

[35] Willam saw his oldest brother from time to time after returning to Utah in 1951. But then Guy retired to California, where he died in 1975.

# 3

# LIFE ON THE CIRCUIT (1927–1934)

When Willam, Lew, their partners, and Chris arrived in Los Angeles to break into vaudeville during the summer of 1927, they were entering a branch of show business in its twilight years. This form of variety entertainment had flourished through the Gay Nineties and the first two decades of the twentieth century, featuring comedians, singers, jugglers and acrobats, dancers, trained animals, skits and pantomimists, magicians, and female impersonators. Twice a day entertainers would go through their acts, each having only fifteen or twenty minutes to capture the public's imagination before giving way to the next feature. After a week's engagement, each act would be off to the next town along the "circuit," as dictated by bookers in "hub" cities, such as New York, Chicago, and Los Angeles.

The primacy of vaudeville as "amusement manna for the masses" remained unchallenged until the 1920s, when motion pictures began to encroach upon the domain of the live performer.[1] Soon the double threat of radio programs, which kept audiences home from the theaters, and motion pictures with sound (beginning with Al Jolson's *The Jazz Singer* in 1927) prompted a decline in attendance at theatres devoted solely to vaudeville.

Newspaper reviews and clippings cited are taken from two sets of family records, unless otherwise noted: (1) three scrapbooks containing vaudeville materials in the Christensen–Caccialanza Collection on deposit at the San Francisco Performing Arts Library and Museum; and (2) loose clippings in Box 1, Folders 4 and 5 and bound scrapbooks, Nos. 1 and 2, in the Utah Ballet Archives, Special Collections, University of Utah Marriott Library, Salt Lake City, Utah. A chronology of vaudeville performances compiled by the author is also available at the San Francisco Performing Arts Library and Museum.

[1] Charles and Louise Samuels, *Once Upon a Stage: The Merry World of Vaudeville* (New York: Dodd, Mead and Company, 1964), 266.

    In response to the public's taste for the new "talkies,"
short motion pictures were added to the line-up of live acts.
"Vaudefilm" was the term coined for this new composite
genre of live acts plus films, and it had swept the country by
the time the Christensens entered show business. So pervasive
was the change that by 1926 only a dozen theaters in America
still offered only "big time" (known and respected) live
entertainers.[2] "The leisurely presented two-a-day all-star
vaudeville bill has gone forever," lamented the entertainment
industry's mouthpiece *Variety* a few months after the
Christensens arrived in Los Angeles. "There may be a pre-
tense of keeping it up a little longer ... [but] the movies have
so badly punished Big Time that Big Time has had to come
down to the movies."[3]
    Even under these disintegrating circumstances, vaude-
ville promised the most likely outlet for the Christensens'
talents. Despite the previously cited examples of balletic
activity between 1910 and 1925, America had few actual ballet
companies at this time. Even the precursors to the New York
City Ballet and American Ballet Theatre would not be
founded for nearly a decade. Catherine Littlefield, one of the
pioneers of American ballet, was teaching at her mother's
ballet school in Philadelphia and would not found the Littlefield Ballet until the mid-1930s. Instead, a few ballet troupes
existed within the framework of opera houses, such as the
Metropolitan Opera in New York and the Chicago Civic
Opera, but even the flourishing San Francisco Opera would
have no *corps de ballet* until 1932. And in 1927 the term "Ballets
Russes" still referred to the original company in Europe under
Diaghilev's dominion, not the competing troupes which
would later tour with the remnants of his repertory.
    In contrast to the relative dearth of independent ballet
companies, vaudeville line-ups had included a variety of
dance acts for decades: "buck and wing" style tap dancers;
exhibition ballroom dancers; skirt dancers; specialty numbers

---

[2] Samuels and Samuels, 265.

[3] "Passing of Vaudeville," *Variety*, September 21, 1927. Not from Christensen family scrapbook.

presenting the dances of foreign cultures; and acrobatic adagio teams with balletic poses. In big-time vaudeville, terpsichorean "class acts" such as Harriet Hoctor's dance numbers on pointe were often included on bills to lend an aura of culture, educational value, and prestige. (No matter that Hoctor's signature stunt was a deep backbend, which she maintained while bouréeing quickly across the stage and then turning in place.) It was not unusual for classically trained dancers to work in the context of the commercial theater; artists as renowned as Fokine and Pavlova had performed at the Hippodrome in New York City. A former Diaghilev dancer, Chester Hale, maintained a ballet troupe at the Capitol Theatre, and in the late 1920s Léonide Massine was leading dancer and ballet master at the Roxy Theatre. Albertina Rasch's dancers traveled the vaudeville circuit; why shouldn't Uncle Pete's protégés do likewise? Based on their experiences in movie prologues and variety revues in Utah, the Christensens were convinced they could present their brand of dancing in a way that would please a wide audience and fit into the varied line-up of a vaudeville bill. Their immediate goal was to make money, and vaudeville was their first, best hope.

In Los Angeles, the Christensens and their partners studied with the former Bolshoi ballerina Julietta Mendez in order to keep up their technique while waiting for their big break. They auditioned for one booker who said he would like to see their act and scheduled them for a performance in a local theater. After the show he suggested a few changes and invited the eager performers to do it again. By the third time the Utahns were asked to perform without pay, they realized they were being used and refused to be taken in by such tactics again. The Le Crist Revue finally got a bona fide engagement, appearing at the Los Angeles Hippodrome the week of August 7, 1927. Next to last on the line-up, their act was billed not as ballet but as a "European Dance Novelty."[4]

---

[4] Copy of program, Hippodrome, Los Angeles, California, Week of August 7, 1927, in Christensen Family vaudeville scrapbook, San Francisco Performing Arts Library and Museum.

Louis Berkoff, whose act with Russian music and dancing had come through Ogden, was in Los Angeles at the time, and he struck a deal with Willam that assured the Christensens ongoing employment. The Le Crist Revue adopted Berkoff's name and acquired bookings as a second Berkoff company, in exchange for 40 per cent of their earnings.[5] So, billed as Russian dancers, Willam, Lew, and their three female partners toured the small-time vaudeville circuits of southern California. They incorporated some Russian character steps taught them by Berkoff into their routine and wore brightly colored costumes with full, Cossack-style pants to reinforce their Russian image.

While billed as the Berkoffs, the Christensens were routed on to Chicago. In the process the brothers lost two of their original partners, Frances Peddlar and Catherine O'Donnell. Anxious to recast the act, Willam sent word of the openings to Mignon Lee, his girlfriend in Ogden, who was one of the advanced students in the family school. Mignon would have been in the act from the start if her conservative father had not disapproved of his daughter going into vaudeville with a boyfriend seven years her senior. (He had also disapproved of her bra-and-harem-pants costume for one of Willam's "Egyptian" ballets.) The second time the invitation came, Mignon was eighteen and was apparently deemed old enough to leave home. Excited at the prospect of life in show business with the Christensens, Mignon and one of Uncle Pete's advanced students, Wiora Stoney, traveled to Chicago to join the group.[6]

---

[5] The contract establishing their partnership specified that Willam would function as road manager (in addition to performing) and that Berkoff would be the act's business manager from September 1, 1927, to September 1, 1928.

[6] According to Willam's memories, Frances Peddlar and Yvonne Mack did not go on to Chicago but stayed in Utah when the act went through there on its way east. Catherine O'Donnell left the act in Chicago, at which point Willam wrote to Mignon and asked her to join them. Elyse Meredith Crockett Chase tells the story differently, claiming that Yvonne Mack went with the group to New York before quitting the act due to knee problems.

**8** Willam and Lew Christensen in Berkoff costumes.
Photograph by Theatrical Studio, courtesy of Special Collections, University of Utah Marriott Library

If Mignon's father had known the circumstances that faced the Christensens in Chicago, he might have prevented his daughter from joining them. Neither their Utah upbringing nor California touring had prepared the Christensens for Chicago's seedy side, where pimps and prostitutes accosted Willam and Lew on the street near their inexpensive boarding house. Prohibition Chicago in the late 1920s was a center for organized crime, the home of Al Capone, and the site of violent gang wars over liquor territory. It was in Chicago during this stormy period that Willam came to see unions as a hindrance to be overcome rather than as benign protectors of a performer's rights. In one theater the Berkoffs were caught in a dispute between a theater manager and the stagehand's union, which wanted the manager to hire another hand. The union man who ran the spotlight, in an attempt to sabotage the show, intentionally aimed the spot away from the action onstage. When Willam and Lew made a big entrance, the light switched to the waiting women, and when the women entered, the spot ignored them in favor of the men standing upstage. Incensed at this mockery of their performance, Willam stopped cold and walked to the edge of the stage. "That's enough," he said firmly to his father, who was conducting the house orchestra, and the dancers walked off. Once backstage the brothers worried that the union stagehands might retaliate by refusing to take down the act's backdrop, but such fears proved groundless. The Christensens were not the target of the union's protest, only pawns in its dispute with the management. Still, the frustrating experience influenced Willam's unfavorable attitudes towards unions for years to come.[7]

The silver lining of the dancers' Chicago experience was their opportunity to study with Laurent Novikoff, a graduate of the Moscow Imperial Ballet School who had performed with the Bolshoi Ballet and Diaghilev's Ballets Russes. One of Pavlova's last partners, Novikoff had danced

---

[7] Interview with Willam F. Christensen, Salt Lake City, Utah, October 7, 1988.

with the famous ballerina at the Salt Lake Theatre in 1925; Uncle Pete had taken Willam and Lew to the performance. Novikoff had his own studio in Chicago, and beginning in 1929 he served as ballet master of the Chicago Civic Opera for four seasons. The Russian was less doctrinaire in his approach to classical technique than Uncle Pete and had a more fluid style of movement than Mascagno. He was particularly good at teaching boys how to handle a partner skillfully in pas de deux work, which would later be one of Lew's strengths.[8] Working with Novikoff lessened the brothers' psychological dependence on Mascagno, who had always been held up to them as the ultimate authority on ballet. Whenever the brothers traveled through Chicago in succeeding years, they made a point of taking class with Novikoff.

The Christensens and their partners learned the ropes of touring in small-time vaudeville, where the life of a performer was far from glamorous. More often than not, the theaters in which they worked had cramped wings, crowded dressing rooms, and stage doors that opened into dirty alleyways. Determined to make a name for themselves, the Utahns met the challenges of life on the circuit with resourcefulness. During cold winter months they put newspapers under their mattresses for added insulation, and when possible they put daybeds in their dressing rooms, to rest between shows. Lew continued to practice the 'cello under his father's tutelage; on train hops between cities he even shared his berth with the instrument to keep it with him.

Like other dancers in vaudeville, the Christensens faced the recurring problem of slippery stages. Stage managers generally disliked the use of resin on their floors, and comedians who needed a slick surface if their act required them to slip and fall could get downright hostile when dancers spread resin across the boards. Fred Astaire solved this problem by sneaking into dark theaters to sprinkle the

---

[8] Ann Barzel, "European Dance Teachers in the United States," *Dance Index* 3 (April–June 1944): 86.

sticky powder on the stage when no one else was about.[9]
Willam's favorite trick was to walk around the stage conversing with other performers, gesticulating with one hand while
he crumbled resin behind his back with the other. As a backup, the dancers placed rubber pads covered with resin
directly on the stage so that they could step on them unob-
trusively while the act was in progress.

Touring small-time theaters billed as the Berkoffs
brought income but not personal fulfillment to the Christensens. Willam, always the most ambitious of the family,
would not be satisfied until the act had earned a respectable
niche in the world of big-time vaudeville, fading though
that world might be. Louis Berkoff's agent in Chicago sent
the Christensens on a Northeastern tour that ended in New
York City, where they hoped to be picked up by one
of the major circuits.

Arriving in New York sometime during the fall of
1928, Chris, his sons, and their partners moved in with two
other dancers from Utah who hoped to find fame on the stage:
Deane and Elyse Crockett. Deane had taken up dancing after
meeting the Christensens as a youth in Ogden; Elyse had been
one of Uncle Pete's students and had performed with Willam
and Lew in L.P.'s revues. After the Crocketts' marriage in
1927, they had moved to Manhattan, where they studied with
different teachers because that was the best way to get a job
in the commercial theater. Deane worked with Fokine while
Elyse took class from Mascagno and performed occasionally
with Chester Hale's group at the Capitol Theatre. During the
fall of 1928 the Crocketts shared their apartment at 616 W.
113th Street with the Christensens, and when Yvonne Mack
(one of the Christensens' original partners) returned to Utah
because of an injured knee, Elyse took her place in the
Berkoff act.

*Variety* acknowledged the Berkoffs' arrival with a
review in its "New Acts" column. "Company apparently all

[9] John E. DeMeglio, *Vaudeville U.S.A.* (Bowling Green, Ohio: Bowling Green University Popular Press, 1973), 173–74.

Russian," ran the description. "Usual hock stepping, knee dropping and spinning present, but of high standard."[10] Encouraged by the article's conclusion that their act was "capable for big time with some work under its belt," the Christensens lived frugally with their fellow Utahns, shared expenses, and waited anxiously for their big break. Having no immediate income, Mignon and Wiora wrote home for money, while Chris and sons received support from Harold, who was running the family school in Ogden. The dancers knew what it was to be hungry; one night when the person fixing dinner accidentally dropped their fried fish onto the top of the garbage, the group devoured it anyway.

While they waited to be picked up by one of the big circuits, the Christensens and their partners took daily class from Mascagno. For his part, the maestro was dissatisfied with the Berkoff format for his protégés. Even if vaudeville must provide the context for their performances, he felt they should appear as *danseurs nobles* in the highest classical tradition, not Russian character dancers. So the Italian offered to manage their act; if they dropped the Berkoff format, he would lend them his name, refine their choreography, and get an agent to book them. Mascagno even promised not to cut his hair until they were successfully launched into big-time careers.

Willam, Lew, Mignon, and Wiora gladly accepted Mascagno's offer and rehearsed their new act diligently. Months passed; Mascagno's hair grew long, and the dancers grew impatient. The Christensens felt trapped; to go after bookings themselves was to risk the wrath of the proud ballet master, but how long would they be expected to wait? When a few scattered engagements over six months produced no extended contracts, Willam took matters into his own hands. He contacted a New York agent named Jack Hart, who was surprised to hear how long the Christensens had been unemployed. In short order, Hart arranged an audition before some

---

[10] Bige, "Berkoff Dancers," *Variety*, October 24, 1928.

circuit bookers in New Jersey. A few days later, word came
that the Christensens and their partners, now billed as the
"Mascagno Four," had been selected for a transcontinental
tour on the Radio-Keith-Orpheum (R.K.O.) circuit that would
include an appearance at the Palace, the most prestigious
theater in vaudeville.[11]

The new act's forte was male virtuosity – tours de
force guaranteed to impress audiences unfamiliar with the
fine points of the balletic tradition. The structure of the act
was based loosely on the format of the traditional grand pas
de deux, with its opening adagio section, female variation,
male variation, and coda full of spectacular technical feats.
Mascagno added an extra adagio section after the female
variation, emphasized the male contribution, and doubled the
formula for two couples. The four entered to a fanfare, and
then Willam partnered Mignon and Lew partnered Wiora in
pointe work and poses that mirrored each other, creating the
symmetrical stage composition found in so many of their
newspaper ads. In a step they called "the fan" the brothers
lifted their partners in a circular sweep over their shoulders
and then brought them down into arabesque on pointe. The
men left the stage while the women did a short variation on
pointe, following which the men returned for the second
adagio section. In the fast-paced finale, Lew performed
multiple pirouettes and *tours à la seconde* while Willam did
*coupés jetés* around him. Then Mignon and Wiora ran to their
partners, who caught them with a flourish for a dramatic
ending.[12]

In addition to traditional ballet steps and positions,
Mascagno inserted a backbend on pointe for Mignon and
Wiora (shades of Harriet Hoctor!). To a drumroll in the music,
the brothers would lower their partners by one hand until

---

[11] The story about getting booked as the Mascagno Four is told in different versions
in Olga Maynard's "The Christensens: An American Dance Dynasty" (*Dance
Magazine* June 1973, 48), Willam Christensen's interview for the KQED biography of
Lew Christensen, and the author's interview with Willam Christensen in Salt Lake
City, Utah, February 20, 1987.

[12] Interview with Willam Christensen, Salt Lake City, Utah, February 20, 1987.

**9**   The Mascagno Four vaudeville act: Willam Christensen, Wiora Stoney, Mignon Lee, and Lew Christensen, in Venetian costumes.
Photograph by Acme, courtesy of Willam F. Christensen

their heads touched the floor. They would let go of the women's hands, the women would blow a kiss to the audience, and the men would raise them up again, to predictable cheering from the crowd. Mascagno may not have wanted the Christensens to appear as Russian character dancers, but he was not against inserting elements guaranteed to appeal to popular tastes. As Harold later admitted, "It was classical ballet hoked up quite a bit."[13]

Mascagno set his choreography to excerpts from ballet music by Delibes, Luigini's *Ballet Egyptien* (which had been

---

[13] KQED interview with Harold Christensen. The backbends were an obvious concession to popular tastes and were not uncommon. Other dancers besides Hoctor employed backbends; Ruth St. Denis's dime museum act also included a full backbend.

on Pavlova's 1921 program at the Salt Lake Theater), and a galop by Johann Strauss. The women wore tutus and pointe shoes, but the men wore tuxedo pants, white shirts open at the neck, and sashes. A critic in Montreal wondered "why the men elected to wear the outfits they did, since these appeared to conceal their real gracefulness."[14] But wearing tights was too risky for the males; they would either be considered sissy (and would thus alienate their audience) or they would be mistaken for acrobats, which happened sometimes anyway. For instance, the critic of the Madison, Wisconsin *Capital Times* complained,

> *The quartet presents some excellent gymnastics in some twenty minutes, but they would have been a much better act if they stopped trying to dance and be graceful. The men do some very finished acrobatic turns and then spoil the effect by some attempt at lily like hand wavings.*[15]

Too graceful for one critic, and not enough for another: the Christensens had to walk a fine line. Their act was based on the classical tradition, but spectacular feats were piled on thick and fast. As Willam later explained, "You couldn't just stand around looking elegant."[16]

The Mascagno Four usually opened the show, setting off a carefully reasoned sequence of acts with alternating styles and escalating excitement. Willam was once highly offended when someone referred to them as a "dumb" act, until he found out later that acts without speech (hence, "dumb") were traditionally used to open or close a show. As the Mascagno Four crossed the continent, advance press touted the four as "Dancers Extraordinaire," the Frenchified

---

[14] *The Gazette*, Montreal, Quebec, August 19, 1929.

[15] *The Capital Times*, Madison, Wisconsin, January 27, 1930.

[16] The foursome also learned how to present themselves by gauging audience response early in a performance. Willam explains, "When we danced the first part of our act, if we got a good hand to start with, we'd hit it with a belt. Then we'd do more of the elegant things. ... If we missed the first hand, then we'd fight like hell for the second hand." *Insight: Willam F. Christensen*, Salt Lake City, Utah: KUED, November 18, 1987.

label supplying a hint of European elegance. Some critics recognized and commented on the classical foundation of the act; more skipped over such technicalities and focused directly on the dancers' turns and the men's virtuosity. The dancers were compared to spinning tops, whirling dervishes, and even Kansas cyclones. Critics often singled out Lew because of his starring role and technical abilities. Columnists also gushed over the dancers' speed. One declared enthusiastically, "Whirlwind is the correct description of the act – more turns are made by the four in twelve minutes than the average person makes in as many years," while another jocularly concluded, "The speed of these youngsters is the kind that takes electric watches to catch."[17] The women's pointe work was singled out less frequently, although many critics mentioned that "toe" work was part of the act. The newspaper emphasis on the male dancing resulted from two factors: the choreography, which Mascagno designed to feature Lew's technique, and the novelty of strong, male, classical dancers when it was more usual to see eccentric dance acts that included women on pointe.

The proper tone that had reigned over Chris's dancing academy in Brigham City informed his sons' relationships with their partners. Despite blossoming offstage romances among the couples, Wiora and Mignon always shared a hotel room, as did the brothers, with no suggestion of physical intimacy out of wedlock. Brought up with notions of chivalry, the Christensen brothers saw their role as "sheltering" their partners, "the girls," from the rougher elements of the theatrical world they encountered during their travels. (In one city, this meant reproving stagehands for using foul language within earshot of the women's dressing room.) But Christensen chivalry was wedded to a patronizing attitude toward the women in the act, whose movement was largely an adornment to the male tours de force. The women were paid considerably less than the men, which Willam justified on the grounds that as the managers of the act the brothers paid all

[17] *The Birmingham Age-Herald*, July 15, 1930; *Portland Telegram*, September 30, 1929.

travel and production costs. The act was their life, and leadership was a distinctly male phenomenon in both, despite Isabell's example of decisive independence during the boys' formative years.

Well-matched in height, Mignon and Wiora had contrasting coloring and personalities. Wiora, a brunette, was sensitive, earnest, and frustrated that her personal interest in Lew produced no serious response on his part. Her insecurity in their relationship sometimes led to temperamental and demanding outbursts that inevitably put Lew off. In contrast, Mignon was a vivacious strawberry blond, with blue eyes and a ready smile. In Mignon Willam found not only a satisfying professional partner but an engaging companion; he valued her sometimes scatterbrained enthusiasm, her good sportsmanship, and her willingness to go along with the group for a good time. Once, during a northern booking, as they prepared to cross the border from Canada back into the United States, a fellow performer asked Mignon to help him smuggle some whiskey back into the country. She strapped the bottle to the inside of her thigh, under a fullish skirt, and considered the challenge an adventure. In addition to a shared commitment to dancing, Willam and Mignon had their Utah upbringings in common. The seven-year difference in their ages was no stumbling block to a serious relationship.

In July of 1929, while playing Cleveland, Ohio, Willam, who was now almost twenty-seven years old, proposed to Mignon. They became quietly engaged but set no specific date for the ceremony. Wiora longed for a similar proposal from Lew, but at age twenty the youngest Christensen was far from ready for commitment. As the act worked its way down the West Coast, the manager of the Pantages theater in Salt Lake City got wind of the romances and proposed a double wedding on the stage during their forthcoming engagement there. That prospect fanned Wiora's hopes, but Willam wired back a polite refusal. The Mascagno Four played Salt Lake City the week of Thanksgiving, 1929, with no extra fanfare other than the usual "favorite son" press that local papers gave them when they came through Utah. After that engagement,

Willam and Mignon slipped off to Ogden, where they were married at the courthouse with Willam's parents and Mignon's father in attendance. When the manager heard about the wedding after the fact, he was put out over the lost publicity stunt. And Wiora, feeling spurned, was upset that Mignon had wed Willam but she still did not have Lew. Her resentment marred the newlyweds' happiness, and the formal honeymoon was postponed. Back on the road, Willam continued rooming with Lew, and Mignon with Wiora, to keep hotel bills down for a few weeks until the couple had saved enough money to live together.

The long R.K.O. tour, which had taken them through New York and Ohio, across Canada, down the west coast, and back across the country through the Rocky Mountains and across the plains states, brought the Mascagno Four back to New York for engagements at the Hippodrome and the Palace in March of 1930. They closed the show at the Hippodrome, and the New York press was favorable, although *Billboard*'s critic speculated that the act would have to open the show at the Palace to be appreciated.[18] That was because standards of performance and admission prices were higher at the Palace than at any other vaudeville theater in the country. The most prestigious of the big time theaters, the Palace had not yet capitulated to the vaudefilm format; in this era it still boasted top name live entertainers, such as Jack Benny and Eddie Cantor. An engagement at the Palace was both a dream to live for and a high-pressure challenge, one so stressful in fact that some established acts refused to appear there.[19] The Mascagno Four would be appearing on the same bill as the comedian W. C. Fields, and their anxiety grew as the occasion drew closer.

On the opening day, Willam and Lew were warming up in the wings when they saw that some stagehands had left a slippery powder on the stage. Willam pointed out that they

[18] Joe Schoenfeld, *Billboard*, March 15, 1930.

[19] Bernard Sobel, *A Pictorial History of Vaudeville* (New York: Bonanza Books, 1961), 88.

might slip on the substance and asked an employee to sweep it off. The latter's superior attitude angered the dancers and fueled a heated argument. Still upset over the incident when it came time to go on, the Mascagno Four danced with an explosive power that stopped the show.[20] The prolonged applause from the nation's most discriminating vaudeville audience signaled the high point of their careers to date. The heady rush of success at the Palace validated the years of struggle since the brothers' tentative Los Angeles debut, and reviews confirmed the high quality of their presentation.[21]

The successful Palace engagement was followed by a string of performances at Fox theaters in and around New York (April and May of 1930) and an interstate R.K.O. tour across five southern states. Theaters were closing because of

---

[20] Interview with Willam Christensen, Salt Lake City, Utah, February 20, 1987. Willam claims that during that Palace engagement, they stopped the show every day but the last.

[21] The reviews of this Palace engagement contain the most telling and sophisticated press coverage of the Mascagno Four act. In *Billboard*, Elias E. Sugarman put the Mascagno Four in the larger context of vaudeville dance acts with the following observations:

> Dancing that is dancing is very rare in vaude. We have plenty of so-called dancing acts that feature rhythmic acrobatics, and frequently it appears there is too much of the eccentric brand better known as hoofing. This act is a thoro-going dance affair; a very good one at that. Two mixed teams comprise the company. Only one number, however, calls for the dancers to work as mixed teams. The greater part of the routine has the men, whose assignments are far more important than those of the girls, working simply and in duo. The girls are also on alone, but their intervals are fewer, briefer, and far less interesting. Not a suggestion of adagioistics. Which is a very interesting phenomenon in a day when there is keen competition in this line, both in offering the largest number of adagio dancers in one grouping and in doing the freakiest acrobatics under the doubtful head of dancing.

Sugarman mentioned costumes and set briefly, commented on the "aesthetic" toe dancing, and drew attention to the "great hand" the Mascagno Four received. But his observations on Lew's "corkscrew-whirling specialty" indicate that Sugarman sensed the Christensen's commitment to artistry rather than flamboyance: "If he had stooped to a coarser brand of showmanship he might have stopped the show with this specialty. But that would not have been dancing, and we have stated that this is a genuine dancing act." "Mascagno Four. Reviewed at the Palace," *Billboard*, April 5, 1930.

the nation's depressed economy, and Mascagno wired that he could get bookings only if the act would take a cut in pay. That did not sit well with the dancers, as Mascagno was paid a hundred dollars a week from their earnings, while the men received, at most, seventy-five dollars each (out of which they paid all costs) and the women, thirty-five. Willam responded, "Maestro, you take the cut because we have to pay for the hotel and buy shoes."[22] Unused to being challenged, Mascagno suggested cutting Willam's pay and raising Lew's and his own. Once again, Willam turned to Jack Hart, who found it unreasonable that Mascagno should receive so much of the act's income. When the situation reached an impasse, the Christensens decided to leave their teacher and form a new act.

The break with Mascagno was more than just a decision forced by economic necessity; it also represented youthful rebellion against an aging authority figure. The fifteen-month tour had taught the Christensens what worked on the vaudeville stage, and their increased experience made them less dependent upon their former mentor. Taking class from Laurent Novikoff in Chicago had opened their eyes to Mascagno's limitations, and success at the Palace had increased their security and sense of self-esteem. Thus began a period of fledgling independence. For a short while the Christensens added two contortionists to their act, Ann Lorraine and Martin La Tosa, and played upstate New York and Pennsylvania as the "Six Spirals." Capitalizing on their strengths, they designed costumes with diagonal black and gold stripes that made them look like corkscrews when they turned. Although the press was good and they were billed as headliners in this tour, the brothers eventually dropped Lorraine and La Tosa and returned to their original balletic format. The name by which they were known for the remainder of their vaudeville years, "Christensen Brothers and

---

[22] KQED interview with Willam Christensen.

Company," is another indication of the act's focus and the women's ornamental, supporting roles.[23]

The split with Mascagno meant that the brothers could no longer use his choreography or his music. Without altering the basic structure that Mascagno had set, they changed individual steps and formations and found suitable music for the new act (including the Intermezzo from Delibe's *Naïla* and Lehar's *The Count of Luxemberg* waltz, which was a staple of L.P.'s teaching accompaniments). They even demonstrated their new choreography in rehearsal for Mascagno, to prove its originality and assure that they would not be sued. Unable to afford an arranger, Willam himself transposed and orchestrated the music, counting the notes of each interval and making allowances for instruments tuned to different pitches.

The Christensens' popularized version of ballet on the vaudeville circuits exemplifies Ernest van de Haag's assertion that mass culture is characterized by two basic premises: "(1) everything is understandable, and (2) everything is remediable."[24] The act made the classical tradition accessible by reducing it largely to stunts that could be understood and appreciated in the same spirit that one applauded circus acrobats. And when experience demonstrated that an element of their act worked against accessibility, the Christensens remedied the situation. Before the start of their second R.K.O. transcontinental tour, the management had an in-house designer upgrade the visual element of the act. Using a Venetian carnival theme, the designer gave the men multicolored diamond-patterned tights, large capes and hats, and the women, long tutus decorated to look like ostrich feathers.

---

[23] This name appears in advertising as early as January 1931. Apparently there was some debate over the advisability of using their own name because of an animal act, The Christensen Stallions, with which they did not want to be confused. The decision to use their own name may have been a result of their growing confidence and a sign that they felt less dependent on outward signs (French names or a teacher's label) to validate the nature of their performance.

[24] Ernest van den Haag quoted by Bernard Rosenberg in "Mass Culture in America," in *Mass Culture: The Popular Arts in America*, ed. Bernard Rosenberg and David Manning White (1957; Free Press of Glencoe, 1962), 5.

A backdrop featured a scene with gondolas and the Grand Canal. The dancers were thrilled over their elegant new costumes, but the men discarded the new tights when they discovered that they were better received in their black tuxedo pants and open white shirts.

By and large, American audiences were not used to the conventions of ballet. When the newly designed act appeared at the Hippodrome in New York, a critic in *Billboard* warned, "Christensen Brothers are taking a chance in trying to sell an act composed entirely of classical dancing."[25] Response to the Christensens depended largely upon the experience of local audiences, and there could be a big difference between expectations in New York or California and those in the heartland of America. The dancers stopped the show in Los Angeles, where *Inside Facts of Stage and Screen* waxed enthusiastic, exclaiming, "It's class and different and they don't have to fear anybody following them."[26] On the other hand, in Toledo a critic apologized for the tepid reception accorded the act in his review of the performance: "Telegram to Christensen Bros., Your ballet dancing is pretty, but Toledoans prefer ankle-breakers, so don't feel hurt about applause."[27] For the most part, however, even observers who had no knowledge of ballet were excited by the act's virtuoso stunts. Walking a fine line between popularization and vulgarization, the Christensen Brothers and Company sold ballet successfully to a broad audience. The *Saint Paul Daily News* reported that although the Christensens were respected by serious followers of dance, they were "also in high favor with audiences who have no further interests in dancing than as a means of entertainment."[28]

---

[25] July 4, 1931.

[26] November 9 or 16, 1929. This is actually a review of the act before the Christensens split off from Mascagno.

[27] Week of August 17, 1931.

[28] St. Paul, Minnesota, week of September 6, 1931.

Despite the seven-year difference in their ages, Willam and Lew enjoyed a smoothly functioning professional partnership with a division of responsibilities based on their respective talents. Lew, with his youthful good looks and impressive stature, was undeniably the act's star performer, after the split from Mascagno as well as before. Willam was the act's moving force offstage; he dealt with agents and managers and fed stories to local reporters. Willam never hesitated to use the press to his advantage. On one tour he spread the word that when their R.K.O. contract had expired, the act would tour "all the principal cities of Europe" and then return to America, where the Christensens would "open a chain of ballet schools from coast to coast."[29] Those plans would never materialize, but they show the inclination and scope of his sometimes extravagant rhetoric.

One professional responsibility Willam and Lew shared was the task of giving daily class. They had heard that Pavlova's technique deteriorated on her long tours and that between tours she returned to serious study to correct faults that crept into her dancing. Despite the act's concessions to popular taste, the Christensens took their technique seriously and worked daily to maintain it. Rehearsal space was limited; to keep in shape on the road they often had to warm up behind the movie screen during the motion picture portion of the show. Silence while the movies were in progress was absolutely necessary, or the stage managers would forbid them to use the stage. So the dancers developed a technique based on soft, deep *pliés*; they learned to do beats such as *entrechats* and double air turns from *grand pliés* rather than the usual *demi-plié* (not a recommended practice today).

Coping with the demands of daily life on the circuit was a challenge in itself. The act played either week-long engagements or "split weeks," in which they performed Monday through Wednesday in one location and Thursday through Sunday in another. At first they made the "jumps" between cities by train, but by the early 1930s the brothers

---

[29] Omaha, Nebraska, *World Herald*, no date, during an engagement the week of December 10, 1931.

were driving between engagements, which more than once meant leaving one city after an evening's final show, driving through the night to their next booking, and performing the next day after little or no rest. To sustain their strenuous performance schedule of three to four shows a day, they ate hearty breakfasts and took food to the theater to snack on. The issue was not keeping weight down but keeping their energy up. Preventing injuries was also a priority because they had no substitutes or understudies. When Willam sprained his right ankle during an engagement in Schenectady, he soaked and wrapped it and danced as well as he could. He made it through the week, but at the price of recurring ankle problems later in his career.

Any leisure time was spent primarily with other performers. A legerdemain artist by the name of Cardini and his wife became their good friends, and from Cardini Lew developed a passion for photography. Cardini taught Lew how to develop film, and often they would set up a darkroom in the hotel where they were staying. Usually, however, there was little time for hobbies or sightseeing; the dancers worked seven days a week, from morning warm-ups to the last show, and saw little of any city other than the alleyway from the hotel (usually one recommended by the circuit management) to the stage door.

Dissatisfaction began to creep into the dancers' whirl-wind lives as the number of performances per day increased. In order to compete with movie houses during the Depression, vaudeville theaters went from a two-a-day format to a continuous run of shows and films. By 1932, the Christensen Brothers and Company act was performing four times a day, and during an engagement at the Hill Street theater in Los Angeles they had to do five shows daily. To make matters worse, the Hill Street manager liked their act so much that he split it in half and used it both to open and close the show. "That meant ten times we warmed up," recalls Willam. "That was where we looked for a way out."[30]

---

[30] Don McDonaugh interview with Willam Christensen, Salt Lake City, Utah, February 28, 1986.

The brothers faced few alternatives. Neither night clubs nor the motion picture industry appeared promising outlets for their talents. Another possibility planted itself in Willam's mind when he and Lew took their partners to a performance of Ted Shawn and a group of Denishawn dancers, probably during the latter's 1930–1931 tour.[31] Exposure to the modern dancers yielded no esthetic revelation; because Willam equated dancing with technique, his primary reaction to Shawn was that the modern dancer was no match for them. However, Willam was impressed by the contrast in their circumstances. The Christensen group had always been just one of many acts sparring for status in a vaudeville line-up, whereas Shawn and his dancers had their own show and did not have to share honors with anyone. This was the beginning of Willam's desire for his own ballet company, although at that time he had no idea how it would be accomplished.

A steady stream of bookings sustained the Christensens and their partners through the early 1930s, but signs of the hard economic realities of the Great Depression unnerved them. In Toledo, the dancers saw the state militia called out to protect a bank from investors trying to break in through the windows. In Omaha they received a telegram from their booking agent saying that theaters where they had been scheduled to play had closed and that they would be rerouted to the South, where theaters were still open. Their agent warned them to "travel light" and have "only one cup of coffee in the morning." Even so, Willam and Lew were

---

[31] Willam recalls this event as being in or around Chicago, shortly after Denishawn's return from the Orient. Actually, Denishawn's Orient tour ended in November 1926, well before the Christensens would have been performing in Chicago. Denishawn's Ziegfeld Follies tour, from September 1927 through May 1928, did not take them to Chicago, and on that tour they were part of a larger show. Because the Christensens performed in Chicago during January, 1931, I assume that the performance Willam remembers was a concert of Ted Shawn and a group of Denishawn Dancers in Chicago on January 18, 1931, or at the University of Illinois at Urbana on January 22, 1931. See Christena L. Schlundt, *The Professional Appearances of Ruth St. Denis and Ted Shawn: A Chronology and Index of Dances, 1906–1932* (New York: The New York Public Library, 1962).

unprepared for the sight that greeted them upon their return to New York: the sidewalk of Forty-Seventh Street lined with the trunks of homeless actors in search of jobs.[32]

Fortunately, the Christensens were off on another tour after a month or two, but Willam wanted steadier employment for personal reasons. During the spring of 1931, Mignon began to have mysterious health problems. She sometimes had trouble spotting when she turned; her eyes oscillated and she tended to lose her balance. During a performance in New England she fainted on stage in the middle of the show. Lew carried her off hastily, pretending it was part of the act, while a confused Willam tried to finish up with Wiora. Although a local doctor could diagnose no condition other than fatigue, that night Mignon's symptoms grew worse: dizziness, nausea, and loss of feeling in the legs. The sporadic recurrence of these symptoms as they toured, combined with the discovery early in 1932 that Mignon was expecting a child, forced the couple to difficult decisions. Uncle Mose had passed away, leaving Aunt Carrie with a well-established dancing school in Portland that could use another instructor. And Harold was in New York, working with Mascagno and improving his technique so that he would be able to replace Willam in the act if necessary. The choice seemed clear: Willam and Mignon would leave vaudeville and move west.

The first two years Willam and Lew were in vaudeville, Harold dutifully ran the Ogden school, teaching, organizing recitals, and providing support for the family as Willam had done before him. At some point that arrangement must have been abandoned, for in 1929 Harold accepted an invitation to rejoin Uncle Fred in Seattle. Harold taught in the Seattle studio during the first part of the 1929–1930 school year, but the partnership soured quickly. Frederic was the least disciplined of the Christensen uncles. In the wake of his divorce from Grace, he took to gambling at a local pool hall. Harold was often left stranded at the ballroom, where he

---

[32] Interview with Willam Christensen, Salt Lake City, Utah, February 20, 1987, and conversation with Willam Christensen, March 25, 1988.

**10** Harold and Lew Christensen atop their apartment building in Queens, early 1930s.
Courtesy of San Francisco Performing Arts Library and Museum

ended up teaching his uncle's classes as well as his own. Fed up with the situation, Harold left Seattle that winter, returned to Ogden for a short period, and then moved with his mother to New York City. They found an apartment in the Forest Hills section of Queens where Willam, Lew, and Chris could also stay between out-of-town bookings.

Now twenty-five years old, Harold took odd jobs to support himself while he concentrated on improving his ballet technique. He studied primarily with Mascagno, for whom he also did some teaching, but he also worked out occasionally at Chester Hale's studio with the Crocketts. Eventually he found a job taking tickets at a Broadway theater that guaranteed him forty dollars a week and his mornings free for ballet classes.[33] His diligent preparation during this period paid off when he replaced Willam in the act during the summer of 1932.

When time for the substitution came, the transition was smooth. Harold took over his brother's role, Elyse Crockett substituted for Mignon, and the choreography remained unchanged. Chris continued to travel with his sons after Harold joined the act, to direct musical matters and settle occasional differences. Because the act's billing and advertising had always featured the "Christensen Brothers" without naming Willam or Lew individually, and because the women's presence was indicated only by "and Company," no change was needed in promotional materials. It was ballet as a family business, and the family carried on.

As time went on, Wiora's unrequited love for Lew became a growing source of strain, especially when it led to emotional outbursts within earshot of theater personnel. Embarrassed by these scenes, Harold and Lew got bookings back to Utah and unceremoniously discharged Wiora and Elyse with the excuse that they needed taller partners. Harold

---

[33] Once when friends from his high school days attended that theater, Harold was embarrassed over his lowly position and took their tickets without admitting that he recognized them. Interview with Harold Christensen, San Anselmo, California, September 23, 1987.

*was* taller than Willam, but the excuse was a transparent ploy. The women were understandably angered by this peremptory treatment; Elyse especially felt betrayed at being stranded in the West without any means of getting back to New York. But to the Christensens, it was easier to find new partners than to deal with the personal problems of Lew and Wiora's relationship. Since the female component of the act functioned chiefly as adornment to the male tours de force, Wiora and Elyse were, to put it bluntly, expendable. Between Uncle Pete's school in Salt Lake and Willam's new set-up in Portland, Harold and Lew would have no problem finding new partners.

By the summer of 1933, Willam had developed a pool of dancers in Portland, and he recommended two well-matched young women for his brothers' act: Ruby Asquith and Agnes Peters. Before coming to study with Willam, Ruby had taken ballet from a former Fanchon and Marco dancer who stressed vaudeville-style stunts such as fast circles of *chaîné* and *piqué* turns. Ruby had strong pointe technique and a soubrette personality that projected well on the stage. The early seeds of romance were planted in the long hours of rehearsal as Harold prepared her to be his new partner.

Agnes, however, did not want to leave Portland, because she was in love with another member of the Christensen family, Carrie's son Victor, who had given up his career on the violin to help his mother run the Christensen Ballroom after Mose's death. So Uncle Pete suggested his protégé in Salt Lake City: Josephine McKendrick. She had taken part in many of his productions, and her relationship to Lew and Harold was somewhat like that of a younger sister. Josephine was only sixteen, but her parents, knowing the Christensen family well, entrusted her safety to Chris and allowed her to join the preparations transpiring in Portland. After a single week of rehearsals, she and Ruby contributed their allotment of luggage, one suitcase each, to the trunk of the Christensen's Cadillac, and the next tour began.

The next year, from the summer of 1933 to the summer of 1934, found the Christensen act tightly booked with four shows a day and few days off. Lew still practiced his 'cello during the long backstage intervals between appearances, although occasionally he would challenge Josephine to sketch with him. (At Ogden High School, Lew had taken an art class from LeConte Stewart, a local painter of some renown, and drawing remained a hobby over the years.) The routine of performances settled into a daily rhythm, starting with morning warm-ups and rehearsals with orchestras to set the tempo of their music. Once performances began, each show had its particular quality. During the first show the dancers were conscious of holding back their energies, preserving their strength. By the second show they were hungry. They would change, leave the theater to eat, and return for the third show, which they danced on a full stomach. The fourth show of the day usually had the best crowd, but by then the dancers were tired. Nonetheless, before leaving the theater, Lew and Harold would take turns leading the four of them in "rehabilitation exercises," a short class that included plenty of small jumps and ended with sixteen *changements* from *grand plié*.

Harold and Lew may have shared teaching duties, but the younger brother was the senior showman and it was Lew who made corrections when necessary. His artistic leadership even at this early stage in the brothers' professional development foreshadowed the relationship he and Harold would share decades later in San Francisco. Lew's exacting standards also manifested themselves at this early stage in his career. Ruby and Josephine found that in dancing four shows a day they went through pointe shoes at an alarming rate. Despite their attempts to save their shoes for performances, Lew would demand that they rehearse all steps full out. In humid climates, their shoes became so drenched with perspiration that at night they would prop them over lightbulbs in order to dry them out.

The costumes and choreography of the vaudeville act changed over the years. Josephine and Ruby wore neither tutus nor ostrich feathers but white chiffon skirts that flowed below the knee and white bodices with floral trim. They fixed their hair in traditional ballet buns, although some producers considered the style too severe and would have preferred

**11**   Harold Christensen and Ruby Asquith in vaudeville performance.
Performance Photograph by Richard Tucker, courtesy of San Francisco
Performing Arts Library and Museum

them in curly bobs. Nylon tights were not yet available, and
silk stockings were an unaffordable luxury, so their legs were
bare under their skirts except when they performed in Boston,
where "opera stockings" were, for moral reasons, *de rigeur*.
These were silk stockings that reached to the thigh and were

held in place by wrapping a penny in the top of each stocking, tying strings around the pennies, and fastening the strings around one's waist. (This created an uncomfortable squeezing sensation when the women dropped into a deep *plié*.) The observance of Blue Laws in Boston had one other effect: since dancing was prohibited on the sabbath, theaters billed the Christensens as acrobats on Sundays.

Back in New York during the summer of 1934, the Christensen Brothers and Company were scheduled for another engagement at the Palace, which now featured a continuous show of movies and live acts. The dancers prepared carefully for the engagement, and Lew was more demanding than usual with his young partner. That week Hassard Short, the director of a new Broadway play still in rehearsal, saw the act at the Palace and invited the dancers to be in his show, *The Great Waltz*. The Christensens were tired of life on the circuit, and *The Great Waltz* would provide steady income while allowing them to study with a new ballet master in town: George Balanchine. They jumped at the chance.

Lincoln Kirstein has commented that when there were few outlets for American entertainers, vaudeville, and particularly the Keith circuit, was the closest thing to a national school for the performing arts.[34] Reflecting on the vaudeville years later in life, the brothers viewed it as a time of maturation, a period in which they gained practical stage experience and learned to cope with the demands of theatrical life. They respected the professionals with whom they toured. "I worked with artists," explained Lew. "Each of those acts – from clowns, comedians, to jugglers had worked to perfect their performances."[35] The Christensens as well learned to polish their performances and focus their vision as they developed the discipline necessary to survive in the highly competitive marketplace of variety entertainment.

---

[34] Interview with Lincoln Kirstein, New York, New York, January 14, 1988.

[35] Renée Renouf, "Lew Christensen Reminisces," *Dance News*, November 1978, 7.

# 4

## WILLAM IN PORTLAND (1932–1937)

The death of Uncle Mose in 1920 left Aunt Carrie a wealthy woman. She continued to run their school in Portland with assistance from Victor, who had given up his career on the violin to help his mother teach ballroom dancing to the children of the city's social elite. Also on the faculty of Carrie's school was her nephew Richard (Dick) Billings, Jorinda's son, who specialized in tap dancing.

The issue prompted by Willam's arrival during the fall of 1932 was whether or not ballet had a rightful place in the school's curriculum. Still pondering the example of the Ted Shawn concert and wondering how he might organize his own ballet company, Willam knew his first step must be to teach, to build up a reservoir of well-trained students. Unfortunately for Willam, his enthusiasm for promoting ballet classes met stiff resistance from his aunt. Carrie and Victor had not seceded from the dancing masters' association in 1925 when L.P., Frederic, and Chris's sons had followed Mascagno out of that organization. Although the ballroom business had declined since the onset of the Depression, Carrie still believed that the future of her Christensen Ballroom lay in social, not theatrical, dance.

Initially, Carrie seemed to be right. When fall classes opened in mid-September, Willam had only three ballet students. He advertised and gained more, slowly, but misfortune plagued the school that year. No sooner had Dick's tap classes started than Jorinda, his mother, died, and he had to leave temporarily for Utah. Then one afternoon as Willam

---

All reviews and newspaper articles cited are found in Scrapbooks 1–3 (Box 7) or clipping folders (Box 5) of the Utah Ballet Archives, Special Collections, University of Utah Marriott Library, Salt Lake City, Utah.

was finishing a class, Aunt Carrie rushed in to announce that the building was on fire. Firemen saved the building from serious damage but had to chop holes in the ballroom floor.[1] In the wake of this destruction, Willam and Dick built a removable wooden platform approximately twenty-eight by thirty feet to cover a portion of the damaged floor. Every time he taught a ballet class, Willam had to assemble the temporary floor by hooking the three sections of the platform together. And when he finished teaching, he had to disassemble the platform and lean the sections against the wall.

Willam's first promising male pupil in Portland was a young ex-lightweight prizefighter named Robert Irwin, whose introductory training consisted of standing behind Willam and imitating his every move during a private morning class before the regular students arrived. With Irwin, Willam set a pattern he would follow the rest of his teaching career: finding athletes and turning them into dancers. (A few years later, Massine would see Irwin dance while the Ballet Russe was in San Francisco and would offer him a contract and a free ticket to Monte Carlo.) Another student whose talent Willam recognized that first year was a pert young redhead named Janet Reed, who was sent to him by another local teacher. As with so many families during the Depression, Reed's mother, a beautician, did not have sufficient cash to pay her daughter's tuition. So in exchange for her daughter's ballet lessons, Mrs. Reed styled Mignon's and Isabell's hair once a week.

After the itinerant existence of the vaudeville years, Portland afforded Willam the chance to establish himself in a community once again. The steps he went through in that process illustrate the methods that would lead to his later successes in San Francisco and Salt Lake City. Attracting talented students (or finding young people with physical strength that could be diverted to ballet), educating parents

---

[1] Letter from Willam F. Christensen to Mignon Lee Christensen, September 25, 1932, in the possession of Willam F. Christensen.

and building audiences, establishing himself institutionally and making advantageous connections within the community, rallying support for his goals, creating performance opportunities, and manipulating the press to his advantage – all were part of Willam's modus operandi as he pressed forward toward the ultimate goal of performance.

Willam's first successful marketing strategy was offering free lecture demonstrations to educate potential students and their parents about ballet. These were followed by a more formal performance billed as "Visitor's Night," a program of ballet excerpts with a twenty-five cent admission fee. To attract a broad audience, Willam and Dick placed a notice in the paper and sent out penny postcard advertisements. Carrie objected on the grounds that people had no money to spend on ballet; twenty-five cents seemed an exorbitant amount when ten or fifteen cents would buy a ticket to the movies. She warned repeatedly that no one would come, but the night of the performance found a line half-way down the street. The capacity crowd witnessed portions of the Dance of the Hours from *La Gioconda*, danced by Willam and his best students on the removable platform at one end of Carrie's ballroom.[2]

Willam took the success of the Visitor's Night as a sign that his vision, not his aunt's, held the keys to a successful future in Portland. But he needed more space, a larger studio with a better floor. The tiresome procedure of setting up the wooden platform every time he taught and taking it down afterwards lodged itself like an irritant under Willam's skin. The floor came to symbolize the constraints he felt working within the confines of Carrie's establishment. He wanted to expand his efforts in a setting more conducive to his needs, and the only way to do so was to break ties with the family school and establish himself elsewhere. Personal ambition eclipsed loyalty to the extended family the following year when Willam and Dick relocated downtown on the top floor of the Selling-Hirsch building, taking their students with

---

[2] Interview with Willam F. Christensen, Salt Lake City, Utah, March 27, 1987.

them.[3] There the cousins had two large studios, and the stern-looking Isabell ran the desk, checking to make sure that students had paid before entering classes.

Having broken ties with Carrie, Willam joined forces with others in the community who could advance his aims. In the process of establishing his new studio, he teamed up with a music teacher and a theater director to establish the Portland Creative Theatre and School of Music, Drama, and the Dance. This ambitious-sounding institution functioned as an umbrella organization that sponsored concerts, small-scale dramatic productions, and performances of Willam's ballet students. Under its auspices, Rouen Faith (a relative of popular band leader Percy Faith) taught music theory and composition and presented his students' compositions in recitals. The drama director, Ruby Page Euwer, brought experience in stage direction, oratory, and broadcasting to the new institution; she taught acting and directed her students in one-act plays. The Portland Creative Theatre provided Willam with a properly "theatrical" context in which to show his students' progress in modest studio demonstrations.

Still in his best performing years, Willam had no outlet for his talents other than the studio of the Creative Theatre; his only opportunities to perform were those he created. In early 1934, a Mrs. Lauterstein, the mother of one of his most talented students, Natalie Lauterstein, suggested that Willam join forces with Jacques Gershkovitch, the conductor of Portland's Junior Symphony. Gershkovitch, a Russian Jew who had emigrated to the United States, claimed to have played in Pavlova's orchestra and did have a fundamental knowledge of the balletic repertory.[4] Gershkovitch proposed that Willam and his students perform portions of Tchaikovsky's *Nutcracker* with the Junior Symphony that

---

[3] Victor was against this break in family ties, and Carrie went so far as to invite Mascagno to come teach in her studio. But the Italian was not available, so Willam and Dick were free to pursue their new enterprise without the threat of competition. *Ibid.*

[4] *Ibid.*

coming June as part of the festivities of Portland's annual Rose Festival.

Willam knew next to nothing about *The Nutcracker* but latched onto the idea eagerly. He studied the music of the second act variations recommended by Gershkovitch – the Russian, Arabian, and Chinese dances, the Mirlitons, and the Waltz of the Flowers. For these he created large group dances that had little to do with the ballet's original scenario. He also created a solo for Janet Reed, who was billed as the "Sugar Plum Fairy, Queen of Jam Mountain," and he danced opposite her as the Nutcracker prince. The royal titles meshed nicely with the context of the performance, which was to be the coronation ceremony of Portland's Rose Queen.

This Rose Festival was Willam's first chance to show Portland he could do things in a big way. He engineered a fabulous press build-up for the event, which was billed as "Russian Ballet" in deference to the common conception that ballet was by nature a Russian art form. Local papers defined "choreography" for the uninitiated amongst Portland's population as "the progressive arrangement of steps used in interpreting the story and music of a ballet," reflecting Willam's narrative orientation. This information was delivered along with the patently false statement that Willam had "inherited" the choreography from his Danish grandfather, "a famous ballet master and musician who saw the original presentation ... in St. Petersburg."[5] Other hyperbolic claims included the description of the Christensens' vaudeville act, which had supposedly toured the United States with a "company of 50."[6]

With such assistance from the press, Willam rode the crest of excitement for the forthcoming festival. Previews stressed the number of performers to participate in the "Nut

---

[5] "Dance Treat Scheduled," *Oregonian*, June 7, 1934, in Portland Scrapbook 1, Box 7, Utah Ballet Archives, Special Collections, University of Utah Marriott Library, Salt Lake City, Utah.

[6] *Ibid.*

Cracker" ballet: "100 ballerinas and feature dancers."[7] Publicity emphasized the size of the event and its attendant spectacle, revealing a pervading "more is better" mentality.
Through Gershkovitch and Mrs. Lauterstein, Willam gained
the informal backing of Portland's Jewish community, and a
host of mothers willingly sewed tutus and appliqued rose
petals onto girls' costumes. The demand for tickets forced the
festival organizers to make extra seats available in the side
portions of the Civic Auditorium, where the coronation
ceremony would take place. Before an audience of five
thousand spectators, his student company made a splashy
debut that culminated in the Waltz of the Flowers. In honor
of the occasion, those flowers were none other than Portland's
specialty, American Beauty Roses. With this attention-getting
production, Willam established his reputation as Portland's
leading ballet teacher.

Shortly after his first successful Rose Festival, Willam
traveled to New York to visit his father and brothers, whose
act was appearing at the Palace. While in New York that
summer (1934), he studied with Fokine. Taking class from
Novikoff had weaned the brothers from their psychological
dependence upon Mascagno; now working with Fokine himself gave Willam a more solid foundation in the reformed
Russian style, especially the flexible torsoes and pliant port
de bras that constituted one aspect of Fokine's choreographic
reforms.[8] Willam accepted Fokine's teachings without reser-
vation; he recalls, "I went hook, line, and sinker for the more
free style."[9]

[7] Advertisement entitled "Russian Ballet," *Sunday Oregonian*, June 3, 1934. This
advertisement promised 350 performers, including 100 instrumentalists, 100 dancers,
and a chorus of 150. The coming event was described as "The first real European
ballet seen in Portland." Utah Ballet Archives (Box 7, Portland Scrapbook 1), Special
Collections, University of Utah Marriott Library, Salt Lake City, Utah.

[8] For an in-depth analysis of Fokine's choreographic reforms, see Lynn Garafola,
*Diaghilev's Ballets Russes* (New York and Oxford: Oxford University Press, 1989),
3–49.

[9] Interview with Willam F. Christensen, Salt Lake City, Utah, March 9, 1987.

**12** Willam Christensen in *Prince Igor* costume, New York, 1934.
Courtesy of Special Collections, University of Utah Marriott Library

After a few weeks, Deane Crockett passed word on that Fokine was pulling together a company for upcoming performances at the Capitol Theatre and could use Willam. So Willam showed up for rehearsal and was immediately put into *Prince Igor*.[10] Unfamiliar with the piece, he picked up the steps without knowing the context and did them as correctly as possible. Dancing past the choreographer in the throng of men, Willam drew the criticism, "You look like an English gentleman." "What am I *supposed* to look like?" he queried Crockett, who responded that Willam was supposed to be "a wild Russian tartar."[11] Willam quickly changed his style.

Fokine's engagement at the Capitol Theatre was only a week long, but it allowed Willam to immerse himself in *Prince Igor* and *Bolero*.[12] He also watched *Les Sylphides* in performance each night. Though the connection was brief, working with Fokine made a lasting impact upon Willam's thinking and his approach to choreography. In the following two years, he would produce his own versions of *Les Sylphides* and *Bolero*. If anything, that summer's experience confirmed Willam's desire for his own company, and Fokine's student troupe provided Willam with a working model. When he reopened the Portland Creative Theatre that fall, Willam announced that he would be forming a Ballet Repertory Company of his most advanced students. He would take the company to New York the following summer to be booked by his old agent, Jack Hart.[13]

---

[10] Willam claims he was one of the three soloists (not the premier danseur, and not in the corps) in this ballet, which he refers to by the name of Borodin's opera, *Prince Igor*, rather than the section, which is technically the *Polovtsian Dances*, as the ballet was called in Diaghilev's company. Interview with Willam Christensen, Salt Lake City, Utah, March 27, 1987.

[11] *Ibid.*

[12] *Ibid.* The length of time Willam was associated with Fokine has been exaggerated by some, including Willam himself, perhaps because of the impact it had on his thinking as a choreographer.

[13] "Ballet Group Planned for Portland Dancers," clipping, no paper credited, October 12, 1934. Utah Ballet Archives (Box 7, Portland Scrapbook 1), Special Collections, University of Utah Marriott Library, Salt Lake City, Utah.

Golden performing opportunities for Willam's would-be company did not present themselves immediately, but he put an optimistic face on the ones that did. His school program the following January (1935) was billed not as a recital but as an "annual midwinter ballet production," despite the complement of tap dances and variety routines contributed by Dick Billing's students. Willam staged two short character works – *Russian Peasant Dance* and *Hungarian Village* – and a version of *Les Sylphides* entitled *Chopiniana* to showcase his star pupils Janet Reed and Robert Irwin. In the latter work, Willam adopted the mood and the basic concept of Fokine's ballet but he modified the structure of the original to meet his specific needs.[14] In place of the solos devised by Fokine, Willam set group dances to display the talents of his students in what was basically a recital showpiece. Ensemble work gave more dancers a chance to be seen and spread the burden of performance. Aside from Reed and Irwin, his student dancers were not advanced enough to carry whole sections of a work individually. In any event, reproducing Fokine's ballet was not Willam's goal; he did not have a photographic memory for steps, but he had the capacity to capture the essence of a style. Later in his career he would work with ballet masters or mistresses who could remember ballets step by step with perfect recall, and although he respected such "reproducers" he never considered himself one of them.[15]

---

[14] Fokine's *Sylphides* was composed of a musical overture (a Prelude) followed by a Nocturne for the ensemble, then four solo dances: a Valse, two Mazurkas, and a Prelude. Then following a Valse pas de deux, the ensemble performed the finale, yet another Valse. (See Peter Brinson and Clement Crisp, *The Pan Book of Ballet and Dance* [London: Pan Books, 1970], 66.) Willam's *Chopiniana* had a Polonaise for the overture, a Nocturne for soloist and ensemble, two Valses for groups rather than soloists, and one Mazurka, again for a small group. The next section, a Prelude, was a pas de deux, followed by the closing section, a Grand Valse for the ensemble. Another version of *Les Sylphides* that Willam had seen before doing his own was the *Chopiniana* Pavlova performed in Salt Lake City in 1921. Pavlova's version also began with a Polonaise and contained nine sections rather than Fokine's eight. Salt Lake Theatre Program, February 22, 1921.

[15] Interview with Willam Christensen, Salt Lake City, Utah, April 17, 1987.

Willam's next performing opportunity was the 1935 Rose Festival, for which he collaborated once again with Gershkovitch and the Junior Symphony. The conductor proposed *Coppélia* as a vehicle for Reed, and this time Willam had something to go on because he remembered seeing Pavlova's abbreviated version in Salt Lake City in 1925.[16] He devised a one-act distillation of the plot, featuring Natalie Lauterstein as Swanilda and Reed as Coppélia. Advance publicity and newspaper articles gave detailed plot summaries to prepare audiences for the story of the village youth Franz who disappoints his fiancée Swanilda by flirting with Coppélia, a mechanical doll. In response to the rush for tickets and the enthusiastic reception of the previous year's *Nutcracker*, the Rose Festival committee decided to present the ballet and Junior Symphony not once but twice during the festival week. Again, the press enticed viewers with promises of costuming and spectacle, and in glowing postperformance write-ups the ballet was declared the "pièce de résistance" of the musical program.[17]

As he had done with *Les Sylphides* in *Chopiniana*, Willam bent the story of *Coppélia* to his own needs, expanding the title role as a vehicle for Reed's talents. Rather than viewing the original work, or its libretto, as a sacrosanct entity to be preserved at all costs, Willam mined it for what he could use, adapting the material freely according to the talent at hand and his own common sense. This pragmatic approach may have resulted from the haphazard manner in which Willam came to know the classics. The Christensens were trained in the language of ballet but were not brought up on its literature; their technical skills were developed far from

---

[16] Salt Lake Theatre Program, February 16, 1925. The same program included a one-act ballet entitled *Snowflakes* with music from *The Nutcracker*, including the Snowflake Waltz, but Willam does not recall this as having informed his first *Nutcracker* stagings.

[17] "Junior Symphony Wins High Praise," *Morning Oregonian*, June 5, 1935. Utah Ballet Archives (Box 7, Portland Scrapbook 1), Special Collections Department, University of Utah Marriott Library, Salt Lake City, Utah.

any opera house setting where they would have had access to the nineteenth-century repertory. Willam became committed to the classics, as he learned about them, but his was not the purist's concern for authenticity.

Despite his busy schedule in Portland, Willam followed his brothers' careers from afar and was especially interested in Lew's continuing development. During their time together in vaudeville Willam had once challenged Lew to do sixteen *tours en l'air* without stopping, betting him five dollars that it was impossible. In Portland Willam received a letter from Lew saying that the older brother owed him five dollars, and Willam paid up.

Family members supported one another in various ways. Chris, Harold, Lew, and Ruby (who was still only Harold's girlfriend at this point) got vaudeville bookings across the country and worked their way to Portland in time to see Willam's 1935 Rose Festival performances.[18] They even picked up Guy in Utah to make it a real family reunion, and Mignon sponsored a studio "tea" in honor of their visit. The brothers and their partners also danced with Willam's student company that summer when the latter was invited to perform at the opening of the Moore Theatre in Seattle, the first appearance of Willam's troupe outside of Portland.[19] The younger brothers' success helped build Willam's reputation in Portland; he made a point of featuring their names on published lists of his students that had gone on to professional careers in dance.[20] On the other hand, Willam helped his brothers through a jobless spell by making them guest artists

---

[18] Josephine McKendrick, Lew's partner at the time, went only as far as Utah, where she stayed due to poor health.

[19] This was technically the reopening of the Moore Theatre when it was taken over by a new manager, Cecelia Schultz. Harold, Ruby, Lew, and one of Willam's Portland students performed a number from *The Great Waltz* and part of the family's traditional vaudeville act.

[20] For example, in the fall of 1934, Willam's status as a teacher was reinforced by a newspaper story reporting that five of his former students (his brothers, their partners, and Wiora Stoney) were now dancing in *The Great Waltz* on Broadway.

on the faculty of his 1935 summer session, which boasted of
advance registrations from Utah, Washington, and California
as well as Oregon.[21] The brothers' efforts were often intertwined, their careers and successes a cooperative project
rather than isolated individual achievements.

Positive reviews from the Moore Theatre engagement
garnered the student group new respect at home. Willam
was now ready to consolidate his position in the community,
and one way to do that was to ally himself with the senior,
not junior, symphony. The Portland Symphony, which had
been founded by Uncle Mose, had the backing of the city's
wealthiest and most influential citizens, who considered
supporting the orchestra a socially acceptable form of community service.[22] For the Moore Theatre opening, Willam
had made the conscious choice to take as his conductor not
Gershkovitch but Mischa Pelz, who worked with the senior
symphony in the absence of its usual conductor Willem van
Hoogstraten. A disappointed Gershkovitch tried to persuade
Willam that the ballet master's future lay in working with
Portland's young people, but Willam had other plans. His
instincts were always to follow the path leading to greatest
opportunity, and it stood to reason that an alliance with the
Portland Symphony would bring increased community backing and more chances to perform. This hunch was confirmed
when Willam and his students were invited to dance with
the Symphony as part of a benefit performance just two
months after their trip to Seattle.

Willam's status as a teacher was validated again that
fall when Natalie Lauterstein, who had gone to New York
after the Moore Theatre opening, received a contract from
George Balanchine at the Metropolitan Opera Ballet. Newspaper announcements for the resumption of classes in the

---

[21] "William F. Christensen Plans Summer Class," *Oregon Sunday Journal*, May 26,
1935, Utah Ballet Archives (Box 7, Portland Scrapbook 1), Special Collections,
University of Utah Marriott Library, Salt Lake City, Utah.

[22] E. Kimbark MacColl, *The Growth of a City: Power and Politics in Portland, Oregon*
(Portland: Georgian Press, 1979), 461.

**13**   Mignon Lee Christensen, early 1930s.
Photograph by Lew Christensen, courtesy of Willam F. Christensen

fall of 1935 celebrated the reopening *not* of the Portland
Creative Theatre but of the "William F. Christensen Ballet
School." The experimental theater had served its purpose and
was now a thing of the past. With the prospect of joint
performances with the Portland Symphony ahead, Willam

had less need of an umbrella organization under which to organize studio performances and lecture demonstrations. He focused his attention on the school bearing his name and expanded the faculty to include Reed, Irwin, and Mignon.

Mignon's early Portland years were devoted to caring for their son William Lee, but as Willam's activities expanded she stepped in to help teach in the school. Her occasional numbness and fainting spells were diagnosed in Portland as multiple sclerosis, a disease about which little was then known. Willam spared no effort to get effective treatment, and Mignon tried experimental cures such as consuming a pound of liver a day when one doctor theorized that the disease was related to an iron deficiency. Mignon's health was uneven and unpredictable, but she did enjoy periods of re-mission in Portland and even performed in some of Willam's ballets in 1936 and 1937, probably in the spirit of supporting the family effort.

The repertory Willam created during his remaining years in Portland reflected the popularity of character ballets during the 1930s. As the ballet historian Katherine Sorley Walker explains, the trend of the day, derived from Fokine and Diaghilev, was generally to *demi-caractère* ballets, "an initial book or scenario and of the expression, through dance, music, and decor, of a story or at least a thematic develop-ment."[23] In contrast to today's technique-oriented, neoclassi-cal repertory, "the creation of character, the grasp of period style, of dramatic inflection and mimetic comedy," took precedence over technique.[24] Willam's Portland repertory fit this pattern neatly; the ballets almost always included an easily understood plot line as well as a prime role for Willam himself. Plot summaries for the ballets were always clearly spelled out in program notes and often appeared in news-paper columns before the day of a performance.

---

[23] Katherine Sorley Walker, *De Basil's Ballets Russes* (London: Hutchinson, 1982), 13.

[24] *Ibid.*

**14**   Zelda Morey, Willam Christensen, and Jacqueline Martin in Willam's
*Visions de Massenet*, 1936.
Photograph by Markham, courtesy of Willam F. Christensen

The three new works Willam produced for a performance with the Portland Symphony in early 1936 exemplified this prevailing esthetic. *Les Visions de Massenet* presented Willam in the role of the composer; lapsing into a reverie while composing, he danced with figures representing instruments of the orchestra.[25] *A Spanish Romance*, set to Rimsky-Korsakov's *Caprice Espagnol*, was built around jealousies in a Spanish cafe. A "handsome gallant" flirted with two ladies, whose jealousy culminated in "a heated mime argument and fight."[26] A drumroll announced the arrival of the hero (Willam), who admired the ladies but was distracted by the arrival of "a ballerina" (Reed). The latter's dancing abated the furore in the cafe and predictably swept all into a colorful finale.[27] *Rumanian Wedding Festival*, set to Georges Enesco's *Rumanian Rhapsody*, was built on the theme of a peasant wedding and included among its predictable characters a shy bride and bashful groom, a peasant girl excited about dressing up for the event, and the comic figure of a mother who brought her overdressed children to the wedding party and was teased by flirtatious young "swains." All three works were populated with broadly drawn figures and depended upon Willam's ability to establish characterization through movement.

During the summer of 1936 Willam went East again, this time to tour briefly with his brothers in Lincoln Kirstein's new company, Ballet Caravan.[28] In New York Willam attended

---

[25] "'Visions of Massenet' Will Open Program," *Oregon Sunday Journal*, February 9, 1936, Utah Ballet Archives (Box 7, Portland Scrapbook 2), Special Collections, University of Utah Marriott Library, Salt Lake City, Utah.

[26] "Spanish Ballet to Be Offered," no paper credited, no date, Utah Ballet Archives (Box 7, Portland Scrapbook 2), Special Collections, University of Utah Marriott Library, Salt Lake City, Utah.

[27] *Ibid.*

[28] In Portland, overblown press reports of Willam's departure alleged that he was going to help Kirstein run the company and even provide ballets for its repertory. Instead, Willam stayed with Harold and Lew in Westport, Connecticut, while Caravan members provided incidental dances for Molière's *Le Bourgeois Gentilhomme* at the Westport Country Playhouse.

a concert at Lewisohn Stadium as the guest of van Hoogstraten, who conducted there regularly each summer. Van Hoogstraten suggested that Willam choreograph Mozart's *Eine Kleine Nacht-musik*, and Willam put his hand to the task that fall.

While working with the Mozart score, Willam under-went a change of orientation as a choreographer. Perhaps because of the music, or perhaps because of his exposure to his brothers' efforts (and insights they might have shared as a result of their work with Balanchine), Willam began to think more seriously about the process of making dances. His self-concept shifted from that of a ballet master fashioning entertaining divertissements or group recital pieces to that of a choreographer concerned with the shape and quality of original movement. His time in the studio involved much trial and error; he experimented with movement passages and changed his mind from day to day as he searched for the steps that would convey the look he sought.[29] The resulting work, *Coeur de Glace* (or, *The Princess with the Frozen Heart*), did include idealized characters in a romantic plot, but it was a breakthrough in that it did not depend upon vaudeville-style stunts, boisterous character dancing, or the massive effect of large-scale spectacle to win his audience over. In retrospect Willam considered it his first serious exercise in concert choreography.

Another ballet Willam set during this period was his version of Fokine's *Spectre de la Rose*, which Willam renamed *L'Amant Reve* ("The Dream Lover"). As in Fokine's original, the ballet was a pas de deux in which a young woman dreamed about her partner at the previous evening's ball, but Willam's version had a significant difference. Fokine's "dream lover" had appeared as an incarnation of the rose held by the girl as she slept, and Nijinsky's leotard was decorated with petals, making him a not quite human, and not very masculine, figure. Willam danced Nijinsky's role

---

[29] Mattlyn Gavers describes Willam's working methods, his tendency to experiment and change movement passages during the Portland years, in the telephone interview dated December 8, 1988.

clad in tux and tails rather than in a leotard with floral motifs. Willam had learned in his vaudeville days that the men were received best when their attire was recognizably masculine, and he continued to reach out to audiences on their own terms. According to Reed, "If he'd come on that stage with a rose petal on, he'd have been lynched."[30] Beyond audience response, Willam's own intolerance for homosexuality left no room for the slightest suggestion of androgynous figures on stage; his ballets were built upon firmly fixed characterizations with very traditional gender roles. As a man making a profession of ballet when such a career choice was almost unheard of, Willam never made an artistic choice that would leave his own masculinity open to question.

By the fall of 1936, Willam had built up a company of respectable size if limited experience. He had a healthy contingent of well-trained male dancers: Robert Irwin, Ronald Chetwood, Earl Riggins, Fred Staver, Robert Franklin, Dan Feely, Alvin Stucki, and Grant Christensen, some developed locally, others forwarded by Uncle Pete in Salt Lake City.[31] The men balanced the company's women – Janet Reed, Norma Nielsen, Merle Williams, Jeanette Harrow, Jacqueline Martin, Zelda Morey, Billie Otis, Mary Corruthers, Mattlyn Gevurtz, and a host of other eager *coryphées*. With this group, Willam felt ready to move forward in a big way. In press releases to local papers he announced grandly that in the next twelve months he would "build an organization equal to any ballet in the country."[32] Such rhetoric was especially ambitious in view of the arrival in America, during Willam's years in Portland, of Colonel W. de Basil's Ballets Russes de Monte Carlo. That company had debuted at the St. James Theatre in

---

[30] Telephone interview with Janet Reed Erskine, November 5, 1988.

[31] Emil Enna, "Christensen Ballet to Feature Male Dancers," *News-Telegram*, October 2, 1936, Utah Ballet Archives (Box 7, Portland Scrapbook 2), Special Collections, University of Utah Marriott Library, Salt Lake City, Utah. Grant Christensen may have been a cousin or distant relation of Willam.

[32] "Christensen Announces New Plans," *Oregon Sunday Journal*, October 11, 1936, Utah Ballet Archives (Box 7, Portland Scrapbook 2), Special Collections, University of Utah Marriott Library, Salt Lake City, Utah.

New York in December 1933 with Massine as artistic director and a roster that included such highly trained and
experienced performers as Alexandra Danilova, Tamara
Toumanova, Irina Baronova, Tatiana Riabouchinska, Nina
Verchinina, Yurek Shabelevsky, David Lichine, André
Eglevsky, and Paul Petroff. The very presence of de Basil's
company might have intimidated Willam, but he was never
one to be deterred by the success of others. Moreover, he
seems not to have lost time worrying over the fact that in
contrast to the touring Russians, he had no clear ties to the
Imperial tradition, no European credentials or obvious mantle
of authority validating his aspirations as a company director.
Willam, a self-motivated entrepreneur, saw de Basil's company as a model and set out to copy it by touring. He hired
a Portland businessman, James S. Richardson, to be his
company's agent and signed a five-year contract.

    Richardson set up offices for the enterprise in Portland
and New York City and even published a cable address to
facilitate inquiries. Willam anticipated a flood of bookings and
doubtless persuaded his unpaid but idealistic and committed
young dancers that fame waited at the doorstep. He focused
on preparing his students to perform and set about building a
touring repertory. That December, he premiered *Coeur de Glace*,
his own version of Ravel's *Bolero*, and *The Bartered Bride*, a
comic character ballet set to music from Smetana's opera.

    The prospect of extensive touring thrilled Willam's
students and stimulated their best efforts in classes and
rehearsals. Willam inspired his dancers' hard work and
sacrifice through the example of his own hard work and his
habitually optimistic rhetoric. He glamorized the situation of
his advanced students, and in so doing he inspired their
loyalty and confidence. Willam's encouraging words were
more than wishful thinking; he had an ability to present past
accomplishments in the best possible light and to see the
potential for achieving great things with the resources at
hand. After all, his former students *had* performed in a hit
Broadway show and were now in the corps de ballet of the
Metropolitan Opera. The power of Willam's positive thinking

convinced his amateur dancers of future glory. He now had the necessary bodies; he had only to continue molding the dancers, forming his repertory, and lining up the necessary bookings to get his show on the road. His immediate goal was similar to his desires in 1927 when he left Utah to break into vaudeville: to get an act together, get it on stage, and gain recognition through touring.

Despite the build-up, the anticipated tour for the spring and summer of 1937 did not materialize. Instead, Willam and the dancers had to be content with staging yet another coronation ceremony for Portland's Rose Festival. Occasionally, academic institutions such as Reed College and the University of Oregon in Eugene sponsored concerts of Willam's dancers, in the spirit of educating their students about ballet. Otherwise, Willam's alliance with the Portland Symphony brought the same types of performing opportunities he had had with the Junior Symphony: periodic appearances in "symphony-ballet concerts" in which the dancers were featured as a special attraction, a bonus enhancing one of the symphony's regular season concerts. With the senior symphony as with the junior, ballet was presented as an adornment to a program that was still essentially a musical event. Other arrangements would be necessary to fulfill Willam's dream of a touring ballet company.

Impatient with Richardson's lack of progress in landing bookings, Willam began to cast about for ways to make his own opportunities. Deane Crockett, who now danced with the San Francisco Opera Ballet, wrote that Adolph Bolm's contract with that institution was not being renewed for the 1937–38 season. Gaetano Merola, the opera's director, was looking for a new ballet master and had hired Serge Oukrainsky on a temporary basis for the fall '37 season. Smelling a major opportunity in the air, Crockett encouraged Willam to come to San Francisco to try to establish himself there.[33]

---

[33] Interview with Willam F. Christensen, Salt Lake City, Utah, March 27, 1987. An unpublished history of the San Francisco Ballet by Russell Hartley also asserts that

In August Willam's troupe was scheduled to perform with the symphony at Portland's Multnomah Stadium as part of the city's "Symphony under the Stars" series. This year the guest conductor brought in for the ballet evening was Efrem Kurtz, the musical director of the Ballet Russe de Monte Carlo who had also toured with Pavlova. Kurtz came to town early for rehearsals and openly expressed his appreciation of Willam's choreography.[34] The conductor was on his way to California, and he promised to put in a good word for Willam with Merola.

Willam felt irresistibly drawn to San Francisco. Ignoring his contract with Richardson, Willam made a quick trip to the Bay Area to meet Merola and Lee Caiti, the man in charge of the ballet school attached to the opera.[35] They encouraged Willam and his students to come down to try out for Oukrainsky, who would be auditioning dancers for the fall season.

Chris could not understand why his son would even consider giving up the Portland school that allowed the family to live so comfortably. Willam was now supporting both parents as well as his wife and son, and going to San Francisco would involve a serious financial risk. Moreover, Richardson threatened to sue Willam for breach of contract if he and his dancers went off to another company.[36] But Willam

---

one of Willam's former Portland students, Betty Joan Dodson, who had joined the Opera Ballet under Bolm, kept Willam apprised of the San Francisco situation. Hartley goes so far as to suggest that Crockett tried to persuade Merola to hire Willam directly following Bolm but that Merola wanted to play it safe and thus hired Oukrainsky on a temporary basis, giving him time for a better appraisal of Willam's fitness for the position. Russell Hartley, "The San Francisco Ballet: A History, 1922–1977," unpublished manuscript, San Francisco Performing Arts Library and Museum.

[34] "Noted Conductor Thrills over 'Chopinade,'" *News-Telegram*, August 7, 1937, Utah Ballet Archives (Box 7, Portland Scrapbook 2), Special Collections, University of Utah Marriott Library, Salt Lake City, Utah.

[35] Caiti's name is spelled variously in the manuscript records available to this author. I have chosen to adopt Hartley's spelling rather than "Ciati," which is also used.

[36] Richardson was upset that Willam got the San Francisco job on his own and did not pay Richardson a commission. Interview with Willam F. Christensen, Salt Lake City, Utah, April 10, 1987.

had aspirations that Portland could not fulfill. He left his family there temporarily while he made an exploratory venture. Late in the summer of 1937, Willam and a core of his best students drove two cars to San Francisco to audition for the San Francisco Opera Ballet.

# 5

# BROADWAY, BALANCHINE, AND BALLET CARAVAN (1934–1936)

The years 1934 and 1935 brought a change of direction in the careers of Lew and Harold: a gradual transition from the world of vaudeville to that of concert dance. That transition unfolded largely according to the dictates of personal finances, a severely limiting factor during this era in which Franklin D. Roosevelt devalued the dollar, dust storms destroyed livestock and crops across much of the nation's interior, and the unemployed looked to government programs such as the Works Progress Administration for jobs. The mid-thirties also presented the Christensens with new social vistas, witnessed Lew's emergence as a star in Balanchine's first American company, and provided the showcase for Lew's first serious choreography. Along the way, the Christensens became part of Lincoln Kirstein's program to Americanize the art of ballet.

In New York during the summer of '34, while Willam performed with Fokine's company at the Capitol Theatre, Harold and Lew were in rehearsals for *The Great Waltz*, which opened at the Center Theatre, September 22, 1934.[1] This lavish

---

[1] Harold and Lew also took class with the Russian choreographer. Lew made a point of learning the solo roles from as many Fokine ballets as he could with an eye to restaging them in the future. He later explained:

> You could be an authority for carrying on his choreography by learning that way. Many dancers I knew at that time knew all the parts … so you knew how to reproduce them if you had to.

(Barbara Newman, *Striking a Balance* [London: Elm Tree Books, 1982], 31.)

According to Harold, Fokine wanted Lew to dance Nijinsky's role, the Golden Slave, in the company's production of *Schéhérazade* (which was performed at Lewisohn Stadium that same month) because Fokine admired Lew's high leaps and deep, soft plié. But when the time came to set the ballet, Fokine's son could not locate Harold and Lew. The lost opportunity did not affect the brothers adversely,

operetta, based loosely on the lives of the Johanns Strauss, father and son, was deemed by the *Times* critic "the most colossal operetta in years," boasting an "orgy of brilliant costumes, whirling scenery and mechanical effects," with a cast of forty-two principals, one hundred singers, fifty-three musicians, and sixty dancers.[2] The Christensen Brothers' act made a sudden leap from its haphazard vaudevillian context to an elaborate stage world of rococo facades, massive chandeliers, and a rising orchestra pit. The show's director, Hassard Short, inserted the Christensens' double pas de deux into his portrayal of Viennese society by revising a scene originally created for a single bride and groom to include two wedding couples. Harold and Lew wore uniforms, Ruby and Josephine wore wedding dresses, and Ruby even delivered a line before the couples left the stage to attend their wedding breakfast.[3]

Alexandra Danilova was the show's ballerina, but the large dance numbers were set by Albertina Rasch, whose "Albertina Rasch Dancers" formed the core of the dancing cast. With choreography for several Broadway plays and Hollywood musicals to her credit, Rasch was well-qualified for *The Great Waltz* assignment.[4] But she had a reputation for being difficult to work with; she was demanding and spoke harshly to her dancers in a vocabulary studded with

---

as they were about to join the cast of *The Great Waltz*. Still, it would be interesting to have reviews describing Lew in the famous role, perhaps with comparisons to Nijinsky. Barbara Cohen interview with Harold Christensen and Ruby Asquith Christensen, San Anselmo, California, December 29, 1976.

[2] Brooks Atkinson, "Opening of 'The Great Waltz' in the Center Theatre of the Rockefeller Group," *New York Times*, September 24, 1934; and Frank W. D. Ries, "Albertina Rasch: The Broadway Career," *Dance Chronicle* 6.2 (1983): 123.

[3] Interview with Ruby Asquith Christensen, San Anselmo, California, September 26, 1987.

[4] See Frank W. D. Ries's series of articles on Rasch, including the one listed in note 2 above; "Albertina Rasch: The Hollywood Career," *Dance Chronicle* 6.4 (1984) 281–362; and "Albertina Rasch: The Concert Career and the Concept of the American Ballet," *Dance Chronicle* 7.2 (1984): 159–97.

obscenities.[5] Rasch was out of town when Short hired the Christensens during the musical's rehearsal period, and when she returned, the Christensens found her a formidable adversary. Perhaps she resented the Christensens' act being imposed upon the show without her approval. In what appeared to the Christensens to be a deliberate attempt at sabotage, Rasch undermined preparations for the wedding scene by tying up Ruby and Josephine in rehearsals for the larger group dances in which they also performed. Personality conflicts rose to the surface one day when Harold addressed her as "Mrs. Rasch" instead of "Madame Rasch," a pointed breach of etiquette. Rasch won this battle of wills: when the show had to be shortened during the final rehearsals, the double wedding scene was greatly abbreviated, and although the couples remained in the scene, Ruby lost her line. The four also lost their semi-private dressing rooms and were moved in with other cast members.

Sharing a dressing room with the sophisticated show girls was in fact a treat for Ruby and Josephine. After years of vaudeville touring and an existence centered chiefly on the Christensens, Ruby and Josephine were now dazzled by the backstage chatter of the Ziegfeld-type beauties. The stage-struck Ruby especially enjoyed watching the show girls apply their makeup and listening to the tales of their glamorous social lives. By pure coincidence, one of the other dancers was Lew's former partner, Wiora Stoney, who had auditioned for the show while taking classes from Rasch. Ruby and Josephine spent leisure time with Wiora, who, to her intense chagrin, ended up as Josephine's understudy for the role of Lew's bride in the wedding scene.

---

[5] Harold and Ruby Christensen's 1976 interview with Barbara Cohen gives examples of the way Rasch verbally abused her dancers. The Christensens were not the only ones who found Rasch's personality unpleasant and rehearsal methods objectionable. In an Oral History Project interview at the Dance Collection, The New York Public Library, Kathryn Mullowny recalled Rasch as "a fat Hungarian Jewess with a cruel voice." Ries's articles give a balanced view of Rasch's personality but do not deny her reputation as a difficult taskmistress.

Rasch's choreography for the show included a Hungarian czardas, a large ballet scene starring Danilova, and the finale in which thirty couples waltzed on the rotating stage.[6] Having been raised on Strauss and trained in social dance forms from an early age, the Christensens did not find the theatricalized folk and social dances set by Rasch much of a challenge. They joked that the show should be called *The Great Two-Step* because of a sequence in which they waltzed to one side (step-step-close) but did the two-step (step-close-step) to the other.[7] But if *The Great Waltz* was not a step forward in the brothers' artistic development, it did provide a steady income for the seventeen weeks they and their partners were on contract. Lew later admitted that, while he "despised" the show, it at least paid the rent.[8] Once the foursome's time commitment to *The Great Waltz* had settled into an orderly pattern of six evening shows and two matinees a week, Lew announced that they were all going to sign up for classes at the School of American Ballet.[9]

Housed in a studio at Madison Avenue and 59th Street (one formerly used by Isadora Duncan), the School of American Ballet had been established by Lincoln Kirstein, Edward Warburg, and George Balanchine with the announced purpose of training young Americans to be ballet dancers. The school was the necessary first step toward Kirstein's larger

---

[6] Ries, "Albertina Rasch: The Broadway Career," 121–22.

[7] Barbara Cohen interview with Harold Christensen and Ruby Asquith Christensen, San Anselmo, California, December 29, 1976.

[8] Newman, 30.

[9] Josephine McKendrick remembers that when Lew began to get restless in *The Great Waltz*, their vaudeville agent lined up a tour for them to Paris. They rehearsed and made plans to acquire passports, but she sprained her ankle, and the brothers decided that they did not want to go to Europe (interview with Josephine McKendrick Collins, Provo, Utah, September 1, 1987). Her story is corroborated by an article in which Harold remembers being offered a contract for six weeks in Paris; see "Petaluma, Ballet, Business, America," *The New Thesaurus*, Summer 1979, 19, 23.

    It also appears that Harold and Lew took classes at the School of American Ballet, at least intermittently, before they were in *The Great Waltz*. But Josephine insists that they did not study there on an ongoing basis, or as a group, until they were in that musical.

vision, the creation of a ballet company composed of Americans. Certainly, Kirstein was neither the first to provide ballet training for young Americans with an eye toward performance nor the first to conceive of an American ballet company. But Kirstein's vision included the development of a new repertory, grounded in American themes; in early conversations with Balanchine he proposed ballets based on the stories of Pocahontas and Custer's Last Stand.[10] The desired repertory would result from collaborations with American poets, painters, and composers. With his wealth, his Harvard education, and his connections in the literary and artistic worlds, Kirstein had the capacity to bring talented people together and the patience to wait out the germination period. These overriding goals shaped his dealings with the Christensen brothers for many years, and Lew especially became a pivotal figure in the working out of Kirstein's ambitions.

Shortly after Balanchine and his business partner, Vladimir Dimitriew, arrived in America in October 1933, John Martin devoted his dance column in the *New York Times* to a discussion of the hoped-for establishment of an American ballet, which now seemed a real possibility "in spite of all the skeptics who said it could never be done." Martin explained of the Kirstein/Balanchine venture: "Only American dancers will be admitted to the courses," and "every effort will be made to develop a distinctly American organization." To those who questioned the choice of a Russian choreographer to direct the desired American institution, Martin pointed out, "Since there has never been an American ballet of this sort, it is obvious that a director must be found elsewhere."[11]

The desired American dancers found their way to Balanchine by a variety of routes and brought diverse backgrounds. Catherine Littlefield and her sister Dorothie brought

---

[10] Kirstein's vision is outlined in a letter to A. Everett Austin, Jr., which is reprinted in "Three Early Letters," *Ballet Review* 24.1 (Spring 1996): 21.

[11] John Martin, "The American Ballet," *New York Times*, October 22, 1933. Chujoy gives the date as 23 October.

a contingent of dancers from their school in Philadelphia. William Dollar came to the School after studying with Michael Mordkin; Elise Reiman had studied with Adolph Bolm when she read about the new school in a magazine. Others learned about the school by word of mouth. Gisella Caccialanza, who in her youth had been one of Enrico Cecchetti's last protégés, was making a living in the corps de ballet at Radio City Music Hall when Serge Lifar, horrified that her consummate training should be put to such use, insisted that she meet Balanchine.

The School of American Ballet opened officially in January, 1934. The Christensens and their partners began regular study there in the fall of that year. They looked with awe upon the young and exacting Balanchine, and they felt keenly Kirstein's scrutinizing gaze as he gauged the students' potential.[12] The foursome's main teacher was Pierre Vladimirov, who had succeeded Nijinsky as a principal danseur at the Maryinsky and had been Pavlova's last partner. A master teacher, Vladimirov gave challenging but satisfying classes and would occasionally astonish the students by murmuring something to the pianist in Russian and bounding around the studio in an excerpt from *Le Spectre de la Rose*.[13] The four considered Balanchine's classes more difficult because he would choose one step and have the dancers repeat it in seemingly endless variations. Ruby realized that their training, which had stressed strength in the legs, quick footwork, and beats, was not what Balanchine was looking for: "We did not have the line, the extension he wanted."[14] Instead, Balanchine demanded greater freedom and fluidity in the legs. "All of a sudden we saw legs like Patricia Bowman's that went up beside the face, and arabesques that never ended. It was quite a change."[15]

In December 1934 the Christensens and their partners were among *The Great Waltz* cast members whose contracts

---

[12] KQED interview with Ruby Christensen.

[13] Interview with Josephine McKendrick Collins, Provo, Utah, September 1, 1987.

[14] KQED interview with Ruby Christensen.

[15] *Ibid.*

expired and were not renewed when the musical was tightened for its extended run. So the foursome returned to vaudeville to make a living while taking class as often as possible at the School of American Ballet. They played the subway circuit (theaters in New York that could be reached by public transportation) and even an occasional nightclub to make ends meet.[16] Although Kirstein later described Lew as "a focus of our stripling seasons," the Christensens played no role in the American Ballet during its first year.[17] Specifically, they did not perform in the company's New York premiere season in March 1935 (for which the repertory included *Serenade, Alma Mater, Errante, Reminiscence, Mozartiana, Transcendence* and *Dreams*). Instead, the brothers and their partners sent Balanchine's dancers an encouraging telegram on opening night and signed it "The Four Christensens," an indication that their identities were still closely tied to the vaudeville act.[18] Their aspirations lay with Balanchine, but the American Ballet's limited financial means simply did not permit him to offer them contracts.[19]

So, during the summer of 1935 the Christensen act worked its way west. As previously noted, Harold and Lew picked up their older brother Guy in Utah, left Josephine there with her family, and took Ruby on to Portland for the family reunion planned by Willam. Meanwhile, Kirstein was pursuing negotiations with the Metropolitan Opera, which had approached him that spring with a residency offer for the American Ballet. While the Christensens were performing at the opening of the Moore Theatre in Seattle, word came that

---

[16] McKendrick recalls that for nightclub performances the women had rubber soles on their pointe shoes, and the contracts specified that waiters could not walk across the floor during the act. Conversation with Josephine McKendrick Collins, Provo, Utah, September 1, 1987.

[17] Lincoln Kirstein, "American Apollo," *Ballet News*, January 1985, 12.

[18] Western Union Telegram, March 1, 1935, in a Christensen family scrapbook, Christensen-Caccialanza Collection, San Francisco Performing Arts Library and Museum.

[19] Kirstein mentions Lew's "audition for a company that, likely enough, would be unable to give him a contract." Kirstein, "American Apollo," 11.

Harold and Lew and their partners had been offered contracts for the Metropolitan Opera Ballet that fall.[20] The following week, the Metropolitan Opera's general manager, Edward Johnson, announced Balanchine's appointment to the post of ballet master.[21]

The invitation to join Balanchine's company meant that Lew and Harold would finally be able to dignify their training and perform classical dance without having to make concessions to popular taste. The career change would bring a cut in pay – Harold would earn only twenty-five dollars a week and Lew, thirty – but their lessons at the School of American Ballet would now be free. So determined were they to make the switch that they burned their vaudeville costumes so they would not be tempted to turn back.[22] But even with the Metropolitan contracts in hand, Harold, Lew, and their partners were not immediately part of Balanchine's American Ballet company. The brothers did not take part in the company's ambitious but ill-fated tour that departed in October and was stranded in Scranton, Pennsylvania, when the booking agency folded. Balanchine actually had two companies at this point.[23] The primary company, which formed the core of the new opera ballet, consisted of the original American Ballet, the twenty-odd dancers who had performed at the Avery and Adelphi Theatres the previous season (including, *inter alia*, Leda Anchutina, Ruthanna Boris, Gisella Caccialanza, Holly Howard, Annabelle Lyon, Kathryn Mullowny, Charles Laskey, Joseph Levinoff, and William Dollar).[24] New dancers

---

[20] "Trio of Dancers Receive Attractive Offer," probably in the *Seattle Star*, July 30, 1935, clipping in Christensen family scrapbook, Utah Ballet Archives (Box 7, Scrapbook 1), Special Collections, University of Utah Marriott Library, Salt Lake City, Utah.

[21] "New Ballet Corps Engaged for the Metropolitan," *New York Times*, August 8, 1935.

[22] Newman, 30–31.

[23] Barbara Cohen interview with Harold and Ruby Christensen, San Anselmo, California, December 29, 1976.

[24] Ruth Eleanor Howard, *The Story of the American Ballet* (New York: Ihra Publishing Company, 1936), 36. Howard lists twenty-three dancers as being "Original Members of the American Ballet Company" and fifty-five dancers under "Present Membership of the American Ballet Company," [37].

such as the Christensens, and some former dancers of the Metropolitan ballet corps, including Lillian Moore, joined this core group to form an expanded company sometimes known as the American Ballet Ensemble.[25] By November, 1935, the full ensemble was immersed in rehearsals for the winter opera season. For Harold and Lew, the long transition was complete; they faced the future in league with Kirstein and Balanchine.

After the American Ballet's aborted tour in October 1935, the Metropolitan Opera House must have seemed a welcome haven. To be in residence at the Metropolitan was to gain secure income on a home stage (averting the uphill struggle of uncertain seasons in strange or inadequate theaters) and to acquire the tradition and prestige of the sponsoring institution. The match seemed ideal: the Met needed a ballet master and an improved corps de ballet, and Balanchine, who had choreographed opera ballets in London, Copenhagen, Monte Carlo, and Paris, had a company that needed opportunities to perform.[26] Edward Johnson announced that the American Ballet had been selected to provide "young blood and a fresh viewpoint," which suggested that Balanchine would be free to supply inventive choreography to the traditional repertory.[27] Kirstein was overwhelmed by the Met's vast scale and luxurious aura; the prospect of his young company performing in the elegant opera house gave the excited young patron a case of "red and gold disease."[28] Expectations ran high; the Christensens were joining the Kirstein-Balanchine venture at a moment of peak enthusiasm and seemingly unlimited potential.

The optimistic bubbles burst as the company discovered their backstage accommodations in an institution that

---

[25] Conversation with Chrystelle Bond, Essen, Germany, June 1988; "New Ballet Corps Engaged for the Metropolitan," *New York Times*, August 8, 1935.

[26] Lincoln Kirstein, "Blast at Ballet," in *Ballet: Bias and Belief* (New York: Dance Horizons, 1983), 185.

[27] "New Ballet Corps Engaged for the Metropolitan," *New York Times*, August 8, 1935.

[28] Lincoln Kirstein, *Thirty Years* (New York: Alfred A. Knopf, 1978), 52.

exalted the voice over all else. At the Metropolitan Opera, dance was considered a necessary evil; it existed chiefly to adorn the action of the operas and was expected to fulfill that subservient role with tact, never distracting from the primary focus of the musical event. This attitude translated into unfavorable working conditions for the ballet troupe. The dancers balked when they saw their costumes: old garments filthy from repeated use because the opera administration did not want to spend the money to have them cleaned. According to Ruby, "The Christensens led a small revolution there. . . . They refused to wear the costumes that itched when you put them on."[29]

The dancers' dressing rooms were also a sore point. The women changed on the fourth floor in a single large room with old mirrors and racks of costumes down the middle.[30] The men's dressing room was up yet another flight of stairs. (They were forced to use the stairs because the elevators were reserved for singers.) The changing rooms had no showers and were usually without running water, so Edward Warburg purchased tubs that could be filled and used for tasks such as removing make-up and body paint. Once the frustrated men took the fire hose off the wall and used it to wash up, only to get into real trouble when the water flooded the costume room beneath them.[31]

Dancers were expected to remain in their changing quarters between entrances and were not allowed to hang around the wings. If they attempted to sneak downstairs to hear a famous singer or a favorite aria they were shooed away by the stage manager and instructed not to come until called.[32] On the other hand, the dancers were often required to "super," to fill out the stage by standing for long periods as supernumeraries, impersonating courtiers, spear-bearers, or

---

[29] KQED interview with Ruby Christensen.

[30] Interview with Josephine McKendrick Collins, Provo, Utah, September 1, 1987.

[31] Newman, 32–33.

[32] Interview with Josephine McKendrick Collins, Provo, Utah, September 1, 1987; KQED interview with Ruby Christensen.

anonymous townspeople. The dancers resented supering because it was beneath their talents and seemed yet another indication of the low esteem in which the ballet was held. Reflecting the general disenchantment, the Christensens joked sourly that at the Metropolitan Opera, the ballet was "the animal act," a term conjuring up vaudevillian images of trained dogs bounding through hoops.

During the winter season of 1935–36, Balanchine staged the ballets for fifteen operas, including *La Traviata*, *Faust*, *Lakmé*, *Tannhäuser*, *Carmen*, *La Juive*, *Die Meistersinger von Nurnberg*, and *The Bartered Bride*.[33] Engaged as principal dancers were two former members of Diaghilev's Ballets Russes: Tamara Geva (Balanchine's former wife) and Anatole Vilzak. Harold, Ruby, and Josephine were simply members of the corps de ballet, but Lew had soloist status.[34] Among his roles that season were the Rektah in *Lakmé*, with Elise Reiman and Doug Coudy, and the Heralds' dance in *La Juive*, with Coudy. Lew's ability to turn, which had been nurtured by Mascagno and highlighted in the vaudeville act, continued to serve him well. Balanchine termed Lew's pirouettes the cleanest he had ever seen and used Lew in a solo that included multiple pirouettes done in quick succession in different areas of the stage.[35] Several years later, when Kirstein published *Ballet Alphabet*, his entry defining pirouettes included Lew's name along with other technicians famous for their turns: Gaetan Vestris, Enrico Cecchetti, Vaslav Nijinsky, and André Eglevsky.[36]

---

[33] Richard Buckle states that Balanchine "made dances for thirteen operas" (Buckle, *George Balanchine, Ballet Master* [New York: Random House, 1988], 97), but *Choreography by George Balanchine: A Catalogue of Works* ([New York: Eakins Press, 1984], 123–34) lists fifteen operas with dances by Balanchine that first season at the Met.

[34] The men whose names were credited in the programs for specific dances were William Dollar, Douglas Coudy, Charles Laskey, and Lew. The list of regularly featured women was much longer, including Leda Anchutina, Ruthanna Boris, Anna Breyman, Gisella Caccialanza, Rabana Hasburgh, Holly Howard, Helen Leitch, Annabelle Lyon, Kathryn Mullowny, Yvonne Patterson, Elise Reiman, and Daphne Vane.

[35] Kirstein, *Thirty Years*, 301; KQED Interview with Harold Christensen.

[36] Lincoln Kirstein, "Ballet Alphabet," *Ballet: Bias and Belief* (New York: Kamin Publishers, 1939; reprint, New York: Dance Horizons, 1983), 354.

The failure of the American Ballet at the Met is generally attributed to Balanchine's artistic choices; the "fresh viewpoint" welcomed by the Met's administration did not include the *danse du ventre* (belly dance) Balanchine inserted in *Aïda* or his unrestrained Bacchanale in *Tannhäuser*. An editorial in *Musical America* complained that Balanchine had replaced the Met's tradition of "bad ballet" with "wrong ballet."[37] The Christensens participated in many of these ill-received divertissements, including the scene in *Aïda* in which the Egyptian princess is entertained in her chambers. Recalls Ruby, "Instead of having darling little children as *Aida's* court, [Balanchine] put the six tallest men in the ballet and had them blackened...and the audiences were horrified."[38] The choreography included a section from *The Prodigal Son* in which the men hold on to each other back-to-back and skitter around with bent knees. The dancers never had a chance to rehearse it with their paint on; on opening night they couldn't recognize each other and had to scramble around the stage to find their partners.[39]

Again because of their height, Harold and Lew were chosen to be boyars in the production of *Le Coq d'Or* the second season. The director instructed the men to wear beards, but Balanchine told them that boyars were clean-shaven, so the dancers showed up for rehearsal beardless. This small example illustrates how the dancers were caught in the middle between conflicting authority figures; the stage manager chastised the dancers for choosing to follow Balanchine, with whom their sympathies naturally lay.

---

[37] "The End of an Unhappy Ballet Experiment at the Opera," *Musical America*, April 25, 1938, 16.

[38] KQED Interview with Ruby Christensen.

[39] Interview with the Christensens, conducted by Francis Mason, Donald McDonaugh, and Don Daniels, in the spring of 1984. This unpublished interview was taped on the occasion of the brothers' visit to New York in conjunction with receiving the 1984 Capezio Dance Award. A transcript has been put on deposit at the San Francisco Performing Arts Library and Museum, San Francisco, California. Hereafter referred to as "Mason Interview, 1984."

Such unresolved conflicts backstage resulted in the dancers being put in untenable situations onstage. The best-known anecdote about Lew at the Metropolitan reflects the confusion that resulted from insufficient communication and cooperation during the period prior to performance. The company was rehearsing *Carmen*, with Rosa Ponselle in the leading role, and Lew was told that he would partner the prima donna in a dance devised by her personal dancing master. Ponselle refused to practice, sending her dancing master instead to sketch out the action. Lew met Ponselle for the first time in performance, and after their dance he started to exit, unaware that anything more was expected of him. To his amazement, Ponselle grabbed him, tossed the wine in her goblet into his face, and then pulled him to her in an embrace and an extended kiss. At intermission, Lew confided sardonically to Kirstein, "I thought she was trying to make me in front of God and everybody."[40]

Having no clout or status in the establishment, the dancers fought back against what they considered ill treatment by sabotaging performances through indifference. According to Harold, "We never memorized a court dance; we'd start out and follow each other. Then we'd bump and someone would fall down."[41] Supering especially brought out their hostilities. Once Harold and Lew were designated as spear bearers for a scene and were told, "When you see fire, you run." They stood on the stage, watched the smoke pouring out, and heard furious whispers to run, but stayed put. After the curtain fell, they were asked angrily why they hadn't run. "Well, we were looking for the fire. We didn't see any fire; we saw smoke."[42] Another time, the men in the

---

[40] Kirstein, *Thirty Years*, 68. In another account of this incident, Lew elaborated on the physical struggle with Ponselle, which he claimed turned into a brawl. See "The Three Brothers Christensen," *Dance*, October 1943, 6–7, 29.

[41] *Ibid*. It may also be that the dancers were not given adequate rehearsal time with the orchestra to stage dances thoroughly.

[42] *Ibid*. Harold also claims that the dancers tried to sneak offstage while supering during long crowd scenes in *Die Meistersinger von Nurnberg*.

company were required to fall and roll around the stage in a fight scene. When the stage manager came on in costume to direct the fight, the dancers dove at him, knocking him over and keeping him rolling throughout the duration of the scene.

And so the dancers got their limited revenge. Some paid acquaintances a dollar a performance to super for them, but Harold rejected that option because he viewed it as capitulating to unjust demands. During the company's second year at the Met, he refused to super and was fired by the opera management. Only when Kirstein and Balanchine persuaded Harold that supering was a necessary compromise that allowed the dancers to achieve their own goals did he apologize and regain his place in the company.[43] Although the management's dissatisfaction with Balanchine's choreography was probably the primary reason the company was let go during its third year at the Met, the dancers' misbehaving (in response to what they considered unfair treatment) may have also played a significant part in the American Ballet Ensemble's dismissal. As Ruby saw it, "the dancers complained and carried on and refused to cooperate until, of course, there was no more any question of Mr. Balanchine's American Ballet working at the Metropolitan."[44]

Against this backdrop of conflict, Lew began to gain stature in the company. He took over some of Anatole Vilzak's leading roles, not without trepidation. Because of Lew's height, he was also chosen (rather than Vilzak) to partner Felia Doubrovska (Vladimirov's wife and a former Ballets Russes ballerina) in Balanchine's *Serenata: 'Magic'*, a *pièce d'occasion* for the Hartford Festival in February of 1936.[45]

---

[43] *Ibid.*

[44] KQED Interview with Ruby Christensen.

[45] A tongue-in-cheek newspaper account of the Festival's impact on Hartford includes an intriguing glimpse of Lew rising to the occasion of his new celebrity with wit and dramatic flair. According to the reporter, he was accompanying Madame Doubrovska to a hotel restaurant, where they were to meet friends for lunch. As they descended a set of stairs, they noticed water leaking from the ceiling – the result of a recent storm. "Being an artist – a very great artist – [Doubrovska] immediately saw all the possibilities of the situation. In a single gesture

Lew also received exposure on the pages of the fashion magazine *Harper's Bazaar*, where he appeared in his *Serenata: 'Magic'* costume alongside models in debutante gowns in a Bonwit Teller ad.[46] But his first real breakthrough as a performer at the Met came later that spring, when he premiered in two new starring roles just two nights apart.

The first was actually a shared role in the sense that Lew and Holly Howard jointly created the figure of the title character in Balanchine's *The Bat*. This was the first independent (non-opera) ballet Balanchine created during the company's residency at the Met, and for it the choreographer selected music from *Die Fledermaus* because the orchestra was already familiar with the score and would not have to be paid for extra rehearsal time. *The Bat* was a frothy diversion evoking the atmosphere of Old Vienna; a poet, masked ladies, Gypsies, coachmen, and Can-Can dancers rounded out the cast in a park setting. Side by side and dressed in black, Lew and Howard impersonated the title character by carrying one large wing each. They separated, interacted with the other figures, and were reunited at the end.[47]

Lew's second major role was that of Orpheus in Balanchine's unconventional staging of *Orpheus and Eurydice*, the ballet master's most daring work at the Met to date. Kirstein and his associates, eager to try out their progressive theatrical ideas, presented the Orphic myth as an "eternal domestic tragedy of an artist and his wife," with "Hell as a

---

she illustrated several kinds of fear and several supplications to the Higher Powers for mercy. Mr. Christensen, also a very great artist, assumed a charming Romanesque pose with cupped hands raised aloft as though to catch every drop, and beneath the shield thus afforded, Mlle. Doubrovska, very gingerly and somewhat like Eliza escaping over the ice, made her way to the two Russians waiting below. These were possibly artists also, for they received the lady as though she had been returned from the jaws of death and one of them kissed her hand over and over again, and so passionately that a strictly American family sitting at the next table … were aghast, and never afterward could properly concentrate upon the business of eating luncheon." Henry McBride, "All Arts United in Hartford," *The Sun*, dateline February 22, 1936.

[46] *Harper's Bazaar*, June 1936, 90.

[47] Nancy Reynolds, *Repertory in Review* (New York: Dial Press, 1977), 45.

**15** Holly Howard, Joseph Lane, Lew Christensen, and Ruthanna Boris in Balanchine's *Orpheus and Eurydice*, 1936.
Photograph by George Platt Lynes, courtesy of Estate of George Platt Lynes and San Francisco Performing Arts Library and Museum

concentration camp," the Elysian Fields as "a desiccated bone-dry limbo of suspended animation," and Paradise as "the astronomical patterns of contemporary celestial science."[48] They were free to experiment with the visual aspects of the production, designed by Pavel Tchelitchew, because Warburg financed the spectacle (while the Metropolitan underwrote the musical side of the production). Balanchine tried the patience of conservative audiences by placing the singers in the pit and having his dancers on stage miming the opera's action.[49]

As the physical incarnation of the sung role, Lew had long acting passages in which he played his lute or suffered over his separation from Eurydice.[50] Ruby recalls that the choreography relied not on Lew's prodigious technique but rather on his stage presence, displaying him as "a man who walked with such beauty and such dignity and carried himself with such poise [that] it was just arresting to watch."[51] The first section of *Orpheus* had not been set fully by opening night (perhaps because the production followed so closely upon the heels of *The Bat*), so at the premiere Balanchine whispered directions to Lew from the prompter's box, talking him through the scene. Balanchine was able to do so in part because of Lew's musicality, his ingrained understanding of musical structure and phrasing derived from hours spent practicing the 'cello as well as the general musical education the Christensen brothers received in their youth.

*Orpheus and Eurydice* may have been a fiasco in the Met's eyes, but it consolidated Lew's new position as a leading male dancer. Balanchine declared with satisfaction that no male performer outside of Russia could match Lew

---

[48] Kirstein, *Ballet: Bias and Belief*, 189.

[49] While this *was* a daring move, Balanchine's separation of the vocal and movement components in *Orpheus and Eurydice* was not without precedent. As early as the 1917–1918 season, the Met had staged Fokine's version of Rimsky-Korsakov's *Le Coq d'Or*, in which dancers mimed the characterization of the singers' roles.

[50] Newman, 37–38.

[51] KQED Interview with Ruby Christensen.

as a *danseur noble*.[52] And surveying the field of that season's significant new performers, John Martin declared of Lew, "His performance of Orpheus, though against almost insuperable odds, stood out as the work of an eminently sincere and unspoiled talent, which will bear close watching."[53] Although the Christensens had originally been hired as part of the extended American Ballet Ensemble rather than the primary American Ballet Company, by the end of the first season at the Met, Lew had secured a place in the inner circle of Balanchine's dancers.

On the personal side, circumstances in the brothers' social lives changed radically during these two years. The romance between Harold and Ruby that had begun in Willam's Portland studio and blossomed on the vaudeville circuit began to fall apart once the two were performing steadily with the American Ballet Ensemble. The eye-opening dressing-room conversations during *The Great Waltz* may have influenced Ruby, alerting her to new social possibilities on the New York scene. Once at the Metropolitan, she gave Harold back his West Point pin and began dating other men. For his part, Harold found soloist Annabelle Lyon very appealing and took her out several times.[54] Without the vaudeville act to keep them together, Harold and Ruby developed separate social lives that would last for the next few years.

While Ruby strove for increasing sophistication, Josephine withdrew emotionally from the company. Josephine had grown up with a privileged position in L.P.'s studio; as one of his favored pupils, she was treated as a member of the extended Christensen clan. She was not used to backstage politics, New York-style, and she disliked the competitive atmosphere of the American Ballet. When it came time to renew contracts, Edward Warburg called her into his office and encouraged her to be more aggressive, but she was

[52] Kirstein, *Thirty Years*, 56–57.

[53] John Martin, "The Dance: Debutantes," *New York Times*, June 14, 1936.

[54] Interview with Harold Christensen, San Anselmo, California, September 23, 1987.

naturally shy and disliked having to push herself forward. She feared she might be expected to exchange sexual favors for good roles, and as a practicing Mormon she felt isolated because she did not drink or smoke. At the end of the first opera season, Josephine returned to Utah for good.

Harold and Lew, whose ties with the Mormon church had been severed effectively by their father's experiences, faced no such quandaries. Unlike Josephine, they fully embraced the experience of working with Vladimirov and Balanchine, if not with the administration of the opera house. Lew and Kirstein developed a fast friendship despite the differences in their backgrounds, education, and sexual orientation. Perhaps Lew, with his limited schooling, was drawn to Kirstein's obvious intellectual acumen, to the aura of confident influence stemming from his superior education and family wealth. For Kirstein, Lew personified a romantic ideal that derived from youthful readings of Robert Louis Stevenson.[55] But the dancer's importance to Kirstein went beyond such personal considerations: Lew's athletic and unmannered style represented to the eager young patron the fulfillment of his hopes for an American style of ballet. As Tchelitchew had observed after costume fittings for *Orpheus and Eurydice*, Lew provided a new prototype of the American prince: *"Beau garçon, mais vrai homme."*[56]

About the same time that Lew's professional, and strictly platonic, partnership with Josephine dissolved, he became interested in Gisella Caccialanza. Already established as a dancer of importance in Balanchine's company when Lew met her, Caccialanza had an unusual background for a twenty-year-old American. Born of Italian parents in San Diego, California, she had been taken to La Scala in 1925, at age eleven, in order to receive superior ballet training. There she attracted the attention of the aging Cecchetti, who devoted

---

[55] Lincoln Kirstein, *Quarry: A Collection in Lieu of Memoirs* (Pasadena: Twelvetrees Press, 1986), 35.

[56] Kirstein, "American Apollo," 13; essentially, "a pretty (or good-looking) boy, but a real man."

**16** Gisella Caccialanza, Enrico Cecchetti, and Magda Cella, La Scala, ca. 1926.
Courtesy of San Francisco Performing Arts Library and Museum

his last years to advancing her technique. During the three years she studied in Milan, Caccialanza received a bronze, a silver, and a gold medal at the year-end class examinations. The master took great personal interest in this prized pupil, showering her with gifts and receiving a special dispensation from the Pope to stand as her godfather at her confirmation ceremony. He invited his young protégé to teas at which she met famous dance personalities, such as Pavlova, Diaghilev, and Lifar. When Gisella returned to the United States, the broken-hearted ballet master gave her a special gift for her fourteenth birthday: a set of posters from the Maryinsky Theatre that listed the exercises for each day's lessons. He urged her to follow the outlined exercises in private study rather than allowing her training to be corrupted in America by teachers he considered incompetent.[57]

Cecchetti's idealistic visions for his protégé's future clashed with the reality of Caccialanza's situation. Needing to earn money, she signed a three-year contract with Albertina Rasch, who called her "The Little One." And so, not unlike the Christensens, Gisella paid her dues to the world of commercial dance. She performed in vaudeville houses, in movie prologues, at the then new Grauman's Chinese Theatre in Los Angeles, and finally at Radio City Music Hall when it opened in 1932.[58] Gisella held Radio City's ballet mistress Florence Rogge in the greatest respect and considered its leading ballerina Patricia Bowman so exalted as to be "untouchable."[59] Gisella was doing five shows a day at the Music Hall when Lifar persuaded her to audition for Balanchine's new school.

---

[57] The interesting tale of Cecchetti's devotion to Caccialanza is best outlined in "Letters from the Maestro: Enrico Cecchetti to Gisella Caccialanza," *Dance Perspectives*, 45 (Spring 1971). The letters are put in context by Sally Bailey, who also gives an overview of Caccialanza's career before and after her studies with Cecchetti.

[58] "Letters from the Maestro," 53.

[59] Interview with Gisella Caccialanza Christensen, San Bruno, California, September 28, 1987. Both Ruby and Gisella remember being excited to meet Patricia Bowman when she took class at the School of American Ballet.

Caccialanza immediately received a scholarship to the School of American Ballet, where the faculty valued her Cecchetti training. Balanchine was always aware of her background and often teased her:

> *He would come into class and say, "Gisella, what day is it today?" I would say, "Friday," and he would say, "Well, what did you do with Maestro Cecchetti on Fridays?" I would say, "Glissades," so he would say, "Well, we'll do those today."* [60]

Caccialanza's movement style was light and bouncy. She projected a sense of joyous ease and modesty while executing technically difficult steps such as double air turns and jumps with multiple beats. [61] Her gift for comedy won her the role of the flapper Heroine in the satirical *Alma Mater* (1935). To show off her *ballon* and Italian training, Balanchine also choreographed the Canzonetta section of *Reminiscence* (1935) for Gisella. [62]

Working with Balanchine, from the first production of *Serenade* to the Hartford and New York premieres, and being part of the core group of dancers he took to the Metropolitan, wrought a change in Caccialanza's priorities and perspective. Now when well-known dancers from the commercial theater came to take class at the School of American Ballet, she felt equal to rather than dazzled by them. Lew Christensen was just another such dancer dropping in to take class. When another dancer teased Gisella about Lew's interested looks in her direction, Gisella replied carelessly, "Let him look." [63] But

---

[60] Quoted in Cobbett Steinberg, "Gisella Caccialanza: A Chronology," *Encore: Archives for the Performing Arts Quarterly* 3 (Winter 1986/87): 12.

[61] Stephen C. Steinberg and Nancy Johnson Carter interview with James Graham-Luján, San Francisco, California, June 24, 1985.

[62] According to James Graham-Luján, the Canzonetta section of *Reminiscence*, which "recalled the airs and graces of Italian ballerinas, evoking their character as much as their gesture," depended on Gisella's "gentle naiveté," her "sincerity and modesty" to prevent the solo from sinking into satire. James Graham-Luján, "Gisella Caccialanza: A Tribute," *Encore: The Archives for the Performing Arts Quarterly* 3 (Winter 1986/87): 8.

[63] Interview with Gisella Caccialanza Christensen, San Bruno, California, September 28, 1987; see also KQED interview with Gisella Caccialanza Christensen.

she could not help noticing Lew's height, his virile style, and the speed with which he could turn pirouettes. The two began dating during preparations for *Carmen* in the fall of 1935.

Lew was naturally reserved and private about his feelings. Neither brusque like Harold nor as loquacious as Willam, Lew maintained an even temper and sometimes seemed cool and distant to those who did not know him well. His courtship with Gisella was long and slow, carried out over lingering Monopoly games and shared meals (usually cooked at home rather than eaten out). The two lived in adjacent buildings one block from the studio, and they could visit each other easily by crossing the roof. Harold caught on to the romance as he noticed Lew going up to the roof more and more frequently, sometimes bringing back a plate of pasta cooked by Gisella's sister Clelia.[64]

The end of the Metropolitan Opera season that spring (1936) left the dancers without employment for the following six months. Seeing the dry spell approaching, Harold contacted theatrical agents and offered them the American Ballet for the summer resort circuit. Harold had no authority to speak for the company and could not even offer the agents free tickets to see them perform, but that did not stop him from trying to persuade the bookers that ballets such as *The Bat* would make lively resort entertainment. Above all, he wanted to keep the company together.[65]

Harold hoped for a continuation of the status quo, but Kirstein's thoughts at this time were pushing into new directions. Or rather, Kirstein was returning to his original,

---

[64] Interview with Harold Christensen, San Anselmo, California, September 23, 1987.

[65] Interview with Harold Christensen, San Anselmo, California, September 22, 1987. Harold claims that a booker for Hershey, Pennsylvania, saw *The Bat* and agreed that it would be more successful than the Ballet Russe, which he claimed had flopped in Hershey. Agents for the RKO and Loews circuits were supposedly interested, even at the price of four thousand dollars a week. According to Harold, "Eddie and Lincoln were happy – Eddie Warburg – but Jack Bender, Doc Bender heard about it. And he said, 'The company is all split up now; they couldn't take it now.' ... They said, 'I guess he's right.' So I didn't even go back to see the agents."

idealistic conception of a ballet company composed of American dancers and grounded in a repertory built on American themes. The American Ballet had gained valuable performing experience at the Metropolitan, but the opera house setting was hardly conducive to the development of new, independent repertory, especially the kind Kirstein envisioned. He needed an experimental laboratory of a company, a small group that could be used to try out his theories. In the meantime, the dancers began the inevitable talk of putting acts together to get summer work. Unlike years past, the Christensens no longer considered vaudeville an acceptable alternative: working with Balanchine had changed their expectations.

Kirstein's published account of this period states that he "decided to organize a small troupe on [his] own and call it Ballet Caravan."[66] The exact details of how that transpired are lost to history. By some accounts, Kirstein just wanted to gather a small group of dancers and have them choreograph at his family's farm in isolation; it would be an experiment independent of the marketplace.[67]

Lew's account of the Ballet Caravan's formation stresses instead the dancers' initiative:

> We were called into the ballet studio at the Met – I think it was Warburg – and told that our contract was through because we only worked six months of the year. So for the other six months we had to find some way to keep going. So Harold and I got together and a few other dancers.... And we would get a pianist, some music and play. We would do our own [ballets]. Lincoln heard about it and thought it would be a hell of a good idea. He organized us and got us booked in little dumps up in New England.[68]

Lew invited Ruthanna Boris to perform in the new ballets; she recalls his relief that Kirstein would allow them to use the SAB studios after hours so that they would not have to

---

[66] Kirstein, *Thirty Years*, 68.

[67] KQED interview with Harold Christensen.

[68] Mason interview, 1984.

rent other space.[69] With Kirstein's interest and financial support, the plans grew more ambitious. The group expanded to include other dancers eager to try their hands at choreography – Eugene Loring, Douglas Coudy, and Erick Hawkins. The summer company was not conceived as a permanent break with Balanchine or the Metropolitan; the dancers saw it simply as a stop-gap measure, a way of earning a living until the next opera season.[70] The creation of ballets on American themes was a secondary goal, a gradual development prompted by Kirstein's constant encouragement, suggestions, and support. Lew later recalled, "All you had to mention was that you'd like to see so-and-so, and Lincoln would bring a ton of books."[71] The formation of Ballet Caravan may have been a case of the dancers and Kirstein "using" each other to their mutual benefit, the dancers, to generate summer employment, and Kirstein, to have the experimental group he desired.

The dancers' first task was to create new ballets. Each member of Ballet Caravan was to choreograph a piece and submit it to the group for consideration in the summer's repertory. Some declined, preferring to be used only as performers. Others made unsuccessful attempts, such as Gisella's solo entitled "Jewels of the Madonna," which even Lew rejected.[72] Erick Hawkins also submitted a ballet that was found wanting; he was actually voted out of the group but was later reinstated.[73] That dismissal was possible because,

[69] Interview with Ruthanna Boris, August 4, 1988.

[70] Gisella went along with the new company that summer because Lew was in it and because she hoped it would earn enough to get by on. Doubtless each participant brought his or her own expectations to the first summer of Ballet Caravan; labeling it a primarily financial proposition may be an oversimplification in some cases. And yet the dancers' need for income during the break between opera seasons was an undeniable motivation for the company's existence.

[71] Mason interview, 1984.

[72] KQED interview with Gisella Christensen.

[73] Barbara Cohen interview with Harold and Ruby Christensen, San Anselmo, California, December 29, 1976.

in contrast to the hierarchical power structures of traditional
ballet companies, Ballet Caravan was conceived as a democracy, a social parallel to its American thematic agenda. In the
early stages, the company voted on important decisions with
the understanding that all dancers had equal rank within the
ensemble. It is unclear how long this democracy lasted;
Kirstein relates that such a policy proved "impractical" and
that the dancers actually asked him to take more responsibility for the direction of the company so that they could
concentrate on dancing.[74] By the time of the first summer
engagements, the company's roster listed Kirstein as Artistic
Director, Coudy as an administrative assistant to Kirstein, and
Lew as Ballet Master. The dancers, listed alphabetically on
the roster rather than designated as soloists or corps members,
included Ruby Asquith, Ruthanna Boris, Gisella Caccialanza,
Rabana Hasburgh, Albia Kavan, Annabelle Lyon, Hannah
Moore, Harold Christensen, Lew Christensen, Erick Hawkins,
Charles Laskey, and Eugene Loring.[75]

   Harold declined to create a work for the new company. Instead, he offered to double as the group's stage
manager. This decision was consistent with the larger pattern
of Harold's life. During his three and a half decades as a
teacher and director of the San Francisco Ballet School, Harold
made many behind-the-scenes contributions to the running
of both school and company, but choreography was not an
area in which he chose to experiment.

   Kirstein's administrative support included hiring
Frances Hawkins to manage the company's summer book-
ings, while the dancers put together their repertory in less
than six weeks. Because of Frances Hawkins' ties to Martha
Graham, the company premiered at Bennington College,
Vermont, where Doris Humphrey and Charles Weidman
were presiding over the third session of the Bennington
School of Dance. With the focus of that summer's activities

[74] Kirstein, *Thirty Years*, 70.

[75] John Martin, "Group from the American Ballet Organizes Summer Tour," *New York Times*, June 28, 1936. Coudy is not listed as a dancer, only as a manager.

on the creation of Humphrey's masterwork *With My Red Fires* and Hanya Holm's first major concert in the Eastern United States, the Caravan's appearance created hardly a ripple in this early bastion of modern dance.[76] But the New England setting provided a comfortable change for the Caravan's dancers, who sat outdoors on the campus lawns as they sewed the final touches on their own costumes, glad to be away from the heat of New York City. They also mingled with the modern dance students, who explained to Gisella why modern dance was superior to ballet technique based on the traditional five turned-out positions of the feet: "We have space, and we can travel, but ballet confines you because you're going sideways."[77] When the company debuted in mid-July, two works by Lew, *Encounter* and *Pocahontas*, led the repertory.[78]

*Encounter*, set to Mozart's "Haffner" Serenade, was basically a plotless ballet inspired by Lew's study with Balanchine. It was also the first of many works in which Lew would explore the limits of illusion. As Harold reflected late in life, "Lew always had an idea that a person would disappear and [re]appear."[79] This early exploration of that theme was built on the similar stage looks of Ruby Asquith and Annabelle Lyon. Lew alternated the ballerinas in such a way as to create the illusion of one dancer; one would dance behind a curtain or screen center stage and the other would dance back out into view, or one would exit one side of the stage and her "twin" would immediately reappear on the other side. The deception carried over into partner work,

---

[76] Sali Ann Kriegsman, *Modern Dance in America: The Bennington Years* (Boston: G. K. Hall & Co., 1981), 53–62.

[77] Interview with Gisella Caccialanza Christensen, San Bruno, California, September 29, 1987.

[78] Nancy Reynold's reference work, *Repertory in Review*, dates the premiere of *Pocahontas* as July 18, 1936, at Bennington. This corrects Cyril Beaumont's *Supplement to the Complete Book of Ballets* (London: C. W. Beaumont, 1942) and Cobbett Steinberg's annotated chronology, "Lew Christensen, An American Original" (*Encore* 1.3, Summer 1984), which both state that the work premiered on August 17, 1936.

[79] Interview with Harold Christensen, San Anselmo, California, September 23, 1987.

**17** Ruby Asquith, Harold Christensen, Annabelle Lyon, and Lew Christensen in Lew's first ballet, *Encounter*, 1936.
Courtesy of San Francisco Performing Arts Library and Museum

thanks to Lew and Harold's family resemblance: Lew and Annabelle would dance, then switch off behind the scenery with Harold and Ruby. Despite such "tricks," *Encounter* represented a departure from the bombastic, stunt-filled style Lew had performed on the vaudeville circuits. The critical response was positive, and the work was revived in subsequent seasons.[80] Lew later lengthened the ballet, using all six movements of Mozart's score and adding a solo for himself.

---

[80] The *Bennington Evening Banner* declared the work "clearly conceived and in most parts brilliant," while the *Boston Post* explained, "There is nothing pretentious about *Encounter*; it is purely decorative, lyrical dancing, delightful in conception and distinctly beautiful in execution." "Dancers Give Fine Program," *Bennington Evening Banner*, July 18, 1936; Reynolds, *Repertory in Review*, 53. *American Dancer* declared the work "most cleverly contrived," explaining that while the work was "almost entirely technical, it nevertheless weaves a little story and refreshing lightness of atmosphere into...the entrances and exits of the dancers." "Ballet Caravan," *American Dancer*, December 1936.

With the creation of *Pocahontas*, Lew fulfilled Kirstein's long held desire for a ballet on this subject. As part of his campaign to develop a repertory based on American themes, Kirstein had devised the ballet's scenario and commissioned the score from one of his Harvard friends, Elliott Carter. Kirstein then encouraged Lew's desires to learn about the historical incident in which Captain John Smith and John Rolfe were captured by Native Americans and then released through the heroic intercession of the princess Pocahontas. Although the program note explained that "no attempt has been made to reconstruct either music or dance from archeological sources," Lew did attempt to devise stylized movements that reconciled classical technique with "some sort of Indian feeling."[81] The result was a confusing amalgam that one Boston critic described as "What Smith, Rolfe, Powhatan, and Pocahontas would have done if they'd known about dissonant brasses and the post-Wigman school of movement."[82] The costumes, designed by Karl Free after period engravings by Theodore de Bry, reminded John Martin of "the old-fashioned cigar-box Indian," with a "pseudo-naïveté" the critic found "irksome," while the British critic Cyril Beaumont found the movement "baroque and pseudoheroic."[83] A strictly classical solo Lew inserted for himself in the role of John Rolfe was also criticized for being out of tune with the overall character of the work.

*Pocahontas* must have had moments that worked, as the reviews were not solidly negative. Ruthanna Boris was praised as the Indian princess, and because it was her first starring role she thought it "the greatest ballet ever done."[84] Carter, uneasy with the colonialist implications of the plot, hoped to make the ballet "a parable of cooperation."[85] That

---

[81] Lew Christensen, quoted in Reynolds, *Repertory in Review*, 55.

[82] John Chapman, quoted in Reynolds, 55.

[83] Quoted in Reynolds, 55.

[84] Boris, quoted in Reynolds, 55.

[85] Allen Edwards, *Flawed Words and Stubborn Sounds: A Conversation with Elliott Carter* (New York: W. W. Norton and Co., 1971), 57, as quoted in Kirstein, *Thirty Years*, 74.

theme was demonstrated visually at the end when Boris, wearing a sheer Elizabethan wedding gown over her still-visible Indian tunic, *bourréed* slowly forward, holding out a large, revolving a globe of the world. "I always felt chills when I did that passage," she recalls.[86] But Lew's choreography for this ballet was hampered by his inability to come to terms with Carter's music. Kirstein had requested a finale that would sound like "an 'American-Indian' version of *Apollo*," and fitting the story to the Stravinskian score was beyond Lew's musical experience at that point. As a result, many viewers found the plot unclear and the characters insufficiently developed. Martin dismissed the entire proceedings as "modernistic and stuffy."[87] The failure of *Pocahontas* was a major blow to the young choreographer, who took it very personally: "Every time I'd walk out on the street, I was convinced everybody was looking at me, thinking 'There's the guy who did that stinker, *Pocahontas*.'"[88] Lew reworked the ballet four times – perhaps because of Kirstein's commitment to its American theme and score – but was never satisfied with the results.[89]

The Caravan's other repertory that first summer included Eugene Loring's *Harlequin for President* and William Dollar's *Promenade*. In the latter, Lew danced "Apollo" opposite Rabana Hasburgh as "Daphne," and Gisella and Harold were "Echo and Narcissus." In Loring's *Harlequin for President*, Lew, Harold, and Charles Laskey impersonated the three

---

[86] Letter from Ruthanna Boris to Debra Sowell, July 28, 1988. *Pocahontas* also had its lighter moments – unintended ones during performances. In the role of King Powhatan, Harold was called upon to sit cross-legged on the stage for long periods. He sometimes fell asleep, and when the dancers nudged him in passing, he would awaken with a comical start. And in one of the later versions, Lew added a "Medicine Man" solo for Erick Hawkins, who would turn and whirl with such intensity that more than once he inadvertently sent his cape flying into the audience.

[87] Quoted in Reynolds, 55.

[88] Stephanie Von Buchau, "Native Dancer," *Ballet News*, May 1982, 26.

[89] In an interview nearly fifty years after the work's debut, Lew was still trying to put the experience of *Pocahontas* behind him: "Such a notorious ballet. I've tried to forget that ballet. Everyone remembers it, and I've tried to forget it. If you ever see Elliott Carter, tell him for me that it *wasn't* his fault. Tell him I said it was my fault." Mason interview, 1984.

"Captains" vying for the presidency, while Gisella danced the role of "Leonora," married to Lew's captain. Ruby, Albia Kavan, and Hannah Moore constituted "The People"; wearing white face paint, they functioned as a chorus of stooges, running from candidate to candidate. (Ruby actually sustained an injury during one energetic performance on a small stage when Lew inadvertently kicked her in the side and broke one of her ribs.) Later in the season, the company added Douglas Coudy's *The Soldier and the Gypsy*, a reworking of *Carmen*, in which Lew was "The Bullfighter" and Gisella, "The Cigarette Girl."

Following the Bennington premieres, Ballet Caravan toured New England by bus, playing movie houses, resort theatres, and college towns. Accustomed to the grueling pace of vaudeville, the Christensens adapted easily to the relatively light schedule of twenty-five performances in seven weeks. One week was spent at the Country Playhouse in Westport, Connecticut, where the company provided the incidental dances for Molière's *The Would-Be Gentleman*.[90] The tour continued into the fall, with more New England performances after Labor Day and a New York debut late in October. In all, the troupe gave thirty-eight performances, met its touring expenses, and succeeded in its goal of keeping the nucleus of dancers together until the opera season resumed in December. With the formation of the Caravan and the resumption of duties at the Met, the structures that would most influence Lew's growth as an artist and provide the context for his development as a choreographer were now in place.

The story of Ballet Caravan, told with an awareness of Lew's contribution in particular, illustrates the significant role an individual dancer may play in the genesis of a company. Erick Hawkins claims that he proposed the scheme of a small summer touring company to Kirstein, was rebuffed, and went

---

[90] Lew choreographed the Turkish scene, and Eugene Loring added stage business to the production, which starred the popular comedian Jimmy Savo. Hawkins's contribution, a divertissement entitled "The Peacock among the Roosters," was nicknamed "the Chicken ballet" by the dancers, who laughed at the way Hawkins had Loring lie on his back and kick his legs in the air. Interview with Harold Christensen, San Anselmo, California, September 22, 1987.

**18** Studio portrait of Lew Christensen, late 1930s.
Photograph by Maurice Seymour, courtsey of Ronald Seymour (The Maurice Seymour Archive) and San Francisco Performing Arts Library and Museum

off to Boston. According to Hawkins, when Lew proposed the same scheme a week later, Kirstein agreed to support the plan. "Lew saved my life," Hawkins claims dramatically, because Lew insisted, out of fairness, that Hawkins be recalled from Boston and included in the group.[91] This anecdote confirms Lew's significance in Kirstein's thinking. Kirstein's personal affection for Lew was matched by faith in the dancer's talent.[92] To Kirstein, Lew was living proof that America could produce a classically trained *danseur* who was the equal of Russian or European dancers. In Kirstein's eyes:

> *It was how Lew danced on stage and behaved off that signified to me a future, and within it a potential for American male dancers.... He combined, in one body, beauty, perfect physical endowment, musicality of a high professional level, a developed acrobatic technique, and an elegance of stage manners which was an exact reflection of his inherent morality.*[93]

Kirstein's commitment to Lew was matched by the latter's willingness to bend his efforts to Kirstein's goals, as evidenced by the creation of *Pocahontas*. "If it had not been for the presence of Lew," Kirstein recalled later in life, "I don't think I would have continued with ballet, during and after our worst trials of the thirties" – the failed tour, the frustrations of the residency at the Metropolitan, and the "lesser disasters" that rocked Kirstein emotionally.[94]

---

[91] Interview with Erick Hawkins, New York, New York, May 25, 1988.

[92] In his later writings about the formation of the Ballet Caravan, Kirstein explained that he was "personally attached to Lew Christensen and to his fiancée Gisella Caccialanza" and that there were other dancers to whom he "felt obligated." Kirstein, *Thirty Years*, 68. Kirstein's account gives a false impression of who danced in the first Ballet Caravan. Of the six dancers listed by Kirstein as those to whom he "felt obligated," only two – Eugene Loring and Erick Hawkins – actually danced in the company that first season. A third, William Dollar, provided a ballet for the group but did not travel with it. Regarding Kirstein's ongoing affection for Lew, see his reminiscences in *Quarry*, 35. There he explains that Lew and a few other men corresponded to his long-held "romantic criteria."

[93] Kirstein, *Thirty Years*, 301.

[94] *Ibid.*

# 6

# APOLLO AND MAC: A GREEK GOD AND A WORKING MAN'S HERO (1937–1939)

Lew's training with Balanchine assumed a personal dimension during the Metropolitan Opera Ballet era as the dancer and the choreographer met daily for a working session before company class. The two would take turns teaching combinations and then picking them apart, analyzing the shape and thrust of the movements. With all his strength as a performer, Lew had never made a detailed study of the classical vocabulary; it was Balanchine who showed him how to analyze its components and structure.[1] This tutorial constituted Lew's finishing course in dance; not only did it hone his skills as a performer (and make him even more useful to Balanchine), but it gave him a working base for teaching and for future independence as a choreographer.

The image of Balanchine training Lew in the studio parallels that of the Muses educating Apollo, and it was the role of Apollo that absorbed Lew's greatest efforts during the American Ballet's second year at the Metropolitan Opera (1936–1937). That year brought little improvement in working conditions for the Met's corps de ballet. Balanchine supplied choreography for five operas and turned his attention to Broadway, where he set the dances for the Rodgers and Hart musical *Babes in Arms*. For the dancers, the most rewarding

---

Unless otherwise noted, reviews and newspaper articles about Ballet Caravan are quoted from the American Ballet Caravan Scrapbooks: Clippings, Announcements, Microfilm, Box 1 (1933–1941) and Box 2 (1941–1942), Dance Collection, The New York Public Library.

[1] Francis Mason interview with Willam, Harold, and Lew Christensen, Ruby Asquith, and Gisella Caccialanza, 1984. Lew also tells of this tutelage in the KQED Interview with Craig Palmer, explaining, "We were analyzing the whole technique itself. It was an education for him and a great education for me."

aspect of the winter season was preparing for a festival of Stravinsky ballets to be presented that spring. The company hoped the festival would raise the ballet's prestige at the Opera and at the same time achieve a popular success. Warburg and Balanchine commissioned a new ballet from Stravinsky and planned to stage ballets to two existing Stravinsky scores, *Baiser de la Fée* and *Apollon Musagète*.

Kirstein initially opposed the idea of a Stravinsky Festival on the grounds that the composer was already well recognized and that using existing scores would not be breaking new ground artistically. But Kirstein's concerns were outweighed by Balanchine's admiration for the Russian composer. The new score, *Jeu de Cartes* (titled *The Card Party* in English), arrived in December, and the American Ballet devoted the winter months to learning and rehearsing the planned works.[2] In *Card Party*, the dancers represented playing cards in a game of poker played according to Hoyle. Lew and Gisella both had secondary roles, he as the King of Hearts and she as the Eight of Hearts, while William Dollar starred as the Joker. In *Baiser*, the story of a young man kissed at birth by a fairy who reclaims him after he has grown and has decided to marry, Gisella received the part of the Bride; Lew danced in the ensemble. But for *Apollon Musagète* Lew was awarded the role of the young god. This role provided greater opportunities for his development as an artist than the previous season's Orpheus and became associated with his name in the history of the Balanchine repertory.

Dancing the role of Apollo constituted a milestone in Lew's career, not just because it was a leading part but because of the way Balanchine taught Lew during the rehearsal period. Day after day Balanchine demonstrated the desired movement, including details as specific as the movement of a finger or the placement of the head, molding Lew's

---

[2] Harold and Ruby did not take part in the Stravinsky Festival, possibly because the festival was independent of the Opera and was a production of the American Ballet rather than of the American Ballet Ensemble.

**19**    Gisella Caccialanza in *Baiser de la Fée* costume, 1937.
Photograph by George Platt Lynes, courtesy of Estate of George Platt Lynes
and San Francisco Performing Arts Library and Museum

movement carefully.[3] Unlike the role of Orpheus, that of Apollo had little room for acting. Balanchine's few interpretive explanations stressed the athletic physicality of the part: "You are a woodcutter, a swimmer, a football player and a god."[4] (When Erick Hawkins suggested that the choreographer explain the Greek myths surrounding Apollo and his relationship to the Muses, Balanchine replied firmly, "He just does my movements."[5]) In the early stages of the rehearsal process, Balanchine left nothing for the dancer to improvise. Only after Lew knew the movement thoroughly did the choreographer allow him to experiment with phrasing, to try "softening or hardening parts of it to make the thing a whole emotional unit," and even then Balanchine was always watching and giving suggestions.[6]

Through Balanchine's example and tutelage, Lew began to understand the nuances of performance, the subtleties of dynamics, phrasing, and mood.[7] As Lew came to terms with the score, he discovered that to do the choreography correctly he had to respond fully to the accents of the music, a difficult but satisfying task. Stravinsky himself came to New York the month before the festival and attended the rehearsals of his works, charging the atmosphere of the company as the festival neared. Both composer and choreographer were pleased with the production, in large part because Lew so satisfactorily conveyed the desired "impression of godhood."[8] Kirstein records that in rehearsals for *Apollon Musagète*, "Lew Christensen was everything one could wish for . . . . At the end of rehearsal, Stravinsky thanked Lew."[9]

---

[3] Barbara Newman, *Striking a Balance* (London: Elm Tree Books, 1982), 34.

[4] "Tiptoe on Parnassus," *Opera News* 2.13 (February 7, 1938): 3.

[5] Interview with Erick Hawkins, New York, New York, May 25, 1988.

[6] Newman, 34.

[7] *Ibid.*

[8] "Tiptoe on Parnassus," 3.

[9] Lincoln Kirstein, *Thirty Years: The New York City Ballet* (New York: Alfred A. Knopf, 1978), 62.

The ballet's image of the young god was neither majestic nor grandiose. Lew's uneffusive personality, unselfconscious good looks, and self-effacing virtuosity fit the "unmannered, untutored boy-man of Balanchine's conception."[10] For visual inspiration, the production's designer Stewart Chaney turned to pastoral scenes by the French neoclassical painter Claude Poussin. Lew's own build, described by Kirstein as "Praxitelean head and body, imperceptibly musculated but firmly and largely proportioned, blond hair and bland air," made him a believable inhabitant of the Poussin-inspired, neoclassical stage picture.[11] He projected the images of the ballet with power but without exaggeration, with cool poise rather than heated strength.[12]

Balanchine had first choreographed *Apollon Musagète* in 1928 for the Ballets Russes as a vehicle for Diaghilev's last *premier danseur*, Serge Lifar, who was not a traditional danseur noble.[13] Now, nine years later, Balanchine had in Lew an Apollo who was tall instead of short, fair instead of dark, and equipped with strong virtuoso technique. The figure of the young god that emerged was less adolescent, less brusque, less idiosyncratic than Lifar's portrayal. Kirstein explained the difference by writing that Lew's "distinguished interpretation" was "more golden baroque, more the Apollo Belvedere than Serge Lifar's dark, electric, archaic animalism."[14] (In addition to gilt leather armor resembling a golden tunic, Lew's ballet slippers and leggings were also golden, and the hair on his head, chest, and legs was gilded so that it shone under

---

[10] Nancy Reynolds, *Repertory in Review* (New York: Dial Press, 1977), 48.

[11] Kirstein, *Thirty Years*, 65.

[12] James Graham-Luján recalls a slight fainting movement done by Lew in this role that was beautiful because Lew's self-assured masculinity could carry it off. Later, when Balanchine set the role on Jacques D'Amboise, the latter asked Balanchine to eliminate that movement on the grounds that it looked effeminate.

[13] Stravinsky's score had been commissioned by Mrs. Elizabeth Sprague Coolidge in 1927. It was first performed at the Library of Congress in 1928, with choreography by Adolph Bolm. Anatole Chujoy, *The New York City Ballet* (New York: Alfred A. Knopf, 1953; Reprint New York: Da Capo Press, 1982), 85.

[14] Kirstein, *Ballet: Bias and Belief* (New York: Dance Horizons, 1983), 196.

**20**   Lew Christensen and Daphne Vane in Balanchine's *Apollon Musagète,*
1937.
Performance Photograph by Richard Tucker, courtesy of San Francisco
Performing Arts Library and Museum

the stage lights.) Despite the ballet's Greek subject matter,
Kirstein used the production to support his Americanizing
crusade, championing Lew in the title role as "an American
dancer with his own individual classical attitude," tall, athletic,
frank, and "wholly unlike the smaller-scaled grace of the
Russian prototype."[15]

The Stravinsky Festival, conducted by the composer
himself (April 27 and 28, 1937), prompted glowing audience
and critical response, with *Card Party* as the audience favorite.
Lew and Gisella, who dawdled backstage before showing up
at a postperformance party the second night, were accorded
a standing ovation by their peers.[16] *Musical America* found the

---

[15] *Ibid.*

[16] Steven Cobbett Steinberg interview with Gisella Caccialanza Christensen for
KQED documentary.

dancers "well-rehearsed" and Lew, "a handsome god."[17] *The Dance* proclaimed him "obviously a dancer with considerable gifts."[18] John Martin, who was not yet a fan of Balanchine choreography, grudgingly conceded that "Lew Christensen as Apollo quite over-rode the handicap of some trying material and made a handsome and dignified figure of the young god."[19] Grace Robert, in *The Borzoi Book of Ballets*, put Martin's reaction in context by pointing out that

> "*several years later, when Ballet Theatre revived the ballet, André Eglevsky, whose performance did not in any way measure up to Christensen's, received the acclaim of the critics, who by that time had been more or less beaten into an acceptance of Balanchine's advanced style.*"[20]

The significance of Lew's Apollo became clear with the acceptance of Balanchine and the passage of time. Writing a dozen years later, George Amberg testified,

> *In* Apollon *Lew Christensen confirmed what he had promised in* Orpheus: *that in him America had a magnificent classical dancer, with flawless technique and a sure grasp of noble style.*[21]

Following the excitement of the Stravinsky Festival, the American Ballet Ensemble once again faced unemployment until the next opera season. Balanchine went to Hollywood to choreograph *The Goldwyn Follies* of 1938, which starred his

---

[17] Oscar Thompson, "New Stravinsky Ballet Achieves World Premiere," *Musical America*, May 10, 1937, 19.

[18] "The American Ballet," *The Dance*, June 1937, clipping in a Christensen family scrapbook, San Francisco Performing Arts Library and Museum.

[19] John Martin, "Stravinsky Leads Ballet Premiere," *New York Times*, April 28, 1937.

[20] Grace Robert, *The Borzoi Book of Ballets* (New York: Alfred A. Knopf, 1946), 31. Marie-Jeanne Pelus, who became Lew's partner in the Caravan not long after the Stravinsky Festival, also recalled Lew as a "marvelous Apollo" – superior to both Lifar and André Eglevsky. Marie-Jeanne also asserted Lew had bad feet that spoiled his line. Paul Magriel and Don McDonagh, "A Conversation with Marie-Jeanne," *Ballet Review* 12.4 (Winter 1985): 68. This criticism has not been echoed by many, although Lew once stated that Mascagno had not stressed the shape of the foot.

[21] George Amberg, *Ballet: The Emergence of an American Art* (New York: New American Library, 1949; reprinted 1953), 82.

current love interest, Vera Zorina. Balanchine's agreement with Samuel Goldwyn stipulated that the film's dancers would be members of the American Ballet, and Gisella was one of the twenty-five dancers who passed the New York screen test and took the train to California. Gisella took her identity as a member of Balanchine's company very seriously; her interest in Lew, although strong, did not deter her from the five-month engagement.

Lew's plans lay in other directions. Kirstein, anticipating the opera's off-season since February, had been making preparations for Ballet Caravan's second summer.[22] In May 1937 he resigned from the Board of Directors of the American Ballet to devote his attention to the Caravan, and Balanchine and Warburg resigned from the board of the School of American Ballet. This parting of the ways, which sounds drastic in the light of subsequent events, indicates that Kirstein had not yet settled on Balanchine as the instrument by which he (Kirstein) would build his dreamed-of company with a repertory grounded in American themes. At this point, the break allowed Balanchine to accept the opportunities that came from Broadway and Hollywood while Kirstein pursued his original vision through Ballet Caravan. Lew, who may have been invited to Hollywood, chose to remain with Kirstein and resume his responsibilities as ballet master of the Caravan. (Opting for the Caravan may also have meant staying with Harold, who probably had not been invited to Hollywood.)

It was a time of difficult decisions. Following the success of the Stravinsky Festival, the American Ballet Ensemble had been invited to return to the Metropolitan Opera for a third year. But Ballet Caravan's touring schedule included

---

[22] In fact, during March, Kirstein explored the idea of an ambitious series of concerts on Broadway, to be held the following December, which would include Ballet Caravan, Martha Graham's company, newly commissioned works by young choreographers, and chamber operas, all accompanied by a fifteen-piece orchestra. The idea was not a viable proposition at the time, but it indicated the direction Kirstein would work toward with Ballet Society during the 1940s. Chujoy, *The New York City Ballet*, 91–92.

engagements that conflicted with the beginning of the fall opera season, making it impossible for the dancers to do both. It was now clear that commitment to the Caravan would require a permanent break with the American Ballet Ensemble. The dancers were forced to choose between the companies, which amounted to choosing between Balanchine and Kirstein.

The Christensens respected Balanchine, but he could offer them no hope for ongoing employment beyond the context of the Metropolitan Opera, a hierarchical and hostile environment. Balanchine himself was piecing together a career based on the random offers that came his way, and he was increasingly preoccupied with matters beyond the Met: Broadway shows, Hollywood musicals, and his infatuation with Zorina. Kirstein, on the other hand, was determined to promote ballet in America, and he had not only the wealth and connections to make that happen but the knowledge and verbal skills to articulate goals toward which the dancers were willing to work. For the dancers, going with Kirstein would mean leaving the indignities of the Met behind. With Frances Hawkins's management and Kirstein's support, the dancers could continue to create new works and tour in a congenial, if not strictly democratic, body. So the Christensens and sixteen other dancers, including Ruby, Ruthanna Boris, Rabana Hasburgh, Albia Kavan, Jane Doering, Douglas Coudy, Eugene Loring, Erick Hawkins, and Fred Danieli, cast their lots with Kirstein.[23]

The reconstituted Caravan rehearsed during May and June of 1937. Harold resumed his duties as stage manager, and Douglas Coudy remained company manager, responsible for the travel arrangements and hotel accommodations for the bookings lined up by Frances Hawkins. Elliott Carter joined the staff as musical director. Marie-Jeanne, a young but

---

[23] Chujoy, *The New York City Ballet*, 94–95. Rabana Hasburgh remained with the Caravan until November and then returned to the American Ballet. Lew later revealed that sometime during this period he was invited to join the Ballet Russe. He decided against it because he found their repertory "kind of tired-looking" and wanted to stay affiliated with Kirstein and Balanchine. Francis Mason interview.

dynamic dancer from the School, was added as a soloist in Gisella's absence.

As one of the original founders of Ballet Caravan, Lew emerged early as a natural leader among the dancers. The source of his authority as ballet master ran deeper than Kirstein's friendship and respect for Lew's abilities as a performer. In addition to being tall and well liked by both the men and women of the company, Lew was recognized as being hard-working and fair. His leadership style was not loud and compelling but quiet and understated. Ruthanna Boris recalls Lew as laconic: "Lew never talked. ... If he was choreographing something, he talked as much as was necessary to get it out of his head and into the person's body."[24] As a ballet master, Lew engendered trust by dividing the rehearsal schedule fairly among the choreographers rather than allocating extra time for his own works at the expense of others. (By contrast, Loring had a reputation for over-rehearsing his own ballets.[25]) While Harold's passions would grow hot over issues and grievances, sometimes offending others in the process, Lew's restraint and self-discipline inspired confidence and loyalty.[26] He also had a no-nonsense attitude that elicited the company's respect and best efforts. Once Fred Danieli and Marie-Jeanne were kidding around during a rehearsal. Lew remained businesslike and held his temper, but the clowning continued. Finally Lew stopped the rehearsal and declared, "Fred, Marie-Jeanne, I'm going to give you a fifteen-minute break. When you come back, I want you to be ready to dance." The message got across. "That

---

[24] Telephone interview with Ruthanna Boris, August 4, 1988.

[25] Peter Conway interview with Fred Danieli, January–April, 1979, Oral History Project, Dance Collection, The New York Public Library.

[26] As Harold explained the differences in their personalities, "Lew had more discipline. I was always a hothead; I fly off the handle too easily. So I couldn't run people. Lew wouldn't do that. Lew would calm down. So Lew right off the bat was given [leadership in Ballet Caravan], and everybody followed him. They believed him." Interview with Harold Christensen, San Anselmo, California, September 23, 1987.

rehearsal turned me into a pro," Danieli later recounted, "because it wasn't that he was mad at me, he was just demanding of me what was necessary to be a dancer."[27]

The summer repertory included three new works: Loring's *Yankee Clipper*, Hawkins' *Show Piece*, and Coudy's *Folk Dance*. A fourth work was promised for the fall. In *Yankee Clipper*, Loring starred as the farmboy who becomes a sailor to see the world. During the voyage he is bullied by the older sailors except one, a friendly figure danced by Lew. The women of the company appeared as "native" dancers in exotic ports of call; Ruby danced a solo in black face representing West Africa.[28]

Hawkins designed *Show Piece* as a divertissement to exhibit the company's technical skills. Lew had a solo "Air" that suited his "nobility of bearing," and Ruby was given a lyrical section titled "Romance" that displayed a new dimension of her usually piquant style.[29] In *Folk Dance*, a suite of Italian, French, and Spanish dances set to music by Emmanuel Chabrier, Harold partnered Helen Stewart in the Siciliano, while Ruby and Loring performed the Saltarello. Ballets from the previous summer were also revived with some casting changes; Ruby inherited the role of Columbine in *Harlequin for President*, to positive critical review.

Ballet Caravan's second summer of New England barnstorming opened in Old Saybrook, Connecticut, in mid-July. Except for a two-night engagement in Philadelphia, where a symphony orchestra accompanied the dancers, the Caravan toured New England towns and performed to piano accompaniment. As before, the company traveled by bus, their lighting equipment and costumes piled in the back where seats had been removed. When the troupe arrived in a new town, the men would unload the equipment while the women took care of the costumes, ironing them and even drying out

---

[27] Conway interview with Fred Danieli.

[28] *Dance Observer* described the choreography of Ruby's solo as "merely very poor Harlem." Mildred Wile, "Ballet Caravan," *Dance Observer*, August–September, 1937.

[29] A.B., "Ballet Caravan," *Dance* October, 1937.

those still damp from the previous performance. As stage
manager, Harold did a majority of the technical work, but
Lew would help him position the battens and hang the
scenery, install the switchboard, secure the stage lights, hook
up electrical wires, and prepare the stage for performance.
During performances, dancers who were not on stage would
run the switchboard for those who were. And when the
engagement was finished, scenery, lights, switchboard, and
five wicker baskets filled with costumes had to be carried back
to the bus and loaded on. Audience size was a constant source
of concern. "We were always counting the audience, always
peeking out to see if there were empty seats," recalls Ruby.[30]
In Keene, New Hampshire, they arrived on a Sunday before
a Monday night opening to find no publicity, either in town
or at the nearby resort; despite last-minute efforts they opened
to an audience of three.[31]

Social subsets existed within the otherwise unified company. The chief division was between those who pursued
sophisticated pleasures such as going to nightclubs after performances, and those with more casual (outdoor or athletic)
tastes. The latter included the Christensens, Marie-Jeanne,
and Erick Hawkins, who used their spare time on the New
England tours to go fishing or sailing.[32] Lew no longer played
the 'cello regularly, but he continued to enjoy photography.

Ruby, her roommate Albia Kavan, Loring, and Coudy
formed a circle that pursued more glamourous pastimes:
dressing up for dinner, lingering over cigarettes and cocktails,
and ballroom dancing in fashionable New York nightclubs.
Harold hated ballroom dancing; it brought back memories of
resented hours spent teaching beginners in the family's dance
studios. But Loring and Ruby were well matched in size and
interests. While Loring was not romantically attracted to
women, he would take Ruby dancing at the Rainbow Room,

[30] Barbara Cohen interview with Harold and Ruby Christensen, San Anselms, California, December 29, 1976.

[31] *Ibid.*

[32] *Ibid.*

where he improvised and she would follow his lead in a foxtrot or tango that would clear the floor as other dancers stopped to admire their skill. When the Caravan played Loring's hometown, Milwaukee, he passed Ruby off as his girlfriend, to his parents' delight.[33]

Following the summer portion of Ballet Caravan's 1937 tour, the company disbanded in mid-August for a brief vacation. Then the dancers returned to classes at the School of American Ballet and began preparations for their winter season, which opened in November. Lew began rehearsals for the work that had been promised the previous spring: *Filling Station*.

Kirstein had proposed ballet libretti to Virgil Thomson for several years, usually to skeptical response. During the summer of 1937, Kirstein once again asked Thomson for a ballet score, this time proposing Lew as the work's choreographer and leading dancer. Thomson saw Lew as a dancer he could work with and agreed to the project.[34] "Lew was probably the best of all the American dancers," he later recalled. "He was certainly the best of the danseurs nobles."[35]

The problem of suitable roles for Lew continued to preoccupy Kirstein: what characters could the American tradition suggest that were heroic in stature, "equivalent to Prince Charming or Prince Siegfried," but translated into "native terms"?[36] The attempt to create in John Rolfe an American hero worthy of Lew's build and technique had failed with the ignominious *Pocahontas*. Lacking an appropriate American legend or ready-made fable, Kirstein, Thomson, and Lew devised a contemporary scenario depicting the various social levels of people stopping by a roadside filling

---

[33] Interview with Ruby Asquith Christensen, San Anselmo, California, September 26, 1987.

[34] Virgil Thomson, *Virgil Thomson* (New York: Alfred A. Knopf, 1967), 275.

[35] Transcript of Virgil Thomson Oral History Interview, interviewed by John Gruen, 36, Dance Collection, The New York Public Library.

[36] Kirstein, *Thirty Years*, 71.

**21**  Lew Christensen as Mac in *Filling Station*, 1937.
Photograph by George Platt Lynes, courtesy of Estate of George Platt Lynes
and San Francisco Performing Arts Library and Museum

station.[37] Lew's heroic role in this slice of American life would be that of a common working man, the filling station attendant.

Lew and Thomson worked out the details of the story and determined the length of each section. Thomson would come to rehearsals, play a section, and often fall asleep while Lew choreographed.[38] Other times Thomson would break out in laughter as he watched the characters and situations Lew devised. Lew asked the composer to make the pas de deux the centerpiece of the ballet but asked him to keep it under five minutes: "I can find things for them to do up to five minutes, but beyond that, they'll have to start doing the same things over again."[39]

The collaboration resulted in a series of broadly drawn characters who entered the station and played out the drama: Mac the attendant, two tumbling truck drivers, a forsaken-looking lost motorist and his family, an inebriated rich couple, a gangster, and a state trooper. Mac's introductory solo established his personal competence through an athletic solo of virtuosic turns, leaps, and beats. The truck drivers (originally Loring and Coudy) roughhoused through an acrobatic routine reminiscent of vaudevillian tumblers. The long-faced motorist provided an ideal role for Harold, whose features could readily assume and project a comical bewildered and henpecked expression. Lew and Harold worked out the characterization of the part together, drawing on their background in popular theatre as they visualized the cigar-smoking tourist in oversized checks as "a cross between W. C. Fields and Caspar Milquetoast."[40] The motorist's wife and obnoxious daughter completed the contingent of middle-class characters. The little girl's antics as she waited to get to the rest room were another bit stolen from popular comedy. (The little

---

[37] Transcript of Thomson interview, 37.

[38] Mason interview, 1984.

[39] Lew Christensen quoted in transcript of Thomson interview, 37.

[40] Interview with Harold F. Christensen, San Anselmo, California, September 23, 1987.

girl originally did a tap dance routine Lew learned from Paul
Draper, but this detail has been lost.[41])

An inebriated upper-class couple dressed for the country club (originally Marie-Jeanne and Fred Danieli) danced the
pas de deux Lew envisaged as the center of the ballet. Their
choreography played with off-balances and missed connections, spoofing the conventions of the classical pas de deux.
The collection of characters on the stage was then galvanized
by the entrance of the gangster (Hawkins), who emptied their
pockets and plunged the scene into darkness for his escape. A
chase scene lit only by flashlights ended in gun shots; the state
trooper (Todd Bolender) brought order to the scene, but only
after the gangster's bullets had finished off the rich girl. Her
body was carried off in a slow funeral march, after which Mac
resumed his air of "business as usual."[42]

The company rehearsed *Filling Station* in theaters and
gymnasiums during the first part of the Caravan's 1937–38
winter tour.[43] Leaving the resort circuit behind, Ballet Caravan
was seeking new audiences in larger cities, broadening the
circle of its activities, and creating a larger frame of reference
for its identity. This tour signaled the beginning of major
engagements; in addition to playing Syracuse, Cumberland,
and Newark, the dancers performed in Washington, D.C.,
New York City, Hartford, and Boston. As the Caravan
reached out to new audiences, it also reached out in new
ways. Kirstein conducted lecture demonstrations (a strategy
more commonly associated with modern dancers than with
ballet companies), with Lew and Marie-Jeanne providing the
movement. The Caravan's cooperative ideal receded in
importance as newspapers pushed Lew and Marie-Jeanne as
the small company's "stars" or cued their audiences which
dancers to watch: "We all know that Lew Christensen and

[41] Mason Interview, 1984.

[42] For a more complete description of the action, see Marcia B. Siegel's *The Shapes of Change: Images of American Dance* (Boston: Houghton Mifflin, 1979), 113–18.

[43] Mason interview, 1984.

Marie-Jeanne are the banner bearers of the troupe and with Ruby Asquith drew special bravos last night."[44]

Kirstein reserved the premiere of *Filling Station* for the company's January engagement at the Wadsworth Atheneum Avery Memorial Auditorium in Hartford, Connecticut, where the School of American Ballet had presented its first public performances three years earlier (in December 1934). The ballet's premiere clinched the Caravan's reputation as purveyors of ballet Americana in the contemporary vein. *Filling Station*'s setting was a world created by modern technology, with imagery drawn from familiar situations to which Americans of varying backgrounds could relate. The comic strip-inspired costumes by Paul Cadmus and the vaudevillian roots of the piece's acrobatics and visual humor also combined to make the ballet's language understandable to a broad audience. *Filling Station* was appealingly up-to-date in its setting and socially aware with its working man hero. Audience reaction at the premiere was wildly enthusiastic, and the critics followed suite. "I may as well say at the outset," declared Anatole Chujoy, "*Filling Station* is a huge success for the Caravan and a personal triumph for Lew Christensen as choreographer and dancer."[45]

As the Caravan's first real hit, *Filling Station* added to the momentum of the winter season. From Hartford the company went to New Jersey and then to Boston, where Kirstein, now on home turf, was able to whip up considerable local enthusiasm for his pet project. The Boston Museum of Modern Art mounted an exhibition of dance-related works and served as the setting for a lecture by Kirstein on the

---

[44] "Bravos Hail Performance of Ballets," *Hartford Daily Courant*, January 7, 1938.

[45] Chujoy admired the ballet's economy of means, the carefully selected characters, the "adroit skill" of the choreography. Mac's own variation was "the finest *pas seul* this young dancer has composed and danced so far," and the *pas d'action* (in which Mac gives the motorist directions) "as clever a bit of choreography as one can desire." Anatole Chujoy, "Ballet Caravan in Filling Station," n.p., clipping in American Ballet Scrapbooks, Dance Collection, The New York Public Library. See also Marian Murray, "'Filling Station' Wins Acclaim Here in Presentation by Ballet Caravan," *Hartford Times*, January 7, 1938.

history of ballet, complete with slides and live demonstration. Private dinners in fashionable circles preceded the lecture. Society columns reported who turned out and what they wore. Ballet Caravan's actual performances in Jordan Hall prompted similar social support. And the press, keyed to nationalist issues by Kirstein's persuasive rhetoric, gave the company's claim to Americanizing a Russian art form serious consideration. The following month Lew's photograph as Mac was on the cover of *Dance,* yet another sign of the Caravan's growing reputation. When the Caravan closed its winter season with performances in New York, John Martin described the group as "a first-rate little ballet company in the making."[46]

By the end of that winter season, Kirstein's venture seemed in full bloom. His theories were being put into action: he had brought together American composers, dancers, and artists to work in full collaboration. The audience was growing, and lecture-demonstrations were educating more viewers. Lew had a fitting leading role, and in May his picture as Mac would be on another magazine cover, *Dance Observer.* The Caravan had a certified hit and bookings for a spring season.

In the meantime, Balanchine's falling out with Edward Johnson at the Metropolitan Opera precipitated the American Ballet Ensemble's final break with that institution at the end of its third year in residence. By April (1938), William Dollar, Kathryn Mullowny, and Gisella were free to join Ballet Caravan as guest artists for the spring tour. Dollar contributed a new work to the Caravan's repertory, *Air and Variations* (set to Bach's Goldberg Variations), with choreography built around Marie-Jeanne, partnered by Lew, as the personification of the musical theme. The enlarged company performed in Virginia, North and South Carolina, and Georgia and

---

[46] John Martin, "Caravan Dancers in Three Ballets," *New York Times,* February 19, 1938. Martin also observed that with Lew Christensen and Loring in the male contingent, the "feminine side of the company [was] put a little in the shade." Martin found more to praise in *Yankee Clipper* than in *Filling Station,* which he considered "not choreographically distinguished." The *New Masses,* however, approved of the "homespun" *Filling Station*; its critic disliked only the rich couple, "intruders, two-dimensional people who don't belong in the more robust working world setting." "Ballet Caravan's 'Filling Station,'" *New Masses,* March 8, 1938.

appeared for the first time outside of the United States in Havana, Cuba. (The Havana engagement proved memorable for Harold because it was the first time he tried to run a stage with a technical crew that did not speak English.) The company returned to New York by boat; the dancers swam in the deckside pool and dove for coins as they traveled north. The tour ended in mid-May with a performance in New Jersey, after which the company disbanded until October.

Although by outward appearances the Caravan seemed to be succeeding in its mission, Kirstein was frustrated by the difficulties involved in promoting his company, especially in competition with de Basil's Ballets Russes. He used the summer of 1938 to compose his polemic *Blast at Ballet*, a pamphlet accusing the entertainment industry's booking managers of conspiring against native ballet companies in favor of imported dancers with famous names and greater glamour. He fired angry salvos at both the audience's and the bookers' tendency to view "Russianballet" as the only authentic form of classical dance. In his railing against the system, Kirstein neglected to mention that when stacked dancer for dancer, Ballet Caravan was not equal to the Ballets Russes in terms of training and experience. De Basil's "baby ballerinas" not only had exotic names – Tamara Toumanova, Tatiana Riaboushinska, Irina Baronova – they also had excellent technique acquired in the Paris studios of former Russian Imperial ballerinas. Moreover, while the Caravan's mission limited it to performing the works of relatively inexperienced choreographers, de Basil's repertory included ballets by choreographers dating to the Diaghilev era: Fokine, Massine, Nijinska, and Balanchine. (That same year was actually a turning point for de Basil, who lost Massine and several leading dancers to a new Monte Carlo company, but the principles underlying this comparison still apply.) Despite Kirstein's good intentions, despite some fine performers (such as Lew), despite the undeniable educational value of the Caravan to its dancers and choreographers, in the battle for public favor the young Americans had no chance.

Lew took this battle very personally, perhaps because *he* did measure up to the Russian- or European-trained dancers. With his limited formal education and a certain intellectual naivete, Lew accepted Kirstein's pro-American stance lock, stock, and barrel. In a sullen statement to a reporter from the *New Yorker*, Lew vented his spleen against audiences who preferred foreign dancers to the homegrown variety.[47] While Lew received his most valuable training from Balanchine, the youngest Christensen absorbed from Kirstein attitudes that would shape his career. Not that Lew accepted Kirstein's every notion; Lew always had an independent streak rooted in his quiet, firm sense of self. But during the half decade from 1934 to 1939, as he worked out his professional identity, Lew would have felt the undeniable power of Kirstein's intellect and the persuasiveness of his passions.

At the bottom of Kirstein's dilemma lay questions of authority and one's connection to the recognized balletic tradition. Traditionally ballet has been an art form dependent

---

[47] Richard O. Boyer, "A Reporter at Large: Americans Dance, Too." *New Yorker*, June 11, 1938, 36. Lew was quoted as criticizing American audiences for being impressed with foreign dancers "just because they can talk French or Russian" and for ignoring "ordinary Americans" who could "spin" just as well. Lew was also quoted as comparing himself favorably with Nijinsky – "He's more plastic but I'm more sharp" – in a passage that seems apocryphal in light of the many accounts of his modesty. Harold denied that Lew ever spoke in such a way and attributes the statement to Kirstein rather than to Lew. Interview with Harold Christensen, San Anselmo, California, September 23, 1987.

In the *New Yorker* article, Lew also criticized Balanchine (although not by name); he censured the latter's working methods in a reference to the 1936 performance of *Serenata: Magic*:

> [Lew] recalled a night when he had performed in a European ballet in Hartford and hadn't even known what the dance was about until he read a description of it in the paper the next day. The proper and American method, he felt, would be to tell the dancers the meaning of everything they were called upon to do.

Apparently, Lew did not like being left in the dark by Balanchine, who was happy to use Lew as a performer but was not interested in interpreting the choreography he asked Lew to do. In the *New Yorker* account, Lew declared that he intended to make his ballets clear to his dancers. The article described Lew as sullen and resentful, suggesting a less sunny side of his disposition than the comforting presence described by Boris. When asked what his next ballet was going to be about, Lew replied grimly, "About death in an automobile."

upon the transmission of knowledge from experienced dancers and choreographers to younger generations. Many American dancers of this era – Catherine Littlefield, Ruth Page, and William Dollar, to name a few – went to Europe to hone their technique. The Christensens, however, accepted Mascagno as a satisfactory link to the grand tradition. In this issue, Harold and Lew initially followed Willam's lead. During the vaudeville years and after, Willam had a family to support (first his parents, then a wife and child), and the point of dancing was to make money. European study would not have been practical, given the family's economic situation and the responsibilities Willam had shouldered. During the mid-1930s, study at the School of American Ballet, and especially his private tutelage with Balanchine, solidified Lew's technical foundation. The question then became, what did European dancers have that he had not, by extension, received? In later years, as the director of his own company, Lew would reject the notion of a repertory grounded in the classics and, looking forward rather than backward, would channel his energy into creating new works.

Ruby made ends meet the summer of 1938 by dancing in the corps de ballet at Radio City Music Hall. She tolerated the environment out of necessity. She had little in common with most of the dancers, whom she did not feel were serious about their artistry, but she had one good friend there in Nora Kaye.[48] The two shared a make-up table and would sneak out when possible to take class with Fokine.

Gisella's relationship with Lew was put on hold as he and Harold spent most of the summer of 1938 in Portland, teaching at Willam's school. The brothers' decision to go to Portland was in essence a decision to go home. Willam had spent the 1937–1938 season in San Francisco, but the family had not yet given up the Portland school. Isabell and Chris (the parents) continued to run it, while others taught. For Lew and Harold, "home" was where their parents were, where the

---

[48] Interview with Ruby Asquith Christensen, San Anselmo, California, September 26, 1987.

family school was, where Willam had established an institution and created an outlet for their skills. Willam's school provided a source of employment for his brothers between Ballet Caravan tours, and their presence during the summer session helped to shore up the family interest in the school's ownership. That summer Lew choreographed a version of *A Midsummer Night's Dream* to be performed at the Multnomah Stadium. While working with Willam's company, Lew became enamored of Janet Reed, whom he cast as Titania opposite himself as Oberon. In keeping with Lew's understated social style, they had no whirlwind romance, just innocent dates to the movies between time spent in the studio. But on the long trip back to New York with Harold, Lew often hummed the melody of Reed's solo or played it on his 'cello.[49]

The Caravan reassembled in the fall of 1938 for its most ambitious season to date: a tour that would take them across the continental United States, down the Pacific coast, back across the southern part of the country, and to New York for a closing engagement in May. The company traveled by train as well as by bus and included a union stagehand who relieved Harold of many of his previous duties. Nonetheless, Harold remembered this tour in terms of stages: the stages in Chicago and San Francisco, which had to be hung with drapes because they were too large for the Caravan's scenery; stages with dry rot that gave the dancers slivers; stages that were dangerously slick because the local crews had waxed them in honor of the dancers' arrival; the stage in New Mexico that had no crossover, which meant the dancers had to leave the theater and cross through an R.O.T.C room to get to the other side; and the theater in a mining town in Arizona where he had to chisel a hole through a cement stage in order to hook up an electrical cable.[50]

---

[49] Telephone interview with Ruby Asquith Christensen, May 10, 1991.

[50] Interview with Harold Christensen, San Anselmo, California, September 26, 1987. This tour has been well documented by Kirstein, who recorded his impressions of the group's experiences for *Dance Magazine*. Kirstein's account includes several references to the Christensens: Ruth Page criticizing Lew's hands in Chicago; Ruby and Harold being interviewed on the radio in Portland; Lew, Gisella, and

One of the tour's major events was the premiere in Chicago that October of Loring's new work, *Billy the Kid*. Loring starred as the frontier boy whose mother's death spurs him to revenge and life as an outlaw. On Lew, Loring created the role of Pat Garrett, the outlaw's friend who ultimately brings Billy to justice. Grace Robert found Lew "the perfect cowboy sheriff, his admirable physique and relaxed movement making him ideal in the part."[51] Kirstein took this a step further, reflecting in later years that in this role Lew resembled the "young John Wayne disguised as the Apollo of Tombstone."[52] Ann Barzel, who attended the premiere and feted the company afterwards, was struck by Lew's impact on the role of Garrett. Garrett is not a typical, mean-spirited sheriff of the Wild West tradition; rather, Barzel sees him as "the kindly guy who tries to guide Billy," a figure of "gentleness" who arrests Billy but without animosity.[53] In a study of landmark works of twentieth-century American choreography, dance critic Marcia Siegel has analyzed Garrett similarly, painting him as a father-figure to Billy. She describes Garrett as "a leader and a pacifier," two roles played by Lew as ballet master of the Caravan.[54] Siegel also observes that when Billy cheats his old friend in a game of cards, Garrett "stops short of a real fight," an interesting parallel to Lew's own tendency to avoid direct confrontation in personal matters.

The Caravan's 1938–1939 cross-country tour concluded with May performances at the Martin Beck Theater, the company's first engagement in one of New York's "legitimate" houses. There the company was sponsored by the short-lived American Lyric Theatre, an organization created

---

Marie-Jeanne giving a lecture demonstration in San Jose; Lew's pirouettes "burn[ing] holes in the floor" and an ovation for Gisella's "sodden grace" as *Filling Station*'s tipsy Rich Girl in Hollywood; and a rowdy Arkansas reception for a romantic waltz danced by Ruby and Erick Hawkins. Kirstein, *Ballet: Bias and Belief*, 59–67.

[51] Robert, *Borzoi Book of Ballets*, 57.

[52] Kirstein, *Thirty Years*, 77.

[53] Interview with Ann Barzel, Winston-Salem, North Carolina, February 15, 1982.

[54] Siegel, 125.

to promote American music, theatre, and dance.[55] During the preparations for this engagement, the stage designer, Robert Edmond Jones, called Harold for the light plot for *Pocahontas*. Unable to put his hands on the plot, Harold drew one from scratch, indicating where each light was to be hung and what color gel to use. When Jones saw the plot, he laughed and sent it on to his assistant, who explained to Harold, "This is all right, except you turned it backwards."[56] That backward light plot betrayed Harold's homegrown theatrical skills and, seen in the broader perspective, is a telling symbol of the group's operating methods. The dancers acquired their knowledge of stagecraft largely by trial and error; while their skills met the needs of the young troupe, they were unpolished and unsophisticated by professional standards.

Although the young company may have lacked sophistication, Kirstein did not view his troupe as an aggregate of amateurs. On the contrary, by affiliating with the American Guild of Musical Artists in 1939, Ballet Caravan was the first American ballet company to achieve union status.[57] Kirstein had a strong personal commitment to unions and pursued possibilities for both Ballet Caravan and the Metropolitan Ballet. In 1938 (or early 1939), he drafted a list of issues

---

[55] Chujoy, *The New York City Ballet*, 117. Ballet Caravan shared the engagement with the musical *Susanna, Don't You Cry*, based on songs by Stephen Foster, and Douglas Moore's opera *The Devil and Daniel Webster*, for which *Filling Station* acted as a curtain-raiser. The Caravan also had two complete evenings in which it presented *Air and Variations*, *Pocahontas*, and *Billy the Kid*. The American Lyric Theatre engagement received considerable press attention. Gisella's photograph graced the cover of *Information about New York* the last week in May. *Pocahontas*, revived at Kirstein's insistence for presentation with orchestra, had mixed reviews, but Lew received praise for his virtuosity in Dollar's *Air and Variations*. *Billy the Kid* was the critics' choice and the audience favorite. Pitts Sanborn, "Brilliant Program in Ballet Caravan," *New York World Telegram*, May 25, 1939; Miles Kastendieck, "The Ballet Caravan Makes Formal Bow," *Brooklyn Eagle*, May 25, 1939; Jerome D. Bohm, "Ballet Caravan Offers Season's Last Program," *New York Herald Tribune*, May 25, 1939; Irving Kolodin, "Ballet Caravan Gives Bill," *New York Sun*, May 25, 1939.

[56] Interview with Harold Christensen, San Anselmo, California, September 22, 1987.

[57] Earlier versions of this manuscript, on deposit at the San Francisco Performing Arts Library and Museum, contain a more complete discussion of efforts at unionization in the dance world of the 1930s.

entitled "Questions Concerning Ballet Field," which he threw down like a gauntlet at AGMA. He challenged the union to prove its competence, charging that "thus far it has shown itself impotent in organizing the dance field."[58] First on the list of Kirstein's concerns was the union's ability to provide maximum employment for American dancers, protecting them against unfair competition from foreign troupes who paid their dancers less, performed for less, and thus found it easier to get bookings. Kirstein also challenged AGMA to require other American ballet companies, especially the Metropolitan Opera Ballet, to bring their wages up to the level of Ballet Caravan's pay, thus eliminating double standards within the profession.

Harold was one of the Caravan dancers appointed by Kirstein to negotiate with AGMA. As company manager, Doug Coudy was probably also involved with this process. Harold had no affection for unions; he saw them as complicating life rather than facilitating it. His chief concern was that impresarios be able to meet their expenses; otherwise, he reasoned, the Caravan would never get engagements. But Kirstein insisted that the dancers be members of a bargaining body, so Harold gave the matter his best efforts. He and a small group of dancers from the company met with an AGMA lawyer in New York, studied other theatrical contracts, and developed a contract for the dancers in Ballet Caravan. When it came time to negotiate salaries, the dancers asked for $50 a week, but Kirstein drew the line at $45. When Ballet Caravan joined AGMA in 1939, the dancers were guaranteed $45 per week when performing and $20 per week during rehearsal periods.[59]

The Caravan's dancers went their separate ways once more in the summer of 1939. Ruby rejoined the corps de ballet at Radio City Music Hall. Harold, who was now thirty-four years old, returned to Portland to teach. This time Lew (who had just turned thirty) went with Gisella and Balanchine's

---

[58] "Questions Concerning Ballet Field," found in Unions Clipping File, Dance Collection, The New York Public Library.

[59] Ann Barzel, "State of the Unions," *Dance Magazine*, October 1947, 16.

ensemble to Hollywood to film the "Slaughter on Tenth Avenue" sequence of Warner Brothers' *On Your Toes*, which also featured Vera Zorina, Eddie Albert, and André Eglevsky.

The great touring days of Ballet Caravan concluded with a ten-week, cross-country sweep from October to December of 1939. The only additions to the repertory were Loring's *City Portrait* and Lew's *Charade, or The Debutante*. The two works contrasted sharply in tone: Loring's was a desperate and disillusioned portrayal of the destructive force of city life on the family, while *Charade* was a whimsical re-creation of a turn-of-the-century coming-out party. This essay in Americana included balleticized versions of the polka, the waltz, the schottische, and the galop, suggesting that Lew was drawing on memories of the dances taught in his father's Brigham City ballroom. The cast of *Charade* featured Marie-Jeanne as the Debutante, Lew as her eligible young suitor, Harold as the Debutante's father (and the ballet's authority figure), and Ruby as the maid. But Gisella stole the show in the role of Trixie, the Debutante's impish younger sister, who, with a lampshade on her head for disguise, enters as a mysterious guest, disrupts the party, and wins the attention of her sister's suitor. John Martin wrote *Charade* off as a "low comedy rumpus."[60] But other New York critics found much to like in Lew's ballet: the "brilliant series of flighty patterns for the younger sister," the spirited "ensemble work that ought to shame the Russian ballet," and Gisella's "superb madcap performance."[61] Ann Barzel compared the two latest additions to Ballet Caravan's repertory by explaining that Loring choreographed "in terms of drama" but that Lew

[60] Reynolds, *Repertory in Review*, 62. In later years Chujoy recalled *Charade* as "an adequate ensemble piece designed to show off the technical prowess of the dancers" with "some excellent dancing and a comic situation or two, and that was all." Chujoy, *The New York City Ballet*, 118.

[61] Irving Kolodin, "Ballet Caravan Gives 'Charade,'" *New York Sun*, December 27, 1939; Walter Terry, "Ballet Caravan Opens Holiday Dance Festival," *New York Herald Tribune*, December 27, 1939; Albertina Vitak, "Dance Events Reviewed," *American Dancer*, n.d., 16, in Christensen family scrapbook, San Francisco Performing Arts Library and Museum.

choreographed "in terms of dance" and wove a "sparkling pattern of dances" using "a wide technical range."[62] *Charade* played well on the road, where audiences enjoyed Gisella's antics.

The Caravan completed its fall 1939 tour by participating in a Holiday Dance Festival at the St. James Theatre in New York. The festival also featured Martha Graham's company, so Harold decided to watch Graham in an attempt to come to terms with her style of movement. Basically, that attempt failed. During the Ballet Caravan years Harold also saw Humphrey-Weidman and Harald Kreutzberg, but the exposure to these artists did nothing to instill in him an appreciation for modern dance.[63] The Christensens had been reared with a strong bias for classical technique; during their formative years Uncle Pete had scoffed openly at the unschooled freedom of the Duncanesque pageantry produced at the University of Utah. The uncles' search for a "scientific" dance technique with discipline and "nomenclature" resulted in an ironclad prejudice for ballet on the part of Willam, Harold, and Lew.

By the end of 1939 the touring Caravan had reached a point of physical and artistic exhaustion. Kirstein did not have sufficient interest to maintain the company once it became clear that his band of American dancers would never generate the excitement and spectacle necessary to put them on par with their touring Russian counterparts. Furthermore, Lucia Chase, a wealthy dance student of Michael Mordkin, was pursuing plans to create a new ballet company (Ballet Theatre) that would include the work of American choreographers and dancers while still appealing to the public's taste for glamour with star dancers in lavish productions. Kirstein was clearly outflanked; the Caravan disbanded once again as he let go of the dream that had sparked its creation.

---

[62] Ann Barzel, "American Ballet Caravan," *Dance*, December 1939, 30–31.

[63] Interview with Harold F. Christensen, San Anselmo, California, September 23, 1987.

Lew had the prospect of another movie contract through Balanchine in the coming months.[64] Clad as a knight in full armor, he danced the male lead, Prince Siegfried, opposite Vera Zorina in an abbreviated version (some say parody) of *Swan Lake* in a new Twentieth Century-Fox film, *I Was an Adventuress*.[65] For Harold, home was now San Francisco, where Chris and Isabell had joined Willam and Mignon. Willam had planned a winter tour for the San Francisco Opera Ballet and needed someone to run the school during the six weeks the company was to be on the road. Harold would fit the bill nicely. Once again the Christensens turned to each other, divided responsibilities and opportunities, and carried on the family business.

As the Caravan disbanded, Loring announced his intention to join Chase's new Ballet Theatre. He encouraged Ruby to join with him, saying that the choreographer Antony Tudor had seen her perform and was interested in her dramatic stage presence.[66] But by this time Ruby and Harold were dating again, and she was not interested in a job that would separate them. When Harold told her that he was going to San Francisco to teach for Willam and humbly admitted he would be pleased if she came, too, Ruby made up her mind to go west.

---

[64] Richard Buckle states in *George Balanchine: Ballet Master* (New York: Random House, 1988), 122, that as soon as *On Your Toes* was completed, Goldwyn lent Zorina to Twentieth-Century Fox for the filming of *I Was an Adventuress* and that by the end of 1939 Balanchine was working on a new musical, *Keep Off the Grass*. Buckle's wording suggests that the ballet sequence for *I Was an Adventuress* was done before 1940. But Cobbett Steinberg's chronology of Lew's career states that Lew did *I Was an Adventuress* in the winter months of 1940. The Playbill for the 1939 Holiday Dance Festival at the St. James Theater includes a brief biography of Lew which states that after this engagement he would leave for Hollywood to partner Vera Zorina in the new film, so I have followed Steinberg's chronology.

[65] This sequence testifies to Lew's self-effacing partnering; while occasional close-ups reveal his handsome face, his focus is always on Zorina as he lifts her back and forth across the stage. The sincerity of the performance is thrown into doubt in the final moments, when Lew trudges stiffly into the lake after the departing swans, his head drooping in mock mourning and his tall figure dwarfing the supposedly distant castle. For further discussion of this sequence, and of Balanchine's other Hollywood films, see Susan Roper, "Balanchine in Hollywood," *Ballet Review* 23.4 (Winter 1995), 48–73.

[66] Interview with Ruby Asquith Christensen, San Anselmo, California, September 26, 1987.

# 7

# WILLAM AND THE SAN FRANCISCO
# OPERA BALLET (1937–1941)

The San Francisco Opera, founded in 1923 by the Italian conductor Gaetano Merola, presented annual seasons that by the
mid-1930s lasted approximately four weeks each autumn. For
wealthy patrons who as "guarantors" subscribed to boxes, the
opening performances signaled the beginning of the fall social
season. Famous singers were imported to lead the local
chorus; productions in the 1930s featured such legendary
names as Lauritz Melchior, Lawrence Tibbett, Ezio Pinza,
Kirsten Flagstad, Lotte Lehmann, and Lily Pons. While prominent singers were imported regularly from the Metropolitan
Opera or from abroad, little attention was given to the
choreographic aspect of the repertory. During the company's
first decade, it had no permanent ballet school or ongoing
ballet troupe beyond the temporary company assembled for
each season. In those ten years, no less than five different
ballet masters provided choreography for productions: Natale
Carossio, Theodore Koslov, Serge Oukrainsky, Ernest Belcher,
and Estelle Reed.[1]

    The completion in 1932 of the War Memorial Opera
House, a neoclassical structure in the city's Civic Center with
a large stage and an elegant interior seating over thirty-two
hundred, inspired Merola to devote greater attention to
details of staging. The following season he hired Adolph
Bolm to direct a ballet school and to provide choreography

---

Most of the reviews cited are found in Christensen family scrapbooks on deposit at
the San Francisco Performing Arts Library and Museum and as part of the Utah Ballet
Archives, Special Collections, University of Utah Marriott Library, Salt Lake City.

[1] Cobbett Steinberg, *San Francisco Ballet: The First Fifty Years* (San Francisco: San
Francisco Ballet Association, 1983), 23.

for the opera's annual seasons. During his tenure from 1933 to 1936, Bolm provided dances for fourteen different operas (including the opera-ballet *Le Coq d'Or*) and mounted twenty-nine ballets (including his modernistic *Ballet Mécanique*). But for unspecified reasons, Merola decided not to renew Bolm's contract after the 1936 season. Léo Staats, ballet master at the Paris Opéra, was suggested as a replacement, but the Opera's management, which was almost all Italian, rejected the notion of bringing in a Frenchman.[2] So Merola rehired Oukrainsky on a temporary basis for the 1937 season and began looking for a permanent new ballet master.

Willam saw the opening in San Francisco as an ideal situation for himself and his Portland company. He was anxious to prove his qualifications for the soon-to-be-empty post, but there were limits to what he could do with Oukrainsky in charge of that fall's performances. Undaunted, Willam and a core of his best students auditioned for the 1937 season. Oukrainsky hired Willam and Janet Reed as soloists and several of Willam's students for the corps: Zelda Morey, Mary Corruthers, Merle Williams, Jacquelyn Martin, Constance Salazar, Mattlyn Gevurtz, Billie Otis, and Ronald Chetwood. Some of the women "Russianized" their names for a touch of glamour: Zelda Morey became Zelda Nerina; and Mary Corruthers, Maria Tovanya. By prearranged agreement, those who received contracts shared their income with those who did not, a testimony to the mutual supportiveness of the group and to the passionate commitment Willam inspired in them.

Once Willam had been hired for the fall, he brought Mignon and their son Lee to the Bay Area. The family, and many of Willam's Portland dancers, settled in Oakland, just a ferry ride across the bay from San Francisco. Willam encouraged a continuing sense of community among the Portland group by having the dancers over on Sunday afternoons to eat or just listen to music and talk about

---

[2] Anonymous interview with Guillermo Del Oro, San Francisco, California, November 9, 1970, San Francisco Performing Arts Library and Museum.

dancing.[3] An inherently social person, Willam loved being surrounded by his dancers, and the informal gatherings provided security for the younger company members away from home for the first time. Willam also intended to keep the dancers he had shepherded down to San Francisco within his own fold; top on his list of things to do was to establish a school in Oakland where he could continue to train his Portland dancers and take on new students for income to support his family. When Lew and Harold visited the Bay Area late that summer, they pitched in to help their brother set up his new studio. They found a rundown ballroom in Oakland that had dressing rooms and a good floor. Together they hauled away a truckload of garbage and cleaned and painted the premises. Harold, ever businesslike, set up the account books for Mignon, who would serve as the school's secretary.

Anxious to impress Merola right away, Willam arranged a performance of his own pupils while his brothers were in town and could participate. On September 17, 1937, the group from Portland, augmented by Harold, Lew, and a few local dancers, performed at the Oakland Women's City Club Auditorium. The program included selections from Willam's Portland repertory as well as Harold and Lew in excerpts from *Encounter*.[4] According to Russell Hartley, a dancer from this period who became the company's unofficial historian, the impact of this revelatory performance was enormous.[5] Willam's dancers were so impressive that members of the San Francisco Opera Ballet (hereafter "SFOB") who had been taking company class from Mildred Hirsch, a local teacher hired to run the ballet school at the time of Bolm's departure, began commuting across the bay to study with Willam instead. This put him in the questionable position of

---

[3] Telephone interview with Jacqueline Martin Schumacher, July 26, 1991.

[4] Marilyn Rae Evans, "The History of the San Francisco Ballet Company from Its Beginnings through 1951" (M.A. thesis, University of Utah, 1960), 25.

[5] Russell Hartley, "The San Francisco Ballet: A History, 1922–1977," unpublished manuscript, San Francisco Performing Arts Library and Museum, 28.

undercutting SFOB's own school, but there was no arguing with the exemplary results of his teaching. Lee Caiti, the school's business manager, resolved the conflict by appointing Willam director of an Oakland "branch" of the school, where he could teach his dancers and any others who enrolled.

Outsiders perceived the dancers from Portland as a close-knit family and their infiltration as something of a "take-over." The dancers Willam had trained and brought with him from Portland were openly loyal to him in a manner that led to strained relations with Oukrainsky. Oukrainsky's supporters later charged that the Portland contingent was disrespectful of the temporary ballet master during rehearsals, sneering and whispering behind his back.[6] Certainly, whether or not Willam openly disparaged Oukrainsky or actively undercut his authority, Willam *was* intent upon strengthening his own position in San Francisco, and that could only be done at the Russian's expense. Now thirty-five years old, Willam was entering the most ambitious era of his career, and he campaigned hard for Oukrainsky's job. The Oakland performance with his brothers and another shortly afterward in Burlingame were intended to demonstrate to the management that he was capable of directing a performing group during the opera's long off-season.

Willam's own performing opportunities that fall were very limited, but his performing skills were of secondary importance at this point. At the time of Bolm's departure, Merola had announced that he intended the Opera Ballet to be "expanded and developed as never before."[7] Only by

---

[6] Interview with Ann Barzel, Winston-Salem, North Carolina, February 15, 1988. James Starbuck also claims that the Portland dancers were disrespectful of Oukrainsky, suggesting they were just tolerating his presence until their own teacher took over. Interview with James Starbuck, Beverly Hills, California, October 15, 1988. Janet Reed does not remember open disrespect shown toward Oukrainsky but explains: "He was old, he was wispy ... he had sort of an impediment of speech, and he was very effeminate." Telephone interview with Janet Reed Erskine, November 5, 1988. Willam's dancers were probably influenced by his intolerance of homosexuality and may have found Oukrainsky hard to accept.

[7] Steinberg, *San Francisco Ballet*, 25.

touring could a company acquire enough engagements to stay together during the ten months of each year they were not rehearsing or performing in operas. So Willam demonstrated his fitness for the still unclaimed position of permanent ballet master by putting together a string of out-of-town performances after the fall 1937 opera season. Although small in scale and not far from San Francisco, these out-of-town engagements fulfilled their purpose.[8] In January of 1938, Willam was named the new director of the San Francisco Opera Ballet School and choreographer for the San Francisco Opera Ballet Company.

Willam's appointment to the post came as part of a reorganization that included the creation of a booking department to arrange tours and assure year-round performing opportunities.[9] The opera even hired a booking agent, Franklyn Smith, to set up engagements for the dance troupe. Merola hoped the plan would enable the troupe to attract and keep prominent dancers. John Martin observed in the *New York Times* that this significant step would represent the first time "a major Western ballet has attempted to support itself by Western touring."[10]

As he assumed the post of ballet master, Willam became newly conscious of his image in the community. Smith persuaded him to cultivate a more exotic *persona* after one of the critics complained that the name "William Christensen" (which he had used until this point) sounded as if it belonged to a sailor. So Willam dropped the second *i* from his name, and press releases presented him as a "young Danish-American artist."[11] (A program as early as March of

---

[8] Evans, 25. Willam Christensen told Evans in an interview in 1960 that he was actually asked by the opera management to put together the out-of-town performances as a trial effort. Under his direction, the dancers performed in Santa Rosa, Santa Cruz, Vallejo, and Petaluma.

[9] Steinberg, 37.

[10] *Ibid.*

[11] Untitled newspaper clipping, probably from the *New York Times*, March 20, 1938, in the San Francisco Ballet Clipping File, Dance Collection, The New York Public Library.

**22**	San Francisco Opera Ballet on the steps of the War Memorial Opera House. Gaetano Merola is 6th from right, standing; Willam is 2nd from right standing. Dean Crockett is second from left, seated on steps.
Photograph by Morton, courtesy of Willam F. Christensen

1938 uses the new spelling, but the press did not adopt the name change uniformly for several years.) It is a telling coincidence that Willam changed his name the very year that Kirstein raged in *Blast at Ballet*, "American dancers have earned the right to be *American* dancers."[12] While Kirstein decried the practice that turned Hilda Munnings into Lydia Sokolova and Lillian Alicia Marks into Alicia Markova, Willam accepted the public's prejudices and was even willing to meet them half-way. Dropping the *i* from his name was a small gesture that would help him to succeed on society's terms.

Willam was less interested in Kirstein's crusade for American ballet than in building a company patterned after

---

[12] Lincoln Kirstein, *Ballet: Bias and Belief* (New York: Dance Horizons, 1983), 242.

the clearly successful Ballet Russe model.[13] Now at last he had a good chance of putting together his desired touring company. Less than two weeks after his appointment as director of SFOB, Willam held auditions to fill out his new troupe.[14] More of his former students came from Portland: Robert Irwin, Earl Riggins, and Norma Nielsen. To these he added talented local dancers such as James Starbuck, Onna White, and Zoe Del Lantis.

Most of the new group's early performances were small-scale appearances, short ballets at social events such as a ball at the Palace Hotel and a Russian Country Fair outdoors at Sigmund Stern Grove. The company offered its first full program in San Francisco under Willam's direction at the Veterans' Auditorium on April 20, 1938. In addition to the ever useful pastiche entitled *Sketches* (which had selections from Gounod's *Faust*, Schubert's *Rosamund*, and Tchaikovsky's *Nutcracker Suite*), Willam presented a one-act *Romeo and Juliet*, *Ballet Impromptu*, and *In Vienna*. The mixed bill indicates the type of balanced program Willam favored throughout his career: one work with drama or pathos to stir the emotions, one "pure dance" work to demonstrate the beauty of balletic movement to the audience, and a lighthearted closer.

The lineup also indicates the range of Willam's activity as a choreographer during this period. His *Romeo and Juliet*, set to Tchaikovsky's Fantasy Overture, distilled Shakespeare's

---

[13] Willam claims that while still in Portland he had seen "the Ballet Russe" perform and had latched onto that company as a model for his own efforts. He had gone backstage to meet the dancers after the show and had taken Danilova to lunch the following day, determined to learn more about how that company was run. According to the chronologies established by Katherine Sorley Walker, de Basil's company did not perform in Portland until 1938, by which time Willam was already established in San Francisco. He may have seen de Basil's company – perhaps under the name Monte Carlo Ballet Russe – in Seattle in January 1935 or perhaps in Eugene, Oregon (as Col. W. de Basil's Ballet Russe), in February 1937. Telephone conversation with Katherine Sorley Walker, London, June 13, 1989.

[14] "Opera Ballet Selecting New Group of Dancers" *San Francisco Call Bulletin*, January 24, 1938, in San Francisco Ballet Clipping File, Dance Collection, The New York Public Library.

play into one act. The story appealed to Willam because he viewed romance as a central fact of life and believed ballet to be an ideal medium for portraying attraction between the sexes. Critics described the style as part dance and part pantomime, with "fiery and judicious" action.[15] *Ballet Impromptu* (also known as *Bach Suite*) constituted Willam's first efforts in an abstract vein; the movement was worked out without dependence upon a narrative line or the type of programmatic intent that had informed his spectacle ballets, such as the large *Nutcracker Suite* in Portland.

In Vienna illustrated Willam's debt to Massine, whose *demi-caractère* ballets Willam openly admired. Willam himself was primarily a *demi-caractère* dancer: always a supportive partner, but shorter and more compactly built than his brothers and possessed of well-developed thighs rather than the elegant lines of a traditional *danseur noble*. Moreover, Willam's company consisted of dancers with diverse personalities and body types; he capitalized on those differences in creating the characters of his pantomimic ballets. Inspiration for *In Vienna* may have come from a variety of sources: Bolm's *Alt-Vien*, Kurt Jooss's *A Ball in Old Vienna*, or even a dance sketch in Uncle Pete's teaching materials entitled "In Old Vienna" that included handsome young men, ballet girls, and exhibition waltzing. In Willam's version, a haughty waiter oversaw his clients: formal matrons, a Flower Girl and a Boulevardier, flirting Hussars, coquettish young ladies, and three cancan dancers. The slight plot unfolded with humorous touches as the characters came and went. All reappeared finally in a ballroom, where a Ballerina (Janet Reed) performed a dizzying *perpetuum mobile* solo.[16] Story ballets that

---

[15] Alexander Fried, "Opera Dancers Bill Ballet Version of 'Romeo and Juliet,'" *San Francisco Examiner*, no date, in San Francisco Ballet Clipping File, Dance Collection, The New York Public Library. Kirstein saw the production when Ballet Caravan came through San Francisco and complimented its compactness and duelling; he found the swordplay superior to David Lichine's in *Francesco da Rimini*. Kirstein, *Ballet: Bias and Belief*, 242.

[16] Set to Johann Strauss's *Emperor's Waltz* and to excerpts from *Die Fledermaus*, Willam's *In Vienna* contained many opportunities for waltzing. Because the brothers

presented a variety of characters and that mixed balletic movement with pantomime and character dancing were Willam's forte during this period. Like so many of his ballets, *In Vienna* profited from Willam's ability to convey personality through movement and betrayed his tendency to depend upon easily understood stereotypes.

One critic pointed out *In Vienna*'s debt to Massine's *Beau Danube* immediately, while another observed that the company's "youthful buoyancy was all that saved [*In Vienna*] from seeming hackneyed."[17] Indeed, in comparison to Kirstein's idealistic use of American themes and his practice of commissioning scores from new composers, *In Vienna* seems retrogressive, looking backward to an era whose material had been previously plumbed and was resultingly found wanting. But *In Vienna* (or *Old Vienna*, as it was sometimes known) was a durable hit for Willam as his company toured the midwest before World War II. No matter what new ballets were on the lineup, impresarios urged Willam, "Include *In Vienna*."[18] The ballet filled the same slot in the company's repertory that Massine's *Le Beau Danube* and *Gaîté Parisienne* did for the Ballet Russe companies; on tours it was the frothy closing ballet with familiar types and accessible music that sent the audience away in good spirits.

Although SFOB's first independent performances under Willam were few and simple, he was beginning to achieve the objective he had been actively working toward since the late Portland years: his own professional touring company.

---

had been raised with ballroom dance training and the popular dance music of their father's generation, few things came to Willam more naturally than such ballroom scenes: "Strauss was in our bones." Interview with Willam Christensen, Salt Lake City, Utah, April 24, 1987.

[17] Marie Hicks Davidson, "Opera Ballet Scores with Varied Program," *San Francisco Call-Bulletin*, and Alexander Fried, "Opera Dancers Bill Ballet Version of 'Romeo and Juliet'," *San Francisco Examiner*, undated clippings in San Francisco Ballet Clipping File, Dance Collection, The New York Public Library. Descriptions of *In Vienna* also suggest images of Massine's *Gaîté Parisienne* transposed to Vienna, although the latter was not seen in the United States until October of that year.

[18] Interview with Willam F. Christensen, Salt Lake City, Utah, April 24, 1987.

That summer *Dance Observer* reported that the San Francisco Opera Ballet, "with the comfortable backing of the Opera Association," was leading regional dance groups in the direction of "regional self-sufficiency, brought about by accepting the barrier of the Rockies as a fortuitous guardian of originality."[19] The article suggests more support from the Opera Association than the dancers actually received. The Opera did pay Franklyn Smith's salary, but, when on tour, the dancers lived on box office receipts, which also went to pay for the bus. Still, Willam had one thing in Merola that Balanchine lacked at the Metropolitan: an opera director who appreciated dance and understood that ballet companies need independent performing opportunities and a year-round existence.

Willam's absence from Portland during the 1937–1938 season did not adversely affect the fortunes of the family's school there. His former pupil Natalie Lauterstein, who had returned to Portland after two seasons at the Metropolitan under Balanchine, was in charge of ballet instruction, and Lew's old vaudeville partner, Wiora Stoney, had joined the faculty. A newspaper article three months after Willam's departure reported that classes were bulging, the studio was planning recital-parties, and Willam was expected to return and stage a concert featuring the local pupils along with his new professional group.[20] That prediction was fulfilled the summer of 1938 when Willam took his new company home to Portland, where, as previously noted, Harold and Lew were teaching between Ballet Caravan tours. As in the past, the dancers performed under the stars at the Multnomah Stadium, this time with Willem Van Den Berg conducting the stadium philharmonic. Apparently their experiences in San Francisco had seasoned Willam's dancers; the *Oregon Daily Journal* reported that the program, consisting of Lew's *Midsummer Night's Dream* and Willam's *Chopinade*, vastly

---

[19] Maxine Cushing, "Dance on the Pacific Coast," *Dance Observer* 5 (June–July 1938): 91.

[20] "Ballet Classes Bulge," *Portland Oregonian*, November 21, 1937.

"outshadowed" the previous two years' performances "in beauty and professional finish."[21]

Back in San Francisco for the fall 1938 season, Willam resolutely faced the challenge of learning to choreograph for operas. A self-described "sponge," Willam over the years made up for the gaps in his training by turning to others with more experience. Initially, he leaned heavily on the San Francisco Opera's stage director Armando Agnini (Gaetano Merola's son-in-law), who had performed with the Metropolitan Opera Ballet all but two seasons between 1918 and 1932.[22] Agnini would explain the traditional staging of the opera and how the dance fit into it, leaving Willam to supply the actual choreography. Willam would also consult with dancers who remembered Bolm's choreography, and through the years he picked the brains of guest conductors and directors who came to San Francisco.

The Christensens' training in social dance and the variety of dance styles taught in Uncle Pete's studio gave Willam a strong background from which to work in setting operatic divertissements. The old-fashioned minuets and quadrilles he had tolerated as a youth were newly relevant as he staged court dances for *Rigoletto* and *Lucia di Lammermoor*. For *Carmen* he drew on the Flamenco technique he had learned years earlier when studying Spanish dancing with Uncle Pete and with a Madame Viola in New York City. In areas where he had no direct experience, Willam found whatever inspiration he could in other sources; in a case of jitters over *Aïda*, he studied photographs of Egyptian art, and for *Lakmé* he picked up details of stance and movement from the dancing of Uday Shankar.[23] Willam's forte as a choreographer for opera, as in his narrative ballets, was his ability to find a gesture or pose that communicated clearly to the audience

---

[21] "Music and Ballet Stir Enthusiasm," *Oregon Daily Journal*, July 19, 1938. In Christensen Scrapbook, San Francisco Performing Arts Library and Museum.

[22] William H. Seltsam, comp., *Metropolitan Opera Annals* (New York: H. W. Wilson Company, 1947), 323, 338, 353, 369, 386, 417, 435, 452, 469, 485, 502, 536.

[23] Interview with Willam F. Christensen, Salt Lake City, Utah, May 1, 1987.

the nationality or personality of the character on stage; he then built upon that gesture or pose a dance in keeping with the needs of the scene or overall work. Willam also turned out peasant dances for *Faust* and *Mefistofeles* and a commedia dell'arte scene for *A Masked Ball*. In the thirteen years he staged opera ballets before moving to Utah in 1951, Willam provided choreography for eighty-four productions of two dozen different operas, often changing his approach to an opera for a new production of it. He learned through experience as he tried to fit into the tradition of operatic dance in San Francisco. Unlike Balanchine and Kirstein at the Metropolitan Opera, Willam did not see the operatic context as an opportunity for choreographic experimentation. He worked hard to meet the Opera's needs, and he aimed to please. As a result, he had a long tenure at the San Francisco Opera, returning as late as 1959 to provide choreography for new productions.

SFOB dancers earned $25 a week during the fall season and made that income last as long as possible. Because the women had to buy pointe shoes out of their wages, rather than being supplied by the company as is now the norm, they coated their shoes with shellac to coax extra performances from them. Like the members of Ballet Caravan, Willam's dancers assisted with the chores involved in travel when their newly organized troupe made its first real tour, following the fall 1938 opera season. Traveling by bus, the company performed its way north to communities in Oregon, Washington, and Idaho, with a program featuring the ballets they had presented in San Francisco: *Ballet Impromptu, Romeo and Juliet, In Vienna*, and *Sketches*. Sometimes Smith arranged for the dancers to stay in homes to cut down on the cost of hotel bills. Getting productions mounted and performances on the stage were the focus of all effort and often exhausted the company's means. "We never earned anything," recalls Starbuck. "Even on that tour, a lot of that money went for costumes and things; [it was] as if 'Don't ask for your salaries, because we're broke.'"[24]

---

[24] Interview with James Starbuck, Beverly Hills, California, October 15, 1988.

Willam gave continually of his own means to pull productions together, and the power of his enthusiasm and determination kept the company together and performing through many difficult periods. But the lack of sufficient funds to pay his dancers adequately eventually drove many to other companies, a recurring problem that would later plague Lew as well. When the Ballet Russe de Monte Carlo came through San Francisco, Willam always opened his studios to them for company class and rehearsals. On the surface he cultivated a policy of good will and cooperation, but he warned his dancers that if they auditioned for the Ballet Russe, they were "out." When Starbuck joined the Ballet Russe after the fall 1938 tour, Willam was angry at what he considered a betrayal. The fact of the matter was that Willam trained good dancers but could not or did not pay them well enough to keep them; available funds tended to go toward the cost of new productions. Perhaps his own vision was so oriented to the stage that he was shortsighted concerning keeping dancers. In contrast to Kirstein, Willam was not union-oriented and had no private fortune or dependable benefactor to underwrite his costs. Consequently, the San Francisco company became a pool of talent that other companies naturally dipped into as they came through town.

Harold was left to run the 1939 summer session of the family's Portland school on his own. Articles announcing his arrival after the Ballet Caravan tour noted that his "professional group classes" were filling up quickly by advance registration.[25] But unlike years past, no Christensen company appeared at the Multnomah Stadium that July. Perhaps Willam was losing interest in the Portland setup, particularly now that he had a going concern in San Francisco. Harold dutifully prepared the students of the William F. Christensen Ballet School for an appearance at the Reed College Bowl, and Chris conducted the string quartet that accompanied the

---

[25] "Renowned Ballet Teacher Arrives," undated clipping from the *Oregon Sunday Journal*, in a Christensen Family Scrapbook, San Francisco Performing Arts Library and Museum.

dancing. When Willam arrived a week before the event to put on the finishing touches, he was shocked to see how weak and pale his father was. In view of Chris's increasingly poor health (he had previously suffered a mild heart attack), the family finally closed the Portland school. Chris and Isabell moved to San Francisco to live with Willam and Mignon.[26]

The outbreak of World War II in Europe affected the fortunes of the San Francisco Opera that year. When Gaetano Merola found himself unable to engage desired European singers, he adjusted the planned season, hired American singers instead, and decided to pair one performance of the short opera *I Pagliacci* with a ballet. Willam proposed a ballet on the myth of Endymion, set to the Rustic Wedding Symphony by Goldmark. But Merola had something more traditional in mind; he countered with the suggestion that Willam produce *Coppélia* instead.[27]

So Willam began gathering the information necessary to stage that ballet. He had owned a piano reduction of Delibe's score since he first left Utah and still had faint images in his mind of the one-act version Pavlova's company had performed in Salt Lake City in 1925. Most likely he had seen the Ballet Russe's abbreviated version in San Francisco the previous February. Willam had, of course, staged a one-act version of *Coppélia* in Portland, but Merola expected the full ballet. In addition to studying the score, Willam turned to Gennaro Papi, an Italian conductor who described how the ballet was staged at La Scala.

One problem hung over Willam's efforts. Although he had a piano score for the full ballet, he could locate the orchestral score for only the first two acts. As Jack Anderson explains in his history of the Ballet Russe de Monte Carlo,

---

[26] Upon returning to California, Willam and Lew worked together briefly prior to the latter's return to Ballet Caravan for its fall 1939 tour. That September, Lew performed with Willam's company in Santa Barbara. Lew was the male soloist in *Chopinade* (equivalent to the Poet in *Les Sylphides*), following which Willam danced the male lead in *L'Amant Reve*.

[27] Interview with Willam Christensen, Salt Lake City, Utah, April 24, 1987. Most of the information about Willam's staging of *Coppélia* is based on this interview.

during this period companies often dropped the last act because it was a divertissement and did not further the plot.[28] To the best of Willam's knowledge, the full score for the third act was not to be found anywhere in America. He was in a quandary, afraid to admit to Merola that he didn't have all the music and unable to proceed without it. Finally, with characteristic resourcefulness, he showed the piano reduction of the third act to his conductor, Fritz Berens, and asked, "Could you orchestrate that so it sounds exactly like Delibes?" Berens obliged, and while the company was in rehearsals Willam casually informed Merola that he had finally found the music for the third act, implying that it had come from abroad.[29] Merola heard the music, liked it, and supported the undertaking.

Because SFOB appeared in only two operas that fall season, *Coppélia* became the major focus of the dancers' efforts. The chance to appear in the opera house on equal terms with the singers constituted an opportunity not to be bungled. Willam cast himself as Franz opposite Janet Reed as Swanhilda, and a junior company consisting of students from the school swelled the ranks of the troupe. Publicity emphasized the size of the spectacle with boasts of a "Company of 60."

On the night of the ballet's only performance, October 31, the president of the Opera Association, Robert Watt Miller, hosted a party instead of attending the production. The dancers were furious over this lack of support and talked of picketing the party after the show. Their indignation in the face of Miller's apathy was vindicated by glowing reviews. Alfred Frankenstein of the *San Francisco Chronicle*, whose coverage of the company to this point had been noncommittal, declared enthusiastically that the company had "grown mightily" since its debut; this production was "entirely professional in all its aspects." He found "zest and bite" in the folk dances while the romantic, lyrical passages were "in the

---

[28] Jack Anderson, *The One and Only: The Ballet Russe de Monte Carlo* (New York: Dance Horizons, 1981), 29.

[29] Interview with Willam Christensen, Salt Lake City, Utah, April 24, 1987.

**23**  Willam Christensen and Janet Reed in Willam's 1939 *Coppélia*.
Photograph by Romaine, courtesy of Willam F. Christensen

great tradition." Janet Reed evinced a "true ballerina's light-ness, technical competence, and dominating personality" while Willam's Franz was "both sensitive and virile." And, compliment of all compliments, "the ensemble of automatons and grotesques in the second act surpassed what the Monte Carlo company did in that scene." The results of this little experiment, Frankenstein concluded, "indicate emphatically that ballet programs might be incorporated in the opera company's future policy."[30] Alexander Fried of the *Examiner* agreed that "by Christensen's taste, his imagination and his skill in group leadership, he raised the Opera Ballet to an

[30] Alfred Frankenstein, "S.F. Ballet Has Its Innings," *San Francisco Chronicle*, November 1, 1939, in Utah Ballet Archives (Box 7, Portland Scrapbook 4), Special Collections, University of Utah Marriott Library, Salt Lake City, Utah.

unprecedentedly high standard." The new production "made everyone regret that the current repertory is not giving the Opera Ballet far more to do."[31]

The success of *Coppélia* was a personal triumph for Willam. He had met and overcome serious production obstacles; his company had shared the boards with the opera on equal terms and received lavish praise; and his own performance as a dancer had been well received. He could claim with pride to be the first twentieth-century American choreographer to set the full-length *Coppélia*.[32] It marked the beginning of palpable success in San Francisco.

Adding to Willam's high spirits was the immediate prospect of three and a half months of touring engagements. By mid-November the company was on the road, headed for the Pacific Northwest once again, this time with new costumes and decors, the full-length *Coppélia*, the group's first souvenir book (with Janet Reed on the cover), and a larger Greyhound bus than the previous year.[33] Also new for this tour was a ballet of social satire, entitled at first *Red Tape* and then *American Interlude*. Set to a commissioned score by a San Francisco composer, Godfrey Turner, *American Interlude* borrowed from Aristophanes' play *Lysistrata*, in which wives refused their husbands all conjugal favors until the men agreed to stop warring. Willam's updated version featured a Communist agitator who persuaded a group of brides to strike against their husbands-to-be. Willam danced the role of a town drunk who inadvertently got mixed up in the action and whose comic maneuvers while trying to light a cigar stole the show.

---

[31] Evans, 41.

[32] Willam's full-length *Coppélia* did have all three acts, but he left out "War" and "Peace" in the earliest performances and added them later.

[33] Steinberg, *San Francisco Ballet*, 37. A jubilant Willam wrote to Harold and Lew in the Caravan upon discovering that their tour paths would be crossing in Seattle. Heady with success, he offered the Caravan's dancers the chance to super in his production of *Coppélia* – a jest he found far funnier than they did. Interview with Willam Christensen, Salt Lake City, Utah, March 27, 1987.

Perhaps no other work demonstrates how thoroughly
Willam distanced himself thematically as well as technically
from modern dance in this period. In New York in the early
1930s, many students of Martha Graham, Doris Humphrey,
Hanya Holm, and Helen Tamiris participated in a vital Leftist
dance movement, performing at Communist Party demonstrations and workers' rallies while Leftist critics debated
whether the movement vocabulary of Graham and Wigman
was too bourgeois for the expression of revolutionary themes.[34]
Willam did not take the Left seriously in the least; the
Communist agitator in *American Interlude* was simply a character representing a course of action sufficiently extreme to
become the object of satire.[35] Turner's dissonant score, which
critics interpreted as reflecting the malaise in American
society, and Willam's more frivolous choreography were
fundamentally mismatched. The presence of the drunk who
stole the show suggests that any serious social comment
would have been undercut by vaudeville-style sight gags. The
same ballet, given a more accessible score by Berens and
retitled *And Now the Brides*, was well received the following
year. Franklyn Smith's 1940–1941 press release reassured
prospective bookers that social commentary was *not* the focus
of *And Now the Brides*. Conceding that the ballet dealt with
current topics, Smith insisted that "primarily, it is *good
entertainment*."[36]

With *American Interlude*, Willam was the first ballet
master of the San Francisco Opera Ballet to create a work to

---

[34] For essays on this fascinating era in American modern dance, see "Of, By, and
For the People: Dancing on the Left in the 1930s," ed. Lynn Garafola, *Studies in Dance
History*, V.1, Spring 1994.

[35] "Native Utahn Returns to Salt Lake With Ballet," no paper given, Salt Lake City,
Utah, November 27, 1939, clipping in Utah Ballet Archives (Scrapbook, Box 4), Special
Collections, University of Utah Marriott Library, Salt Lake City.

[36] Press Release, "Season 1940–1941," San Francisco Ballet Clipping File, Dance
Collection, The New York Public Library. The new version gave Harold the central
role of the Agitator, but Harold was uncomfortable with the farcical treatment of the
ballet's theme and was relieved when Willam gave the part to someone else. Harold
disliked the work because he felt, "it was not thought out choreographically."
Interview with Harold Christensen, San Anselmo, California, September 23, 1987.

a newly commissioned score.[37] But Willam was not particularly interested in collaborating with the cutting edge of the musical world. Instead, he leaned toward nineteenth-century ballet music and preferred scores with traditional tonality to the atonal experimentation that characterized much twentieth-century composition.[38] Over the years, Willam's choice of scores reflected his hesitancy to challenge the listening habits of ballet-goers; he tended to choose music he knew his audience would find pleasing. Unlike Kirstein, Willam did not actively seek out young painters and musicians with whom to collaborate in the spirit of Diaghilev. Not only did Willam not have Kirstein's financial resources with which to pursue such a costly policy, he did not share Kirstein's involvement in the broader world of arts and letters. For example, Willam boasted among friends that he had choreographed *Romeo and Juliet* without reading the play.[39] One day an author brought a book to Willam's office and suggested that Willam might want to make a ballet of it. Not taking the idea seriously, Willam mentioned to Harold in passing that "some writer fellow" had dropped by. When Harold investigated, it turned out the author had been Theodore Dreiser presenting Willam with a copy of *Sister Carrie*.[40]

---

[37] Steinberg, *San Francisco Ballet*, 37.

[38] Interview with Willam Christensen, Salt Lake City, Utah, April 10, 1987. When asked by leading Salt Lake newspaper *The Deseret News* in 1980 to list his favorite musical recordings, Willam included ballet music by Delibes and Tchaikovsky; Stravinsky's *Petrouchka, The Firebird*, and *Baiser de la Fée* (but not the *Rite of Spring*); Aaron Copland's *Appalachian Spring* and *Billy the Kid*; Darius Milhaud's *Le Boeuf sur le Toit*; Bizet's *Symphony in C*; Carl Orff's *Carmina Burana*; and a recording entitled *Pas De Deux* conducted by Richard Bonynge. Willam also commented, "I wish we could get complete recordings of all the music by those extreme romanticists who for so many years gave us a 'golden age' of ballet – people like Minkus, Drigo, and so on; they are passe today, but with some judicious cutting there is still much to enjoy in their work." "A Collection of Ballet Music – How Suite It Is!" *Deseret News*, February 29, 1980.

[39] Stephen C. Steinberg and Nancy Johnson Carter interview with James Graham-Luján, San Francisco, California [n.d., Interview H].

[40] Conversation with Harold Christensen, San Anselmo, California, September 25, 1987.

Harold and Ruby arrived in San Francisco in early 1940, just as Willam was preparing for his company's first foray into the Midwest. As so often happened over the years, Harold supported Willam's desire to tour by stepping in to teach during his brother's absence. (Harold's presence made it possible for the brothers' old friend, Deane Crockett, who had joined Willam's teaching staff in San Francisco, to join Willam on the road.) Harold came with the understanding that he would teach twenty-eight classes a week for the six weeks the company was to be gone.[41] Seeing the situation as strictly temporary, he moved into Willam's apartment and began teaching immediately. Ruby took a room at a boarding-house for young women on Van Ness Avenue but listed her permanent address as "New York City" in the *Dancer's Almanac and Who's Who* that year.[42]

The continuation of the 1939 tour in early 1940 was SFOB's most ambitious project to date. The grassroots tour of the Midwest included performances in Arkansas, Colorado, Illinois, Iowa, Kansas, Missouri, Nebraska, Oklahoma, Texas, Wisconsin, and Wyoming.[43] In Little Rock, Willam's company got extra publicity when the Southern heavyweight boxing champion Bob Sikes showed up backstage to watch a re-hearsal and was coaxed into a pair of tights for a few *pliés*.[44] The company's most rewarding reception that winter was in Chicago, where the critics enthused over *Coppélia*. Positive reviews garnered on tours built the company's reputation and consolidated its position in San Francisco. But Willam paid dearly for the press attention; even with Smith's advance

---

[41] "Petaluma, Ballet, Business, America," *New Thesaurus*, [Petaluma, California], Summer 1979, 23.

[42] Ruth Eleanor Howard, ed., *Dancer's Almanac and Who's Who* (New York: Dancer's Almanac and Who's Who, 1940), 2.

[43] This list is a composite of states cited by Evans, 43–44, and Steinberg, 38.

[44] The sports columnist who covered the event took down quotations geared to make ballet palatable to the sports-minded. "Ballet in its fundamental form is athletics strictly. It's coordination of the eye, timing, and muscle," explained Franklyn Smith in terms any boxer could understand. Ben Epstein, "Gazette Sport Gazing," clipping in San Francisco Ballet Clipping File, Dance Collection, The New York Public Library.

bookings SFOB often lost money on the road. Willam, eager for exposure and glory, would take the company to cities where Smith had lined up engagements "on speculation," meaning that rather than being guaranteed a certain fee, the company would receive a percentage of the box office. When such gambles led to debt, the ballet turned to the Opera Association to pay unmet expenses, and Willam turned to Harold for extra money from the school to tide his family over. Willam accepted the financial risks inherent in touring as part of the necessary cost of keeping the company together. Harold, however, deplored financially unsound propositions; he disapproved of touring under those circumstances and pleaded with Willam to change his tactics.

When the company returned to San Francisco in the spring of 1940, Harold and Ruby stayed to participate in the troupe's summer appearances. Willam restaged Lew's *A Midsummer Night's Dream* for an outdoor performance at Sigmund Stern Grove that June, thinking perhaps that the plot would be especially appropriate to the *al fresco* setting.[45] Lew also performed *al fresco* that summer, but in St. Louis rather than San Francisco. While other Ballet Caravan veterans performed *A Thousand Times Neigh!* six times a day for the Ford Motor Company at the New York World's Fair, Lew and Gisella danced in the summer season of the St. Louis Municipal Opera. Lew was hired as both a leading dancer and a choreographer, the latter thanks to positive reviews of *Charade* in the New York press. As the production team's ballet master, he shared choreographic responsibilities with Al White, Jr., who provided jazz and tap routines. In typical summer stock fashion, they turned out dances for eleven productions in less than three months.

Most of the musicals and light operas presented in St. Louis's outdoor theater included numbers by both White's

---

[45] For this production, Willam cast himself as Oberon opposite Janet Reed as Titania. Lew had cast Natalie Lauterstein – a short but powerful technician – in the role of Puck, and Willam acted similarly in assigning that role to Ruby. Harold was Lysander, one of the bewitched lovers.

Dancing Ensemble and Lew's Corps de Ballet, each listed separately in the programs. If a musical had no ballet number, music was often interpolated to create a ballet scene. The extent to which Lew and White collaborated on specific scenes is unknown, but Lew was probably chiefly responsible for the "Air de Ballet" and commedia dell'arte pantomime in *Naughty Marietta*; the Ballet "Tambourine Chinois" in *Apple Blossoms*; a group waltz in *Rio Rita*; a Peasant Dance and Festival Dance for *The Chocolate Soldier*; a collegiate football ballet for *Good News*; the "Love's Dream" ballet in *Knickerbocker Holiday*; the ballet scene in *East Wind*; the "Valse de Fleur" in *Rosalie*; the "Ballet Imaginary" in *Babes in Arms*; and the Kathi Lanner ballet in *The Great Waltz*.[46] While Lew apparently stuck to the classical side of things, the summer must have served as a vivid reminder of his pre-Balanchine days in the popular theater. Engaged as the season's leading ballerina, Gisella shared starring dance roles with guest artists brought in for specific repertory: Thalia Mara, Nina Stroganova, and Vivien Fay.

While Lew was in St. Louis, his father's health declined seriously. A hike in the hills behind San Francisco aggravated Chris's heart condition. After that he attempted less and less activity, finally spending most of his days resting in bed. One Saturday that summer, Harold took Ruby with him to visit his parents at Willam's house. As the couple conversed with Isabell in the living room, Chris entered the room, greeted them, and slumped to the floor. Harold and Ruby carried Chris back to the bedroom, then ran two blocks to the nearest drugstore hoping to get medicine that might revive him. By the time they returned home, Chris had died of a heart attack. The usually stoic Isabell was disconsolate; Harold and Willam shared their mother's grief but did not notify Lew at once of their father's passing. They understood the pressure Lew was under to produce a steady stream of choreography in St. Louis and feared the news would render him unable to work.

---

[46] Programs, the St. Louis Municipal Opera, 1940 Season.

At the end of that difficult summer, Harold and Ruby decided to get married over the Labor Day weekend. Ever mindful of the school's schedule, they picked the date – Saturday, August 31 – so that they could have a three-day honeymoon rather than a two-day one. Neither her family nor his could afford a lavish wedding; moreover, Harold, who rarely showed his emotions in public and was self-conscious in the extreme about matters of the heart, wanted no fuss over the ceremony. So Willam, Mignon, and Isabell gave the couple a party that Friday evening, and on Saturday morning the two went alone to City Hall. To their surprise, one of the dancers in the company, Earl Riggins, showed up and declared himself their best man. So Harold and Ruby were married with one friend in attendance before driving to Lake Tahoe for the holiday weekend. Upon their return they focused on teaching and preparing for Willam's next landmark production, *Swan Lake*.

Willam had found a new source of inspiration in San Francisco's Russian colony. He often went to observe the ballroom dancing at an officer's club patronized by expatriate White Russian soldiers; there aging balletomanes who had been young officers in St. Petersburg before the Revolution shared their memories of productions at the Maryinsky with him. In 1940, the centennial of Tchaikovsky's birth, they pressed Willam to stage *Swan Lake*, not the isolated second act danced by the Ballet Russe de Monte Carlo, but a full-length, four-act production. A committee of Russian émigrés, headed by the Prince and Princess Vasili Romanoff, formed a Tchaikovsky Centennial Committee. Dedicated to preserving Russian culture in San Francisco, they offered financial backing for *Swan Lake* and support in the form of publicity and production design.[47]

---

[47] This scenario provides an excellent example of George Amberg's assertion that White Russian exiles promoted ballet out of nostalgia for the Imperial tradition. As connoisseurs of that tradition, they did not appreciate Diaghilev's cosmopolitan modernism. In the case of *Swan Lake*, as when he worked for the San Francisco Opera, Willam tried hard to please his sponsors. Amberg, *Ballet: The Emergence of an American Art* (New York: New American Library, Mentor Books, 1953), 41.

Willam had seen the ballet's second act, but he was unfamiliar with the rest of the ballet, which was then hardly known in America. He embarked on a thorough study of the score, and the Russians described the action of the three unfamiliar acts: the placement of the characters on stage, the dramatic interaction, and pantomime. When Willam was sure he could stage the ballet, he went to Merola for permission to perform in the opera house two weeks before the regular fall season opened. Merola flatly refused; the ballet could not appear *before* the opening of opera season. In desperation Willam went over Merola's head and approached Robert Watt Miller, the president of the Opera Association, who as a wealthy socialite knew the Prince and Princess Romanoff. Only when Willam pleaded for the chance to try, promising to take complete financial as well as artistic responsibility for the project, did Miller grant permission.[48]

With Miller's approval, progress on the production began in earnest. Two Russians, Eugene Orlovsky and Nicolas Pershin, designed the scenery. *Swan Lake*'s sponsors did not have the finances necessary to create a lavish production, or even to hire a union crew to execute their designs. To evade detection, the set designers rented a loft and painted drops for the ballet behind locked doors. Charlotte Rider, a union designer who had helped SFOB on previous occasions at below-union wages (and who designed the costumes for *Swan Lake*), put an unearned union stamp on the scenery so that it could be used in the opera house.

The presence of Lew in San Francisco that fall was a great boon to Willam's production. Not having Ballet Caravan to return to, Lew had joined his brothers in San Francisco following the St. Louis summer season. He was automatically cast as Prince Siegfried, which meant that the first American full-length production of *Swan Lake* would appropriately star the dancer who had won recognition as the leading American *danseur noble* during the Caravan's tours.

---

[48] Interview with Willam Christensen, Salt Lake City, Utah, February 20, 1987.

Which of the company's leading female dancers would be cast in the ballet's double leading role posed a problem. Today's audiences expect to see a single ballerina master the subtleties and project the appropriate movement styles of both the vulnerable Odette (the Swan Queen with whom Siegfried falls in love) and the arrogant Odile (the counterfeit Swan Queen or Black Swan, who deceives him); it is part of the challenge and psychological excitement of the ballet. But Willam's audience in 1940, which had little knowledge of the complete work, did not share our preconceived notions of its performance traditions. No single dancer in Willam's company was strong enough to dance the combined role, so it was divided.[49] Janet Reed, who was the company's Prima Ballerina, was cast as Odile because she had virtuoso technique and could perform the thirty-two *fouettés* of the Black Swan pas de deux with brio. The role of Odette was given to Jacqueline Martin, who was taller than Reed and thus easier for Lew to partner in the legato second act pas de deux. Rather than basing the prince's confusion on the physical similarity between Odette and Odile, Willam relied on program notes explaining that Rothbart had thrown a spell over the guests assembled at the ball and used his powers of enchantment to deceive the prince.[50] Another aspect of the 1940 production that would surprise today's audiences was the gold (not black) costume Reed wore for the Black Swan Pas de Deux.

Harold appeared as the prince's friend Benno. He danced in a pas de trois in the first act, and he and Zoya Leporsky lead the Czardas in Act Three.[51] Associates remember Harold as magnificent in the Czardas; he and Leporsky

---

[49] Telephone interview with Janet Reed, August 5, 1991. Actually, the roles of Odette and Odile were originally intended for two dancers, but it has long been customary for one dancer to perform both roles because the characters must resemble each other so closely. Cyril W. Beaumont, *Complete Book of Ballets* (New York: G. P. Putnam's Sons, 1938), 440.

[50] Program notes for *Swan Lake* in the San Francisco Ballet Clipping File, Dance Collection, The New York Public Library.

[51] Steinberg, *San Francisco Ballet*, 41. Janet Reed affirms that Harold danced the Czardas magnificently.

**24**  Lew Christensen and Jacqueline Martin in Willam Christensen's 1940
*Swan Lake*.
Photograph by G. Ludé, courtesy of San Francisco Performing Arts Library
and Museum

roused the audience to cheers in what must have been one of the finest roles of his career. Ronald Chetwood was Rothbart, Ruby danced one of the four Cygnets in Act II, and featured SFOB soloists such as Onna White and Harold Lang enriched the cast. Willam did not dance in this production; all his creative energies went to overseeing the project. Apparently he gave Lew quite a bit of latitude concerning Siegfried's choreography. As he rehearsed with Martin, Lew changed Willam's choreography for the second act pas de deux, substituting Balanchine's version, which Lew had performed earlier that year with Vera Zorina in *I Was an Adventuress*.[52]

Parties within and without the opera questioned Willam's wisdom in choosing to stage such a complex work. The *Chronicle*'s critic, Alfred Frankenstein, asked how Willam could possibly attempt *Swan Lake* when he had never seen the complete ballet. And Theodore Koslov, who had directed the Opera's ballet troupe in 1926–27, sent word from Los Angeles that it was sacrilegious for an American company to attempt to mount the Russian classic. Once again Willam's activities raised the issue of authority and authenticity: how could one outside the living tradition legitimately stage such a ballet? Innately confident, Willam was not deterred by others' misgivings. By analyzing the score, using his memories of the second act as danced by the Ballet Russe, and following the staging remembered by his Russian friends, he succeeded in creating a production that was similar in outline to the Petipa-Ivanov staging, even though the specific choreography, the actual steps, were very much his own. (Years later when he saw the Royal Ballet production, Willam was pleased to see the characters just where he expected them.[53])

Willam's version of *Swan Lake* stressed the tragic side of the tale. In the final struggle between good and evil, represented by Siegfried's love for Odette versus the evil influence of Rothbart, evil triumphed. "Siegfried falls prostrate as the girls glide away in the distance as swans," states

---

[52] Telephone interview with Jacqueline Martin Schumacher, July 26, 1991.

[53] Interview with Willam Christensen, Salt Lake City, Utah, April 24, 1987.

the program note, adding no promise of postmortal reunion for Siegfried and Odette. As always, Willam encouraged his dancers to accentuate the dramatic aspects of the plot, punctuating rehearsals with the admonition, "Yearn, yearn!"

The first full-length production of *Swan Lake* in the United States premiered to a full opera house on September 27, 1940, climaxing the celebration of the Tchaikovsky centennial.[54] Despite the irregularities of casting and costuming that might raise eyebrows today, Willam's *Swan Lake* elicited decidedly positive critical response and prompted more comparisons with the Ballet Russe. The *San Francisco Call-Bulletin* rather naively asserted:

> If San Francisco Ballet can sustain the high order of artistry set last night at the Opera House we are independent of Messrs. S. Hurok and others who make a great ballyhoo about bringing the original "Russian" classics to the wild west.[55]

Even Theodore Koslov, who had traveled from Los Angeles to witness the heretical attempt, sent Willam a congratulatory wire.[56]

In retrospect, what is one to make of Willam's landmark "American" productions of *Coppélia* and *Swan Lake*? No films exist by which the choreography may be analyzed or evaluated. It is perhaps more important to acknowledge that Willam was able to stage these classics successfully, from outside the recognized tradition, precisely because they were unknown quantities to most of his audience. (On tour, one critic referred to *Swan Lake* as Tchaikovsky's "practically-never-seen four-act toe-tragedy."[57]) As cultural historian Douglas Tallack notes, "Autonomy has its spatial and temporal

---

[54] "Tchaikowsky to Be Honored with 'Swan Lake' Performance," *Opera and Concert*, August 1940, 9.

[55] Marie Hicks Davidson, "'Swan Lake' Performance Applauded," *San Francisco Call-Bulletin*, September 28, 1940.

[56] Interview with Willam Christensen, Salt Lake City, Utah, April 24, 1987.

[57] Gilbert Brown, "S.F. Opera Ballet Hit in 'Swan Lake'." [Seattle, Washington] *Star*, November 20, 1940.

co-ordinates."[58] In the relative cultural isolation of San Francisco in the late 1930s and early 1940s, Willam was free to experiment without fear of comparisons because the Ballet Russe did not do these works in complete form. This combination of circumstances favored Willam's desire for personal recognition while allowing him to operate as the free agent he always preferred to be.

As it had the previous winter, SFOB toured the Pacific Northwest before Christmas and the Midwest during January and February. Thus began a second phase of Willam's pioneering efforts with *Swan Lake*: introducing American audiences to a full-length version of this masterwork. His ability to present such an impressive and *recherché* Russian classic raised SFOB's stock with the critics immensely, who gratified Willam with more complimentary comparisons with the Ballet Russe de Monte Carlo.[59] But his prized new production developed problems on tour. The scenery created by the Russians behind closed doors did not hold up well because the paint they had used wrinkled and flaked off when the drops were folded. The shortcut intended to save the ballet company money turned out to be a costly mistake. Even more

---

[58] Douglas Tallack, *Twentieth-Century America: The Intellectual and Cultural Context* (London and New York: Longman, 1991), 13.

[59] The Seattle *Times*'s reporter Richard Hays singled out many of the company's principals and soloists for praise, including Lew, Jacqueline Martin, Janet Reed, Ruby, Harold, and Ron Chetwood, and declared that "the organization being developed by William Christensen and his brothers is not only a credit to America but a rival of the best that Europe offers." Richard E. Hays, "American Ballet Enchants Crowd," *Seattle Times*, on press poster, "San Francisco Opera Ballet, 1940–1941," from the collection of Willam F. Christensen. Gilbert Brown of the Seattle *Star* made new comparisons with the Ballet Russe, asserting that "Lew Christensen and Ronald Chetwood, Janet Reed, Ruby Asquith and Jacqueline Martin deserve to be every whit as famous and well known to balletomaniacs as David Lichine, Roland Guerard, Irina Baronova, Zorina, and Tatiana Riabouchinska of the Russian dance aggregation." Brown, "S.F. Opera Ballet Hit in 'Swan Lake.'" At the same time, Brown recognized the difficulties inherent in making such comparisons and admitted, "The combined enormity of regional pride in the west and snobbish conceit in the east make it somewhat difficult to arrive at any sound relative judgements in such matters as these, but it is my artistic feeling that San Francisco's ballet must now be given equal artistic rank with the best that America can offer today in this line."

serious, while the troupe was in Seattle Lew received a wire calling him back to New York immediately; he was wanted by John Houseman to supply choreography for a new Broadway show, *Liberty Jones*. The call to New York, where Gisella was living with her mother and sister and taking class at SAB, was more compelling than Lew's commitment to his brother's company; most likely it also offered better pay. He left for New York right away, leaving Willam to redistribute his brother's roles for the rest of the winter's engagements.[60]

After Lew's departure, Willam depended less on *Swan Lake*, opening in many cities in the Midwest with *Coppélia* and *In Vienna* instead. Perhaps he relied so heavily on *Coppélia* and *In Vienna* because he felt that a humorous ballet with a successful romance and mechanical dolls, followed by a lighthearted depiction of Viennese society, would be more palatable to Americans unfamiliar with ballet than a tragedy such as *Swan Lake* in which the forces of evil triumphed over true love. Willam's tours were not only a means of keeping the company together; they were part of his crusade to popularize ballet. He always wanted to please his audiences, to convert them to ballet as a form of theatrical entertainment. *Swan Lake* was undeniably a great ballet, but, in the ironic jargon of vaudeville, would it play in Peoria? Certainly, *Coppélia* was better suited to young audiences. The company frequently performed for school groups on tour and appeared regularly in Young People's Concerts at the War Memorial Opera House, so having a ballet that appealed to children was a must. In Willam's memories of these touring years, *Coppélia* stands out as his "lucky ballet," while *Swan Lake* is associated with problems and mistakes.[61]

Willam's touring policy and his repertory confirm that he not only patterned his company after the Ballet Russe

---

[60] "Ballet Member Leaves on Eastern Call," hand-dated clipping, probably from the *Salt Lake Tribune*, January 17, 1941, located in a Christensen Scrapbook, San Francisco Performing Arts Library and Museum. The article also states that because of Lew's departure, the company could not fill its expected engagement in Salt Lake City.

[61] Interview with Willam F. Christensen, Salt Lake City, April 24, 1987.

model, he actually sought to challenge its hegemony as a purveyor of Russian ballet. His repertory now included two evening-length classics as well as works similar to Massine's character ballets (*In Vienna*) and ballets patterned after Fokine's *Les Sylphides* and *Le Spectre de la Rose* (*Chopinade* and *L'Amant Reve*). By presenting that repertory on long tours, Willam was challenging the Ballet Russe de Monte Carlo on its own turf.[62] But realistically, Willam's troupe could not measure up to the Russians' experience or their popularity. After its 1941 winter tour, SFOB secured a *two*-night engagement at the War Memorial Opera House rather than a single evening. They presented a newly designed *Swan Lake* as well as *Coppélia*, preceded by the San Francisco premiere of *And Now the Brides*. Critical response was positive, but the opera house was not filled both nights, as it usually was for the week-long visits of the Monte Carlo company.

Neither could Willam compete with the Ballet Russe in terms of star power, especially after Lew's return to New York. The *San Francisco News* pointed out the local company's forte:

> *It is true that the San Francisco Opera Ballet lacks stars of the quality of Massine, Danilova, and Baronova, but it has what the Monte Carlo Ballet has never had, and that is a* corps de ballet *that knows the meaning of ensemble work.... This city has one of the best looking and best dancing ballets on the American stage today. Critics to the north, south, and east have so acclaimed it. Let it no longer be the prophet without honor in its own city.*[63]

Willam desperately wanted the allegiance of his community and support for his dancers, but like Kirstein, he could not overcome the mass audience's preference for the touring Russians. Well-polished ensemble work would not fill the opera house.

---

[62] "The whole thing was very brave of Willam," reflects Ann Barzel; "it was as if he challenged his audiences, 'What's this "Ballet Russe de Monte Carlo"? Here's the San Francisco Ballet! And *Swan Lake* – yes, we do that, too.'" Interview with Ann Barzel, Winston-Salem, North Carolina, February 15, 1988.

[63] Steinberg, 38.

During the spring and summer of 1941, while Americans watched the European war and wondered how long the United States would remain neutral, Willam kept his company together by arranging small performances around the Bay Area. The two previous years, the start of the fall season had signaled an opportunity to mount a new production, first *Coppélia* and then *Swan Lake*. But this year the dancers had only the opera season to look forward to. Willam realized that as long as his company was under the jurisdiction of the Opera Association, its scope and opportunities would be limited. His company needed independence from the Opera Association; he needed patrons that would support the cost of maintaining a company and mounting new productions. That meant that he needed to tap the wealthy power structure of San Francisco's upper crust, for whom supporting the opera was socially acceptable but for whom dance remained of minimal importance.

When Janet Reed became friends with an influential socialite, Tirey L. Ford, Willam asked her to show Ford a document that outlined plans for a civic ballet company. Ford lent his assistance to the plan, and by mid-November a board of twenty-one directors had submitted articles of incorporation to the California Secretary of State. The directors included men from the Opera Association, including Nion R. Tucker and Robert W. Miller, and other prominent businessmen and bankers, such as L. M. Giannini of the Bank of America family. On November 14, 1941, The *San Francisco Examiner* reported the incorporation of the San Francisco Civic Ballet Association, a nonprofit institution to "cultivate a greater appreciation for ballet and all other forms of musical and dramatic entertainment."[64]

With the Civic Ballet Association behind him, Willam finally felt able to move forward in a big way, and he threw himself optimistically into preparations for a company independent of the Opera. The first Sunday morning in December

---

[64] "Ballet Group Formed," *San Francisco Examiner*, November 14, 1941, in San Francisco Ballet Clipping File, Dance Collection, The New York Public Library.

he met with Hal Keith, a former Stanford student who was studying ballet, to put together a new souvenir program booklet. As they were laying out photographs, dramatic news of the bombing of Pearl Harbor flashed from the radio. Sure that the report was a trick, a takeoff of Orson Welles's "War of the Worlds," they called the *Examiner*. The unwanted confirmation sent Willam into shock. "I don't remember going back and assembling the book or anything. . . . We just walked down the street."[65]

The bombing of Pearl Harbor and America's entry into the war threw Willam's life into disarray and naturally put the very existence of his new company in jeopardy. He had already started losing men to the draft. Franklyn Smith had departed after lobbying unsuccessfully for the company to enrich its repertory by acquiring works by other choreographers.[66] Now the troupe disintegrated even further as three of the most valuable performers left. Jacqueline Martin married and returned to Portland, where she opened a ballet school. Ronald Chetwood left for New York to perform in musical comedies. And Janet Reed, seeking better performing opportunities, accepted an invitation to join a new company, Eugene Loring's Dance Players. Sobered at the prospect of war and crushed that his ardently desired company should be one of the first casualties, Willam reluctantly put plans for the San Francisco Civic Ballet on hold.

---

[65] Interview with Willam F. Christensen, Salt Lake City, Utah, April 17, 1987.

[66] Jacqueline Martin Schumacher states that Smith and Willam had a falling out when Smith advocated inviting guest choreographers to expand the company's repertory beyond Willam's ballets. Telephone interview, July 26, 1991.

# 8

# IN THE SHADOW OF WAR (1941–1945)

During the fall of 1940, as Willam premiered and toured his production of *Swan Lake*, headlines from abroad reported dramatic developments in the war overseas. Hitler's Luftwaffe pounded London in the Battle of Britain; Italy launched a full-scale attack on Greece by land, sea, and air; and Japan formally joined the Axis pact three days after invading French Indochina. In late October, Secretary of War Henry L. Simpson drew the first number in America's draft lottery. In December, as President Roosevelt declared America an "arsenal of democracy" ready to supply arms to European nations battling the Axis dictators, Lew hurried back to New York to choreograph his first Broadway play, a political allegory advocating strong measures in the defense of liberty.[1]

That dramatic allegory was Phillip Barry's *Liberty Jones*. Produced by the Theatre Guild, the play depicted the plight of a sick young woman (Miss Jones) dying of neglect. The traditional doctors of Medicine, Letters, Law and Divinity summoned by her Uncle Sam failed to heal her, and in her bewilderment she danced with three menacing foreigners (Stalin, Mussolini, and Hitler). Liberty's uncle then called on Tom Smith, an idealistic hero who first tried appeasement and then realized he must fight the three totalitarians who threatened Liberty's life. Smith's battle secured Liberty's life but ended in his own death.

For this new show, Lew collaborated with Paul Bowles, who had supplied the score for Loring's *Yankee Clipper*, in creating the occasional dances that were sprinkled throughout the play. Lew and Elise Reiman, one of his former

---

[1] Headlines taken from *Chronicle of the 20th Century*, Clifton Daniel, Editor in Chief (Mount Kisco, N.Y.: Chronicle Publications, 1987), 514–18.

partners from the American Ballet, led the dancing chorus. Lew's contribution to the show received positive reviews, but the production (which also featured attractive settings and costumes by Raoul Pène du Bois) could not transcend the heavy-handed symbolism of the script.[2] After out-of-town openings in New Haven and Philadelphia, *Liberty Jones* enjoyed less than a three-week run on Broadway. By the end of February 1941, Lew was out of a job.

In the meantime, Kirstein was in negotiations with his friend Nelson Rockefeller, who had been appointed Coordinator of Inter-American Affairs by President Roosevelt. Rockefeller's position authorized him to arrange cultural exchanges and to send American artists to South America as a goodwill gesture. Rockefeller, who would later be criticized for spending money "on ballets, not bullets," agreed to sponsor a six-month tour of South America for the American Ballet Caravan.[3] The State Department gave a generous grant for touring expenses with the understanding that Kirstein would cover the cost of mounting the necessary productions.

Kirstein assembled a diverse company that combined former collaborators and new talent. Balanchine was, of course, his chief choreographer, but works by Antony Tudor, Eugene Loring, William Dollar, and Lew also figured in the repertory. Doug Coudy was appointed stage manager, and Lew reassumed his former Ballet Caravan position as ballet master. The performing group of thirty-six dancers included members of the former American Ballet and Ballet Caravan

---

[2] Apropos of Lew's choreography, the *Morning Telegram* reported, "Lew Christensen has contrived dances that blend into the picture and that illuminate it at the same time. His own dancing and that of the men and girls he has trained is a pleasure to watch. The choreography as well as the spoken lines in the party scene are likely to remain long in this audience's memory." (George Freedley, "Theatre Guild Offers Philip Barry's 'Liberty Jones' at Shubert Theatre," *Morning Telegram*, February 7, 1941.) Likewise, The *New Yorker* reported that "Paul Bowles and Lew Christensen have provided just the right kind of music and dancing," and *Variety* found the dances "effective" and competently danced. (Woolcott Gibbs, "Through a Glass Darkly," *New Yorker*, February 15, 1941; Bone, "Liberty Jones," *Variety*, n.d., in Liberty Jones Clipping File, Billy Rose Theatre Collection, The New York Public Library.)

[3] Lincoln Kirstein, *Ballet: Bias and Belief* (New York: Dance Horizons, 1983), 77.

as well as Ballet Theatre, the Philadelphia Ballet, the Metropolitan Opera Ballet, the Ballet Russe de Monte Carlo, and students from the School of American Ballet.[4] Lew, Gisella, Dollar, and Marie-Jeanne filled most of the leading roles.

A key newcomer to the administrative entourage was James Graham-Luján, a Scottish-Mexican-American who had translated several plays of Federico García Lorca. Graham-Luján had studied ballet briefly in Texas before coming to New York in the early '30s. In the city intermittently during that decade, he had taken class with Fokine and had even performed briefly with the Metropolitan Opera Ballet, after Balanchine's tenure there. Tux and tails for dinner dress, expensive diction lessons that left him with the hint of a British accent, and his relationship with Lorca provided Graham-Luján with an entrée into an exclusive circle that included not only Kirstein, Bowles, and Paul Cadmus but also the young American novelist Glenway Wescott (who regularly sent red roses to Gisella at performances), the photographer George Platt Lynes, and Monroe Wheeler, a publisher affiliated with the Museum of Modern Art.[5] Kirstein had Graham-Luján translate the company's programs into Spanish and hired him as assistant director for the tour.

Rehearsals began in March, with the departure date set for early June. Lew reassumed the title role of *Apollon Musagète*, but he was not cast in Balanchine's new creations for this tour: *Ballet Imperial* and *Concerto Barocco*. That may have been because Balanchine had found inspiration in other dancers while Lew was in the West performing and touring with Willam's company. By contrast, Gisella, who had remained in New York, was the second ballerina in *Ballet Imperial*. Lew reprised the role of Pat Garrett in *Billy the Kid* and created the role of the football hero in William Dollar's

---

[4] Anatole Chujoy, *The New York City Ballet* (New York: Alfred A. Knopf, 1953; New York: Da Capo, 1982), 135.

[5] Interview with Gisella Caccialanza Christensen, San Bruno, California, September 28, 1987; Stephen C. Steinberg and Nancy Johnson interviews with James Graham-Luján, [n.d., Interview C]; and the author's telephone interview with James Graham-Luján, July 29, 1991.

*Juke Box*, a ballet featuring contemporary social dances. Lew also oversaw rehearsals of *Filling Station* and *Charade*. For this tour, he altered *Filling Station* to incorporate a new ending suggested by Balanchine: as the mourning characters carried the "dead" rich girl off the stage, she came to and gaily waved good-bye to the audience.[6] The change brought the tone of the total work in line with the comic strip style of the production. That Lew actually made the change indicates his willingness, at this point in his career, to defer to Balanchine's judgment.

Lew's only new creation for the South American tour was a collaboration with José Fernandez entitled *Pastorela*. This ballet distilled a traditional, six-hour Mexican Nativity play known as *El Concilio de los Siete Diablos* (The Council of Seven Devils) into a thirty-minute opera-ballet.[7] The use of this material was a gesture intended to show that Latin American traditions could inform the composition of a modern ballet and that the North Americans who produced it were interested in the culture of their neighbors to the south. Bowles, with whom Lew had just worked on *Liberty Jones*, created *Pastorela*'s score by drawing on the memories of a company member, José Martínez, whose father had participated in an authentic *pastorela*.[8] Fernandez added authentic touches such as a cockfight between St. Michael and Lucifer and a hat dance at the end.[9] Lew himself took the role

---

[6] Marcia Siegel attributes this change to Balanchine's readiness to "sacrifice reverence for the dead in the interests of comedy," *Shapes of Change* (Boston: Houghton Mifflin, 1979), 118. Siegel also questions the date of the change. Kirstein's reference to the "new trick ending which Balanchine had suggested to Christensen" would imply that the change was made during rehearsals for the South American tour, thus during the spring of 1941.

[7] Cyril W. Beaumont, *Supplement to Complete Book of Ballets* (London: C. W. Beaumont, 1942), 136.

[8] Bowles' biographer, Christopher Sawyer-Lauçanno, reports that Kirstein was not happy with Bowles' original score for *Pastorela* and thus demanded that Bowles collaborate with Martínez. *An Invisible Spectator: A Biography of Paul Bowles* (New York: Weidenfeld and Nicolson, 1989), 229.

[9] Nancy Reynolds, *Repertory in Review: Forty Years of New York City Ballet* (New York: Dial Press, 1977), 69.

of Lucifer. Dressed in black as a *charro*, the traditional Mexican horseman, he proved his versatility as a performer with this role. No longer the cool Greek god or the approachable boy next door, Lew electrified audiences in a fiery solo that exuded passion and machismo.[10] Certainly, male dancing dominated the spectacle of *Pastorela*; aside from the role of Gila the cook (danced by Gisella), all the major roles in this ballet were for men. According to Fred Danieli, Lew was a role model for boys at the School of American Ballet during this period; perhaps it seemed fitting that he should set a work to show off the company's men.[11] But more likely it was an assignment from Kirstein that fell to Lew because Balanchine was not interested in choreographing a cultural goodwill gesture. Indeed, Graham-Luján suggests that *Pastorela* was one of the "crumbs" that Balanchine allowed Lew while protecting his own position as primary choreographer with the creation of *Ballet Imperial* and *Concerto Barocco*.[12] This marked the first time Kirstein's Ballet Caravan and Balanchine's American Ballet had officially joined forces since the split in 1937. The new troupe paired Kirstein's two driving concerns: the creation of a company for Balanchine to direct and a dance laboratory in which American repertory (in the broadest sense) might be generated. By delegating *Pastorela* to Lew, Balanchine maintained the upper hand in this merger of diverse talents.[13]

---

[10] This was not the only role in which Lew's stage presence exuded a sensual touch. Graham-Luján relates, "A prominent writer in Buenos Aires, María Rosa Oliver, considered that in *Apollo* Lew was perfection, but an impersonal perfection as the god, whereas he had great sex appeal as Pat Garrett in *Billy*." Letter to the author, September 4, 1991.

[11] Peter Conway interview with Fred Danieli, January–April 1979, Oral History Project, Dance Collection, The New York Public Library.

[12] Stephen C. Steinberg and Nancy Johnson Carter interview with James Graham-Luján, November 6, 1985.

[13] Balanchine watched *Pastorela* from the wings and made snide remarks about the piece to Graham-Luján, whose reaction was, "When [Balanchine] took the trouble to make fun of something, you knew it was a thorn in the flesh." Graham-Luján declined to pass the supercilious comments along out of respect for Lew's feelings. Stephen C. Steinberg and Nancy Johnson Carter interview with James Graham-Luján, [n.d., Interview H].

As tour preparations proceeded, Lew and Gisella were cast as the leading couple in *Time Table*, a new ballet by Tudor that depicted the anguish of wartime partings.[14] Although *Time Table*'s setting was World War I, the issue of separation prompted by military service seemed increasingly timely as Americans witnessed the conflicts overseas. Perhaps Lew and Gisella sensed the possibility of extended separation in their future; it was during this period that they decided to marry. Indeed, the prospect of the United States entering World War II spurred many weddings, in the dance community as well as in society at large. William Dollar and Yvonne Patterson announced their intention to marry before the South American tour, and on the tour itself the dancers saw Paul Draper on his way to wed the former American Ballet dancer Heidi Vosseler.[15] Caught up in similar currents, Gisella and Lew were married on May 10, 1941, four days after Lew's thirty-second birthday. Both of their families were on the West Coast, so Kirstein (who had just entered into a marriage of convenience with Fidelma Cadmus, the sister of the painter who had designed *Filling Station*) acted as best man.[16] The Broadway columnist Dorothy Kilgallen reported after the fact, "Lew Christensen, the ballet star, and Giselle, the ditto, were City Hall elopers over the weekend."[17] The South American tour doubled as the couple's honeymoon. Balanchine, who shared hotel rooms with Graham-Luján and regaled him at night with tales of sexual exploits, took it upon himself to offer Gisella marital advice in the early stages of the tour.

---

[14] Tudor did not have time to finish *Time Table* before the group left for South America, so he gave Lew instructions and let him finish the work while the company was en route. Peter Conway interview with Fred Danieli, January–April 1979, Oral History Project, Dance Collection, The New York Public Library.

[15] Untitled clipping from *Dance*, June 1941; "Paul Draper to Wed Dancer on Monday," *New York Times*, June 21, 1941; both found in clipping files on the 1941 South American Tour, Dance Collection, The New York Public Library.

[16] Graham-Luján asserts that Kirstein married because his parents promised him more money if he did. Telephone interview with James Graham-Luján, July 29, 1991.

[17] Dorothy Kilgallen, "The Voice of Broadway," *New York Journal American*, May 12, 1941.

Just before leaving New York, Lew sprained his ankle and was unable to perform in the open dress rehearsals at Hunter College that showed off the company's new repertory.[18] His ankle healed on the way to Brazil, where the company opened in Rio de Janeiro with *Serenade, Filling Station,* and *Ballet Imperial.* Kirstein found that in Rio, American movies had paved the way for *Filling Station;* audiences were able to identify the character types and understand their antics.[19] Reviews were positive. In Buenos Aires, one columnist singled out *Filling Station* as an example of what could happen when a group of young Americans let "a little fresh air into the stately halls where the ballet used to live."[20] *Charade* (called *Adivinanza* on tour) generated less comment. Lew's greatest triumph as a dancer during the five-month tour came in the role of Apollo. As he prepared for his South American debut in the role, Lew was so nervous that he trembled as Gisella sewed on his gilt leggings and arranged his golden curls. But, as Kirstein has recorded, Lew's "turns exploded and his beats fairly cracked. The ovation was something to live for."[21] When local dance pupils presented Balanchine with a wreath of bay leaves during the extended applause, Balanchine passed it on to Lew.

As ballet master, Lew shared with Balanchine the task of teaching daily class, a job he performed with great seriousness. According to Graham-Luján, the youngest Christensen had a passion for proper technique: "Correct dancing was terribly important to Lew, one of the most important things in his life."[22] Near the beginning of the tour a group of dancers rebelled against Lew's expectations of them in class, claiming that he was "too demanding" as a teacher. For a week the group (led by John Kriza) held

---

[18] Kirstein, *Ballet: Bias and Belief,* 82.

[19] *Ibid.,* 80.

[20] Ray, "The Mulberry Bush: Tradition of the Ballet," *Buenos Aires Herald,* July 20, 1941.

[21] Kirstein, *Ballet: Bias and Belief,* 83.

[22] Interview with James Graham-Luján, San Francisco, California, March 4, 1988.

alternate classes in the theater's foyer.[23] But Lew's authority was usually respected, and the dancers generally found him sympathetic to their concerns. When the company traveled by cattle boat up the west coast of Peru, they had trouble sleeping at night because the cattle in the hold underneath the dancers' cabins shifted sides of the boat with each swell of the water. "It felt like a chorus of horses tap dancing all night," recalls Danieli. None of the dancers could sleep, but it was Lew who voiced their complaints.[24]

Lew and Gisella participated in the adventures shared by the company as a whole, adjusting to raked stages and high altitudes, enduring unforseen travel delays resulting from wartime shortages, flying over the Andes in Boeing transport planes when a snowstorm closed the railroad lines, and meeting the dancers, musicians, and artists that welcomed the company along its route. (Lew accompanied Balanchine and Graham-Luján when the latter, supplied with a letter of introduction from the family of García Lorca, met the Spanish composer Manuel de Falla in the Argentine city of Córdoba, where he had taken refuge after the Spanish Civil War.[25]) In Buenos Aires, Lew, Dollar, Kirstein, and Balanchine watched a ballet class held in that city's large Teatro Colón. After performing in Lima, Peru, Lew and Gisella joined Balanchine and the orchestra conductor, Emanuel Balaban,

---

[23] *Ibid.*

[24] Peter Conway interview with Fred Danieli, January–April 1979, Oral History Project, Dance Collection, The New York Public Library.

[25] In his biography of Balanchine (*George Balanchine: Ballet Master* [New York: Random House, 1988]), Richard Buckle describes this meeting as an encounter of "two men of genius" and muses, "How one would like to know what they talked about" (135). Graham-Luján's down-to-earth account clarifies that *he* was the one with the letter of introduction, thanks to his relationship with García Lorca's family. "Lew came along because we were pals, and Mr. Balanchine came along because I couldn't have got rid of him." The punctual visitors were kept waiting "a long time" by de Falla. "Mr. Balanchine was always sniffing, and it wasn't impressive. Lew, of course, was very impressive – quiet and poised and dignified and beautiful." When de Falla finally greeted them, he spoke French with Balanchine. They discussed a possible production, but nothing came of it. Stephen C. Steinberg and Nancy Johnson interview with James Graham-Luján, San Francisco, California, [n.d., interview C].

for a side trip (in an unpressurized plane) to see the Incan ruins of Machu Picchu. When the company was unable to travel as a whole from Peru to Ecuador because of hostilities between the two countries, Lew was one of the leading dancers who was flown to Quito for a special lecture-demonstration. Still an avid photographer, he took pictures of the places they visited and especially of townspeople in villages the company passed through. As time went on, travel complications, budgetary concerns, and the growing threat caused by the European war forced Kirstein to cut short the anticipated six months in South America. The American Ballet Caravan returned to the United States in October instead of December 1941. Having no prospects for future bookings, Kirstein disbanded the company. Lew and Gisella's honeymoon was over.

Following the South American tour, Lew was forced into a holding pattern as he faced the eventuality of being drafted. His draft status during the early months of 1942 fluctuated between 1A (immediate induction) and 3A (fit for induction, but granted a temporary reprieve).[26] Lew's frequently changing status rendered him unable to secure on-going employment and placed a severe economic burden on the couple that winter.

Opportunity knocked in the form of an invitation from Eugene Loring, who was trying to carry on the tradition of Ballet Caravan. With the financial backing of Mrs. Winthrop B. Palmer, Loring formed a new company and named it Eugene Loring's Dance Players, Inc. Company publicity stressed the group's "All American" identity, and the repertory followed the tradition of *Billy the Kid* in that the ballets contained a strong narrative or dramatic element. In addition to reviving *Billy*, *City Portrait*, and *Harlequin for President*, Loring created *The Man from Midian* (based on the life of Moses) and *Prairie*, after Carl Sandburg's poem. Loring invited Lew to join the new group as a guest artist for the

[26] Interviews with Gisella Caccialanza Christensen, San Bruno, California, September 29 and 30, 1987.

company's New York debut at the National Theater in April 1942. Lew was the only choreographer other than Loring to contribute a work to that season. During this troubled time in which he was struggling to find stability while facing the draft, Lew choreographed *Jinx*.

The creation of *Jinx*, a mysterious mood ballet whose story centers on a malevolent clown, sprang from Lew's fascination with the circus world. In it he saw parallels to his own experiences in vaudeville. In both forms of entertainment the performers contributed their own specialty to a varied bill, and in each case they lived in "a world within a world," traveling from place to place but carrying their environment with them.[27] Before choreographing the new ballet, Lew read about the genesis of the modern circus and the traditions surrounding circus clowns. The score of *Jinx*, Benjamin Britten's *Variations on a Theme by Frank Bridge*, came Lew's way after the composer had tried unsuccessfully to interest Balanchine in it. Lew sensed a haunting quality in the music and concocted the story of a circus troupe plagued by misfortune and prone to superstition. He cast himself as the Jinx, an unsmiling clown whose presence unnerves the other members of the troupe because he always seems to be on hand when disaster strikes.

Lew discussed his ideas for the new ballet with Graham-Luján, who was also in New York and had dealings with Dance Players. (Mrs. Palmer hired him to lecture for the dancers on various dance-related topics.) Lew and Graham-Luján had become pals on the South American tour, and Lew trusted the other man's friendship. To Graham-Luján, Lew now revealed an aspect of his personality that found expression in his choreography in these early years: Lew was something of a loner, slow to form emotional attachments and often doubtful of others' friendship for him. Although he had a devoted wife and spent much time surrounded by friends who admired his talent, Lew felt emotionally isolated from other people. Around those he did not know well he acted

---

[27] Craig Palmer interview with Lew Christensen for KQED Documentary.

cool and distant, reserving the warmer side of his personality for longtime associates. Lew confided to Graham-Luján during the preparations for *Jinx*, and repeatedly in later years, "In the end, you're always alone."[28] Just as *Filling Station* ended with the nonplussed filling attendant alone on stage, in *Jinx* the curtain came down on the isolated title character.

Beyond the solitary figure of the title role, Lew populated *Jinx* with stock circus characters: tightrope walkers, equestrians, a Bearded Lady, a Strong Woman, a Tattooed Lady, and the Ringmaster, who functions as a symbol of control. The unhappy Jinx admires a beautiful tightrope walker (Janet Reed), but she rejects his attention in favor of her equestrian boyfriend. Suspected of sinister intent by the other performers, the Jinx is an isolated figure in this closed community; only the Bearded Lady understands his loneliness and feels compassion for him.[29] When an accident befalls the tightrope walker, the Ringmaster whips the scapegoat clown to death. (Graham-Luján wanted the rejected Bearded Lady to kill the clown instead, but Lew stuck to his original intent.[30]) Ultimately, the clown's ghost rises and terrorizes the company anew. Thus Lew's Jinx goes beyond the common "sad clown" stereotype, one who wears a painted smile that hides a breaking heart, to become a truly malevolent figure. In terms of the ballet repertory of that era, *Jinx* also goes a step further than *Petrouchka*, whose waving, resurrected figure mocks the dominating puppeteer but is never as eerily sinister as the Jinx.

The critics recognized *Jinx* as a foray into new emotional territory for Lew. In the *Times*, John Martin marveled that the good-humored "Mac" of *Filling Station*, the creator of

---

[28] Graham-Luján repeats this statement, sometimes alternately worded ("At the end, you're all by yourself"), in the series of interviews with Stephen C. Steinberg and in the interview with the author, July 29, 1991.

[29] William Huck, "Jinx," *Performing Arts: The Theatre and Music Magazine for California and Texas*, San Francisco Ballet Program Book/Magazine 2.1 (January 1988): 16. Huck's brief description and analysis of *Jinx* are insightful and particularly helpful in outlining the sections of the ballet as they relate to Britten's score.

[30] Telephone interview with James Graham-Luján, July 29, 1991.

the frothy *Charade*, should contribute "this curiously powerful and inturned bit of drama." Finding the mood of the ballet at the same time repellent and fascinating, Martin declared it "utterly without precedent in the field of ballet" and observed that Lew's presence dominated the stage.[31] Walter Terry observed that the element of fear which unified the drama (and increased in intensity through the piece) contrasted ironically with the "seemingly joyous lives" of the circus performers; he found that *Jinx* "disclosed a greater maturity both in movement invention and in emotional content" than Lew's previous works.[32] Lew's ability to match movement to music also elicited praise from the critics, who discussed the score's suitability as if it had been composed to the choreographer's specifications.[33] Lew set a dance for the tightrope walker to the opening statement of the theme and then used the variations for the different circus acts. For example, the funereal movement served as the Bearded Lady's lament at the Jinx's death. Britten, then living in New York, approved of Lew's use of his score and authorized a two-piano reduction (the work was originally written for string orchestra) so that Loring's Dance Players could perform the work when they did not have the luxury of orchestral accompaniment.

Shortly after the premiere of *Jinx*, Lew was invited to accompany Balanchine to Argentina, where the choreographer had been invited to stage works at the Teatro Colón in Buenos Aires. Unfortunately, Lew's draft status prevented his leaving the country, so he stayed behind and awaited the inevitable.[34] The prospect of Lew's induction, coming tragically at the height of his powers, troubled the entire family.

---

[31] John Martin, "Dance Players Give 'Jinx,'" *New York Times*, April 25, 1942.

[32] Walter Terry, "Dance Players Present 'Jinx' in N.Y. Debut," *New York Herald Tribune*, April 25, 1942.

[33] Douglas Watt of the *Daily News* stated that the music "perfectly underscor[ed] the action" (April 25, 1942); and Martin wrote of a later production that although the score was not originally intended for dancing, "Christensen has made excellent use of it for his purposes"; "City Ballet Gives Its First Novelty," *New York Times*, November 25, 1949.

[34] Ann Barzel, "A Gallery of American Dancers: Lew Christensen," *Dance*, June 1942, 12–13, 36.

In a desperate attempt to preserve his younger brother's career, Harold approached the draft board in San Francisco and offered himself to be drafted in Lew's stead. After all, Harold pointed out, *he* had attended West Point and would thus be of greater use to the military than his ballet-dancing brother. The offer was sincere and magnanimous, the attempt genuine, but the Army declined. In fact, the attempt backfired because Harold's offer drew Lew's case to the attention of the authorities in New York, where Lew was still unable to get work because of his fluctuating status. Finally, unwilling to stand the uncertainty any longer, he reported to his draft board in November and told them to take him on the spot. He was inducted November 11, 1942.

That same month saw the publication of a new periodical, *Dance News*, which addressed the seriousness of the dance world's situation as companies lost their men. The editors called for open discussion of an issue being discussed behind closed doors: "whether dancers should be exempt from military service, or at least deferred until the non-dancers' reserve is near exhaustion."[35] "Of all organizations, ballet companies are the ones who will be affected the most," predicted *Dance News*, because "the loss of men in a ballet company can be tantamount to a closure," as the collapse of the Littlefield Ballet had demonstrated the previous winter.[36] Ballet companies should take a lesson from Hollywood, the paper urged, and share the few men who were still available. It complained that companies had not altered their announced repertories realistically in view of the reduced number of male dancers. "Whatever happens," warned the paper, "it is a major problem, perhaps a catastrophe." The December issue reinforced this gloomy prediction by listing men drafted from each company, including "Lew Christensen, of the Ballet Caravan and San Francisco Ballet...at Camp Breckenridge, Ky."[37]

---

[35] "Dancers and the Draft," *Dance News*, November 1942, 1.

[36] *Ibid.*

[37] "Army Claims Dancers," *Dance News*, December 1942, 1.

The reality of war nearly sounded the death knell for Willam's glorious plans in San Francisco. The charter for a Civic Ballet signed so optimistically the month before Pearl Harbor was now a hollow document. The prominent citizens who had agreed to be Willam's backers now devoted their energies to the Red Cross and war relief efforts instead. To make matters even worse, Willam could not fall back on the sponsorship of the Opera because that institution faced the possibility of closure. Anticipating a decrease in attendance, the Opera's management now considered a touring ballet company a luxury it could no longer afford (especially as Willam's tours had, in the past, often lost money).[38] In the spring of 1942, the Opera's president, Robert Watt Miller, announced that operatic productions would continue "by means of series of economies in which all branches of the Association have cooperated."[39] The most drastic of those economies was the decision to discontinue the year-round Opera Ballet and its school.

Willam went in desperation to Mrs. Nion Tucker, whose husband was on the Opera's board of directors and was specifically chairman of the ballet. Mrs. Tucker held out little hope for keeping the ballet company going, but she suggested that Willam speak to one of the most interested board members, Mrs. Julliard (Geraldine) McDonald. Employing all his powers of persuasion, Willam convinced Geraldine McDonald to lend her name to his cause; they would form a guild to keep the company together until the end of the war allowed them to move forward as planned.

---

[38] Willam did not give up on the civic company idea immediately; the April 1942 issue of *American Dancer* ran a short feature on the San Francisco Opera Ballet, calling it "America's First Civic Ballet" and previewing the company's spring season at the Opera House. ("America's First Civic Ballet," *American Dancer*, April 1942, 9.) This description was not accurate, as Dorothy Alexander's Concert Group, founded in 1929 in Atlanta, Georgia, was renamed the Atlanta Civic Ballet in 1941. In any event, Willam's hopes for a viable civic company in San Francisco had collapsed by the end of 1942.

[39] Arthur J. Bloomfield, *The San Francisco Opera, 1923–1961* (New York: Appleton-Century-Crofts, 1961), 71.

Realizing that the ballet could not be supported by a coterie of wealthy patrons, Willam aimed instead for a larger group of subscribers who would pay the relatively affordable sum of ten dollars a year. Prospective members were promised lecture-demonstrations, open classes and rehearsals, and social occasions such as teas and receptions at which to meet the dancers.[40] Through the guild, Willam would be able to educate his audience as he established a broader base of support for his newly independent company.

The loss of the school on top of the diminution of the company was more than Willam and Harold could accept. The school was the family's only source of stable income. If the Opera would not maintain the studio at 236 Van Ness Avenue, which was so conveniently situated across from the War Memorial Opera House, the brothers would have to acquire it somehow and run it themselves. Mrs. McDonald set up a luncheon meeting for the brothers to meet with the Opera's representatives and work out a solution. In March 1942, the San Francisco Opera offered to turn its ballet school over to the Christensens for a total of $900.

That amount seemed astronomical to Willam; he assumed they would have to borrow the money from one of the wealthy patrons. Running the school on a disciplined financial basis had never been Willam's forte; since taking over the company and school in 1938 he had concentrated on training dancers and had left administrative matters to his old friend from vaudeville days, Deane Crockett. But Harold, who found Crockett's haphazard policies inefficient, had made a point of educating himself about the school's affairs after making the commitment to stay in San Francisco in 1940. Now Harold came up with a plan that enabled the brothers to buy the school outright. The school had a bank account separate from the Opera, and that account had $600. Technically, the money may have belonged to the Opera, but the school's name was on the account, and the Opera's management did not seem to know or care about it. Ignoring legal

---

[40] "San Francisco Ballet Company," *American Dancer*, April 1945, 11.

fine points, Harold wrote a check closing out that account and added three hundred dollars of their own money to it to clinch the deal. By May the brothers were the owners of their own school.[41]

In view of the official break with the Opera, the company dropped "Opera" from its name to become the San Francisco Ballet, and the school became the San Francisco Ballet School. Harold was firm with his older brother about how things should be run; now that they both had a vested interest in the school, procedures needed to be tightened up. Crockett had been drafted into the Air Force, so the brothers agreed that Willam would retain directorship of the company, such as it was, and Harold would become director of the school.

Harold immediately set about reforming his institution. He consolidated classes, standardized monthly fees, increased the number of times per week the intermediate-to-advanced students came, and lengthened hour-long classes to one-and-a-half hours.[42] He instituted class rolls where before there had been only haphazard signup sheets and hired a capable secretary who made sure schedules were posted and observed. (Despite the new secretary, Isabell "ran the desk" for several more years, collecting checks from students and not allowing into classes those who had not paid.) Harold had less drive for glory than Willam but more administrative sense. He could be a stickler for detail where procedural issues were concerned, and at times his unbending commitment to policy offended those around him. But under his uncompromising leadership the school became the anchor of the brothers' enterprise, their source of steady income and of dancers for the company. Programs listed Harold as the School Director and included a school mission statement with wording that added to the company's prestige:

> *The San Francisco Ballet Company, following the tradition of great European ballet companies of an earlier period, maintains its*

---

[41] Interview with Harold Christensen, San Anselmo, California, September 25, 1987.

[42] *Ibid.*

*own ballet school where talented students may have an opportu-*
*nity to study in a professional atmosphere.*[43]

Willam continued to push for performing opportunities and adjusted his activities to meet wartime conditions.
Heavy curtains for the studio blacked out evening rehearsals
and classes in compliance with dim-out regulations, and air
raid wardens presided over all performances in the War
Memorial Opera House. The San Francisco Ballet continued
to perform in operas, but the shortage of men forced Willam
to dress the taller women in travesty and use them in men's
roles. For a restaging of *Coppélia*, he put the female "men" in
hats, paired them with women for the Czardas and the
Mazurka in lines perpendicular to the apron of the stage, and
put a real man in the front couple of each line. Similar tactics
in court dance sequences for operas such as *Don Giovanni*
and *Rigoletto* pleased Merola, who thought the women in
travesty more elegant looking than men dancing gavottes
and minuets.[44]

As Willam lost his men to the draft, he was constantly
on the lookout for new ones to train. When he heard about
Peter Nelson, a football player who had expressed some
interest in dancing, Willam took personal charge of Nelson's
training. (Years later, Nelson would run a successful New
York studio.) Another athlete-turned-dancer was Joaquin
Felsch, a skier who became a soloist and later married a
company dancer, Celena Cummings. In his desperate need
for male dancers, Willam took in anyone he could mold and
use to his ends: "If you looked like you were breathing well
and had some rhythm, you'd be in."[45]

Willam also avoided putting all his eggs in one basket.
To increase his personal financial security during the war

[43] Program, War Memorial Opera House, San Francisco, California, September 25, 1942.

[44] Interview with Willam Christensen, Salt Lake City, Utah, April 17, 1987.

[45] Interview with Willam Christensen, Salt Lake City, Utah, April 24, 1987.

years he found other outlets for his choreographic skills in case the company folded altogether. He staged Ice Revues in Berkeley, presenting excerpts from *The Nutcracker* and *Coppélia* on a wooden platform in the center of the ice.[46] Strong skaters carried the dancers, undoubtedly in nicely positioned lifts, to the platform stage to perform their variations. In this chilly environment, the dancers had to work extra hard to keep their muscles and feet warm. Willam was also invited to choreograph a new musical, *The Rose Masque*, a reworking of *Die Fledermaus* in musical theater style. In addition to setting the choreography, Willam played a pantomime role in the production, both in San Francisco and in Los Angeles. As *The Rose Masque* settled into an extended run in Los Angeles, Willam found a replacement for his own role just in time to return to San Francisco to prepare the ballets for the fall opera season. With so many irons in the fire, his immediate family and his mother to support, and little time for home life, Willam began to feel overextended. He felt torn in too many directions and dealt with the stress by starting to smoke cigarettes.

As Harold was the backbone of the school, Ruby became the company's leading ballerina during the war years. Having lost Janet Reed and Jacqueline Martin, Willam was more than ever dependent upon his sister-in-law to fill leading female roles. Fortunately, her performing experience in New York and with Ballet Caravan made Ruby a sufficiently glamorous figure to be accepted by San Francisco's balletomanes. Moreover, her strong technique and dramatic flair matched the demands of Willam's technically challenging *demi-caractère* ballets. She could carry off the steely hauteur of the princess in *Coeur de Glace* or portray a resourceful Swanilda in *Coppélia*. Ruby was also the premiere danseuse in *The Rose Masque*, the corps of which featured most of Willam's company. During the 1940s Ruby began teaching in the family school, where she acquired a reputation for giving

---

[46] These productions actually mixed skating and dancing; in *Coppélia* Willam himself appeared on skates as the crotchety Dr. Coppélius. Robert W. Larkin, "Turning Ice Skates into Dance Shoes," *New York Times*, July 24, 1977.

**25** Ruby Asquith in *Bluebird Pas de Deux* costume, early 1940s.
Photograph by Romaine, courtesy of Willam F. Christensen

challenging pointe classes; SFB ballerinas of later eras, including Cynthia Gregory, acknowledge the strong foundation
Ruby provided in this area of women's technique.[47]

Ruby performed in several of Willam's opera ballets,
sometimes joining the other company women in ensemble
numbers (such as marching while beating a drum in *Daughter
of the Regiment*) and sometimes featured in principal roles (as
in *La Traviata*, *Aïda*, and *Carmen*). In *Aïda* she received extra
pay ($15 instead of $10) for wearing a skimpy bra-and-panties
costume and having the rest of her body covered with
glycerin and painted gold.[48] Her soubrette stage personality
enlivened Willam's 1942 creation, *Winter Carnival*, a tale of
romance in the Swiss Alps with music by Johann Strauss.
Inspired perhaps by the experience of choreographing Ice
Revues in Berkeley, Willam incorporated skating movements
into the balletic vocabulary of this work. Frederick Ashton's
skating ballet, *Les Patineurs*, had debuted in London five years
earlier, but it had not yet been seen in the United States.[49]
The *Chronicle*'s critic, Alfred Frankenstein, compared *Winter
Carnival* not to *Patineurs* but to Massine's depictions of the
high life, including *The New Yorker* and *Saratoga*.[50] He also
singled out Ruby for praise:

---

[47] Another ballerina who pays tribute to Ruby's pointe technique and her ability to
teach pointe work is Jocelyn Vollmar. Interview with Jocelyn Vollmar, San Francisco,
California, March 1 and 3, 1988; interview with Cynthia Gregory, New York, New
York, January 10, 1989.

[48] On one occasion when the chorus master, Kurt Herbert Adler, pushed his way
roughly through the dancers backstage, exhibiting his usual lack of respect, his
expensive dinner jacket brushed against Ruby's paint and came away gold and
greasy – a fact she still remembers with mischievous delight. Interview with Ruby
and Harold Christensen, San Anselmo, California, March 2, 1988.

[49] The Vic-Wells Ballet, predecessor of the Royal Ballet, premiered Ashton's *Patineurs*
in February 1937, but Willam had no opportunity to see that company and did not
know Ashton's ballet first hand. He may have read about *Patineurs* before doing his
own skating ballet as he recalls following the Vic-Wells company and claims that he
read Richardson's *Dancing Times* regularly after his move to San Francisco (Don
McDonagh interview with William Christensen, Salt Lake City, Utah, February 27,
1986). Ballet Theatre performed the American premiere of *Patineurs* in New York in
October 1946.

[50] Cobbett Steinberg, *San Francisco Ballet: The First Fifty Years* (San Francisco: San
Francisco Ballet Association, 1983), 39.

**26**  Willam Christensen and Ruby Asquith in *Winter Carnival* costumes, 1942.
Courtesy of Special Collections, University of Utah Marriott Library

> *Perhaps the finest feature of the work was the utterly delightful dancing of Ruby Asquith as the skating star. Miss Asquith is a magnificent character dancer, and her interpretation was as scintillant, crystalline, deft and finely modeled as the most fanatical balletomane could demand.*[51]

*Winter Carnival* required Willam to experiment with his dancers in the studio and epitomized the way in which he drew on his dancers for inspiration. "Try this turn and see

---

[51] *Ibid.*

if you can make it look as if you are on skates," he would
ask.[52] Willam tried for the most brilliant, exciting combinations his dancers could achieve, but if they could not perform
exactly what he wanted he would modify his demands.
Rather than coming to a rehearsal with his ideas fixed, he
tried different combinations in the studio to see what he could
draw out of each dancer. When choreographing, Willam
usually wanted all his dancers around him, not only those on
whom he might be setting a small section at the moment,
because he would have those watching from the sidelines try
a passage to see what they might do with it. Unlike choreographers who worked only behind closed doors, Willam the
extrovert came to life when others watched him teach or
choreograph, as if the very act of working with his dancers
were in itself a performance. He demonstrated the pantomime
bits with detail and humor, creating vivid images that his
students worked hard to emulate. Ruby recalls his outstanding gift of mimicry: "Whatever the character in the ballet, he
could do it better than anybody else in the company. His
whole body would take on the look."[53] Ruby sees this aspect
of Willam's talents as having strongly influenced Onna White,
a member of the company during this period who went on
to choreograph for musical theater and films, winning recognition for her work in *The Music Man*, *Mame*, and *Oliver*.[54]

Without Franklyn Smith to arrange bookings, and
with the complications that wartime conditions brought to
travel, Willam was forced to reduce, temporarily, the scope
of his touring ambitions. In 1943, the company performed
only in the Bay Area. To avoid the complications of nighttime
blackouts, he organized a series of late afternoon appearances
for his leading dancers. These "Ballets Intimes" were small-
scale performances, the balletic equivalent of chamber music,
held in the Garden Court of the Palace Hotel. But as the

[52] Interview with Ruby and Harold Christensen, San Anselmo, California, March 2, 1988.

[53] *Ibid.*

[54] *Ibid.*

December holiday season approached, Willam felt the desire to do something on a grander scale. He and Harold discussed the holiday tradition of *Hansel and Gretel* at the Metropolitan Opera in New York and decided to implement a Holiday Dance Festival in San Francisco with a danced version of the opera. A stagehand warned that the opera *Hansel and Gretel* had never been popular in San Francisco and was sure to lose money, but Willam went ahead with the plan and borrowed the Opera's sets and costumes.[55] He devised a ballet-pantomime with vocal accompaniment; the singers remained out of sight while dancers portrayed the story on stage. The production starred Ruby as Gretel, the former American Ballet Caravan dancer Beatrice Tompkins (who had followed her soldier-husband to the Bay Area) as Hansel, Earl Riggins as the children's Father, and Mattlyn Gevurtz as the old Witch. (Willam saved himself for the leading male roles in *Chopinade* and *Winter Carnival*, which were also on the holiday program.) Unfortunately, time proved the stagehand right. *Hansel and Gretel* was not well received, perhaps because the extended pantomime of Willam's version, which followed the opera quite literally, gave it a static quality. The production lost money and did nothing to advance his reputation.

By the 1943 holiday season, Willam was forty-one years old and past his prime as a performer. Surgery for torn cartilage in his left knee impaired his strength and flexibility in that joint and hampered his ability to perform. Moreover, much of his time was taken up with teaching, choreographing, arranging performing opportunities, and supporting guild functions—administrative matters that left little time for maintaining his own technique. Willam preferred to limit himself to character parts and might have stopped performing altogether but for the extreme shortage of men. Instead, he continued to fill romantic leads as well as the character roles that came so naturally to him. For performances he wore a toupee to cover his receding hairline, and in the weeks prior

---

[55] Interview with Willam Christensen, Salt Lake City, Utah, May 1, 1987.

to an appearance, he practiced lifts with the heaviest girls in the pas de deux class.[56]

In no other era, from his vaudeville days to the end of his active career, did Willam's determination to get a show on the boards meet such formidable obstacles. But he had no choice other than to carry on. Not to perform, not to continue staging productions, on whatever scale possible, was to admit the defeat of his company in the face of wartime conditions. So despite those conditions, Willam put together an ambitious spring season of five performances at the War Memorial Opera House in May of 1944. The season's centerpiece was a patriotic ballet prompted by America's involvement overseas, *The Triumph of Hope*. The ballet's librettist and designer was Jean de Botton, a French muralist who had been the official court painter at the coronation of George VI in England. A local department store magnate, Paul Verdier, backed the production. Verdier's store, City of Paris, provided fabrics for the costumes, and his support allowed Willam to pay the dancers a minimal rehearsal fee: "$5.00 a night, not to exceed five nights."[57] The dancers, who were used to little or no remuneration for their efforts, considered this sum a windfall.

De Botton's libretto called for four scenes, set to the first and third movements of César Franck's *Symphony in D minor* as well as the composer's "Les Eolides" and "Le Chausseur Maudit." Willam's challenge was to set de Botton's paean to American liberty in a series of scenes depicting Man, Woman, the Child Hope, Satan, and personifications of the forces of good and evil. He cast Ruby as Woman, Riggins as Man, and reserved the role of Satan for himself, thinking perhaps that the devil would need a very convincing portrayal to provide the necessary dramatic conflict.

De Botton couched his homage to America in abstract language and high-flown rhetoric: "the titanic struggle

---

[56] Telephone interview with Janet Reed Erskine, November 5, 1988.

[57] Interview with Jocelyn Vollmar, San Francisco, California, March 1, 1988; and Russell Hartley, "The San Francisco Ballet: A History, 1922–1977," 46, unpublished manuscript, San Francisco Performing Arts Library and Museum.

between the creative and destructive forces," "supreme conflict for the annihilation of the forces of both Divine and human creations," "constructive forces headed by the spiritual love of the Child Hope," and so forth. The ambitious production included four large backdrops designed by de Botton, a complete orchestra, costumes for fifty dancers, and special lighting effects. War shortages cramped the production's style in some areas: the libretto called for the Child Hope to descend from the sky to the stage along a rainbow, and Satan was meant to be blown into the sky, but the steel wire necessary for both tricks was not available. In both cases dummies had to be used rather than the real dancers, to predictably weakened effect. But the greatest weakness of *The Triumph of Hope* was that its abstractions were not easily made coherent in dance, or perhaps that Willam's gifts as a choreographer of narrative ballets could not fulfill the demands of de Botton's philosophical libretto. The critics made unflattering comparisons to Massine's symphonic ballets *Les Présages* and *Le Rouge et Le Noir*, observing that in *The Triumph of Hope* the depiction of grandiose themes too often sank into obvious trivialization or curious abstractions. In fact, Willam's charisma as a performer in the role of Satan undermined de Botton's intended message; one critic observed, "It was Satan who really triumphed in the matter of providing excitement and holding interest, for the handsome and agile demon... directed one of the most wondrous orgies ever staged at the Opera."[58]

While Willam, Harold, and Ruby struggled and sacrificed to hold together the family enterprise in San Francisco, Gisella faced trials of her own in New York. The wrenching sorrow caused by Lew's departure after only six months of marriage was intensified by her feelings of loss as a Balanchine ballerina. The American Ballet had not been reformed following the 1941 South American tour, and Balanchine had no company of his own to which Gisella could

---

[58] Marjory M. Fisher, "San Francisco Sees New Ballet," *Musical America* clipping hand-dated 3/5/44, 34.

belong. Gisella probably felt the loss of a Balanchine company even more than Lew had; she had been with the choreographer before meeting Lew, had chosen to dance with Balanchine during part of the time Lew was in Ballet Caravan, and had never joined Loring's Dance Players. Lew and Gisella's marriage was based on deep personal commitment but did not presuppose identical career choices; she went her own way as a professional during most of her performing years.

During the fall that Lew was inducted, Gisella became marginally involved in the war effort. She danced a pas de deux by Balanchine at U.S.O. headquarters in New York and was featured as a celebrity at a rally to encourage the collection of scrap metal.[59] But Gisella's chief concern at this time was to find employment to supplement Lew's army compensation. Aid came from Kirstein, who arranged for her hiring by the New Opera Company. Balanchine, assisted by William Dollar, was supplying the choreography for the group's fall season, and his *Ballet Imperial* was performed as a curtain raiser. Gisella was also featured in *The Fair at Sorochinsk*, *La Vie Parisienne*, and *The Queen of Spades*.[60]

Following the opera season Gisella teamed up with Charles Laskey, a former associate from Ballet Caravan days. Laskey choreographed an act for the two of them appropriate for nightclubs or similar commercial theater bookings. Then their agent came through with an offer from an unexpected source: Gisella was offered the role of "Laurey" in the dream sequence of *Oklahoma!*[61] The offer was not for the show's premiere but for the Theatre Guild's road company, which

---

[59] The unknown pas de deux, to music by Prokofiev, is listed in *Choreography by George Balanchine: A Catalogue of Works* (New York: Eakins Press Foundation, 1983), 158; photograph caption of "Win the War Rally," no paper, n.d., Gisella Caccialanza scrapbook, San Francisco Performing Arts Library and Museum.

[60] Cobbett Steinberg, "Gisella Caccialanza: A Chronology," *Encore* 3 (Winter 1986/ 87): 17.

[61] "Gisella [Caccialanza] and Charles Laskey have been given the leading dancing roles in the Theatre Guild's road company of 'Oklahoma!' Tour opens in New Haven October 14," *Daily News*, September 30, 1943.

was to begin its tour in New Haven that October (1943). Gisella felt bound to honor her partnership with Laskey and refused to take the role unless he were also hired, so both were taken into the road cast.

Agnes de Mille, who was tied up in rehearsals for her next show, *One Touch of Venus*, had little to do with the touring company's production of *Oklahoma!* She did not even see the balletic dream sequence until the dress rehearsal, by which time Gisella had bleached her hair blond for the part. When De Mille saw Gisella and Laskey at the dress rehearsal, she was shocked by the look of her choreography; although both dancers were fine technicians, neither had the dramatic style De Mille felt was necessary for the roles. Deciding that it was too late to retrain Gisella, De Mille insisted on a replacement and ended up using her agent's fiancée, Dania Krupska.[62] Laskey was harder to replace because most able-bodied men were off fighting. Less committed to the original partnership than Gisella, Laskey stayed with the show.[63] Left high and dry, Gisella had no reason to remain in New York, so Willam offered her a place in his struggling company.

With her hair dyed dark again, Gisella arrived in San Francisco that fall and took a small apartment on Hayes Street not far from Harold and Ruby. She began teaching in the family school, and when Willam was called to the telephone during company class, he would ask Gisella to finish teaching for him.[64] In the 1943 Holiday Festival season, she starred in *Chopinade*, which played as a curtain-raiser to *Hansel and Gretel*. During Lew's absence, Gisella became an integral part of the Christensen effort in San Francisco.

---

[62] Letter from Agnes de Mille Prude to Debra H. Sowell, December 3, 1989. De Mille explains, "I've always felt badly about the treatment Gisella had received. It stemmed from the way that the Guild had simply bypassed me and I was too busy, too distraught with the new show to watch out for my own interests. Gisella was hurt as a result."

[63] Interview with Gisella Caccialanza Christensen, San Bruno, California, September 30, 1987.

[64] *Ibid.*

Throughout the war the San Francisco Arts Commission had funds with which to sponsor dance performances, but Willam's company was repeatedly passed over in favor of out-of-town touring companies, first the Ballet Russe de Monte Carlo and then Ballet Theatre.[65] The commissioner in charge was known to be skeptical of the local troupe, and the failure of *Triumph of Hope* in the spring of 1944 reconfirmed his financial policy. Willam was struggling to gain the respect of his own audience and civic leaders, and he knew that in the wake of *Hansel and Gretel* and the de Botton ballet he needed a big success to restore his reputation in the community. For the 1944 Holiday Dance Festival Willam shied away from heavy philosophical statements and returned to the late nineteenth-century repertory, which he had come to accept as a rich vein to be mined. He decided to stage a full-length version of *The Nutcracker*.

In practical terms, *The Nutcracker* had many commendable features. Not only was the story related to the Christmas holiday, but the complete score was available. Walt Disney's animated motion picture *Fantasia*, released four years earlier, had included cartoon figures dancing to Tchaikovsky's Nutcracker Suite and had made it one of the best known pieces of classical music in America.[66] Willam heard a recording of the Nutcracker Suite in a large San Francisco department store and noticed that people came out humming Tchaikovsky's melodies; the observation convinced him that the score had the potential for a popular success.[67] Moreover, mounting a *Nutcracker* was not tantamount to starting from scratch; he had choreographed excerpts of the ballet in Portland for the Rose Festival and had previously staged a greatly abridged version for San Francisco Children's Theatre.[68]

---

[65] "Taxpayers Help to Book Ballet in San Francisco," *Dance News*, February 1945, 3.

[66] Jack Anderson, *The Nutcracker Ballet* (New York: Mayflower Books, 1979), 197. The existence of *Fantasia* also raises the possibility that the demonic orgy Willam created for *The Triumph of Hope* owed some debt to the movie's *Night on Bald Mountain* sequence.

[67] Interview with Willam Christensen, Salt Lake City, Utah, May 1, 1987.

[68] Interview with Willam Christensen, Salt Lake City, Utah, April 24, 1987.

Willam and Harold called upon the leaders of the Children's Theatre, who were well-connected socially in the community, and asked for their support in mounting a complete *Nutcracker*. Willam promised to accept full responsibility for the production, and Harold guaranteed them a percentage of the box office if they would use their connections to publicize the event. Once that backing was assured, Willam got permission to perform in the opera house, which was usually dark between Christmas and New Year's. One satisfying aspect of the company's break from the Opera was that Willam was now free to negotiate with the opera house himself rather than getting Merola's permission first.

Willam had doubtless seen the abbreviated *Nutcracker* toured by the Ballet Russe de Monte Carlo. That version consisted of a single act that included a short party scene, the snow scene, and the second act divertissements in the Kingdom of Sweets leading up to the Sugar Plum Fairy pas de deux.[69] The battle between toy soldiers and mice, the growing Christmas tree, and many other aspects of the ballet's original staging were missing from the Ballet Russe production and were as yet unknown to Willam. As he had done for *Swan Lake*, Willam drew on the knowledge of San Francisco's expatriate Russian community, picking up details of staging from their memories of productions at the Maryinsky before the Revolution. (The first time he heard the music that accompanies the magical growth of the Christmas tree, Willam remarked that it seemed a shame that such marvelous music was reserved for a tree.[70]) When Balanchine and Danilova came through San Francisco with the Ballet Russe that fall, Willam invited them to his apartment one night and asked them questions he still had about the ballet's original staging. Balanchine, who would not choreograph his own *Nutcracker* until 1954, talked through the ballet with enthusiasm, growing more and more excited over the prospect of a full-length

---

[69] Jack Anderson, 108.

[70] Russell Hartley, "The San Francisco Ballet: A History, 1922–1977," 47, unpublished manuscript, San Francisco Performing Arts Library and Museum.

production as the night wore on. One aspect of the ballet to which they introduced Willam for the first time was Mother Ginger (also known as Mother Buffoon), the gargantuan lady whose skirts hide children that run out and dance as part of the second act divertissements. Danilova, who was hoarse from a cold, jumped into the conversation frequently to demonstrate steps she remembered. But Balanchine understood that Willam wanted to know details of staging, placement of characters on stage and actions that advanced the plot, rather than steps; he cautioned the ballerina, "Let him do his own steps."[71]

Willam cast Gisella in the leading role of the Sugar Plum Fairy and himself as her Cavalier.[72] Earl Riggins appeared as the King of the Mice, and an up-and-coming young dancer from the school, Jocelyn Vollmar, was paired with Joaquin Felsch for the roles of the Snow Queen and Snow Prince. Ruby was on maternity leave, so other company stalwarts fleshed out the cast: Lois Treadwell (Clara and the Merliton variation); Russell Hartley (Mother Buffoon); Celena Cummings (Ballerina, Waltz of the Flowers); Mattlyn Gevurtz (Chocolate); and Onna White (Arabian). Antonio Sotomayor, a South American painter living in San Francisco, contributed the scene designs, which were painted as cheaply as possible by stagehands. Hartley, who had studied painting, performed double duty on this production, designing the production's 143 costumes (and constructing many of them) while taking two classes a day and attending rehearsals.

Constructing the costumes on a budget of $1000 was one of the major challenges of this holiday festival. One fabric the company had in abundance was red velvet; when the Cort Theatre had been destroyed two years earlier, Hartley had

---

[71] Anderson, 112.

[72] When Willam's knee gave him trouble during *Nutcracker* performances, he cut the male variation of the grand pas de deux, thrusting the burden of the performance upon Gisella. This made such an impression on her that later, when Lew choreographed his own version of the ballet, she persuaded him to give the ballerina a chance to rest during the grand pas de deux. Interview with Gisella Caccialanza Christensen, San Bruno, California, September 30, 1987.

purchased its curtains at Goodwill Industries for ten dollars. As a result, many of the party guests in Act I wore red velvet jackets. For the rest of the costumes, Hartley got around the restrictions of wartime rationing by sending the dancers around the city to purchase fabric by the ten-yard limit.[73] Full of enthusiasm for this project, the dancers and many "ballet mothers" helped make the costumes and props. Peter Nelson created the wands carried by the Snowflakes, and most of the ballerinas (Cummings, Vollmar, and Gisella) sewed their own tutus.[74] Depending upon volunteer labor predictably led to a number of snafus: one afternoon Onna White attempted to stitch up part of her costume while still wearing it and had to be cut loose from the sewing machine. As the date of the opening neared, Hartley sewed late into the night and often slept in the costume shop, nestled in spare yards of red velvet, in order to get an early start the next morning.[75]

In contrast to the failure of the 1943 Holiday Festival (featuring *Hansel and Gretel*), the 1944 Festival sold out in advance and generated sparkling reviews. The *Chronicle* recognized the significance of San Francisco seeing the first full-length *Nutcracker* produced in the United States and acknowledged the beauty of the large ensemble dances as well as the divertissements from the familiar suite. The *Examiner* reflected upon Willam's ability to produce such a work in wartime:

> It is remarkable how Director Willam Christensen and his young troupe keep up their excellent standards. When he trains individual dancers to a high pitch, he risks losing them to the national troupes. And the Army takes first call of his young men. Nevertheless, the Nutcracker production is full of color, freshness, and dancing entertainment.[76]

---

[73] Steinberg, *San Francisco Ballet*, 51.

[74] Interview with Gisella Caccialanza Christensen, San Bruno, California, September 30, 1987.

[75] Many of these details about the costumes are taken from Russell Hartley's unpublished history of the company, 48–49.

[76] Steinberg, *San Francisco Ballet*, 51.

**27** Willam Christensen and Gisella Caccialanza in Willam's 1944 *Nutcracker*.
Courtesy of San Francisco Performing Arts Library and Museum

The success of *The Nutcracker* gave new momentum to Willam's plans for the company. Following the holidays, the company set off on a two-month tour of the West and Midwest with Gisella as leading ballerina while Ruby continued her leave of absence. In the various towns and cities where they appeared, the dancers lived on a shoestring and were lodged in private homes or small hotels. Traveling by train rather than by bus was a new luxury for the dancers, but riding the rails presented its own difficulties. Because it was wartime, servicemen crowded the passenger compartments and war materiel had top priority in freight cars. On one connection between engagements, the company members made it to the next city but their scenery and costumes were left behind because the army had commandeered their baggage car. On another journey, the conductor advised Willam to have his dancers disembark and run up to the dining car while the train was in station rather than having the company parade through cars full of girl-hungry soldiers. Facing men in uniform was a strain on the men as well as the women in the company; male dancers felt disapproval for pursuing an activity as seemingly frivolous as dancing while their peers were in combat.

Ruby's maternity leave ended in personal tragedy: a son stillborn because she had received too much anesthetic.[77] After her recovery, Ruby returned to the company and resumed many of her leading roles. But this presented Willam with a diplomatic dilemma. He now had two sisters-in-law as leading female dancers, and only one could legitimately be billed as the company's prima ballerina. He could not slight Ruby, whose talents and dedication had pulled SFB through the difficult early war years, but Gisella required some sort of special billing as she was more recently from New York, which gave her greater celebrity status in the eyes of the public. Willam resolved the situation tactfully by giving each a blown-up photograph in the company's souvenir program; he listed Ruby as "Prima Ballerina of the San Francisco Ballet," and Gisella as "Guest Prima Ballerina."

---

[77] Interview with Ruby Asquith Christensen, San Anselmo, California, March 2, 1988.

Harold was pleased to have another faculty member who had worked with Balanchine, not to mention Cecchetti. Harold's artistic views had been influenced by Balanchine during the time he was in the American Ballet, and he frequently held up Balanchine's ways of doing things to Willam as a model, a model in which Willam was not interested. Willam most decidedly did not like being compared to, or contrasted with, Balanchine by his younger brother. With Gisella's arrival, the San Francisco Ballet School had one more Balanchine-trained dancer on its staff, and Harold appreciated the subtle psychological leverage it gave him in guiding school policy. Although in later years the School's Balanchine connection would be attributed to Lew's influence, Harold also had a hand in establishing that direction early on.

Both Willam and Harold sacrificed to keep the company going and in so doing founded the independent San Francisco Ballet, free of domination by the Opera. Although most histories trace the company's founding to its first performances with the San Francisco Opera under Adolph Bolm in 1933, the San Francisco Ballet, per se, did not exist until Willam took responsibility for directing an independent entity. The family's combined efforts – Willam's choreography and continued presence on stage after the peak of his performing years, Harold's support in running the school and supplying student dancers for the company, and Ruby and Gisella's teaching and performing – enabled the company to maintain a presence in the community. With support from the guild and from the dancers, who performed for little or no pay, supered in operas, and took odd jobs on the side to support themselves, the Christensens were able to do as a family what Balanchine, without Kirstein, was not: keep their own company going despite the extraordinary pressures brought about by World War II. Near the end of the war, *American Dancer* held up Willam's group as a model civic company, praised its broadly based guild, and described Willam's *modus operandi* so that others might follow his example.[78]

---

[78] "San Francisco Ballet Company," *American Dancer*, April 1945, 10–11, 36.

Meanwhile, in the army, Lew received training in radio communications, was assigned to the signal corps, and received a promotion to the rank of staff sergeant in February 1943. When calling cadence, he would choreograph elaborate marching drills, putting the soldiers through convoluted patterns before bringing the squads together smoothly at the finish.[79] But he seldom spoke about his civilian career as a ballet dancer, doubtless fearing teasing from the other soldiers in an environment that stressed macho strength and courage. A feature story in the Army newspaper *Blood and Fire* revealing Lew's background treated it as a case for *Ripley's Believe it or Not* and reported:

> *Sgt. Christensen is so reticent about his personal affairs and achievements that it was almost six months after he'd been in the company before anyone knew that he was a ballet dancer, let alone that he'd been First Dancer at the Metropolitan Opera House in New York.*[80]

When word got around that Lew was indeed a dancer, he was dubbed "the long-haired one" in recognition of his appreciation for classical music.[81]

Lew was sent to the European theater as communications chief of the 254th infantry division. He wrote home to Gisella of trudging across France, avoiding Nazi troops, and spending a Christmas Eve with the cattle in a French manger. He sent her handmade cards upon which he drew a burro christened "Rosario," a reminder of the couple's honeymoon on the South American tour. Lew often sketched as a form of relaxation, and during the war his cards provided a creative outlet as he composed verses for occasions such as family birthdays. His letters to Gisella downplayed the grim reality of his war experience. Lew landed the unenviable assignment of collecting dead and dismembered bodies after battles, and

---

[79] Telephone interview with James Graham-Luján, July 29, 1991.

[80] The entire article from the Army newspaper is reproduced in Dorothy Barrett, "The Three Brothers Christensen," *Dance*, October 1943, 7, 29.

[81] Stephen Steinberg interview with Gisella Christensen for KQED documentary.

**28**　Lew Christensen in military uniform, Esslingen, Germany, 1945.
Courtesy of San Francisco Performing Arts Library and Museum

he learned to recognize the smell of death. The finely tuned
human body had once been the medium of Lew's creativity
as a choreographer; now he faced the wasted corpses of his
fellow soldiers. His hair went prematurely gray.

In January 1945 Lew was discharged as a noncommis-
sioned technical sergeant and was awarded a commission as
part of the first Military Government Battalion.[82] The Battle
of the Bulge had turned the tide of war in favor of the Allies,
and Lew joined the push to cross the Rhine River and occupy
Germany. Now ranked as a lieutenant, Lew served as one of
the occupying forces. His innate sense of fairness qualified
him for a position administering a small German city. He
saw the horrors of the extermination camps, found cast-off

---

[82] Certificate of Service, Army of the United States, included with Lew Christensen's
discharge papers in the possession of Gisella Caccialanza Christensen, San Bruno,
California. My understanding of the technical information contained in Lew's
military certificates has been aided greatly by military historian Philip M. Flammer,
Lieutenant Colonel USAF (R) and Professor of History, Brigham Young University.

German uniforms in the streets, and had to decide when to administer justice to offenders within his jurisdiction. Accepting the commission prevented Lew from being transferred to the Pacific but meant committing to a longer stay in Europe than he might have faced otherwise. After the war ended in August 1945, he spent nearly another full year overseas. Every month, every week Lew spent without dancing made it more unlikely that he would ever regain his prewar technique. In his heart, Lew may have put his career in ballet behind him forever. Near the end of the war he chanced to meet Kirstein on the German border. The two had once made great plans for the future of ballet in America; now their talk was desultory, and Lew expressed doubts that he would ever dance again.[83]

---

[83] Kirstein, *Thirty Years*, 88.

# 9

## BALLET SOCIETY AND WILLAM'S DREAM COMPANY (1946–1948)

Lew returned from Germany in early July 1946. After the initial excitement of the reunion with Gisella and his family had subsided, he faced the question of his future career. Four years had passed since Lew had danced professionally. While he had escaped serious injury during combat, trudging across France had destroyed his once finely tuned leg muscles. At age thirty-seven Lew was too old to regain his former strength as a dancer. He might essay a comeback, but never again could he be the artist he had once been. One of Lew's army buddies had offered him a job in the friend's family business; it was something to fall back on if a career in ballet proved impossible.[1] But just as L.P. had been drawn back into the circle of family musical activities after the mill accident crushed his hand, Lew was drawn back to ballet by the strong influence of his older brothers. Willam had great plans for the future of ballet in San Francisco and an undying belief in Lew's talent. Before the war, Lew's presence had lent stature to Willam's production of *Swan Lake*. Now Willam hoped his brother would someday figure prominently in the future of his company. Gisella, who was still performing, also encouraged Lew to return to the realm of ballet.[2] When Lew filled out his official discharge papers at Camp Beale that August, in the blank for occupation he entered "choreographer."

Willam could not offer his youngest brother work in San Francisco right away; the Bay Area company was still

---

[1] Interview with Ruby and Harold Christensen, San Anselmo, California, March 2, 1988.

[2] Interview with Gisella Caccialanza Christensen, San Bruno, California, September 29, 1987.

feeling the effects of the war. That fall, performances were limited to the opera season; there would not even be a holiday festival in December. Immediate opportunity for Lew lay not in San Francisco but in New York, where Kirstein and Balanchine were putting together another company.

Ballet Society, as the new Kirstein–Balanchine venture was called, constituted a change in orientation from Kirstein's goals for Ballet Caravan. Rather than touring the country with a repertory drawing on American history and folklore, Ballet Society would perform periodically in New York City and would present a variety of new works by Balanchine and developing choreographers. Performances would be open only to subscribers, who for fifteen dollars a year would qualify for lecture demonstrations and exhibitions, a journal (*Dance Index*), and performances that mixed dance works with straight orchestral compositions and lyric theatre presentations. Kirstein's plan echoed Willam's approach to the San Francisco Ballet Guild during World War II in that it was based upon a large pool of small contributors rather than a few wealthy patrons, but Kirstein's ambitions were broader and further reaching. For example, Ballet Society commissioned Gian Carlo Menotti's *The Telephone* and gave its premiere on a nonballet program that included the composer's *The Medium*.

In putting together his new company, Kirstein added new dancers from the School of American Ballet to a nucleus of performers from his former companies: William Dollar, Fred Danieli, Todd Bolender, Marie-Jeanne, Beatrice Tompkins, Elise Reiman, Gisella, and Lew. Company leadership included Balanchine as artistic director, Leon Barzin as musical director, and Kirstein as secretary. The position of ballet master fell to Lew, as it had in Ballet Caravan. Lew had an exceptional memory for choreography; nearly twenty years after first dancing *Apollo* he still knew the ballet well enough to train an entire cast of dancers new to the work.[3] And while Kirstein may have given up the ideals that fueled the Caravan,

---

[3] Telephone interview with James Graham-Luján, July 29, 1991.

he still clung to his faith in Lew personally as a key examplar of the new American male classicist. Graham-Luján asserts that during the years following the American Ballet's residency at the Met, Kirstein kept Lew's lyre from *Orpheus* as a kind of good luck talisman, always taking it with him when he moved to a new apartment.[4] Before the war, Lew had demonstrated his loyalty to Kirstein's goals with the creation of works such as *Pocahontas* and *Pastorela*. Kirstein returned that loyalty.

Being ballet master once again put Lew on familiar terrain as he assumed the dual challenge of rebuilding his own technique and assisting Balanchine with company class and rehearsals. Pierre Vladimirov tried to discourage Lew from attempting a comeback on the grounds that he would be only an "ordinary" dancer in second-rate roles.[5] But Lew did regain enough strength to perform as a soloist in Ballet Society's early seasons. In the company's debut program, November 1946, Lew and Gisella both danced in the premiere of Balanchine's *Four Temperaments* at the Central High School of Needle Trades. Lew partnered Elise Reiman in the Second Theme, a role that required skillful presentation and manipulation of the ballerina in a variety of evolving positions. Whatever the state of Lew's own technique at this point, deft partnering characterized by an understated grace remained one of his strengths as a *danseur*. In January 1947, Lew filled the role of the Rooster in Balanchine's *Renard*, figured among the eight soloists in *Divertimento*, and restaged his opera-ballet *Pastorela* in keeping with Ballet Society's stated purpose of encouraging lyric theatre. He chose a twelve-year-old boy from the school, Jacques D'Amboise, to dance the role of St. Michael opposite himself as the devil. "I remember how patient he was with me," recalls D'Amboise, who was intrigued with the Mexican footwork.[6]

---

[4] Stephen C. Steinberg and Nancy Johnson interview with James Graham-Luján, San Francisco, California, [n.d., interview C].

[5] KQED interview with Harold Christensen.

[6] Interview with Jacques D'Amboise, New York, New York, January 12, 1989.

Gisella was still in her prime as a performer and enjoyed a succession of substantial roles in Ballet Society. In *The Four Temperaments*, she and Francisco Moncion presented the Third Theme.[7] Like Lew, she was one of the eight soloists in Balanchine's *Divertimento*, and in Todd Bolender's *Zodiac* she created the central role of the Earth. She was also cast as the Bride in Dollar's *Highland Fling*, a reworking of the *La Sylphide* plot in which the Groom remained faithful to his Bride rather than running off with the tempting Sylph. Walter Terry praised Gisella's wedding dance and described her style: "performed with joyous feet, released body energy, and an air of delight."[8]

For the May 1947 season, Gisella joined Beatrice Tompkins and Tanaquil LeClerq as soloists in Merce Cunningham's *The Seasons*. Gisella was initially puzzled that Cunningham, a recently departed soloist from Martha Graham's company, should be asked to choreograph a work for Ballet Society. "I can't do your kind of dancing," she warned him at the outset of rehearsals, but the choreographer reassured her she would be fine.[9] Gisella found the work a challenge rhythmically because of the changing patterns of counts. She called *The Seasons* the "knitting ballet" because "if you dropped a stitch you were gone – if you dropped a count you were gone. You did nothing but count."[10] (Counting stitches was, of course, a familiar image in a day when many dancers knitted their own tights.) Gisella, Tompkins, LeClerq, and Cunningham himself led the ensemble in the abstracted suggestion of the passing seasons from winter to

---

[7] Fred Danieli asserts that the "straight up and down" posture of the Third Theme ballerina in *The Four Temperaments* is a reflection of Gisella's Cecchetti background. "Celebrating *The Four Temperaments*," *Ballet Review* 15.1 (Spring 1987): 41. Another possible Christensen contribution to the movement material of this ballet is the spinning cello image, as Balanchine was well aware of Lew's training on that instrument.

[8] Quoted in Nancy Reynolds, *Repertory in Review* (New York: Dial Press, 1977), 80.

[9] Interview with Gisella Caccialanza Christensen, San Bruno, California, September 29, 1987.

[10] *Ibid.*

fall. Cunningham later credited Gisella's lightness and bird-like jump with being one of the factors that made *The Seasons* a success.[11]

Lew's one choreographic essay for Ballet Society, *Blackface*, ended in abject failure. The work was prompted by Lew's new consciousness of racial issues, an awareness sparked by his experiences in the army. Unfortunately, his choice of the minstrel show format as a vehicle for decrying racism backfired. Graham-Luján recalls a transitional moment in the ballet, after the preliminary minstrel setup, when one of the minstrels tried to rub the paint off another and realized that it would not come off: "It was a chilling moment, when people were expecting froth."[12] Gisella, sitting with Lincoln in the audience on opening night, witnessed the ballet's tepid reception. Ever-encouraging, Kirstein leaned over and reassured her, "Tell Lew not to worry; the next one will be better."[13] But the critics were not so kind. Terry accused Lew of garbling this translation of the minstrel show into ballet, "omitting the bravado, the wit, and the gaudy glitter of the original form."[14] Louis Horst in *Dance Observer* found the set by Robert Drew "naturalistically dull," the score by Carter Harman "dull and unhappily orchestrated," and Lew's choreography "null, dull, and void."[15] Chujoy more reflectively observed that *Blackface* "would have been more in place on a program of the Ballet Caravan than of Ballet Society" and labeled its effect on the program "rather retardative."[16]

---

[11] Telephone conversation with Merce Cunningham Foundation Archivist David Vaughan, New York, New York, May 26, 1988.

[12] Stephen C. Steinberg and Nancy Johnson interview with James Graham-Luján, San Francisco, California, [n.d., interview J].

[13] Beth Witrogen McLeod, "Gisella Caccialanza Christensen: A Ballet Legend," San Francisco *Gazette*, September 1987, 19; and interview with Gisella Caccialanza Christensen, San Bruno, California, December 9, 1987.

[14] Quoted in Reynolds, *Repertory in Review*, 81.

[15] L. H., "Reviews of the Month – Ballet Society," *Dance Observer*, August–September 1947, 78.

[16] Anatole Chujoy, *New York City Ballet* (New York: Knopf, 1953; rpt. New York: Da Capo, 1982), 172.

By the beginning of the 1947–1948 Ballet Society season, Lew was in his late thirties and injury-prone.[17] His dancing could not live up to its former reputation.[18] Most difficult for Lew, perhaps, was facing the reality that he was no longer useful to Balanchine as an instrument. Balanchine derived creative inspiration from dancers with extraordinary technical or expressive capabilities, and Lew was past that point in his performing career. Vladimirov's prediction was coming true in that during that season Lew was given secondary parts: the Puppeteer and Devil in Danieli's *Punch and the Child* (while Herbert Bliss danced the Father and Punch) and the Major Domo in Balanchine's ballet-cantata *The Triumph of Bacchus and Ariadne* (in which Nicholas Magallanes and Tanaquil LeClerq were featured in the title roles). With the failure of *Blackface*, Lew's future in Ballet Society held distinctly limited promise.

Lew's position within the company evolved inevitably as he aged and as younger dancers came up through the School. In the prewar Caravan, his abilities as a performer, his endowment of musicality and virtuoso technique, had lent weight to his authority as the group's ballet master. Now his own dancing took second place to helping Balanchine run the company.[19] Lew also taught company class frequently for Balanchine. The biographical sketch for Lew in Ballet Society programs (which was probably written by Kirstein) suggests that his value to the company now lay not in his performing

---

[17] Lew later explained: "I tried to dance again, but those army years had taken their toll, and I kept hurting myself." Stephanie von Buchau, "Native Dancer," *Ballet News*, May 1982, 26.

[18] D'Amboise, who had often heard Lew spoken of at the School of American Ballet during the war, was disappointed when he finally saw Lew dance: "I thought he was very energetic, crisp, and sharp, but he wasn't that fantastic. I expected someone to float around in the air. Everybody told me, 'Oh, he hasn't danced for four years; he's been in the army. You should have seen him before.'" Interview with Jacques D'Amboise, New York, New York, January 12, 1989.

[19] He later explained, "I'd get to class whenever I could, do my own dancing, and rehearse something we'd already done to a point where he could correct it and get it onstage." Barbara Newman, *Striking a Balance* (London: Elm Tree Books, 1982), 39.

abilities but in his training, which Kirstein hoped would be passed on to future generations of dancers at the School.[20]

On the personal side, Lew and Gisella settled in a cold water flat in midtown Manhattan. Their living conditions left much to be desired: their bathtub doubled as a kitchen table when its removable top was in place, and the small icebox would overflow if Gisella forgot to run home to empty the drain between rehearsals.[21] "No one had any money. It was a fight for existence," Lew recalled later in life.[22] Neither Lew nor Gisella was of a disposition to strike out on a new path or initiate a move to look for better opportunities; instead, they focused on supporting Kirstein and Balanchine in their latest effort.

Harold visited New York and was upset at seeing his talented younger brother in these circumstances. Harold did not share Lew's vision of building Balanchine's company; instead, Harold saw his brother as Balanchine's majordomo, delivering pointe shoes to the ballerinas and bringing in sandwiches for lunch.[23] Harold felt that Lew had too much talent to be spending his time in servitude to Balanchine and pressed Lew to join Willam and himself in San Francisco. After returning to the Bay Area, Harold wrote to Lew and offered to match and better any salary offered by Kirstein if Lew would come to California.[24]

The summer Lew returned from Germany, Willam spent twelve weeks in Pittsburgh, choreographing eight musicals (much as Lew had done in St. Louis in 1940).[25] The job

---

[20] Ballet Society Program, January 13–14, 1947.

[21] Michael Harris, "The San Francisco Ballet Makes a Leap Forward," *State of the Arts in San Francisco*, a Special Series reprinted from the *San Francisco Chronicle*, 1986, 16.

[22] Barbara Newman, *Striking a Balance* (London: Elm Tree Books, 1982), 39.

[23] Interview with Harold F. Christensen, San Anselmo, California, December 3, 1987.

[24] Telephone interview with James Graham-Luján, July 29, 1991.

[25] Unfortunately, the Civic Light Opera of Pittsburgh no longer has any records of that season, so it is impossible to list with certainty the productions choreographed by Willam.

brought needed income but left Willam disenchanted with the grueling pace of summer repertory. As soon as one show opened he began rehearsals for the next, often working with the dancers after evening performances until two in the morning. Willam longed to be in San Francisco, where Mignon had recently given birth to their second child, a daughter they named Roxanne. He declined an invitation to return to Pittsburgh the following summer.[26]

Willam enjoyed a period of increasing personal recognition in San Francisco during the postwar years. In the spring of 1946 he was invited to join the prestigious Bohemian Club, a privilege usually reserved for wealthy and powerful white males. Talent, not wealth, provided Willam's entree to the gentlemen's club; he joined as an artistic member. For six years Willam staged the association's annual burlesque theatricals, "High Jinx" and "Low Jinx," at the men's summer camp at Russian River. In town, the club provided a place where Willam could go for drinks and casual conversation with other influential men, including potential patrons of the ballet. Willam thrived on the bonhomie and good-natured ribbing as he associated with the city's elite on a first-name basis.

Further recognition came in the media in the fall of 1946. In September, *Opera and Concert*, which regularly covered Willam's activities in San Francisco, briefly spotlighted the three Christensens and their recent activities.[27] And in November, *Dance* magazine included Willam's views about dance in America in a forum that also contained statements by Anton Dolin, Frederick Franklin, Patricia Bowman, and Martha Graham.[28] Willam's statement was actually written

[26] Interview with Willam Christensen, Salt Lake City, Utah, April 24, 1987.

[27] "S.F. Ballet Activities," *Opera and Concert*, September 1946, San Francisco Ballet Clipping File, Dance Collection, The New York Public Library. This short article actually refers to Willam's company as the "San Francisco Civic Ballet," indicating that although the organization chartered just before Pearl Harbor had fallen through, Willam was still clinging to the illusion of civic support for his efforts.

[28] Willam Christensen, "The Opportunity Is Close at Hand," *Dance*, November 1946, 12, 35–36.

by Graham-Luján, who had gotten to know the West Coast wing of the family while being stationed at a Bay Area hospital during the latter part of the war. (In ghostwriting this piece, Graham-Luján contributed his services *gratis*, just as other members of the community were prevailed upon over the years to support the local ballet company in one way or another.) Under Willam's name, Graham-Luján spoofed the pioneers of modern dance ("With Isadora Duncan all Hellas broke loose") and advocated a very conservative approach to building repertory through reliance on the classics. "Within traditional ballets, the abilities of a company's artists may be affirmed," the article insisted. "The repetition in performance of *Swan Lake*, *Raymonda*, *Sylphides*, and *Coppelia* means that audiences will eventually be able to appreciate nuance and degrees of ability.... On classic ballet let tomorrow's repertory be based."[29] While Willam doubtless approved the sentiments expressed, he was probably less interested in the content of the statement than in the public relations value of appearing in print alongside the other contributors.

Another exciting opportunity was an invitation to produce ballets for the 1947 season of a Chicago group called the United States Opera Company. The invitation represented a further broadening of opportunities for Willam, a reassuring expansion of his reputation. *Dance News* reported that he would be in Chicago for seven weeks with a handful of his leading dancers: Celina Cummings, Jocelyn Vollmar, Onna White, Peter Nelson, and Richard Burgess.[30] Ruby was not invited to Chicago because she was expecting another child, a personal choice of which Willam did not approve. "Cows can have babies," he sometimes scoffed, insinuating that ballerinas should reserve themselves for their art.[31] But Harold and Ruby had their own ideas about what they wanted in life; they became parents of a healthy daughter, Heidi, the following January (1947). And at the last minute,

---

[29] *Ibid.*, 36.

[30] "Willam Christensen to Stage in Chicago," *Dance News*, January 1947, 2.

[31] Telephone interview with Ruby Asquith Christensen, May 10, 1991.

the invitation to Chicago fell through, so Willam remained in the Bay Area and focused his efforts on improving the fortunes of his company there.

Since the end of the war Willam's thoughts had turned to reestablishing the Civic Ballet, whose hopeful start had been cut off by the bombing of Pearl Harbor. Willam's use of the term *Civic Ballet* in 1946 did not imply the connotations that label developed in the 1950s, when it came to mean a small amateur or semiprofessional company, generally run by a prominent local teacher, showcasing the talents of advanced student dancers in small-scale performances for the benefit of the community.[32] Instead, Willam's use of the term *civic* stemmed from his fervent wish for community funding, the kind the symphony and the opera enjoyed in San Francisco.[33] The document drawn up one month before America entered World War II had promised Willam the support of many of the city's leading citizens. Willam wanted that philanthropic support in addition to dependable funding from the city's coffers, especially the Arts Commission budget that sponsored outside touring companies. Geraldine McDonald, still his chief patron and president of the Ballet Guild, urged San Franciscans to support ballet for the sake of civic pride: "We would be known as the only city besides New York which had completed the trilogy of culture – symphony, opera, and ballet."[34]

Willam's potential backers let him know that before they would support a full-blown effort to develop a bigger and better ballet company in San Francisco, he would need to find a competent manager for the desired troupe. By the

---

[32] For a more complete description of the term *Civic Ballet*, as it acquired its current meaning in the late 1950s, see Anatole Chujoy, *Civic Ballet* (New York: Dance News, 1958).

[33] Willam may or may not have been consciously looking back to the tradition of ballet within the context of civic opera companies; both Bolm in Chicago and Littlefield in Philadelphia had operated within the context of local civic opera organizations. With the war, Willam's company had been freed of its subjection to the San Francisco Opera, but in addition to that independence he wanted equal status.

[34] Quoted in Steinberg, *San Francisco Ballet*, 52.

middle of 1946 Willam had found the perfect candidate: Irving Deakin. Deakin had been in the Bay Area numerous times as the advance agent for dance companies touring under the auspices of Sol Hurok, notably the Ballet Russe de Monte Carlo and Ballet Theatre. As an "advance man" Deakin would come to town before the company's arrival to manage publicity and business arrangements, including the hiring of extra musicians and stagehands. Through his work for Hurok, which was arranged by contract on a season-by-season basis, Deakin had acquired a firm grasp of the business side of American dance. But Deakin's experience and assets went far beyond business arrangements; he was also an author, editor, and music critic. By 1946 he had published two books on dance: *To the Ballet* (1935), and *Ballet Profile* (1936). Moreover, he and his wife Natasha owned a large collection of recorded ballet music, and he had originated the first ballet radio program in the United States over WQXR in New York. Deakin had valuable connections in the dance world and strengths in areas in which Willam felt weak. Perhaps Willam saw Deakin as the means to his long-desired end of a glamorous touring company. Willam's goals had not changed significantly since the Portland days, but he now had more *savoir faire*; he understood the importance of allying himself with someone who had the connections and expertise he lacked, even though it would diminish the autonomy he had hitherto enjoyed in San Francisco.

Willam met with Deakin during one of the latter's trips to San Francisco and proposed that Deakin join him in putting together the new Civic Ballet. Deakin was intrigued with the possibilities provided by the intended setup. The ballet would be a nonprofit enterprise, which, he observed in a letter to Adolph Bolm (formerly Deakin's father-in-law), offered "greater possibilities for experimentation and development than would ever be possible in the more purely commercially-minded ballet companies."[35] With financial support from the community and the use of Willam and his

---

[35] Letter from Irving Deakin to Adolph Bolm, June 28, 1946, Irving Deakin Correspondence, Folder 39, Dance Collection, The New York Public Library.

dancers, Deakin would direct the fortunes of company that would balance the classical repertory with new works by diverse choreographers, in productions whose costuming, scenery, and lighting would draw upon "the full resources of the modern theatre."[36] Deakin knew of the Christensens' sacrifices to keep a company going in San Francisco and had heard favorable reports of Willam's previous efforts. "Even in spots quite remote from San Francisco, where they have played, I have heard only fine things about the San Francisco Ballet," Deakin confided to a business acquaintance. "I have great faith in its potentialities."[37]

From his vantage point inside the Hurok organization, Deakin was well aware of the politics and power plays behind the major touring ballet companies. Hurok, who had managed Ballet Theatre since 1941, maintained control of the pre- and post-opera ballet season at the Metropolitan Opera House, with the result that Ballet Theatre performed in that prestigious house while Sergei Denham's Ballet Russe de Monte Carlo (which Hurok dropped in 1942) resorted to the City Center Theatre. While Hurok's management had initially been considered a boon to Ballet Theatre's fortunes, over time his relations with the company's management soured.[38] In April 1946, Hurok and Ballet Theatre announced a parting of the ways, and Hurok was left without a major ballet company

---

[36] "Outline of Plan and Policy," Irving Deakin Correspondence, Folder 43, Dance Collection, The New York Public Library.

[37] Letter from Irving Deakin to Alexander Haas, May 29, 1946, Irving Deakin Correspondence, Folder 38, Dance Collection, The New York Public Library.

[38] Hurok ruffled feathers by advertising the American enterprise as "the greatest in Russian ballet" and raised Lucia Chase's ire with his insistent promotion of guest artists over regular company members. At a time when Chase preferred to compare the company to an integrated symphony in which each instrument had its proper and important place, Hurok insisted that "the guest star principle had been responsible for American interest in ballet." Sol Hurok, *Sol Hurok Presents: A Memoir of the Dance World* (New York: Hermitage House, 1953), 167. Hurok was also accused of meddling with the company's artistic freedom, forcing his tastes upon their programming. For example, he insisted upon a production of *The Firebird* during the 1945–1946 season because he believed in the drawing power of the Russian story and score.

to present at the Metropolitan that fall. Scrambling to find another attraction, he patched together a company with Alicia Markova, Anton Dolin, André Eglevsky, and defectors from Ballet Theatre, but the group's preliminary tour proved disastrous due to complications with transportation and electrical shortages. For the 1946–1947 season, Hurok renewed his former ties with de Basil's Original Ballet Russe, which had spent most of the war years touring in South America, and supplemented that company's repertory with works from the Marquis de Cuevas's International Ballet. The resulting "attraction" boasted famous names, but the worn productions lost substantial amounts of money on tour. Hurok severed his ties with de Basil for the last time, and in November 1947 the impresario gave up his longstanding contract with the Metropolitan Opera House.

During this period of managerial turmoil, Massine contemplated forming his own company. *Dance News* responded to that idea with an emphatically negative editorial, asking incredulously, "Five Ballet Companies in U.S.?" Recognizing the existence of the Ballet Russe de Monte Carlo, Ballet Theatre, de Basil's Original Ballet Russe, the Marquis de Cuevas' Ballet International, and the possible new company projected by Massine, the paper insisted, "The American public cannot possibly support five ballet companies, or even three. All of them cannot hope to compete with each other and survive."[39] But Deakin saw future opportunity in the confusion. As he contemplated the proposed San Francisco company in early 1947, he predicted:

> *There are sound reasons to believe the presently crowded ballet picture will be clarified by the closing within the next couple of years of some of the companies now touring. It should therefore be apparent that the national opportunity is great, provided we are in a position to take advantage of it when the former presents itself.*[40]

---

[39] "Five Ballet Companies in U.S.?" *Dance News*, January 1946, 4.

[40] "Outline of Plan and Policy," Irving Deakin Correspondence, Folder 43, Dance Collection, The New York Public Library.

Deakin may have concluded that Ballet Theatre would fold without Hurok's management; just as likely, the poor success of the Original Ballet Russe in 1946–1947 might have suggested that company's eventual demise. Time essentially proved Deakin correct about the future availability of booking dates. De Basil took the Original Ballet Russe to Europe after the spring of 1947, the Marquis de Cuevas took over the Nouveau Ballet de Monte Carlo in 1947 and transferred his attentions to European touring, and the dancers of Ballet Theatre experienced a long layoff in the fall of 1948. (The existence of Kirstein's subscription-only Ballet Society was not even an issue in Deakin's thinking; he was looking at the market for touring companies.) As Deakin viewed the situation in 1947, no matter who dropped out of the running, the collapse of one or more of the established companies would signify an opening in the dance scene, and a prepared San Francisco troupe could step in and take over available booking dates.

So Deakin and Willam drew up plans for the new company, conspiring to put together a package that would win the support of the revitalized San Francisco Civic Ballet Association. In the new hierarchy Deakin held the title of general manager, while Willam was not artistic director but artistic collaborator.[41] Putting Deakin at the head of the organization signaled that the planned company was more than just another incarnation of the struggling troupe of dancers Willam had directed since the late 1930s. Moreover, while Willam was crucial to the success of the scheme, the new company's repertory would have to be enriched by other choreographers, and guest artists would add the glamour necessary to transform the San Francisco Civic Ballet from a strictly local troupe to a company with national, perhaps someday international, standing. After years of struggling to

---

[41] The stationery of the San Francisco Civic Ballet Association listed Deakin at the top as General Manager and then Willam as Artistic Collaborator. Sources since then have generalized or assumed that Willam was Artistic Director, including Steinberg's history of the San Francisco Ballet, *Fifty Years*, which states as much on page 53.

run the San Francisco Ballet with minimal support, Willam accepted the new arrangement (essentially a demotion) with grace. While Deakin was still on contract to Hurok, Willam wrote him an encouraging letter and admitted, "This Ballet of ours has been too much for me to handle alone so you have no idea how grateful I will be when you arrive upon the scene."[42]

Irving and Natasha Deakin committed themselves unstintingly to the new opportunity. They gave up their apartment in New York and moved their belongings, including a vast collection of books and records, to San Francisco in early April 1947. The San Francisco Civic Ballet Association, Inc., was formally organized, with George Washington Baker as president, Nion R. Tucker and Clarence R. Lindner as vice presidents, James K. Lochead and D. V. Nicholson as treasurer and secretary, respectively, and a board of fifty directors. The officers and board assured Willam and Deakin that they, the board, would support the company financially if it met three requirements. The new company would have to perform in the War Memorial Opera House, be accompanied by the San Francisco Symphony, and engage guest artists of international stature.[43] Deakin put his energies to meeting the board's requirements: lining up dates with the Symphony, engaging guest artists, and querying outside choreographers about their availability. He also organized a fundraising performance for the association's new board members and prevailed upon his good friend Anton Dolin to speak as guest of honor. Generating more funds immediately was necessary because the $100,000 the board had promised to provide in order to get the company off the ground was not enough for the operating scale Deakin envisioned.[44]

---

[42] Letter from Willam Christensen to Irving Deakin, March 4, 1947, Irving Deakin Correspondence, Folder 43, Dance Collection, The New York Public Library.

[43] Interview with Willam Christensen, Salt Lake City, Utah, May 1, 1987.

[44] As early as July 1946, Deakin warned Baker that the $100,000 setup money promised by the board would not be enough to sustain a first-class company. Report to Mr. Baker, July 4, 1946, Irving Deakin Correspondence, Folder 39, Dance Collection, The New York Public Library.

Deakin pulled a major coup for the new company's premiere, which was set for two nights in early November (1947). With permission from Hurok, Deakin hired Dolin and Alicia Markova, who were touring with their own small company under Hurok's management, to perform jointly with Willam's dancers at the opera house. (Hurok later characterized the joint engagement as the "highlight" of Markova–Dolin's tour that year.[45]) Deakin also went to work lobbying the city's Arts Commission, which had used its symphony-ballet budget to sponsor Lucia Chase's Ballet Theatre in annual appearances since 1943 despite some feeling that local tax money ought to support local dancers.[46] "Lucia, through MCA, is pulling every possible string to get the Art Commission booking for Ballet Theatre," wrote Deakin to Dolin in June. "It's still in the air." When Deakin did succeed in wresting the Commission's $5,000 gift from the grip of Ballet Theatre, Willam relished the psychological victory as much as the monetary prize.

Such maneuvering was a necessary part of getting the new company into the public's eye and winning the allegiance of ballet audiences. Once the November dates had been confirmed with Markova–Dolin, Deakin wrote gleefully to Hurok, "This will knock the Monte Carlo season here... square in the eyes, if we can pull it off. We will be in the Opera House here just a week before the Monte Carlo season opens."[47] Timing was crucial because the dance audience was not perceived as being strong enough to patronize two companies in a row.

While still in the early stages of building the new company, Deakin was not above hiring a union scene painter in Oakland who would execute designs of nonunion artists at below-union fees. When it came time to hang the drops at

[45] Hurok, 199.

[46] Jack Loughner, "Taxpayers Help to Book Ballet in San Francisco," *Dance News*, February 1945, 3.

[47] Letter from Irving Deakin to Sol Hurok, July 29, 1947, Irving Deakin Correspondence, Folder 51, Dance Collection, The New York Public Library.

the opera house, Deakin simply claimed the company was using borrowed sets or found a similar excuse. "If the scene designers' union moved in on us," he rationalized to Bolm, "we should have to close up shop, because we simply cannot afford to pay $1,000 a drop as a designer's fee."[48]

The board of directors was not yet moving forward with a strong fund-raising program, so Deakin got credit on the board members' names and went on putting together his premiere season. The first night at the opera house would feature Markova–Dolin in Dolin's *The Lady of the Camellias*, the *Black Swan Pas de Deux*, and Rosella Hightower's *Henry VIII*, while Willam's dancers would perform a new work by Adolph Bolm, *Mephisto*. On the second night, Markova–Dolin would present Bronislava Nijinska's *Fantaisie*, the companies would appear together in the Markova–Dolin staging of *Giselle*, and Willam and his dancers would conclude the evening with *Parranda*, his new work to Morton Gould's *Latin American Symphonette*. When Bolm proved difficult in negotiations, Deakin pleaded for his cooperation in light of the importance this opening season would have in establishing the new enterprise: "Everything, but *everything*, is being staked on these performances."[49]

Word of the ambitious new company got around during the summer of 1947. The Chicago critic Claudia Cassidy observed that the dance scene in Chicago was "becalmed" while San Francisco moved ahead, and in New York Walter Terry suggested the new company as a possible "contender for the American Ballet crown."[50] In September, *Dance* magazine ran a long feature article on the Christensens and their plans for San Francisco, including praise for Harold

---

[48] Letter from Irving Deakin to Adolph Bolm, August 20, 1947, Irving Deakin Correspondence, Folder 54, Dance Collection, The New York Public Library.

[49] Letter from Irving Deakin to Adolph Bolm, October 2, 1947, Irving Deakin Correspondence, Folder 59, Dance Collection, The New York Public Library.

[50] Claudia Cassidy, "On the Aisle," *Chicago Sunday Tribune*, June 29, 1947; and Walter Terry, "Four New Dance Organizations Sprout Both Here and Abroad," *New York Herald Tribune*, July 6, 1947.

and the school. In November, *Opera and Concert* highlighted the impending debut of the new SFCB with a prophetic sense of its potential future impact:

> For the first time, a major ballet company is being municipally sponsored and encouraged. This is a step without precedent and, in all probability, will mean a turning point in the somewhat checkered career of the American dance. . . .
>
> Now, with the City of San Francisco taking the lead . . . it is expected that other large cities will likewise establish their own ballet companies. Thus, in time, a network of firmly established, financially secure, major dance groups will be serving large regional sections of the country.[51]

A few last-minute snags threatened to disrupt the opening performances. The carefully constructed chandeliers for Willam's *Parranda* were destroyed in an accident and had to be hurriedly remade in a day.[52] And the sets for *Lady of the Camellias* mysteriously did not arrive; Mrs. McDonald dashed around to friends' and neighbors' homes to borrow appropriate-looking furniture and props to create a bedroom for the final scene.[53] But all was assembled in time, and a standing-room-only crowd, "aglow with civic consciousness," packed the opera house both nights.[54] Glittering patrons adorned the Golden Horseshoe. "Exciting and almost as dressy as opera opening night," reported the gossip columns, who chronicled the outfits worn by prominent citizens and reported their entr'acte activities.[55] Underscoring the social importance of the occasion, and lending ballet the exalted status usually reserved for the symphony and the opera, was one of the most helpful things the newspapers could do for the new company.

---

[51] Frank Russell, "First Municipally Sponsored Civic Ballet in Formal Debut," *Opera and Concert*, November 1947, 8.

[52] Interview with Willam Christensen, Salt Lake City, Utah, May 7, 1987.

[53] Mildred Brown Robbins, "From Where I Sit: It Takes All Types to Make a Ballet Audience," *San Francisco Chronicle*, November 13, 1947.

[54] Marie Hicks Davidson, "Colorful Ballet Hailed by S.F.," *San Francisco Call-Bulletin*, November 12, 1947.

[55] "The Notebook," *San Francisco Examiner*, November 13, 1947.

The critics were as supportive as the gossip colum- nists. Their comments on the consummate artistry of Markova and Dolin in *Giselle* were balanced by praise for Vollmar as Myrtha and by the observation that the performance would not have succeeded without the well-trained corps de ballet as the Wilis. And Willam's *Parranda*, which starred Vollmar as the Young Woman, Richard Burgess as the Young Man, Ruby as a Confetti Vendor, Peter Nelson as her estranged lover, and a large cast of diverse characters in a Southern Caribbean festival, won praise as warm as Bolm's *Mephisto* and warmer than that accorded to Dolin's *Lady of the Camellias* or Nijinska's *Fantaisie*.[56] Thanks to Deakin's extensive net- work, reviews appeared as far abroad as London, where an article in *Dancing Times* noted the company's official debut and rousing reception.[57] To cap it off, the *Examiner* ran an editorial stating that the Arts Commission's "daring" risk had paid off; the San Francisco Civic Ballet had "scored an unpre- cedented success" in the "hard test of the glaring footlights," and the company's fund-raising campaign now deserved the support of "every good San Franciscan."[58] Willam was walking on air.

Deakin moved swiftly to build success on success. He hired Tamara Toumanova to star in the next series of Arts Commission performances, buying Paul Petroff out of his contract with Hurok to partner the ballerina.[59] Deakin also queried Frederick Ashton about his availability; the British

---

[56] Ruby's talents were appreciated by Markova and Dolin, who invited her to appear as a soloist with their company in Seattle. Willam, however, persuaded Ruby to decline the offer in the interest of the SFCB. How would it look, he argued, if she appeared as his leading ballerina on their next tour to Seattle after she had been seen there as only a soloist with Markova–Dolin?

[57] "San Francisco," *Dancing Times*, January 1948, 195.

[58] "Civic Ballet Comes of Age," *San Francisco Examiner*, November 19, 1947.

[59] Actually, Deakin first hired Eglevsky from the Marquis de Cuevas's company, but when de Cuevas retracted his permission for Eglevsky to appear in San Francisco, Deakin turned to Hurok, who had the Nana Gollner–Paul Petroff troupe under contract. Deakin's relationship with Hurok was a key factor in the short-lived success of the San Francisco Civic Ballet.

choreographer expressed sincere interest in creating a new work for the young company, but his Covent Garden schedule prevented his leaving London, so Deakin invited John Taras to contribute a ballet instead.[60] The company's second set of performances, in February 1948, ran not two but four nights. Some of the ballets were were carried over from previous seasons (Willam's *Sonata Pathétique*, *Parranda*, *Mephisto*, *Swan Lake*, and *Coppélia*, with Toumanova as Swanilda), some were virtuosic grand pas de deux (*Black Swan*, *The Nutcracker*, *Don Quixote*), and one was a contribution by Simon Semenoff (*Gift of the Magi*). Taras's *Persephone*, set to Schumann's Symphony No. 1 in B flat Major, was included on the program to placate symphony members who disliked playing only "ballet music." The season opened on Thursday, February 5, and nearly ended prematurely due to lack of funds. The board of directors had not come up with sufficient money to pay the dancers and stagehands, so Deakin threatened to go before the curtain Saturday night, explain the situation to the audience, and cancel the performance. To prevent such an embarrassment, Geraldine McDonald persuaded the president of Wells Fargo to open the bank for her that Saturday afternoon. From her own account she withdrew enough cash, in combinations of bills dictated by Deakin, to pay the performers and crew. She took the money in a sack to the opera house, where Deakin sat on the stage and made the necessary disbursements before curtain time.[61]

The critical and popular success of the San Francisco Civic Ballet's second season left Willam jubilant once again, but this time his optimism was clouded by worry over the company's financial straits. The situation was confusing and

---

[60] Letter from Frederick Ashton to Irving Deakin, October 12, 1947, Irving Deakin Correspondence, Folder 62, Dance Collection, The New York Public Library.

[61] Mrs. McDonald's generous act has become part of SFB company lore; the amount she withdrew is rumored to have been $12,000. Most accounts suggest that she paid the dancers after the company had folded, but Natasha Deakin clarifies that the dancers were paid on a Saturday afternoon in order to prevent that evening's performance from being cancelled. Telephone interview with Natasha Deakin, July 5, 1991.

contradictory. On one hand, Deakin was exploring further booking possibilities with Hurok. Acting as if SFCB were not teetering on the edge of bankruptcy, Deakin offered Hurok SFCB with his choice of guest stars: Toumanova or Markova–Dolin. SFCB had already been invited to appear at the Hollywood Bowl that summer; Deakin suggested that a "respectable tour" following the fall opera season would constitute the ideal arrangement.[62]

On the other hand, demands from the company's creditors were growing increasingly urgent. The Arts Commission money had gotten the ballet off to a start, but the board of directors had not fulfilled its promised role by raising funds. Most likely, the board felt Deakin had done too much too quickly; the initial plan had called for slow, careful development, with the first year devoted to planning and preparation rather than star-studded performances.[63] By March the amount owed Capezio for shoes was almost a thousand dollars, and the scene painter threatened suit if the company did not pay its obligations immediately. Even Deakin was forced to remind the association in writing that he had not received several months' pay.

Deakin put on a good face for his negotiations in Los Angeles over the Hollywood Bowl booking, but he was operating without a firm base of support. The dilatory board in San Francisco could not seem to bring itself to raise the money needed to maintain the operation Deakin had put together so successfully. D. V. Nicholson, the association's secretary, finally put the situation in writing. "The time has come, in my judgement, when the officers and directors of the San Francisco Civic Ballet Association must make a final decision as to the future of this enterprise," he warned. Noting

---

[62] Letter from Irving Deakin to Sol Hurok, March 17, 1948, Irving Deakin Correspondence, Folder 72, Dance Collection, The New York Public Library.

[63] According to one article, the three-year plan for the company devoted the first year to preparation, the second to producing new works, and the third to full-fledged seasons. Irving Deakin, "Plans Are Being Made for a Permanent Ballet Group to Function in S.F.," *San Francisco Chronicle,* undated clipping in the San Francisco Ballet Clipping File, Dance Collection, The New York Public Library.

that the troupe's initial seasons had broken attendance records, a clear indication that San Franciso was ready to support ballet, he called for the board to either "assume financial leadership" as promised, or "abandon the enterprise, advise the underwriters to pay their notes, and either pay, repudiate, or ask our friends to help clear the remaining indebtedness."[64]

In a last-ditch attempt to force the board into providing meaningful support, Deakin arranged for SFCB to be invited to perform in New York City that fall. The official invitation, in the form of a telegram from Grover Whalen, chairman of New York's Golden Anniversary Committee, arrived April 1. Baker sent a letter to his board the next day, calling for action in light of the debts at hand and the extraordinary opportunity in view. Hurok would finance the company's New York performances, but the company must pay its own travel costs. And they must first pay off the company's existing deficit of $59,000, "a very modest figure indeed in the theatrical world," Baker pointed out.[65] (In this respect the Civic Ballet was in line with the San Francisco Opera, whose deficit the previous year had been $55,000.[66]) In retrospect, simple arithmetic shows that a donation of eleven hundred dollars from each of the officers and board members listed on the association's stationery would have more than made up the deficit. Still, the reluctant board held back.[67]

---

[64] Letter from D. V. Nicholson to George Washington Baker, Jr., March 29, 1948, Irving Deakin Correspondence, Folder 73, Dance Collection, The New York Public Library.

[65] Letter from George Washington Baker to the Officers and Directors of the San Francisco Civic Ballet Association, Inc., April 2, 1948, Irving Deakin Correspondence, Folder 75, Dance Collection, The New York Public Library.

[66] Arthur J. Bloomfield, *The San Francisco Opera, 1923–1961* (New York: Appleton-Century-Crofts, 1961), 86.

[67] In addition to the officers noted above and the Treasurer, James K. Lochead, the Directors listed on the SFCB Association's stationery were Mrs. Roger Laphan, Jr., Mrs. Thomas Carr Howe, Mrs. Lawrence Fletcher, Mrs. George W. Baker, Jr., Edward D. Keil, L. M. Giannini, Harry D. Collier, W. P. Roth, George T. Cameron, James B. Black, William W. Crocker, John F. Forbes, Sidney M. Ehrman, Frank Clarvoe, Mrs. Richard Tobin, Mrs. David Bouverie, Mrs. William P. Roth, Alexander F. Haas, John Rosekrans, E. Raymond Armsby, Dr. Ralph Soto-Hall, Mrs. Nion R. Tucker, Mrs. Marcus F. Koshland, Mrs. Jerd F. Sullivan, Mrs. Robert Watt Miller, Mrs. Stanley

Called into a meeting with Deakin and Baker, Willam stared in disbelief as Deakin hurled epithets and accusations at the president; the alliance that had brought Willam's greatest dream to life was now disintegrating before his very eyes.[68] Willam still had hope for the company's future, but Deakin had come to the realization that the board was not going to honor its commitment, and he felt used and betrayed. Ultimately, SFCB's collapse stemmed not from this confrontation between Baker and Deakin but from the board's lack of respect for their president. Although Baker had previously held the office of national chairman of the March of Dimes, his position in San Francisco society was based on his marriage to a daughter of the Ghirardelli chocolatiers, and his leadership did not inspire the confidence of his board. As Deakin's wife Natasha wrote to a friend, "So long as Baker is at the head it is a dead duck and he won't resign and nobody has enough courage to kick him out, they are all in the same circles and they still have to have social amenities observed."[69] Abandoning the ballet and its debts was less problematic to the social figures on Willam's board than openly challenging Baker's leadership. Because of their shortsightedness, the San Francisco Civic Ballet folded. Willam's appeal to civic pride, his attempt to promote ballet as a means of elevating the city's cultural level, failed because at midcentury, San Francisco, and the United States at large, had no dependable system of arts funding that extended to dance. Willam's company was left to teeter precariously on the whims of an elite minority that ultimately declined to support his ambitions.

---

Powell, Mrs. Wood Armsby, Mrs. George Pope, Jr., Mrs. Andrew B. Talbot, Mrs. Edmunds Lyman, Edmond D. Coblentz, Tracy Cummings, Charles E. Moore, Brayton Wilbur, Charles Page, George Montgomery, Mrs. Kenneth Monteagle, Mrs. Julliard McDonald, Mrs. M. C. Sloss, Mrs. Starr Bruce, Mrs. Sheldon Cooper, Mrs. Ryer Nixon, Mrs. Dunne Dailey, Mrs. Powers Symington, Mrs. John S. Logan, Mrs. Frank R. Girard, Robert Watt Miller, Mrs. Dorothy Liebes, Allard A. Calkins, and Mrs. Frances A. Elkins.

[68] Interview with Willam Christensen, Salt Lake City, Utah, May 1, 1987.

[69] Letter from Natasha Deakin to Franz Allers, May 12, 1948, Irving Deakin Correspondence, Folder 78, Dance Collection, The New York Public Library.

So the most glorious phase of Willam's career ended in crushing disappointment, due to forces completely beyond his control. The SFCB Association declared bankruptcy and paid its creditors a fraction of the amount owed them. "Which seems rather a dirty deal on all the poor little people who extended credit on the names," reflected Natasha Deakin, "and after the 'names' took their bows the little people who cannot afford to contribute such substantial amounts are the real benefactors of the ballet."[70] Deakin threatened suit for nonpayment of his salary and left the state in bitter disgust. "I have severed my association with the San Francisco Civic Ballet," he informed Anatole Chujoy, editor of *Dance News*. "Its history may one day make interesting reading for those who are really interested in ballet."[71] And to Hurok he reported, "There is a remote possibility that Christensen and the local dancers will continue in some small way, with the school and occasional local charity performances. But that is all."[72]

---

[70] *Ibid.*

[71] Letter from Irving Deakin to Anatole Chujoy, June 7, 1948, Irving Deakin Correspondence, Folder 79, Dance Collection, The New York Public Library.

[72] Letter from Irving Deakin to Sol Hurok, July 6, 1948, Irving Deakin Correspondence, Folder 80, Dance Collection, The New York Public Library. In his memoirs, Hurok later wrote that the San Francisco Civic Ballet had "promised much in the way of a civic supported ballet company of national proportions. ... Its closing was the result of the lack of that most vital element, proper subsidy. These things shock me." Hurok, 199.

# 10

## REGROUPING (1949–1951)

The collapse of the San Francisco Civic Ballet drove Willam's spirits to their lowest point in his career. The venture had come so close to succeeding that his pain at its failure was exquisite. The illustrious but short-lived SFCB had proven Willam's dreams possible and at the same time confirmed his worst fears: that even with all the ingredients for a successful company in place, San Francisco was not yet willing to support ballet. If his dream could not materialize in San Francisco, where he had excellent social connections and had earned respect in the community, where did it have a chance? Admitting the venture's defeat was tantamount to giving up his long-cherished desire for a large touring company. Willam may have appreciated the irony of the situation that fall when Deakin's prediction about an impending vacancy in the dance field came true: Ballet Theatre cancelled its fall 1948 tour and announced a suspension of all activities until January, 1949.[1] As Deakin had foretold, the timing would, indeed, have been perfect for a San Francisco company to step into the open spot and take over the cancelled bookings, but such speculation was useless.

  Additional factors complicated Willam's depression. SFCB's bankruptcy had hurt his personal credit, and the dancers who had other options left to find better-paying positions. Jocelyn Vollmar, who had seemed such a promising young prima for the company, left to join the nascent New York City Ballet as a principal dancer.[2] Even more serious was a sudden downspin in Mignon's health. After several

---

[1] "Via the Grapevine," *Dance Magazine*, September 1948, 8.

[2] Anatole Chujoy, *The New York City Ballet* (New York: Da Capo Press, 1982), 207. After a season with NYCB Vollmar went to Ballet Theatre.

years of partial remission, her multiple sclerosis worsened following the birth of their second child. Confined to a wheelchair, Mignon was now unable to perform many basic tasks. Willam arranged for part-time nursing care and assisted around the house as he was able to. The doctors could offer little help and held out no hope of a cure.

Another man might have given up on San Francisco altogether, but that was not Willam's nature. For one thing, he still had the basis of a skeletal operation there. He was still the choreographer for the San Francisco Opera, he still had the nominal backing of Mrs. McDonald and the Ballet Guild, and he and Harold still had the school. So Willam carried on out of habit, operating on the level he had established before the Civic Ballet. During the summer of 1948, his remaining dancers, billed as the "Willam Christensen Ballet," performed at Stern Grove and in Marin County. Ruby starred in a revival of *Coppélia*, with Willam filling the character part of Dr. Coppélius. The opera season brought welcome income for the dancers that fall, but the winter slipped by without a holiday festival season.

The San Francisco Ballet School, under Harold's committed leadership, was now more than ever the bedrock of the brothers' fortunes, their single source of dependable income in the wake of the Civic Ballet bankruptcy. Fortunately, the school benefited financially from the G. I. Bill, which paid tuition for veterans returning from the war, and returning men helped to replenish the ranks of male dancers. By the late 1940s, three to four hundred students filled classes from elementary to advanced levels of ballet technique. In addition to pointe classes and classes specially geared to male technique, students could choose supplementary coursework in partnering and adagio, variations from the standard repertory, and Spanish "Classical, flamenco, and regional" styles.[3] The curriculum also included preballet instruction for children ages four to seven years.

[3] "Ballet School," *Balletomane* (San Francisco Ballet Guild) 1.1 (Summer 1949): n.p.

During the final days of Willam's SFCB, Lew and Gisella were in New York, preparing for Ballet Society's first performances in its new home, the City Center of Music and Drama. Both had roles in the New York premiere (March 1948) of Balanchine's *Symphony in C*, which the choreographer had created in Paris the previous year and presented under the name *Le Palais de Cristal*. Lew and Elise Reiman led the fourth movement, while Balanchine set the leading female role in the third movement on Gisella.[4] Balanchine recognized Gisella's natural balon; he once sighed appreciatively to an associate, "She jumps like Nijinsky."[5] The third movement, designed for jumpers, drew on her gift. But during a rehearsal for the New York premiere, as Gisella bounded across the studio, her Achilles tendon snapped with a reverberating pop. Fearing that the injury signaled the end of her career, Gisella began a long period of recuperation while Lew performed in the ballet that March.

April brought the premiere of Balanchine's next collaboration with Stravinsky: *Orpheus*. Lew had first come to prominence in the role of Orpheus in Gluck's *Orpheus and Eurydice* at the Metropolitan Opera twelve years earlier; this time the leading role went instead to Nicholas Magallanes. By this point in his career, Lew was no longer the automatic candidate to portray Greek gods and heroes, and, in fact, he had lost much of his desire to perform.[6] Harold's repeated invitations to join the family business in San Francisco began to exert a stronger pull.

In years past Lew had looked to his brothers for teaching jobs to tide him over during layoffs and periods

---

[4] Nancy Reynolds, *Repertory in Review: Forty Years of the New York City Ballet* (New York: Dial Press, 1977), 84. The Balanchine Catalogue lists John Taras, not Lew, as leading the fourth movement with Reiman, but the Ballet Society Program, March 22, 1948, shows Lew and Reiman leading the fourth movement. Perhaps Lew and Taras shared the role.

[5] Balanchine quoted by James Graham-Luján, "Gisella Caccialanza: A Tribute," *Encore* 3.4 (Winter 1986/87): 7; Reynolds, 85.

[6] Steven C. Steinberg and Nancy Johnson interview with James Graham-Luján, San Francisco, California, [n.d., interview J].

between tours. Now Harold wanted Lew in San Francisco for good. In the aftermath of the SFCB fiasco, the family ballet business needed a strong shot in the arm. Lew's presence would lend prestige to both the school and the company. His taste and training would steer the company's repertory in a new direction, which would bring about changes Harold saw as timely and desirable. According to Harold's somewhat contradictory rationale, Lew was both a family resource that needed tapping and a favored sibling who needed to be protected from exploitation from Balanchine. Because Harold controlled the school, and, by extension, its income, he had a great deal of say in decisions of finance and administration. Hiring Lew fell under that rubric.

Willam, of course, was always eager to improve the family school and company. In one sense, if ever he needed the talents of his youngest brother, it was after the calamitous collapse of his dream company. And in the past, Lew's temporary presence had been a boon, especially to the 1940 *Swan Lake*. But Willam was still feeling the financial effects of the SFCB bankruptcy, and he may have also sensed that Harold wanted to bring Lew as an eventual replacement rather than to support the existing company structure.[7] So this time, before Willam was willing to divide the school's income three ways instead of two, he felt that Lew should "buy into" his brothers' partnership. Willam was very conscious of the three hundred dollars he and Harold had scraped together in 1942 to buy the school, and over the years they had made personal sacrifices while pouring their own money into productions. Still smarting from the SFCB bankruptcy, Willam insisted upon a material contribution from Lew.

Harold was aghast at Willam's demand; he felt that Lew's talent warranted automatic acceptance. For that matter, Harold argued, they should pay Lew to contribute his talents to the family business, especially as Lew and Gisella had no

---

[7] Graham-Luján claims that Harold clearly wanted Willam "out" and wanted Lew as his partner in the San Francisco enterprise instead. *Ibid.*

savings and no way of buying in. But Willam insisted, so Harold devised a workable compromise: all three brothers would receive the same salary, $250 a month, but Lew would forfeit the savings bond the other two received for a period of eight months, after which he would be considered a partner in full.[8]

Lew and Gisella weighed Harold's proposal with a sense of its far-reaching implications. Balanchine's company was just making the transition from Ballet Society to the New York City Ballet, but even with the name change the dancers would have only two short seasons a year and little immediate financial security. Between Gisella's injury and Lew's waning technique, their future as performers appeared limited at best. Lew could continue to assist Balanchine in running his company, between layoffs, but Lew's own role would always be subservient. In New York, he would clearly remain in Balanchine's shadow. His chances to choreograph might even be limited to Balanchine's cast-off opportunities, as had been the case with *Pastorela* (the "cultural goodwill gesture" for the South American tour) and *Jinx* (whose score went Lew's way because it did not interest the Russian). In contrast, San Francisco held the promise of family support and freedom in which to experiment. During the summer of 1948, Lew and Gisella moved to the Bay Area and began to invest in a future there.[9]

Thus began a period in which the three brothers truly worked together to create finished dancers. All three stressed the importance of musical awareness; beyond that, each brother had his own specialty, his individual strength and gift in working with students.

Harold's gift resided in his ability to train beginning and intermediate students, especially the pre-adolescent girls

---

[8] Interview with Harold Christensen, San Anselmo, California, September 22, 1987.

[9] It has not been possible to pinpoint the exact date of Lew and Gisella's move to San Francisco. By the spring of 1949, Lew was coproducing a season with Willam. Given Harold's penchant for order, Lew probably began teaching at the San Francisco Ballet School in the fall of 1948 or in January of 1949.

**29**   Harold, Willam, and Lew Christensen, ca. 1950.
Photograph by Cristof, courtesy of San Francisco Performing Arts Library
and Museum

who sensed the nurturing spirit behind his firm manner. He
analyzed the fundamental aspects of ballet technique and
understood how to break down the components of each step
or position and build it into the students' bodies through
constant repetition. With his perfect turn out and perpetually
straight posture, Harold presented the ideal model for young
dancers as he demonstrated the five basic positions of the
feet, *pliés*, and other rudiments of technique. In class he gave
plentiful corrections to individual students, usually dropping
to one knee to mold a leg or foot with his hands while offering encouragement. He stressed turn out, a pulled up torso,
and exact placement of each body part, and he used his dry
wit to impress important points upon his students. For
example, once upon hearing that a man had jumped out of a
window and died, Harold quipped, "If he had just had a good

*plié*, he wouldn't have been hurt when he touched the ground."[10]

Harold rarely gave the impression of being physically relaxed or at ease. Especially to those who knew of his days at West Point, all six feet two inches of him seemed to be constantly standing at attention. When demonstrating a step he had a habit of pulling in his stomach muscles, lifting his ribs, and then reaching for his pants as they threatened to slide down his slender frame. The students mimicked the grab for the pants, but along the way they also absorbed the straight back and pulled up position.

Willam pushed his students to master virtuoso steps and stunts, such as a dramatic circle of leaps and turns around the stage or a sparkling line of *brisées volées*, but his special concern was the dancers' stage presence. Willam demanded temperament from his dancers; his definition of artistry included the revelation of personality. His teaching reflected the aesthetics of his choreography, with its narrative orientation, and he drilled the necessity of theatrical projection into his dancers while they were still students. Even simple classroom excercises were to be performed with an awareness of one's intended audience. "Finish! Finish!" Willam would shout if a student came out of an enchaînement without a properly polished ending and a smile. Willam's students learned how to think like performers, and many of the pupils at the school participated in the opera season, either as dancers or as supers. Performing constituted an integral part of their training, and Willam was able to maintain a company of sorts because he used unpaid students in mounting productions. As Harold was the backbone of the school, Willam embodied the spirit of the company. He did not reveal to his remaining dancers the full degree of his despair over the collapse of the Civic Ballet project. Instead, his habitual enthusiasm kept company classes lively and vigorous, with

---

[10] Interview with Nancy Johnson, San Francisco, California, December 9, 1987. This interview is the best single source on the brothers' differing teaching styles, and I acknowledge my debt to Johnson in this section.

exercises that got students moving through space with a sense of purpose and fulfillment. In the postwar years, his teaching methods and his personal example in the classroom inspired young men such as Roland Vasquez and Gordon Paxman to use their G. I. Bill benefits to study at the San Francisco Ballet School.

To distinguish between the brothers, the students called Harold, "Mr. Christensen" (or, behind his back, "the General"), and Willam, "Mr. C," or, if older and more familiar with him, "Boss." From the time the youngest brother arrived, he was known by all simply as "Lew." Given stewardship over the advanced students, he set to work offering them new technical challenges. The dancers fell immediately for Lew's handsome looks and admirable technical abilities as he demonstrated in class. The youngest Christensen held an appeal that Willam and Harold could not match: he was still a performing artist; he possessed impressive New York connections; and he was just enough closer in age to his students that they could identify with him. The advanced students hungrily absorbed what he had to offer. "We used to eat, sleep, and drink ballet with Lew," recalled one in that group. "We'd go out and have coffee after class and talk about technique."[11] Less exuberant than Willam, Lew proved demanding in his own quiet way: thoughtful, often serious, sometimes quite intense, but possessing a wit that allowed him to deflect tension with a well placed quip.

While Willam stressed style and delivery, Lew concentrated on extending his students' technical range. More demanding in the classroom than Willam but less dogmatic than Harold, Lew worked through the balletic vocabulary, systematically exploring the possibilities inherent in various steps as he incorporated them into classroom exercises at the barre and in center. In doing so, he was, consciously or unconsciously, repeating the process Balanchine had gone through during his early years in New York, and perhaps even reliving the tutorial he had received from Balanchine.

---

[11] Interview with Dick Carter, San Francisco, California, March 8, 1988.

Thinking through the possibilities of the balletic movement vocabulary, and determining the most effective way of instilling that vocabulary in the bodies of his students, reflected the analytical side of Lew's nature. He spent long hours discussing technique with Harold and Gisella, then taught with exacting standards. He demanded a new precision of the students, "the cleanest possible execution of every step" recalls Nancy Johnson, who was part of the advanced student group that worked hard to get the new look Lew desired.[12] For example, his students now began wrapping the working foot around the ankle of the supporting foot in *sur le coup de pied* position. And from Lew, they learned about using the foot against the floor in jumps, whereas, Johnson recalls, under Willam they "just jumped" and "whoever jumped best did the jumping parts."[13] In contrast with Willam's emphasis on communicating emotion to the audience, Lew made fun of dancers who "spilled their guts" on stage or wooed the audience.[14]

The students also perceived a difference in Willam's and Lew's approaches to choreographing. Willam generally staked out the dramatic action of a ballet first, establishing the general blocking, and then worked out the actual steps the dancers would do. If a company member could not do what he desired, he experimented until he found a movement the dancer could do that gave the effect he wanted. For Lew, even with a narrative work such as *Jinx*, the steps came first. He cared first and foremost for the shape and execution of his choreography; any narrative intention or expression of character had to be layered over the movement he devised.[15]

---

[12] Interview with Nancy Johnson, San Francisco, California, December 9, 1987.

[13] Stephen C. Steinberg and Nancy Johnson interview with James Graham-Luján, San Francisco, California, [n.d., interview G].

[14] Stephen C. Steinberg and Nancy Johnson Carter interview with James Graham-Luján, San Francisco, California, [n.d., interview C].

[15] Stephen C. Steinberg and Nancy Johnson interview with James Graham-Luján, San Francisco, California, September 30, 1985, [interview D].

Teaching the advanced class allowed Lew to work with bodies that were ready for technical challenges but still malleable enough to be trained according to his desires as a choreographer. He reshaped the stiff and proper bearing drilled into the beginners by Harold and molded the advanced students to his needs as he began to choreograph in his new setting. Lew was well aware that in Paris, two years earlier, Balanchine had set *Serenade* on advanced students because he found the Opéra's professionals incapable of giving the work the look he wanted.[16] Now in San Francisco Lew developed a nucleus of advanced students who would become instruments for his purposes as a choreographer. At the same time, by taking over the upper classes, he was essentially creating the company of the future, especially as Willam's older, experienced dancers either retired or moved on to better-paying positions.

Despite Deakin's dire predictions, Willam and Lew managed to mount a two-night season with what was left of the company in April 1949. These performances, not at the opera house but in the nearby Hayes Street Auditorium of the Commerce High School, signaled the rebirth of the San Franciso Ballet after the previous year's debacle. Willam revived John Taras's staging of *Les Sylphides* (a remainder from the SFCB repertory) and created *Danza Brillante* to Felix Mendelssohn's First Piano Concerto. The concerto, like the rest of the musical accompaniment that season, was heard in a two-piano redaction; low funds permitted only the simplest staging. Lew personally built the boxes to be used as set pieces in his restaging of *Jinx*, which featured Roland Vasquez in the title role. Lew's other contributions included a technically oriented étude, *Vivaldi Concerto*, for his advanced students, and a lecture demonstration starring Ruby entitled *The Story of a Dancer*. The narration for the latter was delivered by Lew in performance but was actually written by his former American Ballet Caravan associate James Graham-Luján, who

---

[16] Letter from Irving Deakin to "John," July 18, 1947, Irving Deakin Correspondence, Folder 50, Dance Collection, The New York Public Library.

was then working on a master's degree in Spanish literature at Columbia University. The monologue drew unexpected guffaws from the audience when Lew's opening line, "Ballet begins at the barre," was construed by some as a reference to liquor.

That same spring (1949), Willam received an unexpected telephone call from the University of Utah with an invitation to stage summer theatricals. The proposal was far more reasonable than the repertory situation he had faced three years earlier in Pittsburgh; the university produced one musical and one opera or operetta each summer in its outdoor stadium with guest artists from New York supported by a local chorus. The director of the Theater Department, Dr. C. Lowell Lees, asked Willam if he would choreograph that summer's productions, *Carmen* and *The Great Waltz* (starring Kitty Carlisle). Willam could bring a few soloists with him but would be expected to use local talent to fill out the dance scenes.

Lees had invited Willam after hearing he was "possibly the fastest working choreographer in the business."[17] Willam accepted chiefly because he needed the income. He won the respect of the university's production team at the first rehearsal, when in less than an hour he watched fifty local aspirants attempt basic steps, divided them into groups of ten, and worked with each group as a unit while giving corrections to individual dancers.[18] With his San Francisco dancers Joan Vickers, Roland Vasquez, and Richard Burgess carrying the leading dance roles, Willam devised choreography that showed the local dancers to best advantage and won warm praise in the productions' reviews. His enthusiasm and diplomacy in dealing with people impressed the Utahns and prompted an invitation to return the following summer.

---

[17] "Dance Chief Rehearses Group at 'U,'" *Deseret News*, Utah Ballet Archives, Box 5, Folder 36, Special Collections, University of Utah Marriott Library, Salt Lake City, Utah.

[18] *Ibid.*

As Willam turned his attention to another fall opera season, Lew returned to New York to help Balanchine prepare for the 1949 New York City Ballet fall season. The exact reason why Lew returned to New York at this time, after having decided to throw in his lot with his brothers, is unclear. Doubtless he saw his position in New York as temporary. He was not needed immediately in San Francisco, where Willam could choreograph the coming opera season without assistance. Balanchine's company was just reassembling after a nine-month layoff; perhaps Kirstein deemed Lew's presence necessary, or at least highly desirable, to pull the group together. Kirstein probably clinched the deal by offering Lew the chance to restage *Jinx*. So, for the first time, Lew was officially named Ballet Master of New York City Ballet. (Balanchine himself was listed as Ballet Master in programs during the company's first season.) Lew resumed his usual duties of teaching and rehearsing and helped prepare the company's fall repertory.

John Martin (of the *New York Times*) remembered *Jinx* as "quite the most distinguished piece" introduced by Eugene Loring's short-lived Dance Players, but he was not enamored of this production. Martin found Francisco Moncion ineffectual in the title role, especially in comparison to Lew's memorable portrayal.[19] According to Martin, the "macabre strength" of this "gripping little horror piece with philosophical overtones" was diluted by the dancers' under-accented dramatic climaxes and less-than-convincing characterizations.[20] A dramatic ballet such as *Jinx* required expressive skills that were not stressed in Balanchine's technically oriented training; only Janet Reed, who had long since absorbed Willam's theatricality, impressed Martin as giving a "completely satisfying performance."[21] Lew revised the ballet the following year, at

---

[19] John Martin, "City Ballet Gives Its First Novelty," *New York Times*, November 25, 1949.

[20] *Ibid.*

[21] *Ibid.*

which time Martin approved of the "stunning, atmospheric, taut new version which [held] the attention unflaggingly."[22]

Lew returned to San Francisco in December 1949, in time to help Willam put the finishing touches on the first Bay Area production of *The Nutcracker* since the premiere of Willam's full-length version in 1944. Willam had not conceived the ballet as a holiday ritual that first season; his initial plan had been to produce new works each December. Holiday festival seasons had been abandoned during the war for lack of men and money; during the Civic Ballet period the idea of the holiday festival had been rejected as a holdover from a previous era. But in 1949, with the Civic Ballet a thing of the past, Harold and Willam presented *The Nutcracker* in a premeditated attempt to establish the ballet as a holiday tradition, one paralleling English pantomimes and the Metropolitan Opera's annual *Hansel and Gretel*.[23] Once again, the Children's Theatre sponsored the ballet, and Harold geared the publicity towards attracting a young audience as a conscious ploy to lure adults into the opera house alongside their children.

From this time on, performances of *The Nutcracker* became an annual holiday occurrence in the Bay Area. (Balanchine would not do his version until 1954, a full decade after Willam's first production and five years after Willam's had initiated a West Coast tradition.) *The Nutcracker* also functioned as a learning experience for student performers advancing through the ranks of toy soldiers and mice, snowflakes and flowers. In the early years, when the company was small, each dancer would have more than one role. Nancy Johnson recalls being a Mother in the first act party scene, then changing into a Soldier costume for the fight scene, changing into a Snowflake costume for the snow scene, changing again for the Merlitons in the second act variations, changing again for the Waltz of the Flowers, and going back

---

[22] John Martin, *New York Times*, February 25, 1950; quoted in Reynolds, *Repertory in Review*, 96.

[23] *The Balletomane* (San Francisco Ballet Guild) 2.3 (Winter 1950): 4.

to her Merliton costume for the finale.[24] Willam would coach
the dancers in the appropriate expression and attitude for
each role, with the result that students with many roles
received multifaceted training in characterization as well as
valuable performing experience.

After the 1949 *Nutcracker*, Lew spent the winter
months in San Francisco once again, working with his advanced class and helping Willam prepare another series of
low-budget winter and spring performances culminating
in one night at the opera house. The family closed ranks,
pulling together to produce a five-night season. Ruby had
retired from the stage with the birth of her second daughter,
Stephanie Lee Christensen, in January (1950). Now Gisella
and Harold returned to the stage to re-create their original
roles in Lew's *Charade*, but Lew cast Roland Vasquez (rather
than himself) in the leading male role. Lew reworked *The
Story of a Dancer* and set it on Jocelyn Vollmar, who was
temporarily back in town after appearances with New York
City Ballet and Ballet Theatre. Willam restaged ballets from
the company's traditional repertory and contributed a new
work, arguably the hit of the season, *Nothing Doing Bar*.

Willam's new ballet satirized Prohibition America.
For the plot he drew inspiration from his experiences living
above a Manhattan speakeasy while studying with Mascagno.
Federal agents had raided the speakeasy, closed it down, and
sealed its door, but a few days later a new opening in the
wall had appeared, and the establishment had carried on. Still
amused by the incident decades later, Willam concocted a
satire involving caricatures of raffish jazz-age saloon habitués:
a bartender, a bookie, two college students (Joe College and
Fannie Flapper), a couple of slummers (the Von Snoopers), a
gangster (Payoff Mo) and his girlfriend (Shady Sadie), a
doorman, and so on. The farce included period dances from
the Charleston to the Black Bottom and built to a climax in
which the gangster bombed the joint. After a brief curtain, the

---

[24] Interview with Nancy Johnson, San Francisco, California, December 9, 1987.

final tableau revealed the characters in a celestialized saloon, wearing halos and drinking glasses of milk. Willam and Lew built the barroom set themselves.

Willam's *Nothing Doing Bar* was only marginally related to Jean Cocteau's 1920 *Nothing Doing Bar*, better known by its French title, *Le Boeuf sur le Toit*. Cocteau, in collaboration with Darius Milhaud, Paul Fauconnet, and Raoul Dufy, had devised a barroom scenario purposely devoid of logical meaning in which stock characters played by circus clowns with oversized cardboard heads moved in slow motion against Milhaud's score of popular Brazilian dance melodies.[25] Instead, Willam's creation to that score bore a family resemblance to Lew's *Filling Station* in its use of popular social dance steps and in the structure of the plot. Both brothers' ballets presented a variety of characters in a setting presided over by a benign authority figure (the bartender and the station attendant), and those characters played out personal dramas (with significant doses of humor) in an overall plot that climaxed in violence.

The earlier success of *Filling Station* may have legitimized American themes in Willam's eyes, but if so, Willam was slow to follow Lew's lead. Willam's sole work with an overtly American setting and contemporary plot material, *American Interlude* (1939, also known as *And Now The Brides*, 1940), had enjoyed a mixed success at best. Since that time, Willam had built his reputation on his productions of nineteenth-century classics (*Swan Lake*, *The Nutcracker*); Massine-inspired depictions of European society (*Old Vienna* and *Winter Carnival*); ballets based on Spanish dance traditions (*Amor Espagnol*, *Blue Plaza*, and *Parranda*); short comedic works derived from European sources (*Le Bourgeois Gentilhomme* and *Dr. Pantalone*); and the occasional non narrative étude-

---

[25] For a collection of period documents describing the creation and performance of this work, see Jean Cocteau, "Le Boeuf sur le Toit," *Drama Review* 16.3 (September 1972): 27–45. Lynn Garafola analyzes Cocteau's approach to this ballet, in which the characters were "moving decor," in *Diaghilev's Ballets Russes* (New York: Oxford University Press, 1989), 102–3.

(*Sonata Pathétique* and *Danza Brillante*). *Nothing Doing Bar* represented his first foray into American popular culture in ten years. It was an American ballet, to be sure, but it differed from *Filling Station* in that it was also a period piece, grounded in a colorful setting ostensibly distant from contemporary concerns.[26]

*Nothing Doing Bar* also demonstrated one aspect of Willam's insensitivity to contemporary social issues. Just as Cocteau's ballet had included a "Negro Boxer" and a "Piccaninny Billiard Player," Willam's had a blackface doorman named "Yo-Yo."[27] In Paris in the 1920s such racial stereotyping had occasioned no comment in the press; but the premiere of Willam's version at the high school auditorium drew a protest from the Labor Youth League, which threatened to picket the opera house performance if the character were played in burnt cork. Lew's army experiences had prompted the serious treatment of racial issues in *Blackface*. By contrast, Willam did not take this charge of racism seriously; instead, he argued that the doorman character was not intended as a racial slur but was simply a caricature, like the other figures in the ballet, based on an established theatrical tradition. A special jury, which included representatives from the National Association for the Advancement of Colored People, concluded that "playing the role in blackface would do no good and that playing it in whiteface would do no harm, artistic or otherwise."[28] For once Willam, who was used to depending upon easily recognized types and stock characters, was forced to come to terms with the meanings behind the stereotypes. He conceded the point, and the doorman appeared without burnt cork at the opera house that May.

[26] When Arlene Croce viewed a production of *Nothing Doing Bar*, performed by the San Francisco Ballet in 1980, she wrote, "And instead of 1950 I'd have guessed the date of Willam Christensen's *Nothin' Doin' Bar*...to be 1938 (because of its resemblance to *Filling Station*)." Quoted from "Americana," in *Going to the Dance* (New York: Knopf, 1982), 315.

[27] James Harding, *The Ox on the Roof* (London: Macdonald, 1972), 77.

[28] Cobbett Steinberg, *San Francisco Ballet: The First Fifty Years* (San Francisco: San Francisco Ballet Association, 1983), 58.

As part of the unified family effort to pull off the limited spring season, Lew partnered Vollmar in *Swan Lake*, Act II, and Celena Cummings in *Parranda* in the one opera house performance that May. Afterward, Alexander Fried noted in the *Examiner* that Lew was "a handsome, able dancer, but not quite the virtuoso one would wish."[29] This condescending review, coming less than a fortnight after Lew's forty-first birthday, may have provided the impetus for his retirement from the stage. In contrast to the highly publicized final performances that punctuate the careers of some dancers, Lew Christensen, the outstanding American *danseur noble* of his generation, hung up his slippers without ceremony or farewell. If Lew had ever been driven by a need for the adulation of an audience, he was now satisfied. Perhaps more to the point, his abilities as a performer no longer measured up to his own high standards. Even so, in this final performance Lew unwittingly influenced a dance student with whom he would someday work as a close associate. Richard Carter was taking ballet lessons as part of his preparation to be a jazz dancer, but after watching Lew cross the opera house stage in powerful leaps even at this late stage in his career, Carter decided to pursue a career in ballet.[30]

The Christensen brothers needed new aspirants, as they continued to lose the dancers they had trained to larger and better-paying companies. That season saw the loss of the emerging soloist Jimmy Hicks, who went on to renown in Ballet Theatre under the name Scott Douglas.[31] Since his early San Francisco days Willam had lost many soloists to larger companies – James Starbuck, Harold Lang, Janet Reed, Mary Burr (to musical theater and Ballet Theatre), and Onna White. More recently, Mattlyn Gavers (née Gevurtz) had gone to Ballet Society (she would eventually become a ballet mistress at the Metropolitan Opera), and Norman Thompson had left

[29] Alexander Fried, "Full House Hails S.F. Ballet," San Francisco *Examiner*, May 15, 1950.

[30] Interview with Richard Carter, San Francisco, California, March 7, 1988.

[31] Performance Chronology, Property of San Francisco Ballet, 1949.

to join Sadler's Wells.[32] Jocelyn Vollmar, who had spent the previous year in New York, would soon leave again, emerging later as a leading ballerina in the Grand Ballet du Marquis de Cuevas and the Borovansky Ballet. In addition to the inevitable lure of New York, economic factors made it impossible for the Christensens to keep their dancers in San Francisco; the brothers had too little money to pay dancers salaries that reflected their true worth. One departing dancer was heard leaving the studio in tears, lamenting, "I'd have stayed if I could just make $25 a week."[33]

To combat this problem, Willam directed much of his energy into the community, raising awareness of the company and drumming up support from the guild. He gave interviews and speeches, formed a second branch of the guild on the peninsula south of San Francisco, and drummed up performing opportunities that kept his dancers before the public at charity events and social gatherings. All his skills with people, his gentlemanly manners, suavity, sense of humor, and ability to shine in a crowd, helped to build the company's foundation of support. Willam had never worked with the assured financial backing Lew had enjoyed in Kirstein's companies; he was used to overseeing, and being ultimately responsible for, all aspects of his company's functioning, and much of his time went to cultivating patrons.

During the brothers' vaudeville years, Willam had been the act's front man while Lew was its uncontested virtuoso. Now, twenty years later, a parallel situation developed. Willam remained the undisputed chief of the San Francisco troupe, but as Lew's students advanced technically they acquired an increasingly significant place in the company. This led to a schism among company members. Many of the dancers trained by Lew were loyal to him personally and to the kind of movement he demanded. Their sense of what mattered in ballet and what style of ballet they wanted to perform differed from that of the older dancers, whose values

---

[32] Beatrice de Baltazar, "Westward the Ballet," *Dance*, September 1947, 41.

[33] Marc Rivette, "Ballet-By-The-Bay," *Opera and Concert*, May 1950, 21.

and performing styles had solidified in Willam's classes. Feelings of fraternal commitment and mutual support still bound the brothers, but undercurrents of jealousy and divisions stirred the dancers and strained even family relations. Lew, who characteristically avoided conflict, tried to persuade Willam that if they ignored the schism it would die down. But Willam was eaten away by a feeling that he was losing control over the company that had once been his alone.

That feeling was aggravated by his awareness that Harold sympathized with Lew's vision of ballet. The two younger brothers saw eye-to-eye on certain matters of training and technique that were not part of Willam's canon. (This, of course, was based on their shared experience of working with Vladimirov and Balanchine at the School of American Ballet.) Moreover, Willam and Lew had fundamental philosophical differences about repertory. Willam continued to maintain that nineteenth-century classics should be the proper underpinning for any ballet company's repertory, while Lew had no interest in doing ballets that had been done before and thought rather in terms of creating new works. The company schism reflected the clashing of the brothers' aesthetic styles: Willam's *demi-caractère* repertory (inspired by his work with Fokine and the example of Massine's narrative ballets) versus Lew's neoclassicism, which was a direct outcome of his work with Balanchine as well as his own efforts to come to grips with the technical possibilities of the balletic vocabulary. In this aesthetic tug-of-war, Harold lined up behind Lew.[34]

Willam went off to the University of Utah a second summer, uneasy over the strength of his position in the company he had nurtured through good times and bad for over a decade. In Salt Lake City he set the dances for

---

[34] Another reason Harold favored Lew as a partner may have been that he had once discovered that Willam was teaching a weekend ballet class in his garage for his daughter and her friends without contributing their tuition to the SFB School's pot. Harold was firmly against the brothers' teaching independently in addition to teaching at the family school; such a course could only weaken the latter. Stephen C. Steinberg and Nancy Johnson interview with James Graham-Luján, San Francisco, California, November 6, 1985, [interview A].

Gounod's *Faust* and for *Promised Valley*, a musical by the local composer Crawford Gates depicting the pioneer settling of Utah. Helen Tamiris had first choreographed *Promised Valley* in 1947, when its premiere celebrated the centennial of the Mormons' arrival in the territory. (According to Maurice Abravanel, Tamiris simply reused the Indian dances she had created for *Annie, Get Your Gun* and didn't create anything new or particularly appropriate for the Mormon saga.[35]) Critics observed that whereas the choreographic high point in the original production had been Tamiris's own solo early in the play, Willam's version more properly built to a climax in the cricket scene, when the arrival of cricket-eating seagulls rescued the struggling settlers from certain famine. Once again Willam earned the respect of the local directors and won praise from audiences and critics. He found the university productions such a positive experience that he began to contemplate the advantages of a permanent position in an academic setting.

While Willam spent his second summer at the University of Utah, Lew once again joined Balanchine's company as ballet master, this time for the 1950 summer season at Covent Garden. Lew shouldered much of the responsibility of preparing the dancers for their first bid for recognition across the Atlantic. In addition to rehearsing the Balanchine repertory, Lew restaged *Jinx* and came out of retirement temporarily to fill the nondancing role of the father in Balanchine's revival of *Prodigal Son*.

Lew helped Balanchine in a variety of ways, depending upon the need of the moment. For example, the skullcaps for *Prodigal Son* needed wreaths around them, but there was no money to commission the work from the wardrobe department, so Lew and Balanchine took the skullcaps to the top of the City Center theater and finished them together on the sly.[36] The two worked together on close terms, and for relaxation they sometimes went to western movies together.

---

[35] Interview with Maurice Abravanel, Salt Lake City, Utah, November 25, 1987.

[36] Barbara Newman, *Striking a Balance* (London: Elm Tree Books, 1982), 39.

But Lew and Balanchine were not personally close. Lew respected his teacher's genius as a choreographer, but he knew Balanchine the man too well to put him on a pedestal. Lew always addressed the Russian as "Mr. Balanchine," a point of formality and respect that pleased the latter. Lew later explained of their relationship that although Balanchine was "a close professional friend," he was not "an intimate friend."[37]

The London season was not a happy period for Lew, although *Jinx* drew fairly positive reviews. Perhaps it was still emotionally difficult for him to accept that he was no longer performing (other than the non dancing appearance in *Prodigal Son*). As a featured dancer Lew had been an inspiration to Balanchine's creative process; as ballet master he was a dependable assistant but no longer of central interest to the choreographer. Moreover, the role of Balanchine's assistant contained built-in frustrations. Janet Reed, who also experienced the transition from favored performer to ballet mistress, later reflected that as a favored dancer for Balanchine, one was "his angel." But when assisting him in another capacity, especially as ballet master or mistress, "he made sure that you did not take too much authority because he had to be the one link with his dancers."[38] So while the summer season raised anew the possibility of Lew's future ties to New York City Ballet, it reconfirmed the constrictions that would surely face him within that company. At age forty-one, Lew had outgrown the role of Balanchine's personal assistant; he wanted his own company and an opportunity to put into practice the knowledge he had gained.

Kirstein still saw in Lew the fulfillment of his ideals for American ballet and hoped that he would remain with the company as backup and heir apparent, ready to take over the reins when Balanchine died. Lew, however, realized that because he was only five years younger than Balanchine, he

---

[37] Craig Palmer interview with Lew Christensen, KQED.

[38] Telephone interview with Janet Reed Erskine, November 5, 1988.

was too close in age to inherit the latter's company. Meanwhile, back in San Francisco, Lew now had a vested interest in the success of the San Francisco Ballet and a group of trained dancers he could work with as he pleased. He and Gisella returned to San Francisco in the fall of 1950 with a new commitment to his work there. He later reminisced, "I had mixed feelings. I was walking away from the center of dance, but at the same time I wanted to be more creative. I wanted to solidify all I had learned."[39] Kirstein felt the loss deeply; later in life he reflected:

> *[Lew] was raised in the West; his West remained a magnet. After the war, I had hoped he would stay in our orbit, implement our company, if there was one, teach in our school when a succession proved necessary. All this might have been possible – except for the Hitler war. We won the war; the West won Lew.*[40]

Cut off from the immediate influence of his former New York associates, Lew felt the need for a collaborator in San Francisco, someone to reduce the sense of artistic isolation he felt at being so far from Kirstein and Balanchine. By early 1951, James Graham-Luján, who had proven a loyal friend since the 1941 South American tour, had finished his graduate work at Columbia. Lew invited him to join the Christensens in San Francisco in a loosely defined advisory capacity. That February, Graham-Luján flew out to lecture at an exhibition of ballet designs at San Francisco's De Young Museum and then stayed on, moving in with Lew and Gisella until he found a place of his own.[41]

---

[39] Stephanie Von Buchau, "Native Dancer," *Ballet News*, May 1982, 26.

[40] Lincoln Kirstein, *Thirty Years* (New York: Alfred A. Knopf, 1978), 302.

[41] Stephen C. Steinberg and Nancy Johnson interview with James Graham-Luján, San Francisco, California, [n.d., interview G]. The exhibition, which was a public relations move to draw attention to the San Francisco Ballet, proves once again Kirstein's personal commitment to Lew's success. Costume designs by Pavel Tchelitchew, Paul Cadmus, and Eugene Berman were culled not only from the Kirstein and Tchelitchew collections of the Museum of Modern Art but also from Balanchine's personal collection. The fact that the exhibition was a joint project of the Ballet Guild and the De Young Museum Society was facilitated by Geraldine McDonald Bodrero's membership on the boards of both institutions.

In many ways, Graham-Luján brought to Lew the same desirable characteristics Irving Deakin had contributed to his partnership with Willam. The Christensens would benefit from Graham-Luján's formal education and concomitant writing skills, his understanding of theatrical life and of the needs of a ballet company, his New York connections, and his own artistic ideas and taste. Having just received a generous disbursement from his family, Graham-Luján was not overly concerned about remuneration for his new work in advancing the cause of the San Francisco Ballet. Only *after* he had arrived in San Francisco was he informed, by Willam rather than by Lew, that he would earn fifty dollars a week.[42] Graham-Luján's talents were put to work writing articles for the Ballet Guild's quarterly newsletter, which ran stories about the company's progress, letters of encouragement from the guild's president (Geraldine McDonald Bodrero, who had recently remarried), and excerpts from favorable reviews of recent performances. With generosity of spirit, Willam promoted Graham-Luján around town, introducing him to supporters and newspaper critics, lining up speaking opportunities for him, and teaching him by example how to ingratiate the ballet into the life of the community.

While Willam contemplated a move to academia, the brothers pulled together one last time to stage a series of performances in San Francisco at the Commerce High School that culminated in a night at the opera house. The 1951 performances would prove to be a watershed season for the family enterprise in San Francisco. For the first time, Lew was listed as a codirector of the company with Willam, and both collaborated with Graham-Luján in the creation of new repertory.

For Willam, Graham-Luján devised the libretto of *Les Maitresses de Lord Byron*, a loosely historical treatment of the poet's relations with key women in his life, set to Liszt's Concerto No. 1 in E Flat Major. Willam's insistence on the

---

[42] Stephen C. Steinberg and Nancy Johnson interview with James Graham-Luján, San Francisco, California, October 7, 1985, [interview D].

role of romance in ballet obtained once again as his choreography traced Byron's amorous relations with a series of women. (The dancers stumbled over the French title and humorously referred to the work as "Lord Byron's Mattresses.") When Alfred Frankenstein reviewed the work at its premiere at the high school auditorium, he characterized *Maitresses* as a ballet without a plot. This distressed Willam greatly. He wanted to pull the ballet from the line-up scheduled for the opera house performance and was furious when he realized that he could not because the publicity for that date had already been printed. Loath to be criticized again, Willam made subtle changes in the ballet, such as renaming Byron's assistant the "Muse of Poetry," and Frankenstein reversed his judgment after the opera house engagement.[43] Willam's reaction was one of jubilant relief; unlike choreographers who never read reviews and claim not to care what the critics say of their work, Willam cared very deeply about the reception of his works and how his talents were perceived in the community. (Two years later, when Willam choreographed *The Creatures of Prometheus*, Alexander Fried's highly critical review in the morning paper made Willam feel "like taking poison," but when Alfred Frankenstein's positive review came out that afternoon, Willam felt fine again.[44]) Willam enjoyed and found reassurance in outward signs of success: positive reviews, recognition and awards, status symbols such as fancy cars, and belonging to a prestigious club.

Graham-Luján displayed an affinity for French titles that season; for Lew he concocted a pretext for classical technique entitled *Le Gourmand*. Lew's creations for his advanced students to this point had been brief choreographic essays, in the manner of musical études, allowing him to explore limited areas and build his students' strength and

---

[43] Interview with Willam Christensen, Salt Lake City, Utah, May 1, 1987; Alfred Frankenstein, "Season's Finale by S. F. Ballet Co.," *San Francisco Chronicle*, May 21, 1951.

[44] Conversation with Willam Christensen, October 7, 1988.

performing skills.[45] Although ostensibly a tongue-in-cheek depiction of a *cordon bleu* banquet, *Le Gourmand* was actually Lew's most technically demanding work to date in San Francisco, a sort of graduation exercise for the advanced students who had come of age under his tutelage. Set to Mozart's Divertimento No. 15, *Le Gourmand* constituted Lew's first full-blown, independent work in the neoclassical style since his departure from New York.[46]

For the pretext of the ballet, Lew and Graham-Luján worked out a libretto in the form of a menu, from *hors d'oeuvres* to dessert, with help from the *maître d'hôtel* of a prominent San Francisco restaurant. The names and identities of the dancers contained hidden puns for insiders: for example, Carolyn George, a strong jumper, was cast as the Filet of Sole *Sauté* Meunière (italics added).[47] George, who would later join New York City Ballet, was partnered by Willam, who danced on stage for the last time at age forty-eight in the role of the Grilled Lobster. For Gisella, who danced the *pêche flambée* of the dessert course, Lew devised a variation on one pointe to protect her still weak Achilles tendon.[48] Lew's leading female students, Nancy Johnson and Sally Bailey, appeared respectively as the "Pheasant in Love with Wild Rice" and a "Plucked Chicken," while others represented side dishes and trimmings in whimsical costumes by New York designer Leonard Weisgard.[49] Costuming provided the key to recognizing the intended delicacies in *Le Gourmand*; the movement itself involved no pantomime or literal depiction of the dishes' supposed identities.

[45] Interview with Nancy Johnson, San Francisco, California, December 9, 1987.

[46] Stephen C. Steinberg and Nancy Johnson interview with James Graham-Luján, San Francisco, California, [n.d., interview G]. It is worth noting in passing that Balanchine used the same Mozart Divertimento one year later for *Caracole* (1952).

[47] Stephen C. Steinberg and Nancy Johnson interview with James Graham-Luján, San Francisco, California, [n.d., interview G].

[48] Olga Maynard, "The Christensens: An American Dance Dynasty," *Dance Magazine*, June 1973, 54.

[49] Steinberg, *San Francisco Ballet*, 59.

**30**  Gisella Caccialanza in *Pêche Flambée* costume from *Le Gourmand*, 1951.
Photograph by Balon, courtesy of Willam F. Christensen

Lew wanted *Le Gourmand* to end with the bloated title character alone on stage, in the same tradition as *Filling Station* and *Jinx*, but Graham-Luján insisted otherwise. With Weisgard's collusion, Graham-Luján devised a trick ending which he felt gave the audience a proper sense of release: the dancers converged on the gourmand, unfolded a portion of his costume, and created the illusion of a tablecloth with the gourmand's head, transformed into that of a pig, at the center. Lew had doubts about this vaudeville-style climax calculated to elicit applause, but he allowed himself to be persuaded by his collaborators. The creation and transformation of images before the audience's eyes had been one of his choreographic preoccupations since his first creation for Ballet Caravan, *Encounter*. In a sense, *Le Gourmand* continued in this vein, except that the transformed image sprang from costuming and props rather than from the bodies of the dancers.

The whole 1951 spring season was a family affair; the brothers depended heavily upon each other, and upon Gisella, to stage their new works and to revive former repertory. In addition to the family cooperation in *Le Gourmand*, Harold, at age forty-six, reprised his role of the befuddled motorist in *Filling Station*, and Gisella re-created her original role, the inebriated society girl, despite her weakened tendon. (She changed the choreography so that all *relevés* were done on her good leg.) To outsiders, the facade of family unity showed no cracks. But relations among family members were strained by the continuing division between Lew's advanced class and the older company members loyal to Willam. The future of ballet always belongs to the young, and Willam's older dancers, who had no intention of learning to dance to Lew's specifications, may have seen the writing on the wall. Willam cast his dancers with a sense of loyalty and expected that loyalty to be returned, while Lew used whoever could best perform his choreography. Sharing the company between brothers meant that dancers could not rehearse with Lew and Willam at the same hour; somehow the personnel had to be divided, and that naturally happened along more-or-less generational lines. Willam felt the tension more keenly than

Lew, whose approach to dealing with the dancers' divided loyalties was to negate the problem by ignoring it. Willam had been considering the advisability of moving to an academic environment since the previous fall; now he pursued the option seriously.

Isabell, who had lived with Willam since her husband's death, felt the tension between her sons. She was concerned over the strained family atmosphere and upset by the thought of the boys splitting up, but in this matter she was powerless. That April, four days after *Le Gourmand*'s premiere, she heard a news report that her cousin, George Albert Smith, who was then president of the Mormon church, had passed away. Isabell suffered a stroke that evening and never regained her full strength.

Tension within the company was not the only reason, or perhaps even the major reason, that Willam made his move. Mignon's doctors had warned that he must simplify their existence or she would collapse. A university setting would eliminate from their lives the upheavals and anxieties associated with a professional company; in addition to the less hectic pace and the non-union environment, a university would provide steady pay, insurance coverage, and medical benefits. Perhaps Willam also sensed that his era of leadership in San Francisco was coming to an end. He let his interest be known and received job offers from Stanford and from the University of California at Berkeley. Either campus would keep Willam near his beloved San Francisco, but in both cases he would teach in the College of Physical Education.[50]

At this, Willam absolutely balked. He could not bring himself to teach ballet alongside track and football. His wholehearted love for ballet included a firm conviction that ballet was a "fine art" and should be accorded respect as such. So Willam telephoned Lees at the University of Utah and

---

[50] Interview with Willam F. Christensen, Salt Lake City, Utah, November 20, 1987. The author has been unable to find supporting evidence for this claim. Sometimes when telling this story, Willam claims that at Stanford he would have been put in the Music Department.

asked him about an offer he had made during Willam's summer sojourns. The question of where Willam would be placed institutionally was the single greatest issue in his thinking, and Lees was willing to be accommodating. At the University of Utah, as at most colleges in the early 1950s, modern dance classes were offered through Physical Education. So Lees devised a plan to hire Willam in the Speech Department, which was placed institutionally in the College of Letters and Sciences. The Speech Department produced musical theater as well as straight drama; in that setting, Willam would be able to choreograph musicals and teach courses in "theater ballet." Willam accepted the offer, choreographed the university summer productions a third summer, and stayed on to join the faculty in the fall of 1951.

Decades later, when asked why he had left San Francisco for Salt Lake City, Willam habitually explained the move as a consequence of his wife's illness. A questioner digging deeper might learn about the failure of the Civic Ballet and Willam's ensuing despair. But what probably drove Willam from the Bay Area was the collapse of his vision of the family ballet business: each member contributing his or her talents and expertise under Willam's orchestration, the whole enterprise fueled by Willam's ambition. Lew was now a fully formed professional in his own right, ready to try his hand at running a company, and his training represented the path to the future. In later years these two brothers would once again be personally close, committed to each other's welfare, and temperamentally more compatible than either was with Harold. But now the San Francisco company was not big enough for both of them; it was time for Willam to move on.

# 11

## WILLAM STARTS ANEW IN
## SALT LAKE CITY (1951–1963)

Willam arrived in Salt Lake City the summer of 1951 largely unaware of the controversy that surrounded his permanent appointment at the University of Utah. The dispute over his role in university productions actually dated to two years earlier when Willam had initially been hired for summer work. At that time Dr. C. Lowell Lees, head of the Speech Department and director of the summer musicals and operas, wanted to hire the modern dance choreographer Charles Weidman instead. Lees was thinking in terms of Broadway rather than the Met; by 1949 Weidman's credits included work on nearly a dozen productions, including *As Thousands Cheer*, *Spoon River Anthology*, and *Sing Out, Sweet Land* (with Doris Humphrey). Opposing Lees was Maurice Abravanel, the recently appointed director of the Utah Symphony Orchestra, who felt that Weidman's style would be wrong for the planned operatic repertory. The conductor lobbied for Willam, whom he had never met, on the grounds that anyone who had staged opera ballets successfully at the San Francisco Opera for over a decade would be able to provide choreography appropriate to the tone of the anticipated productions.[1]

Abravanel's opinion carried weight because he brought such a wealth of professional experience to Utah. The Greek-born, Swiss-trained musician had studied with the conductor Bruno Walter, had worked closely with the composer Kurt Weill for many years (Abravanel conducted the first performance of *The Seven Deadly Sins* and the Paris premiere of

---

[1] Abravanel's version of the controversy surrounding Willam's hiring at the University of Utah is contained in the transcript of the author's interview with Maurice Abravanel, Salt Lake City, Utah, November 25, 1987.

Weill's "Little" *Mahagonny* suite), and had made his conducting debuts at the Berlin State Opera, the Paris Opéra, and the
Metropolitan Opera by the age of thirty-three.[2] In addition to
his work in opera, Abravanel had worked with Weill on
Broadway and knew the dance world from the inside; he had
been Balanchine's conductor for the choreographer's short-
lived but artistically significant Les Ballets '33 and had
also conducted for Markova–Dolin.[3] When Abravanel went
to Utah in 1947 to assume what he initially considered a
temporary post, he found talented and committed instrumentalists with whom he felt he could make a truly professional
orchestra. Abravanel chose to stay in Salt Lake City, where
he built the Utah Symphony into a strong cultural force in
the western United States and then won national recognition
through touring and recordings.[4]

The dispute over whom to hire to choreograph the
1949 summer festival ended in Willam's favor when Gail
Plummer – the manager of the university's theater, Kingsbury
Hall – remarked that the Christensens came from Brigham
City. Abravanel latched onto this at once. Someone from Utah
would understand the values of the local population, which
was still over sixty per cent Mormon, and would be able to
work well with the state's young people.[5] Willam got the job,
and his success in 1949 won over Lees and prompted the
second summer invitation.

---

[2] For a complete account of Abravanel's career, see Lowell Durham, *Abravanel!* (Salt
Lake City: University of Utah Press, 1989).

[3] Abravanel claims that when he was a young assistant conductor at the Metropolitan
Opera in 1934, he was the only conductor that Balanchine felt made the dancers look
good. Interview with Maurice Abravanel, Salt Lake City, Utah, November 25, 1987.

[4] For an overview of the Utah Symphony, its growth under Abravanel and national
reputation, see "Utah Symphony Orchestra" in Robert R. Craven, ed., *Symphony
Orchestras of the United States: Selected Profiles* (New York and Westport, Conn.:
Greenwood Press, 1986), 407–11.

[5] *Statistical Information on The Church of Jesus Christ of Latter-day Saints and Church
University Needs.* Presented to National Advisory Committee of Brigham Young
University Development Program, April 1958. Special Collections, Harold B. Lee
Library, Brigham Young University.

Lees wanted a choreographer year-round, and he wanted someone like Willam with an established reputation and plenty of professional experience. But his plans to lure Willam to Utah on a permanent basis faced opposition from several quarters. The political climate militated against hiring a big-name artist at an institution run by state tax money because Governor J. Bracken Lee was committed to cutting taxes and keeping down state costs. Moreover, a group of local dance teachers protested against Willam's hiring, doubtless fearing competition should he decide to teach privately on the side. But the stiffest opposition came from within the university itself, where the modern dance faculty had very legitimate concerns. Lees had proposed to the head of the modern dance program, Elizabeth Hayes, that dance be taken out of Physical Education, placed institutionally with the other arts, and given its own department, with Willam at its head.

This plan had Hayes's faculty up in arms, for they were well aware of Willam's prejudice against modern dance. During his two summer visits he had made deprecating remarks about modern dance similar to the witty put-downs published under his name in the 1946 *Dance Magazine* article. Hayes and colleagues such as Virginia Tanner had worked hard to build a respected program and had just succeeded in establishing a dance major. Their financial situation was still precarious. Receiving no funding for concerts from the administration, they relied heavily on ticket sales and token support from student body funds. Their program had promise but was not yet strong enough to endure competition from another dance form – not to mention from Willam – for student interest, audiences, and box office proceeds. If the university suddenly embraced ballet, they reasoned, modern dance might lose the interest of both students and audiences, and even the meager funding they received would be in serious jeopardy.[6] Accepting Willam as the administrator of their program would be certain suicide. They openly protested Lees's plan.

---

[6] Interview with Elizabeth Hayes, Salt Lake City, Utah, November 15, 1988.

Hayes countered by suggesting that since Lees wanted to have a choreographer for his musicals, he could hire Willam and put him in the Speech Department (as the Theatre Department was known during much of the 1950s). A. Ray Olpin, the university president, supported this solution, despite the cost-cutting political climate. Olpin understood that Willam had kept a ballet company going in San Francisco by producing finished dancers from local young people rather than by depending upon imported dancers from New York. If Willam could train dancers in California, he could surely train them in Utah, too. So Willam joined the University as a full-time faculty member in the Speech Department as of the fall of 1951.[7]

It was a time of mixed emotions for forty-nine-year-old Willam, who viewed the move as his retirement from the world of professional dance. Although in one sense he was retreating from the emotional pressures and financial uncertainty of that world, by nature he was not a quitter. And Willam arrived in Utah with a wealth of professional experience to share. He had been tempered emotionally by years of concern over Mignon's condition. The Willam who returned to Utah in 1951 was more mature, and more cautious, than the impetuous young Portland ballet teacher who had gone to San Francisco in hopes of inheriting Serge Oukrainsky's post. His performing career was behind him, but he came fully armed with the knowledge of how to train dancers and how to build and run a company. Willam still had the drive and the desire to use that knowledge, to build up a program in his new setting based upon the full range of his experience in San Francisco.

---

[7] Willam's new position was unusual because, by and large, modern dance programs in departments or colleges of Physical Education dominated dance activity in America's universities during this era. But his appointment was not totally without precedent: Texas Christian University had hired David Preston to teach ballet in 1949 and had been the first university in the United States to place its Dance Department in the College of Fine Arts. Letter from Nancy Carter, Secretary of Department of Ballet and Modern Dance, Texas Christian University, to Debra H. Sowell, April 26, 1989.

The irony of being hired as a professor when he had never even gone to college, and had pulled his youngest brother out of high school, did not prevent Willam from jumping into his new setting with every appearance of confidence. He bravely informed reporters that he intended to build good dancers in the fertile soil of Utah's cultural climate, with its tradition of pioneer dancing and church social dance events.[8] Willam's professional orientation distanced him from certain traditional concerns of modern dance educators, particularly that of finding a desirable balance between the mastery of movement technique and the development of creativity and freedom of expression.[9] In Willam's mind, skill development took top priority; his goal was a conservatory-style program modeled upon European ballet academies, with technique classes ranging from beginning to advanced levels and supplementary training in character dance and pantomime. He drew on his memories of Mascagno's descriptions of Italian training and probably upon Gisella's descriptions of her training at La Scala as well. For several years he required students of different levels to wear tunics of a different color for each level, just as Gisella remembered doing at La Scala.[10] Willam's success in the academic environment stemmed from the harmonious match between his abilities and the university's expectations. Apparently he faced no pressure to "publish or perish"; a fact sheet in his personnel file includes titles of productions staged instead of works published. By

---

[8] James Fitzpatrick, "The Dancing Master," no paper, clipping in University of Utah Ballet Archives, Box 8, Scrapbook 3, Special Collections, University of Utah Marriott Library, Salt Lake City.

[9] Richard Kraus and Sarah Chapman, *History of the Dance in Art and Education*, 2nd ed. (Englewood Cliffs, N.J.: Prentice-Hall, 1981), 258.

[10] Diana Muriel Cole, "Utah Ballet – A Unique Development in the World of Dance," (master's thesis, University of Utah, 1971), 75. Cole reports that beginning classes always wore black leotards and pink tights. Intermediate classes wore tunics: Intermediate III wore pale blue, Intermediate II wore hot pink, and Intermediate I wore yellow. Only members of the "company class" were allowed to select their own attire for class. Gisella recalls that during her training at La Scala, dancers wore color-coded tunics according to class level; interview with Gisella Caccialanza Christensen, San Bruno, California, September 29, 1987.

the end of 1953 Willam had been advanced in rank from associate professor to full professor, a clear indication that his
efforts were looked upon favorably by the university administration. The students ignored professorial titles and referred
to him with a mixture of respect and affection as "Mr. C."

As Willam made the switch from a family-run school
and company to a state-supported university, he understood
the necessity of patience. Remembering one of Uncle Frederic's
favorite sayings, "Don't get too fast too quick," Willam kept
the students' early appearances simple and waited until his
new dancers had acquired greater skills before attempting
serious productions. At the end of his first academic year,
he presented the students not in concert but in a lecture-
demonstration, admitting frankly, "This program is my beginning. It is neither ostentatious nor glorified. It points the
direction."[11] At the same time, Willam was open and friendly
with the press. He granted interviews to reporers, shared the
glories of his past achievements, warned his new audience
that developing a high-caliber company would take years,
and expressed the hope that the people of Salt Lake would
bear with him while the process took its course.[12]

That process began in earnest Willam's second full
year in Salt Lake City (1952–1953) when he formed a student
performing group, the University Theatre Ballet (hereafter
UTB), and planned a five-night season for the end of that
school year. By Christmas a group of balletomanes had
formed the Utah Ballet Society under the leadership of Enid
(Mrs. Walter) Cosgriff, the wife of a local banker. A lawyer
from the university drew up the group's charter, proving once

---

[11] Cole, 13. Excerpts included in the lecture-demonstration represented three different styles of ballet: the classical (*Waltz of the Flowers* from the *Nutcracker*), the
dramatic ("a mysterious stranger comes into a girl's life, only to leave her," set to
Schubert's *Wanderer Fantasy*), and the dance pantomime (a "demi-mondaine" story
"à la Slaughter on Tenth Avenue" to music of Gershwin). Jim Fitzpatrick, "Debut
of Ballet Whets City's Appetite," *Salt Lake Tribune*, May 1952 clipping in University
of Utah Ballet Archives, Box 5, Folder 36, Special Collections, University of Utah
Marriott Library, Salt Lake City.

[12] Fitzpatrick, "The Dancing Master," *ibid.*

again that Willam's new academic setting had built-in benefits. In the best Mormon pioneer tradition, members of the
Society supported the dancers in direct and practical ways,
such as bringing homemade dinners to the students during
rehearsal periods when the dancers were too busy to go out
for food.

One of Willam's major challenges was to change the
mind-set of dancers who had been trained in local studios
and were geared to a recital format in which each dancer was
automatically given a solo. Willam reformed these expectations, making a polished corps his first objective and the
group to which his student dancers aspired.[13] With the corps
in place, Willam hired guest artists to fill principal roles and
add a touch of glamour to the student company's annual
spring seasons. In UTB's early years, guest stars such as Leon
Danielian from the Ballet Russe, and Nancy Johnson, Gordon
Paxman, and Sally Bailey from the San Francisco Ballet attracted supportive audiences for the students' performances.
Guest artists also provided models of finished artistry for the
students and balanced the company's repertory by bringing
with them other choreographers' works: in 1954 André
Eglevsky of New York City Ballet performed Balanchine's *Pas
De Trois* (Minkus) with Johnson and Bailey, and in 1955 Lew
brought the whole San Francisco Ballet to present his still new
*Con Amore*. (In order to make that engagement economically
feasible, most of Lew's company slept on Mrs. Cosgriff's floor.)

During his first several years at the University of
Utah, Willam revived the most successful ballets of his San
Francisco Ballet period rather than producing new works.
Between 1953 and 1957 he restaged his abbreviated version
of *Swan Lake, Romeo and Juliet, Old Vienna, Divertimenti* (a
pastiche of Tchaikovsky ballet excerpts), *Nothing Doing Bar*,
and *Parranda*. Willam doubtless altered these ballets to suit
the capabilities of his student performers, but this dependence
on past repertory provides a clue to his priorities. For some
choreographers, having a company is the necessary means to

[13] Nigel S. Hey, "Professor in Ballet Slippers," *Dance Magazine*, May 1963, 52.

the desired end of creating new works, whereas in Willam's case, having suitable repertory was a necessary step toward his desired end of having a ballet company. The difference is one of emphasis. Generally speaking, Willam enjoyed chore- ographing, but for him this was a period of training new dancers rather than one of dealing with new issues as a choreographer.

When the question of UTB performances first arose, the university Music Department assumed that its student orchestra would accompany the student dancers. But Willam refused to present his company with anything but the best accompaniment available; in his mind, that meant collaborat- ing with the Utah Symphony. He insisted on the best possible music both as a matter of principle and in realistic recognition that his still unfinished dancers needed that kind of support to lift the quality of the spectacle. "If I had first-rate dancers, I could do that [ballet] with two pianos," he once commented to Abravanel. "But I don't; I need an orchestra."[14] Fortunately, Willam had Abravanel's support from the beginning. Implicit in the maestro's decision to settle in Utah and foster musical culture in that state had been a commitment to opera and ballet as well as symphonic music.

As Willam began his career in academia, Abravanel became Willam's closest tie to the professional world he had left behind. Abravanel had also made the commitment to stay in Utah and could understand Willam's decision to come to Salt Lake City. Their mutual respect deepened quickly into a solid friendship. Each knew the other's field well enough to have an informed respect for his friend's accomplishments. Abravanel openly praised Willam's talents, comparing his ability to devise movement appropriate to the capabilities of his dancers with that of Balanchine. Interacting with the maestro filled Willam's need for professional association; no longer could he drop by the Bohemian Club and be sure of camaraderie with artists and gentlemen. Abravanel's

---

[14] Interview with Maurice Abravanel, Salt Lake City, Utah, November 25, 1987.

presence in the cultural outpost of Salt Lake City lessened Willam's sense of isolation and loss in leaving San Francisco.

Cutting his ties with San Francisco was the most painful aspect of accepting the full-time position in Utah, and in fact Willam did not make a clean break. He maintained his membership in the Bohemian Club until 1953. And just as he had kept the Portland school running during his first two years in San Francisco, Willam initially maintained his ties with the San Francisco Opera. Lew, conditioned by his experiences at the Metropolitan, disliked choreographing for the opera and gladly ceded that unpleasant task to Willam after the 1951 season. Willam viewed the opera much more favorably. His initial success in San Francisco had come through the opera establishment, as had his position in society. He returned to San Francisco each summer from 1952 through 1957 and again in 1959 to set the ballets for the fall operas, some years handling the job alone, some years splitting the responsibility with Lew. In 1953, Willam even staged an ambitious production of Beethoven's *The Creatures of Prometheus*, which shared the bill with Strauss's *Electra* but was overshadowed by the success of that opera.[15]

During these California stays, Willam depended on substitutes and teaching assistants to keep his program running at the university. To help carry the load of technique classes, he hired a British dancer, Barbara Barrie, who had performed with the Opéra Comique in Paris and René Blum's Ballet de Monte Carlo in the late '30s and with the International Ballet in London during the '40s. The Salt Lake television personality Ron Ross also danced and assisted Willam with teaching and productions in the early years at the university. With such support, Willam was able to keep one finger in the pie in San Francisco.

Shortly after settling in Salt Lake, Willam began teaching on the side at Purrington's dance studio just south of the

---

[15] "San Francisco Opera Visits Los Angeles," *Musical America*, November 15, 1953, in Willam F. Christensen Clipping File, Dance Collection, The New York Public Library.

**31** Willam Christensen conversing backstage with Bené Arnold, *Creatures of Prometheus*, 1953.
Photograph by Tracy, courtesy of Willam F. Christensen

university. Mignon helped with secretarial duties to the extent she was able. Willam justified this "moonlighting" by citing the high cost of his wife's medical care, but another factor provided just as much incentive. As long as Willam was limited to a pool of students whose training was gained solely, or mostly, during the university years, he would never have dancers sufficiently skilled to make up a company of able performers. He no longer had the luxury of Harold and the SFB School behind him, supplying a steady stream of well-trained dancers. By teaching privately, Willam was able to find promising bodies, train them as he wished while they were still young and flexible, and then add them to his company when they were old enough to matriculate. Two of the university's most influential figures, Lowell Durham (a professor of music and dean of the College of Fine Arts) and Sterling McMurrin (dean of the College of Letters and Science), were aware of Willam's off-campus activities because they had daughters taking class from him at Purrington's studio. Fearing that other professors, and especially his own dean, might take a dim view of his unsanctioned extracurricular activities, Willam explained to both men his need for extra income and bodies trained at a young age. Both were sympathetic, but McMurrin did not like the atmosphere of the dingy basement studio, so he approached Olpin with the proposal that Willam be allowed to teach his younger students right on campus through the Extension Division. (That university department, later renamed the Division of Continuing Education, administered courses for adults and workshops for young people.) Olpin approved, and Willam was able to transfer his private teaching to the university, which simplified the logistics of his teaching schedule and facilitated his self-imposed task of building a creditable ballet company in Salt Lake City. The Extension Division courses were announced in the university's catalogue for the first time during the 1954–1955 academic year.[16]

---

[16] Cole, 22.

As Willam and Abravanel exchanged stories and shared memories of their past achievements, Willam naturally spoke of the evening-length ballets he had staged in San Francisco. Abravanel decided that when Willam's student company was ready, the two friends, with their respective forces, would produce the *Nutcracker* in Salt Lake City. Willam waited four years and watched his dancers progress. As the women improved, he increased the difficulty of their repertory and shortened the skirts of their costumes. By 1955, he judged the company ready for a holiday *Nutcracker*, assuming that guest artists would fill the primary roles. Lew had purchased a new production in San Francisco the previous year and had offered Willam the old SFB costumes and décors by Antonio Sotomayor. With the promise of support from the symphony, everything was in place until a controversy at the university nearly cancelled the planned production. Plummer, the manager of Kingsbury Hall whose chance comment had helped in Willam's hiring, had decided that the ballet would lose money because in Salt Lake City the Christmas holidays were traditionally a slow time for theatre. Determined to prevent a fiasco, he wrote to President Olpin that the production would fail. Plummer won Mrs. Cosgriff over to his position and persuaded the university's theatre committee to drop the production. Abravanel and Willam protested that the university had given its word and that the Symphony's December schedule had been arranged around the *Nutcracker* commitment. Abravanel even suggested that if the university would not sponsor the *Nutcracker*, Willam's dancers and the Symphony could perform the ballet at the old Orpheum Theatre downtown. This incensed Olpin, who considered the ballet group university property, so the administration took the *Nutcracker* under consideration one more time.[17] Ultimately, the university agreed to a contract

---

[17] My description of the controversy surrounding this first Utah *Nutcracker* is based on numerous conversations and interviews with Willam and on the interview with Maurice Abravanel, Salt Lake City, Utah, November 25, 1987. Abravanel stresses that to produce the *Nutcracker*, the university was forced to enlarge Kingsbury Hall's orchestra pit to make room for the symphony.

with the Utah Symphony in which the orchestra essentially subsidized the ballet. The players received slightly less than their usual pay, the orchestra management received no overhead or administrative fee, and Abravanel, in a heroic gesture that extended many years, conducted all *Nutcracker* performances free of charge.

In San Francisco, Harold and Lew protected the interests of the family institutions by selecting children for *Nutcracker* casts only from the company school. But in Utah, Willam turned his *Nutcracker* into a project of community (rather than just university) interest by drawing on children from several different Salt Lake dance studios. From Lew's company he borrowed Sally Bailey and Conrad Ludlow, to dance the Sugar Plum Fairy and Cavalier, and filled the rest of the parts with a cast of over seventy-five local dancers. Among that number was Willam's daughter Roxanne, who appeared as one of the children in the party scene and re-appeared in Act II as one of the clowns under the voluminous skirt of Mother Buffoon. The large cast brought with it the interest of family and friends, who snapped up tickets for the week of performances, allowing Willam to add an extra matinee and still boast of sold-out houses.[18] His opponents were proven decidedly wrong by the tremendous response, and *The Nutcracker* became a holiday tradition in Salt Lake City, as it had in San Francisco.

During the controversy leading to that *Nutcracker*, Mrs. Cosgriff withdrew her support from the student company, but a new patron soon stepped forward: Glenn Walker Wallace. The daughter of a wealthy Salt Lake banker, Mrs. Wallace had studied piano, voice, and dance in Boston during her youth and maintained her interest in music through conspicuous philanthropy. Her husband, John M. Wallace, was chairman of Walker Bank and a former mayor of Salt Lake City. Mrs. Wallace had supported the small Salt Lake

---

[18] Conrad B. Harrison, *Five Thousand Concerts: A Commemorative History of the Utah Symphony* (Salt Lake City: Utah Symphony Society, 1986), 212; interview with Willam Christensen, Salt Lake City, Utah, May 1, 1987.

Symphony as early as 1924, and through her support the Utah Symphony was founded in 1939. A hard working fund-raiser, Mrs. Wallace served as the Symphony's vice-president until 1947 and then as its president until 1952.[19] Dividing her time between Utah and California, Mrs. Wallace's idea of going to the ballet was to attend the Ballet Russe when she was on the West Coast. But as Willam's program grew and his dancers improved, Mrs. Wallace became a key benefactor of the student company.

Cooperation among the three brothers continued despite the distances involved. In order for Willam to return to help Lew with the fall opera seasons, Harold would step in and teach Willam's classes in Salt Lake City.[20] Lew allowed his dancers to perform as guest artists with Willam's company; or, as seen from the other side, Willam provided Lew's top dancers with an extra source of income and additional performing experience. As Willam's dancers graduated and had no local professional ballet company to employ them, several went to Lew; for example, in 1957, Wayne Brennan and Gerrie Bucher joined the San Francisco Ballet for the company's Far East tour. Fraternal cooperation helped Willam put a professional face on his university performances because the brothers "shared" guest artists; each hired Danielian in '53 and Eglevsky in '54. Willam even imported Lew's conductor, Earl Bernard Murray, for the annual May concerts. Sharing dancers and conductors meant coordinating performance schedules; throughout the 1950s, Lew presented his *Nutcracker* before Christmas, and Willam presented his the week following.

Mutual support also extended to nitty-gritty, behind-the-scenes work. When Willam staged *The Creatures of Prometheus* in San Francisco, the ballet was not accorded a lighting rehearsal because all available stage time was given

---

[19] "Glenn Walker Wallace Dies, Longtime Crusader for Arts," *Deseret News*, December 31, 1988.

[20] Cole asserts that Lew, Harold, and SFB dancer Janet Sassoon were "often guest teachers." Cole, 31.

to the opera appearing on the same bill. The opera's stage director assumed that the ballet performance would have to be cancelled and told the dancers to go home, but Lew (who knew the lights his brother wanted) saved the night by going up to the bridge and cuing the lights for the first performance himself.[21] In view of such devoted cooperation, it is little wonder that those who knew nothing of the strains within the San Francisco Ballet at the time of Willam's departure accepted the notion that his move had been prompted only by his wife's deteriorating health. Differences between family members were never aired in public. As Ann Barzel later recalled, the common perception when Willam left San Francisco was that another ballet job had opened in the West and the Christensens were "dividing the spoils," like members of the Rothschild family each taking over a different European city.[22]

After the 1955 *Nutcracker*, Willam continued to recycle ballets from his most successful San Francisco repertory, but in 1957 he began to choreograph new works again. Between 1957 and 1963 he created several new ballets of significant length. When Abravanel suggested that Willam choreograph Mendelssohn's *Italian Symphony*, Willam responded with *Crown of Joy*, a ballet populated by Grecians, Dionysus, Fauns, the Three Graces, and an assortment of "Sprites" (Water, Wood, and Flower). To music of Ibert, Willam created *Caprice De Paree* (later known as *Les Bijoux du Mal*), a dramatic ballet about a prostitute and a jewel thief who vie over a string of stolen pearls while the happier world around them is represented by a succession of *gens qui passent*: a wedding party, a circus parade, cancan dancers, and so on. To the music of Mozart, he created the plotless works *Symphonia* and *Variations in Contrast*. A "ballet buffo" in 1960 called *La Fille Naive*, with a story fashioned by Willam himself, centered on a young girl who hides an escaped prisoner from a general

---

[21] Interview with Willam Christensen, Salt Lake City, Utah, October 7, 1988.

[22] Interview with Ann Barzel, Winston-Salem, North Carolina, February 15, 1988.

and his bumbling soldiers. With its provincial farmhouse setting reminiscent of *La Fille Mal Gardée*, *La Fille Naive* was in itself rather naive; the plot combined romance, vaudeville style sight gags involving the soldiers, and a *deus ex machina* ending revealing the escapee to be a nobleman. Two years later Willam choreographed the more sinister *Garden of Evil* (Shostakovitch), a contemporary reworking of the Faust theme in which the devil figure woos the female protagonist and causes her to go mad. The 1963 *Toxcatl* exemplified the support Willam was able to draw upon in the university environment: Gaylen Hatton, a graduate student in music (and the husband of dancer Marianne Johnson Hatton), composed the score, while theatre professor Keith Engar worked out the libretto about an Aztec fertility rite, with assistance from the Anthropology Department.

Willam won the interest of Salt Lake City musicians when he set a ballet for his students to Stravinsky's *Octet for Double Woodwind Quartet* in 1957. Entitled *Something in the Wind*, the ballet involved four couples and changing moods as the dancers wore white gloves, black gloves, and then gloves of varying colors.[23] When invited to stage this work for New York City Ballet the following year, Willam recognized the compliment but feared the consequences. Now accustomed to gauging his efforts to a student level, he feared he had lost touch with professional standards and the expectations of New York audiences. In the event, Willam's apprehensions were justified. *Octet* (as the work was renamed for NYCB) was received as a minor work and damned with faint praise. Walter Terry declared it "tidily fashioned and quite harmless."[24] John Martin more graciously conceded that while *Octet* would "set no worlds afire," it was nevertheless "a smart and engaging piece of choreography, [with] very nice invention, fresh manipulation of the group, and general

---

[23] Nancy Reynolds, *Repertory in Review: Forty Years of the New York City Ballet* (New York: Dial Press, 1977), 192.

[24] "New York City Ballet," *New York Herald Tribune*, December 3, 1953.

geniality."[25] Perhaps the ballet's weakest point, when seen on Balanchine's home turf, was that Willam's choreography did not satisfactorily convey the richness and complexity of Stravinsky's music. Martin observed, "There may well be more in the score than this choreographic small talk would suggest."[26]

Willam left New York smarting under *Octet*'s tepid reception. Still, his failure to take New York by storm at this late date in his career did not adversely affect his fortunes in Salt Lake City. In Utah his efforts were received appreciatively by a community whose dominant population combined political conservatism with idealistic notions of beauty. Willam considered his beliefs a private matter and did not affiliate with the LDS church until the mid-1990s, but through the years he accommodated its influence with the same tact that had helped him promote ballet in San Francisco's social circles. His father's Brigham City experiences with the church were left to the past; no good could come from resurrecting the old controversy, and Willam was far too savvy and self-disciplined to indulge in a personal crusade that might threaten his professional goals. His Utah upbringing had effectively prepared him to live in the predominantly Mormon environment of Salt Lake City. While Willam resented losing talented female dancers to marriage and pregnancy, the plots of his narrative ballets reinforced conservative family values. Moreover, his idealistic rhetoric about the beauty and refinement associated with ballet as an art form were seen as consonant with a statement from one of the Latter-day Saint Articles of Faith: "If there is anything virtuous, lovely, or of good report, or praiseworthy, we seek after these things."[27] From an LDS viewpoint, the development of an accomplished

---

[25] Martin quoted in Reynolds, 192.

[26] *Ibid.*

[27] Joseph Smith, "The Articles of Faith of The Church of Jesus Christ of Latter-day Saints," reprinted in *The Pearl of Great Price* (Salt Lake City: The Church of Jesus Christ of Latter-day Saints, 1981), 61.

ballet troupe in the Mormon capital confirmed again the pioneer vision of the latter-day Zion in which the desert would
"blossom as the rose."[28] Utah would continue to provide a
supportive host community for Willam's efforts.

Willam and Mignon's son, William Lee (who went by
"Lee"), rebelled against ballet training as a boy and did not
stay long with the family after its move to Utah. Instead, he
joined the army at age eighteen during the Korean conflict.
Roxanne, however, loved to dance and took ballet through
the Division of Continuing Education program in her youth.
She performed as a child in *The Nutcracker* and worked her
way into the company when she was old enough to enter the
university. Roxanne benefited from her father's profile in the
community and the last years of her mother's mobility. One
of her favorite childhood memories is of going to postperformance parties with them and falling asleep on mink coats
piled up on beds in back rooms.[29] During the family's early
years in Salt Lake City, Mignon maintained her outwardly
cheerful demeanor, grieving privately as her multiple sclerosis began to restrict her mobility. As she lost the ability to
walk, Willam often carried her around the house. He also had
a pool installed in their backyard so that the family could
swim together. But despite such attentions, family life was
organized around the demands of his performing group. His
standard response when asked by Mignon if the family might
do some activity was, "My dear, I would love to – after the
show."[30]

Willam pushed forward his program from year to
year, adding classes and making requirements for the ballet
degree instituted in 1955 ever more rigorous. By 1962, a
University of Utah student desiring to major in ballet entered
the program on probation and had to earn "major status" by

---

[28] Isaiah 35:1; see Chapter 1.

[29] Interview with Roxanne Christensen Selznick, Salt Lake City, Utah, August 27,
1990.

[30] *Ibid.*

the end of his or her sophomore year. Students took daily technique classes and performed in UTB productions while also filling requirements in beginning and advanced character dance, pantomime, pas de deux, choreography, ballet history, dance history, anatomy, and zoology, in addition to taking a year of French and courses in music, theater, and art.[31] Ballet students also performed in the musicals and opera productions that Willam choreographed as part of his departmental obligations, with the result that students gained experience in a variety of genres.

Despite his openness to other theatrical forms, Willam habitually steered students away from modern dance. When his dancers asked Willam if they should take modern dance along with ballet, he always encouraged them to stick with ballet, asserting that they could switch to modern later if they wanted to. He saw ballet as the more demanding, and hence preferable, form of training, and if he realized that there might be arguments for taking modern dance instead, he never let on. This stance was not atypical in the 1950s and 1960s. The pioneers of modern dance had initiated the separation from ballet in their quest for new movement vocabulary and greater freedom of expression; Willam simply did his part to maintain the gulf separating the two forms. The experimental climate that would allow modern choreographers to set works on major ballet companies and would witness ballet stars performing in experimental ensembles did not yet exist. From the vantage point of the 1990s, when contemporary dance companies employ dancers skilled in both ballet and modern dance technique, Willam's singleness of vision seems a waste of the resources at hand. In addition to Virginia Tanner's widely acclaimed creative dance program for children, the University of Utah spawned two highly successful modern dance companies in this era, Repertory Dance Theatre and the Ririe-Woodbury Dance Company. In a climate of mutual cooperation and cross-over training, an open-minded Willam

---

[31] Cole, 74–75.

might have entered into a dynamic period of experimentation. But the focus that made Willam successful as a promoter of ballet was characterized by narrowness of vision, an assumption of the superiority of ballet over other theatrical forms. Although he learned over time to soft-pedal both his intolerance of homosexuality and his biases against modern dance, every once in a while he would let slip a statement showing his true feelings. Years later, reflecting on his experience with modern dance, he admitted, "When they just had the pianist and drum on stage and improvised, I'd get bored as hell."[32]

The proof of Willam's teaching lay in the developing skill and artistry of his students. In his first decade at the University of Utah, he nurtured talents that would go on to national recognition: Michael Smuin and Kent Stowell both performed in his 1955 *Nutcracker*, and Finis Jhung was Franz in Willam's first Utah *Coppélia* (1958). Even in conservative Salt Lake City, Willam continued to attract and train strong male dancers. Not known nationally but of importance locally were the talents of Ron Ross, Phil Keeler, Josef France, Wayne Brennan, Rowland Butler, John Hiatt, Rocky Spoelstra, Christopher Fair, and Gary and Steven Horton (whose father Dr. W. H. Horton was a cochairman of the Utah Ballet Society and one of UTB's major supporters). Among the women, Janice James rose through the ranks to dance the Sugar Plum Fairy with Jacques D'Amboise as her Cavalier and was invited by the NYCB star to join Balanchine's company in 1963. Other women prominent locally were Kay Ford, Carolyn Anderson, Karen Cheney Shores, Marianne Johnson Hatton, Nila Speck Horton, and Victoria Morgan (who went on to Lew's company). One of his most dependable performers in those early years was Barbara Hamblin, who now chairs the University of Utah's Ballet Department. Sandra Birch Allen, the mainstay of Brigham Young University's ballet program for decades, was another early company member who has extended Willam's influence to several generations of ballet students.

---

[32] Interview with Willam Christensen, Salt Lake City, Utah, November 20, 1987.

**32** Willam Christensen demonstrating a lift with University of Utah students Kent Stowell and Carol Ann Price.
Courtesy of Special Collections, University of Utah Marriott Library

As his dancers improved, Willam expanded the activities of the student company. In 1958 he broke the limited pattern of May and December concerts by adding a spring engagement in southern Utah (Cedar City); two years later he added UTB's first out-of-state *Nutcracker*, performed in Idaho prior to opening in Salt Lake City. At age fifty-eight, Willam was still pushing for a greater audience, looking for opportunities to tour and to gain recognition; the academic setting had become the new means to his original end. At the same time, the role of ballet within the department itself grew stronger over the years; the department's name was changed from "Speech" to the "Department of Speech and Theatre Arts" in 1956 and then to the "Department of Speech, Theatre Arts, and Ballet" in 1961.[33]

---

[33] Cole, 19, 30, and 54.

Slowly Willam acquired colleagues whose combined talents constituted a strong production staff. In 1959 Gordon Paxman left the San Francisco Ballet, where he had been one of Lew's leading male soloists and the company's ballet master, to join Willam in teaching and administering the student company. In 1962, another one of Lew and Harold's trusted assistants, the SFB ballet mistress Bené Arnold, moved to Salt Lake City to teach ballet privately and go back to school. Arnold was inevitably drawn into the circle of Willam's productions; she helped set *Con Amore* on UTB for the May 1963 season and eventually joined the university faculty. In 1962, Willam's department also hired set designer Ariel Ballif, who brought experience gained in professional productions along the East Coast and at Brandeis University.

With these individuals and the continued support of Abravanel, Willam had all the major elements he needed to stage ambitious productions. His advanced students could now teach lower-level technique classes in the Extension Division, which allowed Willam to devote more of his time to advancing the company. In 1962 a local benefactor donated the full orchestral score of *Swan Lake* to UTB, probably an indication that Willam hoped to stage the complete ballet in Utah. Willam was thinking in terms of large productions again; he optimistically informed a local reporter that he wanted to enlarge the shallow stage of Kingsbury Hall by sixty-five feet to the rear.[34] That fall the university catalogue listed UTB's company class for the first time and added a course entitled "Production." And the next year, Willam's pioneering efforts at the University of Utah attracted nationwide attention in a feature story in *Dance Magazine*.[35] In response to this laudatory profile, other dance teachers wishing to establish ballet programs in university settings wrote to Willam to inquire how he had structured his

---

[34] Richard O. Martin, *Salt Lake Tribune*, December 26, 1961, 12; quoted in Cole, 57.

[35] Hey, 48.

curriculum.[36] After a dozen years in Salt Lake City, Willam had proven the wisdom of Olpin and Lees' bold hiring decision. He had won solid recognition for the University of Utah and had brought his student company as close to being a professional troupe as he could within an academic setting.

---

[36] Interview with Willam Christensen, Salt Lake City, Utah, May 1, 1987. Correspondence in the Utah Ballet Archives, Box 11, Special Collections, University of Utah Library, Salt Lake City, contains examples of such requests for information, from dance teachers on the East and West coasts. Ruthanna Boris also inquired about the University of Utah program when she set up her dance program at the University of Washington. Telephone interview with Ruthanna Boris, October 7, 1988.

# 12

## LEW TAKES OVER THE SAN FRANCISCO BALLET (1951–1960)

Shortly after Willam's departure for Utah, representatives from the Bohemian Club visited Lew's class with an eye toward inviting him to join their organization. Lew all but ignored them. The youngest Christensen was neither interested in nor capable of being the kind of company director Willam had been: a meeter and greeter, a social presence in the community, the debonair artist mixing with patrons at parties and exclusive gatherings. The brothers' leadership styles reflected their sharply contrasting personalities. Willam had paved the company's way in San Francisco with his warmth, confidence, and loquacious charm. In this respect, everything that Willam was, Lew was not. As a *danseur noble*, Lew had commanded the attention of entire opera houses, but he was quiet and retiring in a crowd and at formal social occasions. In interviews he deflected personal questions and focused on his work instead of his feelings. Just as Lew had allowed his older brother to "front" for the vaudeville act during their years as partners, he now delegated many public appearances and speaking engagements to Graham-Luján. Lew also cut down on the "charity ball" performances Willam had encouraged to keep the dancers in the awareness of the city's social set. Lew disapproved of the dancers being asked to perform on inappropriate floors and decided instead to hold out for professional performance opportunities.

As the administrative structure of the family business mutated following Willam's departure, Harold retained his control over the school and over most financial matters (including the company's box office income). Lew, who had formerly shared the title of co-director with Willam, was now the sole director. Because Lew relied on Graham-Luján for advice on artistic matters, the latter was named artistic director. Lew knew his own weakest area to be his formal education, and Graham-Luján provided the necessary support in that area. Lew respected his colleague's knowledge and may have even seen him as a link to Kirstein's world in New York. In Ballet Caravan, Lew had had the luxury of working with artistic collaborators, and Graham-Luján provided a partial continuation of that support in San Francisco. He suggested designers for costumes and sets, and he provided the libretti for most of Lew's ballets between 1951 and 1956, although he did not always claim them on the program because he feared a steady stream of Christensen–Graham-Luján works would make the company appear artistically impoverished. Graham-Luján also picked up some of the slack created by Willam's departure by fraternizing with the critics and working with the guild, which raised money to cover the cost of new productions.

When Lew inherited the directorship of the San Francisco Ballet from his older brother, he also inherited performing opportunities that Willam had lined up before leaving. In addition to choreographing the fall opera season that first year, Lew collaborated with other Bay Area artists on *The Standard Hour,* a series of thirteen half-hour television programs sponsored by Standard Oil that featured San Francisco's performing arts institutions. Each week's program included a variety of numbers contributed by solo instrumentalists, opera singers, the San Francisco Symphony, and the San Francisco Ballet. In his first concerted effort for television, Lew learned to choreograph for the camera lens, taking into consideration camera angles and toning down large movements and gestures that were appropriate for the big opera stage but not for the more intimate scale of the television screen. The resulting repertoire consisted of short ballets (six to ten minutes to fit into the half-hour variety format) or excerpts of longer works: a *commedia dell'arte* pantomime, a version of Rossini's *Boutique Fantasque,* excerpts from *The*

*Nutcracker* and *Les Sylphides*, and so on.[1] Each ballet was handsomely costumed and filmed with complete décor in a large auditorium across the bay in Richmond, where the latest technical equipment had been installed. Lew worked tirelessly to meet the creative challenge of turning out fresh choreography week after week, rising early for long days of filming beginning with 6:00 a.m. makeup calls. When the shows aired in the fall of 1952, Ruby and Harold bought a television set just so that they could watch the series. In the final analysis, Standard Oil found the innovative series too costly to continue, but SFB benefited from the exposure gained in that pilot series. After the broadcast of the thirteen segments, the *Chronicle* reported that *The Standard Hour* had "succeeded in removing the 'mink and mothball odor' that many Americans associated with ballet and opera."[2]

In the midst of what was arguably the company's busiest fall since Willam's touring days, two misfortunes touched the brothers' lives. In September 1951, their mother, Isabell, who had been living with Harold and Ruby since Willam moved to Utah, was hospitalized following a second stroke. The brothers knew her death was imminent. It was a hard time for all three but especially for Lew, who had an unusually strong fear of death and dreaded his mother's passing. Lew's army experiences had not hardened him to death; instead, he rarely talked about dying and could not bring himself to attend funerals. During Isabell's final hours, Harold forced Lew to accompany him to the hospital.[3] Together they sat by their

---

[1] Interview with Nancy Johnson Carter, San Francisco, California, December 11, 1987; Cobbett Steinberg, *San Francisco Ballet: The First Fifty Years* (San Francisco: San Francisco Ballet Association, 1983), 107. Steinberg reports that Lew also choreographed a Walpurgis Night Ballet from *Faust* but that the flesh-colored costumes made dancers Sally Bailey and Nancy Johnson appear nude on the screen, so the work was considered unsuitable.

[2] Steinberg, *San Francisco Ballet*, 107.

[3] Interview with Harold Christensen, San Anselmo, California, September 25, 1987. Virginia Johnson also comments that Lew talked about death with her only once during their many years' association, and Ruby confirms that Lew rarely if ever attended funerals. Interview with Harold Christensen and Ruby Asquith Christensen, San Anselmo, California, March 2, 1988.

mother's bed and held her hands as she expired. That ordeal over, Lew left the usual family responsibilities to Harold, who traveled to Salt Lake City with his mother's remains. Isabell was buried in a family plot next to her husband, Chris.

Less painful but still a major source of concern and stress was the loss of the studio on Van Ness Avenue. The building that had housed the brothers' efforts since Willam's early days in San Francisco was changing hands and would no longer be available for either the school or the company. In November, the brothers transferred their operations to the Theatre Arts Colony on Washington Street (between Polk Street and Van Ness Avenue), where they shared rehearsal studios with a resident theatre company. The Theatre Arts Colony, with its courtyard, garden, and polished woodwork, had a pleasing ambience and adequate studio space, but it lacked sufficient space for offices and the storage of sets and costumes.[4] The brothers and their dancers enjoyed the building's atmosphere and worked around its drawbacks. Gisella's sister Clelia, whose husband had recently passed away, ran the desk.

Having a new location underscored the changes wrought by Willam's departure as Lew took over the company. Unlike the even-tempered, generally upbeat Willam, Lew was susceptible to moods. He usually kept problems bottled up inside himself, forcing even Gisella to guess what was troubling him, until he had worked through a solution and was ready to confide in others or settle the problem openly. His dancers grew to appreciate his self-control, as he would seldom break into a rage or lambaste a performer. On the other hand, he was not effusive and used praise sparingly; his dancers could not hope for constant positive reinforcement and assurances of his approval. During periods of quiet, perhaps melancholic introspection, Lew would play his 'cello for hours at a time or doodle elaborate designs and caricatures. Perhaps he found comfort and release in music, as did

---

[4] Steinberg, *San Francisco Ballet*, 147; interview with Nancy Johnson Carter, San Francisco, California, December 11, 1987.

his father, Chris, who had retreated to playing the violin when the family lost its property in Brigham City.

Lew was more reserved in the classroom and rehearsal studio than his older brother. Whereas Willam would call out corrections or encouragement throughout a combination, Lew watched his dancers quietly after giving them instructions and gave corrections only when they had finished. He generally came to a rehearsal already knowing the movement he wanted to set and maintained strict discipline, demanding the dancers' focused attention. Lew would teach new choreography one step or short phrase at a time, having the dancers go back to the beginning of the sequence after each addition. He felt that if the dancers concentrated, they would not need to ask questions. Not all the dancers accustomed to Willam's gregarious ways felt comfortable working with Lew; when Finis Jhung joined the San Francisco Ballet, he found Lew cold and aloof in comparison to Willam.[5]

Although their careers seem parallel in many respects, Willam and Lew had different aims in life, at least in San Francisco. Bristling with confidence, Willam wanted the best ballet company in America. He was never daunted or intimidated by the success of others and always thought in terms of seizing opportunities to build the company at hand. But Lew, who recognized the towering nature of Balanchine's genius, admitted only to more modest goals. Over the years, Lew would discourage the extravagant claims of his own P.R. agents, claiming, "I don't want the best company in the world. I just want a damn good company."[6]

Willam always focused on getting a show together and getting it on the boards. As a choreographer he was generous to his dancers, giving them movement that flattered their abilities. Lew was more exacting in his technical demands and insisted upon dancers coming up to his standards of execution. On one occasion the *Bluebird Pas de Deux* was

---

[5] Interview with Finis Jhung, New York, New York, May 16, 1988.

[6] Interview with Harold Christensen, San Anselmo, California, December 3, 1987.

scheduled as part of an evening's performance, but the male dancer who was to appear had not mastered the choreography to Lew's satisfaction. Rather than changing the choreography to suit the dancer's abilities, Lew pulled the piece from the program.[7] Lew also cared about his dancers' weight; he monitored their diets when the company toured and had scales placed prominently in the lobby outside the studios.[8] On Lew's birthday, the dancers would bring him a lean steak instead of a birthday cake.

With Willam's departure, Geraldine McDonald Bodrero's personal involvement with the ballet quickly declined. Willam had made the guild president's job more of an adventure: he showed her the designers' sketches, invited her to costume reviews, and asked her opinion on matter of style and taste. Willam valued Mrs. Bodrero's sophistication and encouraged her involvement in company affairs. Lew, however, had his own ideas, and he did not turn to Mrs. Bodrero for advice. Perhaps Lew felt a need to establish his authority over the company; at least initially, his actions made it clear that he was the new boss and that things would be done his way. It must be remembered, too, that in the 1950s the San Francisco Ballet was still essentially a family business, a for-profit concern that provided for Lew and Harold's families (thanks largely to the school). Tuition from the school supported the company, whose existence brought prestige to the school. The company itself had no board of directors, no independent administrative wing, no comptroller, no development or publicity departments, and only minimal secretarial help. The only "board" was the board of the Ballet Guild, whose responsibility was to raise funds for new productions. The guild would pay for the construction of sets and costumes and then "lend" them to the company for performances.

One reason Lew depended less upon Mrs. Bodrero was that he had a firm ally, an abiding source of professional

---

[7] Interview with James Graham-Luján, San Francisco, California, March 4, 1988.

[8] Conversation with Virginia Johnson, Corte Madera, California, March 2, 1988.

support, albeit at a distance, in Lincoln Kirstein, whose interest in Lew's professional activities and welfare did not end when the latter moved west. Even before Willam left and Lew took over as company director of the San Francisco Ballet, Kirstein aided Lew, and thus, indirectly, his company, from afar. The revival of *Filling Station* in San Francisco in February 1951 was possible because Kirstein loaned Lew the original Paul Cadmus scenery and costumes for that ballet. And an exhibition entitled "Ballet Design," jointly sponsored by the De Young Museum and the SFB Guild, featured items from the personal collections of Balanchine and Kirstein, on loan from the Museum of Modern Art. At approximately the same time as Willam's departure for Salt Lake City, Kirstein and Lew announced an exchange policy between their respective companies; New York City Ballet and San Francisco Ballet would exchange soloists and repertory.[9] The following year (April 1952), Balanchine sent Vida Brown to San Francisco to set *Serenade*, and Alexandra Danilova led the company in that work's premiere at the War Memorial Opera House.

The exchange policy might best be described as a formalization or institutionalization of the Kirstein–Christensen friendship. Lew and Graham-Luján saw it as a way of lifting SFB's status in its home city; being connected with the New York City Ballet could only add prestige to the local troupe, and positive reviews of SFB dancers in the New York press would add a touch of glamour to the company's personnel. The exchange policy was, certainly, less crucial to the fortunes of the New York City Ballet, but it temporarily fulfilled Kirstein's purpose of keeping Lew within NYCB's orbit. Kirstein wanted Lew as ballet master for Balanchine's company again and was holding the post open: during 1950, 1951 and most of 1952, NYCB programs and printed company rosters listed no ballet master when Lew was not with that company but often listed Vida Brown as "Assistant to the

---

[9] Cobbett Steinberg, "Lew Christensen: An American Original," *Encore* 1.3 (Summer 1984): 9.

Ballet Master." When it came to running a company, Kirstein
and Lew shared a certain temperamental compatibility that
neither shared with Balanchine. Jacques D'Amboise relates that
unlike Balanchine, after the war Lew was "very military and
strict."[10] Kirstein's writings about the School of American Ballet
also employ military metaphor, and he has explained of the
company, "I've always had the idea – particularly after my
Army experience – that we were conducting a military operation."[11] Lew's ongoing ties to New York City Ballet after World
War II doubtless stemmed more from his solid friendship with
Kirstein than from his professional relationship with Balanchine.

Kirstein saw his hopes fulfilled in October 1952, when
Lew accepted the post of NYCB's Administrative Director.
Press releases in New York and San Francisco explained that
Lew would be "in direct charge of the company" and would
"also mount works of his own."[12] Lew's announced plans
included a new work, *Gloriana*, to Edward Elgar's *Enigma
Variations*, in honor of the forthcoming coronation of Elizabeth II.
The following month, Lew's name was added to the company's roster, which now listed George Balanchine, artistic
director; Jerome Robbins, associate artistic director; Leon
Barzin, musical director; Lincoln Kirstein, general director;
and Lew Christensen, administrative director. The inclusion
of Robbins as associate artistic director and the placement
of Lew's name after Kirstein's suggest that Robbins would
second Balanchine in contributing new works to the repertory, while Lew's role would be to assist in the running of
the company, as he had done as ballet master in Ballet
Caravan and Ballet Society.

Lew could legitimately take on responsibilities in
New York while heading the San Francisco Ballet because the
latter had such a limited performing schedule. Following the
unusual opportunities afforded by *The Standard Hour* series,

[10] Interview with Jacques D'Amboise, New York, New York, January 12, 1989.

[11] "Conversations with Kirstein – I," *New Yorker*, December 15, 1986, 45. Later in the
same interview Kirstein compares the School of American Ballet with West Point.

[12] George Freedley, "Off Stage – And On," *New York Morning Telegraph*, October 15,
1952.

the company had reverted to the pattern of limited engagements that came its way seasonally: a few performances of *The Nutcracker* in December, a brief spring season in April, occasional performances sprinkled around the Bay Area, and a midsummer open-air performance in Stern Grove, followed by the dependable but artistically unsatisfying fall opera season. Opera productions excluded, the San Francisco Ballet performed in the War Memorial Opera House only three nights in all of 1952 and gave a grand total of eleven performances the entire year. With such limited opportunities in California, Harold running the school, and Willam returning to take over opera duties every fall, Lew was free to go to New York. Thus began a two-year, bicoastal period during which he divided his time between San Francisco and New York.

Lew's appointment to administrative positions in both companies facilitated the exchange program between New York and San Francisco. The spring of 1953 witnessed the full flowering of the program when the San Francisco Ballet staged Balanchine's *Concerto Barocco* and *A La Françaix* and the New York City Ballet produced *Filling Station* and Lew's latest creation, *Con Amore*. Both the year and circumstances within NYCB favored the revival of *Filling Station*, which had premiered in the Ballet Caravan repertory fifteen years earlier. The talents of eighteen-year-old Jacques d'Amboise afforded Lew a Mac who could fill the technical demands of the role Lew had originated at the peak of his own powers. Presented as an example of the company's roots from the Ballet Caravan era, *Filling Station* delighted the audience and met with an overwhelmingly positive response from the critics.[13] John

---

[13] As if concerned that the audience would find the revival dated or backward-looking in the context of the company's more recent repertory, Kirstein gave an almost apologetic curtain speech on the first night of *Filling Station*, explaining the ballet's significance as "the first work to be commissioned completely – score, decor and choreography – by the Ballet Caravan." John Martin, "Ballet Revives 'Filling Station,'" *New York Times*, *Filling Station* Dance Clipping File, Dance Collection, The New York Public Library. The ballet's program note also presented *Filling Station* as, if not a museum piece, at least an example of Ballet Caravan's repertory "to indicate the origins of the repertory of the New York City Ballet." New York City Ballet program, September 1, 1954.

Martin found the "spirited and hilarious farce" a "thoroughly good show" and a "first-rate little piece in its modest way."[14] Walter Terry welcomed *Filling Station* in comparable glowing terms, and Robert Sylvester asserted that Lew's work was "funnier and [had] more pantomime value than, for instance, the sainted 'Fancy Free.'"[15] Janet Reed attracted a large share of the honors for her portrayal of the inebriated socialite, and the role of Mac thrust d'Amboise to new prominence within the company.

Within a month of the successful revival of *Filling Station* came the NYCB premiere of Lew's newest work, *Con Amore*, starring SFB dancers Sally Bailey and Nancy Johnson as guest artists. The New York appearance of Lew's students provided the impetus behind the new ballet. Bailey and Johnson had risen from Lew's advanced class to become soloists in the company; they were strong technically and ready for starring roles, but they needed reviews from the New York press to be taken seriously as performers in San Francisco. So Graham-Luján created a libretto with two leading female roles with the goal of getting East Coast exposure for San Francisco's ballerinas. (Graham-Luján, who remembered Balanchine's vivid tales of his amorous conquests, sent the ballerinas to New York with a warning to Balanchine to "leave them alone."[16]) It was a sign of Balanchine and Kirstein's trust in Lew that they agreed to feature two of his dancers in a work performed by the New York company.

The tone and structure of *Con Amore* resulted from careful strategy. Lew and his librettist decided that a humorous work had the best chance of immediate audience acceptance.

---

[14] Martin further observed that while *Filling Station* might be no more than a vaudeville-style cartoon of a ballet, "it came over on its own terms." John Martin, "Christensen's Ballets Take the Chief Honors," *Filling Station* Dance Clipping File, Dance Collection, The New York Public Library.

[15] Robert Sylvester, "Filling Station Comic Triumph," *Filling Station* Clipping File, Dance Collection, The New York Public Library.

[16] Interview with James Graham-Luján, San Francisco, California, March 4, 1988.

Graham-Luján conceived the broad outlines of the libretto after hearing a recording of Rossini's operatic overtures. As classical music, the overtures were "respectable" but still accessible, and their style suggested a lighthearted work rooted somehow in the nineteenth century. Leafing through a copy of Cyril Beaumont's *Complete Book of Ballets*, Graham-Luján happened on a photograph of Lucile Grahn in Jules Perrot's *Catarina, ou La Fille du Bandit* and decided the long-legged Bailey would look good in such a costume.[17] One of the overtures included "knocking" passages, which to Graham-Luján suggested a bedroom farce with successive entrances of lovers, a scenario Graham-Luján decided would be appropriate for the beautiful and elegantly proportioned Johnson. Lew complained at first that a succession of three allegro compositions would not allow sufficient contrast between sections, but once he had accepted Graham-Luján's basic vision of the ballet, the two settled quickly upon the details and staging of *Con Amore*'s tongue-in-cheek examination of love and human foibles.[18]

In the ballet's first scene, "The Amazons and the Bandit," a thief (danced by Leon Danielian in the San Francisco premiere) stumbles upon the forest encampment of martial Amazons, who execute drills and maneuvers that may have been inspired by Lew's army experience. Led by their Captain (Bailey), the women first capture the intruder, then succumb to the charms of his male physique, and finally threaten him with their muskets when he refuses their advances. The Bandit bares his chest to their weapons, but at the critical moment the decor changes to the boudoir of Scene Two, "The Master's Return," in which the Fashionable Lady (Johnson) sends off her husband and receives three suitors in turn: a sophisticated man-about-town, a steamy sailor, and a reluctant poet. Each hides at the entrance of the next, but they

---

[17] Cyril W. Beaumont, *Complete Book of Ballets* (New York: G. P. Putnam's Sons, 1938), opp. 254.

[18] Interview with James Graham-Luján, San Francisco, California, March 4, 1988.

eventually emerge to force the lady to choose between them, at which moment her husband reappears. The two plots resolve in Scene Three, "A Triumph of Love," in which the Bandit escapes from the Amazons into the Fashionable Lady's boudoir and touches off a mêlée of trysts and reconciliations. A shower of arrows from a feminine, garland-bestrewn Cupid matches up unlikely couples: the Bandit with the Fashionable Lady, her Husband with the Amazon Captain, and the timid student with Cupid herself.[19] *Con Amore*'s farcical use of timeworn conventions allowed Bailey and Johnson to integrate their training from both Willam and Lew: Willam's emphasis on theatrical projection helped them convey the exaggerated and silly aspects of the plot and underscore the "comedic points" inherent in Lew's choreography.

Reviewing the New York premiere of *Con Amore* in *Dance News*, P. W. Manchester admitted,

> *I would have sworn beforehand that this was precisely the kind of ballet which could not amuse me in any circumstances, but Lew Christensen's simple hearted gaiety and very genuine ability to tell a story in dancing is disarming, and* Con Amore *romps merrily along its unimportant but entertaining way.*[20]

Manchester deemed the work "an unexpected bonus," coming as it did at the end of the season.[21] (The New York premiere came late in the spring season because Bailey and Johnson were needed for April performances in San Francisco.) John Martin praised the West Coast ballerinas' performances as well as *Con Amore*'s ingenuity and wit, its style, and the movement's phrasing and sense of flow: "One cannot recall any other Christensen ballet with so nice an

---

[19] Graham-Luján wanted the ballet to end with Cupid and the student re-creating Canova's *Cupid and Psyche*, but Lew refused. Perhaps he considered it too arcane or esoteric. Lew accepted suggestions from his collaborator to a point, but his own taste always prevailed in the choreography itself. Stephen C. Steinberg and Nancy Johnson interview with James Graham-Luján, San Francisco, September 9, 1985, [Interview G].

[20] P. W. Manchester, "New York City Ballet," *Dance News*, September 1953, 10.

[21] *Ibid.*

approach."[22] Picked again by Lew for the leading male role, that of the Bandit, d'Amboise garnered more accolades from the press; Manchester declared him "the most promising male talent anywhere on the American ballet horizon."[23]

Lew may have had the chance to set these works on NYCB because in March Balanchine and his new wife, Tanaquil LeClerq, had left for Italy, where the choreographer set opera ballets for Milan's La Scala and Florence's Teatro della Pergola. In Balanchine's absence that spring, NYCB presented not only Lew's *Filling Station* and *Con Amore* but also the premieres of Todd Bolender's *The Filly* and of Robbins's *Afternoon of a Faun* and *Fanfare*. In his position as administrative director, Lew was part of the backup team that kept the company going and even supplied new repertory in Balanchine's absence. As a member of that team, Lew's contribution to the company was unquestionably positive. In a summary essay at the conclusion of the spring season, Martin declared that NYCB should "circle the genial brow of Lew Christensen with a laurel" because his two ballets, "unquestionable hits," had added "a definite brightness to the season." Martin accorded neither *Filling Station* nor *Con Amore* the status of "masterpiece," but he found both more satisfying than the season's other novelties (*Fanfare*, *Afternoon of a Faun*, and *The Filly*).[24] Media recognition of Lew's talents rose to its highest since before the war. An article in *Newsweek* that April highlighted the exchange program and Lew's role in both companies.[25]

By all outward signs, Lew seemed to have the ideal arrangement. The exchange policy continued to strengthen the San Francisco Ballet: in 1954 ranking NYCB dancers Maria

[22] John Martin, "Christensen's Ballets Take The Chief Honors," *New York Times*, *Filling Station* Clipping File, Dance Collection, The New York Public Library; John Martin, "Coast Ballerinas Guests at Center," *New York Times*, *Con Amore* Clipping File, Dance Collection, The New York Public Library.

[23] P. W. Manchester, "New York City Ballet," *ibid.*

[24] John Martin, "Christensen's Ballets Take the Chief Honors," *ibid.*

[25] "Dance: City Exchange," *Newsweek*, April 20, 1953.

Tallchief and André Eglevsky made guest appearances in Balanchine's one-act version of *Swan Lake* and the *Sylvia Pas de Deux*. In exchange, Lew revised *Con Amore* for NYCB, making greater technical demands on Balanchine's dancers with new choreography deemed more "brilliant and intricate" than that of the original version.[26] In San Francisco, the dancers' greatest fear was that Lew would relocate in New York permanently.[27] But his post in New York did not provide Lew the opportunity to choreograph on Balanchine's company. The *Gloriana* ballet announced when he was appointed Administrative Director never made it into production. Instead, Robbins's *Fanfare*, with its score by Benjamin Britten, constituted the company's celebration of Queen Elizabeth II's coronation. One attraction of being connected with NYCB had been the prospect of having funding at his disposal for the creation of new works, but *Con Amore*, Lew's major creation of this period, was put together not in New York but in the nearly poverty-stricken San Francisco company. Apparently, not even the overwhelmingly positive reviews earned by *Filling Station* and *Con Amore* in 1953 while Balanchine was in Italy gave Lew carte blanche to stage new works for NYCB the following year, when Balanchine was in town and producing *Opus 34*, *The Nutcracker*, *Western Symphony*, and *Ivesiana*.[28]

---

[26] John Martin, "Ballet Presents New *Con Amore*," *New York Times*, March 12, 1954. It seems that Lew was able to adjust his choreographic style more successfully to the skills of NYCB dancers than Willam would be, a few years later, in *Octet*. Doubtless, Lew's background with Balanchine gave him an edge over his brother in this respect.

[27] Sometime during this general period, Lew was also considered for or offered the post of ballet master at the Metropolitan Opera. According to Willam and Harold, Dorothy Kilgallen leaked news of the planned appointment, and Tudor fought it, successfully, by lobbying for the job to go to Zachary Solov. Kirstein concurs about the Met's offer to Lew but does not remember when it took place. This author has not been able to find a reference to the intended appointment in Kilgallen's column, "The Voice of Broadway."

[28] Balanchine's decision to add *The Nutcracker* to NYCB's repertoire has been attributed to Sadler's Wells' triumph in full-length ballets in America, particularly the success of *The Sleeping Beauty* during its New York debut season in 1949. According to Buckle, Kirstein and Baum encouraged Balanchine to do a full-length work, and Balanchine came up with the idea to do *Nutcracker* (Buckle,

Whether Lew himself declined to put other San Francisco creations from this period on view in New York or was prevented from doing so by others within NYCB is open to conjecture. But it seems in retrospect that Lew's opportunities in New York were fated to be limited, especially since Robbins had secured the slot of secondary choreographer. As had been the case in Ballet Society, Lew's primary focus at NYCB would be to assist Kirstein in running a company in which Balanchine's repertory always and inevitably would have top priority.

On the personal side, too, Lew now faced a different situation than when he and Gisella had contemplated his career choices after the war. In November 1953, Gisella give birth to their son, Chris Edward Christensen. She recalls that while their only child was being delivered, Lew was in the garage making papier-mâché mouse heads for the *Nutcracker*.[29] Gisella was less willing to consider a permanent move to New York now that she had a child to raise as well as her mother and sister living on the West Coast. (Her mother actually lived with the family for long periods of time.) Perhaps the specter of the old cold-water flat haunted Gisella; she felt they could live better as a family in the West. Now retired from the stage, Gisella would not be directly involved with Balanchine's company. In San Francisco she at least had the satisfaction of teaching at the Lakeside branch of the SFB School and passing on her Cecchetti training to a new generation of dancers. Convinced of her husband's gifts as a choreographer, Gisella also suspected Balanchine of guarding

---

Balanchine: Ballet Master, 200). It is not inconceivable that Lew suggested or was instrumental in endorsing the selection of *Nutcracker*, especially in view of the fact that the ballet had succeeded well upon its San Francisco premiere in 1944 and had been a holiday tradition in the West since 1949. New York-oriented dance writing tends to obscure this fact; witness Dale Harris's claim that before Balanchine's version of *Nutcracker*, "the work had never made much impact on American audiences before." Dale Harris, "America on Its Toes," *Town & Country*, November 1988, 238.

[29] Interview with Gisella Caccialanza Christensen, San Bruno, California, September 30, 1987.

his own territory. Mingled with her respect for Balanchine was the fear that he was capable of using Lew without providing him with opportunities to develop his own creative gifts. By 1954 it was clear that San Francisco, not New York, offered the road to future opportunities.

Lew's position in New York lapsed quietly as he refocused his efforts on building the San Francisco Ballet. His name was removed from NYCB's company roster in 1955. In a concerted attempt to build the home audience, SFB offered four "Dollar Ballet" nights at the opera house in April '54. The number of annual performances, not including the opera season, began to mount again, from the drastic low of 11 in 1952 to 30 in 1955.[30] In 1954, Lew added four new works to the company's repertory: a neo-Romantic ballet entitled *The Dryad*; a Viennese wedding celebration during the wine-making season, set to music by Mozart, named *Heuriger*; a retelling of the story of Paris and the golden apple entitled *The Masque of Beauty and the Shepherd*; and a new *Nutcracker*. The following year Lew restaged Balanchine's *Le Renard* and created *The Tarot*, which was inspired by the allegorical figures on fortune-telling cards and was set to Tchaikovsky's *Mozartiana*.

Lew was often asked why he did not stage a *ballet blanc* from the traditional repertory, *Giselle* or *Swan Lake*, as Willam had done. Lew's refusal to produce such works was less a gesture of defiance than a sign of his modesty. Rather than attempting ambitious stagings of the classics with his small company (and risk inviting comparisons with productions of larger, better-funded groups), Lew created *The Dryad* as a "white ballet" fitting the capacity of his troupe. The idea of building a work around a tree spirit came to Graham-Luján when Kirstein sent Lew a backdrop no longer useful to New York City Ballet. The drop, designed by Dorothea Tanning

[30] Alfred Frankenstein, "The San Francisco Ballet," *Dance Magazine*, April 1955, 21. The log of performances belonging to the SFB lists only twenty-five for that year, so Frankenstein may be stretching the truth.

for Balanchine's *Bayou*, depicted a Louisiana swamp dominated by a large tree. Balanchine had suggested to Lew
separately that Franz Schubert's Fantasy in F Minor had
potential as a ballet score. The chief drawback of the music,
in Lew's opinion, was a waltz in the middle that he referred
to pejoratively as "Old Vienna" (a clear reference to Willam's
ballet). Lew was not interested in a score that even hinted at
schmaltz. But Graham-Luján, inspired by the slightly sinister
atmosphere of the drop and an element of melancholy in the
music, concocted a story about a hunter who disturbs a tree
eternally inhabited by a powerful dryad. The waltz could
provide the musical setting for a sort of "witches' rout," a
dance of the dryad's sister spirits, reminiscent of the wilis in
the second act of *Giselle*. Originally, the central role was
intended for Maria Tallchief when she came on exchange
from New York, but as Lew worked out the ballet he derived
such inspiration from Nancy Johnson's sinuousness and
dramatic strength that all thoughts of using Tallchief were
dismissed.[31] At the end of *The Dryad* the tree became transparent, revealing the bodies of other unsuspecting men murdered by the malevolent spirit. This sort of closing visual
transformation, which had begun with the trick ending of
*Le Gourmand*, became a hallmark of the Christensen–Graham-
Luján repertory during this period. *Heuriger*, which starred
Sally Bailey and Gordon Paxman as the bride and groom,
contained another such final image: a human maypole created
by lifting Sally Bailey in the middle of the corps de ballet,
whose circling members held the other end of ribbons coming
from her hand.

   *Beauty and the Shepherd* was thrown together hurriedly
for a performance at Stern Grove and surprised everyone with
its success. A retelling of the Judgment of Paris story to music
by Gluck (a pastiche assembled by Lew's new conductor, Earl
Murray), the work provided ballerina roles for the goddesses
Hera, Juno, and Aphrodite, a cameo for Nancy Johnson as

---

[31] Stephen C. Steinberg and Nancy Johnson interview with James Graham-Luján,
San Francisco, December 9, 1985.

Helen of Troy, and a significant male role for Lew's new leading danseur, Conrad Ludlow. Like *The Dryad* and *Heuriger, Beauty and the Shepherd* ended with a transformation before the audiences's eyes: the warriors' shields became the side of a ship, spearlike poles turned to oars and a mast (complete with sail), and Johnson was lifted in a pose simulating a ship's figurehead. On one hand, this transformation was a matter of expediency: the outdoor setting at Stern Grove, for which *Beauty and the Shepherd* was created, allowed for little scenery in the traditional sense, so Lew used the props of the story to create a living set piece. Like the other final transformations, it reflected the delight of Lew the sketcher, Lew the doodler, in playing with all the visual elements at his disposal. But beyond these considerations, the final pose in *Beauty and the Shepherd* provides a telling clue to the source of Lew's inspiration during this period: the image suggests a similar transformation in Balanchine's *The Prodigal Son*, when members of the cast assemble on stage to create the image of a sailing ship.

    As Lew's choreographic output increased in San Francisco, his opus naturally came under critical scrutiny. The San Francisco critics sensed the change in company style as Lew's repertory at first supplemented and then replaced Willam's; Alfred Frankenstein observed mid-decade, "In 1950 the company's productions began to take on a new character – a lightness, a subtlety, a whimsicality and sophistication they had never had before."[32] Inherent in discussions of Lew's style was the question of his debt to Balanchine, an issue that dogged Lew for the remainder of his career. Obviously, Lew had acquired professional artistry from his work with Balanchine; he had also absorbed the master's teaching methods and his attitudes as a choreographer. As he worked with students in San Francisco, Lew quoted Balanchine often, holding him up as the final authority on matters of technique. Hallmarks of the Balanchine style – the speed, athleticism, and density of the choreography; chains of dancers in interlacing

---

[32] Frankenstein, "The San Francisco Ballet," *Dance Magazine*, April 1955, 19–21.

figures; even patterns of interaction between soloists and groups of corps members reminiscent of *Concerto Barocco* or *The Four Temperaments* – found their way into Lew's early San Francisco creations. Once he unintentionally used a series of movements from *Concerto Barocco* in one of his new ballets; only after the work was completed did Lew realize the source of the phrase.[33]

But Lew did not want to be a mere imitator of Balanchine. Although Lew's ballets inevitably betrayed his artistic inheritance, he rejected the term "neoclassical" as descriptive of his work, insisting always that he worked in the field of "classical" ballet.[34] He resented the suggestion that his works imitated Balanchine's style and grew frustrated when critics jumped to facile conclusions about Balanchine's influence. Late in life Lew stated categorically that he did *not* think about Balanchine when he choreographed, his ballets did *not* look like Balanchine's, and that *no one* could match Balanchine's genius.[35] Unlike Balanchine, Lew's creative gift was not the ability to reinvent the classical vocabulary or to break down the barriers of tradition with a new syntax enlarging the formal or expressive possibilities of dance as a medium. Given his unquestioned talent as a performer, perhaps innovative genius as a choreographer would have been too much to ask. Instead, Lew absorbed Balanchine's innovations and turned them to his own uses, employing them according to his own musical training, his native wit, and his frequent interest in narrative structures. Graham-Luján, grappling with the issue of Lew's debt to Balanchine in a 1956 essay, attributed any similarity in the two men's works not to "plagiarism" but rather to Lew's having adopted Balanchine's "approach and intent."[36]

---

[33] Stephen C. Steinberg and Nancy Johnson interview with James Graham-Luján, San Francisco, California, [n.d., interview I].

[34] Telephone interview with Leon Kalimos, December 28, 1988.

[35] Stephanie Von Buchau, "Native Dancer," *Ballet News* 3.1 (May 1982): 27.

[36] James Graham-Luján, "Lew Christensen: Music, Wit and Theatre," *Impulse: The Annual of Contemporary Dance* (San Francisco: Impulse Publications, 1955), 23–25.

The well-publicized exchange policy between SFB and NYCB doubtless contributed to the perception that the San Francisco company, and Lew himself, were simply extensions of Balanchine's influence. But finances played a vital role in shaping this aspect of SFB's repertory. Balanchine was generous with his repertory; he trusted Lew as a ballet master and did not charge exorbitant sums for the use of his ballets, which allowed SFB to produce works by at least one choreographer other than Lew at a reasonable cost. Aside from NYCB, Lew seems to have kept apart from the New York dance community; when Ballet Theatre came to town, Graham-Luján's attempts to get Lew to attend their performances were usually futile.[37] Some evidence suggests, however, that Lew was open to influences other than Balanchine and would have liked to expand SFB's repertory with works by other choreographers. Erick Hawkins claims that in the mid-fifties, Harold and Lew came to his New York studio and invited him to choreograph a work for their company.[38] Likewise, when Merce Cunningham went to California to teach at the Halprin-Lathrop summer school in 1956, his announced itinerary included setting a new piece on SFB.[39] Neither of these projects came to fruition, probably for lack of funding. Money was always a key issue and a limiting factor; Tudor might have been invited except that he was too expensive for company finances. De Mille was out of the question on other grounds; Lew harbored a grudge against her as a result of Gisella's *Oklahoma!* experience and called her ballets "run of de Mille." Overall, Lew definitely did not see his new company as a collective for choreographers the way Ballet Caravan had been. It became and would remain his project, his opportunity, and his vehicle.

---

[37] Stephen C. Steinberg and Nancy Johnson interview with James Graham-Luján, San Francisco, November 6, 1985. Cal Anderson concurs that Lew was not interested in seeing other companies when they came to town. Interview with Cal Anderson, San Francisco, California, December 1, 1988.

[38] Interview with Erick Hawkins, New York, New York, May 25, 1988.

[39] "Halprin-Lathrop Announce Course," *Dance News*, January 1956, 9.

In the mid-fifties, one of the dancers, Leon Kalimos, offered to try setting up bookings for the company. A few trial runs to nearby cities proved satisfactory, so Kalimos bought into the brothers' partnership and took over the financial end of the company's management. This, of course, could only have been accomplished with Harold's blessing. Harold was fond of quoting, "The man who signs the checks has the power."[40] Harold objected when some funds raised by the guild were put in an account with checks requiring Lew and Graham-Luján's signatures rather than his own.[41] This threatened Harold's control over company finances and may ultimately have wrought Graham-Luján's demise as Lew's collaborator. Harold began to promote Kalimos instead as a support to the brothers' enterprise. Kalimos was a Greek American with experience in business and importing. As a skilled ballroom dancer, he first became interested in ballet when he saw another dancer do a pirouette. He joined a group of GIs using their post-war benefits to pay for evening classes at the San Francisco Ballet School, and before long Willam had him performing. Kalimos created the role of the bartender in *Nothing Doing Bar*, an apt bit of casting as Kalimos had owned and operated a Geary Street bar called "Leon's."[42] Although his primary professional experience stemmed clearly from the commercial world, Kalimos also knew the company from a dancer's point of view and understood the demands of performance situations.

The school remained Harold's domain, and its running required enormous ongoing effort. During Lew's bicoastal period, Harold's daily attention to the school provided stability and a sense of continuity for the local dancers. In 1956 his commitment was put to the test when the building on Washington Street changed hands, and once again the

---

[40] Stephen C. Steinberg and Nancy Johnson interview with James Graham-Luján, San Francisco, October 7, 1991.

[41] Stephen C. Steinberg and Nancy Johnson interview with James Graham-Luján, San Francisco, October 7, 1985.

[42] "Notes on a Ballet Program," *Balletomane*, 2.1 (Spring 1950): n.p.

brothers were forced to find a new facility. Harold scoured the neighborhoods of San Francisco in hopes of finding space appropriate for dancers' needs. After an extended search he and Lew settled on a two-story parking garage on Eighteenth Avenue. The garage's location in the Richmond district, far from the opera house, was not ideal, but the structure had large open spaces that could be converted to studios.

Having found a possible new home, the main question remained how to pay for it. The guild sponsored productions, but it was hardly in a position to buy the brothers a new building. Once again Harold came through. He produced a stash of government bonds he had bought over the years with the school's proceeds. With Kalimos as a partner, the Christensens expended all their resources to acquire and remodel the building. They converted the upper level into three studios, one slightly raised so that it could be used as a stage for small, in-house performances. Harold personally constructed the risers and bleachers to be used for such events. The ground floor was converted into company offices and storage areas for costumes and scenery. Thanks largely to Harold's administrative commitment, the family business carried on in its new setting.

Lew's concentrated efforts in San Francisco paid off with greatly increased performance opportunities for the company during the second half of the decade. The company's first big break came in 1956 when Anatole Chujoy suggested to Ted Shawn that he invite SFB to perform at Jacob's Pillow, the annual summer dance festival in the Berkshires. Lew took the East Coast debut seriously as a way to shed the company's image as a troupe of only regional interest. In previous years Shawn had imported the National Ballet of Canada, the Celtic Ballet of Scotland, and Ten Dancers from the Royal Danish Ballet, and all had received touring offers as a result of their successful performances.[43] Prior to SFB's three-week residency, Kalimos made the round of booking agents in New York to assure that the company's

[43] Steinberg, *San Francisco Ballet*, 84.

**33** Lew Christensen, Ted Shawn, and James Graham-Luján at Jacob's Pillow, 1956.
Photograph by Stephen, courtesy of San Francisco Performing Arts Library and Museum

performances at the Pillow would yield maximum exposure and, hopefully, pay off with offers for more engagements.[44]

Jacob's Pillow had just that effect. Representatives from the New York critical establishment, and Walter Terry in particular, raved over SFB's youthful dancers. Lew's achievements as a teacher and ballet master received unstinted praise in the press. His abilities as a choreographer drew more mixed comments; some writers found *The Dryad* and *The Tarot* less satisfying than *Jinx*, *Con Amore*, and *Masque of Beauty and the Shepherd*. SFB's very capable rendering of Balanchine's *Concerto Barocco* and *Apollo* drew attention to the exchange policy (mentioned in reviews as if it were still being actively implemented) and added to the company's status. At the close of the three-week season, the State Department announced that it had selected the San Francisco Ballet to represent the United States as cultural ambassadors on an eleven-nation tour of Asia.

Lew and Graham-Luján had a falling-out after the Jacob's Pillow engagement, and the latter left the company. A short press release divulged only that Graham-Luján had resigned because the two did not see eye to eye in unspecified matters of company policy. Because the company was basically a family concern, Lew got his way and his associate left.[45] Rather than replacing Graham-Luján with a new Artistic

---

[44] Telephone Interview with Leon Kalimos, December 28, 1988.

[45] According to Ruby, Graham-Luján had promised Leonard Weisgard (who had designed the costumes for *Le Gourmand*) that he would be commissioned to design Lew's next ballet, but Lew had other plans. Neither was willing to compromise on the point. Telephone conversation with Ruby Asquith Christensen, January 27, 1992. Graham-Luján's departure may also have been spurred by disagreements over the financial arrangements explained above. Harold, already feeling "out of the loop" by the close manner in which Lew and Graham-Luján collaborated on company projects, may not have been able to tolerate the bank account that did not require his signature. Also, Harold had a strong protective streak toward his little brother. Whenever he felt that one of Lew's professional associates was encroaching on Lew's rightful domain in any way, Harold's protective instincts rushed to the fore. Some combination of these factors may have affected Graham-Luján's position with the company. Later in life, Graham-Luján reflected that while at first Harold had supported him, eventually Harold withdrew that support: "I think it was Harold who fired me." Stephen C. Steinberg and Nancy Johnson interview with James Graham-Luján, San Francisco, November 6, 1985.

Director, Lew assumed complete leadership of the company. He also announced that Lincoln Kirstein would fill Graham-Luján's role as a part-time "artistic collaborator."[46] While Kirstein later denied that he ever functioned officially in such a capacity, company members recall his periodic visits.[47] According to Richard Carter, "[Kirstein] came out quite often from New York to watch the company and offer suggestions." He offered advice on details of costuming and staging for subsequent productions such as *Beauty and the Beast* and *Danses Concertantes*.[48]

Any drama inherent in Graham-Luján's departure was overshadowed by the negotiations and preparations for the State Department tour. Robert Schnitzer, who administered the International Exchange Program under the auspices of ANTA (the American National Theatre and Academy), wanted the San Francisco Ballet to tour Asia with a production of *Swan Lake*, supporting Alexandra Danilova in the starring role.[49] Willam would have jumped at the chance, but Lew declined the invitation on those terms; if his company toured, they would perform their own repertory. Schnitzer agreed to Lew's conditions because SFB seemed the ideal company for this tour. With its West Coast location, San Francisco acted as a gateway to America for many immigrants from the Far East and had a large Asian population (although SFB itself did not). SFB's repertory contained staples of the Balanchine canon, but the San Francisco troupe was smaller and thus more mobile than Balanchine's own company.

---

[46] "Graham-Luján Out," *Variety*, October 31, 1956, in "San Francisco Ballet" Clipping File, Dance Collection, The New York Public Library. Further proof that Kirstein was to somehow replace Graham-Luján is found in a letter from the latter to Lucia Chase, dated October 24, 1956. Graham-Luján wrote, "Here is a clipping that will tell you that I'm no longer associated with the Christensens. We parted quite amicably but definitely. The work I've had to do here was joyous, so I have no regrets on that score. Lincoln K is to take my place here." ABT Records, 1936 to ca. 1967, Correspondence File 761, The New York Public Library Dance Collection.

[47] Interview with Lincoln Kirstein, New York, New York, January 14, 1988.

[48] Interview with Richard Carter, San Francisco, California, March 7, 1988.

[49] Telephone interview with Leon Kalimos, December 28, 1988.

New York City Ballet had already been chosen to tour Northern Europe, and Ballet Theatre was touring Southern Europe and the Middle East.[50] It somehow seemed appropriate that the San Francisco Ballet be the first American ballet company to tour Asia under State Department sponsorship.

Lew and Kalimos plunged into preparations. Kalimos devised contracts in numerous languages, ordered specially shaped wicker baskets for the costumes to fit securely in the luggage holds of their chartered plane, acquired lightweight aluminum cables and compact copper lighting boards, and tracked down information on the electrical current used in each country with assistance from Harold. Willam handled all the choreography for the opera season that fall, while Lew prepared the repertory and dancers for their departure in early January 1957.

Lew worked out programming and rehearsed the repertory, which included his *Con Amore*, *Jinx*, *Beauty and the Shepherd*, *Nutcracker Act II*, *The Tarot*, *The Dryad*, plus Balanchine's *Concerto Barocco* and *Renard*. Although he refused to have his company back up Danilova in *Swan Lake*, Lew understood the need for a "big name" artist on a tour of this magnitude and invited Leon Danielian to join them. Danielian was nearing the end of his career as a principal dancer of the Ballet Russe de Monte Carlo; he had appeared with SFB a few years earlier when he created the role of the Bandit in *Con Amore*. Danielian accepted the invitation to revive that role and to star in virtuoso divertissements from the international repertory (the *Don Quixote* and *Black Swan* pas de deux) that were an expected element of touring ballet presentations during the 1950s. Conrad Ludlow, Richard Carter, and Gordon Paxman would lead the rest of the male contingent. On the women's side, Nancy Johnson, Sally Bailey, Christine Bering, and Virginia Johnson all had positive reviews from the Jacob's Pillow engagement. Jocelyn Vollmar's return to SFB gave Lew a ballerina of international standing: after

---

[50] Walter Terry, "Ballet on Good Will Tours," *New York Herald Tribune*, August 19, 1956.

touring Europe, North Africa, and South America with the Grand Ballet du Marquis de Cuevas and Australia as the prima ballerina of the Borovansky Ballet, Vollmar had decided to return to her home company. She stayed with SFB for the rest of her career.

Representatives from the State Department coached the dancers in their roles as international goodwill ambassadors. The International Exchange Program under whose auspices the dancers were to appear was a conscious effort to spread American influence and goodwill during the Cold War. Company members were instructed to be on best behavior at all times, to be friendly to the people they met in each nation but not to talk politics, to bow first to the royal box if a head of state were in the audience, and so on. A battery of inoculations fortified the dancers against the diseases they might encounter in their travels. Before departure, each woman received forty pairs of pointe shoes, a number that seemed astronomical to the members of the struggling troupe.

The tour itself brought a mixture of adventures and honors.[51] In Manila, near the beginning of the tour, the local management had oversold the quonset hut-style theatre by four thousand tickets, and unseated patrons staged a near riot trying to occupy the building. In Cambodia, the company had to travel through the jungle by bus and then erect its own stage to perform for the village of Kampong Cham. In Burma, a Russian circus cancelled one of its own appearances to attend SFB's performance. In India, one of the dancers was given a baby cobra as a souvenir while visiting a zoo. (It was not allowed on the plane.) Everywhere, Lew and the dancers were fêted at dinners and receptions, and in many countries, after the Americans had performed, their hosts entertained them with performances of local dance traditions long into the night. The performance schedule allowed time for

---

[51] My description of SFB's international tours is indebted to Steinberg's section "International Touring, 1957–1959," *San Francisco Ballet*, 86–87, as well as to records at San Francisco Performing Arts Library and Museum.

sightseeing and receptions, so Lew and Leon arranged side trips for the dancers to see historical sites such as Angkor Wat.

The only serious hitch as the tour unfolded was the discovery that India did not plan to pay travel costs that had been worked into the budget. As a result the company was temporarily stranded in Bombay, reports of which caused large headlines in San Francisco. Harold conferred with reporters and frantically contacted congressmen in an effort to bring the company's situation to national attention. Lew remained calm and sheltered the dancers from the financial problems, which were resolved by shortening the original itinerary. As *Dance News* pointed out, such fiascos came with the pioneering nature of the tour: "No other company sponsored by the State Department has toured over this route before, and it fell to these dancers to absorb the shocks of trail blazing."[52] Despite this glitch, ANTA was more than satisfied with the political payoff reaped by the dancers' polished performances and their sterling behavior offstage. During the company's travels, the dancers performed repeatedly for dignitaries and heads of state: the king of Thailand, Madame Chiang Kai-shek, the king of Cambodia, the governor-general of Hong Kong, the prime minister of Burma, and President Magsaysay of the Philippines.[53] Even building the stage for their own performance in Kampong Cham was considered an impressive demonstration of the Yankee spirit of determination and hard work. On the basis of this tour, ANTA selected the San Francisco Ballet for two more international tours: South America in 1958 and the Middle East and Africa in 1959.

The four-month South American tour was less glamorous and more grueling than the Asian tour had been. Lew and the company made their way through Venezuela, Colombia, Ecuador, Peru, Paraguay, Uruguay, Argentina, Brazil, Costa Rica, Nicaragua, Honduras, El Salvador, Guatemala, and Mexico in a series of short engagements and

---

[52] "SF Troupe Asian Snafu Is Being Straightened Out," *Dance News*, March 1957, 1.

[53] Steinberg, *San Francisco Ballet*, 87.

**34** Lew Christensen and SFB dancers entertained by Philippine President Ramón Magsaysay.
Courtesy of San Francisco Performing Arts Library and Museum

one-night stands. In Quito and Bogotá, where it was feared some dancers might pass out while performing at the high altitude, oxygen tanks and litters waited in the wings.[54] The tour brought back memories of American Ballet Caravan's similar odyssey in 1941; Lew even encountered people he had met on that first trip. Also, as in the early days, the dancers did much of the physical labor necessary to set up performances. Michael Smuin, who joined the company for the second tour, recalls:

> *We'd load the equipment into the plane, fly into a town, unload the equipment into a truck, go to the theater, and we boys would*

---

[54] Interview with Jocelyn Vollmar, San Francisco, California, March 1, 1988; telephone interview with Leon Kalimos, December 28, 1988.

*unload the truck, put down the floor, put up the boom, focus the lights, hang the curtains, take out the props, get the costumes out and hang them. After the performance, the scenery and lights would go back in the crates (we even made the crates), and we'd load the truck, and then, we'd go out and have dinner.*[55]

Unlike many of their stops in Asia, most of the cities in South America where SFB performed had seen ballet, and some were quite sophisticated in their tastes. Thus, it was reassuring when the *Dance News* correspondent in Brazil reported, "It was good to see again in Rio a well directed and homogeneous company after so many haphazard seasons of guest artists and divertissement programs."[56]

Back in San Francisco, Kalimos and Harold hung a world map in the foyer of the school and stuck a pin in each city where the company performed. Harold supported the company intellectually, but he did not realize the difficulties of international touring, and he tended to resent the extra income and recognition that touring brought to the company but not the school. Lew felt it was important that Harold share in the experience of international touring, so Lew actually left SFB during a portion of its South American tour and had Harold fly down to travel with the dancers.

The third ANTA tour took Lew and his company to the Middle East and northern Africa. In just over three months they gave 76 performances as they worked their way through Greece, Turkey, Lebanon, Iran, Ethiopia, Eritrea, the Sudan, Egypt, Syria, and Libya. Unforeseen incidents and regional tensions complicated their travel: two men in the company came down with meningitis, forcing a delay while all the dancers were tested for the illness. When they resumed their journey without rescheduling permission to fly over Iraq, fighter pilots forced the company's plane down over Baghdad. In Beirut, a general strike caught the company by surprise; two dancers blithely out shopping were whisked

---

[55] Michael Smuin quoted in Steinberg, *San Francisco Ballet*, 87.

[56] *Dance News*, September 1958, 13.

back to their hotel past gunfire and burning streetcars. The audience for their performance that night was small and tense, and the dancers feared a spontaneous outbreak of violence at the climax of *Filling Station*, when the stage went dark and the gunshot rang out. Taking no chances that night, Lew brought the lights back up much more quickly than usual.

Despite such tensions, the State Department considered the tour an artistic and political success. In Egypt, the wife of President Gamal Abdel Nassar made her first public appearance since that country's revolution to attend SFB's performance. In Addis Ababa, Emperor Haile Selassie awarded Lew and each company member a gold medal, despite current propaganda about Ethiopa's negative feelings toward America.[57] A critic in Istanbul praised the dancers' professionalism with a prediction anticipating the future prominence of American ballet on the international scene:

> *It would not be a wild dream to anticipate West Berlin, Rome, Paris and London audiences cheering the San Francisco Ballet one day. . . . It is very likely that the world might speak in the future of American ballet just as it now speaks of Russian, French, and British ballet.*[58]

State Department post reports from all three tours stressed the dancers' excellence in public relations work as they met people in each country, adjusted good naturedly to unplanned delays and inconveniences, and occasionally gave unscheduled, free performances for mass audiences. In Greece, the company visited a boys school, and Lew played games with the children. In Burma, Conrad Ludlow played chess with members of the Russian Circus staying in the same hotel. In Turkey, company members picked up a few words of Turkish and impressed local citizens by buying traditional instruments and dancing in the streets. In their conscious

---

[57] Press Release, "1959 Tour," San Francisco Ballet Company, April 23, 1959, in "San Francisco Ballet" Clipping File, Dance Collection, The New York Public Library.

[58] *Ibid.*

efforts to reach out in friendship, the dancers were the willing emissaries of the State Department, which set itineraries according to political expediency. Ann Barzel, a member of the committee that selected cultural attractions to represent America abroad, recalls that Lew's dancers were held in the highest estimation by ANTA because they were "exemplary in their relationships with foreign groups."[59]

Subsidized touring brought new economic stability to the company. It provided money to put more dancers on contract and thus helped Lew to keep the dancers he had trained (although Ludlow did join NYCB after the Asian tour). Lights and electrical equipment purchased with touring funds were put to good use in subsequent home performances. Perhaps most important, having guaranteed opportunities to perform gave Lew the means and the reason to create new ballets.

Circumstances forced Lew to work in a variety of styles. As the company's only resident choreographer during this era, he was obliged to think in terms of balanced programming. He created works to open and close evenings and divertissements to round out touring programs. For the company's silver anniversary in 1958 he needed an accessible story ballet that would appeal to families. His solution was an original fairy-tale ballet, *Beauty and the Beast*. Part of the ballet's mass appeal would be elaborate costumes and sets designed by a new collaborator, Tony Duquette. The latter's career in design touched many areas: interior decoration, fabric design, advertising campaigns, even jewelry for the Duchess of Windsor. His theatrical credits included stage and film experience (*Kismet* and *Lovely to Look At*) as well as the San Francisco Opera's production of *Der Rosenkavalier*.[60] Perhaps most importantly, Duquette was a socially acceptable designer, one considered chic by members of the guild's board.[61] His extensive contribution to the overall look of

---

[59] Interview with Ann Barzel, Winston-Salem, North Carolina, February 15, 1988.

[60] "Tony Duquette," *Dance Digest*, July 1958, 294–95.

[61] Interview with Cal Anderson, San Francisco, California, December 1, 1988.

*Beauty* foreshadowed Lew's heavily dressed ballets of the 1960s.

The score for *Beauty* consisted of excerpts from Tchaikovsky's symphonies and orchestral suites, deftly pieced together by the company conductor, Earl Murray.[62] *Beauty*'s form lived up to the grand tradition of multi-act story ballets. It presented the contrasting worlds of Beauty (Nancy Johnson) with her father and greedy sisters in opposition to the Palace of the Beast (Richard Carter) and the animals constituting his entourage (which included Virginia Johnson, Michael Smuin, and Kent Stowell). A grand pas de deux, ballabiles, and second act divertissements adorned the tale, which included themes of sorrow and loss as well as the discovery of unexpected inner beauty and love. *Beauty* was such a popular success that it played with the *Nutcracker* that year as part of the holiday season and stayed in the repertory for ten years.

Another narrative work from this period designed by Duquette was Lew's 1958 *The Lady of Shalott*. The invitation to choreograph *Shalott* came Lew's way from the University of California at Berkeley, which had commissioned Sir Arthur Bliss, then Master of the Queen's Music in Britain, to compose a new ballet for the opening of Albert Hertz Memorial Hall. Lew worked from a piano score while Bliss completed the orchestration, which the dancers did not hear in full until opening night. The libretto was based on the poem by Alfred, Lord Tennyson, in which a lady weaves a tapestry in her tower and is permitted to view life outside her seclusion only in a mirror. Vollmar danced the title role, and Richard Carter, that of Sir Lancelot. Lew's challenge in this work was to choreograph a pas de deux expressing their attraction to each other while the Lady remained in her tower and Lancelot looked on from a distance. Drawing on his exposure to

---

[62] In addition to Tchaikovsky's First, Second, and Third Symphonies and the First, Second, and Third Orchestral Suites, Murray used excerpts from *The Storm*, Opus 76. A portion of the *Theme and Variations for Piano*, Opus 19, No. 6, was added in 1982, by Denis de Coteau. Steinberg, *San Francisco Ballet*, 195.

**35** Kirstein backstage at the opening of Lew's *Beauty and the Beast*, 1958. Courtesy of San Francisco Performing Arts Library and Museum

Kabuki theater in Japan, Lew devised a pas de deux that was really a pas de quatre: a man in black representing Lancelot's shadow partnered Vollmar in her tower, while Carter danced with a woman in black representing Vollmar's shadow.

To balance these elaborately produced story ballets, Lew revived his technically oriented 1949 *Vivaldi Concerto* (renamed *Balletino*), and for the 1959 tour he created *Sinfonia*, a neoclassical work performed in leotards to music by Boccherini. For the third tour Lew choreographed a virtuoso pas de trois, *Divertissement d'Auber*, as an alternative to the usual grand pas de deux. The *Auber* pas de trois taxed the dancers' stamina with its display of strength and speed; it remained a touring staple through the sixties and climaxed many lecture demonstrations.

The 1950s proved to be a richly productive period for Lew. He worked through his Balanchine heritage as he attempted to find his own style as a choreographer, with the loyal support of an important collaborator for the first two-thirds of the decade. The group of advanced students he had taken on in 1949 matured into instruments capable of expressing his evolving artistic vision. Graham-Luján recalls that Lew's first real happiness and satisfaction as a choreographer in San Francisco came when he set the pas de deux for *Masque of Beauty and the Shepherd*, because Johnson and Ludlow could do whatever he asked of them.[63] Still at the peak of his energies as a choreographer, Lew had freedom to experiment in San Francisco while benefiting artistically and financially from the international tours.

Kirstein came to San Francisco for the premiere of *Beauty and the Beast* and tried once more to lure Lew back to New York.[64] This time Lew firmly declined. He now had a fully professional company in San Francisco and the immediate prospect of the third international tour. Perhaps Lew felt less need for Kirstein's support than he had in the past; on tour Lew experienced more recognition, in the form of medals

---

[63] Stephen C. Steinberg and Nancy Johnson interview with James Graham-Luján, San Francisco, November 6, 1985.

[64] Conversation with Willam F. Christensen, Salt Lake City, Utah, May 1, 1987. According to Willam, he, Lew, and Kirstein skipped a postperformance reception and went for highballs instead. Over drinks, Kirstein offered Lew $20,000 a year if he would return to NYCB, a sum that seemed very high to Willam in 1958.

and honors, than he had ever known in San Francisco. The ANTA tours also brought SFB a wealth of performing experience. After the meager number of non-opera appearances in the early fifties, SFB gave 77 independent performances in 1957, 90 in 1958, and 95 in 1959. The dancers became seasoned professionals in a sense that had been impossible with only intermittent Bay Area performances. The opportunities to work and the income for the dancers provided by touring allowed Lew to pursue the goal for which he had severed his ties with New York City Ballet: to run his own company and build his own repertory.

# 13

## THE FORD FOUNDATION GRANTS (1960–1963)

*"Lincoln Kirstein is my best and oldest friend, next to my brothers. And my next best friend is McNeil Lowry. ... He saved the ballet in San Francisco."* [1]

*Lew Christensen*

In March 1957, W. McNeil Lowry, director of Higher Education for the Ford Foundation, received approval from that institution to initiate an exploratory study of the state of the arts in America. Lowry's ultimate objective was nothing less than an ambitious program of philanthropy to benefit creative and performing artists and institutions throughout the United States – a program of systematic support on a level nearly unthinkable in the days prior to the National Endowment for the Arts.

As a first step towards his objective, Lowry assumed the challenge of familiarizing himself firsthand with arts organizations around the country. In the first eighteen months of his exploratory program, he and his staff visited 175 cities. He interviewed artists to discover trends in their fields and brought leading figures to New York for informal roundtable discussions, at which he took note of their problems and aspirations. [2] Lowry had no authority to give immediate financial aid to most of the organizations with which he was becoming familiar. His annual budget of two million dollars was restricted to surveying the field and establishing profiles of artistic activity, modest grants-in-aid to talented

---

[1] Olga Maynard, "The Christensens: An American Dance Dynasty," *Dance Magazine*, June 1973, 54.

[2] Interview with W. McNeil Lowry, New York, New York, May 9, 1988.

individuals, and pilot or demonstration projects to test ways of implementing more far-reaching support once the exploratory phase was completed.

In the course of his field work, Lowry studied Abravanel's progress with the Utah Symphony and Willam's accomplishments at the University of Utah. Lowry was impressed that Willam, rather than allowing himself to be "trapped" by the circumstances of his wife's illness and the limited training opportunities available in most university settings, had established a performing group and extended his influence to younger dancers through the university's Extension Division.[3] Willam took Lowry's inquiries seriously; here, at last, was a New Yorker who was sincerely interested in dance west of the Hudson River. Lowry could give Willam no immediate financial assistance, but he kept Willam in mind as the exploratory period progressed.

In San Francisco, Lowry admired the soundly operated SFB School and company, which was then in the era of its international tours. He observed Harold's and Lew's teaching with excitement and discussed with them the issue of advanced training for gifted students, as he had already done with Kirstein and Balanchine. How were the best dance students around the country to be found and their talents developed to a professional level?[4]

Lowry's immediate interest in dance related to *professional* companies and the training of *professional* dancers; he perceived the regional "civic ballet" movement, which was spreading from the southeastern U.S. to other portions of the country, as a largely amateur activity resulting in performances the equivalent of advanced school recitals.[5] He found the process by which talented dancers might end up in a professional company unconscionably haphazard: "Only the

---

[3] *Ibid.*

[4] Memo to the Ford Foundation Records Center, from W. McNeil Lowry, August 3, 1959, Ford Foundation Archives, PA59-465.

[5] W. McNeil Lowry, ed., *The Performing Arts and American Society* (Englewood Cliffs, N.J.: Prentice-Hall, 1978), 11.

accident of word of mouth or the hazard of a New York or San Francisco audition could put even the most gifted on the road to a professional career."[6] Between those two cities, Lowry acknowledged the existence of only two groups: "the small semiprofessional company of Willam Christensen" and "the commercially chartered company directed by Ruth Page in Chicago largely as a complement to the opera."[7]

In 1959, under the category of pilot projects permitted by the terms of the exploratory grant, Lowry fashioned a scholarship program for gifted ballet students. Those east of the Mississippi River would be invited to pursue advanced studies at the School of American Ballet (SAB), and those west, at the San Francisco Ballet School. The following academic year (1960–61), fifteen students, including Suzanne Farrell, received scholarships to SAB; thirteen, including Cynthia Gregory, went to San Francisco.[8]

The terms of the pilot grant had immediate implications in the brothers' lives as they canvassed their territory in search of well-trained ballet students. They began with the West Coast; together, or individually with Leon Kalimos, Lew and Harold held audition classes first in major cities in California, Oregon, and Washington, and then extended their efforts to Utah and Texas. Auditioning large numbers of dancers allowed the brothers to be increasingly selective about the students they accepted; both shared Balanchine's ideal of slender, long-legged dancers and made judgments based on body type as well as technical mastery. The audition process also brought to their attention boys and young men, providing the SFB School with the greatest infusion of male

---

[6] *Ibid.*

[7] *Ibid.*

[8] Elizabeth Kendall, *Dancing: A Ford Foundation Report* (New York: Ford Foundation, 1983), 22. Kendall states that "eight or nine" students attended the San Francisco Ballet School that year, but a list entitled "Students Accepted, Enrolled, and Terminated" in papers regarding the Ford grants to the school at the San Francisco Library and Museum for the Performing Arts includes the names of thirteen students who began the program during the 1960–1961 academic year.

talent it had experienced since postwar GI Bill days. Lew and Harold paid for these new luxuries with their time, energy, and diplomacy. When luring away another teacher's promising student to their own school in San Francisco, they tried to stress the honor that accrued to that teacher in the event.[9]

The Ford Foundation scholarship students in San Francisco tended to receive less money than comparable students in New York because Lew and Harold did not believe students should be given a free ride. The brothers stretched the Ford money as far as it would go. For example, they would meet with the parents of students accepted into the program and explain that families should continue to pay as much as they could toward the dancer's training. Dancers were even encouraged to take part-time jobs on the side to supplement their scholarship money. When Lowry questioned this, Lew explained that that was how he and Harold had worked their way into Balanchine's company. Lew believed firmly in the work ethic and did not want his dancers to adopt the attitude that the world owed them a living.[10] Lew also valued self-discipline and viewed ballet training as a means by which many young people, even those with no professional aspirations, could develop that trait in their lives.

Sharing honors with the School of American Ballet as a finishing school for professional dancers greatly boosted SFB's morale and reputation. Certainly, the Ford money contributed to the financial stability of the school, but in strictly

---

[9] Harold and Lew soon concluded that to improve the standard of ballet in the United States, they must improve teaching on the local level in addition to providing advanced experience to a select few. In 1961, the Christensens inaugurated two-week summer workshops for teachers, supported by Ford money, as Balanchine had done in New York the previous summer. The brothers gave classes in teaching methods and provided pointers in technical theater for the teachers, many of whom were involved in civic ballet companies. The following summer, forty-three teachers from a dozen different states and even the Philippines gathered for such instruction. To keep in touch with these teachers and others visited on the road, SFB initiated a publication entitled *Ballet Herald*. Memo from W. McNeil Lowry, to Ford Foundation Records Center, September 15 and 17, 1961, Ford Foundation Archives, PA59–465.

[10] *Ibid.*

economic terms, the scholarship money was a mixed blessing. Scholarship funds were to support only student travel, tuition, and/or living expenses; none could be applied to the general operating costs of the SFB School itself. And to qualify for Ford money, the brothers had to give up ownership of their school as a private enterprise and turn it into a not-for-profit institution. This would prove to be a significant turning point in the brothers' lives; applying for nonprofit status signaled the end of the family ballet business and set the San Francisco company and school on a course that would ultimately result in the family's loss of control over both institutions. At this juncture, as Harold and Lew transferred control of their school to the guild, the only way they could benefit economically was to declare the loss as a tax write-off.[11]

Harold's behind-the-scenes contributions to the stability of the family enterprise in San Francisco have never received due recognition. Harold deferred to Lew on artistic matters – not always without argument but always with an awareness of the esteem in which his brother had been held as a Balanchine performer.[12] On the other hand, Harold possessed an instinct for finances that both Willam and Lew lacked, and his instincts were always tuned to the benefit and preservation of the institution he directed. Harold's fiscal conservatism benefited Lew because the financial stability of the school directly supported the company. Income from student tuition paid Lew's salary as well as Harold's. During the early '60s, when Bené Arnold assisted Lew as the company's ballet mistress, her salary was paid by the school, where she carried a heavy teaching load in addition to "volunteering" further hours each day rehearsing the company and typing cast lists, rehearsal hours, and program information. School funds paid building and maintenance

---

[11] Letter from Lew Christensen, to Miss Lavelle, March 18, 1971, Ford Foundation Archives, PA64–92.

[12] Interview with W. McNeil Lowry, New York, New York, May 9, 1988.

**36** Studio portrait of Harold Christensen.
Photograph by Henri McDowell, courtesy of San Francisco Performing Arts
Library and Museum

expenses for the company as well as the school and covered SFB's insurance costs.[13] Over the years, Harold salted away any extra school income in a savings account against the proverbial rainy day and protested, but capitulated, when those savings were put toward company deficits in the late '60s.[14]

Because he was never the performer Lew was, some have assumed that Harold's career as a teacher was a decision made by default, the only option open to him within the framework of the family business. Although by teaching Harold did fill a need, it was not a role he disliked. Many of his students testify that he loved to teach, that he was in his element in the classroom studio, where he could mold beginning and intermediate students according to his specific ideals of posture and placement. Despite his military bearing and strict attention to detail, Harold joked with and teased his students. "He adored his students," recalls Virginia Johnson, "and he was always smiling, joking, and laughing. He loved to tease."[15] If he had to change a lightbulb in the girls' dressing room, the type of light janitorial duty Harold assumed in addition to teaching, he would call out, "Shut your eyes; I'm coming in."[16] Harold would make himself available to the students before and after classes and was in some ways more approachable than was Lew, who sequestered himself in his office at the back of the building and whose primary concern was the company.[17] Harold's commitment to building the company expressed itself in training young dancers for his brother's future use; when he found a new student with a perfect fifth position, Harold would take the student in and proudly show Lew.

---

[13] Memo Ford Foundation Records Center, from W. McNeil Lowry, August 3, 1959, Ford Foundation Archives, PA59–465.

[14] Interviews with Harold Christensen, San Anselmo, California, December 4, 1987, and March 2, 1988.

[15] Conversation with Virginia Johnson, Corte Madera, California, March 2, 1988.

[16] *Ibid.*

[17] Interview with Robert Gladstein, San Francisco, California, November 30, 1988.

**37**   Harold Christensen teaching, ca. 1962.
Photograph by Bill Cogan, courtesy of San Francisco Performing Arts
Library and Museum

During summers, which were traditionally a slack
time for the company, Lew would spend extended periods
with his family at their cabin near Santa Cruz, listening to
music, sketching, and planning new works. This time for re-
plenishment was necessary for Lew as a choreographer, but
Harold's responsibilities as director of the school permitted
no such luxury. He took only two weeks of vacation a year,
one at the end of the winter term, and one at the end of the
summer (during which he prepared for the fall term). Harold
had a strong work ethic and dealt with others according to
the strict standards of his own unyielding integrity. Once a
class started late because a photographer had come to take

a publicity shot of one of the dancers and the teacher had decided to turn the situation into an object lesson for her students. Harold, seeing only the interruption in the schedule, scolded the teacher for the delay. This unbending commitment to form sometimes offended those with whom he worked, but no one could question Harold's dedication or his tireless efforts to further the school and the company.

After the international tours of the late 1950s, Lew focused on strengthening the presence of his company in its home city. He was fond of observing that the only places the San Francisco Ballet had not been engulfed in applause were Antarctica, Timbuktu, and San Francisco.[18] On tour, Lew had been hosted by dignitaries, feted at receptions, and decorated by heads of state. Now he faced the more mundane challenge of drumming up enough local performing opportunities to earn the dancers' pay and to keep the company together. He risked losing his experienced dancers if he could not provide work for them; they now knew their worth and were accustomed to both the income and performing implied by extended contracts.[19] The major stumbling block to lining up regular seasons was that SFB had only intermittent access to the opera house because the symphony and opera company had higher priority in scheduling the building. So Lew and Kalimos tried a new venue: the Alcazar Theatre, a midsized legitimate drama house in the city's theater district. More intimate in scale and ambience than the opera house, the Alcazar was more easily filled, and its stage did not dwarf the small company. Kalimos instituted the company's first subscription series while Lew created new repertory for the new setting: *Danza Brillante*, to Mendelssohn, and *Esmeralda: Pas de Deux*. The Balanchine connection continued with SFB's premiere of that choreographer's *Pas de Dix*, and Maria

---

[18] Cobbett Steinberg, "Lew Christensen: An American Original," *Encore* 1.3 (Summer 1984): 13.

[19] Suki Schorer claims that Lew assigned roles by seniority so as not to give his most experienced dancers cause to leave, and that in so doing he discouraged younger, less experienced dancers. Interview with Suki Schorer, New York, New York, May 13, 1988.

Tallchief and Jacques D'Amboise appeared as guest artists. The support from NYCB continued to be a tremendous asset during this period as Lew handled the artistic direction of the company with little or no assistance, especially after Bené Arnold left San Francisco for Salt Lake City in 1962. Busy with teaching, rehearsing most of the repertory, auditioning Ford Foundation students, doing lecture demonstrations, and even building scenery on the side, Lew was content to leave administrative and financial decisions totally to Kalimos.[20]

A second spring season at the Alcazar (1961) enabled Lew to present another Balanchine ballet, *Symphony in C*, as well as two new works of his own. *St. George and the Dragon*, set to Hindemith's *Kammermusick No. 1 for Wind Quartet*, depicted three St. Georges rescuing three damsels from three dragons, simultaneously, with the rather cubist twist that each trio was presented to the audience at a different angle.[21] But the hit of that season was *Original Sin*, a tongue-in-cheek retelling of the Adam and Eve story with an original jazz score by John Lewis. Complete with angels, flaming swords, and an elaborately costumed bestiary, *Original Sin* starred Michael Smuin as the serpent and presented a provocative Adam and Eve (Roderick Drew and Sally Bailey) in nude-colored unitards.[22] Adam arose as if coming to life from clay in the Garden of Eden, named the animals (from walrus and ape, lamb and leopard, to zebra, lion, and camel) in dances of twos and threes, and then paused to rest by the gnarled roots of a tree. As he rested, Eve (hiding behind the tree since the beginning of the ballet) emerged from Adam's "rib" and joined him in a dance of highly charged sexual discovery, the two dancers shifting positions of bodily contact until the serpent entered offering the fruit of temptation. Foreshadowing the sexual openness to come later in the decade, *Original Sin*

---

[20] Michael Smuin recounts the heavy list of Lew's responsibilities, concluding, "It seemed like he just did everything." KQED Interview with Michael Smuin.

[21] Steinberg, "Lew Christensen: An American Original," 13.

[22] My description is indebted to Cobbett Steinberg's discussion of *Original Sin* in *San Francisco Ballet: The First Fifty Years* (San Francisco: San Francisco Ballet Association), 98.

was by far the most erotic of Lew's balletic romances, but its significance lay beyond its risqué foreplay. Although the new work was less obvious an essay in Americana than *Pocahontas* or *Filling Station*, Lew saw the jazz-inspired ballet as "an American idea adapted to American music rather than an imported European idea."[23] This brand of Americana guaranteed box office success; the ballet was reviewed in *Time* magazine, and the five scheduled performances stretched to fourteen.

In 1960, during the usual summer lull in company activity, a group of the dancers appeared in works by Michael Smuin and Jeannde Herst at the Contemporary Dancers Center in a program entitled "Ballet '60." This, Harold decided, was not in the company's best interest; if company members wanted to try their hand at choreography, they should be encouraged to do so within the SFB organization or through the SFB School. The following summer, with Harold's encouragement and Lew's blessing, the "Ballet '61" series was held on SFB's own premises on 18th Avenue, using the raised studio as a stage. The Ballet '60s series developed into an annual event closely associated with the company, although it began as an experimental offshoot of SFB's activities.

The stability so hopefully established by the two spring seasons at the Alcazar evaporated when the property's owner decided to replace the theater with a hotel. Kalimos kept the company on contract by arranging three weeks at another of San Francisco's legitimate theaters, the Geary, the following spring (1962) and filling the remaining time with a "bus and truck" tour, on which company members spent long hours on a bus between engagements. Another obstacle to lining up season dates in San Francisco was the increasing difficulty of securing members of the San Francisco Symphony to accompany productions, due to conflicts in performance scheduling. Eventually Lew came to an agreement with the Oakland

---

[23] *Ibid.*

Symphony and its conductor, Gerhard Samuel, who obligingly scheduled his symphony's concerts so as to keep that group available for the ballet. Active in contemporary music circles, Samuel found Lew receptive to the idea of using new compositions. At his suggestion, Lew chose an atonal score by Ernst Krenek for the major effort of the 1962 spring season, *Jest of Cards*.

While in Balanchine's *Card Party* the play of the deck had been carefully worked out "according to Hoyle," Lew's *Jest of Cards* presented a grim, "existential" game in which the cards were "shuffled about by life, thrown into the 'nothingness' of the stage wings, only to discover that death, the Joker, was the trump card."[24] Lew created the role of the bounding Joker for Smuin's compact physique and worked out the visual aspects of *Jest of Cards* with Duquette (with whom he had previously collaborated on *The Lady of Shalott* and *Beauty and the Beast*). The element of visual design assumed a key role in Lew's ballets of this period, perhaps because of Kalimos's taste and Duquette's influence with the board of the guild. In *Cards* Lew and Duquette explored the idea of choreographed scenery, creating shuffling drops as well as towering kings, queens, and jacks – richly robed dancers on stilts. Duquette enjoyed the chance to work on a project he considered so avant-garde: "I was always thinking in terms of the Ballets Russes and Bakst." When he expressed such an outlook to Lew, the latter replied with a chuckle, "You have a generous view of things."[25] But *Jest of Cards* proved a major hit for the company, and *Life* magazine named it "one of two important ballet events of the spring," the other being the Balanchine/Stravinsky *Noah and the Flood*.[26]

---

[24] Steinberg, *San Francisco Ballet*, 98.

[25] Telephone conversation with Tony Duquette, January 5, 1989.

[26] "Deck of Dancing Cards," *Life*, June 8, 1962, 91. Balanchine's *Card Party*, in which Lew had danced in the 1937 Stravinsky Festival, must have suggested some ideas to Lew as he choreographed *Jest of Cards*. On the other hand, it is worth pointing out that Lew did *Original Sin* a year *before* Balanchine did his take on Genesis, *Noah and the Flood*. Perhaps in some cases the influence worked both ways.

**38** Michael Smuin looks on while Lew Christensen arranges Fiona
Fuerstner's headpiece for *Jest of Cards*, 1962.
Photograph by Henri McDowell, courtesy of San Francisco Performing Arts
Library and Museum

By the spring that saw the creation of *Jest of Cards*,
Lew's company was strong in good dancers. He had lost
Conrad Ludlow and Suki Schorer to New York City Ballet,
and Richard Carter and Nancy Johnson had gone to San Diego

to found a company, but Lew still had Vollmar as the company's leading ballerina and other proven dancers from the international touring years: Sally Bailey, Roderick Drew, Fiona Fuerstner, Virginia Johnson, Frank Ohman, Terry Orr, Michael Smuin, Kent Stowell, and Paula Tracy. SFB was not short on men; Robert Gladstein had graduated from the school into the company, and Finis Jhung had come from Willam's program in Utah. In addition, many of the Ford Foundation scholarship students, such as Cynthia Gregory, had progressed to the point that they could be used in performances.

Immediately following the season at the Geary Theater, a strong SFB traveled to Seattle to perform at the World's Fair. It did not, however, return in the same strength. Several of Lew's top dancers, having no performing opportunities other than the "Ballet '62" workshop to look forward to during the coming months, put their World's Fair pay toward transportation to New York City. One by one they approached Lew at the end of the run to tell him they were leaving: Michael Smuin and Paula Tracy, Kent Stowell, Frank Ohman, Finis Jhung, and Jeffreys Hobart. Roderick Drew agreed to stay with SFB through a performance at Stern Grove that summer, but then he, too, left for New York.

Lew took the departures very personally, even though he understood his dancers' desires to try their fortunes in the nation's dance capital. Lew and Harold had raided dance schools throughout the West to build their own school and company, persuading other teachers that their pupils' achievements would bring honor to their home schools. Now Lew found himself in the position of the discarded master, and it hurt. The subsequent successes of those very dancers in New York City Ballet (Stowell and Ohman), American Ballet Theatre (Smuin and Tracy), and the Harkness and Joffrey companies (Jhung and Drew) did, indeed, confirm Lew's reputation as a teacher and build his reputation in the East while he remained in San Francisco. But this was little comfort in comparison with the overpowering sense of loss. Lew telephoned Carter in San Diego to tell him the bad news.

"Have you got fifty cents?" asked Lew sourly. "I'll sell you a ballet company, cheap."[27]

Lew's dancers left because they needed steady employment in order to earn a living. Lowry diagnosed the situation in San Francisco early in his research:

> *Ultimately they must put the dancers on annual contract or they will continue simply to be a pool raided by the New York City Ballet Company and Ballet Theatre. This is particularly difficult when they train a good male dancer.*[28]

It was clear that without the funds necessary to pay his dancers well, year-round, Lew would always lose them to better opportunities. He and Kalimos retaliated by scheduling more bus and truck tours, which, although grueling, at least kept the company together. In 1963 they provided the dancers forty-week contracts, an achievement the *New York Times* critic Allen Hughes pronounced "extraordinary in the American dance world."[29]

By 1963, Lowry had completed the exploratory phase of his program and was ready to make direct grants to dance companies. New York City Ballet and the School of American Ballet were to be the chief beneficiaries, not only because of Balanchine's prominence as a choreographer but because of an extensive nationwide scholarship program to be administered through SAB. Beyond New York, Lowry was interested in cities that had (1) professionals qualified to run a company, (2) a nucleus of dancers organized in a nonprofit organization, and (3) enough financial backing from local citizens to match Ford money and insure the future of a company. Parties

---

[27] Telephone interview with Richard Carter, December 6, 1988. Personal finances may also have added to Lew's woes; James Ludwig asserts that after mounting the 1962 spring season, Lew and Harold were deeply in debt and getting by on loans against their property. Interview with James Ludwig, San Francisco, California, December 2, 1988.

[28] Memo to the Ford Foundation Records Center, from W. McNeil Lowry, September 15 and 17, 1961, Ford Foundation Archives, PA59–465.

[29] Allen Hughes, "The San Francisco Ballet Grows Rapidly," *New York Times*, May 5, 1963.

desiring a grant were instructed to submit proposals to the Ford Foundation showing their needs and how grant money would be spent.

As Lowry continued his trips across the country, he met with Lew and Kalimos in San Francisco to help them put together a realistic grant proposal. Kalimos envisioned an elaborate, multimillion dollar setup, but Lowry brought him back down to earth after seeing the actual figures of annual support from SFB's guild. The Ford Foundation was limited, in part, by a company's ability to raise funds in its home city, and private patrons in San Francisco did not support dance on the same scale as either the opera or the symphony.

The situation was somewhat different in Salt Lake City, where Willam's company had reached as professional a level possible in its academic setting. He had chosen that setting at a time in his life when he needed stability and security, a haven from the pressures and politics of the world of professional ballet. Now, at age sixty-one, Willam told Abravanel that he felt "bottled up." The production support Willam received from his department was purchased at a cost; he was still expected to choreograph musicals and operas in addition to running the student ballet company. The Department of Speech, Theatre, and Ballet was no longer big enough to contain Willam's aspirations; he wanted more freedom to tour and more opportunities for his dancers. Willam confided to Abravanel, "I have to get out of the university."[30]

Willam began to talk in terms of paying engagements for the University Theatre Ballet (UTB). His student company performed annually in the *Nutcracker*, the May concerts, and the summer theatre festivals, with occasional short tours to Idaho and Southern Utah. A subset of UTB had even toured South America, subsidized by the U.S. State Department, with the university's production of *Annie, Get Your Gun*.[31] The dancers wanted to have a professional company, in Utah, in

---

[30] Interview with Maurice Abravanel, Salt Lake City, Utah, November 25, 1987.

[31] Nigel S. Hey, "Professor in Ballet Slippers," *Dance Magazine*, May 1963, 52.

which they could earn a living after they had graduated. That idea made all the sense in the world to Willam, whose entrepreneurial streak had him itching to line up more bookings.

As Willam contemplated the possibility of directing a touring company again, he was well aware of the Ford Foundation's plans for future arts funding. On a trip to the East, he eagerly explored the possibility of his student group receiving a grant. Lowry had followed Willam's activities with interest for several years and had settled on him as a professional worth backing, but UTB's university affiliation disqualified it from consideration. As long as Willam's troupe was part of a university program, it could not receive Ford Foundation assistance. If, on the other hand, Willam could transform his group into a professional company, with non-profit tax status, he had a good chance at the money.

Faced with this tantalizing prospect, Willam called together the board of the Ballet Society, minus Mrs. Wallace who was in Beverly Hills, and explained the situation. When he added that the local community would have to raise "a few thousand dollars" to match the Ford grant, Willam was rewarded with astonished stares; the Salt Lake support group had never been engaged in serious fund-raising. So Willam called Mrs. Wallace in California and received her resolute promise of support.[32] Under Mrs. Wallace's determined leadership, the Ballet Society reorganized itself and was incorporated as a nonprofit organization, the Utah Ballet Society, specifically designed to support the development of greater performing opportunities for Willam's company.[33]

The process of negotiating the company's separation from the university proved more complicated. The administrators who had braved controversy to bring Willam to Salt Lake and had supported the growth of his program were offended that he would even consider taking it off campus.

---

[32] Robert J. Welsh interview with Willam F. Christensen, Ballet Studio, University of Utah, October 9, 1975.

[33] Susan White, "Utah Civic Ballet and Ballet West: A Preliminary Study, 1964–1976," M.A. thesis, University of Utah, 1982, 9.

Ballet performances had become a source of pride for the university, and both the annual *Nutcracker* and the May concerts with guest artists from New York brought welcome revenue in ticket sales.[34] The administration valued the program Willam had built and did not want to lose it. The plan to go professional met with such stiff resistance from administrators that Willam feared losing his job if he pushed too hard.

In a stance typical of his expansive thinking, Willam did not intend to quit teaching at the University of Utah; he just wanted to add the responsibilities of directing a professional company to the load he was already carrying. He could not afford to cut himself off completely from the university; he needed the campus's physical facilities and the steady supply of dancers provided by the Extension Division and by the college-level classes. Moreover, being part of a degree-earning program was an attraction that had brought him some of his best performers, dancers who wanted a college education. For instance, Anne Burton, who was originally from Georgia, left New York City Ballet after touring with that company in 1962 and enrolled at the University of Utah so that she could get a college degree while continuing to dance.

Lowry visited Salt Lake City, met with Willam, Mrs. Wallace, and President Olpin, and helped work out a compromise that would allow the dancers to qualify for a grant without completely disrupting the university's successful ballet program. The dancers would be professional in the sense of being paid to perform. In addition to directing this professional group, Willam would remain on the faculty and would continue to oversee the Extension Division (later, Division of Continuing Education) program. The university would retain ownership of the *Nutcracker* production (although this was later bought by the nonprofit Utah Ballet Society). Company classes and rehearsals would be held in the university's ballet studios, and the university, rather than

---

[34] Hey, 52.

the company, would pay Willam's salary. To insure that Willam got the support he needed in Salt Lake, Lowry impressed upon Mrs. Wallace the necessity of raising matching funds and building a strong financial base in Utah.

Confidential letters notifying both Willam's and Lew's companies that they had received Ford Foundation grants arrived early in December 1963. The official announcement was not made public until December 16, at which time a storm of controversy reverberated through the American dance world. Nearly $6 million of the $7.7 million appropriated for dance by the Ford Foundation went to institutions presided over by Balanchine and Kirstein: New York City Ballet and the School of American Ballet. (This figure is somewhat deceptive, as $1.5 million of that amount was earmarked for scholarships around the country, but even that scholarship program was to be administered by SAB.[35]) The remaining approximately $1.8 million was divided between Lew's San Francisco Ballet ($644,000), the National Ballet of Washington, D.C. ($400,000), the Pennsylvania Ballet ($295,000), Willam's "Utah Ballet," ($175,000), the Houston Ballet ($173,750), and the Boston Ballet ($144,000).[36]

Lowry, anticipating the impact his multimillion dollar program would have in dance circles, had given advance notice to major papers to allow them to prepare adequate coverage, but not even Lowry guessed the storm of protest the Ford grants would elicit. Allen Hughes of the *New York Times* declared that by obviously favoring the Balanchine–Kirstein institutions, the Ford Foundation had upset the usual "checks and balances" of the dance economy, and Walter

---

[35] Lowry insists that this manner of interpreting the figures is deceptive because only $2,000,000 was earmarked for NYCB, and that amount was to stretch over ten years, as with the other companies' grants. The School of American Ballet received $2,425,000 in addition to the $1,500,000 in local and regional scholarship money it was to administer. These three figures total $5,925,000 – clearly a lion's share of the prize.

[36] "Presstime News: Historic Bonanza For Ballet in America," *Dance Magazine*, January 1964, 3–4. An authoritative source of information on the Ford Foundation grants is Kendall, *Dancing: A Ford Foundation Report.*

Terry of the *New York Herald Tribune* asserted that the "flagrant favoritism" shown would lead to "an unhealthy monopoly."[37] Dorothy. Alexander, a leader in the regional ballet movement, received the news of the Ford Foundation's "one-dimensional view of dance in America" with "a sense of impending disaster," while Sol Hurok found the lack of a grant for Ballet Theatre "astonishing."[38] (According to Lowry, Lucia Chase was invited to apply for one of the grants but American Ballet Theatre failed to provide the Ford Foundation with sufficiently detailed financial information during the application period.[39]) Perhaps the most dramatic response came from the modern dance pioneer Ted Shawn, who accused the Ford Foundation of "warping and distorting the world of dance in America away from its organic development" since the days of Isadora Duncan and Ruth St. Denis. "Please, Mr. Lowry," he urged, "Do not be another Pontius Pilate, do not wash your hands, shrug 'What is truth?,' and allow the true American dance to be crucified on a cross of Ford Foundation gold!"[40]

A recurring theme of the protests was not only that modern dance, a genuine "American" contribution to theatrical dance, had been ignored, but that only one style of ballet received the legitimizing support of Ford Foundation money. Critics protested that the grant money would, in effect, institutionalize Balanchine's style as the approved model of classical dancing in America. If such was Lowry's intent, Lew's lingering connection to New York City Ballet stood him in good stead: his company received the largest amount after the New York City Ballet and School of American Ballet. But Willam was no Balanchine disciple. His concept of ballet had been formed in an essentially pre-Balanchine era, his training

---

[37] Hughes and Terry are quoted in "Ford Foundation Controversy Pros and Cons," *Dance Magazine*, January 1964, 38, 82.

[38] *Ibid.*, 36.

[39] Interview with W. McNeil Lowry, New York, New York, May 9, 1988.

[40] Letter from Ted Shawn to W. McNeil Lowry, reprinted in "Ford Foundation Controversy," 36.

defined by Mascagno and Novikoff and his tastes honed on Fokine and Massine. His family connection to Lew cannot be ignored as a strategic reason why Willam's essentially student company received a Ford grant (and a small one, at that); however, those who argue that the money went only to NYCB and "Balanchine satellite" companies show complete misunderstanding of Willam's troupe and its repertory. Of the thirty-six ballets presented by UTB between 1952 and 1963, over two-thirds were choreographed by Willam himself, another ten percent were works by his brother Lew, and the remainder consisted of contributions from guest artists such as Jacques D'Amboise and restagings of standard repertory (Fokine's *Les Sylphides* and virtuosic excerpts from Petipa's ballets such as the grand pas de deux from *Don Quixote*).[41] UTB programs featured Balanchine choreography only when guest artists such as André Eglevsky performed excerpts from the NYCB repertory or when Lew's dancers performed SFB repertory on the same bill as Willam's students.

*After* the 1963 Ford Foundation grants, Balanchine ballets did indeed enter the regular repertory of Willam's newly professional company, starting, appropriately, with *Serenade* in 1964. But Balanchine's influence never overwhelmed the personal nature of Willam's company; rather, the Utah Civic Ballet (as it was christened) acquired Balanchine ballets gradually, adding *Concerto Barocco* in 1965 and *Symphony in C* in 1968. Willam's own ballets, designed to meet the talents and needs of his dancers, always greatly outnumbered those of other choreographers. When Balanchine works did enter Utah Civic Ballet's repertory, they were used to compose balanced programs. In a typical concert, a neoclassical Balanchine work such as *Concerto Barocco* would appear alongside a comedy by Lew (*Filling Station* or *Con Amore*) and one of Willam's dramatic ballets (*Creatures of Prometheus* or *Les Bijoux du Mal*) or a virtuoso piece (Willam's *Pas de Six*).

---

[41] Statistics compiled from Cole's chronicle of UTB performances. Diana Muriel Cole, "Utah Ballet – A Unique Development in the World of Dance," M.A. thesis, University of Utah, 1971.

Willam's balanced approach was also evident in the
guest artists he hired from 1964 through 1968, the five years
the Utah Civic Ballet was in existence as such (before its
name change to Ballet West). Jacques D'Amboise, Marnee
Morris, and Melissa Hayden, all of NYCB, appeared with
UCB during those five years (D'Amboise repeatedly), but so
did ABT's Scott Douglas and Lupe Serrano (twice), Toni
Lander and Bruce Marks, and the Harkness Ballet's Roderick
Drew and Panchita de Peri. Willam even rented the entire
ABT production, sets and costumes, of *Firebird* when he
decided to choreograph his own version in 1967. To cite
Willam's company as proof that Ford money went only to
Balanchine and Balanchine "satellite" companies is to misrep-
resent Willam's tastes as an artist and his intent as a company
director.[42]

Winning the Ford Foundation grant brought attention
to Willam's company at home as well as in the national press,
validated his efforts in the sight of local leaders and potential
benefactors, and vindicated those who had gone out on a limb
to bring him to the university in the first place. The controversy over the grant recipients that played out in the New
York press and national dance periodicals had little impact
on Willam, but his own teapot tempest stirred in Salt Lake
City. In a local newspaper article about the newly professional
company, Willam tactfully and generously recognized the
important role the university had played and would continue
to play in the success of the new professional company.
Willam felt that giving credit to the university was the
honorable thing to do, and when his remarks appeared in the
paper he felt that he had smoothed over the bad feelings
generated in the process of going public: "I felt good because
we were in harmony again."[43]

[42] Lowry even claims that in 1963 Kirstein did not approve of Ford Foundation
money going to Willam's company. "He was shocked that I cared about what was
going on in Utah, being the kind of elitist that he was." Later, Kirstein reversed that
opinion and agreed that Lowry had acted wisely in endowing the Utah Civic Ballet.
Interview with W. McNeil Lowry, New York, New York, May 24, 1988.

[43] Interview with Willam F. Christensen, Salt Lake City, Utah, July 2, 1988.

But Mrs. Wallace called Willam on the carpet, furious that he had spoken out in such terms because she feared it would hurt their chances of raising the necessary matching funds ($100,000 in five years). Wallace countered Willam's article with a strident press announcement claiming, "The Utah Ballet Company is a completely independent entity, and is not affiliated with the University of Utah. Its financing will be accomplished through the Ford Foundation and through contributed matching funds."[44] As if to underscore the break with the university, the Utah Civic Ballet made its debut performance not in Kingsbury Hall, where the student company had always performed, but in the auditorium of Skyline High School, which had a larger stage.[45] While Mrs. Wallace set her sights on community fund-raising, Willam was left to deal with the residual resentment on campus, which lingered several years.[46]

---

[44] *Salt Lake Tribune*, December 22, 1963, quoted in White, 9.

[45] The inaugural concert of the Skyline High School auditorium had been an appearance by the Royal Winnipeg Ballet, so the Utah Civic Ballet had a respectable precedent for performing on that stage. "Royal Winnipeg Ballet Initiates Skyline High Stage," *Salt Lake Tribune*, February 13, 1963.

[46] Gordon Paxman asserts that the cloud of that controversy hung over Willam's efforts and presence on campus for many years, really until the company had severed its university ties completely and stopped performing in Kingsbury Hall, which did not happen until the year Willam retired. Telephone interview with Gordon Paxman, November 29, 1989.

# 14

## SAN FRANCISCO BALLET IN THE 1960s

The 1963 Ford Foundation grant, which provided much needed financial backing to Lew and Harold's institutions in San Francisco, did not erase the brothers' professional concerns. Grant money helped to cover the costs of new productions and dancers' salaries, and that brought the company a limited security. But other challenges spanned the decade of the 1960s, namely, the periodic loss of well-trained dancers and the company's lack of a home theater. The latter forced SFB out of town for performance opportunities; after the international tours of the late 1950s, the '60s was a decade of extensive domestic touring. For Lew and his company, touring meant rising very early and driving all day to the destination where they would perform that evening, sometimes arriving just in time for a snack before dancing a full program. Dancers had assigned seats on the bus, with location determined by seniority in the company. Some decorated their windows or added personal touches to make the vehicle in which they spent so many hours seem more like home.

By 1960, performing in San Francisco Opera productions had provided bread-and-butter money for Christensen dancers for over two decades, but the marriage of convenience was wearing thin. Merola's successor, Kurt Herbert Adler, evinced little of his predecessor's fondness for ballet. Lew's grudge against opera ballet in general (developed during the years at the Metropolitan) was intensified when Adler cut carefully planned choreography in last-minute rehearsals.[1] Given that the funding SFB received from the city

---

[1] Interview with Robert Gladstein, San Francisco, California, November 30, 1988.

was less than half the amount either the opera or the symphony received, Lew probably did not feel he owed the opera company any favors, yet he was called upon regularly to help stage the opera's annual Fol-De-Rol benefit performances without remuneration.[2] The greatest drawback of SFB's dancing in the fall opera season was that it hampered Kalimos's ability to plan tours. In 1962, after the disastrous exodus of dancers following the World's Fair engagement, Lew and Kalimos announced that that year would be the last time the San Francisco Ballet would be available for the opera. Although Lew did occasionally provide choreography for opera productions after 1962, the fall months were given to stateside touring in subsequent years. Some years, as a sort of compromise, one subset of the company toured with repertory from the summer experimental season, while another group remained behind to dance in the operas.

In the absence of a home theater, the building on 18th Avenue doubled as the school and a small performance facility, where the "Ballet '60s" productions were staged on the raised studio with an audience of two hundred on Harold's bleachers. Because the company's opportunities for exposure in San Francisco were so limited, the summer series took on greater significance in the annual round of performances. The "Ballet '60" series became SFB's experimental arm, experimental in the sense that it featured the works of as-yet unproven choreographers. Over the years, its repertory included works by Smuin and Herst, Kent Stowell, Robert Gladstein, Jocelyn Vollmar, Terry Orr, Ron Poindexter, Frank Ordway, Thatcher Clarke, Carlos Carvajal, John McFall, Ronn Guidi, Stuart Hodes, and many others. Lew himself used the workshop as a laboratory, devising within its framework *Prokofiev Waltzes* (1961), *Bach Concert* (1962), *Dance Variations* (1963), *Il Distratto* (1967), *Three Movements for the Short Haired*

---

[2] "The Hotel Tax Is Divvied Up: Who Got What," *San Francisco Chronicle*, August 24, 1967, Russell Hartley Scrapbooks, 1967, San Francisco Performing Arts Library and Museum.

(1968), and *The Magical Flutist* (1968). A chief benefit of the series was that it provided choreographers the opportunity to create new works without risking failure in the high-stakes environment of the opera house. Ballets judged successful in this try-out were then considered for programming during the regular season. Although in the 1960s the company was still an essentially Christensen concern, with a repertory dominated by Lew's ballets and supplemented by Balanchine, the Ballet '60s series earned SFB a reputation for nurturing and promoting its own talent.

Just after the announcement of the Ford Foundation grant, SFB received another dispensation of good fortune. Margot Fonteyn and Rudolf Nureyev had been scheduled to perform at the White House in early 1964, but the assassination of John F. Kennedy in November 1963 forced the cancellation of that engagement. So the president of the ballet guild, James Ludwig, who knew Fonteyn personally, invited the couple to perform with SFB during their now free period. Fonteyn accepted, on terms generous to the company. After appearing in San Francisco's War Memorial Opera House, the company and its guest stars toured to St. Louis and Chicago. Lew generally disliked depending on guest artists because he wanted his company to be strong enough to stand on its own merits, but he recognized the value of Fonteyn and Nureyev's box office appeal. The tour netted the company a healthy sum ($64,000, according to Ludwig), which Kalimos put toward the company's anticipated debut at Lincoln Center the following year.[3]

Following the appearances with Nureyev and Fonteyn, Lew oversaw a winter tour of one-night stands, a spring season at the Geary Theatre, a fall tour of one-night stands, and a holiday season at the Opera House, during

---

[3] Interview with James Ludwig, San Francisco, California, December 2, 1988. Lew invited Nureyev to give company class one day while they were in Chicago, a fact Kalimos holds up as proof that Lew did not resent the Russian's ability to overshadow American dancers in box office draw. Telephone interview with Leon Kalimos, December 28, 1988.

which ABC-TV filmed his version of the *Nutcracker*.[4] Other
than the unresolved issue of a home theater, which the company was working around, Lew's position looked good by
1965. In a report published that year, the Rockefeller Panel
cited SFB as a model for other dance companies.[5] And rumors
circulated early in 1965 that Lew had another offer to return
to New York City Ballet. While he probably did not entertain
the prospect seriously, leaks to the press reinforced his
importance on San Francisco's cultural scene, and Ludwig
went so far as to assure local papers that Lew would not leave
until a proper replacement could be found.[6]

Lew did have his eye on New York, not for his own
employment, but for SFB's debut at Lincoln Center after
nearly fifteen years under his leadership. After a two-month
spring tour, the company would perform in the home of
Balanchine's company, the New York State Theater, where it
would draw the full attention of New York's critical establishment. What Lew hoped to gain from this personally can
only be guessed. For better or for worse, New York represented the pinnacle of talent and influence in American dance,
the crucible in whose theaters reputations were made or
broken. Although one might argue with a system according
any single city, even one with New York's unique institutions
and cultural norms, such validating power, the undeniable

---

[4] The performance of the *Nutcracker* filmed by ABC featured Cynthia Gregory and
David Anderson as the Sugar Plum Fairy and her Cavalier, and Virginia Johnson
and Terry Orr as the Snow Queen and King. The filming, done December 22, 1964,
commenced at 8:30 p.m. and continued until 4:30 the next morning. The show aired
on New Year's Day in 1965 in the United States and was later televised abroad.
Cobbett Steinberg, *San Francisco Ballet: The First Fifty Years* (San Francisco: San
Francisco Ballet Association, 1983), 107.

[5] Rockefeller Panel Report, *The Performing Arts: Problems and Prospects* (New York:
McGraw-Hill Book Company, 1965), 46. The report explained that SFB was really
two companies, the larger troupe, and the subset of the company that put on the
summer season and toured with the summer repertory each fall. The report also
drew attention to the SFB School, which had an enrollment of 400 and gave student
recitals.

[6] "Stumbled into Jim Ludwig," unattributed clipping, Lew Christensen Clipping File,
Dance Collection, The New York Public Library.

perception was that a successful New York engagement would be the highest form of validation SFB could earn. Praise from New York's critics would grant his company a seal of approval that affirmed the quality of Lew's choreography and his contribution as a company director.[7] Before leaving the Bay Area, the dancers presented the ballets with which they hoped to take New York by storm: *Life* and *Lucifer*.

The original impetus for *Life* came from Kalimos, who clipped a picture of a Pop Art painting from the newspaper and dropped it on Lew's desk.[8] Kalimos considered it his job not only to shelter Lew from administrative and business concerns but also to stimulate Lew's creative processes and prod him to new works. This was especially important since Lew no longer had the artistic stimulation James Graham-Luján had provided earlier. Lew liked the notion of doing a work incorporating Pop Art images and conferred with Cal Anderson, a commercial artist who had designed SFB publications and who generously supported the company. Anderson recommended that Lew hire a New Yorker, perhaps Roy Lichtenstein or Andy Warhol, to design the sets. But negotiations in that direction fell through, so Anderson took on the task himself.

Lew set this cynical statement about modern society to two pieces by Charles Ives: *Halloween* and *The Pond*. The San Francisco columnist Herb Caen had taken a few potshots at SFB, so Lew enlisted Caen to write the libretto in hopes of changing the writer's attitude toward the company.[9] The ballet traced the four ages of modern man: Incipiency

---

[7] Arlene Croce takes a hard look at New York's power to canonize dance companies in "Stuttgart's Ballet, New York's Myth," *Afterimages* (New York: Alfred A. Knopf, 1977), 344–55.

[8] Cal Anderson clarifies that the clipping was of a work by Mel Ramos, who painted realistic nudes and women in bathing suits, and who was not, in Anderson's opinion, strictly a Pop artist. Lew, however, considered the painting as being in a Pop vein and used it as a point of departure for the new work. Interview with Cal Anderson, San Francisco, California, December 1, 1988.

[9] Craig Palmer interview with Lew Christensen for KQED documentary.

("children should be obscene but not absurd"), Virility ("fraught with sex and violence and all the other good things of life"), Maturity ("the age of anxiety has given way to the age of tranquilizers"), and Resignation ("happy is the man who can adjust to unreality, for he shall inherit the world of television").[10] Lew wanted to name the work *The Great Society* as a pointed reference to Lyndon Johnson's political ideals, but Lew's collaborators persuaded him that the new president's vision should not be satirized before it had had a chance to succeed, so they settled upon the title *Life: A Do-It-Yourself Disaster.*[11]

For the decor Lew requested a series of shifting panels, which Anderson filled with blown-up comic book characters, Warholesque S&H Green Stamps, and IBM punch cards. Images in the choreography itself included young kids chewing bubblegum and playing menacingly in the streets; a motorcycle gang in leather jackets who molest a girl and kill her boyfriend (the letters on the back of the jackets spelled "H-A-T-E" when the men turned upstage); a mourning widow who goes mad while those around her wear two-faced masks; and an elderly man before a television station out of which emerges a cross-section of American characters, including beauty queens, mop-haired musicians, and figures from commercials. *Life* presented a compendium of American figures, fragments of contemporary culture in a framework designed to give order through chronological sequence, but it did not provide answers to the social problems it pointed out. The ballet contained many blatant messages, the motorcyclists' "H-A-T-E" being perhaps the least subtle, but critics found fault with the production on the grounds that the ele ments did not come together to present a convincingly "biting commentary" on the "frenzied emptiness" of modern life.[12]

---

[10] Steinberg, *San Francisco Ballet*, 99. My description of *Life* is indebted to Steinberg's account of the work.

[11] Interview with Cal Anderson, San Francisco, California, December 1, 1988. The work was also performed under the title *Life: A Pop Art Ballet.*

[12] Steinberg, *San Francisco Ballet*, 99.

For the second new work, *Lucifer*, Lew went over several Hindemith scores with his conductor Gerhard Samuel. The composer's *Concert Music for Strings and Brass Instruments* appealed to Lew because of its contrasting timbres. Reuben Ter-Arutunian, a New York designer better known for his collaborations with Martha Graham and George Balanchine, created a backdrop of stained glass, a clear ladder from which Lucifer towered over the action on stage, and mammoth crystal wings. *Lucifer* drew its imagery from Milton's epic poem, *Paradise Lost*, but Lew underplayed the narrative of the devil's fall from heaven, using the idea as a pretext for a basically nonnarrative ballet. R. Clinton Rothwell, wearing a red mask, starred as Lucifer, opposite David Anderson as St. Michael and a chorus of angels, led by Sally Bailey and Cynthia Gregory. Russell Hartley, in his column in *Dance Magazine*, suggested that *Lucifer*'s strength lay in the "elegant, detached, and spiritual abstractions result[ing] in a glittering display of choreographic symmetry."[13] The ballet's weakness lay in the final confrontation between St. Michael and Lucifer, a literal tussle that ended in the latter's fall from grace (down the lucite ladder) in a shaft of bright light which represented God. Critics found the title figure inadequately characterized and objected that the choreography contained little suggestion of pride and insufficient Satanic struggle to substantiate the ballet's title and supposed source. As a choreographer, Lew could not have it both ways; either he had to re-create the drama inherent in the ballet's pretext (through more dramatic movement, not necessarily through reliance on mime or literal confrontation), or he must give up the outward tokens of that source (the wings, the ladder, the shaft of light).[14] To deflect

---

[13] Russell Hartley, "San Francisco Bay Area News," *Dance Magazine*, April 1965, 79.

[14] When Lew explained his approach to choreography in *Dance Magazine*, during SFB's engagement at Jacob's Pillow, he stated that a plot in a ballet is like a colored gel that one places in front of a stage light. It changes the way the audience looks at the movement. The movement itself was what interested Lew most. It seems that he sometimes used plots as a gel for himself or as a springboard for a work. But in the case of *Lucifer*, having used the springboard, he abandoned it because it was not what interested him most as a choreographer. Lew Christensen, "Story and Story-Less Ballets," *Dance Magazine*, July 1956, 24–25.

expectations of an obvious narrative, Lew retitled the work *Concert Music for Strings and Brass Instruments.*

Following the local premiere of these works, the company headed south for the long bus tour that would culminate in Manhattan during Easter week (1965). After six weeks of one-night stands, the dancers arrived in New York exhausted but excited about their Lincoln Center debut. A large contingent of the SFB Guild's board flew in for opening night festivities, to enjoy the company's anticipated triumph. Thinking perhaps to impress the New York critics with the company's contemporary savvy, Lew and Kalimos scheduled both *Life* and *Lucifer* for the opening performance. For pure bravura, they added *Divertisement d'Auber,* now a three movement ballet with the virtuoso trio as its centerpiece. As the week progressed, the company also presented *Beauty and the Beast*; *Fantasma,* a neo-Romantic ballet about a Wanderer and a Mistress of the Mansion set to Prokofiev waltzes; *Shadows,* a mysterious mood ballet that played with lighting effects as the leading female figure, surrounded by couples, searched for her shadow partner (score by Hindemith); *Sinfonia,* a neoclassical exercise to Boccherini with dense phrasing and Balanchinesque touches; and *Caprice,* a lighthearted closer about flirtations in a Viennese park, set to music by Franz von Suppé. The only non-Christensen work presented was Ron Poindexter's jazz ballet, *The Set.*

Audiences responded favorably to the company, but the critics found fault with the repertory and objected to the heavy preponderance of Lew's own works. The retitled *Lucifer* still brought criticism that its movement reflected little of Milton's themes of Satan's proud struggle and dramatic fall. (Ter-Arutunian's crystal wings, which rose from the shoulders of the angel-dancers at the beginning of the ballet to hang in midair, prompted unfortunate comparisons to handlebar mustaches.) Rather than being hailed as an innovative breakthrough, *Life* was seen as naive and was criticized for lacking a clear point of view. While the critics generally acknowledged the dancers' strong performing abilities, more than one suggested that costuming and scenery overwhelmed

Lew's choreography, particularly in elaborately produced works such as *Life* and *Beauty and the Beast*. The heavily dressed ballets appeared dependent upon externals, the decorative elements masking lackluster choreography. P. W. Manchester even raised the issue of the Ford Foundation grants, asserting, "On this showing it is impossible not to wonder on exactly what basis of merit did the Ford Foundation ... decide that San Francisco Ballet was deserving of $664,000."[15]

Overall, critical response reflected the direction in which the company had veered since the late 1950s. The lack of an in-house artistic advisor following Graham-Luján's departure may have prompted the subsequent emphasis on the elements of visual design, notably in Lew's collaborations with Duquette. Kalimos was undeniably committed to supporting Lew as an administrator, but Lew needed both administrative support *and* knowing artistic collaborators, not one at the expense of the other. That SFB could not afford both seriously weakened his efforts and affected his reputation as his choreography was put on national display.

Perhaps Lew should not have looked to New York for validation; perhaps he should have been content filling a cultural niche in his home city and in the western communities to which SFB toured. But Lew had made his reputation as a dancer in New York, and he still had important relationships with figures such as Balanchine and Kirstein. He cared about how his former colleagues viewed his work. That desire for acceptance caused Lew and his associates much disappointment as their bid for recognition brought unexpectedly negative results. Lew was further demoralized when company members slipped away to audition for other companies in the city, some even missing his rehearsals to do so. At the

---

[15] P. W. Manchester, "San Francisco Ballet: Too Little, Too Late," *Christian Science Monitor*, April 22, 1965. See also Allen Hughes, "Ballet: Coast Visitors," *New York Times*, April 14, 1965; Walter Terry, "2 New Ballets for New York," *New York Herald Tribune*, April 16, 1965; and Doris Hering, "San Francisco Ballet, New York State Theater, April 13–18, 1965," *Dance Magazine*, June 1965, 30, 32–33.

end of the tour the company disbanded for the summer, and Cynthia Gregory and Terry Orr left Lew to join American Ballet Theatre.[16]

During the months following the Lincoln Center debut, Lew's personal life took a sharp downward turn. Added to his discouragement over the company's New York reception was a new and very serious problem with his health; he was diagnosed as having prostate cancer and was hospitalized for treatments. When it became clear that he would not be able to create a new work for the dates set aside at the opera house the following January, Kalimos telephoned Balanchine and explained the company's plight. Balanchine offered SFB his *Scotch Symphony*, sending both the costumes and a ballet mistress to set the work on Lew's dancers.

So directly was the San Francisco Ballet a reflection of Lew's life and work that his productivity, or lack thereof, directly affected the company's fortunes. Rather than lining up an extended winter tour for the early months of 1966, Kalimos scheduled a sprinkling of opera house performances between mid-February and late April. Because the symphony had first choice on dates in the opera house, SFB was able to schedule only Saturday evening and Sunday matinee performances, a situation that was far from ideal.[17] As Lew recovered, he took a room at a motel near the opera. He would walk over and watch rehearsals as long as his stamina held out and then return to the room to rest. By May he had created a small ballet, *Pas de Six*, to music of the nineteenth-century

---

[16] Cynthia Gregory relates that she had auditioned for Balanchine the previous summer but that he hesitated to offer her a job when Lew depended on her so much. "I can't do this to my old friend Lew Christensen," demurred Balanchine; "I've taken too many dancers from him, and I feel terrible about it." Balanchine got around the issue by promising that if Gregory decided to leave SFB on her own, she would have a place in his company. When SFB was in New York, rehearsing the week before its State Theater debut, Gregory saw ABT perform and decided she liked the theatricality of that company; hence her decision to join ABT instead of NYCB. Interview with Cynthia Gregory, New York, New York, January 10, 1989.

[17] A.B., "Ballet Gets Leftover Dates for Spring," no paper, Russell Hartley notebooks, 1966, San Francisco Performing Arts Library and Museum.

Danish composer Hans Christian Lumbye, but that summer the choreographer's workshop season ("Ballet '66") unfolded without a contribution from him. The number of SFB performances dipped that year to 78, down markedly from 122 performances in 1965. That spring and fall the company made ends meet by doing lecture-demonstrations, sometimes three a day, sponsored by Title III funding in California schools.

To fill the vacuum caused by Lew's illness, Harold hired two highly distinguished teachers for the school: Anatole Vilzak and Ludmilla Schollar. Both had been trained at the Imperial School of Ballet in St. Petersburg and had danced leading roles at the Maryinsky Theater. Vilzak had joined Diaghilev's Ballets Russes as a premier danseur and, over the years, had appeared with Ida Rubinstein, René Blum's Ballets de Monte Carlo, and Balanchine's American Ballet at the Metropolitan Opera House, before joining the faculty at the School of American Ballet. Schollar, Vilzak's wife, had gained comparable performing experience, with Diaghilev, Rubenstein, and Bronislava Nijinska, before teaching in New York. Together Vilzak and Schollar provided the Christensens' students with a direct link to the classical tradition as epitomized by their former teachers, Cecchetti and Fokine.

Another sign of new life following Lew's illness came in the form of resuscitated fund-raising efforts. Over the years, Lew, Kalimos, and some of the leading dancers had formed the habit of eating a light supper after performances at the famous San Francisco restaurant Trader Vic's. The owner, Vic Bergeron, respected SFB and offered Kalimos a free fund-raising luncheon.[18] Kalimos took Bergeron up on the offer in November 1966 and used the highly publicized luncheon to announce the beginning of a ten-year fund-raising campaign. Money was desperately needed to revamp the worn-out 1954 *Nutcracker* production, whose costumes were in tatters, as well as to meet the qualifications of the Ford Foundation grant. Balanchine, who had supported Lew from afar by

[18] Telephone interview with Leon Kalimos, December 28, 1988.

lending him repertory, came to California to show his support for the San Francisco Ballet in person. Ray Bolger flew up from Los Angeles to add more star power to the occasion, and with photographers and reporters primed, guild president Ludwig announced a campaign to raise $2 million.[19]

Lew went to New York early in 1967 to meet with scene designer Robert O'Hearn about the projected new *Nutcracker*. (While in the city, Lew taught at the School of American Ballet, where he was always a welcome guest.) Following that summer's workshop performances, SFB lost another group of leading dancers to New York companies: David Anderson, Henry Berg, Zola Dishong, Betsy Erickson, Robert Gladstein, Sue Loyd, and Nancy Robinson.[20] This cut seriously into Lew's pool of experienced dancers just as the fund-raising drive kicked off at Trader Vic's was making his new *Nutcracker* a reality. As he had done in the past, Lew replenished the ranks of the company with advanced students from the school. For the opening night of the new production that December, to celebrate the conclusion of this long-overdue project, he brought Melissa Hayden and Jacques D'Amboise from NYCB to dance the Sugar Plum Fairy and her Cavalier. Harold and Ruby's son, Harold Christensen, Jr., appeared as Drosselmeyer's Assistant, thus extending the family performing tradition into the fourth generation on Harold's line.[21]

---

[19] Arthur Bloomfield, "S. F. Ballet Launches 10-Year 'Dream Realization' Plan," *San Francisco Examiner*, November 22, 1966.

[20] Russell Hartley, "The San Francisco Ballet: A History, 1922–1977." Unpublished manuscript, San Francisco Performing Arts Library and Museum, 114.

[21] Harold, Jr., had little enthusiasm for ballet and had to be coaxed by his parents to appear on stage. His oldest sister, Heidi, likewise became disenchanted with ballet lessons at a young age. Only the second daughter, Stephanie, loved to dance and took lessons enthusiastically until her early teens. According to Ruby, Stephanie stopped dancing when she was disappointed over not receiving a desired role in *The Nutcracker* one year. Interview with Ruby Asquith and Harold Christensen, San Anselmo, California, March 2, 1988. In the mid-1990s, married and living in Milwaukee, Stephanie served on the board of the Milwaukee Ballet, and her daughter studied at the Milwaukee Ballet School.

Lew was intrigued with the possibilities of making dancers appear or disappear by the use of light, particularly colored light on costumes of the same color. One evening in the early 1960s, in the school's studios on 18th Avenue, he and Richard Carter experimented long into the night with the company's portable lighting equipment, a useful legacy from the years of international touring. When Carter tried to explain that a red light on a red costume would not make a dancer disappear, Lew insisted on toying with the gels himself, investigating the range of possibilities in creating illusions. The effects Lew discovered that night found their way into three ballets of this decade: *Shadows* (1961), *Fantasma* (1963), and *Il Distratto* (1967).[22] The last used black light on costumes of white and black to accentuate different portions of the body. In one movement, the audience could perceive only the dancers' upper torsoes and arms; in the next, only their legs. The high point was a double pas de deux in which two women, each supported by an unseen man in black, danced on opposite sides of the stage, one woman visible only from the waist up, and the other from the waist down. Lew designed their movements to give the eerie effect of one dancer somehow separated into two distinct parts that nonetheless executed movements as if a single figure.

Lew's first summer workshop piece since 1963, *Il Distratto* was designed initially as an exercise for some of the company's less experienced dancers, but he later reworked the ballet and presented it during regular seasons. In 1968 it entered the repertory of the City Center Joffrey Ballet, along with *Jinx*. The same New York critics who had found fault with Lew's repertory in 1965 saw the humor in *Il Distratto* (retitled *Distractions*) and even picked up allusions to Balanchine choreography that had passed unnoticed in San Francisco. P. W. Manchester found *Distractions* "an absolutely delightful send-up of ballets in black leotards," while Walter Terry declared the irreverent ballet "a brilliant satire on

---

[22] Interview with Richard Carter, San Francisco, California, March 7, 1988.

[Lew's] own master," Balanchine.[23] Doris Hering dissected Lew's sources more thoroughly, seeing the spoof on such revered works as *Serenade, Concerto Barocco,* and *The Four Temperaments.*[24] If nothing else, *Il Distratto* proved that Lew could distance himself from Balanchine's influence enough to do a knowing parody of the latter's style.

Gisella saw in *Il Distratto* the essence of Lew's personality: the ballet's straightforwardly classical opening section paralleled Lew's calm surface manner, while movement puns as the ballet unfolded mirrored his understated, often unexpected witticisms.[25] A passage Lew added later to the ballet included a young man trying to find a woman on stage; the man reaches into a huddle of female dancers, and each time he pulls out a hand, the wrong woman emerges. After several tries, he pulls out a hand which turns out to be the end of a plastic arm, and the group melts away without comment. Carter saw the unexplained limb as a visual example of Lew's quipping humor; he would make a comment or drop an enigmatic phrase and leave it to those around him to figure it out, or not, as they were able. Lew's taste in this area differed markedly from Willam's predilection towards easily understood mime, a case in point being the ending of Willam's *Nothing Doing Bar,* in which the resurrected barroom characters, wearing halos, hold their glasses of milk up to the audience clearly as if to say, "Look what we're drinking now!"

The critical observation that Lew's choreography lacked a clear or focused point of view surfaced repeatedly in reviews of his works over the years. The original *Jinx* did not spell out to the audience whether the living clown was indeed a malevolent figure or just the target of the circus players' superstitions. (In this case, Lew's refusal to point a

---

[23] P. W. Manchester, "New York Newsletter," *Dancing Times,* May 1968, 409; Walter Terry, "World of Dance," *Saturday Review,* March 23, 1968.

[24] Doris Hering, "Clowns, Mannequins, Amazons, Sylphs, Naiads, Birds . . . And the City Center Joffrey Ballet," *Dance Magazine,* May 1968, 70.

[25] Interview with Gisella Caccialanza Christensen, San Bruno, California, September 29, 1987.

blaming finger rescued the ballet from melodrama and added to its sinister mystery.) Lew's *Danses Concertantes* was a ballet within a ballet in which the dancers represented both performers and audience. Jack Anderson noted of the 1959 production that Lew "let viewers decide for themselves" whether the slight plot line was just a pretext for dancing or a more pointed "comment on the 'shows' that socialites often put on at opera openings."[26] And during the 1965 New York engagement, the single most common critical response to *Life* was that the elements did not come together to create a clear message or to indicate the choreographer's point of view. Some of his former dancers now see Lew as having been ahead of his time, presenting images without commenting on them, in a manner anticipating today's MTV. Less sympathetic observers might conclude that as a choreographer, Lew was not always capable of bringing together the disparate elements of his works and fusing them into a cohesive statement. A third possibility, one reflecting his personality, is that the reticence that kept Lew from emotional involvement in heated conflict took the form of this detachment in his work.

Throughout the late 1960s, and really until the end of his career, Lew's works also showed a detachment from the issues troubling American society. His late '60s ballets gave no hint that Americans were involved in a highly controversial war in Vietnam or that San Francisco's own Haight-Ashbury district had spawned the "hippie" counter-culture of drugs and experimental lifestyles. Lew's decision to stage *Life* had resulted from the stimulus of a visual image dropped on his desk by Kalimos; the production was not born of a strong inner urge on Lew's part to make a statement about American society and the growing television culture. Lew's collaborators during this period saw him as essentially conservative, with a strong sense of propriety stemming from his Mormon upbringing and a tendency to close his eyes to

---

[26] Cobbett Steinberg, "Lew Christensen: An American Original," *Encore* 1.3 (Summer 1984): 13; and Jack Anderson, *New York Times*, March 3, 1983, quoted in Steinberg, "Lew Christensen: An American Original," 13.

contemporary problems.[27] (This was in itself ironic, given Lew's complete lack of contact with the church during most of his life.) Commentary on contemporary issues was left to the company's younger choreographers such as Carlos Carvajal, Robert Gladstein, Michael Smuin, and John McFall, whose works found their primary outlet in the "Ballet '60s" series. For example, one of Carvajal's 1966 summer creations, *Voyage Interdit*, combined rock music and sound effects with psychedelic colors to create the effect of a surrealistic drug trip.[28] Thus, one important by-product of the summer series was that it did not just spawn *more* works to be considered for regular seasons, it gave birth to very different *kinds* of works, which brought needed variety to the company's repertory.

The nature of national funding patterns for dance in the United States changed significantly between 1951, when Lew inherited the company-plus-guild structure established by Willam, and the late 1960s. Harold and Lew had reluctantly given up private interest in the school and the company in order to qualify for Ford Foundation assistance. In the mid-sixties, the creation of the National Foundation for the Arts and Humanities, and the National Endowment for the Arts that stemmed from it, triggered the era of federal funding. Companies were forced to become increasingly sophisticated in applying for grants and in accounting for their use of funds.

In San Francisco, the company and the guild were still two separate entities. Lew and Kalimos retained control over

---

[27] Russell Hartley points out that because of Lew's Mormon background, he "had clear cut guide lines of what was right and in good taste." ("The San Francisco Ballet: A History, 1922–1977," unpublished manuscript, San Francisco Performing Arts Library and Museum, 128.) Lew's conductor during this period, Gerhard Samuel, also states that Lew was "a very conservative person" who was sometimes accused of closing his eyes to what was going on around him. (Telephone interview with Gerhard Samuel, January 2, 1989.)

[28] This sort of work went beyond Lew's interest in "Americana" ballets; four years later he openly disapproved of Carvajal's psychedelic take on the Creation, *Genesis '70*, which caused one portion of the audience to walk out while the other stayed and cheered.

company finances, which sometimes led to friction with guild board members who raised money to keep the company afloat. Kalimos functioned better as an individual than as a committee member; with secretarial help from his wife, former company dancer Wana Williams, Kalimos handled the business end of the company as a one-man show. By the late 1960s, this form of management proved inadequate. Guild board members complained that Kalimos did not account accurately for funds already spent or give them sufficiently detailed financial projections for future company productions.[29] On the other hand, Kalimos had difficulty scheduling performances because of the dearth of dates available at War Memorial Opera House and the company's lack of any other home theater. (The problem of competing for dates at the opera house was not fully alleviated until the opening of Louise M. Davies Symphony Hall in 1980.) Also, although certain patrons generously stepped forward to meet the company payroll in times of desperation, overall the guild's funding fluctuated with an instability that made it hard for Kalimos to plan seasons.[30] Frustration arising from lack of communication on these issues and pressure from the guild's board led to Kalimos's resignation in January 1969.

With Kalimos's departure Lew lost a loyal friend who had sheltered him from business concerns and had prodded

---

[29] Board meeting minutes and other papers indicating guild frustrations over the financial administration of the company may be found in the Louise Henrick Collection, San Francisco Performing Arts Library and Museum. Sally Bailey indicates that Kalimos was forced to resign because he was so used to "robbing Peter to pay Paul" that he "couldn't give a decent financial report" and the board finally lost patience with his lack of accountability. (Telephone interview with Sally Bailey, October 25, 1989.) There is also some evidence that Harold resented Kalimos at times, either because of the financial control Kalimos wielded or because of his working relationship with Lew. The two shared the same office on 18th Avenue. (Interview with James Ludwig, San Francisco, California, December 2, 1988.)

[30] James Ludwig reports that key San Francisco patrons such as Harold Zellerbach, Lola Prentice, Debbie Copeland, Doris Magowan of the Merrill Trust, the Jewetts, the Driscolls, and the Carvers saved the company several times by meeting ongoing operating expenses. Interview with James Ludwig, San Francisco, California, December 2, 1988.

him to new choreography during slow periods. No replacement was hired to pick up the slack. Rather than moving in the direction of an increasingly sophisticated administrative structure, which Lew clearly needed to support his creative efforts, the San Francisco organization took a step backwards. Pat TeRoller, the well-intentioned wife of the guild president, Derk TeRoller, took over the management of the company on a volunteer basis. At the same time, the guild's board expressed its desire that Lew assume a more forceful role in directing the company's fortunes.

In this, they showed little understanding of Lew's personality. Dealing with matters of organizational administration lay decidedly outside the scope of Lew's interest and frustrated his efforts in handling the company's artistic direction. The winter Kalimos left, Lew lost two more dancers and had to cancel a major spring tour even though the company had just received an NEA grant to make the tour possible. He found a Finnish guest artist, Matti Tikannen, and managed to salvage part of the performance schedule. But the absence of strong administrative support, combined with the company's still aggravating lack of a home theater, interfered with Lew's creative powers. Some associates remember these as dark days for Lew, who may have suffered from depression. He choreographed no new ballets during 1969 and 1970.

# 15

## BALLET WEST (1964–1971)

In Salt Lake City, Willam balanced his desire to promote the Utah Civic Ballet in the community with respect for the university structure in which he still functioned. On campus, ballet classes and rehearsals were carefully scheduled in such a way that students could reasonably complete the requirements for a baccalaureate. Dancers attended other courses before daily company class at 11:00 a.m. and had afternoon time for academic work before returning to the studio for rehearsals.[1] For the first two years, any out-of-town appearances took the form of brief tours for which dancers were officially excused from other classes. Willam's setup actually contained significant parallels to his brothers' situation in San Francisco. As Lew benefited from the students taught by Harold at the SFB School, Willam depended on the regular influx of new freshmen who came prepared with solid training from the ballet program he had established through the Division of Continuing Education. The university also provided Willam a corollary to SFB's "Ballet '60s" series for experimental choreography; works created by M.A. students were performed by company members and presented annually in Kingsbury Hall on a "Choreographer's Showcase" program.[2] The most successful of the Master's projects entered the company's repertory and were taken on tour.

---

[1] Telephone interview with Bruce Caldwell, May 2, 1991.

[2] The first "Young Choreographers' Workshop" was actually held in the university's ballet studio on First South Street, with ballets by four MFA students, three of whom were company members. The workshop moved to Kingsbury Hall the fall of 1965 and thereafter appeared under various titles: "Discover Showcase '66," "Showcase." In 1969, the showcase season was given the official status of "Contemporary Season," and a smaller production of student works in the ballet studio took back the title "Choreographer's Workshop." Susan White, "Utah Civic Ballet and Ballet West: A Preliminary Study, 1964–1976," M.A. thesis, University of Utah, 1982, 40.

After the 1963 Ford Foundation grant, Willam spent less time choreographing departmental productions such as the summer musicals for which he had initially been hired. The summer of 1966, instead of appearing in a musical the ballet presented its own production, *Coppélia*. Willam chose this old favorite because the performances were to be given in a theater downtown whose stage was deeper than that of Kingsbury Hall; the dancers would be able to perform the mazurka straight toward the audience, as he felt was proper. P. W. Manchester saw the production and wrote to Willam afterwards praising the ballet's expressive element and the company's excellence in character dances such as the czardas and the mazurka. "It was also interesting for me to see the last act divertissement performed as it was set out in the original 1870 libretto," commented Manchester. "Not even the Royal Ballet does this in its entirety so you have truly made a valuable contribution to ballet history in restoring it."[3] Manchester understood the magnitude of Willam's contribution to American dancers in providing them a chance to get university degrees while pursuing serious ballet training: "To give young dancers this chance, their education and a vocation at the end of it, that is something worth working for. I hope Salt Lake City and the state of Utah realize how blessed they are."[4]

The high school auditorium in which UCB gave its debut performance in the fall of 1964 did not draw large audiences. From the start, it was considered a temporary resting place; the Ballet Society had supported a successful $17 million bond issue in 1962 for the construction of a county auditorium complex that would include a suitable new theater to house the company. Unfortunately, plans for the large auditorium were scrapped in 1964. Seeing no viable alternative, the company returned to Kingsbury Hall, where

---

[3] Letter from P. W. Manchester to Willam Christensen, August 3, 1966, University of Utah Ballet Archives, Box 10, Folder 24, Special Collections, University of Utah Marriott Library, Salt Lake City. New York City Ballet did not do its complete *Coppélia*, choreographed by Balanchine and Danilova, until 1974.

[4] *Ibid.*

**39**  Ballet West on the steps of Kingsbury Hall, ca. 1968. Standing, left to right: Kenneth Mitchell, Sandra Allen, Rowland Butler, John Hiatt, Barbara Hamblin, Gary Horton, Shirley Nelson, Wayne Brennan, Phil Keeler, Rocky Spoelstra, Tomm Ruud, Anne Burton, Norman Preston. Steated, Left to right: Carolyn Anderson, Nila Speck, Linda Reynolds.
Photograph by Robert Clayton, courtesy of Willam F. Christensen

they performed for over a decade. This left Willam with the problem of a shallow stage and very small wings. When he and Bené Arnold decided to add Balanchine's *Symphony in C* to the young company's repertory, Francia Russell was brought to Salt Lake City to set the ballet. Russell was aghast when she saw the size of Kingsbury Hall's stage. "How are you going to get this ballet on here?" she asked doubtfully, to which Arnold grimly replied, "With a can opener."[5] Willam was a pragmatist rather than a purist in such matters, with a "make-do" philosophy and "can-do" attitude that allowed

---

[5] Interview with Bené Arnold, Salt Lake City, Utah, August 29, 1989.

him to move forward despite obstacles others might have seen as insurmountable. He was also open to unconventional solutions. For example, to deepen the performing space for the second act variations in *The Nutcracker*, he opened a set of double doors at the very back of the stage area that existed for loading and unloading scenery. In the space behind these doors, actually outside the theater, a temporary platform was constructed for the throne from which Clara presided over the kingdom of the sweets. (A small electric heater was installed to lessen the chill of the frosty December evenings.) Willam's steamroller confidence was wedded to a charisma that made his commitment to the company contagious, especially when he dealt with female supporters. Arnold always counseled the Ballet Guild leaders to enlist Willam as the final speaker at their luncheons because he had a gift for sending the women away feeling happy, uplifted, and recommitted to supporting the ballet.

Willam never neglected his university responsibilities, but his heart was with the company as it grew in strength and professionalism. His forté was envisioning the big picture, not working through the countless details that brought it to life. In addition to teaching, Arnold served as the company's ballet mistress; Willam was very fortunate to have in her an experienced, hardworking colleague with a keen memory who shared his vision and gave unstintingly of her time. Because Willam often had to be home in the evening to care for Mignon (they could not afford twenty-four-hour nursing care), Arnold ran evening rehearsals and faithfully called afterwards to report on the dancers' progress. Willam also relied heavily on Gordon Paxman to oversee the ballet program on campus and deal with administrative matters. In 1966, the modern dance faculty agreed to merge with the ballet faculty to create a single department in the College of Fine Arts. This seeming turnabout on the part of the modern dancers was prompted by their desire to leave the College of Physical Education and their increased strength and confidence, which was bolstered by the receipt of a grant from the Rockefeller Foundation. Their decision to join the ballet faculty (thus consolidating the place of dance in the university) was dependent on the administration's assurances that Willam would not be the department chairman, so that role fell to Paxman. The latter's willingness to assume administrative burdens and his equity in handling the affairs of the joint department freed Willam to focus on the company.[6]

Promoting Utah Civic Ballet in the community meant dealing with Glenn Walker Wallace. From the outset, Willam was artistic director of the company, while Mrs. Wallace was president of the Ballet Society (and later, president of the company's board of directors). As chief patron, Mrs. Wallace saw herself as the cofounder of UCB and enjoyed much public credit for the company's existence. This constituted another departure from the Christensen tradition of ballet as family business, and it irked Willam because he knew Lowry had chosen the Utah company for a grant because of *him*, not his chief patron. But like Lew in San Francisco, Willam had to raise matching funds in order to keep his Ford Foundation grant, and he was dependent upon Mrs. Wallace to spearhead the fund-raising effort. When they did not see eye to eye on matters of company policy and planning, Willam had to employ all his skills of diplomacy and negotiation. His philosophy in dealing with problems or a controversy was, "Never be afraid of a fight, but you choose the battleground, and consider the cost."[7] To alienate Mrs. Wallace would have cost Willam the company, so he bent his diplomatic skills toward cooperation and accommodation. The Wallaces funded several key productions, so Willam had no choice but to share with them the credit for his company's existence.

In the summer of 1966, UCB's board of directors hired a new company manager, Alan Behunin. Moving in the direction of more sophisticated financial planning, Behunin

---

[6] At the end of Paxman's tenure as chairman of the merged department, no replacement acceptable to both camps could be found. Thus, the dancers split into two departments again, sharing the university's dance building but running independent programs.

[7] Telephone interview with Alan Behunin, October 7, 1991.

**40** Ballet West President Alan Hall and Willam Christensen with patrons Glenn Walker Wallace and Berenice Jewett Bradshaw, early 1980s. Courtesy of Willam F. Christensen

instituted the first subscription ticket sales. He and Willam agreed on an obvious strategy for increasing the dancers' opportunities to perform: the company must tour more. Of the seven companies who received the 1963 grants, the Utah Civic Ballet was the only one not located in a major metropolitan area. From the outset, Lowry had considered Willam's nascent company a prime candidate for touring; regular tours would give the company a larger base of support and would provide beneficial side effects such as introducing new audiences to ballet. Throughout his career, Willam always pushed for new audiences, more opportunities for his dancers to perform, and recognition in new quarters. Now that he had a genuine company again, and enthusiastic support from Behunin and the assistant company manager, Steve Horton, touring was a viable option.

Like Lew's company, Willam's dancers participated in grassroots bus tours consisting of short residencies or one-night stands. In so doing, they introduced thousands of Utahns to live ballet performances. Supported by Title I funds from the Elementary and Secondary Education Act, the company gave lecture-demonstrations (which usually culminated in a performance of *Con Amore*) in schools around the state. Often a local service group, church group, or ladies' club would sponsor a performance the same evening. The company was welcomed warmly by ranchers, farmers, small-town merchants, and academicians in college towns; church groups, women's clubs, and local service organizations entertained the dancers at buffet suppers, while businessmen donated hotel and restaurant facilities.[8] Willam also built audiences for ballet by making films of the company available, free of charge, to schools, dance clubs, and other groups.[9] During the 1966–1967 season, UCB presented 114 programs (including 32 lecture-demonstrations) for 90,000 people, which constituted approximately one-eighth of the state's population.[10]

But that was not enough. Willam and Behunin wanted to plan month-long tours instead of ones lasting just a week or two. The thorniest problem was how to work around the university schedule. America's involvement in Viet Nam forced the issue of university matriculation; as long as the men in the company were enrolled as students, they were exempt from the draft. So Behunin met with university officials and worked out a solution: a touring quarter, during which the dancers would get academic credit for performing. To sweeten the deal for the university, the Ballet Society established scholarships for dance students.[11] In the spring of 1968, the company set out on its first six-week tour, which

---

[8] Jack Anderson describes the welcome UCB received in his article "There's More Than Sand and Sagebrush Here," *Dance Magazine*, August 1967, 42–43.

[9] White, 26.

[10] *Ibid.*, 29; Anderson, "There's More Than Sand and Sagebrush Here," 42.

[11] Telephone interview with Alan Behunin, October 7, 1991.

covered over five thousand miles and included performances in six intermountain states.

Another approach to creating performing opportunities was to capitalize on the students' free summer months, which coincided with the peak tourist season at Utah's state parks. During the summers of 1967 and 1968, UCB enjoyed two-week residencies at the threshold of Zion National Park. With its steep cliffs, narrow canyons, gigantic buttes, and multihued strata of sandstone and shale, the park provided a dramatic setting for an outdoor summer festival. A rough-hewn stage on the riverbank presented the dancers in front of one of Zion's most majestic rock formations, the Great White Throne.

Pasture land abutted the performing area, and to the dancers' amusement, cows lined up at the fence behind the sparsely filled seating area to listen to *Swan Lake, Act II.* At one performance a calf even slipped into the audience and had to be chased out. Another night a swarm of migrating flying ants besieged the stage area; attracted by the bright lights and white tutus, they descended upon the dancers in mid-performance.[12] Such outdoor hazards, combined with unpredictable rainstorms, persuaded Willam and Behunin that however dramatic the rock formations, Zion National Park was not the best setting for a summer festival. They considered other options and ultimately settled upon Aspen, Colorado, which already had an established summer music festival. There the company found a new home for its summer seasons beginning in 1970.

In 1968, UCB gave a benefit performance for the Nevada Multiple Sclerosis State Committee in Reno's new Pioneer Theatre Auditorium.[13] The slogan of the evening was "The Utah Civic Ballet Dances That Others May Walk," but

---

[12] Seated at the back of the amphitheater, Willam could not see the ants and wondered why his dancers seemed muted and lifeless. Afterwards he strode down to the stage, discovered the ants, and heaved a sigh of relief that the dancers had made it through the ballet without screaming. Interview with Willam Christensen, Salt Lake City, Utah, January 4, 1989.

[13] White, 32.

that hope remained unfulfilled in Mignon's case. While Willam's troupe progressed and expanded its activities, his wife's condition became progressively worse. Now confined to her bed or wheelchair, Mignon required twenty-four-hour attention and assistance. Willam spent many hours shuttling her back and forth to hospitals and doctors' offices. Nurses watched over Mignon during the day and stayed through the night when he was out of town with the company.

The loss of muscular control is a cruel fate for a dancer. Mignon grew quieter and experienced understandable mood swings, anger and frustration over her deteriorating condition, jealousy that she could no longer share in the excitement of Willam's career, and even concern that her illness prevented him from accomplishing all that he should with his company. She still loved the world of ballet, but from an ever-receding vantage point. She passed the days watching television, while a German housekeeper prepared ample meals and kept the household functioning on a strict schedule.[14]

Willam dealt with Mignon's illness, the emotional strains as well as the logistical problems caused by living with an invalid, by trying to carry on as if she were not ill. That is, while making sure that her every medical need was met, Willam tried to keep her involved in his professional life by inviting dancers to the house for meals and including Mignon in conversations about the company. At performances, Willam would often be seen wheeling her into Kingsbury Hall and lifting her into an aisle seat. When possible, he arranged for them to travel together, with the inevitable nurse in tow. Having their daughter Roxanne in the company kept her within his sphere of influence when Mignon's illness limited her physical ability to function actively as a parent. As always, rather than focusing on the negative, Willam concentrated on the positive and the possible; associates confirm that he never complained and rarely took others into his confidence about the difficulties of the ongoing medical situation. Medical bills were a constant drain on family finances, but Willam always

---

[14] Interview with Roxanne Christensen Selznick, Salt Lake City, Utah, August 27, 1990.

managed to make ends meet and still buy the latest models of his favorite imported sports cars, an indulgence since his San Francisco days.

Willam had little time for hobbies, other than watching an occasional western on television. All his energies were directed to running the company and keeping his household functioning. Much of his satisfaction in life derived from the progress of his company. Not having the luxury of finished performers to choose from, he selected dancers with presence and potential and molded them to his needs. His company included a variety of body shapes and sizes, not just the lanky, long-limbed ballerinas favored by his brothers and Balanchine. (Once when Harold came to teach in Salt Lake City, he quipped that if he were being paid by the pound, he'd make a fortune there.[15]) Also, Willam always had company members who specialized in mime roles. One of his greatest strengths as a company builder remained his ability to attract men to ballet and train them to the point of performance. In Utah he continued his practice of finding male athletes and turning them into dancers; a pair of gymnasts, the Fuller twins, were a case in point. The year Willam's company went public, its sixteen paid dancers included more men than women (nine to seven); and as the company grew, the number of men never lagged far behind that of the women.

Willam's strength as a company director was knowing how to work with the dancers available to him. To overcome the diversity of body types, he and Arnold focused on polishing ensemble work, rehearsing the corps de ballet relentlessly so that the overriding image presented in performance would be that of a perfectly unified ensemble. The other reason the company was able to progress despite the variety of body types and levels of technique was that as a choreographer, Willam valued and even highlighted individuality. While Lew found his chief inspiration in music, Willam built his ballets around his dancers' personalities. He also encouraged his dancers to personalize their roles, allowing

---

[15] Telephone interview with Gordon Paxman, November 29, 1989.

them to decide details of the movement such as the tilt of the head or the shape of a hand. He drew out their emotions, criticizing passionless movement with comments such as, "This is drier than the Sahara Desert."[16] In rehearsals, he was more apt to correct the dancers' characterization, energy level, and facial expressions than their line or technique.[17]

Given this emphasis on expression, it is not surprising that narrative works remained Willam's forte. The ballets he created for UCB included a reworking of his 1953 *Creatures of Prometheus* and a new ballet to Ravel's *La Valse*, both of which employed narrative structures to provide pretexts for dancing. In *La Valse* ghostly apparitions in a deserted country mansion showed their displeasure when live waltzers invaded the mansion's ballroom. Another story ballet performed often during this period was Willam's *Les Bijoux du Mal*, a reworking of the *Caprice de Paree* created earlier for the student company, in which the role of the greedy prostitute provided a vehicle for the expressive powers of Janice James, who had returned to Utah after a brief period with NYCB.

As the company progressed, Willam depended less on guest artists and filled principal roles with his own dancers, notably Carolyn Anderson, Barbara Hamblin, Janice James, John Hiatt, Ben Lokey, Tomm Ruud, and Rocky Spoelstra. The partnership of James and Ruud especially caught the public imagination and gave Willam a leading couple with strong box office appeal. This brought Willam great personal satisfaction because he wanted more than just a group of dancers on which to choreograph. He craved a company on the traditional model, with corps de ballet, soloists, and glamorous principal dancers. His goal was to introduce audiences to the grand tradition of ballet and to the conventions of nineteenth-century classicism he so loved. That love included the music he associated with the grand tradition: "Let these basketball players hear a little Tchaikovsky," he would quip from time to time.

---

[16] Telephone interview with Bruce Caldwell, May 2, 1991.

[17] *Ibid*.

As UCB toured in the Intermountain West, Willam insisted upon using "first- string" casts for each performance rather than allowing less experienced dancers to try new roles in small town appearances. This "best foot forward" policy paid off in the short term as the company built its reputation, but it was short-sighted concerning the development of new talent because dancers develop artistry through performing experience. Essentially, Willam was out to sell ballet to as many Americans as he could reach, and no performance was unimportant in his eyes. He held to his ideal of ballet's mass appeal and was not above occasional hucksterism. When he met Arthur Fiedler, the longtime director of the Boston Pops, Willam asked the conductor, "How do you make it on two dollars a ticket?" Fiedler replied with a smile, "I make it on the popcorn." Later, when Willam and Behunin studied company finances, Willam would ask jokingly, "Where can I sell popcorn?"[18]

UCB's touring in the Intermountain West brought the company to the attention of Don Galvin, program coordinator for Arts and Humanities of the Federation for Rocky Mountain States. The Federation had been founded in 1966 by the governors of seven western states (Arizona, Colorado, Idaho, Montana, New Mexico, Utah, Wyoming, and later Nevada) to promote economic growth in the region. The Federation's leaders recognized that in order for their states to attract business and industry, they needed to provide cultural advantages as well as a favorable economic climate. Although each state might not be able to support its own symphony, opera, and ballet company, the states could improve their cultural offerings by sharing resources.

The Federation granted UCB $7,500 to support its six-state tour in the spring of 1968. The money was a great boon to the Salt Lake-based company, but it raised issues of regional commitment versus civic pride. Or, as Willam summed up the situation, "Cities have egos." Even if the Federation decided that Willam's company should become

---

[18] Telephone interview with Alan Behunin, October 7, 1991.

the primary provider of ballet performances in the Rocky Mountain region, would the citizens of Denver feel that a troupe named "Utah Civic Ballet" was really *their* ballet company? Would inhabitants of Reno and Phoenix feel a sense of commitment to a company whose very name distanced itself from their concerns? If the Utah Civic Ballet were now going to serve a larger area than its home state, should its name not reflect its true constituency?

That same year, while in New York for meetings, Behunin met Clive Barnes, then one of the most influential dance critics in America. When Behunin asked Barnes for advice on promoting UCB, the latter spoke bluntly to the issue of the company's name. As long as it had "civic" in the title, Barnes insisted, it would be considered an amateur regional troupe.[19] So Willam finally abandoned the label under which his San Francisco company had reached its greatest (albeit short-lived) heights. As he and others brainstormed alternatives, they considered the example set by the multimillionaire Howard Hughes, who had recently bought a struggling local airline and had renamed it "Air West." Thinking that Hughes might support their cause if they followed his lead, they came up with "Ballet West."[20] It was short, catchy, and not tied to any one state. The board approved, and the Federation of Rocky Mountain States announced the change officially in December 1968.

The Federation's professed goal, announced along with the name change, was to create for the company "a permanent in-residence program with all the major cities of the Rocky Mountain area."[21] By rotating through the major cities of each state in week-long "seasons," the company could afford to keep the dancers on longer contracts. The University of Utah would remain the company's official school, but other institutions would be considered for associate status.

---

[19] *Ibid.*

[20] *Ibid.*

[21] Michael Fox, "Utah Civic Ballet Regroups – Becomes New Ballet West," *Salt Lake Tribune*, December 1, 1968.

To prove the regional intent of the new company, its inaugural performance was given not in Utah but in Loretto Heights, Colorado (near Denver), because Loretto Heights College had a dance program interested in jumping on the Ballet West bandwagon. The name change crowned Willam's efforts in Salt Lake City and symbolized the enlarging circle of his influence.

This period of increasing momentum late in Willam's career coincided with Lew's darkest hours in San Francisco: the loss of his company manager; the lack of a home theater; and the period of withdrawal during which he choreographed no new works. During the transitional year in which UCB became Ballet West, Willam's company gave 76 major public performances and made 84 other appearances, including lecture-demonstrations.[22] In that same time period, the struggling San Francisco company gave only 50 performances. Ballet West actually benefited from SFB's bad fortune; when Lew was forced to cancel the original itinerary of his 1969 spring tour, Willam's company inherited SFB's performance dates in Arizona.

The rotating residencies announced along with Ballet West's name change did not materialize, but the Federation brought Willam's company increased prominence and financial stability, making it a respectable ally for San Francisco's more prestigious but beleaguered company. That May, Willam, Lew, and Behunin met secretly to discuss the possibility of merging the two brothers' companies. The three worked out a mutually beneficial plan in which the brothers would share a company with forty dancers on year-round salaries. During the fall season, the company would be under Willam's jurisdiction in Salt Lake City, and during the spring season, Lew would oversee the same group in San Francisco. For the *Nutcracker* season and summer workshops the company would split in two, so that each city could plan its own performances. Each city would retain its school and build a local corps de ballet to supplement productions requiring

---

[22] White, 41.

more than forty dancers. High salaries and an attractive retirement program would induce dancers to remain in the West, and the companies would benefit by ordering toeshoes in greater volume and sharing the cost of scenery and costumes for new productions. In essence, the brothers sought to join their assets to create a stronger company than either could acquire individually.[23]

Some cooperation did follow in the ensuing months. That summer, SFB's "Ballet '69" series presented Tomm Ruud's *MOBILE*, a trio with a highly sculptural quality in which a man balanced two women in slowly evolving positions (the title was an acronym for "Moving Objects Behaving in Linear Equipose"). In the fall, Lew's *Lady of Shalott* entered Ballet West's repertory, and *Il Distratto* followed that winter. But the merger itself never happened. If cities had egos, so did companies' boards of directors. Perhaps the backers who exercised influence over Lew's company did not want their ballet to lose its identity to an upstart troupe from the hinterlands.[24] Or some may have felt that each brother's repertory was tailored to his own environment and would not play well in the other's hometown. In any event, the days of arranging business by family ties were past. Willam's company would not provide the solution to Lew's problems in San Francisco.

While Willam broadened the sphere of his activities, he remained sensitive to conservative audience tastes in his own state. Rather than being exhilarated by controversy, he was concerned in the spring of 1969 when Ballet West's premiere of Richard Kuch's pessimistic *Chaos*, whose production

---

[23] The details of this plan are spelled out in a "Confidential Report to Mrs. Wallace and Mr. Cameron," from Alan Behunin, contained in the Utah Ballet Archives, Box 21, Folder 30, Special Collections, University of Utah Marriott Library, Salt Lake City. Russell Hartley also leaked word of the merger plan in his regular *Dance Magazine* column covering Bay Area news in August 1969.

[24] This is Behunin's opinion of why the proposed merger never took place. Willam also believes that the plan fell through because the merger would not work at the board level. Interview with Willam F. Christensen, Salt Lake City, Utah, January 4, 1989.

had been funded by a grant from the National Endowment for the Arts, displeased local audiences and drew negative reviews. To reassure his public, Willam responded the following year with a production of *Cinderella*, to Sergei Prokofiev's 1945 score. As the first complete production of this work by an American company, Ballet West's *Cinderella* gave Willam a final "first" to add to the list of classics that had established his reputation in San Francisco (*Coppélia, Swan Lake*, and *The Nutcracker*). It is indicative of Willam's interests that his landmark productions took their inspiration from traditional sources rather than from contemporary society. *Cinderella* reflected Willam's forte in delineating characters, his gift for portraying humor with a light touch, and his commitment to the role of romance in ballet. This "first" was less in advance of national trends than his revivals of nineteenth-century classics had been: the National Ballet in Washington, D.C. premiered Ben Stevenson's version of the Prokofiev *Cinderella* later the same month.[25] Regardless of such considerations, *Cinderella* proved an ideal programming choice for the family-oriented community; just the announcement that the company planned to stage the ballet brought an increase in subscriptions that year.[26]

In 1971, Willam turned sixty-nine and officially retired from the University of Utah. His switch to emeritus status did not attract much attention because he maintained a connection with the university through the Division of Continuing Education. His efforts that year focused on a new project: he planned to set Ballet West on the world stage with an international tour.

---

[25] The listing of Prokofiev *Cinderellas* in the Dictionary Catalogue of the Dance Collection of The New York Public Library indicates Willam's, which premiered April 1, 1970, as the first American production and includes Ben Stevenson's production for the National Ballet, which premiered in Lisner Auditorium on April 24, 1970. Foreign productions listed that preceded Willam's version include those by Rostislav Zakharaov (Moscow, 1945), Constantin Sergeev (Leningrad, 1946), Sir Frederick Ashton (London, 1948), Jean Combes (Strasbourg, 1959), Franjo Horvat (Sarajevo, 1960), Wazlaw Orlikowsky (Paris, 1963).

[26] Jack Anderson, "Ballet West in 'Cinderella,' Kingsbury Hall, Salt Lake City, April 1–3, 1970," *Dance Magazine*, June 1970, 20.

The Utah Symphony had received an invitation to perform at the Athens Festival in 1968 through the intervention of Mr. and Mrs. Christopher Athas, a prominent couple in Salt Lake City's Greek community. Following the concerts in Athens, the symphony had toured Europe, earning glowing reviews that had raised the group's prestige at home immeasurably. Abravanel had thus shown the way, and Willam was anxious for the ballet to follow in the symphony's footsteps. When Mrs. Athas arranged for a similar invitation for Ballet West to perform in Athens the summer of 1971, Willam devoted all his efforts to this new opportunity.[27]

At Jacques D'Amboise's suggestion, Willam invited an impresario named Paul Szilard to handle the trip. Szilard showed Ballet West's board that by scheduling performances (at higher fees than usual) in summer folk festivals around the Continent, Ballet West could tour Europe for six weeks for little more than it would cost to perform in Athens for two weeks. In theory, such a tour would raise the company's stature by thrusting it into the international arena. The projected budget of $161,000 concerned Ballet West's board of directors, even though it was extremely modest considering that American Ballet Theatre had spent over three times that amount for a European tour of the same length.[28] Fundraising proved difficult until a private donor, the local philanthropist Dean Eggertsen, stepped forward to make up the difference created by the additional four weeks, and the tour began to take shape.[29]

Szilard suggested two precautions to ensure a successful tour. First, Ballet West's name was temporarily changed to "Ballet West U.S.A." to clarify its home for European audiences. Second, Ballet West needed guest artists to attract

---

[27] Details of the invitation, as well as a detailed account of the tour, are found in Michael Rozow, Jr., "The General Formulation and Summarization of Ballet West U.S.A.'s 1971 European Tour," M.A. thesis, University of Utah, 1972, 27.

[28] *Ibid.*, 50.

[29] *Ibid.*, 4–5. Eggertsen, who was on the company's board that year, donated $79,000, effectively making the tour possible.

audiences, stars with proven box office strength. Willam and Szilard agreed on D'Amboise and Karel Shimoff (formerly of NYCB and London Festival Ballet) as the company's leading couple. They also "borrowed" Lynda Meyer from Lew's company to dance leading roles and serve as a backup to Shimoff and Janice James. For repertory, Willam selected his lucky favorite, *Coppélia*, the ever-serviceable *Swan Lake* (*Act II*), his version of the *Paquita Pas de Deux*, and a technical show-case entitled *Bravura*; three works by Balanchine (*Serenade*, *Tchaikovsky Pas de Deux*, and *Symphony in C*); two by D'Amboise (*Irish Fantasy* and *Meditations*); and one each by Lew and by Tomm Ruud (*Con Amore* and *MOBILE*). The large-scale works required more women than were currently in Ballet West, so Willam augmented the company with dancers from the school, including his daughter Roxanne. A single male dancer was added from the school: Jay Jolley, who, like Bart Cook, another male dancer trained by Willam in this period, would go on to New York City Ballet.

Ballet West's summer residency at Aspen that year (June 13 to July 3) doubled as a dress rehearsal period as the company and its guest stars polished the ballets to be taken overseas. D'Amboise reset major portions of *Coppélia*'s second act and added solo variations for himself and Shimoff in the third act. Bené Arnold drilled the corps to perfection and even standardized the shades of makeup the women would wear. While the managers and production crew finalized all travel arrangements, the dancers geared up and adjusted psycho-logically to a new level of professionalism.

To Willam, the prospect of a European tour sym-bolized more than a chance to see countries he had never visited. To perform in Europe, the cradle of Western classical dance, meant exposure to critics familiar with the finest accomplishment of the classical tradition. In Willam's mind, positive reviews garnered in that arena would prove the worth of his company beyond any doubt. Aside from the value of quotable reviews, the European tour held great emotional and psychological significance for Willam. He had left the cosmopolitan center of San Francisco for the culturally isolated Salt Lake City, where it was easy to feel that one's efforts were overlooked or ignored by the New York-oriented dance community. A successful European tour, he reasoned, would bring his company to the attention of that establishment. As if the act of performing overseas in itself indicated that a company was "world class," Willam assumed that a European tour would somehow lift Ballet West from the category of a secondary regional troupe to the top rank of American companies. Perhaps an element of sibling rivalry also entered Willam's thinking. Lew had attracted a lot of attention by taking SFB abroad in the late 1950s; now it was Willam's turn.

By the end of the summer Aspen residency, Willam and his dancers were primed for Europe. But as the company and its entourage prepared to return to Utah, Mignon caught pneumonia. Willam, nearly overcome by conflicting emotions, drove his wife and the attending nurse from Aspen back to Salt Lake City at top speed. Mignon was hospitalized immediately, and the doctors informed Willam gravely that her passing was imminent.

For decades Willam had met Mignon's ever-increasing needs. Now he was torn between his love for her and the European tour that represented (in his mind) the pinnacle of his company's achievements. As the departure date approached, Mignon lingered on in Intensive Care. Ultimately, Willam and Roxanne had no choice but to stay behind while Ballet West began the long-awaited tour. Willam bade farewell to the company at the airport with tears streaming down his cheeks.[30]

In yet another example of family solidarity, Lew stepped in to act as Ballet West U.S.A.'s temporary artistic director. He accompanied the dancers to Greece while Willam added bitter disappointment to his already heavy burden of anxiety. Mignon passed away on August 1, 1971, at age 62. The funeral was held three days later, and in lieu of flowers the family suggested donations to a memorial fund in

---

[30] Interview with Willam Christensen, Salt Lake City, Utah, January 4, 1989.

Mignon's honor whose proceeds would fund scholarships for dancers. A few days after the funeral, Willam and Roxanne joined Ballet West in Verona.

Although Willam had missed seeing the company dance in Greece and Yugoslavia, he oversaw performances in Italy, Spain (Santander and San Sebastian), Switzerland (Geneva), and France (Vichy, Aix-les-Bains, St. Jean de Luz, and Biarritz). Ballet West U.S.A. did not perform in major cultural capitals; rather than dancing at the Paris Opéra or Milan's La Scala, it appeared mainly at summer festivals in smaller cities. In Split, Yugoslavia, they danced on the plaza of Diocletian's Palace, and in Geneva they appeared in a large skating arena. It might be argued that Ballet West had traded the American provinces for European ones. Nevertheless, the company's reviews were filled with quotable superlatives, not only for the guest artists but also for the "irreproachable ensemble."[31] And coverage in *The New York Times*, *The Chicago Tribune*, and *The San Francisco Chronicle* netted the company an estimated $25,000's worth of free publicity.[32] While winning the Ford Foundation grant and taking his student company professional was unquestionably Willam's single most important accomplishment in Utah, Ballet West's 1971 European tour was undoubtedly the high point of Willam's life in ballet.

---

[31] J. Mirosevic, "An Exceptional Ballet Experience," *Vecernji List* (Croatia), August 11, 1971; from collection of 1971 tour reviews, translated, acquired by the author from the Ballet West press office in the late 1970s. The most discriminating critic to review the company in Athens, Oleg Kerensky, did point out that audiences "should not expect a very original or thought-provoking repertoire, nor dancing of the polish and virtuosity associated with New York City Ballet," but he conceded that Ballet West was "lively and likeable" and would "give a lot of pleasure in Europe." Oleg Kerensky, "Ballet West: Lively and Likable," unattributed clipping, August 1971, in collection noted above.

[32] Rozow, 48.

# 16

## RECOGNITION AND TRANSITIONS
### (1971–1978)

Professionally, Willam rode the crest of the Summer 1971 European tour the following season as Ballet West repeated its touring repertory in home performances that showed new polish and verve. The company even received more funding from the Ford Foundation, this time a cash reserve grant totaling $287,461. But in his personal life, the gregarious Willam (now sixty-nine years old) passed a lonely fall. It was the first time he had come home from a tour without Mignon to greet him and share the excitement of his success.

Willam needed people around him; he needed to receive the affection and warmth he offered to others. Given that he was not cut out for the solitary life, it was inevitable he would remarry. With his standing in the community, he could have married for wealth, finding a woman whose means matched his taste for specific luxuries: imported cars, dinners at the country club, and post-performance parties. But much of his career had been spent struggling to maintain the proper balance of power with female patrons, showing gracious appreciation for their economic support of his enterprises without allowing them to dictate to him in artistic matters. Consciously or not, he avoided a second marriage that might put his personal life in a similar balancing act. At a Christmas party that December he met Florence Goeglein, a widow whose son was performing arias as part of the evening's entertainment. Florence had majored in vocal music in college, and she listened with interest to Willam's reminiscences of the San Francisco Opera. Music was their first common ground.

Willam invited Florence to attend a performance of Ballet West's *Nutcracker* that New Year's Eve, a thoroughly

**41**   Willam Christensen and Florence Goeglein, 1973.
Photograph by Robert Clayton, courtesy of Willam F. Christensen

fitting beginning to their romance. Florence, who had lost her husband to cancer, understood something of the ordeal Willam had been through during the years of Mignon's illness. A member of the local Mormon community, Florence struck Willam as being fun, caring, well rounded, honest, a good sport, and "charming as hell." In the following months, Willam's dancers noticed a new excitement in his manner and enthusiasm in his work. He obviously enjoyed having a woman on his arm again at performances and special occasions, and his self-confidence overrode any qualms he might have had about a relationship with someone nearly fifteen years younger than he. They were married on June 30, 1973.

Back in San Francisco at the end of the 1960s, Lew struggled within SFB's administrative vacuum. The possibility of merging SFB and Ballet West had come to naught, a failure which was probably in the best interests of both companies in the long run. But in the meantime, without Kalimos as company manager, Lew was left to rely on the volunteer efforts of the guild president's wife, Pat TeRoller. The Ballet Guild had let its expectations be known: Lew was to assume more direct control of the company's day-to-day management. Like an author with writer's block, Lew was unable to produce new works. Yet unlike times past when SFB was in a pinch, he did not turn to Kirstein and Balanchine for repertory. Instead, in comments to the press, Lew insisted that he wanted the San Francisco company to have its own look. In a gesture of independence, he relied on "in-house" choreographers, members of the company such as Carlos Carvajal who had developed their creative skills through the Ballet '60s series.[1] And for the spring 1970 season, Lew brought former company member Michael Smuin from ABT to set a new work, *Schubertiade*. The return of Robert Gladstein, from ABT, for the 1970 *Nutcracker* season and Gladstein's appointment as ballet master in 1971 also helped keep the company going.

Some attributed Lew's lack of productivity to the company's need for a home theater, but the underlying causes ran far deeper. Basically, the organizational structure of his company was hopelessly outdated and no longer adequate to function in the professional arena. The two-part company-plus-guild system established by Willam in 1942, when the ballet's annual budget ran to perhaps a few thousand dollars, was woefully inadequate by 1971, when that budget hovered around half a million dollars.[2] The intervening decades had seen a major increase in the professionalism of the company

---

[1] Lew and Carvajal actually had a falling out over the latter's *Genesis '70*, a psychedelic version of the creation of the world. Hartley theorizes that Lew brought Michael Smuin to set a piece the next year as a direct result. Carvajal left the company to found San Francisco Dance Spectrum, but he returned to choreograph *New Flower* for SFB's 1972 spring season. Hartley, "The San Francisco Ballet: A History, 1922–1977," unpublished manuscript, San Francisco Performing Arts Library and Museum, 126–28.

[2] Robert Commanday, "S.F. Ballet Reorganization," *San Francisco Chronicle*, July 16, 1971.

as well as the number of yearly performances. The stakes were now much higher, but the company-plus-guild structure had no built-in system of checks and balances. Issues of power and control underlay the question of proprietorship. Although Lew and Harold had exchanged their business interest in the school and company for nonprofit status, they maintained total control over both institutions, in the family tradition, expecting the guild to raise supporting funds without dictating matters of artistic or financial policy.

The guild's board of directors felt that their contribution to SFB's solvency earned them a greater say in determining how company money was allocated. Lack of communication was a major problem, in part because Lew was not an outwardly verbal person and was not as gifted in dealing with patrons as was Willam. Lew complained that he needed more advance information from the guild to enable him to plan seasons.[3] Perhaps the major reason the company seemed stalled was that Lew needed more administrative support to handle matters such as promotion, season scheduling, touring arrangements, and so on. Mrs. TeRoller's appointment had originally been announced as a temporary measure, but after a year-and-a-half the situation had not changed.

This impasse brewed for months before Lew confronted the situation squarely. The company continued to limp along, and in 1971 Lew's creativity picked up slightly. He spent the month of February in Helsinki staging *Con Amore*, *Il Distratto*, and *Fantasma* for the Finnish National Opera Ballet.[4] For SFB's spring season he created *Airs de Ballet*, to music by André Grétry, to showcase the French training of guest artist Violette Verdy. (This abstract work was a series of playful pas de deux and pas de trois for five dancers that remained in the company's repertory throughout much of the decade.) But ignoring the organizational problems did not make them go away. That year the

---

[3] *Ibid.*

[4] Cobbett Steinberg, "Lew Christensen: An American Original," *Encore* 1.3 (Summer 1984): 15.

National Endowment for the Arts let it be known that SFB would not qualify for federal money until it had streamlined its organizational structure and established its financial dealings on firmer footing.

The NEA ultimatum forced a decisive step. That July, Lew, who had always eschewed controversy, stunned his associates by firing Pat TeRoller. Derk TeRoller immediately resigned as president of the guild. Under the direction of longtime company patron Harold Zellerbach, a committee of former guild board members mobilized to explore the possibility of a merger between the company and the guild. That summer, while the committee studied ways to reorganize the company along more modern lines, Lew left town. In Washington, D.C., he set the dances for the American stage premiere of Handel's opera *Ariodante*, for the inaugural season of the John F. Kennedy Center for the Performing Arts.[5] While in Washington, Lew caught wind of disturbing rumors that a member of the guild's board was trying to replace him as company director.[6] The threat was not carried out, but it showed cracks in the Christensens' hegemony in San Francisco. Meetings with McNeil Lowry and with June Arey of the National Endowment for the Arts helped convince Lew of the importance of cooperating with SFB's pending reorganization.

Negotiations with the committee under Zellerbach's direction recommenced upon Lew's return to the Bay Area. A management study resulted in the formation that fall of the San Francisco Ballet Association with authority over all aspects of company activity. Governing powers of the Ballet Association were invested in a nine-member executive committee that included former guild directors plus Harold and Lew. The brothers were placed on seven-year renewable contracts by the association, which spelled out their duties and provided pension plans for their retirement. A press

[5] The production featured Beverly Sills, Tatania Troyanos, and Donald Gramm. Steinberg, "Lew Christensen: An American Original," 15.

[6] Interview with Gisella Caccialanza Christensen, San Bruno, California, December 9, 1987.

release clarified that the Christensens no longer had the authority to "fire" members of the board.[7] The new SFB Association began functioning that October, signaling the final dismantling of the Christensen's family ballet business in San Francisco.

Lew and Harold were now employees of the institutions they had formerly owned and controlled. Paradoxically, by relinquishing control they actually gained new financial security. Earlier that year Gisella had been hospitalized for three months with a severe case of peritonitis, and she and Lew had been caught without sufficient insurance to pay the medical bills. So Lew welcomed the financial benefits of being on contract; for the first time the brothers were assured of insurance and retirement pensions. The company benefited from its new organizational stability as well. The number of performances began to pick up again, from the lows of 51 performances in 1968, 49 in 1969, 46 in 1970, and 58 in 1971, to 94 in 1972.

Following the organizational restructuring achieved in 1971, the directors of the SFB Association began to build up an increasingly sophisticated administrative framework for Lew and Harold's efforts. In addition to company manager Timothy Duncan, a general manager (William R. Baer), public communications director (Craig Palmer), and development coordinator (Ann Gralneck) fleshed out the staff by the end of 1972. The company's spring season boasted four world premieres, all by local choreographers, including a new work by Lew, *Tingel-Tangel-Taenze*. But artistically, SFB was not yet out of the quagmire. The season drew mixed reviews, and revivals of Lew's earlier works (*Filling Station, Jinx, Con Amore,* and *Divertissement d'Auber*) elicited stronger praise than his latest creation. Descriptions of *Tingel-Tangel-Taenze*, a collection of waltzes and polkas to music by Strauss and Lumbye set in a nineteenth-century Viennese ballroom, suggest a dilution of Lew's choreographic vision. The Lew who had left New York in the early 1950s, trained in Balanchinian

---

[7] San Francisco Ballet Press Release, October 29, 1971.

neoclassicism and steeped in Kirstein's rhetoric of American ballet, had studiously avoided anything remotely resembling his brother's *Old Vienna*.[8] And while Lew's actual choreography for *Tingel-Tangel-Taenze* probably bore no resemblance to his brother's warhorse, it did adopt the outward trappings, complete with flirtatious episodes. The work soon fell from the repertory.

By early 1973, Lew was losing the desire and the ability to oversee the company's artistic direction single-handedly. At age sixty-three, he had less energy than did Willam at seventy-one. Perhaps at the urging of the SFB Association's executive committee, Lew decided to take on an assistant director. He flew to New York, auditioned dancers to build up the company, and conferred with Michael Smuin, who was now a principal dancer and choreographer with American Ballet Theatre.

If Lew had to take on a partner, hiring Smuin came close to keeping SFB in the family. After all, Smuin's longtime association with the Christensens dated to his training under Willam at the University of Utah, where he had danced leading roles in Willam's student productions. Smuin had participated in SFB's international tours of the late 1950s and had been instrumental in founding the "Ballet '60" series. After leaving SFB in 1962, he and his wife, Paula Tracy, had formed a nightclub act in New York, hitting glamorous night spots and touring widely before settling down to perform with ABT.[9] At age thirty-four, Smuin was still performing, but he knew that his future lay in other directions. He accepted Lew's offer to become SFB's new associate artistic director.

Smuin's appointment filled part of the void created by the departure of Leon Kalimos. Lew needed someone with energy and enthusiasm to stimulate the dancers, perhaps even to stimulate his own efforts, and to help promote the

---

[8] Stephen C. Steinberg and Nancy Johnson interview with James Graham-Luján, San Francisco, California, December 9, 1985.

[9] For an overview of Smuin's career, see John Gruen, "Smuin Sets Sail on Broadway," *Dance Magazine*, January 1988, 52–57.

company. In contrast to Lew's seeming withdrawal from the issues facing American society, Smuin was very much in touch with contemporary culture. Smuin's arrival was like fresh water bringing new life to a quietly stagnating pond. The dancers relished the thought of new artistic challenges and found new energy as the dynamic younger man took over physically demanding responsibilities such as teaching company class. At the same time, fifteen new company members were hired to reverse the effects of the West Coast–East Coast migration that had plagued SFB in years past. This influx of new talent was built around a nucleus from ABT: Paula Tracy, Betsy Erickson, and Vane Vest (who had appeared in SFB's 1972 *Nutcracker* season), Diana Weber, Naomi Sorkin, and Bojan Spassof. Other newcomers hailed from companies and schools around the country: the Harkness Ballet, National Ballet, Pennsylvania Ballet (Sean Lavery), the Joffrey Ballet School, and smaller companies in Los Angeles, St. Louis, and Chicago.[10] This move constituted a marked departure from the tradition of replenishing the company with advanced students from Harold's school. Certainly, with the new dancers and associate artistic director from ABT, Lew's company could no longer be considered a satellite of New York City Ballet. The retirement of Jocelyn Vollmar after the 1972 *Nutcracker* season, combined with the radical changes in personnel, signaled the beginning of a new era in SFB's history.

Smuin's youth, vitality, and exuberant self-confidence balanced Lew's more subdued personal style and aging wisdom. The partnership was a marriage of opposites in terms of personality and theatrical styles, and yet Lew could identify with Smuin's experience in commercial theater, having traveled the vaudeville circuit and choreographed musical comedies himself. Both understood the importance of entertaining an audience. At times, Smuin's brashness must have been irksome; in one newspaper interview, he carelessly declared, "I respect Lew a lot, he's not the hayseed some

---

[10] "New Dancers from American Ballet Theater [sic] Debut in San Francisco Ballet Spring Season," San Francisco Ballet Association Press Release, April 7, 1973.

people think, but there's a limit to what he could do alone."[11] Nonetheless, Lew confided to Gisella that he had found the right person to take over the company someday, and he began to prepare Smuin for that eventuality.

As Lew and Smuin worked out their partnership, they discussed their vision of the kind of company SFB should be. In the March 1973 *Dance News*, the two announced their intention to create a "new look" for the San Francisco company. "We've always worked well together," claimed Lew. "Now we're going to build up a relationship like that of Balanchine and Robbins, or Petipa and Ivanov in St. Petersburg."[12] They were not yet clear just how the "new look" would evolve; perhaps it would be a combination of Lew's Balanchinian neoclassicism and Smuin's theatricality. Lew assured the *Dance News* reporter:

> We don't want to look like anybody else or be patterned on anybody else, although our company will always be similar to Balanchine – trained in a high, pure classic style, and aiming always to look good and execute well.[13]

The first example of that "new look" was *Cinderella*, a work already in process when Smuin arrived. Michael joined Lew in choreographing this sumptuously produced fairy tale to Prokofiev's score, SFB's first evening-length ballet in fifteen years.[14] If *Cinderella* demonstrated anything about the

---

[11] Arthur Bloomfield, "S.F. Ballet Plans Big Leaps Forward," *San Francisco Examiner*, February 28, 1973.

[12] Herbert Kupferberg, "Christensen and Smuin Tell Plans for 'New Look' in San Francisco," *Dance News*, March 1973, 6.

[13] *Ibid.*

[14] One reporter described the working partnership in this shared creation: "Instead of dividing up the score piece by piece, they were collaborating simultaneously, so that at any given instant both choreographers' work would be evident, but in different dancers. The blend was extremely successful. And at the Opera House run-throughs, while the highly cooperative stage-hands were struggling with the 24 hanging pieces and massive open-curtain scene changes, Christensen huddled with the orchestra while Smuin stayed at the back with the light man and gave orders through his remote-control microphone." Paul Hertelendy, "Cinderella's Miracle, *Tribune* [Oakland, California], June 9, 1973, Russell Hartley Scrapbook.

company's future artistic direction, it was that the element of visual design would continue to play a large role, as it had in Lew's collaborations with Duquette.

The board was pushing for large-scale productions, so Lew had the backing to do a work he had contemplated for years: *Don Juan*. Anatole Vilzak, who had created the title role in Fokine's 1936 *Don Juan*, first planted the seed of this work in Lew's mind.[15] Lew became fascinated with the imaginary figure and did extensive reading on the Don Juan tradition. Focusing on the seventeenth-century play by Tirso de Molina, Molière's drama, and Lorenzo Da Ponte's libretto for Mozart's *Don Giovanni*, Lew structured a four-part ballet composed of three seductions and the Don's demise. Elaborate and historically accurate sets designed by Ming Cho Lee (a designer associated with New York City Opera productions) included a massive three story convent around which Lew devised chases requiring split-second timing by the dancers. For the score, Lew rejected both Gluck's ballet and Strauss's lush tone poem, settling instead on Spanish classical guitar music by Joaquin Rodrigo (the *Concierto de Aranjuez* and excerpts from *Fantasia para un Gentilhombre*). This choice complemented the visual effect of the period sets and reflected Lew's sense of understatement. The Don's nefarious deeds were played out against an aural backdrop that belied the violence on stage, the contrast adding dramatic tension to the whole. The title role was created by Attila Fizcere, a newcomer to the company who had defected from Hungary to the Royal Winnipeg Ballet in 1970. Great energy went into every aspect of the production; K. Dunkley was even brought from the Dance Notation Bureau in New York to notate the choreography.[16]

---

[15] Paul Hertelendy, "Ballet Produces Biggest 'Cinderella' of All," *Tribune* [Oakland, California], June 3, 1973, Russell Hartley Scrapbook, 1973.

[16] Dunkley actually did double duty on this trip; he also set Doris Humphrey's *The Shakers* on SFB because Smuin was pushing to incorporate modern dance in the company repertory. "S.F. Ballet June Season," *Dance News*, June 1973, in Russell Hartley Scrapbook, 1973.

**42**  Michael Smuin, George Balanchine, Lew Christensen, and SFB dancers at the premiere of *Don Juan*, 1973.
Courtesy of San Francisco Performing Arts Library and Museum

Kirstein and Balanchine flew to San Francisco for the premieres of *Cinderella* and *Don Juan* that June. Kirstein, ever Lew's ally, praised Lew's *Don Juan* to the skies in an interview on a local radio station: "It is one of the finest pieces of theater, whether dancing or opera or drama, that I have ever seen in Europe or America . . . What I saw was of the first ascendancy and brilliance."[17] As if the exchange policy of the 1950s were still in force, Kirstein offered to take both *Cinderella* and *Don Juan* into NYCB's repertory the following year, giving SFB two Balanchine works in trade. But Balanchine remained noncommital. The weight of *Don Juan*'s massive sets made shipping the production to New York a very costly proposition,

---

[17] Robert Commanday, "Something Is Bugging Mr. Kirstein," *San Francisco Chronicle*, June 19, 1973, Russell Hartley Scrapbook, 1973.

so the idea was dropped.[18] Two Balanchine works entered SFB's repertory for the first time the following year, but not as part of a two-way exchange.

Smuin's hiring prompted rumors that Lew was about to resign, which was not at all the case. Lew never stepped down as SFB's artistic director; he just pulled back from the day-to-day running of the company as his stamina and physical strength diminished. Nonetheless, Lew remained an important figurehead. During periods when he seemed unapproachable, such as after posting the cast list for a new ballet and then retreating to his office for days to wait out any storms of controversy, the dancers referred to him with affectionate irony as the "Great White Father."[19]

A month before the premieres of *Cinderella* and *Don Juan*, the three Christensen brothers received one of the most prestigious honors bestowed in the professional dance world: the *Dance Magazine* Award. Granted annually to individuals in recognition of their contribution to dance in America, the 1973 award was shared by the Christensens and Rudolf Nureyev. All three brothers were genuinely pleased about the honor, and many of their associates felt it was long overdue.

The brothers and their wives flew to New York to be honored that May. Before a capacity crowd at the Regency Hotel, *Dance Magazine* editor William Como praised Nureyev's genius as a performer and lauded the Christensens' decades of dedication to ballet in America. Janet Reed added personal insights into the greatness of the Christensens' contribution, noting particularly the number of wonderful male dancers they had trained. To long applause, an elated Willam, ever the family leader, stepped forward to accept the award and

---

[18] Interview with Gisella Caccialanza Christensen, San Bruno, California, December 5, 1987. Very likely the set's weight became a convenient excuse to cover up the fact that Balanchine did not want his company to produce Lew's *Don Juan*. Kirstein's continuing support of Lew's choreographic efforts appears to have been an area of disagreement between Kirstein and Balanchine. Gisella recounts, "Mr. Balanchine talked to me about everything in the ballet except taking it back to New York, which I think aggravated Lincoln a little bit."

[19] Telephone interview with Sally Bailey, October 25, 1989.

express the brothers' gratitude for this honor. As Willam stepped back, Lew added a sardonic tag line to the proceedings: "There's one little item I think my brother Bill forgot to mention. This is, I think, the only family that has two ballet companies. Also, two deficits."[20]

In fact, Ballet West did not have a deficit in 1973. The company ended its fiscal year with $140,000 in reserve, thus qualifying for the third year of its latest Ford Foundation matching grant.[21] But Lew's company was in serious financial difficulty. The SFB Association created in 1971 had elected as chairman Steve Zellerbach, son of Harold Zellerbach, and had spent vast sums to produce new repertory (including the 1973 *Don Juan* and *Cinderella*) in hopes of attracting larger audiences. The ambitious 1974 spring season, which presented company premieres of Balanchine's *The Four Temperaments* and *La Sonnambula*, Bournonville's *Flower Festival at Genzano: Pas de Deux*, Lester Horton's *The Beloved*, Michel Fokine's *Les Sylphides* (staged by Danilova) and *Dying Swan* (danced by Natalia Makarova), John Cranko's *Legende* and *Taming of the Shrew: Pas de Deux*, and Smuin's *Mother Blues* and *Pulcinella Variations*, played to critical acclaim and large audiences. But by that summer the enterprise was heavily in debt. The National Endowment for the Arts Dance Panel voted against granting funds to the company on the grounds that it was not financially secure.[22] Steve Zellerbach was replaced by Maggie Carver, who made the association's financial solvency a top priority. Many members of the board favored the idea of declaring bankruptcy and disbanding the company, assuming perhaps that another company could be formed in the future on a more stable base.

To Lew, that idea was simply not an option. The San Francisco Ballet was the greatest single project of his professional life. His concern was not only for himself and for what

[20] "Foreign Genius and Native Talent," *Dance Magazine*, July 1973, 63.

[21] Susan White, "Utah Civic Ballet and Ballet West: A Preliminary Study, 1964–1976," M.A. thesis, University of Utah, 1982, 60.

[22] Telephone interview with Richard E. LeBlond, Jr., March 9 and 14, 1988.

he had built; it was also for the dancers, who would be left stranded if the company were dissolved. (He did not believe in dancers being left to go on welfare, or as he would say, "on the dole," between contracts or between seasons.[23]) The issue came to a head in September as the board met to settle on a course of action. Knowing that the decision to declare bankruptcy required a unanimous vote of the board, Lew went to the meeting determined to save SFB. "I have only one vote," he told Gisella, "and it's for the dancers."

The board did not declare bankruptcy at its September 19 meeting, but it sent out an alert that unless $500,000 could be raised in eleven days, both the company and the school would be forced to close.[24] Rather than sitting by and watching their company fold, the dancers, led by Gladstein, mounted a "Save Our Ballet" (S.O.B.) campaign and took it to the people of San Francisco. Some manned telephones in a direct appeal to potential donors, while others performed on the streets, in department store windows, and even during the half-time of a '49er's game. Streets were closed to traffic and given over to S.O.B. block parties, and S.O.B. buttons and balloons appeared around the city. Mayor Joseph Alioto and Governor Ronald Reagan called for support from the people of California while telegrams expressing concern over the company's future poured in from across the country. Over six thousand people attended a special S.O.B. day at Marine World-Africa USA, where the dancers performed an adaptation of Lew's *Beauty and the Beast* with live elephants and tigers. Michael Smuin even rode a tricycle in a race against a chimpanzee – and won.

The S.O.B campaign was a desperate act, a vigorous display of determination in which Smuin was involved to an extent that Lew's age and health did not permit. The very

---

[23] Robert Commanday, "S.F. Ballet Reorganization," *San Francisco Chronicle*, July 16, 1971, Russell Hartley Scrapbook, 1971.

[24] The following description of the S.O.B. campaign is indebted to Cobbett Steinberg's account in *San Francisco Ballet: The First Fifty Years* (San Francisco: San Francisco Ballet Association, 1983), 111–13.

visible physical efforts of Smuin and the dancers forced the SFB Association board to rally to the company's side.[25] Inspired greatly by the spirit of renewal that had accompanied Smuin's arrival, the dancers agreed to diminished contracts and offered to dance five extra *Nutcracker* performances without pay that year. Initial efforts brought such response in terms of community involvement that the eleven-day deadline was extended by two weeks. Smuin flew to Washington, D.C., to lobby for more funding from the N.E.A., which gave the company $40,000. By the middle of October, the company had raised enough money to secure its existence; the dancers embarked on their planned Hawaiian tour and began *Nutcracker* rehearsals.

One important outcome of the S.O.B. campaign was the association's hiring of an arts consultant, George Alan Smith. Smith studied the San Francisco institution and recommended that the association hire a professional arts administrator full time, a paid president who would see that the company and school were run with fiscal responsibility. Having a paid president would give the association a chief executive officer who could meet on equal footing with presidents of businesses and corporations, which was a psychological advantage in fund-raising. In January 1975, the association surprised the dance world by hiring Dr. Richard E. LeBlond, Jr., as its new president and general manager. A former academician, LeBlond had a doctorate in sociology from the University of Michigan, where he had specialized in issues relating to funding and administration of the performing arts. At the time of his hiring, LeBlond was working for

---

[25] Telephone interview with Richard E. LeBlond, Jr., March 9 and 13, 1988. LeBlond, who inherited responsibility for the company's financial situation following the "S.O.B." campaign, cautions against a "mythology" that has grown up about its effectiveness. He points out that it is risky to admit that an institution is on the brink of folding because many patrons want to give only to a winning team. Moreover, many of the contributions that came in during the campaign were advances on money the company would have received anyway the following spring, which made his work that much harder the next year. But LeBlond agrees that the dancers' bold move provided a sort of emotional blackmail that forced the board to come forward with support.

Barbara Weisberger's Pennsylvania Ballet; he also brought
to San Francisco valuable experience gained as president of
the Association of American Dance Companies and as cochairman of the N.E.A. Dance Panel.

LeBlond's hiring proved yet another turning point
in the fortunes of the San Francisco Ballet. He developed a
professional fund-raising program and drew up a five-year
plan for the company's financial solvency. LeBlond's plan
won the confidence of the city's financial community and
wiped out the company's debt in less than two years rather
than the anticipated five. The financial stability achieved
through LeBlond's reforms brought Lew a new freedom from
concern over SFB's future. For the first time in his San
Francisco career, he was able to plan new works with the
assurance that he would have enough funding to see them
mounted.

While Lew adjusted to the company's organizational
changes, Harold remained actively involved in teaching and
in auditioning scholarship students. In 1972, Harold's fortieth
anniversary as director of the San Francisco Ballet School, he
personally auditioned a thousand students in seven Western
states, selecting three hundred for the school's summer
session (of which eighty received Ford Foundation scholarships).[26] While Ruby remained on Harold's faculty as a
teacher of pointe classes into the early 1970s, the majority of
her professional teaching took place in a private school in
Mill Valley, a community just across the Golden Gate Bridge
which was nearer the couple's home in San Anselmo.

In the institutional restructuring of the early 1970s, the
school, like the company, came under the direction of the SFB
Association. The final issue of Harold's tenure as school
director came to be guarding the school's interests against
what he considered the encroaching needs of the growing
company. The converted garage on 18th Avenue could barely
contain the two institutions. Over time a fourth studio was

[26] "San Francisco Ballet School Opens 40th Summer Session on July 19th," San
Francisco Ballet Press Release, Russell Hartley Scrapbook, 1972.

**43**   Harold Christensen teaching, 1972.
Courtesy of San Francisco Performing Arts Library and Museum

added downstairs, and administrative offices were moved
into apartments leased by the company in the building next
door. Still, the use of space and the allocation of studio time
became a bone of contention between Harold on one hand

and Lew and Smuin on the other. Harold, who naturally had
to work his scheduling around time constraints imposed by
public education, wanted rights to the studio space beginning
as soon as young dancers could arrive after school. He felt
that company class should begin early and that company
rehearsals should be finished by late afternoon. Lew and
Smuin were loathe to ask the dancers to come too early,
and they wanted rehearsal space for the company during late
afternoons and evenings. One day Harold had a run-in with
Smuin when the latter kicked a class out of one of the studios
in order to use the space for a rehearsal.[27] With the creation
of the SFB Association and a new reliance on outside grants
for company funding, income from the school became a less
important factor in keeping the company financially solvent.
Thus, Harold lost the clout he had formerly wielded in such
discussions.

At the turning point in SFB's fortunes, just before
LeBlond arrived and put the company on firmer financial
footing, the SFB Association began retirement negotiations
with Harold.[28] By January 1975, he was seventy-one years old.
Health problems had begun to diminish his effectiveness as
a teacher, and the board felt that a new, younger leader would
be better able to accomplish the school's mission.[29] Harold
retired that spring, and company regisseur Richard Cammack
took over his position, initially on a trial basis. Lew was
not pleased to see his brother negotiated out of his job, but
under the new administrative structure Lew, too, was a hired
employee and could no longer dictate personnel policy.

---

[27] Interview with Harold Christensen, San Anselmo, California, December 4, 1987.
Ruby confirms that shortly before Harold was asked to retire, he had a serious
argument with Michael Smuin over the use of studio space. She assumes that Smuin
went to the Board and stated that he could not work with Harold. Conversation with
Ruby Asquith Christensen, October 22, 1989.

[28] Telephone interview with Richard E. LeBlond, Jr., March 9 and 14, 1988.

[29] Smuin had also gone on record, shortly after his arrival, as desiring younger
teachers who had just retired from performing. Arthur Bloomfield, "S.F. Ballet Plans
Big Leaps Forward," *San Francisco Examiner*, February 28, 1973.

Harold keenly resented his forced retirement, perhaps because he never got over the fact that the school and company he and his brothers had originally bought and built up as a private enterprise were no longer under their control. Also, teaching had given Harold a sense of power; the classroom was the arena in which he exercised control and held forth. Without his teaching and his position as head of the school, he was left without a platform from which to express his opinions, which expression was a very real need on his part. As health permitted, Harold taught briefly in Ruby's studio, working with the advanced students. But various maladies, including the eventual onset of prostate cancer, sharply curtailed his activities. Harold felt estranged from the SFB School, and as his physical condition worsened, he stopped attending company performances.

In Salt Lake City, Willam choreographed few new ballets in the 1970s. Instead, he indulged in greater touring ambitions. Paul Szilard, the impresario who had arranged Ballet West U.S.A.'s 1971 European tour, persuaded Willam that the company should return to Europe soon, before their name was forgotten by the public. Willam and Szilard cooked up a second tour for 1974, enlisting Violette Verdy and Helgi Tomasson as guest stars and going all the way to London to reserve Sadler's Wells theater. But the required funding never came through; neither the Wallaces nor Eggertsen, the philanthropist who had underwritten the first European tour, chose to support the costly project. Szilard, left in the lurch, sent letters of profuse apology to the guest artists and to the theaters where he had lined up engagements.

Greatly disappointed by the tour's failure to materialize, Willam felt frustrated by what he considered a lack of support nearly on par, in his mind, with the collapse of the 1947–1948 San Francisco Civic Ballet. But his focus on building the company's reputation through touring was shortsighted in view of a less glamorous but more critical issue requiring his attention. After pouring money into companies built around key artistic directors, the Ford Foundation wanted assurance that those companies would not wither at the death or retirement of their founders. As Willam aged, both his local board and Ford Foundation program officer Marcia Thompson urged him to think of his company's long-range welfare. They persuaded him to select an assistant director to whom the reins of the company would eventually pass.

Willam did not confer with his brothers about whom to select. He assumed they would suggest a Balanchine dancer, and he wanted to make this decision without their advice. In the fall of 1973 he brought a Yugoslavian dancer, Milorad Miskovitch, to Ballet West as an artistic collaborator. This choice reflected Willam's artistic differences with Lew and his tendency to favor the old Ballet Russe tradition. Miskovitch had danced with Col. de Basil's Original Ballet Russe and the Grand Ballet de Monte Carlo, had been a leading dancer in Roland Petit's Ballets de Paris in the late 1940s, and had appeared as a guest artist with the London Festival Ballet before forming his own company in the mid-1950s. At Ballet West, Miskovitch functioned primarily as a ballet master. He lasted only six months with the company because he clashed with Bené Arnold, who enjoyed Willam's complete loyalty.

Willam also invited Jacques D'Amboise, whom he respected and trusted deeply, to consider the position, but D'Amboise was not ready for that type of career move.[30] So Willam conferred seriously with his professional associates, including Mattlyn Gavers, one of his dancers dating to Portland days who was now on the University of Utah faculty. One name that came up in conversations repeatedly was that of Bruce Marks, whom Gavers had known when she was a ballet mistress at the Metropolitan Opera. Marks and his wife, Toni Lander, had appeared with the company as guest artists over the years, and Willam appreciated Marks's theatrical flair. More importantly, Willam prized Lander's gifts as a

---

[30] Interview with Jacques D'Amboise, New York, New York, January 12, 1989. D'Amboise claims that both Willam and Lew offered him their companies but that he wanted to continue performing.

ballerina and as a teacher; he thought she would be an excellent influence on Ballet West.[31] The couple was then living in Copenhagen and performing with the Royal Danish Ballet, but Willam had heard rumors that they wanted to return to the United States to rear their children. Willam called Marks and discussed the offer, and in August the official announcement was released. Marks and Willam would share the company's artistic directorship for two years, after which Willam would retire and Marks would assume sole control.

"I decided to join Ballet West because I think the company as Mr. Christensen has built it, has the most potential of any ballet company in America," announced Marks when the appointment was made public.[32] As the two-year transition period began, Marks attracted the sort of publicity to which Willam had long grown accustomed. Utah Governor Calvin L. Rampton declared June 16, 1976, "Bruce Marks and Toni Lander Day." Two nights of performances to celebrate Marks's and Lander's arrival featured soloists from the Royal Danish Ballet in performance with Ballet West.[33] Just as Willam had impressed Utahns upon his arrival by showing off guest artists from his San Francisco company, Marks now attracted press attention and impressed audiences with guest artists from Denmark.

As Marks took control of Ballet West and proved impatient to lead the company in new directions, Willam found it harder to give up authority than he had anticipated. While he always supported Marks in public, those who knew Willam best realized that he was not happy with the transition. In Willam's eyes, Lew's transition had worked out much better; Lew and Smuin had choreographed *Cinderella* jointly,

---

[31] Willam confirmed years later that without Lander he would not have brought Marks to Ballet West. Telephone conversation with Willam F. Christensen, November 5, 1991.

[32] White, 72.

[33] *Ibid.*, 75.

and they seemed to have a real partnership.[34] Willam and Marks enjoyed no such collaboration and developed no close personal relationship. The two years passed all too quickly, and as the date of his announced retirement (June 1, 1978) approached, Willam did not want to step down. It was painfully difficult to give up the daily association with the dancers, the backstage involvement as new productions were born, the glamour and anticipation of opening nights, and the press attention to which he was accustomed. Perhaps hardest of all for Willam, the habitual leader, was losing his position as "Boss," the name by which his San Francisco dancers had once called him. A complete break with the company was unthinkable; as he stepped down the company announced that he would remain an advisor to the board.

The final great irony of Willam's tenure with Ballet West was that after years of struggling to produce works on the shallow stage of Kingsbury Hall, he retired just as the city finished preparing a new home for the company. At the instigation of Mrs. Wallace, the old Orpheum Theatre, which had been built as a vaudeville house by her father in 1913, was restored and refurbished as a home for Salt Lake City's performing arts companies. Ballet West was principal tenant but was to share the theater with the Utah Opera, Repertory Dance Theatre, and the Ririe-Woodbury Dance Company.

Renamed the Capitol Theatre, Ballet West's new home provided rehearsal studios, storage areas for costumes and scenery, and administrative offices and meeting rooms, allowing the company to centralize its efforts and house its assets under one roof. Transferring operations to the new location signified the company's final break with the university and suggested an ever-increasing level of professionalism. *Dance Magazine* published a feature article on the company and its new home, observing that Ballet West was "Moving into the Majors."[35] But Willam did not benefit from this long-awaited

---

[34] Telephone interview with Sondra Sugai, November 1, 1989.

[35] Olga Maynard, "Ballet West: Moving into the Majors," *Dance Magazine*, February 1979, 79.

44   Bruce Marks, right, looks on as Maestro Maurice Abravanel, Utah Symphony President Wendell Ashton, and Willam Christensen cut a cake at a symphony celebration.
Courtesy of Willam F. Christensen

step because the company did not make the move until the fall of 1978, four months after his retirement. This left the rueful Willam somewhat in the position of Moses, who, after shepherding the children of Israel through the wilderness for forty years, stayed behind and watched Joshua lead them into the promised land.

# 17

## THE FINAL YEARS

Lew never officially retired; he just abdicated more and more responsibility to Michael Smuin. Although the latter had come to San Francisco in 1973 in a supporting role, in 1976 the partnership became an equal one. Smuin was appointed co-director with the understanding that all decisions regarding policy and programming would be agreed upon by both men. Lew took a back seat in the day-to-day running of the company and openly expressed support for his co-director's efforts. Because Smuin carried the heavier burden, he received a larger salary than did Lew, who retreated ever further into the role of company figurehead.[1]

With Smuin in place to help run the company, Lew reserved his remaining strength for choreographing. In the spring of 1976, SFB produced an all-Stravinsky program to celebrate the twenty-fifth anniversary of Lew's tenure as SFB artistic director. For those with a sense of history, the choice of Stravinsky was an oblique reminder of Lew's success as Apollo in Balanchine's 1937 Stravinsky Festival. SFB revived Smuin's *Pulcinella Variations* and Lew's 1959 *Danses Concertantes* and acquired Balanchine's *Agon*. In this context, Lew created his first new work in three years: *Stravinsky Pas de Deux*, set to the composer's *Four Norwegian Moods*, a little-known composition dating from 1942.

---

[1] Harold said of Lew in a 1976 interview: "Now since the new group took [SFBA] over, Lew doesn't give a damn. Lew has just given up. He's not fighting." (Barbara Cohen Interview with Harold Christensen and Ruby Asquith Christensen, San Anselmo, California, December 29, 1976.) On a visit to San Francisco in 1977, Lowry also detected that Smuin was the power behind company planning and that Lew had lost his will to run things. Lowry was disappointed by this turn of events and felt, as did many of Lew's friends, that Lew needed to be more assertive. (Interview with W. McNeil Lowry, New York, New York, September 16, 1988.)

Less than nine minutes long, *Stravinsky Pas de Deux*
followed the general plan of the grand pas de deux, with its
entry and partner work, solo variations, and bravura closing
section. To highlight the technical capabilities of two dancers
new to the company, Susan Magno and Keith Martin, Lew
incorporated more tours de force than usual, but with a light
touch; in a witty moment suggesting the image of a juggler
rolling a ball along his arms, Magno rolled her head up one
of Martin's arms, across his back, and down the other, while
*bourréeing* in circles behind him. *Stravinsky Pas de Deux*
pleased audiences and critics with its "elegant, playful,
spirited, and technically demanding" variations.[2] It stayed
in the company's repertory and earned favorable reviews during SFB's New York performances in 1978 at the Brooklyn
Academy of Music. Although Smuin's *Romeo and Juliet* led the
company's programming in that engagement, Tobi Tobias, in
a later article in *Dance Magazine*, declared Lew's short work
"the most intelligently made item on the agenda."[3] Arlene
Croce also declared *Stravinsky Pas de Deux* "choreographically
the most distinguished work of the season."[4] Reflecting on
Lew's oeuvre, she summed up her feelings with the observation that although his thoughts seemed to "wander" in some
of his works, Lew's was "a choreographic mind of no small
distinction." She concluded, "The Christensen ballets hold a
provocative secret. They ought to be much better known
than they are."[5]

Such praise vindicated Kirstein's longtime support of
Lew as a choreographer. It may also have given Kirstein the
ammunition he needed to have New York City Ballet acquire
another Christensen ballet, which had not happened since *Con*

---

[2] Cobbett Steinberg, "Lew Christensen: An American Original," *Encore* 1.3 (Summer 1984): 15.

[3] Tobi Tobias, "Brooklyn Celebrates Ballet in America," *Dance Magazine*, January 1981, 69.

[4] Arlene Croce, "The San Francisco Version," in *Going to the Dance* (New York: Alfred A. Knopf, 1982), 135.

[5] *Ibid.*

*Amore* in 1953. Now, nearly thirty years later, *Stravinsky Pas de Deux* (renamed *Norwegian Moods*) was the only work by an outside choreographer to be included in NYCB's 1982 Stravinsky Centennial Celebration.[6]

While Lew's ballets were not often seen in New York, his repertory did spread in the West, notably to Willam's company, which contained six of Lew's works by 1976. By Lew's death in 1984, *Filling Station* had been staged by six other companies, and *Con Amore*, by eight.[7] By the late 1970s, the Pacific Northwest Ballet (led by the former Christensen, as well as Balanchine, dancer Kent Stowell) and the Honolulu City Ballet both had productions of Lew's *Nutcracker*, which he traveled to touch up annually.[8] In early 1978 there was even talk of Lew going to France at the invitation of Violette Verdy to set his *Nutcracker* on the Paris Opera Ballet.[9] But that same year, the weakness and chest pains that had limited his productivity were diagnosed as congestive heart failure. His doctor gave him one year to live.[10]

---

[6] Lew feared that *Norwegian Moods* would not be well received in the context of Balanchine's company. According to Gisella, he said, "Nothing will please New York, but I don't want to let Lincoln down, so I'm going to offer the *Norwegian Moods*.... [New York] never liked me and they never will with Balanchine there ... but I'm prepared for it. It doesn't matter." When the work received an ovation and good write-ups, Lew was so surprised that "he couldn't get over it." Interview with Gisella Caccialanza Christensen, San Bruno, California, December 9, 1987. It is unclear why Lew would have feared the worst in 1982 after this ballet received such good reviews in 1978. Gisella may be confusing that original New York presentation with the 1982 showing.

[7] Steinberg, "Lew Christensen: An American Original," 17. According to Steinberg, by the time of Lew's death, *Filling Station* had been staged by Ballet Caravan, San Francisco Ballet, New York City Ballet, Ballet West, Pacific Northwest Ballet, and Kansas City Ballet. By the same time, *Con Amore* had been produced by the Joffrey Ballet, Ballet West, San Francisco Ballet, New York City Ballet, the National Ballet, Chicago Opera Ballet, Ballet Oklahoma, Cincinnati Ballet, and the Finnish National Opera Ballet.

[8] Arthur Bloomfield, "National TV and a trip to Spoleto in the Ballet's Future," *San Francisco Chronicle*, January 8, 1978, Russell Hartley Scrapbook, 1978.

[9] *Ibid.*

[10] According to Lew's son Chris, Lew's heart condition began suddenly and was probably caused by a virus. Lew may have also inherited a susceptibility to heart disease from his father, who had died of a heart attack at age sixty-five.

In fact, Lew lived not one but six more years and witnessed the resolution of many important issues in his life's work. He choreographed two final ballets, saw his son Chris find a career in music, witnessed the construction and completion of the new facility to house the school and company, and participated in the celebration of SFB's 50th anniversary.

Lew's musical tastes reverted to the Baroque masters for his final creations: *Scarlatti Portfolio* (1979) and *Vivaldi Concerto Grosso* (1981).[11] Set to seven Scarlatti piano sonatas orchestrated by Benjamin Lees, *Scarlatti Portfolio* consisted of a series of *commedia dell'arte* sketches, complete with ribald humor and bawdy movement jokes. Lew identified the episodic nature of successive *commedia dell'arte* scenes with the variety format of his own vaudeville experiences.[12] The seven sections of *Scarlatti Portfolio* included what he described as an "off-the-beaten-path" pas de deux between Arlequin and Columbine in which the focal point is the latter's long, easily pulled hair; a travesty sketch in which the rich but ugly Franceschina (played by a man) wears a veil and manipulates a large false bosom by pulling strings in an attempt to attract a husband; and Arlequin's virtuoso "duet" with a white hula hoop. The latter, which was choreographed for the considerable technical skills of David McNaughton, combined classical feats with dexterous manipulation of the hoop; in 1979 it earned the bronze medal for choreography at the International Ballet Competition in Jackson, Mississippi. McNaughton, who performed the hoop solo at the competition, won the silver medal in the senior men's division, which was the highest prize won by an American that year.[13] In *Scarlatti Portfolio*, Lew combined, one final time, the classical technique he prized with elements of popular culture, completing a succession of ballets with a similar mixture, dating back to

[11] Stephanie von Buchau, "Native Dancer," *Ballet News*, May 1982, 27.

[12] My description of *Scarlatti Portfolio* is indebted to William Huck's article "Scarlatti Portfolio," *Performing Arts* [Programs III and IV] 2.1 (January 1988): SFB-2.

[13] Cobbett Steinberg, *San Francisco Ballet: The First Fifty Years* (San Francisco: San Francisco Ballet Association, 1983), 169.

*Filling Station*, including *Charade*, *Beauty and the Beast*, *Danses Concertantes*, *Original Sin*, *Jest of Cards*, and *Life*.

If *Scarlatti Portfolio* looked back to Lew's comedic and character ballets, the 1981 *Vivaldi Concerto Grosso* completed the line of abstract works in a neoclassical vein that began with his 1936 *Encounter* and included *Sinfonia*, *Divertissement d'Auber*, and *Symphony in D*.[14] *Vivaldi* employed fourteen dancers (a leading couple and a corps of twelve) in fast-paced first and third movements sandwiching a languorous pas de deux. When pressed to comment on his last work, Lew said matter-of-factly, "I wanted to see if I had the strength to do it."[15] With characteristic modesty, he played down his own choreography and spoke, as Kirstein often did, in terms of craftsmanship rather than artistry: "I'm not trying to save the art of ballet or the world. Ballet is just a craft I know."[16]

By the late 1970s, SFB was in better condition than ever, economically stable, drawing large audiences, and performing about 140 times a year. The Christensen–Smuin partnership seemed to be working. Generally speaking, Lew's repertory kept the dancers grounded in the classical tradition, while Smuin's ballets stretched the boundaries of that tradition. Big-name guest artists from New York and European companies, and the addition of ballets by Maurice Béjart, John Cranko, Jerome Robbins, and Sir Frederick Ashton, challenged the dancers and added a brightness to the seasons. The company's reputation enjoyed a pronounced renaissance in the local press as critics who had deplored the stagnation of the late 1960s and early 1970s now praised the company in glowing tones. "Of all our major performing organizations, the Ballet has become the most adventurous, consistent and rewarding ticket in town," declared the formerly acerbic

---

[14] *Ibid*. For more description of *Vivaldi Concerto Grosso*, see "Lew Christensen's Contemporary Ballets," in Steinberg, *San Francisco Ballet*, and Janice Ross, "Lew Christensen, An American Original," *Dance Magazine*, December 1981, 66–69.

[15] Ross, "Lew Christensen: An American Original."

[16] *Ibid*., 69.

Heuwell Tircuit.[17] If Lew felt overlooked or undervalued when the focus of public and critical attention was riveted upon his partner's *Romeo and Juliet* in 1978, he did not let on. When asked by a reporter how he felt about Smuin's success, Lew affirmed, "Wonderful, wonderful. That's the point, the spirit of cooperation and development in the company. By helping each other we expand each person's work."[18] In fact, Lew made his final stage appearance in the non-dancing role of Friar Lawrence in Smuin's *Romeo*, which was televised in 1978 as part of the PBS *Dance in America* series.

One of the most personally satisfying developments Lew lived to witness was the career of his son, Chris. Whereas the other brothers had insisted that their children take dance lessons, Lew and Gisella had not; Chris was the only child in the family's fourth generation who never actually studied ballet. Paradoxically, he was the one whose career eventually mirrored the multigenerational family tradition most closely. (Shortly after Ballet West's European tour, Willam's daughter Roxanne stopped dancing, finding the life of a professional dancer too narrow and restricting.) In his youth, Chris often watched his mother teach intermediate and advanced classes at the SFB School's Lakeside Branch, and when waiting for his parents at the main building on 18th Avenue, he would pass the time by playing in the scenery and the *Nutcracker* props. Chris felt comfortable backstage at the opera house and developed a lasting love for *The Nutcracker* at an early age. In his teens, he traveled occasionally with SFB on its West Coast tours, acting as an extra stagehand and helping with the lighting equipment. His serious music study began with flute lessons and a rigorous grounding in music theory at the

[17] Heuwell Tircuit, "The Season of the S.F. Ballet – 'Romeo,' and Five Premieres," *San Francisco Sunday Examiner and Chronicle*, January 8, 1978, Russell Hartley Scrapbook. *Newsweek* also drew attention to the rebirth of SFB's glory, comparing the company's history to the story of Cinderella; this artistic stepchild was saved at the stroke of midnight by the S.O.B. campaign and was now at the ball to stay. Hubert Saal, "Cinderella Story," *Newsweek*, May 9, 1977, Russell Hartley Scrapbook.

[18] Beth Witrogen, "Ballet Keeps Artistic Director on His Toes," *San Francisco Examiner*, May 17, 1978, Russell Hartley Scrapbook.

San Francisco Conservatory, followed by a focus on composition as he completed his bachelor's degree at the University of California at Berkeley. After graduation, he became interested in conducting, inspired by the example of his grandfather, who had conducted the Christensen brothers' vaudeville act. It is fitting that Chris has inherited his grandfather's violin.

When a small company, the San Francisco Dance Theatre, asked Lew's former music director, Earl Murray, to conduct a repertory season for them in the early 1980s, Murray recommended Chris instead. Denis de Coteau, the conductor of SFB's new resident orchestra, attended one of those performances and subsequently hired Chris as an assistant conductor. Chris showed a natural affinity for conducting for dance; to his father's delight, Chris conducted not only Lew's *Nutcracker* but also his *Stravinsky Pas de Deux, Variations de Ballet*, and *Vivaldi Concerto Grosso* between 1982 and 1985. After Lew's death, Chris went on to engagements with the New York City Ballet (1985–1986), the Joffrey Ballet (1987), the National Ballet of Canada (1988), Ballet Arizona (1988–1989), the Houston Ballet (1990), Pittsburgh Ballet Theater (1989–1991), the Sacramento Ballet (1991–1992), and the Milwaukee Ballet (1995). Of all these, his time with the New York City Ballet was the most personally meaningful, as his father's former colleagues welcomed him warmly and some members of the orchestra still remembered playing for Lew.[19] In 1989, Chris completed a Doctorate of Musical Arts at Stanford, with a dissertation on Prokofiev's *Cinderella*. While composition remains Chris's primary interest, he also works with former SFB ballet mistress Virginia Johnson to promote Lew's repertory.

Working with SFB during his father's final years, Chris watched Lew adjust to changes in the company's operations as LeBlond expanded SFB's marketing and development program. Though grateful for the financial security brought by LeBlond, Lew never quite adjusted his thinking to the new scale on which the company operated. He and

---

[19] Letter from Chris Christensen to the author, November 15, 1996.

**45** Chris Christensen.
Photograph by William Acheson, courtesy of Chris Christensen

Gisella could not get over being picked up by a limousine at their home in San Bruno and chauffeured into the city for special company occasions. And Lew marveled that by the early 1980s the organization was large enough to require twelve telephone lines.[20]

SFB's administrative offices filled three converted apartments in the building next to the studio that had once been a parking garage. The operation was growing in size and numbers, but it lacked a decent facility in which to expand. Office space was at such a premium that LeBlond worked out of a front bedroom, while the company manager functioned in a kitchen, plugging his typewriter into an electric stove that doubled as a filing cabinet.[21] Studio space was likewise cramped and overcrowded; low ceilings forced dancers to duck their heads at the top of high lifts, and the company's fifty dancers shared meager changing facilities (and a total of two showers) with hundreds of students from the school.

Studies for a new building began in 1979. A San Francisco architect and ballet subscriber, Beverly Willis, was chosen to design the first building in the United States to be built specifically to meet the needs of a major ballet company. With cooperation from city officials, the SFB Association acquired land directly behind the War Memorial Opera House, signaling the company's return to the city's Civic Center after thirty-one years on 18th Avenue. A fact-finding team studied dance facilities in Stuttgart, Paris, New York, and Toronto, then interviewed SFB's dancers to determine their needs.[22] In the May 1982 groundbreaking ceremony for the new building, Willam and Harold looked on as Lew turned the first shovelful of dirt with the same spade that had been used to break ground for the Golden Gate Bridge.

---

[20] Interview with Chris Christensen, San Bruno, California, December 9, 1987.

[21] Stewart McBride, "San Francisco Ballet, Cinderella of Dance, Sheds Rags for Riches," *Christian Science Monitor*, December 29, 1983, San Francisco Ballet Clipping File, Dance Collection, The New York Public Library.

[22] Steinberg, *San Francisco Ballet*, 148.

**46** Willam, Lew, and Harold Christensen at the groundbreaking for the new SFB building, 1982.
Courtesy of San Francisco Performing Arts Library and Museum

SFB's new building was completed late in 1983, just in time to move in before the end of the company's fiftieth anniversary year. The four-story, $13.8 million building included separate floors for the school and the company and contained a total of eight rehearsal halls, two of which could be joined to re-create the dimensions of the Opera House stage for blocking and dress rehearsals. Other desirable features included high ceilings (twelve feet for the school, fifteen feet for the company), canted mirrors, special lighting to avoid fluorescent glare, scientifically placed barres, sprung floors chosen by the dancers from twelve different mock-ups, a lounge and changing facilities with over thirty showers, exercise machines and facilities for physical therapy, storage rooms for props and toeshoes, a library, and generous office space with plenty of conference rooms. Lew was overwhelmed by the new building and never felt truly at home in the luxury of his new environs, but he rejoiced in the stability and community respect the edifice symbolized: "While other companies begin and fold, ours is permanent. It should be a cornerstone for American classical ballet for centuries."[23]

Lew participated in the celebration of SFB's golden anniversary that year, but Smuin's energy was behind the week of gala performances that brought all three Christensens back to the stage of the War Memorial Opera House to receive cheering ovations. In May of 1984, friends and company benefactors gathered to honor Lew on his seventy-fifth birthday, which proved to be his last. The image of Mac, in the *Filling Station* costume, decorated the large cake. Lew made an unusually emotional speech, thanking his associates and especially the dancers who had stayed with the company through its difficult years. Lew's pace had slowed dramatically by his seventy-fifth birthday. When the brothers went to New York to receive the Capezio Award that spring,

---

[23] Lew Christensen, "Tribute in Concrete," *San Francisco Ballet Magazine*, November 1983, 4. Another factor that shored up the ballet's security in this era was the opening of the $35-million Louise M. Davies Symphony Hall in September 1980. Once the symphony had its own performance space, the San Francisco Ballet found it significantly easier to schedule performances in the War Memorial Opera House.

Willam and Harold were alarmed to see that Lew could not walk from Lincoln Center to their nearby hotel without stopping to rest along the way. With a weakened heart working at fifty to seventy-five percent capacity, Lew had good days and bad.[24] Two days at work might be followed by two more spent at home recuperating. Less than a year earlier, he had given de Coteau seven scores to study for future use, but by the spring of 1984 it had become clear that Lew would not be able to choreograph another complete work. He set his sights instead on revamping his *Nutcracker* on the grounds that the company's 1967 production was worn out. Lew spent less and less time in the new building and began to find himself "outside the loop" in the making of company decisions.

As Lew's health worsened, and as the number of his working hours decreased, Smuin's influence over company policies and artistic direction grew inevitably stronger. New dancers hired by Smuin were naturally loyal to the director who was responsible for their position in the company and who made the majority of casting decisions. SFB's younger generation had little understanding of Lew's significance in the earlier decades of their own company, let alone the early days of American ballet. Lew's understated manner was partly responsible for their ignorance. Unlike Willam, he never promoted himself by recounting the glories of his past accomplishments. If others did not know enough about his past to respect him, Lew would not go out of his way to clue them in. Instead, he spent time with people who knew him well: LeBlond; Timothy Duncan, SFB's general manager; and Richard Carter, who had become the company's technical director. At times he withdrew into his office, where he spent hours listening to music.

By the early 1980s, Lew felt uncomfortable with the degree to which he had lost control over the company. Time and time again he found programs printed without having passed his desk for prior approval. He became angered that decisions about casting and programming were made without

---

[24] Telephone interview with Chris Christensen, November 20, 1991.

his consent, usually on the excuse that he was too tired or too sick to be bothered. "It makes me more tired and sick when I find out later that something was done that I didn't like," he would complain to LeBlond.[25]

Lew's anger was not directed against LeBlond; rather, it was the working partnership with Smuin that was beginning to fray. Lew sought out LeBlond because the latter had become a trusted confidant. By putting the company on solid financial ground, the administrator had relieved Lew of long-standing economic worries and had earned his complete trust. Lew saw LeBlond as the knight who had slain the company's financial dragons. With his extensive education and informed taste, LeBlond may have even provided Lew with a quasi-Kirstein figure in San Francisco. When a financial planner volunteered his services to help Lew arrange his affairs in the early 1980s, Lew appointed LeBlond the executor of his estate, entrusting the administrator with the security of his family and the future of his repertory.[26]

In addition to his frustration at being passed over when Smuin made artistic decisions, Lew became concerned about the quality of the company's dancing, which he felt was in jeopardy.[27] He was delighted with SFB's magnificent new building, but he wanted it to house a superior ensemble. Lew felt that the school was not doing its job of preparing students

---

[25] Telephone interview with Richard E. LeBlond, Jr., March 9 and 14, 1988.

[26] The financial advisor, Roy Tolan, volunteered his time as a favor to LeBlond but confirms that Lew attracted such gifts because he was loved in the community. A prominent San Francisco law firm drew up Lew's will free of charge, marshalling its forces to complete the task in record time because Tolan, seeing Lew's weakened condition, feared that he might die any day. Telephone interview with Roy Tolan, November 11, 1991.

[27] Richard E. LeBlond, Jr., with Meg Madden, *From Chaos to Fragility: My Years at the San Francisco Ballet Association* (Dubuque, Iowa: Kendall/Hunt Publishing Co., 1988), 131. Clearly, LeBlond is not an impartial witness of company affairs and of Lew's attitudes toward the shape the company was in because those issues developed into key concerns in LeBlond's power struggle with Smuin. However, Gisella confirms LeBlond's claims; Harold also expressed similar concerns about the company's evolving style and Lew's feelings on that subject.

**47** Lew Christensen and Michael Smuin, ca. 1982.
Photograph by Ira Nowinski, courtesy of Ira Nowinski and San Francisco
Performing Arts Library and Museum

for the company adequately, and he was particularly concerned about the quality of male dancing.[28] Although Lew
generally paid little attention to critics, he may have taken
note when Anna Kisselgoff wrote, after seeing the company
perform at Wolf Trap in 1982, that the influx of dancers from
Ballet Theater had shifted SFB's style away from the
Balanchine esthetic: "There is none of the attack common to
Balanchine dancers. The technique can even go occasionally
slack: More knees have to be stretched, more feet pointed,
more pirouettes polished."[29]

The concerns Lew expressed privately among friends
were echoed more forcefully by other members of the American dance community. In 1983, the Dance Advisory Panel of
the National Endowment for the Arts warned SFB that it
needed to improve the quality of new works and repolish
some of its standard repertory (including the Balanchine ballets). To give the warning meaning, the panel recommended a
ten percent cut in the company's funding.

In early 1984, Dance/USA, a newly formed organization of professional ballet and modern dance companies, held
its first national conference in San Francisco. The dancers,
administrators, and directors who came to San Francisco for
the meetings (which included most of the NEA Dance Panel)
visited SFB's new building and raved about its features. But
SFB's performances elicited a far different response. The
Dance Panel's report that year informed the company that
since standards had obviously continued to deteriorate, they
were cutting SFB's grant by an additional thirty percent.[30]

Thus, the final summer of his life, Lew faced the grim
possibility that his company was deteriorating and that his
handpicked successor might not be the best candidate for the
job. It was not too late to effect a change because Smuin's
contract was up for renewal, and he was making negotiations

---

[28] LeBlond, 131.

[29] Anna Kisselgoff, "As the San Francisco Ballet Nears 50," *New York Times*,
September 12, 1982.

[30] LeBlond, 135.

difficult for the Ballet Association by refusing to attend meetings. Smuin demanded a large salary increase and insisted on receiving at least one dollar more than LeBlond as a token that the board valued its chief choreographer over its chief administrator.[31] Smuin also demanded increased funds for more rehearsal time and more lavish company productions.[32]

In the past, when LeBlond and Duncan had had problems dealing with Smuin, they had gone to Lew, who as a revered father figure exerted a calming influence and was able to bring opposing sides together. But this time Lew could not resolve the conflict; his poor health led to depression and to a lack of emotional energy that lessened his ability to deal with contention in the company.[33] Moreover, the differences that surfaced in Smuin's contract negotiations were inflated by a growing sentiment that his artistic policies were no longer in the company's best interest. The loss of NEA funds must have been seen as a serious matter by LeBlond, who also had donors in the community to satisfy. At issue was the tone of Smuin's choreography, which was aimed at a popular audience and whose flashiness sometimes offended notions of good taste. A strong case in point was Smuin's 1979 *A Song for Dead Warriors*, scenes from the life of a contemporary Native American struggling against the corruption of white society. Audiences responded enthusiastically to *Warrior*'s

---

[31] For a discussion of this controversy that takes a more sympathetic view of Smuin's side, see Holly Brubach, "Room Enough to Move," *Atlantic Monthly*, May 1988, 62–74. The chief weakness of Brubach's account is her failure to recognize the role Lew played in Smuin's dismissal. Brubach paints the controversy as a power struggle between Smuin and LeBlond, observing, "What is remarkable is not that [LeBlond] may have acted with malice aforethought but that the board, when pressed, chose its administrator over its artistic director – or, rather, its administrator's vision of the San Francisco Ballet over its artistic director's" (66). This summation ignores the fact that the board's decision reflected the artistic judgments of the company's senior artistic director, Lew.

[32] When Smuin tells the story of his departure from SFB, he stresses that he wanted more money for the company; he does not mention wanting to earn more than LeBlond. For Smuin's version of the story, see John Gruen, "Smuin Sets Sail on Broadway," *Dance Magazine*, January 1988, 56.

[33] Letter from Chris Christensen to the author, April 4, 1992.

use of film, music, dance, drama, and special effects; its dramatically explosive vignettes; the hard-hitting male dancing of the work's disco sequence; and the sheer force with which Smuin delivered the ballet's overtly political message. The critics, however, found *Warrior's* rhetoric cliché-ridden and propagandizing, its emotions melodramatic, its staging overdone.[34] In contrast to *Warrior*, Lew's *Scarlatti Portfolio*, with all its bawdy *commedia*-inspired humor, was deemed a model of restraint. Also, Smuin's undeniable gift for the commercial theater brought him opportunities to choreograph for Broadway (Duke Ellington's *Sophisticated Ladies*, 1981), television (a series of PBS dance specials, including *Young American Artists in Performance at the White House*, 1982) and cinema (*The Cotton Club*, 1984).[35] Some members of the board expressed the concern that such freelance work on projects outside of San Francisco interfered with Smuin's ability to function as a full-time artistic director.

Ultimately, what turned key figures against Smuin was not his freelancing but his poor judgment in programming. The final blow, in Lew's mind, came that July, when SFB was invited to perform in Los Angeles and Pasadena as part of the 1984 Olympics Festival. Rather than presenting any aspect of its repertory in depth, SFB's program (which Lew's supporters insist was determined unilaterally by Smuin) consisted of excerpts of over a dozen ballets in a cut-and-paste melange that did justice to no single work. That format had worked well for the company's fiftieth anniversary gala the year before in San Francisco, where audiences understood the context of the bits and pieces presented. But when seen in Los Angeles in comparison with the programs of Merce Cunningham, Pina Bausch, and the Royal Ballet, the San Francisco Ballet came off looking glitzy and superficial. Snippets of Balanchine (the opening of *Serenade*, a section of *Stars and Stripes*) and snatches of Lew's ballets (the drunken

---

[34] Steinberg, *San Francisco Ballet*, 115. Steinberg explains the genesis of *A Song for Dead Warriors* and gives a balanced account of its reception.

[35] For more on his opportunities away from San Francisco, see Gruen, 56.

pas de deux from *Filling Station*, the hoop solo from *Scarlatti Portfolio*, part of *Il Distratto*) were intertwined with selections from Smuin's *To the Beatles*, *A Song for Dead Warriors*, Mozart's *C Minor Mass* (considered a trivialization of the score), and a romantic pas de deux that degenerated into a striptease. *Los Angeles Times* critic Martin Bernheimer described the fare as ranging "from the innocuous to the offensive" and charged that the company "dabbled" in

> neoclassical maneuvers, in tap-dance gimmicks, in show-biz glitz, in narrative ritual, in mixed-media experiments, in pop indulgences, in hippety-hop satires, in mystical pretension, in modern dance poses, in candy-coated profundity, and, of course, in borrowed Balanchine.

Rather than providing something for everyone, the eclectic sampling, concluded Bernheimer, "left the discomforting impression that, despite the considerable talent involved, the San Francisco Ballet values kitsch over art."[36] And the *Christian Science Monitor* summarized SFB's program as "an evening of glitz, glitter, and blatant sensuality – an embarrassment not only to the company but to its country."[37]

When LeBlond returned from the Olympics performances, Lew stormed into his office with a fistful of reviews and eyes filled with tears of anger and frustration. "I never thought I'd agree with Martin Bernheimer," he exclaimed, "but this time I think he was right."[38] The signs that serious change was needed in the artistic direction of the company had grown too loud to ignore. In Lew's mind, the future of his company was at stake. The idealistic prediction he and

[36] Martin Bernheimer, "A Silly San Francisco Sampler," *Los Angeles Times*, July 27, 1984, Russell Hartley Scrapbooks.

[37] David Wilck, "Olympic Arts: The Night the San Francisco Ballet Turned Superficial," *Christian Science Monitor*, August 13, 1984, San Francisco Ballet Clipping File, Dance Collection, The New York Public Library. Also quoted in Brubach, 65.

[38] Telephone interview with Richard E. LeBlond, Jr., March 9 and 14, 1988. Gisella tells the same story; Lew was livid over the company's presentation and reception at the Olympics.

Smuin had issued in *Dance News* at the outset of their partnership, that SFB would always be "trained in a high, pure classic style," had not come to pass. Lew recognized Smuin's dynamism and talent but felt betrayed by the way the partnership had evolved. He called LeBlond and Duncan to a meeting at his home that August to consider alternatives.

Lew himself no longer had the physical or psychological strength to effect sweeping reforms. Even if he had, the structure of the SFB Association placed responsibility for artistic as well as administrative issues ultimately under the control of the chief executive officer, LeBlond. When LeBlond and Duncan arrived at Lew's home to confer with him, they found that he had already discussed SFB's situation with Lincoln Kirstein. Kirstein recommended that the association replace Smuin with NYCB's Helgi Tomasson, who was ready to retire from the stage and was being courted by the Royal Danish Ballet. Lew was familiar with Tomasson's work and accepted Kirstein's recommendation.[39] LeBlond and Duncan agreed to take the necessary steps to move in that direction.

This decision generated a heated power struggle between Smuin and LeBlond and a divisive controversy between Smuin's supporters and those who wanted him replaced. In late August, two days before Smuin's contract expired, the SFB Association posted a press release announcing that Smuin had resigned and that the association had accepted his resignation.[40] Smuin immediately denied the story and claimed that he was being forced out. The next day,

---

[39] LeBlond, 149. Gisella also states that Kirstein recommended Helgi to Lew; see Beth Witrogen McLeod, "Gisella Caccialanza Christensen: A Ballet Legend," *San Francisco Gazette*, September 1987, 19. Lew's son Chris confirms that after Lew and Kirstein discussed the matter by telephone, Kirstein wrote Lew a letter recommending Tomasson. Telephone interview with Chris Christensen, November 20, 1991. At some point, Lew also telephoned Tomasson and discussed his concerns about the quality of training at the SFB School. Janice Ross, "San Francisco Ballet: The California Dream at Sixty," *Dance Magazine*, February 1983, 60.

[40] "Executive Committee Accepts Michael Smuin's Resignation," Press Release, San Francisco Ballet Association, August 29, 1984. LeBlond may have felt justified in claiming that Smuin had resigned when Smuin refused to go through the necessary steps to renew his contract.

his supporters appeared at the new building with pickets, chanting his name. Smuin, who still looked to Lew as a father figure, found it hard to believe that his partner had turned against him and alleged that others, ostensibly LeBlond, were putting words in Lew's mouth.[41]

Initially, the SFBA Executive Committee and Board of Trustees unanimously accepted Smuin's "resignation" and the motion to find a new artistic director.[42] But the open controversy stoked by Smuin's supporters eventually caused a split in the board and an angry proxy battle to replace its existing members with a slate of Smuin supporters. Thus Lew spent the final weeks of his life embroiled in a battle that threatened to destroy the organization he was trying to preserve. Currents of contention polarized working relationships in the new building and strained the association's board to near breaking point as Lew pressed forward slowly with plans to revise his *Nutcracker*.

Lew's quiet resolve to find a new partner was tested when Smuin supporters pressed him for statements in support of his co-artistic director, who had indisputably helped rescue the company in its time of financial crisis and whose ballets were very popular with one segment of the ballet-going public.[43] But Lew was angered by the wording of an open letter to the board by the Committee to Restore Michael Smuin (which operated independently of Smuin), in which Smuin was credited with being "the man who made the Ballet what it is today."[44] Had he been in good health, with the calm patience of his youth, Lew might have let such rhetoric pass. But in his weakened state, Lew was easily upset, and when a reporter called him at home one night Lew voiced his true

---

[41] Michael Harris and Robert Commanday, "Ballet Co-Director Wants Smuin Out." *San Francisco Examiner*, September 28, 1984, San Francisco Ballet Clipping File, Dance Collection, The New York Public Library.

[42] Telephone interview with Timothy Duncan, November 20, 1991.

[43] Interview with James Ludwig, San Francisco, California, December 2, 1988.

[44] Harris and Commanday, "Ballet Director Wants Smuin Out."

feelings about the Smuin situation.[45] Aside from overlooking Lew's contribution to making the company what it was, the grandiose claims of Smuin's backers ignored LeBlond's organizational contribution, which had restored the company's fiscal integrity in the wake of the Save Our Ballet campaign. As Lew perceived the situation, it was LeBlond's skill as a fund-raiser that had made Smuin's productions possible. It might even be argued that the ambitious spring season devised by Smuin the year before LeBlond's arrival had brought about the company's near demise in 1974.

On September 20, 1984, bowing to the extraordinary pressure exerted by Smuin's advocates, the Board of Trustees agreed to extend his contract through the spring 1985 season and to appoint him principal guest choreographer the following two years. LeBlond saw this compromise as a step backwards but was bound to implement his board's decision. Lew, however, made one last attempt to influence SFB's future artistic direction. Weakened by the effects of his illness and less cautious than he might have been in earlier years, Lew declared outright, in interviews with reporters from a local newspaper the following week, that Smuin should leave for the sake of the company.[46]

On the morning of October 9, Lew arose and prepared to drive to an important meeting in the new building, determined to face the revived turmoil there head on. But he never left the house; he suffered a massive heart attack in the shower and died shortly thereafter. According to his wishes, his body was cremated. At an emotional memorial service in the new building, stunned dancers, associates, and family members put aside their differences temporarily to pay tribute to a respected artist in the fourth floor studio that bore

---

[45] Chris Christensen believes that Lew's poor health and his depressed spirits were chief factors behind his negative comments about Smuin at this time. Letter to the author, April 4, 1992.

[46] Harris and Commanday, "Ballet Co-Director Wants Smuin Out," and Alan Ulrich, "Co-Director Says Ballet's Future Here Threatened," *San Francisco Examiner*, September 27, 1984, cited in LeBlond, *From Chaos to Fragility*, 155.

his name. With remarkable emotional control, Gisella spoke calmly to the dancers, encouraging them on as she felt Lew would have done. Letters and flowers poured in, and Kirstein himself wrote the tribute that appeared in *Ballet News*.

Gisella asked LeBlond and Duncan to scatter Lew's ashes around San Francisco, as he had wished. The grief-stricken associates spread one-third of the ashes around the park behind the stage door of the Opera House, sprinkled another portion in the garden court of the company's new building, and threw the remainder from the top of Twin Peaks over the city below.

Harold's final years passed in much pain and disability resulting from a prolonged battle with cancer. As long as he was mobile, he maintained his straight posture and formal manner. Harold's mind remained alert; he read novels and played options on the stock market while Ruby continued to teach and oversee her ballet studio not far from the couple's Marin County home.

As Harold lost strength, he was forced to use a wheelchair, and finally he became bedridden. Harold kept his pain to himself and suffered in stoic silence, as one might expect from the brother whose personal discipline most reflected his mother's iron will. He read the *Wall Street Journal* daily until his arms became too weak to hold the paper up. When he could no longer read novels, he listened to books on tape. Occasional visits from former associates cheered his last days. He also received one final award. The recognition Harold had received previously had usually been shared with his brothers (the 1973 *Dance Magazine* Award and the 1984 Capezio Award). But in 1987 he was singled out by the San Francisco Arts Commission for his "distinguished work and achievement in dance." Unfortunately, Harold was in the hospital at the time of the celebratory banquet; LeBlond accepted the award for him.

Harold hated being hospitalized, so Ruby arranged for home care and temporarily turned her studio over to an assistant as Harold neared the end of his time. He passed away quietly at home on Monday, February 20, 1989, at age

**48**  Harold Christensen takes a bow at the SFB Golden Anniversary Gala, 1983.
Photograph by John Markowski, courtesy of John Markowski and San Francisco Performing Arts Library and Museum

eighty-four. Like Lew, Harold was cremated; his memorial
was held in the San Francisco Ballet building in early March.
Tributes and obituaries stressed the magnitude of his contribution in training generations of dancers during the thirty-
three years he directed the San Francisco Ballet School. On a
more personal note, Willam confirmed Harold's unsung generosity. While the other two brothers had enjoyed greater
limelight, Harold had always been in the background, giving
his time and effort in thankless tasks that kept the school
functioning over the years.

Because Willam tended to equate success with position, he was initially lost without a company to preside over
when Bruce Marks assumed control of Ballet West. Willam
now faced a new challenge: looking on in diplomatic silence
as Marks took the company in new directions. Marks never
related to the LDS community with the same understanding
that Willam had. In the 1960s, when planning repertory to
be included in school lecture-demonstrations, Willam had
favored *Con Amore* over *Filling Station* because of the latter's
intoxicated pas de deux, which he feared might be construed
by young audiences as glorifying drunkenness.[47] In this,
Willam showed tact and a keen sensitivity to the practices of
Mormonism. Marks, in contrast, cared less about local traditions than about the artistic content of his repertory.[48] Early
on, he challenged the religious community with the radically
different approach to spirituality exhibited in his African
Islam-inspired *Sanctus* (1979). And Marks cared more about
the dancers' technique than their ability to project emotions
to the last row of the balcony. Willam grew concerned by
what he considered a lack of personality coming across to the
audience, but he could do nothing about it.[49]

In the early years of the brothers' careers, Willam more
than once provided the context in which Lew danced, taught,

[47] Minutes of Management Meeting, August 14, 1967, Utah Ballet Archives, Box 12,
Folder 6, Special Collections, University of Utah Marriott Library, Salt Lake City.

[48] Telephone interview with Bruce Caldwell, May 2, 1991.

[49] Caldwell, 1991.

or choreographed. In 1980, this situation was reversed when Lew and Smuin invited Willam to restage his 1950 *Nothing Doing Bar* for SFB during a celebration honoring the career of Darius Milhaud, the composer of the ballet's score.[50] *Nothing Doing Bar* ran five nights in the War Memorial Opera House and was included in the company's programming the next fall at the Brooklyn Academy of Music. The New York reviews gave Willam something to crow about, especially when Tobi Tobias declared his one contribution to the SFB lineup "a little gem in the context of a dubious repertory."[51]

In Salt Lake, teaching remained the one avenue open to Willam, and this became his primary outlet, the last tangible means by which he could promote ballet in Utah. Neither a hip replacement in 1981 nor a broken ankle nearly a decade later deterred him from this self-imposed mission. A year-and-a-half after his formal retirement, a group of friends and patrons formed the Willam F. Christensen Foundation and Academy, which sponsored Willam's continued teaching in a variety of settings. His one hope was to be affiliated with Ballet West through a training school or junior company, but various efforts in that direction proved disappointing. So in 1986, Willam opened a new Christensen Center in the Salt Lake suburb of Murray. With the help of his teaching staff there, he produced elaborate student recitals that included reworkings of one of his old favorites, *Old Vienna*. But Willam's heart was not in the suburbs; it was downtown, where Ballet West enjoyed its new quarters in the Capitol Theatre. In the fall of 1991 he joined the staff of the Ballet West Conservatory, where he seems to have come home to stay. At the time of this writing, he teaches advanced classes three evenings a week and maintains some involvement with the Ballet West *Nutcracker*.

---

[50] "Willam Christensen Returns to San Francisco Ballet as Guest Choreographer," Press Release, San Francisco Ballet Association, February 8, 1980.

[51] Tobi Tobias, "Brooklyn Celebrates Ballet in America," *Dance Magazine*, January 1981, 69.

**49** Willam Christensen demonstrates a moment from *Nothing Doing Bar*, 1980.
Courtesy of San Francisco Performing Arts Library and Museum

Before his brothers' deaths, Willam called Lew and Harold every Sunday. Although diametrically opposed in their tastes in repertory, Willam and Lew were close personally in their later years and enjoyed talking through their problems at length. Lew's death, and later Harold's, left Willam with an increasing sense of loneliness. His life gained an added sense of purpose when the SFB Association named him their company's artistic director emeritus following Lew's death. Granted, the position was largely honorary because Willam, then eighty-two years old, was based in Salt Lake City and could have little to do with the daily running of the company. But Willam had a long-standing relationship with Smuin; the appointment was designed to smooth upset feelings and ease the transition as the latter completed one last year with the company. During the transition period, Willam's intermittent presence in San Francisco kept awareness of the Christensen tradition alive and reinforced the memory of Lew's contribution. Willam's emotional support also boosted the board's morale when he seconded their decision to hire Tomasson.[52] Finally, Willam lent his interest and experience to the refurbishing of *The Nutcracker* that had been Lew's final project.

The Christensens lived to see their companies and school grow into solid and lasting institutions. Arlene Croce observed in 1980 that with the establishment of those companies, "the Christensens' lifelong mission is fulfilled."[53] Paradoxically, the brothers lived to see their achievements celebrated by the larger dance establishment and minimized by their immediate successors. By 1984, Lew's contribution to the history of SFB had been obscured by Smuin's more visible leadership. Likewise, company histories of Ballet West composed during Bruce Marks's tenure emphasized the role played by Mrs. Wallace, at Willam's expense, because the

---

[52] Interview with Richard E. LeBlond, Jr., March 9 and 14, 1988.

[53] Arlene Croce, "Americana," in *Going to the Dance* (New York: Alfred A. Knopf, 1982), 312.

Wallaces still had money to give.[54] Marks also made dispar-
aging comments to associates about the state of Ballet West
when he came, insinuating that the company was nothing
until he reformed it.[55] In their later years, both Willam and
Lew felt a growing desire to preserve the story of their lives
and have their histories understood. When in New York to
receive the Capezio Award during the spring of 1984, they
met with W. McNeil Lowry in his private New York office
and reviewed the circumstances of their lives while Lowry
took copious notes. The brothers reminisced with a sense of
urgency, as if they were unhappy with the direction their
careers had taken at the last and wanted to preserve the
memory of their earlier accomplishments.[56]

Ultimately, Utah gave Willam what he needed most:
recognition. While he may not have enjoyed Lew's celebrity
as a performer, it can never be said that Willam was not
honored for his achievements in his home state. He received
two honorary doctorates (Utah State University, 1973, and
the University of Utah, 1978), medals and awards from local
and state institutions, membership in honorary societies,
recognition from national dance organizations, and numerous
certificates of appreciation. When a financially beleaguered
Ballet West threw its own "S.O.B." campaign in 1987, newspaper ads included photographs of the company's beloved,
aging founder. His eightieth, eighty-fifth, and ninetieth birthdays occasioned large celebrations sponsored by longtime
associates and company patrons. His contribution to the

---

[54] Company programs in the late 1980s listed Willam as "Founder" but gave Mrs.
Wallace top billing as "Founder, Honorary Life Chair and Special Advisor to the
Board." Both were also listed with over forty other trustees, and for a while Willam
was an "Artistic Advisor" to the board. While Willam never made a public fuss over
the inordinate amount of credit that went to his chief patron, it was a thorn in his
side until she passed away in December 1988.

[55] Christine Temin, "A Man with a Plan," *Boston Globe*, Clipping file, Harvard
Theatre Collection. Temin also states that "one longtime observer of American Ballet
says Marks likes to give the impression that Ballet West barely existed before he took
over.... Willam Christensen *made* him [Marks], and then he turned around and
pushed Willam out of the picture."

[56] Interview with W. McNeil Lowry, New York, New York, September 16, 1988.

dance program at the University of Utah was set in stone with the construction of a new dance building on campus: the Alice Sheets Marriott Center for Dance. In this spacious building designed specifically for the needs of ballet and modern dance students, the primary performing space is the Hayes/ Christensen Theatre. Its name, which symbolizes the strong dual tradition that has coexisted since Willam's arrival in 1951, will remind future generations of students of the committed founders of their programs. In the spring of 1991, the Hayes/Christensen Theatre was the scene of a celebratory Christensen Tribute. Ruby and Gisella came from the Bay Area to join Willam in receiving recognition for the family's contribution to dance in America. The university's student ballet company, supplemented by guest artists from Ballet West, performed trademark Christensen ballets, and old friends, including Lowry, flew in to show their support.[57]

The Christensen brothers demonstrated enormous commitment to their chosen profession; indeed, their ongoing expenditure of mental, physical, and emotional energy shows just how demanding a life in ballet can be. In Willam's case, that commitment seems to have bordered on madness at times. Although the critics never praised him as a choreographic genius, his ability to keep a company running under the most adverse circumstances attracted attention over time. Not long after the collapse of the San Francisco Civic Ballet, when Willam resuscitated a small performing group, the *San Francisco Chronicle* lauded his ability to find his dancers something to do:

> *"Genius" might be a better word than "gift" to apply to the latter aspect of Christensen's activities. Logically speaking, it isn't in the cards for San Francisco to possess a major ballet company year in and year out, but Christensen keeps it going.*[58]

---

[57] The program consisted of *Nothing Doing Bar, Con Amore*, and a new work by Willam, *Cotillion*. The latter included balleticizations of social dance forms learned in the brothers' youth – the waltz, polka, and mazurka – with effective stage groupings and suggestions of relationships between the main characters.

[58] Quoted in Steinberg, *San Francisco Ballet*, 57.

In a survey of ballet in America published that same year, George Amberg paid a similar tribute to Willam's "methodical work" and "invaluable contribution" in San Francisco:

> *In the confused and constantly shifting ballet picture in America today the San Francisco Ballet is a telling example of what admirable results can be achieved in a modest frame with personal and artistic integrity and singleness of purpose and direction.*[59]

"They could call us fools or pioneers, but we did things with a dream, not knowing the result of the dream," reminisced Willam in an interview not long before Lew's death.[60] Indeed, Willam thought in terms of dreams, and his expansive rhetoric persuaded others to share and support his dreams. Any summation of his contribution to the history of ballet in America must take into account his confidence, his charisma, and the dedication with which he promoted ballet as an art form capable of entertaining a broad audience. Individuals make choices, and the choices Willam made were nearly always to promote, to expand, to popularize, to build and go forward.

Harold's choices tended toward solidifying, consolidating, and protecting the brothers' institutions in San Francisco. Harold did not speak in terms of dreams or allow his thoughts to follow flights of fancy. Rather, his natural inclination was to make sure that his brothers' dreams were built upon financially realistic foundations. A pragmatist with a strict sense of attention to detail, Harold did not capture the public imagination. As director of the school, his contribution was less visible than Willam's or Lew's, and hence less appreciated. When Lew died, Gisella was invited to join the San Francisco Ballet Association's Board of Trustees, but Ruby received no such honor upon Harold's death, perhaps because Harold had been retired nearly a decade by that time.

---

[59] George Amberg, *Ballet, The Emergence of an American Art Form* (New York: New American Library, 1949), 70.

[60] Bill Christensen KQED interview transcript for Lew Christensen Biography, 24, San Francisco Performing Arts Library and Museum.

The identification of the institution with the man was no longer strong. Because our society pays greater homage to performers than to teachers, Harold's reputation will always be eclipsed by the achievements of his older and younger brothers.

If Lew thought in terms of following a dream, he was not as openly romantic about it as Willam was. When pressed by an interviewer for reflective comment on the success of his career, Lew shrugged off serious self-appraisal:

> *I guess if you consider working with dance for fifty years a success, I'm a success. Some of my ballets were good, some were bad. I never tried to make a masterpiece, and I don't have a favorite among them.*[61]

Asked later if his long career in dance had made him happy, Lew replied in a similarly unglamorous vein, "I don't know what happiness is. Is it a lack of sadness? Is it keeping occupied? Is it working and worrying? You explain to me what happiness is, and maybe I could tell you if I'm happy or not."[62]

Like Willam, Lew received recognition and honors in his final years. In May 1978, the San Francisco Bay Area Dance Coalition honored him for his "outstanding contribution to dance."[63] In 1982 Lew received an honorary doctorate from John F. Kennedy University in Orinda, California, an award he found especially gratifying because Willam had enjoyed an honorary doctorate for nearly a decade. In 1983 Lew became the first recipient of an award established by his company's Board of Trustees, the Lew Christensen Medal.[64]

But the recognition that probably meant the most to Lew was in the writings and published statements of Kirstein

---

[61] Beth Witrogren, "Ballet Keeps Artistic Director on His Toes," *San Francisco Examiner*, May 17, 1978.

[62] Von Buchau, 27.

[63] Witrogen, "Ballet Keeps Artistic Director on His Toes."

[64] Steinberg, "Lew Christensen: An American Original," 17.

and Balanchine. Lew lived to see in print how his dancing had been regarded by the two men whose opinions mattered to him most. In the 1978 edition of *Thirty Years: The New York City Ballet*, Kirstein explained Lew's seminal influence in confirming his (Kirstein's) early vision of an American ballet company and establishing the prototype of the new American *danseur*. He spelled out Lew's significance in the history of the company's male members: when talented young boys graduated from school to company, Kirstein mentally placed them in a schema which he termed "an apostolic succession in our history which I date from Lew Christensen through Jacques D'Amboise."[65] Exactly when Kirstein finally gave up on the notion of Lew returning to New York and inheriting Balanchine's company is unclear – perhaps during the down-swing of the late '60s and early '70s. But when Peter Martins joined NYCB, Kirstein took his arrival as "the fulfillment of an ideal of heroic male dancer" whose image had been established, for him, by Lew.[66]

---

[65] Kirstein, *Thirty Years*, 303. Kirstein's essay, "Alec: Or the Future of Choreography" (first published in *Dance News Annual*, 1953; reprinted in *Ballet: Bias and Belief* [New York: Dance Horizons, 1983], 97–106), gives a glimpse of how Kirstein envisioned Lew's role in the company earlier on. Kirstein describes the training of an imaginary young male dancer, Alec, who winds up as an assistant to NYCB's administrative director, Lew. "Lew Christensen, who had been a skillful performer himself, realized in Alec a variant of himself at half his age. It was Christensen indeed who proposed to Alec the music for his first full-length ballet.... Christensen assigned him a few dancers and a few rehearsal hours from the company's working time.... [Balanchine] would have seen Alec around backstage, but would certainly not know his name. But Christensen asked him to look at the finished [ballet]...." Perhaps the most striking feature of this essay, seen from the perspective of what it betrays of Kirstein's artistic judgment of Lew as a choreographer, lies in the implied comparison of Lew and Alec, a "variant of [Lew] at half his age." Alec is not an original choreographer: "Everything he thought and did came from some attributable source that he frankly traced and acknowledged." Alec's choreography is described as well crafted, neat, and harmonious, but not groundbreaking. On the other hand, Kirstein judged Alec competent and found him "of use to the profession." How much of this reflected Kirstein's critical judgment of Lew as a choreographer may only be guessed. In *Thirty Years*, Kirstein wrote that Lew had proven to be "a dance designer of taste, ingenuity, and humor" (301).

[66] Kirstein, *Thirty Years*, 306.

Balanchine's influence in Lew's life was a mixed blessing.[67] Working with Balanchine gave Lew the training he needed to excel as a dancer, and Balanchine's repertory provided Lew with roles that established him as *the* leading American *danseur noble* of his day. This was particularly important in an era when most Americans still considered ballet primarily a foreign art form. But ultimately Lew chose an independent route, one that required him to create his own repertory as part of his responsibilities as a company director. As a choreographer, he could never equal Balanchine's fecund abstract invention, and Lew never claimed to. So for the rest of his life, Lew struggled with the critics' charges that his ballets were derivative of his master's works. Given the inevitability of Balanchine's influence on Lew's style, it is perhaps more productive to view Lew as a key disseminator of Balanchinian neoclassicism, its first important exponent in the American West. Balanchine did not lavish Lew with praise to his face, but he confirmed repeatedly that Lew's Apollo had set a standard for the performance of that role. The master's respect for the student was reaffirmed in an interview that was published in the *New Yorker* four months after Balanchine's death. Balanchine confirmed that Lew had indeed been the finest male dancer among his peers in his youth, and that even in today's more crowded field, Lew would be "one of the best."[68] After years of harboring some insecurity about his relationship to Balanchine, Lew was moved to tears by this tribute.

In view of the Christensens' multigenerational involvement and undeniable importance in the history of American ballet, they have been termed an "American dance dynasty." Despite its alliterative appeal, this label does not match the

---

[67] James Graham-Luján writes, "If Mr. Balanchine had not been along, Lew would truly have been the head of the company – for his ability to remember every step of every ballet, for his musicality, and because the world favors beautiful people." Letter to the author, September 4, 1991.

[68] W. McNeil Lowry, "Conversations with Balanchine," *New Yorker*, September 12, 1983, 63. When asked about Eugene Loring and William Dollar, Balanchine denied that either of them compared with Lew as dancers.

reality of the Christensens' lives. Implicit in the concept of a dynasty is a family in a major capital that rules with absolute power. Although a large diaspora of students spread the Christensens' influence throughout much of the western United States, and a smaller percentage of Christensen dancers went on to reknown in prominent New York companies, the Christensens did not rule over the fortunes of twentieth-century American ballet from an acknowledged center of power. Rather, it is appropriate to celebrate the Christensen saga for what it does represent: a broad slice of American dance history, a variety of attitudes and achievements from Grandfather Lars's vision of dance as volunteered entertainment to his sons' social dancing schools, from the third generation's ballet companies run as family businesses to public institutions well housed in major cities in the western United States. The Christensen legacy reflects each brother's individual personality, his unique gifts, and the somewhat divergent opportunities that shaped the style of their teaching and choreography. Without Willam's drive and deeply rooted ambition, the others might have followed different career paths. But strong family ties led to combined efforts, and in their intertwining careers they shared an attitude of dedication and personal sacrifice. Ultimately, each needed his own domain, a company or school to administer, an institution to direct according to his own ideals. That Willam and Lew remained close later in life, following the professional tensions at the time Willam left San Francisco for the University of Utah, is a testament to the profound family loyalty binding the brothers. The Christensens left an enduring legacy through the students they taught, the companies they formed or kept alive, and the lives they touched through their commitment to dance.

# APPENDIX A

## CHOREOGRAPHY BY WILLAM CHRISTENSEN

My sources in compiling the following include (1) Willam Christensen's Scrapbooks on deposit as part of the Utah Ballet Archives, Special Collections, the University of Utah Marriott Library; (2) the San Francisco Ballet program files, at the San Francisco Performing Arts Library and Museum; (3) Cobbett Steinberg's *San Francisco Ballet: The First Fifty Years*; (4) Nancy Reynolds' *Repertory in Review*; (5) documents in Willam Christensen's faculty personnel file at the Records Management Office of the University of Utah; (6) the Maurice Abravanel Program Collection, Special Collections Department, the University of Utah Marriott Library; (7) Diana Muriel Cole's thesis, "Utah Ballet – A Unique Development in the World of Dance"; (8) Susan White's thesis, "Utah Civic Ballet and Ballet West: A Preliminary Study, 1964–1976," and Bill Wright of the Christensen Centre, Murray, Utah. These sources correct the inadequate and often incorrect listing of Willam's choreography published in Arnold Haskell's first issue of *The Ballet Annual* (1947). Because no archival material exists for the season Willam choreographed in Pittsburgh during the summer of 1946, those works cannot be included. Incomplete evidence suggests that Willam also choreographed specialty numbers for the San Francisco Opera Guild's Opera Ball and Fol De Rol programs in 1950 and 1953.

Multiple productions of the same opera are entered only once, with later productions listed at the end of the entry, along with information about principal dancers or cast changes. If, however, Willam choreographed an opera in Salt Lake City subsequent to doing the same opera in San Francisco, I have given the Utah production a separate listing. For some works, alternate casts are indicated by slash marks between the names of dancers sharing a role.

1. Vaudeville act, "The Christensen Brothers," Radio-Keith-Orpheum circuit, 1930–1932 (and possibly 1932–1934).
Cast: William and Lew Christensen, Mignon Lee, Wiora Stoney. Later Cast: Harold and Lew Christensen, Ruby Asquith and Josephine McKendrick (1932–1934).

2. *Nut Cracker* (Excerpts)
Music: Peter Ilyich Tchaikovsky
Costumes and Scenery: Harriet Meyer
Premiere: 12 June 1934, Portland Junior Symphony Association, Civic Auditorium, Portland, Oregon.
Principal Dancers: Sugar Plum Fairy, Queen of Jam Mountain, Janet Reed; Marie, Natalie Lauterstein; Nutcracker, William Christensen; Chinese Dance, Vivian Emery and Donald Sharp; Russian Trepak, Jeanette Harrow and Robert Irwin; Arabian Dance, Mattlyn Gevurtz.

3. *Chopiniana* or *Chopinade* (After Fokine)
Music: Frederic Chopin
Premiere: 16 January 1935, Portland Creative Theatre and School of Music and Dancing, Grant High School Auditorium, Portland, Oregon.
Cast: 37 dancers, including Janet Reed and Robert Irwin, Merle Williams, Zelda Morey, Norma Nielson.
California Premiere: 17 September 1937, Women's City Club, Oakland, California.
Costumes: J. C. Taylor
Company: San Francisco Opera Ballet
Cast: 15 dancers, including Janet Reed, William Christensen, Merle Williams, Zelda Morey.

4. *Hungarian Village Festival*
Music: Franz Liszt, Hungarian Rhapsody No. 2
Premiere: 16 January 1935, Portland Creative Theatre and School of Music and Dancing, Grant High School Auditorium, Portland, Oregon.
Cast: 16 dancers, including Merle Williams, Robert Irwin, Natalie Lauterstein, William Christensen.

5. *Coppélia* (One-Act Version)
Music: Leo Delibes, with Liadov's "Music Box" interpolated for the dance of Pierrot and Pierrette.
Costumes: Harriet Meyer
Premiere: 4 June 1935, Portland Junior Symphony Association, Civic Auditorium, Portland, Oregon.
Company: The William F. Christensen Repertory Ballet
Cast: 82 dancers, including: as Coppélia, Janet Reed; Swanilda, Natalie Lauterstein; Franz, William Christensen; Dr. Coppélius, Earl Riggins.

6. *Klinka* or *Kalinka*
Music: Russian Folk Music
Premiere: 29 July 1935, Moore Theatre, Seattle, Washington
Dancers: Natalie Lauterstein, William Christensen
Note: This work may have been based on a dance taught by Lars Peter Christensen and was probably very similar to the *Russian Peasant Dance* (choreographer not listed) performed on the same program as *Chopiniana* and *Hungarian Village Festival* in Portland on 16 January 1935.

7. *Les Visions de Massenet*
Music: Jules Massenet, "Phedre" Overture, Meditation from *Thaïs*, "March" and "Fête Boheme" from *Scenes Pittoresque*. Arranged by Mischa Pelz.
Costumes and Scenery: Harriet Meyer
Premiere: 29 February 1936, Municipal Auditorium, Portland, Oregon.
Company: The William F. Christensen Ballet
Cast: 37 dancers, including: as the Ballerina, Janet Reed; Thaïs, Merle Williams; Massenet, William Christensen.

8. *A Spanish Romance*
Music: Nikolai Rimsky-Korsakov, *Capriccio Espagnol*
Costumes: Harriet Meyer
Premiere: 29 February 1936, Municipal Auditorium, Portland, Oregon.
Company: The William F. Christensen Ballet

Cast: Norma Nielson, Jacqueline Martin, Frances Corruthers, Mattlyn Gevurtz, Ronald Chetwood, Earl Riggins, Merle Williams, Zelda Morey, William Christensen.

9. *A Roumanian Wedding Festival*
Music: Georges Enesco, Roumanian Rhapsody No. 1 in A Major
Costumes: Harriet Meyer
Premiere: 29 February 1936, Municipal Auditorium, Portland, Oregon.
Company: The William F. Christensen Ballet
Cast: Bride, Merle Williams; Groom, Robert Irwin; Mother, Jacqueline Martin; and ensemble of 48.
California Premiere: *Rumanian Wedding Festival* or *Rumanian Rhapsody* (A Comedy Ballet in One Act)
California Premiere: 17 September 1937, Women's City Club, Oakland, California.
Scenery and Costumes: J. C. Taylor
Cast: 16 dancers, including: as the Bride, Merle Williams; Bridegroom, William Christensen; A Rumanian Mother, Jacqueline Martin; Her Children, Lois Hoffschneider, Constance Salazer.
Utah Premiere: 3 May 1960, Kingsbury Hall, University of Utah, Salt Lake City.
Company: University Theatre Ballet.

10. *Royal Ballet* for Portland Rose Festival
Note: Extant newspaper articles about this event are unclear and contradictory as to the music, which may have been excerpts from Tchaikovsky's *Nutcracker* but may also have been excerpts from Smetana's *The Bartered Bride*.
Premiere: 10 June 1936, Multnomah Civic Stadium, Portland, Oregon.
Company: The William F. Christensen Ballet
Cast: 53 dancers, including Merle Williams, Mary Corruthers, Frances Corruthers, Jacqueline Martin, Norma Nielson, Janet Reed, Zelda Morey, Jeanette Harrow, Billie Otis, Mignon Lee, Constance Salazar, Celene Radding, Fred Staver, Earl Riggins, Robert Irwin, Ronald Chetwood, Dan Feely.

11. *Coeur de Glace (The Princess With the Frozen Heart)*
Music: Wolfgang Amadeus Mozart, *Eine Kleine Nachtmusik*
Costumes and Scenery: J. C. Taylor
Premiere: 15 December 1936, Municipal Auditorium, Portland, Oregon.
Company: William F. Christensen Ballet
Principal Dancers: Janet Reed, William F. Christensen
California Premiere: 26 May 1942, Veterans Auditorium, San Francisco.
Principal Dancers: Ruby Asquith, Willam Christensen.

12. *L'Amant Reve (The Dream Lover)*
Music: Carl Maria von Weber, Invitation to the Dance
Costumes: J. C. Taylor
Premiere: 15 December 1936, Municipal Auditorium, Portland, Oregon.
Cast: The Maiden, Janet Reed; The Dream Lover, William F. Christensen

13. *Ballet from The Bartered Bride*
Music: Bedřich Smetana
Costumes: J. C. Taylor
Premiere: 15 December 1936, Municipal Auditorium, Portland, Oregon.
Company: The William F. Christensen Ballet
Cast: 31 dancers.
California Premiere, under the title *The Bartered Bride: Three Dances*: 4 June 1938, Stern Grove, San Francisco. Prior to the official San Francisco premiere, the work was performed 9 April 1938 at the San Francisco Symphony's Young People's Concert, War Memorial Opera House.
Costumes: J. C. Taylor
Cast: 22 dancers, including Janet Reed, Ronald Chetwood, Deane Crockett, Jeanne Hayes, James Starbuck, Jacqueline Martin.
Utah Premiere, under the title *Dances From The Bartered Bride*: 5 May 1953, Kingsbury Hall, University of Utah, Salt Lake City.

Scenery: Vern Adix
Company: University Theatre Ballet

14. *Bolero*
Music: Maurice Ravel
Costumes: J. C. Taylor
Premiere: 15 December 1936, Municipal Auditorium, Portland, Oregon.
Company: The William F. Christensen Ballet
Cast: Gypsy Favorite, Norma Nielson; Carmen, Merle Williams; ensemble of 42.

15. *Promenade and Minuet*
Music: Christoph Willibald von Gluck
Premiere: 9 June 1937, Rose Festival Coronation Ceremony, Multnomah Civic Stadium, Portland, Oregon.
Company: The William F. Christensen Ballet
Cast: Jeanette Harrow, Jacqueline Martin, Billie Otis, Mignon Lee, Fred Staver, Ronald Chetwood, Earl Riggins, Robert Irwin.

16. *Gigue Variations*
Music: Christoph Willibald von Gluck
Premiere: 9 June 1937, Rose Festival Coronation Ceremony, Multnomah Civic Stadium, Portland, Oregon.
Company: The William F. Christensen Ballet
Cast: Zelda Morey, Mary Corruthers, Jeannette Harrow, Celene Radding, Jacqueline Martin.

17. *Bourrée Fantasque*
Music: Emmanuel Chabrier
Premiere: 9 June 1937, Rose Festival Coronation Ceremony, Multnomah Civic Stadium, Portland, Oregon.
Company: The William F. Christensen Ballet
Cast: Ballerina, Natalie Lauterstein; Troubadours, Ronald Chetwood and Robert Irwin.

18. *Tarantella*
Music: Ottorino Respighi, after Gioacchino Rossini

Premiere: 9 June 1937, Rose Festival Coronation Ceremony, Multnomah Civic Stadium, Portland, Oregon.
Company: The William F. Christensen Ballet
Cast: Norma Nielson, Margaret Bergstrom, Constance Salazar, Lorraine Lammosson, Mignon Lee, Robert Franklin, Earl Riggins, Fred Staver.

19. *Grand Ballet Finale: The Grand Waltz*
Music: Cornelius Rubner
Premiere: 9 June 1937, Rose Festival Coronation Ceremony, Multnomah Civic Stadium, Portland, Oregon.
Company: The William F. Christensen Ballet
Cast: Merle Williams, Margaret Bambery, Billie Otis, Robert Irwin, Ronald Chetwood, Earl Riggins, and an ensemble of 26.

20. *Dance Divertissements*
Music: Helen Green, *Nightingale's Dream*; Arthur Honegger, *Hoyden*; Anonymous, *Fandanguillo de Aracena*; Johannes Brahms, *Czardas*.
Premiere: 17 September 1937, Women's City Club, Oakland, California.
Cast: Virginia Russ, Betina Noyes, Laura Post, Zoya Leporsky, Peggy Bates, Ronald Chetwood.

21. *Sketches* (A Suite of Divertissements)
Music: Charles Gounod, from *Faust*, and Franz Schubert, from *Rosamunde*.
Premiere: 12 November 1937, Santa Rosa High School Auditorium, Santa Rosa, California. San Francisco premiere: 20 April 1938, Veterans Auditorium.
Company: San Francisco Opera Ballet
Cast: 9 dancers, including Janet Reed, Willam Christensen.
Note: In succeeding years Willam added excerpts from Tchaikovsky's *Nutcracker*, Russian folk music, divertissements from Respighi's *Rossiniana* and Delibes' *Coppélia*, and a divertissement from Bizet's *L'Arlésienne*. This work, in modified versions, was also variously titled *Scènes de Ballet* (1942) and *Divertimenti* (1951).

22. *Capriccio Espagnol*
Music: Nikolai Rimsky-Korsakov, *Capriccio Espagnol*
Costumes: J. C. Taylor
Premiere: 13 December 1937, Santa Cruz High School Auditorium, Santa Cruz, California. This work may have resembled #8 above, *A Spanish Romance.*
Company: San Francisco Opera Ballet
Cast: 10 dancers, including: as The Smuggler, Deane Crockett; Toreador, James Starbuck; Gypsy Girls, Merle Williams, Zelda Morey, Laura Post.


23. *Romeo and Juliet* (Ballet in Three Scenes)
Music: Peter Ilyich Tchaikovsky
Costumes: Helen Green
Scenery: Charlotte Rider
Premiere: 3 March 1938, Memorial Auditorium, Sacramento. San Francisco premiere: 20 April 1938.
Company: San Francisco Opera Ballet
Cast: 28 dancers, including: as Juliet, Janet Reed; Romeo, Willam Christensen; Mercutio, James Starbuck; Paris, Deane Crockett; Tybalt, Ronald Chetwood; Benvolio, Grant Cristen; Nurse, Zoya Leporsky.
Utah Premiere: 4 May 1954, Kingsbury Hall, University of Utah, Salt Lake City.
Company: University Theatre Ballet.
Cast: Romeo, John Ray; Juliet, Kay Ford; Capulet, Don Steele; Mercutio, Michael Stevens; Paris, Hy Somers; Benvolio, Phil Keeler; Tybalt, Ron Ross.


24. *Ballet Impromptu* (A Bach Suite)
Music: Johann Sebastian Bach, Suite No. 2 in B Minor
Premiere: 20 April 1938, Veterans Memorial Auditorium, San Francisco.
Company: San Francisco Opera Ballet
Cast: 16 dancers, including Janet Reed, Merle Williams, Deane Crockett, James Starbuck, Ronald Chetwood.

25. *In Vienna* or *In Old Vienna*
Music: Johann Strauss, *Emperor's Waltz* and excerpts from *Die Fledermaus*.
Costumes: Helen Green
Setting: Charlotte Rider.
Premiere: 20 April 1938, Veterans Memorial Auditorium, San Francisco. (Premiere of Scene One: 3 March 1938, Memorial Auditorium, Sacramento.)
Company: San Francisco Opera Ballet
Cast: 22 dancers, including: as the Ballerina, Jacqueline Martin; A Young Huzzar, Robert Franklin; Waiter, James Starbuck; a Boulevardier, Ronald Chetwood; A Huzzar, Deane Crockett; His Love of the Moment, Laura Post.
Utah Premiere: *Old Vienna*, 4 May 1954, Kingsbury Hall, University of Utah, Salt Lake City.
Company: University Theatre Ballet.
Cast: Ballerina, Pat Jeppsen; Waiter, Phil Keeler; Ladies of the Boulevard, Patsy Robbins and LaRae Wagstaff; Boulevardier, Ron Ross; Flower Girl, Nancy Gold; Hussar, Hy Somers; Sweetheart, Dorothy Brown.
Later Production: *Old Vienna*, 14 July 1989, Murray Park Amphitheater, Murray, Utah; Christensen Centre (school).


26. *Andrea Chénier*
Music: Umberto Giordano
Opening Night: 7 October 1938, San Francisco Opera, War Memorial Opera House, San Francisco.
Later Production: Fall 1950 season.


27. *Don Giovanni*
Music: Wolfgang Amadeus Mozart
Opening Night: 10 October 1938, San Francisco Opera, War Memorial Opera House, San Francisco.
Later Productions: Fall 1940 season; Fall 1943 season; Fall 1945 season; Fall 1947 season; Fall 1948 season; Fall 1949 season; Fall 1952 season; Fall 1953 season; Fall 1959 season.

28. *Martha*
Music: Friedrich von Flotow
Opening Night: 12 October 1938, San Francisco Opera, War
Memorial Opera House, San Francisco.
Later Production: Fall 1944 season.

29. *Die Meistersinger von Nürnberg*
Music: Richard Wagner
Opening Night: 14 October 1938, San Francisco Opera, War
Memorial Opera House, San Francisco.
Later Productions: Fall 1948 season; Fall 1959 season.

30. *La Forza del Destino*
Music: Giuseppe Verdi
Opening Night: 28 October 1938, San Francisco Opera, War
Memorial Opera House, San Francisco.
Principal Dancer: Janet Reed
Later Productions: Fall 1943 season; Fall 1944 season; Fall
1946 season; Fall 1948 season; Fall 1954 season.

31. *Le Coq d'Or*
Music: Nikolai Rimsky-Korsakov
Opening Night: 3 November 1938, San Francisco Opera, War
Memorial Opera House, San Francisco.
Later Productions: Fall 1942 season; Fall 1955 season.

32. *Faust*
Music: Charles Gounod
Costumes: J. C. Taylor
Premiere: 6 May 1939, One in a series of Concerts for Young
People, War Memorial Opera House, San Francisco.
Company: San Francisco Opera Ballet.
Cast: 21 dancers, including as Helen of Troy, Janet Reed.
Note: The program note explains, "In using the Ballet music
from the Opera *Faust*, Mr. Christensen has not followed the
opera story but rather has used the music for a setting and
design for a classical ballet."

33. *Rigoletto*
Music: Giuseppe Verdi

Opening Night: 23 October 1939, San Francisco Opera, War Memorial Opera House, San Francisco.
Later Productions: Fall 1940 season; Fall 1941 season (4 October 1941 in Portland, Oregon, and 19 October 1941 in San Francisco); Fall 1943 season; Fall 1944 season; Fall 1945 season; Fall 1946 season; Fall 1947 season; Fall 1948 season; Fall 1949 season; Fall 1952 season.

34. *La Traviata*
Music: Giuseppe Verdi
Opening Night: 30 October 1939, San Francisco Opera, War Memorial Opera House, San Francisco.
Principal Dancers: Merle Williams, Willam Christensen
Later Productions: Fall 1942 season, featuring Ruby Asquith and Willam Christensen; Fall 1943 season, featuring Beatrice Tompkins and Willam Christensen; Fall 1945 season, featuring Ruby Asquith, Willam Christensen; Fall 1946 season, featuring Jocelyn Vollmar, Peter Nelson; Fall 1947 season, featuring Ruby Asquith, José Manero; Fall 1948 season, featuring Ruby Asquith, Peter Nelson; Fall 1953 season, featuring Sally Bailey, Gordon Paxman; Fall 1957 season.

35. *Coppélia*
Music: Léo Delibes
Costumes: Helen Green
Scenery: Charlotte Rider
Premiere: 31 October 1939, War Memorial Opera House, San Francisco.
Company: San Francisco Opera Ballet
Cast: 55 dancers, including: as Swanilda, Janet Reed; Franz, Willam Christensen; Dr. Coppélius, Earl Riggins; Burgomeister, Deane Crockett.
Utah Premiere: 12 May 1958, Kingsbury Hall, University of Utah, Salt Lake City.
Company: University Theatre Ballet
Cast: Swanilda, Marianne Johnson/Sharon Givan; Coppélia, Nancy Gold/Shirley White; Franz, Finis Jhung; Dr. Coppélius, Ron Ross.

36. *American Interlude*
Music: Godfrey Turner
Costumes: Helen Green
Scenery: Charlotte Rider
Premiere: 16 November 1939, War Memorial Opera House, San Francisco.
Company: San Francisco Opera Ballet
Note: This work was set to new music, rechoreographed, and presented as *And Now the Brides* the following year. See #43.

37. *A Midsummer Night's Dream*
Music: Felix Mendelssohn
Costumes: J. C. Taylor and Charlotte Rider
Scenario: Based on Shakespeare's play.
Premiere: 23 June 1940, Stern Grove, San Francisco
Company: San Francisco Opera Ballet
Cast: 27 dancers, including: as Oberon, Willam Christensen; Titania, Janet Reed; Puck, Ruby Asquith; Bottom, Norman Thomson; Lysander, Harold Christensen.

38. *Swan Lake*
Music: Peter Ilyich Tchaikovsky
Costumes: Charlotte Rider
Scenery: Eugene Orlovsky and Nicolas Pershin
Premiere: 27 September 1940, War Memorial Opera House, San Francisco.
Company: San Francisco Opera Ballet
Cast: 41 dancers, including as Prince Siegfried, Lew Christensen (guest artist); Odette, Jacqueline Martin; Odile, Janet Reed; Von Rothbart, Ronald Chetwood.

39. *Lakmé*
Music: Léo Delibes
Opening Night: 14 October 1940, San Francisco Opera, War Memorial Opera House, San Francisco.
Principal Dancers: Janet Reed, Norman Thomson, Frank Marasco

Later productions: Fall 1944 season, featuring Ruby Asquith, Earl Riggins, Frank Nelson; Fall 1946 season, featuring Onna White, Joaquin Felsch, Peter Nelson.

40. *A Masked Ball*
Music: Giuseppe Verdi
Opening Night: 23 October 1940, San Francisco Opera, War Memorial Opera House, San Francisco.
Later Productions: Fall 1944 season; Fall 1953 season; Fall 1957 season.

41. *Carmen*
Music: Georges Bizet
Opening Night: 25 October 1940, San Francisco Opera, War Memorial Opera House, San Francisco.
Principal Dancers: Emita De Sosa, Lew Christensen
Later Productions: Fall 1941 season, featuring Maclovia Ruiz; Fall 1942 season, featuring Maclovia Ruiz; Fall 1943 season, featuring Betty Parades, Mattlyn Gevurtz, Earl Riggins, and Joseph Carmassi; Fall 1944 season, featuring Ruby Asquith, Mattlyn Gevurtz, Earl Riggins; Fall 1945 season, featuring Ruby Asquith, Solana; Fall 1946 season, featuring Lois Treadwell, José Manero, Rosalie Prosch; Fall 1948 season, featuring Ruby Asquith, Vadja Del Oro, José Manero; Fall 1949 season, featuring Geraldine Vasquez, Joan Vickers, Roland Vasquez; Fall 1953 season, featuring Sally Bailey, Gordon Paxman; Fall 1955 season, featuring Nancy Johnson, Conrad Ludlow; Fall 1959 season, featuring Nancy Johnson, Richard Carter.

42. *Aïda*
Music: Giuseppe Verdi
Opening Night: 30 October 1940, San Francisco Opera, War Memorial Opera House, San Francisco.
Principal Dancers: Janet Reed, Lew Christensen
Later Productions: Fall 1942 season, featuring Ruby Asquith; Fall 1944 season, featuring Ruby Asquith; Fall 1945 season, featuring Ruby Asquith; Fall 1947 season, featuring Ruby

Asquith; Fall 1949 season, featuring Celena Cummings; Fall 1950 season, featuring Celena Cummings; Fall 1952 season, featuring Sally Bailey; Fall 1955 season, featuring Nancy Johnson and Conrad Ludlow; Fall 1956 season, featuring Nancy Johnson and Conrad Ludlow; Fall 1957 season, featuring Nancy Johnson and Richard Carter; Fall 1959 season, featuring Nancy Johnson, Sally Bailey, Richard Carter, Roderick Drew.

43. *And Now the Brides*
Music: Fritz Berens
Costumes: Helen Green
Scenery: Charlotte Rider
Premiere: 15 November 1940, Burlingame High School Auditorium, Burlingame, California.
San Francisco premiere: 26 April 1941, War Memorial Opera House.
Company: San Francisco Opera Ballet
Cast: 23 dancers, including: as The Bride, Janet Reed; Bridegroom, Ronald Chetwood; Agitator, Harold Christensen; Drunk, Willam Christensen.

44. *Tarantella*
Music: Ottorino Respighi
Premiere: 29 June 1941, Stern Grove, San Francisco.
Cast: 14 dancers, including Jean Dalziel and Norman Thomson
Note: This may have been related to #18.

45. *Tannhäuser*
Music: Richard Wagner
Opening Night: 8 October 1941, San Francisco Opera, War Memorial Opera House, San Francisco.
Principal Dancer: Janet Reed

46. *The Daughter of the Regiment*
Music: Gaetano Donizetti
Opening Night: 16 October 1941, San Francisco Opera, War Memorial Opera House, San Francisco.

Later Productions: Fall 1942 season, featuring Ruby Asquith and Ronn Marvin; Fall 1952 season.

47. *Scenes de Ballet* (A Suite of Divertissements)
Note: See #21, *Sketches*.
Music: Ludwig van Beethoven, from *Ecossaises*; Peter Ilyich Tchaikovsky, from *Swan Lake*, *Nutcracker*, and *Sleeping Beauty*; Franz Schubert, from *Rosamunde*; Modest Mussorgsky, from *Sorochintzky Fair*.
Premiere: 26 May 1942, Veterans Auditorium, San Francisco.
Company: San Francisco Ballet
Cast: 43 dancers, including Zoya Leporsky, Earl Riggins, Ruth Reikman, Deane Crockett, Ruby Asquith, Norman Thomson, Willam Christensen.

48. *Six Dances from The Nutcracker Suite*, on Ice and Stage, with William Swallender
Music: Peter Ilyich Tchaikovsky
Premiere: 14 August 1942, East Bay Iceland (Berkeley Festival Association's "Review of Revues"), Berkeley, CA.
Company: San Francisco Ballet and skaters.
Principal Dancer: Ruby Asquith

49. *Winter Carnival*
Music: Johann and Josef Strauss, arranged by Fritz Berens.
Costumes and Scenery: Betty Bates de Mars
Premiere: 25 September 1942, War Memorial Opera House, San Francisco.
Company: San Francisco Ballet
Cast: 35 dancers, including: as Officer of the Alpine Guards, Willam Christensen; A Skating Star, Ruby Asquith; The General, Earl Riggins.

50. *Amor Espagnol*, with Elena Imaz and Maclovia Ruiz
Music: Jules Massenet, ballet music from *Le Cid*.
Costumes and Scenery: Charlotte Rider
Premiere: 25 September 1942, War Memorial Opera House, San Francisco.

Company: San Francisco Opera Ballet
Cast: 30 dancers, including: as Dolores, Elena Imaz (guest artist); The Matador, Earl Riggins; Marcarena, Maclovia Ruiz (guest artist).

51. *The Bartered Bride*
Music: Bedřich Smetana
Opening Night: 16 October 1942, San Francisco Opera, War Memorial Opera House, San Francisco.
Principal Dancers: Ruby Asquith, Barbara Wood, Alice Kotchik, Earl Riggins.

52. *Lucia di Lammermoor*
Music: Gaetano Donizetti
Opening Night: 18 October 1942, San Francisco Opera, War Memorial Opera House, San Francisco.
Later Productions: Fall 1943 season; Fall 1944 season; Fall 1945 season; Fall 1947 season; Fall 1949 season; Fall 1950 season; Fall 1957 season.

53. *Faust*
Music: Charles Gounod
Opening Night: 21 October 1942, San Francisco Opera, War Memorial Opera House, San Francisco.
Later Productions: Fall 1944 season; Fall 1947 season; Fall 1949 season; Fall 1955 season.

54. *Die Fledermaus*
Music: Johann Strauss
Opening Night: 26 October 1942, San Francisco Opera, War Memorial Opera House, San Francisco.
Principal Dancer: Ruby Asquith

55. *Sonata Pathétique*
Music: Ludwig van Beethoven
Costumes: Cliff Jones
Premiere: 18 February 1943, Garden Court, Palace Hotel, San Francisco.

Company: San Francisco Ballet
Cast: 12 dancers, including Ruby Asquith, Frank Marasco.


56. *Nutcracker: Divertissements*
Music: Peter Ilyich Tchaikovsky
Premiere: 4 March 1943, Garden Court, Palace Hotel, San Francisco.
Company: San Francisco Ballet
Cast: 11 dancers, including Ruby Asquith, Mattlyn Gevurtz, Earl Riggins, Rosalie Prosch, Lois Treadwell, Frank Marasco.


57. *The Rose Masque*
Music: Johann Strauss
Opening Night: 23 August 1943, Curran Theatre, San Francisco.
Dancers: 17 members of San Francisco Opera Ballet; Premiere Danseuse, Ruby Asquith; Premier Dancer, Frank Marasco. Willam appeared in the pantomime role of the Aide de Camp.
Note: This musical theater version of *Die Fledermaus* was directed by Reinhold Schunzel.


58. *Samson et Delilah*
Music: Camille Saint-Saëns
Opening Night: 7 October 1943, San Francisco Opera, War Memorial Opera House, San Francisco.
Principal Dancer: Beatrice Tompkins
Later Production: Fall 1949 season, featuring Joan Vickers.


59. *Hansel and Gretel* (A Ballet Pantomime with Solo Voices and Symphony Orchestra)
Music: Engelbert Humperdinck
Costumes: Goldstein and Company
Scenery: San Francisco Opera Company
Premiere: 26 December 1943, War Memorial Opera House, San Francisco.
Company: San Francisco Ballet
Cast: 67 roles

Principal Dancers: Hansel, Beatrice Tompkins; Gretel, Ruby Asquith; Mother, Celena Cummings; Father, Earl Riggins; Witch, Mattlyn Gevurtz.
Principal Singers: Hansel and Sandman, Mary Ellen Markham; Gretel, Lois Hartzell; Mother, Claire Mae Turner; Father, Edward Wellman; Dew Fairy and Witch, Jeannette Hopkins.

60. *Triumph of Hope*
Music: César Franck, from Symphony in D Minor, *Les Eolides*, and *Le Chasseur Maudit*.
Scenery and Costumes: Jean de Botton
Premiere: 18 May 1944, War Memorial Opera House, San Francisco
Company: San Francisco Ballet
Cast: 48 dancers, including: as Man, Earl Riggins; Woman, Ruby Asquith; Satan, Willam Christensen; Icarus, Joaquin Felsch.

61. *Prince Siegfried*
Music: Peter Ilyich Tchaikovsky
Costumes: J. Paget-Fredericks and Charlotte Rider
Premiere: 18 May 1944, War Memorial Opera House, San Francisco.
Company: San Francisco Ballet
Cast: 24 dancers, including: as Prince Siegfried, Willam Christensen; Odile, Ruby Asquith; Von Rothbart, Joaquin Felsch; Wolfgang, Russell Hartley.
Note: The program indicates that this was a "new staging of the Third Act of Swan Lake." The choreography may or may not have been substantially different from that of item #38.

62. *Le Bourgeois Gentilhomme* (A Ballet Pantomime), with Earl Riggins and André Ferrier
Music: Jean-Baptiste Lully, *Le Bourgeois Gentilhomme*, and André Grétry.
Costumes: Goldstein and Company
Premiere: 19 May 1944, War Memorial Opera House, San Francisco

Company: San Francisco Ballet
Cast: 30 dancers, including: as The Lovers, Ruby Asquith and Willam Christensen; Monsieur Jordan, André Ferrier; Tailor, Earl Riggins; Ballet Master, Joaquin Felsch; Muphti, L. Harlan McCoy.

63. *Nutcracker*
Music: Peter Ilyich Tchaikovsky
Costumes: Russell Hartley
Scenery: Antonio Sotomayor
Premiere: 24 December 1944, War Memorial Opera House, San Francisco.
Company: San Francisco Ballet
Cast: 126 roles; principal dancers included: as Clara, Lois Treadwell; Drosselmeyer, Robert Thorson; King of the Mice, Earl Riggins; Snow Queen, Jocelyn Vollmar; Snow Price, Joaquin Felsch; Sugar Plum Fairy, Gisella Caccialanza; Her Cavalier, Willam Christensen; Mother Buffoon, Russell Hartley; Ballerina, Waltz of the Flowers, Celena Cummings; Chocolate, Mattlyn Gevurtz; Arabian, Onna White; Merliton, Lois Treadwell.
Note: Lew Christensen presented new versions of *The Nutcracker* for the same company in 1954 and 1967.
Utah Premiere: 27 December 1955, Kingsbury Hall, University of Utah, Salt Lake City.
Company: University Theatre Ballet
Principal Dancers: Guest artists Sally Bailey and Conrad Ludlow.

64. *Pyramus and Thisbe*
Music: Fritz Berens
Costumes: Russell Hartley
Premiere: 2 September 1945, Marin Music Chest, Forest Meadows, Dominican College, San Rafael, California. Premiere title: *Once Upon a Time, or Why Mulberries are Purple.*
Company: San Francisco Ballet
Cast: 9 dancers, including: as Thisbe, Jocelyn Vollmar; Pyramus, Robert Hansen; The Lion, Willam Christensen.
San Francisco premiere: 27 December 1945.

65. *Blue Plaza*, with José Manero
Music: Aaron Copland, *El Salón México*
Costumes and Scenery: Antonio Sotomayor
Premiere: 26 December 1945, War Memorial Opera House, San Francisco.
Company: San Francisco Ballet
Cast: 24 dancers, including: as El Pelado, José Manero (guest artist); The Flower Vendor, Ruby Asquith; El Hacendado, Robert Thorson; His Daughter, Onna White.

66. *Tales of Hoffmann*
Music: Jacques Offenbach
Opening Night: 4 October 1945, San Francisco Opera, War Memorial Opera House, San Francisco.
Later production: Fall 1949 season.

67. *Boris Godounoff*
Music: Modest Mussorgsky
Opening Night: 27 September 1946, San Francisco Opera, War Memorial Opera House, San Francisco.
Later Productions: Fall 1948 season, featuring Rosalie Prosch, Peter Nelson; Fall 1953 season, featuring Gordon Paxman; Fall 1956 season.

68. *Dr. Pantalone* (Pierrot's Allergies)
Music: Domenico Scarlatti, arranged by Fritz Berens.
Costumes: Geraldine Cresci
Premiere: 10 August 1947, Stern Grove, San Francisco.
Company: San Francisco Ballet
Cast: 7 dancers, including: as Dr. Pantalone, Marcus Nelson; Columbine, Joan Vickers; Pierrot, James Curtis; Harlequin, William Hay.
(Unofficial Premiere at Recital of Junior Ballet Group, 14 February 1947, Marines Memorial Theater. Cast: as Pierrot, Joaquin Felsch; Nurse, Sally Whalen; Maids, Lois Treadwell and Joan Vickers; Columbine, Jocelyn Vollmar; Harlequin, Peter Nelson; Dr. Pantalone, Marvin Krauter.)

69. *Parranda*
Music: Morton Gould, *Latin American Symphonette*
Costumes and Scenery: Antonio Sotomayor
Premiere: 12 November 1947, War Memorial Opera House,
San Francisco.
Company: San Francisco Civic Ballet
Cast: 25 dancers, including: as A Young Woman, Jocelyn
Vollmar; A Young Man, Richard Burgess; El Colonel Toribio,
José Manero; A Confetti Vendor, Ruby Asquith.
Utah Premiere: 17 May 1956, Kingsbury Hall, University of
Utah, Salt Lake City.
Cast: Woman, Miriam Harding; Man, Ron Ross; Colonel, Phil
Keeler; Vendor, Kay Ford; Policeman, Wayne Brennan; Dock
workers, Michael Smuin, Finis Jhung, Jay Kirk, Gary Horton;
plus Ladies, Mulattos, Beatas, and Skeletons.

70. *Romeo and Juliet*
Music: Charles Gounod
Opening Night: 18 September 1947, San Francisco Opera, War
Memorial Opera House, San Francisco.

71. *The Marriage of Figaro*
Music: Wolfgang Amadeus Mozart
Opening Night: 5 October 1947, San Francisco Opera, War
Memorial Opera House, San Francisco.
Later Production: Fall 1950 season.

72. *Falstaff*
Music: Giuseppe Verdi
Opening Night: 14 September 1948, San Francisco Opera, War
Memorial Opera House, San Francisco.
Later Production: Fall 1956 season.

73. *Vivaldi Concerto*
Music: Antonio Vivaldi, Piano Concerto in B Minor
Premiere: 4 April 1949, Commerce High School Auditorium,
San Francisco.
Company: San Francisco Ballet

Cast: 15 dancers, including Janet Sassoon, Nancy Johnson, Sally Bailey, Jane Bowen, Alton Basuino.

74. *Danza Brillante*
Music: Felix Mendelssohn, Piano Concerto No. 1
Costumes: Jimmy Hicks
Premiere: 25 April 1949, Commerce High School Auditorium, San Francisco.
Company: San Francisco Ballet
Cast: 13 dancers, including Celena Cummings, Joan Vickers, Sally Whalen, Carolyn George, Rosalie Prosch.
Utah Premiere: 11 April 1959, College of Southern Utah Auditorium, Cedar City, Utah.
Company: University Theatre Ballet.

75. *The Great Waltz*
Music: Johann Strauss, Jr. and Sr.
Costumes: Sereta T. Jones
Scenery: Vern Adix
Opening Night: 4 July 1949, University of Utah Summer Festival, Stadium Bowl, Salt Lake City.
Dancers: Joan Vickers, Janice Day, Roland Vasquez, Richard Burgess, and an ensemble of 17.

76. *Carmen*
Music: Georges Bizet
Costumes: Sereta T. Jones
Scenery: Vern Adix
Opening Night: 15 July 1949, University of Utah Summer Festival, Stadium Bowl, Salt Lake City.
Later University of Utah Production: 13 July 1961.
Principal Dancers: Janice James, Rocky Spoelstra.

77. *The Nothing Doing Bar*
Music: Darius Milhaud, *Le Boeuf sur le Toit*
Costumes: Grace MacOuillard
Scenery: Louis MacOuillard

Premiere: 11 March 1950, Commerce High School Auditorium, San Francisco.

Cast: 10 dancers, including: as Joe the Bartender, Leon Kalimos; Punchie, Robert Frellson; The Van Snoopers, Carolyn George, Vernon Wendorf; Fannie Flapper, Joan Vickers; Joe College, Alton Basuino.

Utah Premiere: 17 May 1956, Kingsbury Hall, University of Utah, Salt Lake City.

Company: University Theatre Ballet

Cast: 10 dancers, including: as Joe, Kent Stowell; Yo-Yo, Michael Smuin; Weasel, Wayne Brennan; Punchy, Kay Kirt; Van Snoopers, Josef France and Carol Wilcox; Fanny Flapper, Nancy Gold; Joe College, Phil Keeler; Shady Sadie, Charlene Callow.

78. *Promised Valley*
Music: Crawford Gates
Book: Arnold Sundgaard
Costumes: Sereta T. Jones
Scenery: Vern Adix
Opening Night: 4 July 1950, University of Utah Summer Festival, Stadium Bowl, Salt Lake City.
Dancers: Joan Vickers, Roland Vasquez, Geraldine Vasquez, Leo Duggan, Carolyn George, Nancy Johnson, and an ensemble of 28.

79. *Faust*
Music: Charles Gounod
Costumes: Sereta T. Jones
Scenery: Vern Adix
Opening Night: 14 July 1950, University of Utah Summer Festival, Stadium Bowl, Salt Lake City.

80. *Divertimenti*, with Lew Christensen (After Petipa)
Music: Peter Ilyich Tchaikovsky, from *Swan Lake*, *Sleeping Beauty*, and *Nutcracker*.
Costumes: Russell Hartley

Premiere: 3 March 1951, Commerce High School Auditorium, San Francisco.
Company: San Francisco Ballet
Cast: 33 dancers, featuring Sally Whalen and Peter Nelson in the Czardas from *Swan Lake*; Nancy Johnson and Richard Burgess in the Black Swan Pas de Deux, *Swan Lake*; Joan Vickers and Peter Nelson in the Blue Bird Pas de Deux, *Sleeping Beauty*.

81. *Les Maîtresses de Lord Byron*
Music: Franz Liszt, Concerto No. 1 in E flat Major
Scenario: James Graham-Luján
Scenery and Costumes: Russell Hartley
Premiere: 17 March 1951, Commerce High School Auditorium, San Francisco.
Company: San Francisco Ballet
Cast: 8 dancers, including: as Lord Byron, Richard Burgess; Countess Guiccioli, Joan Vickers; Count Guiccioli, Leo Duggan; Caroline Lamb, Carolyn George.

82. *The Merry Widow*
Music: Johann Strauss
Costumes: Sereta T. Jones
Scenery: Vern Adix
Opening Night: 9 July 1951, University of Utah Summer Festival, Stadium Bowl, Salt Lake City.
Dancers: Sally Bailey, Barton Mumaw, and an ensemble of 25.

83. *Tales of Hoffmann*
Music: Jacques Offenbach
Costumes: Sereta T. Jones
Scenery: Vern Adix
Opening Night: 19 July 1951, University of Utah Summer Festival, Stadium Bowl, Salt Lake City.
Principal Dancers: Sally Bailey, Barton Mumaw

84. *The Snow Queen*
Music: Marcel Tyrell
Costumes: Winifred Bowers

Scenery: Vern Adix
Opening Night: 11 January 1952, Young People's Theatre, Kingsbury Hall, University of Utah, Salt Lake City.

85. *Kiss Me, Kate*
Music: Cole Porter
Costumes: Winifred Bowers, Jon Beck Shank
Scenery: Vern Adix
Opening Night: 7 July 1952, University of Utah Summer Festival, Stadium Bowl, Salt Lake City.
Dancers: Sally Bailey, Rudy Tone, and an ensemble of 36.

86. *Samson and Delilah*
Music: Camille Saint-Saëns
Costumes: Winifred Bowers, Jon Beck Shank
Scenery: Vern Adix
Opening Night: 17 July 1952, University of Utah Summer Festival, Stadium Bowl, Salt Lake City.
Dancers: Sally Bailey, Rudy Tone, and an ensemble of 36.

87. *Mefistofele*
Music: Arrigo Boito
Opening Night: 20 September 1952, San Francisco Opera, War Memorial Opera House, San Francisco.
Later Production: Fall 1953 season.

88. *Swan Lake, Act II*, with Barbara Barrie (After Petipa and Ivanov)
Music: Peter Ilyich Tchaikovsky
Scenery: Ron Crosby
Premiere: 5 May 1953, Kingsbury Hall, University of Utah, Salt Lake City.
Company: University Theatre Ballet
Cast: Guest artists from the San Francisco Ballet included: as Odette, Sally Bailey; Siegfried, Gordon Paxman. Local dancers: Benno, John Malotzi; Von Rotbart, Ron Ross. Ensemble in Waltz, Hunters scene, Pas de Quatre, Pas de Dix, Coda and Finale.

89. *Le Chausseur Maudit*
Music: César Franck
Scenery: Vern Adix
Premiere: 5 May 1953, Kingsbury Hall, University of Utah, Salt Lake City.
Company: University Theatre Ballet
Cast: Girl, Kay Ford; Mother, Jo Olsen; Hunter, Ron Ross; Priest, Edwin Peay; Priest of Death, John Malezzi; ensemble of Girls in the Square, Church-Goers, and Spirits of Torment, 23 dancers.

90. *Naughty Marietta*
Music: Victor Herbert
Costumes: Sereta T. Jones
Scenery: Vern Adix
Opening Night: 6 July 1953, University of Utah Summer Festival, Stadium Bowl, Salt Lake City.
Dancers: Pierrette, Sally Bailey; Pierrot, Gordon Paxman; Ensemble of 21.

91. *La Traviata*
Music: Giuseppe Verdi
Costumes: Sereta T. Jones
Scenery: Vern Adix
Opening Night: 15 July 1953, University of Utah Summer Festival, Stadium Bowl, Salt Lake City.
Dancers: Ensemble of 21.

92. *The Creatures of Prometheus*
Music: Ludwig van Beethoven, *The Creatures of Prometheus*
Scenario: Salvatore Viganò, adapted by James Graham-Luján
Scenery: Armando Agnini
Premiere: 25 September 1953, War Memorial Opera House, San Francisco.
Company: San Francisco Ballet
Cast: 41 roles, including: as Prometheus, Gordon Paxman; Fire, Virginia Johnson; Woman, Nancy Johnson; Man, Ray Barallobre; Athena, Patricia Johnston; Terpsichore, Bené Arnold; Aphrodite, Sally Bailey; Bacchus, Conrad Ludlow.

Utah Premiere: 12 April 1966, Weber State College, Ogden.
Company: Utah Civic Ballet

93. *Turandot*
Music: Giacomo Puccini
Opening Night: 11 October 1953, San Francisco Opera, War
Memorial Opera House, San Francisco.
Later Productions: Fall 1954 season; Fall 1957 season.

94. *Oklahoma!*
Music: Richard Rodgers
Book and Lyrics: Oscar Hammerstein II
Costumes: Sereta T. Jones
Scenery: Vern Adix
Opening Night: 10 July 1954, University of Utah Summer
Festival, Stadium Bowl, Salt Lake City.
Dancers: Dream Curly, Gordon Paxman; Dream Laurey,
Connie Coler; Dream Jud, Ron Ross; ensemble of 22.

95. *Aïda*
Music: Giuseppe Verdi
Costumes: Sereta Jones
Scenery: Vern Adix
Opening Night: 26 July 1954, University of Utah Summer
Festival, Stadium Bowl, Salt Lake City.
Dancers: Sally Bailey and an ensemble of 41.
Later Summer Festival Production: 26 June 1966; 39 dancers.

96. *Joan of Arc at the Stake* (with Lew Christensen)
Music: Arthur Honegger, *Jeanne D'Arc au Bûcher*
Opening Night: 15 October 1954, San Francisco Opera, War
Memorial Opera House, San Francisco.

97. *Divertimento* (with Lew Christensen)
Music: Peter Ilyich Tchaikovsky
Premiere: 10 May 1955, Kingsbury Hall, University of Utah,
Salt Lake City.
Company: University Theatre Ballet, with San Francisco
Ballet.

Note: Willam choreographed the first two sections of the ballet, which were set to music from *Swan Lake*. Lew contributed the third, "Mozartiana," which was danced by members of his company. The final two sections were excerpts from *The Nutcracker* and were performed by UTB. Portions may have been similar to #80.

98. *South Pacific*
Music: Richard Rodgers
Book: Oscar Hammerstein II and Joshua Logan
Costumes: Sereta T. Jones
Scenery: Vern Adix
Opening Night: 4 July 1955, University of Utah Summer Festival, Stadium Bowl, Salt Lake City.
Dancers: Patt Jeppson, Bonnie Jo Nelson, Charlene Callow, Carol Ann Price, Beverly James, Phil Keeler, Jay Kirk, Michael Smuin.

99. *Tchaikovsky Ballet* or *Divertimenti from Tchaikovsky Ballets*
Music: Peter Ilyich Tchaikovsky, the Grand Waltz, Czardas, and Black Swan Pas de Deux from *Swan Lake*, and the Chinese Dance, Russian Dance, and Waltz of the Flowers from *Nutcracker*.
Opening Night: 13 July 1955, University of Utah Summer Festival, Stadium Bowl, Salt Lake City.
Company: University Theatre Ballet
Dancers: Guest Artists Sally Bailey and Conrad Ludlow, with an ensemble of 34.
Note: This may have been very similar to #96, *Divertimento*.

100. *Macbeth*
Music: Giuseppe Verdi
Opening Night: 27 September 1955, San Francisco Opera, War Memorial Opera House, San Francisco.
Later Production: Fall 1957 season.

101. *Concerto*
Music: Johann Sebastian Bach, Concerto in A Minor for Violin and Orchestra.

Scenery: Vern Adix
Premiere: 17 May 1956, Kingsbury Hall, University of Utah, Salt Lake City.
Company: University Theatre Ballet
Cast: Kay Ford, Ron Ross, Nancy Gold, Cheri McMillan, Sue Gibbons, and ensemble of 12.

102. *The King and I*
Music: Richard Rodgers
Lyrics and Book: Oscar Hammerstein II
Costumes: Sereta T. Jones
Scenery: Vern Adix
Opening Night: 2 July 1956, University of Utah Summer Festival, Stadium Bowl, Salt Lake City.
Principal Dancers: Kay Ford and Ron Ross

103. *Madame Butterfly*
Music: Giacomo Puccini
Costumes: Sereta T. Jones
Scenery: Vern Adix
Opening Night: 11 July 1956, University of Utah Summer Festival, Stadium Bowl, Salt Lake City.
Principal Dancers: Phil Keeler, Gary Horton, Finis Jhung, Michael Smuin, Robert A. Sharp.

104. *Il Trovatore*
Music: Giuseppe Verdi
Opening Night: 16 September 1956, San Francisco Opera, War Memorial Opera House, San Francisco.
Principal Dancers: Sally Bailey, Conrad Ludlow

105. *The Elixir of Love*
Music: Gaetano Donizetti
Opening Night: 12 October 1956, San Francisco Opera, War Memorial Opera House, San Francisco.

106. *Salome*
Music: Richard Strauss

Costumes: Sereta T. Jones
Scenery: Vern Adix
Opening Night: 17 July 1957, University of Utah Summer
Festival, Stadium Bowl, Salt Lake City.
Dancers: University Theatre Ballet

107. *Crown of Joy*
Music: Felix Mendelssohn, 4th Symphony in A Major
Scenery: Vern Adix
Premiere: 7 May 1957, Kingsbury Hall, University of Utah,
Salt Lake City.
Company: University Theatre Ballet
Principal Dancers: Dionysus, Michael Smuin; Leader of Greek
Women, Miriam Harding; Silenus, Ron Ross; Chosen Sprite,
Nancy Gold.

108. *Something in the Wind*
Music: Igor Stravinsky, Octet for Double Woodwind Quintet
Costumes: Sereta T. Jones
Scenery: Vern Adix
Premiere: 8 May 1957, Kingsbury Hall, University of Utah,
Salt Lake City.
Company: University Theatre Ballet
Cast: Charlene Callow, Sharon Givan, Carol Ann Price, Zoe
Terzetta, Joseph France, Finis Jhung, Kent Stowell, Gary Horton.
New York Premiere: Renamed *Octet*; 2 December 1958; New
York City Ballet; Barbara Walczak, Edward Villella, Dido
Sayers, William Weslow, Roberta Lubell, Robert Lindgren,
Judith Green, Richard Rapp.
San Francisco Premiere: *Octet*; 6 February 1965; San Francisco
Ballet; Sue Loyd, Terry Orr, Virginia Johnson, Lee Fuller,
Joan deVere, David Anderson, Cynthia Gregory, R. Clinton
Rothwell.

109. *Caprice De Paree*
Music: Jacques Ibert
Costumes: Sereta T. Jones
Scenery: Vern Adix

Premiere: 8 May 1957, Kingsbury Hall, University of Utah, Salt Lake City.
Company: University Theatre Ballet
Leading Dancers: Lady, Charlene Callow; Thief, Ron Ross.
Revived by Utah Civic Ballet in 1966 as *Les Bijoux du Mal.*

110. *Song of Norway*
Music: Edvard Grieg
Costumes: Sereta T. Jones
Scenery: Vern Adix
Opening Night: 6 July 1957, University of Utah Summer Festival, Stadium Bowl, Salt Lake City.
Dancers: Charlene Callow, Sharon Givan, Carol Ann Price, Ron Ross, Jay Kirk, Joe France, Gary Horton, Fred Schwab, Kent Stowell, Finis Jhung, Michael Smuin, and ensemble of 12.

111. *Carousel*
Music: Richard Rogers
Lyrics and Book: Oscar Hammerstein II
Costumes: Sereta T. Jones
Scenery: Vern Adix
Opening Night: 5 July 1958, University of Utah Summer Festival, Stadium Bowl, Salt Lake City.
Principal Dancers: Zoe Terzetta, James DeBolt, and members of University Theatre Ballet.

112. *Der Rosencavalier*
Music: Richard Strauss
Costumes: Sereta T. Jones
Scenery: Vern Adix
Opening Night: 17 July 1958, University of Utah Summer Festival, Stadium Bowl, Salt Lake City.
Dancers: University Theatre Ballet

113. *Symphonia*
Music: Wolfgang Amadeus Mozart, Haffner Symphony No. 35, Divertimento in B flat.

Costumes: Sereta T. Jones
Scenery: Therald Todd
Premiere: 4 May 1959, Kingsbury Hall, University of Utah.
Salt Lake City.
Company: University Theatre Ballet
Dancers: Guest Artist Janet Sassoon and ensemble of 24.

114. *Brigadoon*
Music: Frederick Loewe
Lyrics and Book: Alan Jay Lerner
Costumes: Sereta T. Jones
Scenery: Vern Adix
Opening Night: 6 July 1959, University of Utah Summer
Festival, Stadium Bowl, Salt Lake City.
Dancers: Zoe Terzetta, Fran Schwab, and members of the
University Theatre Ballet.

115. *Il Trovatore*
Music: Giuseppe Verdi
Costumes: Sereta T. Jones
Scenery: Vern Adix
Opening Night: 15 July 1959, University of Utah Summer
Festival, Stadium Bowl, Salt Lake City.
Dancers: Gypsy Dancer, Patricia Knight; Gypsy Leader, Jay
Kirk; Fran Schwab, Zoe Terzetta, Janice James, Shirley White,
Fred Schwab, Finis Jhung, Wayne Brennan, Gary Horton.

116. *Orfeo ed Euridice*
Music: Christoph Willibald von Gluck
Opening Night: 15 September 1959, San Francisco Opera, War
Memorial Opera House, San Francisco.

117. *Variations In Contrast*
Music: Wolfgang Amadeus Mozart, *Eine Kleine Nachtmusik*
(Movements I, II, and IV) and *Adagio and Fugue for String
Orchestra.*
Scenery: Vern Adix
Premiere: 3 May 1960, Kingsbury Hall, University of Utah,
Salt Lake City.

Company: University Theatre Ballet
Leading Dancers: Shirley White and Rowland Butler; 5 soloists; 13 corps de ballet.

118. *Adagio, Ensemble*
Premiere: 3 May 1960, Kingsbury Hall, University of Utah, Salt Lake City.
Company: University Theatre Ballet
Cast: Rocky Spoelstra, Janice James, Marianne Hatton, Tony Scott, Miriam Harding, Peggy Powell, Fred Schwab, Fran Schwab, Barbara Blanchard, Jay Kirk, Marilyn Evans, Camilla Kennell.

119. *La Fille Naive*
Music: Daniel-François-Esprit Auber
Premiere: 3 May 1960, Kingsbury Hall, University of Utah, Salt Lake City.
Company: University Theatre Ballet
Cast: Youth, Gordon Paxman; La Fille Naive, Marianne Hatton; Mother, Camilla Kennell; Four Sisters, Marilyn Evans, Janice James, Fran Schwab, Kay Stevenson; General, Jay Kirk; Four Soldiers, Rowland Butler, Fred Schwab, Tony Scott, Rocky Spoelstra; Courriers, Patrick Hunt and Robert Miya.

120. *Annie, Get Your Gun*
Music: Irving Berlin
Book: Dorothy and Herbert Fields
Costumes: Sereta T. Jones
Scenery: Vern Adix
Opening Night: 1 July 1960, University of Utah Summer Festival, Stadium Bowl, Salt Lake City.
Dancers: University Theatre Ballet

121. *Die Fledermaus*
Music: Johann Strauss
Costumes: Sereta T. Jones
Scenery: Vern Adix
Premiere: 12 July 1960, University of Utah Summer Festival, Stadium Bowl, Salt Lake City.

Dancers: Janice James, Wayne Brennan, and University Theatre Ballet.

122. *Destry Rides Again*
Music and Lyrics: Harold Rome
Costumes and Scenery: Vern Adix
Premiere: 30 June 1961, University of Utah Summer Festival, Stadium Bowl, Salt Lake City.
Dancers: 26 members of University Theatre Ballet.

123. *Bells Are Ringing*
Music: Jule Styne
Book and Lyrics: Betty Comden and Adolph Green
Costumes: Sereta Jones
Scenery: Vern Adix
Opening Night: 3 October 1961
Dancers: University Theatre Ballet

124. *Garden of Evil*
Music: Dimitri Shostakovitch
Costumes and Scenery: Angelo Caravaglia
Premiere: 1 May 1962, Kingsbury Hall, University of Utah, Salt Lake City.
Company: University Theatre Ballet
Cast: Fast, Phil Keeler; Lucifer, Wayne Brennan; Innocence, Sally Carlton; Her Protectress, Gisela Guenther; and ensemble.

125. *Blue Bird Pas de Deux* (After Petipa)
Music: Peter Ilyich Tchaikovsky
Premiere: 1 May 1962, Kingsbury Hall, University of Utah, Salt Lake City.
Company: University Theatre Ballet
Leading Dancers: Shirley White, Rowland Butler

126. *Tannhäuser*
Music: Richard Wagner
Costumes: Sereta T. Jones

Scenery: Vern Adix
Opening Night: 26 June 1962, University of Utah Summer
Festival, Stadium Bowl, Salt Lake City.
Principal Dancers: Janice James, Gordon Paxman.

127. *The Music Man*
Music and Lyrics: Meredith Wilson
Costumes: Sereta T. Jones
Scenery: Vern Adix
Opening Night: 5 July 1962, University of Utah Summer
Festival, Stadium Bowl, Salt Lake City.
Principal Dancers: Shirley White, Rowland Butler.

128. *Blue Tournament*
Music: George Frideric Handel, *Water Music Suite* and
*Fireworks Music*
Costumes and Scenery: Ariel Ballif
Premiere: 7 May 1963, Kingsbury Hall, University of Utah,
Salt Lake City.
Company: University Theatre Ballet
Cast: "Allegro," two soloist couples and an ensemble of nine;
"Andante and Bourree," 4 couples; "Hornpipe," Wayne
Brennan, Bill Evans, Rocky Spoelstra; "Adagio," Shirley White,
Janice James, Wayne Brennan, Bill Evans, Rocky Spoelstra.
Revived by Ballet West in 1971 under the title *Le Cour d'Azur*.

129. *Toxcatl*
Music: Gaylen Hatton
Scenery: Ariel Ballif
Scenario: Keith Engar
Premiere: 7 May 1963, Kingsbury Hall, University of Utah,
Salt Lake City.
Company: University Theatre Ballet
Leading Dancers: Chosen One, Gordon Paxman; His Beloved,
Janice James.

130. *Manon*
Music: Jules Massenet

Costumes: Sereta T. Jones
Scenery: Vern Adix
Premiere: 25 June 1963, University of Utah Summer Festival, Stadium Bowl, Salt Lake City.
Dancers: University Theatre Ballet

131. *Kismet*
Music and Lyrics: Robert Wright and George Forrest (based on themes of Alexander Borodin)
Book: Charles Lederer and Luther Davis
Costumes: Sereta T. Jones
Scenery: Vern Adix
Premiere: 5 July 1963, University of Utah Summer Festival, Stadium Bowl, Salt Lake City.
Principal Dancers: Shirley White, Rowland Butler.

132. *La Valse*
Music: Maurice Ravel
Costumes and Scenery: Ariel Ballif
Premiere: 10 September 1964, Skyline High School, Salt Lake City.
Company: Utah Civic Ballet

133. *Pas de Six*
Music: Otto Nicolai, *The Merry Wives of Windsor*
Costumes: Ariel Ballif
Premiere: 29 April 1965, Kingsbury Hall, University of Utah, Salt Lake City.
Company: Utah Civic Ballet
Dancers: Carolyn Anderson and Gary Horton; Anne Burton and Rowland Butler; Barbara Hamblin and Phillip Keeler.

134. *West Side Story*
Music: Leonard Bernstein
Book: Arthur Laurents
Costumes: Sereta T. Jones
Scenery: Vern Adix

Opening Night: 8 July 1966, University of Utah Summer Festival, Stadium Bowl, Salt Lake City.
Dancers: Utah Civic Ballet.

135. *Romantica*
Music: Anton Dvorak
Costumes: Ronald Crosby
Premiere: 4 May 1967, Kingsbury Hall, University of Utah, Salt Lake City.
Company: Utah Civic Ballet
Cast: Carolyn Anderson, Barbara Hamblin, Janice James, John Hiatt, Kenneth Mitchell, Tomm Ruud.

136. *Firebird*
Music: Igor Stravinsky
Premiere: 25 October 1967, Kingsbury Hall, University of Utah, Salt Lake City.
Company: Utah Civic Ballet
Cast: Firebird, Janice James; Ivan Tsarevich, Kenneth Mitchell; The Beautiful Tsarevna, Dianna Cuatto; Kastchei, Rocky Spoelstra.

137. *Bravura*
Music: Emmanuel Chabrier
Premiere: 10 February 1969, Merced College, Merced, California
Company: Ballet West
Cast: Carolyn Anderson, Ben Lokey, and ensemble of 16.

138. *Mother of Us All*
Music: Virgil Thomson
Opening Night: 1 May 1969, University of Utah Opera Company

139. *La Bayadère, Act IV* (After Petipa)
Music: Ludwig Minkus
Premiere: 1 October 1969, Kingsbury Hall, University of Utah, Salt Lake City.
Company: Ballet West
Cast: Janice James, Tomm Ruud, and an ensemble of 16.

140. *Cinderella*
Music: Sergei Prokoviev
Costumes and Scenery: Kenneth McClelland
Premiere: 1 April 1970, Kingsbury Hall, University of Utah, Salt Lake City.
Company: Ballet West
Cast: Cinderella, Carolyn Anderson/Barbara Hamblin/Janice James; Prince, Tomm Ruud/John Hiatt.

141. *Paquita Pas de Deux* (After Petipa)
Music: Ludwig Minkus
Premiere: 31 March 1971, Kingsbury Hall, University of Utah, Salt Lake City.
Company: Ballet West
Cast: Janice James and Tomm Ruud
Note: *Paquita Pas de Deux* is listed as part of the company repertory in the 1969-1970 Souvenir Program, but I have not found evidence that it was performed before the date given above. Newspaper articles confirm that the work received its Salt Lake City debut in March 1971.

142. *Mozartiana*
Music: Peter Ilyich Tchaikovsky
Costumes: Sarah B. Price
Premiere: 22 March 1972, Kingsbury Hall, University of Utah, Salt Lake City.
Company: Ballet West
Principal Dancers: Vicki Morgan/Janice James, John Hiatt/ Tomm Ruud.

143. *Jubilee*
Music: Dimitri Shostakovitch
Premiere: 20 February 1974, Kingsbury Hall, University of Utah, Salt Lake City.
Company: Ballet West
Principal Dancers: Janice James, Tomm Ruud.

144. *Woman Remembered*
Music: James Prigmore
Costumes: Ron Hodge
Scenery: David Barber
Scenario: Byron Meadows
Premiere: 8 October 1976, Kingsbury Hall, University of Utah, Salt Lake City.
Company: Ballet West

145. *Fur, Feathers, and Fins*
Music: Camille Saint-Saëns
Premiere: 15 July 1988, Murray Park Amphitheater, Murray, Utah.
Company: Christensen Centre (school)
Principal Dancers: Michelle Wright, Richard Richards, Leah Elzner, Rita Snyder.

146. *Maggie's Dream*
Music: George Gershwin
Premiere: 13 July 1990, Murray Park Amphitheater, Murray, Utah.
Company: Christensen Centre (school)
Principal Dancers: Michelle Wright Armstrong, Ted Johnson, Kaelynn Antczak, Beth Olsen.

147. *Orpheus*
Music: Jacques Offenbach
Premiere: July 1990, Murray Park Amphitheater, Murray, Utah.
Company: Christensen Centre (school)
Principal Dancers: Joe Dewey, Alison Northrup, Michelle Armstrong, Tiffany Nielsen

148. *Cotillion*
Music: Josef Strauss and Johann Strauss Jr.
Costume: David Heuvel

Lighting: Deward Wilson
Scenery: Ronald Crosby
Premiere: 25 April 1991, Hayes/Christensen Theatre, Alice
Sheets Marriott Center for Dance, University of Utah, Salt
Lake City.
Company: Utah Ballet
Principal Dancers: Guest artists Dianna Cuatto, Mark
Borchelt.

149. *Overture de Ballo*
Music: Arthur Sullivan
Premiere: 11 June 1993
Company: Ballet West Conservatory

# APPENDIX B

## CHOREOGRAPHY BY LEW CHRISTENSEN

The following list is based on data from several sources, including (1) the San Francisco Ballet program files, on deposit at the San Francisco Performing Arts Library and Museum, (2) Lew Christensen's program files and scrapbooks in the Christensen-Caccialanza Collection, also at the San Francisco Performing Arts Library and Museum, (3) Nancy Reynolds' *Repertory in Review*, (4) Cobbett Steinberg's *San Francisco Ballet: The First Fifty Years*, and (5) Steinberg's abbreviated Title List (unpublished) of works by Lew Christensen. I have relied heavily on the last two for information on Lew Christensen's choreography for San Francisco Opera productions. Later productions of operas previously choreographed are not given separate entries; instead, they are added to the entry the first time the opera appears. Information on the musicals choreographed in St. Louis during the summer of 1940 is particularly scarce and has been gleaned from scrapbook clippings. Incomplete evidence also suggests that Lew choreographed specialty numbers and finales for the San Francisco Opera Guild Fol De Rol programs, 1954–1957 and 1960–1963.

1. *Encounter*
Music: Wolfgang Amadeus Mozart, Serenade in D Major, K. 250, "Haffner," 1776.
Women's costumes: traditional
Men's costumes: after the drawings of J. G. von Schadow
Premiere: 17 July 1936, College Theatre, Bennington, Vt.
Company: Ballet Caravan
Cast: Ensemble of 12.

2. *Pocahontas*
Music: Elliott Carter (1936; commissioned by Ballet Caravan)
Scenario: Lincoln Kirstein
Costumes: Karl Free, after the engravings of Theodore de Bry

Premiere: 18 July 1936, College Theatre, Bennington, Vt.
Company: Ballet Caravan
Cast: Princess Pocahontas, Ruthanna Boris; King Powhatan, her father, Harold Christensen; Captain John Smith, Charles Laskey; John Rolfe, Lew Christensen; Priest, Erick Hawkins; Indians, 6 women.

3. *Filling Station*
Music: Virgil Thomson (1937; commissioned by Ballet Caravan)
Scenario: Lincoln Kirstein
Costumes and Scenery: Paul Cadmus
Premiere: 6 January 1938, Hartford, Conn.
Company: Ballet Caravan
Cast: Mac, the attendant, Lew Christensen; Roy and Ray, truck drivers, Douglas Coudy, Eugene Loring; The Motorist, Harold Christensen; His Wife, Marjorie Moore; His Child, Jane Doering; The Rich Girl, Marie-Jeanne; The Rich Boy, Fred Danieli; The Gangster, Erick Hawkins; The State Trooper, Todd Bolender.
West Coast Premiere: 17 February 1951, Commerce High School Auditorium, San Francisco.

4. *A Midsummer Night's Dream*
Music: Felix Mendelssohn
Scenario: Based on Shakespeare's play.
Premiere: 18 July 1938, Multnomah Civic Stadium, Portland, OR. Company: The William Christensen Ballet
Cast: Titania, Janet Reed; Oberon, Lew Christensen; Puck, Natalie Lauterstein; Lysander, Ronald Chetwood; Hermia, Zelda Morey; Demetrius, Harold Christensen; Helena, Jacqueline Martin; Bottom, William Christensen.

5. *Charade, or The Debutante*
Music: American songs and social dances, including melodies by Stephen Foster and Louis Gottschalk, and variations on "Good Night, Ladies," arranged by Trude Rittman (1938)
Scenario: Lincoln Kirstein

Costumes: Alvin Colt
Premiere: 17 October 1939, Lancaster, Pa.
Company: Ballet Caravan
Cast: Blanche Johnson, the debutante, Marie-Jeanne; Trixie, her younger sister, Gisella Caccialanza; Mr. Johnson, their father, Harold Christensen; Minnie, the maid, Ruby Asquith; Wilmer J. Smith, a young man, Lew Christensen; 7 female guests; 6 male guests.
West Coast Premiere: 25 April 1950, Commerce High School Auditorium, San Francisco.

6. *The American Way*
Opening Night: 3 June 1940, St. Louis Municipal Opera

7. *Naughty Marietta*
Music: Victor Herbert
Opening Night: 17 June 1940, St. Louis Municipal Opera

8. *Apple Blossoms*
Music: Fritz Kreisler and Victor Jacobi
Opening Night: 24 June 1940, St. Louis Municipal Opera

9. *Rio Rita*
Music: Harry Tierney
Opening Night: 1 July 1940, St. Louis Municipal Opera

10. *The Chocolate Soldier*
Music: Oscar Straus
Opening Night: 8 July 1940, St. Louis Municipal Opera

11. *Good News*
Music: Ray Henderson
Opening Night: 15 July 1940, St. Louis Municipal Opera

12. *Knickerbocker Holiday*
Music: Kurt Weill
Opening Night: 22 July 1940, St. Louis Municipal Opera

13. *Anything Goes*
Music: Cole Porter
Opening Night: 29 July 1940, St. Louis Municipal Opera

14. *East Wind*
Music: Sigmund Romberg
Opening Night: 5 August 1940, St. Louis Municipal Opera

15. *Rosalie*
Music: Sigmund Romberg and George Gerschwin
Opening Night: 12 August 1940, St. Louis Municipal Opera

16. *Babes in Arms*
Music: Richard Rogers
Opening Night: 19 August 1940, St. Louis Municipal Opera

17. *The Great Waltz*
Music: Johann Strauss, Sr. & Jr.
Opening Night: 26 August 1940, St. Louis Municipal Opera

18. *Liberty Jones*
Music: Paul Bowles
Opening Night: 5 February 1941, Theatre Guild, New York City

19. *Pastorela*, a Ballet-Opera in one act, with José Fernandez
Music: Paul Bowles, from traditional songs, orchestrated by Blas Galindo; words by Rafael Alvarez.
Scenario: José Martinez
Costumes: Alvin Colt, from original sources.
Premiere: 27 June 1941, Teatro Municipal, Rio de Janeiro, Brazil. (Also presented in an open dress rehearsal, 27 May 1941, Little Theatre of Hunter College, New York.)
Company: American Ballet Caravan
Cast: Hermit, John Kriza; St. Michael, Charles Dickson; Lucifer, Lew Christensen; Indian, Fred Danieli; 6 shepherds; 3 devils; Gila, the cook, Gisella Caccialanza; 4 women.

20. *Jinx*
Music: Benjamin Britten, *Variations on a Theme by Frank Bridges*
Premiere: 24 April 1942
Company: Dance Players
West Coast Premiere: 25 April 1949, Commerce High School Auditorium, San Francisco.

21. *Blackface*
Music: Carter Harmon (1947; using themes of Stephen Foster)
Costumes and Scenery: Robert Drew
Premiere: 18 May 1947, Ziegfeld Theater, New York
Company: Ballet Society
Cast: Interlocutor, Fred Danieli; Mr. Tambo, Paul Godkin; Mr. Bones, Marc Beaudet; White Girl, Beatrice Tompkins; Colored Couple, Betty Nichols, Talley Beatty; 3 White Couples; 3 Creole Couples.

22. *La Gioconda*
Music: Amilcare Ponchielli
Opening Night: 3 October 1948, San Francisco Opera, War Memorial Opera House, San Francisco.
Principal Dancer: Sally Whalen

23. *The Story of a Dancer*
Music: George Frideric Handel, *Water Music Suite*
Premiere: 4 April 1949, Commerce High School Auditorium, San Francisco.
Company: San Francisco Ballet
Cast: 22 dancers; Women's pointe section led by Ruby Asquith.
Narrated by Lew Christensen; scenario probably by James Graham-Luján.
Revised and retitled *Prelude: To Performance*, 1 February 1950, with Jocelyn Vollmar in the Ballerina role.

24. *Vivaldi Concerto*
Music: Antonio Vivaldi, transcribed by Raul Paniagua

Premiere: 4 April 1949, Commerce High School Auditorium, San Francisco.
Company: San Francisco Ballet
Cast: 15 dancers, including Janet Sassoon, Nancy Johnson, Sally Bailey, Jane Bowen, Alton Basuino.

25. *Divertimenti* (with Willam Christensen, after Petipa)
Music: Peter Ilyich Tchaikovsky
Costumes: Russell Hartley
Premiere: 3 March 1951, Commerce High School Auditorium, San Francisco.
Company: San Francisco Ballet
Cast: 33 dancers, including Sally Whalen and Peter Nelson in the Czardas from *Swan Lake*; Nancy Johnson and Richard Burgess in the Black Swan Pas de Deux from *Swan Lake*; Joan Vickers, Peter Nelson in the Bluebird Pas de Deux from *Sleeping Beauty*.

26. *Le Gourmand*
Music: Wolfgang Amadeus Mozart, Divertimento No. 10 in F Major.
Scenario: Lew Christensen and James Graham-Luján, with assistance from M. Paul Ferrier, Maître d'Hotel of the Mark Hopkins Hotel
Scenery and Costumes: Leonard Weisgard
Premiere: 31 March 1951, Commerce High School Auditorium, San Francisco.
Company: San Francisco Ballet
Cast: 15 dancers, including M. Le Gourmand, Alton Basuino; Un Viel Homard Grillé, Willam Christensen; Un Filet de Sole, Carolyn George; Une Poule Déplumée, Sally Bailey; La Pêche Flambée, Gisella Caccialanza.

27. *Bittersweet*
Book: Noel Coward
Opening Night: 30 July 1951, Gene Mann's Summer Operetta Festival, War Memorial Opera House, San Francisco.

28. Standard Hour Television Series
This project consisted of 13 sequences filmed during the fall and winter of 1951 and aired in the fall or 1952. Choreography included excerpts from *Nutcracker*, *Lew Sylphides*, *Faust*, *Boutique Fantasque*, and a commedia dell'arte sequence.

29. *Carmen*
Music: Georges Bizet
Opening Night: 20 September 1951, San Francisco Opera, War Memorial Opera House, San Francisco.
Principal Dancers: Joan Vickers, Geraldine Vasquez, Roland Vasquez
Later Productions: 16 October 1960, Greek Theatre, University of California, Berkeley; co-choreographed with Michael Smuin, 20 September 1962; Principal Dancers: Sally Bailey, Robert Gladstein.

30. *Romeo and Juliet*
Music: Charles Gounod
Opening Night: 21 September 1951, San Francisco Opera production, War Memorial Opera House, San Francisco.
Later Production: 2 May 1961.

31. *La Forza del Destino*
Music: Giuseppe Verdi
Opening Night: 28 September 1951, San Francisco Opera, War Memorial Opera House, San Francisco.
Later Production: 8 October 1963.

32. *Boris Godounoff*
Music: Modest Mussorgsky
Opening Night: 2 October 1951, San Francisco Opera, War Memorial Opera House, San Francisco.
Later Production: 21 September 1961.

33. *La Traviata*
Music: Giuseppe Verdi
Opening Night: 5 October 1951, San Francisco Opera, War Memorial Opera House, San Francisco.

Later Productions: co-choreographed with Michael Smuin, 13 May 1961; Principal
Dancers: Jocelyn Vollmar, Roderick Drew; 4 October 1963.

34. *Rigoletto*
Music: Giuseppe Verdi
Opening Night: 20 October 1951, San Francisco Opera, War Memorial Opera House, San Francisco.
Later Productions: 17 September 1954; 30 September 1961.

35. *The Nutcracker*, with Willam Christensen
Music: Peter Ilyich Tchaikovsky
Premiere: 23 December 1951, War Memorial Opera House, San Francisco.
Company: San Francisco Ballet
Note: Lew choreographed the Dance of the Snowflakes and the Waltz of the Flowers; the rest was Willam's production.

36. *Hansel and Gretel*
Music: Engelbert Humperdinck
Premiere: 30 December 1951, Pacific Opera Company, War Memorial Opera House, San Francisco.

37. *American Scene*
Music: Carter Harman
Scenario: James Graham-Luján
Scenery and Costumes: Russell Hartley
Premiere: 14 September 1952, Stern Grove, San Francisco
Company: San Francisco Ballet
Cast: Mamma, Patricia Johnson; Papa, Leon Kalimos; Sister, Virginia Johnson; Sister, Nancy Demmler.

38. *Con Amore*
Music: Gioacchino Rossini, Overtures to *La Gazza Ladra*, *Il Signor Bruschino*, and *La Scala di Seta*.
Scenario: James Graham-Luján
Scenery and Costumes: James Bodrero
Premiere: 10 April 1953, Veterans Auditorium, San Francisco

Company: San Francisco Ballet
Cast: 18 dancers, including as Captain of the Amazons, Sally Bailey: The Bandit, Leon Danielian; The Lady, Nancy Johnson.

39. *The Festival*
Music: Wolfgang Amadeus Mozart
Costumes: Eloise Arnold
Premiere: 5 September 1953, Marin Dominican College, San Rafael, California. San Francisco Premiere: 13 September 1953, Stern Grove.
Company: San Francisco Ballet
Cast: 21 dancers, including Sally Bailey, Gordon Paxman, Nancy Demmler, Virginia Johnson, Conrad Ludlow, Leon Kalimos, Carlos Carvajal.

40. *Heuriger*
Music: Wolfgang Amadeus Mozart, *Les Petits Riens*, *German Dances*
Scenario: James Graham-Luján
Costumes: Eloise Arnold
Premiere: 10 April 1954, Memorial Auditorium, Stanford University, Stanford, California. San Francisco premiere: 30 April 1954.
Company: San Francisco Ballet
Cast: 22 dancers including as the Bride, Sally Bailey; Bridegroom, Gordon Paxman; Uncomfortable Conscience, Nancy Demmler; Temptation, Constance Coler.
Note: This work was a revised version of *The Festival*.

41. *The Dryad*
Music: Franz Schubert, Fantasy in F Minor, Opus 103, Orchestrated by Felix Mottl.
Scenario: James Graham-Luján
Costumes: Joseph St. Amand
Scenery: Dorothea Tanning
Additional Effects: Russell Hartley
Premiere: 28 April 1954, Berkeley Community Theater, Berkeley, California. San Francisco premiere: 29 April 1954.

Company: San Francisco Ballet
Cast: 21 dancers including: as The Dryad, Nancy Johnson; A Murdered Boy, Glen Chadwick; A Young Man, Gordon Paxman.

42. *Beauty and the Shepherd* (also called *A Masque of Beauty and the Shepherd*)
Music: Christoph Willibald Gluck
Costumes: Russell Hartley
Premiere: 29 August 1954, Stern Grove, San Francisco.
Cast: 20 dancers including: as Hera, Constance Coler; Athena, Bené Arnold; Aphrodite, Louise Lawler; Paris, Conrad Ludlow; Helen, Nancy Johnson.

43. *Lucia di Lammermoor*
Music: Gaetano Donizetti
Opening Night: 23 September 1954, San Francisco Opera, War Memorial Opera House, San Francisco.
Later Production: 15 September 1961.

44. *The Portuguese Inn*
Music: Luigi Cherubini
Opening Night: 24 September 1954, San Francisco Opera, War Memorial Opera House, San Francisco.

45. *Manon*
Music: Jules Massenet
Opening Night: 28 September 1954, San Francisco Opera, War Memorial Opera House, San Francisco.
Principal Dancers: Nancy Johnson, Sally Bailey, Gordon Paxman, Conrad Ludlow

46. *The Marriage of Figaro*
Music: Wolfgang Amadeus Mozart
Opening Night: 12 October 1954, San Francisco Opera, War Memorial Opera House, San Francisco.

47. *Joan of Arc at the Stake*, with Willam Christensen
Music: Arthur Honegger, *Jeanne D'Arc au Bûcher*

Opening Night: 15 October 1954, San Francisco Opera, War Memorial Opera House, San Francisco.

48. *The Nutcracker*
Music: Peter Ilyich Tchaikovsky
Scenario: James Graham-Luján, based on the E. T. A. Hoffmann story
Costumes and Scenery: Leonard Weisgard
Premiere: 18 December 1954, War Memorial Opera House, San Francisco
Company: San Francisco Ballet
Cast: Drosselmeyer, Gordon Paxman; Clara, Suki Schorer; King of the Mice, Carlos Carvajal; Snow Queen, Sally Bailey; Snow Prince, Gordon Paxman; Sugar Plum Fairy, Virginia Johnson; The Cavalier, Conrad Ludlow; Rose in Waltz of the Flowers, Nancy Johnson.

49. *Renard* (after George Balanchine)
Music: Igor Stravinsky
Scenario: Igor Stravinsky
Costumes and Scenery: Esteban Francés
Premiere: 19 May 1955, Ventura High School Auditorium, Ventura, California. San Francisco premiere (with voices): 28 May 1955, War Memorial Opera House.
Company: San Francisco Ballet
Cast: 4 dancers, 4 singers: The Fox, Conrad Ludlow; The Rooster, Carlos Carvajal; The Cat, Christine Bering; The Ram, Fiona Fuerstner.

50. *The Tarot*
Music: Peter Ilyich Tchaikovsky, *Mozartiana*
Costumes: Eloise Arnold
Premiere: 7 August 1955, Stern Grove, San Francisco
Company: San Francisco Ballet
Cast: 11 dancers, including Virginia Johnson, Fiona Fuerstner, Bené Arnold, Constance Coler, Nancy Johnson, Conrad Ludlow, Richard Carter, Carlos Carvajal.

51. *Louise*
Music: Gustave Charpentier
Opening Night: 23 September 1955, San Francisco Opera, War Memorial Opera House, San Francisco.
Principal Dancer: Nancy Johnson

52. *Don Giovanni*
Music: Wolfgang Amadeus Mozart
Opening Night: 30 September 1955, San Francisco Opera, War Memorial Opera House, San Francisco.
Later Productions: 16 October 1962.

53. *Andrea Chenier*
Music: Umberto Giordano
Opening Night: 4 October 1955, San Francisco Opera, War Memorial Opera House, San Francisco.
Principal Dancers: Nancy Johnson, Conrad Ludlow

54. *Emperor Norton*
Music: Vernon Duke (based in part on Jacques Offenbach)
Scenery and Costumes: Antonio Sotomayor
Special Costume Effects: Russell Hartley
Premiere: 8 November 1957, War Memorial Opera House, San Francisco.
Company: San Francisco Ballet
Cast: 22 dancers, including: as The Emperor, Gordon Paxman; Bummer, Matilda Abbe; Lazaruss, Suki Schorer.

55. *Lady of Shallott*
Music: Arthur Bliss
Scenario: Arthur Bliss, after the poem by Alfred, Lord Tennyson
Scenery and Costumes: Tony Duquette
Premiere: 2 May 1958, Hertz Hall, University of California, Berkeley, California. San Francisco premiere: 24 May 1958.
Company: San Francisco Ballet
Cast: 20 dancers, including: as The Lady of Shallott, Jocelyn Vollmar; Sir Lancelot, Richard Carter; Village Belle, Fiona Fuerstner; Red Knight, Kent Stowell.

56. *Beauty and the Beast*
Music: Peter Ilyich Tchaikovsky, arranged and orchestrated by Denis de Coteau and Earl Bernard Murray.
Scenery and Costumes: Tony Duquette
Premiere: 23 May 1958, War Memorial Opera House, San Francisco.
Company: San Francisco Ballet
Cast: 100 roles, including: as Beauty, Nancy Johnson; Beast-Prince, Richard Carter; Beauty's Father, Julien Herrin; Beauty's Sisters, Bené Arnold and Gerrie Bucher; Rose Waltz, Sally Bailey and Kent Stowell; Bird, Virginia Johnson; Stags, Jerome Brannin, Michael Smuin, Kent Stowell.

57. *Sinfonia*
Music: Luigi Boccherini, Symphony in A Major
Scenery and Costumes: Tony Duquette
Premiere: 6 January 1959, Hogan Junior High School Auditorium, Vallejo, California.
San Francisco Premiere: 19 December 1959, War Memorial Opera House.
Company: San Francisco Ballet
Cast: 20 dancers, including Fiona Fuerstner, Sally Bailey, Jocelyn Vollmar, Richard Carter.

58. *Divertissement D'Auber* (Pas de Trois)
Music: Daniel-François-Esprit Auber, from overtures to *Bronze Horse, Crown Diamonds, Fra Diavolo, Black Diamond.*
Costumes: Tony Duquette
Company: San Francisco Ballet
Premiere: 6 January 1959, Hogan Junior High School Auditorium, Vallejo, California.
San Francisco Premiere: 19 February 1960.
Cast: Jocelyn Vollmar, Richard Carter, Fiona Fuerstner

59. *Caprice*
Music: Franz von Suppé, from Overtures to *The Beautiful Galatea, Boccaccio,* and *Tantalusqualen.*
Scenery and Costumes: Tony Duquette

Premiere: 6 January 1959, Hogan Junior High School Audi-
torium, Vallejo, California.
San Francisco Premiere: 12 February 1960.
Company: San Francisco Ballet
Cast: 25 dancers, including Virginia Johnson, Jocelyn Vollmar,
Richard Carter.

60. *Danses Concertantes* (after George Balanchine)
Music: Igor Stravinsky, *Danses Concertantes*
Scenery and Costumes: Tony Duquette
Premiere: 13 October 1959, War Memorial Opera House, San
Francisco.
Company: San Francisco Ballet and San Francisco Opera
Cast: 22 dancers, including Nancy Johnson, Roderick Drew,
Sally Bailey, Kent Stowell, Jocelyn Vollmar, Richard Carter,
Virginia Johnson, Michael Smuin, Fiona Fuerstner, Julien
Herrin.

61. *Danza Brillante*
Music: Felix Mendelssohn, Octet in E Flat for Strings, Op. 20
Costumes: Tony Duquette
Premiere: 26 February 1960, Alcazar Theatre, San Francisco
Company: San Francisco Ballet
Cast: 20 dancers, including Jocelyn Vollmar, Sally Bailey,
Roderick Drew, Kent Stowell.

62. *Esmeralda: Pas de Deux*
Music: Cesare Pugni, from *Esmeralda*
Costumes: Antonio Sotomayor
Premiere: 11 March 1960, Alcazar Theatre, San Francisco
Company: San Francisco Ballet
Cast: Jocelyn Vollmar, Richard Carter

63. *Aïda*
Music: Giuseppe Verdi
Opening Night: 30 September 1960, San Francisco Opera, War
Memorial Opera House, San Francisco.

Principal Dancers: Jocelyn Vollmar, Sally Bailey, Roderick Drew, Julien Herrin.
Later Productions: 3 November 1961; Principal Dancers: Sally Bailey, Jocelyn Vollmar, Kent Stowell, Roderick Drew; 13 September 1963.

64. *Variations de Ballet*, with George Balanchine
N.B. This ballet was a reworking of Balanchine's *Pas de Dix*, presented earlier that year by SFB, with additional sections by Lew inserted.
Music: Alexander Glazounov, from *Raymonda*
Premiere: 11 October 1960, War Memorial Opera House, San Francisco.
Company: San Francisco Ballet
Cast: 20 dancers, including Jocelyn Vollmar, Roderick Drew, Sally Bailey, Julien Herrin.

65. *Così Fan Tutte*
Music: Wolfgang Amadeus Mozart
Opening Night: 9 November 1960, San Francisco Opera, War Memorial Opera House, San Francisco.

66. *Original Sin*
Music: John Lewis
Scenario: Kenneth Rexroth
Scenery and Costumes: John Furness
Premiere: 10 March 1961, Alcazar Theatre, San Francisco
Company: San Francisco Ballet
Cast: 17 dancers, including as Adam, Roderick Drew; Eve, Sally Bailey; Temptation, Michael Smuin; Raphael, Robert Gladstein; Lucifer, Robert Vickrey.

67. *St. George and the Dragon*
Music: Paul Hindemith, *Kammermusik No. 1 for Wind Quintet*
Scenery and Costumes: Maurine Simoneau
Premiere: 31 March 1961, Alcazar Theatre, San Francisco.
Company: San Francisco Ballet

Cast: 9 dancers, including as St. George, Kent Stowell, Frank Oman, Robert Gladstein; The Princess, Fiona Fuerstner, Virginia Johnson, Eugenia Van Horn; The Dragon, Michael Smuin, Terry Orr, Finis Jhung.

68. *Shadows*
Music: Paul Hindemith, *Educational Music for Instrumental Ensembles*, Op. 44, and *Trauermusik*
Premiere: Ballet '61, San Francisco Ballet Theater, San Francisco.
Company: San Francisco Ballet – Ballet '61.
Cast: 10 dancers, including Jocelyn Vollmar, Kent Stowell.

69. *Prokofiev Waltzes*
Music: Sergei Prokofief
Costumes: Maurine Simoneau
Premiere: 4 August 1961, San Francisco Ballet Theater, San Francisco.
Company: San Francisco Ballet – Ballet '61.
Cast: 8 dancers: Jocelyn Vollmar, Sally Bailey, Fiona Fuerstner, Virginia Johnson, Kent Stowell, Robert Gladstein, Finis Jhung, Terry Orr.

70. *Blood Moon*
Music: Norman Dello Joio
Opening Night: 18 September 1961, San Francisco Opera, War Memorial Opera House, San Francisco.
Principal Dancer: Roderick Drew

71. *Un Ballo in Maschera*
Music: Giuseppe Verdi
Opening Night: 12 October 1961, San Francisco Opera, War Memorial Opera House, San Francisco.

72. *Jest of Cards*
Music: Ernest Krenek, *Marginal Sounds*
Scenery and Costumes: Tony Duquette
Premiere: 17 April 1962, Geary Theatre, San Francisco.

Company: San Francisco Ballet
Cast: 25 dancers, including as The Joker, Michael Smuin; Fiona Fuerstner, Kent Stowell, Sally Bailey, Jocelyn Vollmar, Cynthia Gregory, Terry Orr, Virginia Johnson, Robert Gladstein.

73. *Bach Concert*
Music: Johann Sebastian Bach, Partita No. 2 in C Minor, Prelude for Lute, "Courante" from Suite No. 2 for 'Cello, "Adagio" and "Toccata" from Toccata in C Major.
Premiere: 10 August 1962, San Francisco Ballet Theater, San Francisco.
Company: San Francisco Ballet – Ballet '62
Cast: 15 dancers, including Sue Loyd, Cynthia Gregory, Jocelyn Vollmar, Robert Gladstein, Nancy Robinson.

74. *Faust*
Music: Charles Gounod
Opening Night: 25 September 1962, San Francisco Opera, War Memorial Opera House, San Francisco.

75. *The Daughter of the Regiment*
Music: Gaetano Donizetti; ballet music interpolated from Donizetti's *La Favorita*.
Opening Night: 18 October 1962, San Francisco Opera, War Memorial Opera House, San Francisco.
Principal Dancers: Jocelyn Vollmar, Robert Gladstein, Terry Orr

76. *Falstaff*
Music: Giuseppe Verdi
Opening Night: 23 October 1962, San Francisco Opera, War Memorial Opera House, San Francisco.

77. *Divertissement D'Auber* (II)
Note: This work was an expanded version of item #58, with the original pas de trois kept as the central section.
Music: François Esprit Auber, from Overtures to *Bronze Horse*, *Crown Diamonds*, *Fra Diavolo*, and *Black Domino*.

Costumes: Tony Duquette
Premiere: 4 February 1963, Phoenix Union High School
Auditorium, Phoenix, Arizona.
Company: San Francisco Ballet
Cast: 18 dancers, including Virginia Johnson, Terry Orr,
Cynthia Gregory.

78. *Fantasma*
Music: Sergei Prokofiev, Waltzes, Opus. 101, arranged by Lew
Christensen.
Scenery and Costumes: Tony Duquette
Premiere: 5 February 1963, University of Arizona Audito-
rium, Tucson, Arizona.
Company: San Francisco Ballet
Cast: 21 dancers, including: as the Wanderer, Robert
Gladstein; Mistress of the Mansion, Jocelyn Vollmar.

79. *Dance Variations*
Music: Vittorio Rieti
Premiere: 14 June 1963, San Francisco Ballet Theatre, San
Francisco.
Company: San Francisco Ballet – Ballet '63
Cast: Sue Loyd, Nancy Robinson, Cynthia Gregory, Ron
Poindexter, David Anderson, Henry Berg.

80. *La Sonnambula*
Music: Vincenzo Bellini
Opening Night: 14 September 1963, San Francisco Opera, War
Memorial Opera House, San Francisco.

81. *Mefistofele*
Music: Arrigo Boito
Opening Night: 19 September 1963, San Francisco Opera, War
Memorial Opera House, San Francisco.

82. *Samson et Delilah*
Music: Camille Saint-Saëns
Opening Night: 26 September 1963, San Francisco Opera, War
Memorial Opera House, San Francisco.

83. *Queen of Spades*
Music: Peter Ilyich Tchaikovsky
Opening Night: 1 October 1963, San Francisco Opera, War Memorial Opera House, San Francisco.

84. *Seven Deadly Sins*, by George Balanchine, revised by Lew Christensen.
Music: Kurt Weill
Scenario: Bertholt Brecht, translated by W. H. Auden and Chester Kallman.
Scenery and Costumes: Reuben Ter Arutunian
Premiere: 9 April 1964, Geary Theater, San Francisco.
Company: San Francisco Ballet
Cast, singers: Anna I, Nina Foch; Mother, Sam Resnick, bass; Father, Milton Williams, bass; Brother I, Thomas Hageman, tenor; Brother II, Patrick Dougherty, tenor.
Cast, dancers: 26 including, as Anna II, Cynthia Gregory.

85. *Life: A Do-It-Yourself Disaster (A Pop Art Ballet)*
Music: Charles Ives, *Halloween* and *The Pond*
Scenario: Herb Caen
Scenery and Costumes: Cal Anderson
Premiere: 30 January 1965, War Memorial Opera House, San Francisco.
Company: San Francisco Ballet
Cast: 28 dancers, including: Incipiency, Barbara Begany and Salicia Smith; Virility, Lynda Meyer and David Anderson; Maturity, Jocelyn Vollmar and Gerald Leavitt; Resignation, Gerald Leavitt.

86. *Lucifer*, also known as *Concert Music for Strings and Brass Instruments*
Music: Paul Hindemith, *Concert Music for Strings and Brass*, Op. 50.
Scenery and Costumes: Reuben Ter Arutunian
Premiere: 20 February 1965, War Memorial Opera House, San Francisco.
Company: San Francisco Ballet

Cast: 18 dancers, including: as Lucifer, R. Clinton Rothwell; St. Michael, David Anderson.

87. *Pas de Six*
Music: Hans Christian Lumbye, *Frederick VII March, Britta Polka, Columbine Polka Mazurka, Concerto Polka for Two Violins,* and *Salute for August Bournonville Galop.*
Costumes: Robert O'Hearn
Premiere: 1 May 1966, Hilmar High School Auditorium, Merced, California. San Francisco premiere: 8 April 1967, War Memorial Opera House.
Company: San Francisco Ballet
Cast: Sue Loyd, Jocelyn Vollmar, Sally Bailey, Robert Gladstein, David Anderson, Lee Fuller.

88. *Symphony in D*
Music: Luigi Cherubini
Scenery and Costumes: Robert O'Hearn
Premiere: 4 March 1967, War Memorial Opera House, San Francisco
Company: San Francisco Ballet
Cast: 32 dancers, including Lynda Meyer, Henry Berg, Sue Loyd, David Coll.

89. *Il Distratto*
Music: Franz Josef Haydn, Symphony No. 60 in C, "Il Distratto"
Costumes: David Barnard
Premiere: 4 August 1967, San Francisco Ballet Theater, San Francisco.
Company: San Francisco Ballet – Ballet '67
Cast: 15 dancers including Jocelyn Vollmar, Ingrid Fraley, Patricia Garland, Cynthia Quick, Krista Scholter, Wendy Holt, Gina Ness, Allyson Segeler, Catherine Warner, Sally Bailey.

90. *Nutcracker* (a new production)
Music: Peter Ilyich Tchaikovsky
Scenery and Costumes: Robert O'Hearn

Premiere: 12 December 1967, War Memorial Opera House, San Francisco
Company: San Francisco Ballet
Number of roles: 191
Cast: Drosselmeyer, Henry Kersh; His Assistant, Harold Christensen, Jr.; Clara, Bridget Mullins; King of the Mice, William Johnson; Queen of Snow, Virginia Johnson; King of Snow, David Coll; Sugar Plum Fairy, Melissa Hayden (guest artist); Cavalier, Jacques D'Amboise (guest artist); Rose, Waltz of the Flowers, Lynda Meyer.

91. *Three Movements for the Short Haired*
Music: John Lewis, *Sketch, England's Carol*, and *Golden Striker*
Costumes: Kageyama
Premiere: 14 May 1968, Presentation Theater, San Francisco
Company: San Francisco Ballet – Ballet '68
Cast: 10 dancers including Jon Engstrom, David Coll, Kenneth Lipitz, Sven Norlander.

92. *The Magical Flutist*
Music: Amilcare Ponchielli, Quartet in B Flat Major for Winds with Piano.
Costumes: Kageyama
Premiere: 10 July 1968, Norse Auditorium, San Francisco
Company: San Francisco Ballet – Ballet '68
Cast: Virginia Johnson, David Coll, Lynda Meyer

93. *Airs de Ballet*
Music: André Grétry, from *Zémire et Azor*.
Costumes: Robert O'Hearn
Premiere: 26 May 1971, Palace of Fine Arts Theater, San Francisco
Company: San Francisco Ballet
Cast: Violette Verdy (guest artist), Philippe Arrona, Sara Maule, Laurence Matthews, Susan Williams.

94. *Ariodante*
Music: George Frideric Handel

Opening Night: 14 September 1971, John F. Kennedy Center for the Performing Arts.

95. *Tingel-Tangel-Taenze*
Music: Johann Strauss, Jr. & Sr., Josef Strauss, and Hans Christian Lumbye
Costumes: Robert O'Hearn
Scenery: Robert Darling
Premiere: 8 March 1972, Palace of Fine Arts Theater, San Francisco
Company: San Francisco Ballet
Cast: 14 dancers including Lynda Meyer, Philippe Arrona, Victoria Gyorfi, John McFall.

96. *Cinderella* (with Michael Smuin)
Music: Sergei Prokofiev
Scenery and Costumes: Robert Fletcher
Premiere: 6 June 1973, War Memorial Opera House, San Francisco
Company: San Francisco Ballet
Number of roles: 88
Cast: Cinderella, Lynda Meyer; Prince, Vane Vest; Father, Gary Moore; Mother, Anita Paciotti; Fairy Godmother, Paula Tracy; Jester, John McFall; Sisters, Anton Ness and Daniel Simmons.

97. *Don Juan*
Music: Joaquin Rodrigo, *Concierto de Aranjuez*, *Fantasia para u Gentilhombre.*
Scenery: Ming Cho Lee
Costumes: José Varona
Premiere: 10 June 1973, War Memorial Opera House, San Francisco
Company: San Francisco Ballet
Cast: 30 dancers, including: as Don Juan, Attila Ficzere; Catalinon, Daniel Simmons; Dona Ana, Diana Weber; Commander, Robert Gladstein.

98. *Stravinsky Pas de Deux* (Also known as *Four Norwegian Moods*)
Music: Igor Stravinsky, *Four Norwegian Moods*
Costumes: Patricia Polen
Premiere: 10 April 1976, Orpheum Theater, San Francisco
Company: San Francisco Ballet
Cast: Susan Magno, Keith Martin

99. *The Ice Maiden*
Music: Igor Stravinsky, *Le Baiser de la Fée*
Scenery and Costumes: José Varona
Premiere: 6 January 1977, War Memorial Opera House, San Francisco
Company: San Francisco Ballet
Cast: 38 dancers, including: as the Ice Maiden, Betsy Erickson; Groom, Tomm Ruud; Bride, Susan Magno.

100. *Scarlatti Portfolio*
Music: Domenico Scarlatti, Sonatas L. 58, L. 465, L. 382, L. 104, L. 64, L. 282, L. 499, orchestrated by Benjamin Lees.
Scenery: Cal Anderson
Costumes: Sandra Woodall
Premiere: 15 March 1979, War Memorial Opera House, San Francisco
Company: San Francisco Ballet
Cast: 16 dancers, including: as Arlequin, David McNaughton; Columbine, Diana Weber; Franceschina, Vane Vest; Isabella, Lynda Meyer; Lucretia, Tina Santos; Pulcinella, John McFall; Pantalone, Anton Ness; Coviello, Jerome Weiss.

101. *Vivaldi Concerto Grosso*
Music: Antonio Vivaldi, Concerto Grosso, Op. 3, No. 11
Costumes: Sandra Woodall
Premiere: 27 February 1981, Blaisdell Concert Hall, Honolulu. San Francisco Premiere: 14 April 1981, War Memorial Opera House.
Company: San Francisco Ballet
Cast: 14 dancers, including Betsy Erickson, Jim Sohm.

# SELECTED BIBLIOGRAPHY

## Interviews and Letters

Tapes and/or transcripts of most of the interviews listed are on deposit at the San Francisco Performing Arts Library and Museum; the remainder are in the author's possession or belong to the Dance Collection of the New York Public Library at Lincoln Center. Interviews noted as being for the KQED Documentary may be found at the San Francisco Performing Arts Library and Museum under the listing "Christensen TV Documentary." The documentary, by Stephen Cobbett Steinberg, was entitled "Lew Christensen: The Triumph of American Dance," and was first aired May 6, 1985.

Abravanel, Maurice. Interview with author. Salt Lake City, Utah. November 25, 1987.

Anderson, Cal. Interview with author. San Francisco, California. December 1, 1988.

Arnold, Bené. Interview with author. Salt Lake City, Utah. August 29, 1989.

Bailey, Sally. Telephone interview with author. October 25, 1989.

Barker, Barbara. Telephone conversation with author. November 20, 1989.

Barzel, Ann. Interview with author. Winston-Salem, North Carolina. February 15, 1988.

Behunin, Alan. Telephone interview with author. October 7, 1991.

Billings, Delome S. Interview with author. Bountiful, Utah. April 23, 1988.

Boris, Ruthanna. Telephone interviews with author. August 4, 1988, and October 7, 1988. Letter to author. July 28, 1988.

Burr, Mary Corruthers. Interview with author. Monterrey, California. December 7, 1987.

Caldwell, Bruce. Telephone interview with author. May 2, 1991.

Carter, Nancy (Texas Christian University). Letter to author. April 26, 1989.

Carter, Richard. Interview with author. San Francisco, California. March 7, 1988. Telephone interview with author. December 6, 1988.

Christensen, Chris. Interview with author. San Bruno, California, December 9, 1987. Telephone interview with author. November 20, 1991. Letters to author. April 4, 1992, and November 15, 1996.

Christensen, Florence. Interview with author. Salt Lake City, Utah. October 21, 1991.

Christensen, Gisella Caccialanza. Interviews with author. San Bruno, California. September 28–30, 1987; December 5 and 9, 1987; and March 7, 1988.

Christensen, Gisella Caccialanza. Interview by Stephen Cobbett Steinberg for KQED Documentary. No date.

Christensen, Harold. Interviews with author. San Anselmo, California. September 22, 23, 25, and 26, 1987, and December 4, 1987.

Christensen, Harold. Interview for KQED Documentary. No date.

Christensen, Harold, and Ruby Asquith. Interview with author. San Anselmo, California. March 2, 1988.

Christensen, Harold, and Ruby Asquith. Interview by Barbara Cohen. San Anselmo, California. December 29, 1976.

Christensen, Lew. Interview by Craig Palmer for KQED Documentary. No date.

Christensen, Lew, Harold, and Willam; Gisella Caccialanza; and Ruby Asquith. Interview by Francis Mason, Donald McDonagh, and Don Daniels. New York, New York. Spring 1984.

Christensen, Ruby Asquith. Interview with author. San Anselmo, California. September 26, 1987. Telephone interviews with author. November 14, 1990, and May 10, 1991.

Christensen, Ruby Asquith. Interview for KQED Documentary. No date.

Christensen, Willam F. Interviews with author. Salt Lake City, Utah. February 20, March 9, March 27, April 10, April 17, April 24, May 1, and November 20, 1987; July 2 and December 16, 1988; and January 4, 1989. Conversations with author. Salt Lake City, Utah. April 27, 1987; March 25, 1988.

Christensen, Willam F. Interviews with Don McDonagh. Salt Lake City, Utah. February 26–28 and March 1, 1986.

Christensen, Willam F. Interview with Robert J. Welsh. Salt Lake City, Utah. October 9, 1979.

Christensen, Willam F. Interview for KQED Documentary. No date.

Cohen-Stratyner, Barbara. Conversation with author. New York, New York. September 13, 1988.

Collins, Josephine McKendrick. Interview with author. Provo, Utah. September 1, 1987. Telephone conversation with author. April 4, 1988.

D'Amboise, Jacques. Interview with author. New York, New York. January 12, 1989.

Danieli, Fred. Interview with Peter Conway. January–April, 1979. Oral History Project Typescript. Dance Collection. The New York Public Library.

De Coteau, Denis. Interview with author. San Francisco, California. March 1, 1988.

De Mille, Agnes. Letter to author. December 3, 1989.

Deakin, Natasha. Telephone interview with author. July 5, 1991.

Duncan, Timothy. Telephone interview with author. November 5, 1991.

Erskine, Janet Reed. Telephone interview with author. November 5, 1988.

Gavers, Mattlyn. Telephone interviews with author. November 8, 10, and 11, and December 8, 1988.

Gladstein, Robert. Interview with author. San Francisco, California. November 30, 1988.

Graham-Luján, James. Interview with author. San Francisco, California. March 4, 1988. Telephone interview with author. July 29, 1991. Letter to author. September 4, 1991.

Graham-Luján, James. Interviews with Steven Cobbett Steinberg and Nancy Johnson. San Francisco, California. June to December, 1985.

Gregory, Cynthia. Interview with author. New York, New York. January 10, 1989.

Hamblin, Barbara. Telephone interview with author. November 29, 1989.

Hawkins, Erick. Interview with author. New York, New York. May 25, 1988.

Hayes, Elizabeth. Interview with author. Salt Lake City, Utah. November 15, 1988.

James, Janice. Telephone interview with author. October 9, 1991.

Jhung, Finis. Interview with author. New York, New York. May 16, 1988.

Johnson, Nancy. Interviews with author. San Francisco, California. December 9 and 11, 1987.

Johnson, Virginia. Interview with author. Corte Madera, California. March 2, 1988.

Jolley, Jay. Interview with author. London, England. June 22, 1989.

Kalimos, Leon. Telephone interview with author. December 28 and 30, 1988.

Kirstein, Lincoln. Interview with author. New York, New York. January 14, 1988.

LeBlond, Richard E., Jr. Telephone interview with author. March 9 and 14, 1988.

Lowry, W. McNeil. Interviews with author. New York, New York. May 9 and 24, and September 16, 1988.

Ludlow, Conrad. Telephone interview with author. September 19, 1991.

Ludwig, James. Interview with author. San Francisco, California. December 2, 1988.

Marks, Bruce. Telephone interview with author. November 7, 1989.

Meyer, Lynda. Telephone interview with author. October 27, 1989.

Mullowny, Kathryn. Interview with Victoria Huckenpahler. Oral History Project Typescript. Dance Collection. The New York Public Library.

Murray, Earl. Interview with author. San Francisco, California. November 29, 1988.

Paxman, Gordon. Interview with author. Salt Lake City, Utah. November 22, 1988. Telephone interview with author. November 29, 1989.

Phinney, Ernest. Telephone interview with author. November 11, 1991.

Samuel, Gerhard. Telephone interview with author. January 2, 1989.

Schorer, Suki. Interview with author. New York, New York. May 13, 1988.

Schumacher, Jacqueline Martin. Telephone Interview with author. July 26, 1991.

Selznick, Roxanne Christensen. Interview with author. Salt Lake City, Utah. August 27, 1990.

Smuin, Michael. Interview for KQED Documentary. No date.

Starbuck, James. Interview with author. Beverly Hills, California. October 15, 1988.

Stowell, Kent. Telephone interview with author. December 23, 1988.

Sugai, Sondra. Telephone interview with author. November 1, 1989.

Thomson, Virgil. Transcript of interview with John Gruen. 1977. Dance Collection. The New York Public Library.

Tolan, Roy. Telephone interview with author. November 11, 1991.

Vasquez, Roland. Interview with author. New York, New York. May 21, 1988.

Vaughan, David. Telephone conversation with author. May 26, 1988.

Vollmar, Jocelyn. Interviews with author. San Francisco, California. March 1 and 3, 1988.

Walker, Katherine Sorley. Telephone conversation with author. London, June 13, 1989.

Watts, Ardean. Interview with author. Salt Lake City, Utah. December 16, 1988.

Weisberger, Barbara. Telephone interview with author. January 2, 1989.

**Ephemera**

American Ballet Caravan Clipping Files. Dance Collection. The New York Public Library.

American Ballet Caravan Scrapbooks: Clippings, Announcements. Microfilm, Box 1 (1933–1941), Box 2 (1941–1942). Dance Collection. The New York Public Library.

Christensen Brothers Clipping File. Billy Rose Theatre Collection. The New York Public Library.

Christensen Family Papers and Scrapbooks. In the possession of Delome Sorenson Billings. Bountiful, Utah. Copies of many of these family documents are also on deposit at the San Francisco Performing Arts Library and Museum.

Christensen–Caccialanza Collection. San Francisco Performing Arts Library and Museum.

*Con Amore* Clipping File. Dance Collection. The New York Public Library.

*Filling Station* Clipping File. Dance Collection. The New York Public Library.

Gisella Caccialanza Christensen Clipping File. Dance Collection. The New York Public Library.

Grant Files. Ford Foundation Archives. Ford Foundation. New York City, New York.

Irving Deakin Correspondence. Dance Collection. The New York Public Library.

Janet Reed Scrapbook. Dance Collection. The New York Public Library.

Letters from Willam F. Christensen to Mignon Lee Christensen. In the possession of Willam F. Christensen. Salt Lake City, Utah.

Lew Christensen Clipping File. Dance Collection. The New York Public Library.

*Liberty Jones* Clipping File. Billy Rose Theatre Collection. The New York Public Library.

Lillian Moore Correspondence with Harold Christensen. Dance Collection. The New York Public Library.

Programs of Ballet Society and New York City Ballet, 1946–1955. Dance Collection. The New York Public Library.

Russell Hartley Scrapbooks. San Francisco Performing Arts Library and Museum.

San Francisco Ballet Clipping File. Dance Collection. The New York Public Library.

San Francisco Ballet School papers. San Francisco Performing Arts Library and Museum.

"San Francisco Opera Ballet Scores," Press poster with reviews, 1940–1941 season. In the personal collection of Willam F. Christensen. Salt Lake City, Utah.

Unions Clipping File. Dance Collection. The New York Public Library.

Utah Ballet Archives. MS 247. Special Collections. University of Utah Marriott Library. Salt Lake City, Utah.

Willam F. Christensen Clipping File. Dance Collection. The New York Public Library.

## Visual Works

*I Was An Adventuress*. Twentieth-Century Fox. 1940.

*Insight: Willam F. Christensen*. Salt Lake City, Utah. KUED. November 18, 1987.

Steinberg, Stephen Cobbett. *Lew Christensen: The Triumph of American Dance*. San Francisco, California. KQED. May 6, 1985.

## Books, Articles, and Manuscripts

Altrocchi, Julia Cooley. *The Spectacular San Franciscans*. New York: E. P. Dutton and Company, 1949.

Amberg, George. *Ballet: The Emergence of an American Art*. New York: New American Library, Mentor Books, 1953.

"America's First Civic Ballet." *American Dancer*, April 1942, 9.

Anderson, Jack. *The Nutcracker Ballet.* New York: Mayflower Books, 1979.

———. *The One and Only: The Ballet Russe de Monte Carlo.* New York: Dance Horizons, 1981.

———. "There's More Than Sand and Sagebrush Here!" *Dance Magazine*, August 1967, 42–45, 72.

Arrington, Leonard J. "Cooperative Community in the North: Brigham City, Utah." *Utah Historical Quarterly* 33.3 (Summer 1965): 198–217.

Atkinson, Brooks. "Opening of 'The Great Waltz' in the Center Theatre of the Rockefeller Group." *New York Times*, September 24, 1934.

"Ballet's Summer Stars." *Newsweek*, July 17, 1937, 30.

Baltazar, Beatrice de. "Westward the Ballet." *Dance*, September 1947, 22–25, 40–41.

Barrett, Dorothy. "The Three Brothers Christensen." *Dance*, October 1943, 7, 29.

Barzel, Ann. "European Dance Teachers in the United States." *Dance Index* 3 (April–June, 1944): 56–100.

———. "A Gallery of American Dancers: Lew Christensen." *Dance*, June 1942, 12–13, 36.

Beaumont, Cyril. *Complete Book of Ballets.* New York: G. P. Putnam's Sons, 1938.

———. *Supplement to Complete Book of Ballets.* London: C. W. Beaumont, 1942.

Bernheimer, Martin. "A Silly San Francisco Sampler." *Los Angeles Times*, July 27, 1984.

Billings, Frank Jack. "Utah's First Inaugural." *Salt Lake Tribune*, January 23, 1977.

Bitton, Davis. "'These Licentious Days': Dancing among the Mormons." *Sunstone* 2.1 (Spring 1977): 16–27.

Bloomfield, Arthur J. *The San Francisco Opera, 1923–1961.* New York: Appleton-Century-Crofts, 1961.

"Le Boeuf sur le toit." *Drama Review* 16.3 (September 1972): 27–45.

Born, George. "Unique in the U.S.–San Francisco Ballet and School." *Opera and Concert*, February 1947, 13.

Boyer, Richard O. "A Reporter at Large: Americans Dance, Too." *New Yorker*, June 11, 1938, 30–37.

Brinson, Peter, and Clement Crisp. *The Pan Book of Ballet and Dance*. London: Pan Books, 1970.

Brubach, Holly. "Room Enough to Move." *Atlantic Monthly*, May 1988, 62–74.

Buckle, Richard, and John Taras. *George Balanchine: Ballet Master*. New York: Random House, 1988.

*Choreography by George Balanchine: A Catalogue of Works*. New York: Viking, 1984.

Christensen, Frederic. "The West's Own Association of Dancing Masters." *American Dancer*, August 1927, 26.

Christensen, Lew. "Story and Story-less Ballets." *Dance Magazine*, July 1956, 24–25.

———. "Tribute in Concrete." *San Francisco Ballet Magazine*, November 1983, 4.

Christensen, Willam. "The Opportunity Is Close at Hand." *Dance*, November 1946, 12, 35–36.

Chujoy, Anatole. *Civic Ballet*. New York: Dance News, 1958.

———. *The New York City Ballet: The First Twenty Years*. New York: Alfred A. Knopf, 1953. Reprint. New York: Da Capo Press, 1982.

Cohen, Barbara Naomi. "Chain Prologs: Dance at the Picture Palaces." *Dance Scope* 13.1 (Fall 1978): 12–23.

Cole, Diana Muriel. "Utah Ballet – A Unique Development in the World of Dance." M.A. thesis, University of Utah, 1971.

Coray, John Louis. "Emma Lucy Gates (Bowen), Soprano." M.A. thesis, Brigham Young University, 1956.

Croce, Arlene. *Going to the Dance*. New York: Alfred A. Knopf, 1982.

Cushing, Maxine. "Dance on the Pacific Coast." *Dance Observer* 5 (June–July 1938): 91.

"Dance: City Exchange." *Newsweek*, April 20, 1953.

Danieli, Fred. "For Five Months...The American Ballet in South America." Dance Collection, The New York Public Library.

"Deck of Dancing Cards." *Life*, June 8, 1962, 91.

DeMeglio, John E. *Vaudeville U.S.A.* Bowling Green, Ohio: Bowling Green University Popular Press, 1973.

Dorris, George. "The Legacy of Hurok." *Ballet Review* 5.1 (1975–76): 78–88.

Dunning, Jennifer. *"But First a School."* New York: Viking, 1985.

Durham, Lowell. *Abravanel!* Salt Lake City: University of Utah Press, 1989.

"Early Organization of West's Association Is Urged." *American Dancer*, January 1928, 16, 27.

Evans, Marilyn Rae. "The History of the San Francisco Ballet Company from Its Beginnings through 1951." M.A. thesis, University of Utah, 1960.

"Ford Foundation Controversy Pros and Cons." *Dance Magazine*, February 1964, 34–37, 82.

"Foreign Genius and Native Talent." *Dance Magazine*, July 1973, 58B–63.

Forsberg, Helen. "Brothers Christensen Plan Working Reunion." *Salt Lake Tribune*, June 18, 1978.

Forsgren, Lydia Walker, ed. *History of Box Elder County*. Utah: [ca. 1937].

Frankenstein, Alfred. "The San Francisco Ballet." *Dance Magazine*, April 1955, 16–21, 65.

Franks, A. H., ed. *Ballet: A Decade of Endeavor*. London: Burke Publishing, 1955; rpt. New York: Da Capo Press, 1981.

Graham-Luján, James. "Gisella Caccialanza: A Tribute." *Encore* 3.4 (Winter 1986/87): 4–9.

———. "Lew Christensen: Music, Wit and Theatre." *Impulse*. San Francisco: Impulse Publications, 1955.

———. "The San Francisco Ballet." *Dance News Annual 1953* (New York: Alfred A. Knopf): 145–57.

Gruen, John. "Smuin Sets Sail on Broadway." *Dance Magazine*, January 1988, 52–57.

Harding, James. *The Ox on the Roof*. London: Macdonald, 1972.

Harris, Dale. "America on Its Toes: The Best Regional Ballet." *Town and Country*, November 1988, 235–42.

Harris, Michael. "The San Francisco Ballet Makes a Leap Forward." *State of the Arts in San Francisco*, A Special

Series Reprinted from the *San Francisco Examiner*, 1986, 16–20.

Harrison, Conrad B. *Five Thousand Concerts: A Commemorative History of the Utah Symphony.* Salt Lake City: Utah Symphony Society, 1986.

Hartley, Russell. *The San Francisco Ballet: A History, 1922–1977.* Unpublished manuscript. San Francisco Performing Arts Library and Museum.

Haskel, Arnold L. *The Ballet Annual.* Vol I. London: Adam and Charles Black, 1947.

Hey, Nigel S. "Professor in Ballet Slippers." *Dance Magazine,* May 1963, 48–52.

Hicks, Michael. *Mormonism and Music.* Urbana: University of Chicago Press, 1989.

Howard, Ruth Eleanor. *The Story of the American Ballet.* New York: Ihra Publishing Company, 1936.

———, ed. *Dancer's Almanac and Who's Who.* New York: Dancer's Almanac and Who's Who, 1940.

Huck, William. "Jinx" and "Scarlatti Porfolio." *Performing Arts: The Theatre and Music Magazine for California and Texas.* San Francisco Ballet Program Magazine 2.1 (Programs I & II, Programs III & IV, January 1988): 16.

Hughes, Allen. "The San Francisco Ballet Grows Rapidly." *New York Times,* May 5, 1963.

Hurok, Sol. *S. Hurok Presents: A Memoir of the Dance World.* New York: Hermitage House, 1953.

Hurok, Sol, and Ruth Goode. *Impresario.* New York: Random House, 1946.

"An Informal Interview with Lew Christensen." *Dance Digest,* February 1958, 49–54; March 1958, 106–11.

Jowitt, Deborah. "Ford vs. the Press." *Dance Critics Association News,* Fall 1989, 4, 14.

Kendall, Elizabeth. *Dancing: A Ford Foundation Report.* New York: Ford Foundation, 1983.

———. *Where She Danced: The Birth of American Art Dance.* Berkeley: University of California Press, 1979.

Kirstein, Lincoln. *Ballet: Bias and Belief, Three Pamphlets Collected and Other Dance Writings of Lincoln Kirstein.* New York: Dance Horizons, 1983.

——. *Thirty Years: The New York City Ballet.* New York: Alfred A. Knopf, 1978.

Kupferberg, Herbert. "Christensen and Smuin Tell Plans for 'New Look' in San Francisco." *Dance News*, March 1973, 1, 6.

Larkin, Robert W. "Turning Ice Skates into Dance Shoes." *New York Times*, July 24, 1977.

Laurie, Joe, Jr. *Vaudeville: From the Honky-Tonks to the Palace.* New York: Henry Holt and Company, 1953.

Leaf, Earl. "Crashing Cecchetti's Class." *Dance*, June 1945, 14.

LeBlond, Richard E., Jr., with Meg Madden. *From Chaos to Fragility: My Years at the San Francisco Ballet Association.* Dubuque, Iowa: Kendall/Hunt Publishing Co., 1988.

Leivick, Laura. "San Francisco Ballet Turns Fifty." *Dance Magazine*, February 1983, 552–60.

"Letters from the Maestro: Enrico Cecchetti to Gisella Caccialanza." *Dance Perspectives*, No. 45 (Spring 1971). Ed. Sally Bailey. Trans. Gisella Caccialanza.

Lowry, W. McNeil. "Conversations with Balanchine." *New Yorker*, September 12, 1983, 52–88.

——. "Conversations with Kirstein – I" and "Conversations with Kirstein – II." *New Yorker*, December 15 and 22, 1986.

——, ed. *The Performing Arts and American Society.* Englewood Cliffs, N.J.: Prentice-Hall, 1978.

MacColl, E. Kimbark. *The Growth of a City: Power and Politics in Portland, Oregon.* Portland: The Georgian Press, 1979.

Magriel, Paul, and Don McDonagh. "A Conversation with Marie-Jeanne." *Ballet Review* 12.4 (Winter 1985): 58–73.

Martin, John. "The American Ballet." *New York Times*, October 22, 1933.

——. "Group from the American Ballet Organizes Summer Tour." *New York Times*, June 28, 1936.

——. "Stravinsky Leads Ballet Premiere." *New York Times*, April 28, 1937.

Maynard, Olga. "Ballet West: Moving into the Majors." *Dance Magazine*, February 1979, 79–87.

———. "A Christensen Seminar." *Dance Magazine*, November 1978: 76–78.

———. "The Christensens: An American Dance Dynasty." *Dance Magazine*, June 1973: 43–56.

———. *Thirty Years: Lincoln Kirstein's The New York City Ballet*. New York: Alfred A. Knopf, 1978.

McLeod, Beth Witrogen. "Gisella Caccialanza Christensen: A Ballet Legend." *San Francisco Gazette*, September 1987, 19.

Mellen, Leona Lucile. "History of the Dancing Masters of America, Inc." *Forward* 18 (November 1930): 5–7.

Milton, Paul R. "Organization in the Dance Field." *Proceedings of the First National Dance Congress and Festival*. New York, 1936.

Moore, Lillian. "American Notes." *Dancing Times*, March 1947, 298.

Newman, Barbara. "Lew Christensen." In *Striking a Balance: Dancers Talk about Dancing*. London: Elm Tree Books, 1982.

Older, Cora. *San Francsico, Magic City*. New York: Longmans, Green & Co., 1961.

Olsen, Erna Persch. "An Historical Study of Physical Education for Women at the University of Utah." M.A. thesis, University of Utah, 1949.

Palmer, Winthrop. *Theatrical Dancing in America: The Development of the Ballet from 1900*. 2d ed. South Brunswick and New York: A. S. Barnes and Co., 1978.

"Passing of Vaudeville," *Variety*, September 21, 1927.

Payne, Charles. *American Ballet Theatre*. New York: Alfred A. Knopf, 1978.

"Petaluma, Ballet, Business, America." *New Thesaurus* [Petaluma, California], Summer 1979.

Renouf, Renée. "Lew Christensen Reminisces." *Dance News*, November 1978, 5, 7.

———. "San Francisco's Ballet." *Dancing Times*, August 1981, 760–61.

Reynolds, Nancy. *Repertory in Review: Forty Years of the New York City Ballet*. New York: Dial Press, 1977.

Ries, Frank W. D. "Albertina Rasch: The Broadway Career." *Dance Chronicle* 6.2 (1983): 95–37.

———. "Albertina Rasch: The Concert Career and the Concept of the American Ballet." *Dance Chronicle* 7.2 (1984): 159–97.

———. "Albertina Rasch: The Hollywood Career." *Dance Chronicle* 6.4 (1984), 281–362.

Rockefeller Panel Report. *The Performing Arts: Problems and Prospects*. New York: McGraw-Hill, 1965.

Ross, Janice. "San Francisco Ballet: The California Dream at Sixty." *Dance Magazine*, February 1993, 56–61.

Rozow, Michael, Jr. "The General Formulation and Summarization of Ballet West U.S.A.'s 1971 European Tour." M.A. thesis, University of Utah, 1972.

Russell, Frank. "First Municipally Sponsored Civic Ballet in Formal Debut." *Opera and Concert*, November 1947, 8.

Sabin, Robert. "Hurok: Adventurer in the Arts." *Dance Magazine*, January 1964, 40–46, 74.

Samuels, Charles and Louise. *Once Upon a Stage: The Merry World of Vaudeville*. New York: Dodd, Mead and Company, 1964.

"San Francisco." *Dancing Times*, January 1948, 195.

San Francisco Ballet Association Three Year Plan, Fiscal '89 to '91. Helgi Tomasson and George B. James, Chairmen, Board of Trustees. September 26, 1988. Appendix A: Brief History of San Francisco Ballet.

"San Francisco Ballet Company." *American Dancer*, April 1945, 10–11.

Sawyer-Lauçanno, Christopher. *An Invisible Spectator: A Biography of Paul Bowles*. New York: Weidenfeld and Nicolson, 1989.

Seltsam, William H., comp. *Metropolitan Opera Annals: A Chronicle of Artists and Performances*. New York: H. W. Wilson Company, 1947.

Siegel, Marcia B. *The Shapes of Change: Images of American Dance*. Boston: Houghton Mifflin Co., 1979.

Sowell, Debra Hickenlooper. "Theatrical Dancing in the Territory of Utah, 1848–1868." *Dance Chronicle* 1.2 (1977–78): 96–126.

Staver, Frederick Lee. "San Francisco Ballet Goes Touring." *Dance*, June 1940, 36.

Steinberg, Cobbett. "Gisella Caccialanza: A Chronology." *Encore* 3.4 (Winter 1986/87): 10–19.

———. *San Francisco Ballet: The First Fifty Years*. San Francisco: The San Francisco Ballet Association, 1983.

Stowe, Dorothy. "An 'Institution' Speaks Up." *Deseret News*, September 16, 1982.

Taper, Bernard. *Balanchine: A Biography*. Rev. ed. New York: Macmillan Publishing Co., 1974.

Terry, Walter. "Four New Dance Organizations Sprout Both Here and Abroad." *New York Herald Tribune*, July 6, 1947.

———. "Initial Ballet Society Works Stress Variety of Form, Style." *New York Herald Tribune*, January 19, 1947.

Thompson, Oscar. "New Stravinsky Ballet Achieves World Premiere." *Musical America*, May 10, 1937.

Thomson, Virgil. *Virgil Thomson*. New York: Alfred A. Knopf, 1967.

Ullrich, Allan. "The Woman Who Shares the Lew Christensen Tribute. *San Francisco Examiner and Chronicle*, April 28, 1985.

"Utah Association Reports on Work." *American Dancer*, February 1928, 26.

Von Buchau, Stephanie. "Native Dancer." *Ballet News*, May 1982, 26.

Wade, Ruthella. "Ballet in America, 1939–45: A Check List." In *The Ballet Annual*, edited by Arnold L. Haskell. London: Adam and Charles Black, 1947.

Walker, Katherine Sorley. *De Basil's Ballets Russes*. London: Hutchinson, 1982.

Werner, M. R. *Brigham Young*. New York: Harcourt, Brace & Company, 1925.

White, Susan. "Utah Civic Ballet and Ballet West: A Preliminary Study, 1964–1976." M.A. thesis, University of Utah, 1982.

Wilk, David. "Olympic Arts: The Night the San Francisco Ballet Turned Superficial." *Christian Science Monitor*, August 13, 1984.

# INDEX

Page numbers in bold indicate illustrations.

**Other titles in the Choreography and Dance Studies series**

This book is part of a series. The publisher will accept continuation orders which may be cancelled at any time and which provide for automatic billing and shipping of each title in the series upon publication. Please write for details.